S0-EGX-027

Speaking of Montana

A Guide to the Oral History Collection
at the Montana Historical Society,
through 1996

Speaking of Montana

A Guide to the Oral History Collection
at the Montana Historical Society,
through 1996

Compiled by:
Patricia Borneman
Jodie Foley
Laurie Mercier
Roberta Opel
John Terreo

Edited by:
Jodie Foley
Dave Walter

MONTANA
HISTORICAL
SOCIETY
PRESS

Helena

Cover images, all from the collections of the Montana Historical Society Photograph Archives, clockwise from bottom left:

Havre Commercial Co. Red Cross girls, Havre, 1917
Montana State Federation of Negro Women's Clubs, photographed by L. H. Jorud, Helena, 1938
Workmen replacing a worn cutterhead at Fort Peck Dam, Fort Peck, 1936
Wise River CCC crew constructing the road to Elkhorn, Beaverhead National Forest, photographed by C. Owen Smithers, 1933
Crow school boys and girls, Crow Agency, 1896
Opening of the Forsyth Bridge, photographed by L. A. Huffman, 1905

Cover and book design by Kathryn Fehlig
Typeset in Times and Serif Gothic
Printed by Bookcrafters, Chelsea, Michigan

©1997 Montana Historical Society Press, P.O. Box 201201, Helena, Montana 59620-1201
All rights reserved.
Printed in the United States of America

98 99 00 01 02 03 04   9 8 7 6 5 4 3 2 1

Library of Congress Cataloging-in-Publication Data
Speaking of Montana : a guide to the oral history collection at the Montana Historical Society / compiled by Patricia Borneman . . . [et al.] ; edited by Jodie Foley and Dave Walter.
    p.   cm.
Includes index.
ISBN 0-917298-53-5 (pbk.)
    1. Montana—History, Local—Sources—Audiotape catalogs.
    2. Montana—Biography—Audiotape catalogs.
    3. Montana—Social life and customs—Sources—Audiotape catalogs.
    4. Interviews—Montana—Audiotape catalogs.
    5. Oral History—Catalogs. 6. Montana Historical Society—Audiotape catalogs. I. Borneman, Patricia. II. Foley, Jodie, 1964– . III. Walter, Dave, 1943–. IV. Montana Historical Society.
F731.S59 1997   97-19548
016.9786—dc21   CIP

Contents

Introduction

Oral histories draw on personal experiences to provide vivid descriptions and reveal human emotions and motivations. They add new dimensions to the historical record, providing future generations a glimpse into the lives of people who may not have initiated historic events, but whose experiences shaped and were defined by those events.

The Montana Historical Society's collection of oral histories creates a rich and varied tapestry, interweaving the varied textures and hues that form the fabric of the Montana experience. Society staff conducted and created summaries for interviews as early as 1916, and in 1970 the Society began collecting tape-recorded oral histories. In 1981 an oral history program was created to systematically research and record Montana's "living history." The program was funded by a Montana Legislative Cultural and Aesthetic Grant until 1991. From that date to the present, the Society's oral history collection has been maintained by the archives staff.

The collection, nearly 1,700 interviews strong, was created primarily as a result of large topical projects, including "Montanans at Work," "Small Town Montana," "Metals Manufacturing in Four Montana Communities," "Women as Community Builders," "Helena Business History," "Native American Educators," "The New Deal in Montana/Fort Peck Dam," "Medicine, Health Care, and Nursing," and "20th Century Montana Military Veterans." In addition to these large society-sponsored projects, the collection includes many individual and donated interviews exploring themes as diverse as ethnic communities, pioneer and homesteading experiences, legislative trends, and the impact of urban renewal on small businesses. Speeches, musical recordings, and conference proceedings, although not technically oral histories, round out the collection and are included because they are historic recordings.

The Montana Historical Society Oral History Program strongly encourages public use of its oral history collection for educational and instructional programs, publications, exhibits, genealogical research, and personal enjoyment. All tapes and accompanying transcripts are available at our facility. Tapes may be borrowed through interlibrary loan, and duplicate copies may be purchased from the Montana Historical Society. Please contact the society archives oral historian for more information.

It is impossible to put together a guide like this without incurring major debts. An internal guide was compiled in the late 1980s by Patricia Borneman, under the supervision of Laurie Mercier, then the oral historian. Borneman labored for over two years to create a descriptive guide to nearly 1,000 oral history interviews. Most of these interviews were conducted between 1981 and 1989 by Mercier, whose foresight and dedication laid a strong foundation on which this oral history collection rests, and upon which we hope to build.

With the help of a computerized cataloging system, talented oral history program assistants Doris Peterson and Roberta Opel, and innumerable volunteer transcriptionists, we have added over 700 interviews to the original guide. The majority of these interviews were conducted by John Terreo, oral historian for the Montana Historical Society from 1989 to 1993.

Additional Society staff support has included that of Dave Walter, Kathryn Otto, Ellen Arguimbau, Connie Geiger, Lory Morrow, Becca Kohl, Kathryn Fehlig, Doug Weber, and Martha Kohl. The project could not have been completed without financial support provided by a Cultural and Aesthetic Grant—for which we are very grateful.

The Montana Historical Society oral history program owes its greatest debt to the narrators who chose to share their stories with us and to the many dedicated volunteers who labored to make those stories accessible. We hope you find these interviews as fascinating and rewarding as we have!

Jodie Foley,
Montana Historical Society Oral Historian
1997

User's Guide

This guide comprises the oral history holdings of the Montana Historical Society Archives, current to 1996. The entries are arranged by project category, and each section includes a descriptive introduction to that project. The subject index identifies interviews concerning particular topics, places, and people, while the index of interviewees will direct the user to interviews with specific people.

The abbreviations used in this guide refer to types of collections in the Montana Historical Society Archives:

OH 215 = Oral History Number 215
SC 1295 = Small Collection Number 1295
MC 64 = Manuscript Collection Number 64
MF 101 = Microfilm Number 101
MM 8 = Multimedia Collection Number 8

Each entry should provide a sufficient description of the individual oral history collection for the user to make a decision regarding its applicability to his or her interest. With some minor variations each entry contains:

—the Montana Historical Society Archives Oral
    History identification number
—the collection title and identity of inter-
    viewee(s)
—a description of the collection contents
—information about the interview: interviewer's
    name, date of interview, place of interview
—the form in which the collection is held: avail-
    ability of a printed summary, transcript, or
    typescript; number of cassette tapes; length
    of interview in hours/minutes.

The absence of a form designation in the entry indicates that such a form does not exist for the item. For example, if an entry shows no "transcript" line, then no transcript exists for the interview.

All locales mentioned in the guide are in Montana unless otherwise specified.

List of Abbreviations

The following abbreviations have been used throughout this guide:

AAUW	American Association of University Women
ASARCO	American Smelting and Refining Company
BIA	Bureau of Indian Affairs
CCC	Civilian Conservation Corps
IWW	Industrial Workers of the World
LWV	League of Women Voters
Milwaukee Road	Chicago, Milwaukee, St. Paul and Pacific Railroad
Mine-Mill	International Union of Mine, Mill and Smelter Workers
NYA	National Youth Administration
PTA	Parent-Teachers Association
REA	Rural Electrification Administration
UMW	United Mine Workers of America
WAAC	Women's Auxiliary Army Corps
WAVES	Women Accepted for Volunteer Emergency Service
WPA	Work Projects Administration
YMCA	Young Men's Christian Association
YWCA	Young Women's Christian Association

Oral History Projects

Helena Business History Oral History Project

Begun in 1986, this ongoing project focuses on the development of Helena businesses from World War I through urban renewal in the 1960s. Montana Historical Society staff and volunteers interviewed people who established or worked in Helena's communications, entertainment, manufacturing, service, grocery, and retail businesses. Narrator discussions include business practices, changing consumer demands, changing technologies, and the impact of the automobile. The project not only reflects changes in the economy of the "Capital City" but also sheds light on the fiscal development of towns across Montana and the West.

OH 1171
BILL DeWOLF AND FREDDY DeWOLF
INTERVIEW

Bill DeWolf and Freddy DeWolf discuss: their parents; their father's grocery stores in Townsend and Helena; the 1930s Depression; the 1935 Helena earthquakes; buying the Union Market in Helena in 1945; the development of chain stores; customers; Chinese vegetable sellers; store operations; urban renewal–related litigation; the effects of state and federal health regulations on their business.
INTERVIEWED BY PATRICIA BORNEMAN, AUGUST 21, 1986, HELENA.
SUMMARY: 5 PAGES
2 TAPES: 1 HOUR, 50 MINUTES

OH 1172
WARD THOMPSON AND VIRGINIA THOMPSON
INTERVIEW

Ward Thompson (b. 1917) and Virginia Thompson describe: Ward Thompson's early life in Butte; his family's relocation to Helena in 1938; his family's paper business; changes in the paper industry; their marriage.
INTERVIEWED BY PATRICIA BORNEMAN, MARCH 23, 1987, HELENA.
SUMMARY: 2 PAGES
1 TAPE: 55 MINUTES

OH 1173
SUSAN EAKER INTERVIEW

Susan Eaker (1900–1992) depicts: her arrival in Helena in 1930; her work as a speech and drama teacher at Helena High School; owning and operating a bookstore on North Main Street; rebuilding her business after a 1951 fire; nearby businesses; changes in the retail book industry; types of books carried; the effects of urban renewal.
INTERVIEWED BY LORETTA LINDELL, SEPTEMBER 6, 1986, HELENA.
SUMMARY: 5 PAGES
2 TAPES: 1 HOUR, 30 MINUTES

OH 1174
THOMAS C. POWER INTERVIEW

Thomas Power (b. 1919) discusses: the Power family businesses in Helena; his involvement in the transportation business, including working for the Community Transit Company from 1948 to 1968.
INTERVIEWED BY LAURIE MERCIER, SEPTEMBER 19, 1986, HELENA.
SUMMARY: 8 PAGES
2 TAPES: 1 HOUR, 55 MINUTES

OH 1175
LEWIS BRACKMAN INTERVIEW

Lewis Brackman (b. 1917) describes: his father's grocery business in Powell, Wyoming, and his connections with the Klein and Borne Company; his family's reloca-

tion to Helena; opening a new grocery business; his work as an automobile mechanic for Capital Ford; the 1935 Helena earthquakes; entering the grocery business with his father; store operations and competitors; the effects of gasoline and food rationing during World War II; labor relations; urban renewal.
INTERVIEWED BY PATRICIA BORNEMAN, JANUARY 29, 1987, HELENA.
SUMMARY: 5 PAGES
2 TAPES: 1 HOUR, 50 MINUTES

OH 1176
WILLIAM R. MILES INTERVIEW
William Miles discusses: the immigration of his grandfather, Frederick Gamer, from Germany to Helena in 1866; his grandfather's ownership of Gamer's shoe stores in Helena; his brewery partnership; his ownership of shoe stores in Great Falls; the National Shoe Retailers of America; helping establish God's Love Mission; the Helena Chamber of Commerce; urban renewal.
INTERVIEWED BY PATRICIA BORNEMAN, NOVEMBER 17, 1986, HELENA.
SUMMARY: 4 PAGES
2 TAPES: 1 HOUR, 20 MINUTES

OH 1177
GEORGE "SHORTY" HUBER INTERVIEW
George Huber (d. 1992) talks about: his father's downtown blacksmith business in Helena; the Central Garage; the Helena Gas and Electric Company; the 1935 Helena earthquakes; other Helena businesses and aspects of the city's history.
INTERVIEWED BY LAURIE MERCIER, NOVEMBER 18, 1986, HELENA.
TRANSCRIPT: 52 PAGES
2 TAPES: 1 HOUR, 40 MINUTES

OH 1178
ROSCOE "ROCK" HAND INTERVIEW
Roscoe Hand (b. 1904) discusses: his parents and his early life in the Wise River area; the 1930s Depression; owning and operating Rock Hand Hardware in Helena; various Helena business establishments.
INTERVIEWED BY LAURIE MERCIER, MARCH 10, 1987, HELENA.
SUMMARY: 6 PAGES
2 TAPES: 1 HOUR, 25 MINUTES

OH 1179
GENE BROWN INTERVIEW
Gene Brown (b. 1926) recalls: being a science teacher and a musician; his experiences as manager of the Marlow Theater in Helena from 1959 to 1962.
INTERVIEWED BY PATRICIA BORNEMAN, MARCH 11, 1987, HELENA.
TRANSCRIPT: 37 PAGES
1 TAPE: 1 HOUR

OH 1180
LaVERNE TRAUFER YUHAS INTERVIEW
LaVerne Yuhas speaks of: growing up in Helena; her father's Helena grocery-business activities—such as home delivery, merchandise pricing, advertising, meat processing, types of merchandise for sale, other grocery stores, and various customers; her father's early work with the Helena Trading Company; her father's partnership with Curt Dehler.
INTERVIEWED BY LORETTA LINDELL, JANUARY 26, 1987, HELENA.
SUMMARY: 10 PAGES
1 TAPE: 40 MINUTES

OH 1181
JOHN TRAUFER INTERVIEW
John Traufer (1899–1986) speaks of: the pioneer activities of his family in Montana; growing up and living in Marysville; Marysville businesses; the Drumlummon Mine; his recollections of Thomas Cruse.
INTERVIEWED BY LORETTA LINDELL, APRIL 1986, HELENA.
TRANSCRIPT: 19 PAGES
1 TAPE: 40 MINUTES

OH 1182
ALBERT LUNDBORG INTERVIEW
Albert Lundborg (b. 1914) reviews: his early life in South Dakota; the 1930s Depression; owning and operating a grocery business in Helena.
INTERVIEWED BY HARRIETT MELOY, JUNE 13, 1986, HELENA.
TRANSCRIPT: 14 PAGES
1 TAPE: 30 MINUTES

OH 1183
JEAN G. WEEKS INTERVIEW
Jean Weeks summarizes the origin and business operations of the Globe Men's Store in Helena from 1890 to 1958.

INTERVIEWED BY HARRIETT MELOY, MAY 18, 1987,
HELENA.
SUMMARY: 5 PAGES
1 TAPE: 55 MINUTES

OH 1184
R. B. RICHARDSON INTERVIEW

R. B. Richardson depicts: his early life in Illinois; his college education and study in actuarial science; serving as a sniper for the U.S. Marine Corps in World War I; relocating to Helena; his work with the Montana Life Insurance Company and its subsequent merger with St. Paul Fire and Marine Insurance in 1957; the 1930s Depression.

INTERVIEWED BY HARRIETT MELOY AND CLARK PYFER,
MAY 14, 1987, HELENA.
SUMMARY: 3 PAGES
1 TAPE: 1 HOUR, 20 MINUTES

OH 1185
GLENN BREED AND EILEEN REDD BREED INTERVIEW

Glenn Breed relates: his military service during World War II; his family; his involvement in civic activities and organizations in Helena. Eileen Breed describes: her parents' ownership and operation of Redd's Grocery and other businesses in Helena; her marriage to Glenn Breed; owning and operating Rodney Street News and Confectionery; various Helena businesses.

INTERVIEWED BY PATRICIA BORNEMAN, SEPTEMBER 17, 1987, HELENA.
SUMMARY: 6 PAGES
3 TAPES: 2 HOURS, 5 MINUTES

OH 1186
MARY FRIEL INTERVIEW

Mary Friel recounts: her early life in Idaho; her relocation to Montana; her experiences during the 1930s Depression; owning and operating a gift shop in Helena; the effects of government regulations on business; urban renewal.

INTERVIEWED BY LORETTA LINDELL, SEPTEMBER 18, 1987, HELENA.
SUMMARY: 4 PAGES
2 TAPES: 1 HOUR, 25 MINUTES

OH 1187
J. HOWARD RETZ INTERVIEW

J. Howard Retz (1911–1988) talks about: his early life in Polson; his education and mortuary training; em-

balming and cremation in Montana; the Montana mortuary industry; Helena funeral homes; the effects of the 1930s Depression on the industry.

INTERVIEWED BY HARRIETT MELOY, APRIL 20, 1988, HELENA.
SUMMARY: 14 PAGES
1 TAPE: 55 MINUTES

OH 1188
BERNICE MITCHELL INTERVIEW

Bernice Mitchell (b. 1902) discusses: her parents and their operation of a Helena confectionery; the 1935 Helena earthquakes; the 1930s Depression; her husband's World War II military service; owning and operating Clafin's Furniture; other Helena businesses; urban renewal.

INTERVIEWED BY LORETTA LINDELL, APRIL 9, 1988, HELENA.
SUMMARY: 4 PAGES
2 TAPES: 1 HOUR, 25 MINUTES

OH 1670
HAROLD L. PAULSEN INTERVIEW

Harold Paulsen describes: his Norwegian parents and childhood in Helena; attendance of Intermountain College in Helena; early employment with Montana Life Insurance Company; experiences in the Air Force during World War II; work as an insurance salesman with Western Life in Helena; involvement with Helena Jaycees, Kiwanis, and Shriners; experiences as a Montana legislator; performing as a singer at churches and community events in Helena.

INTERVIEWED BY PAUL VERSON, APRIL 25, 1996, HELENA.
TRANSCRIPT: 32 PAGES
2 TAPES: 2 HOURS

OH 1671
JOHN DELANO INTERVIEW

John Delano—a longtime Montana Legislative lobbyist—discusses: growing up in Billings; his education at the University of Montana; selling life insurance in the 1950s for Blue Cross; work for the Alumni Association at the university; serving in the legislature and on the Girl's Vocational School Board in Helena and St. Peter's Hospital Board; lobbying for the University of Montana, Montana Railroad Association, and his company John Delano and Associates; work with the Timber Industry, tobacco companies, and on various environmental regulation cases.

INTERVIEWED BY PAUL VERDON, MARCH 14 AND APRIL 9, 1996, HELENA.
TRANSCRIPT: 24 PAGES
3 TAPES: 1 HOUR, 15 MINUTES

OH 1672
JOSEPH MAIERLE INTERVIEW
    Joseph Maierle describes: his Croate-Slovenian parents; his childhood in East Helena and Helena; attendance of Mount St. Charles School; employment as an engineer including work with the Montana Highway Department, the Montana Water Board, designing bridges in Iran during World War II, and his own national and international consulting business, Morrison-Maierle; design and construction of Koocanusa Bridge at Libby Dam and the interstate highway through Wolf Creek Canyon; environmental engineering; work with the board of Carroll College.
INTERVIEWED BY PAUL VERDON, APRIL 4, 1996, HELENA.
TRANSCRIPT: 20 PAGES
2 TAPES: 2 HOURS

Medicine, Health Care, and Nursing in Montana Oral History Project

The primary goal of this project was to document the experiences of longtime physicians, nurses, nurse educators, emergency medical technicians, and lay health care providers in serving the medical needs of Montanans in the twentieth century. Interviewees discuss the impact of weather, distance, and road conditions on treatment; the role new technologies, drugs, and regulations played in expanding services; recruitment of health care professionals to the state; nursing education opportunities in Montana and the region; and home care remedies and treatments prior to modern medicine.

OH 1217
HERBERT TOWNSEND INTERVIEW

Herbert Townsend (b. 1906) describes: his early life in Stevensville, Dillon, and Missoula; health care during his childhood; the 1930s Depression; employment with Dr. C. R. Thornton (founder of the Thornton Hospital); service in the U.S. Army during the 1930s; courses in veterinary medicine; service in the U.S. Navy in the Pacific Theater during World War II; work as a carpenter; his ranch; work in a sawmill; the electrification of the Seeley Lake area in the 1950s; employment with Broken Arrow Ranch; the development of Seeley Lake from the 1930s through the 1980s; the local timber industry; his environmental concerns.
INTERVIEWED BY JOHN TERREO, SEPTEMBER 20, 1990, SEELEY LAKE.
SUMMARY: 19 PAGES
2 TAPES: 1 HOUR, 20 MINUTES

OH 1300
BEATRICE KAASCH INTERVIEW

Beatrice Kaasch (b. 1912)—a Fergus County native—discusses: her ancestry and early childhood; homesteading; the 1930s Depression; nursing school; nursing techniques; her job as a science instructor at St. James, St. Vincent, and St. John hospitals and at Carroll College in Helena; her various nursing positions; changes in nursing education; her work as president of the Montana State Board of Nursing; rural health care; nursing

credentials.
INTERVIEWED BY JOHN TERREO, NOVEMBER 16, 1989, LAUREL.
TRANSCRIPT: 89 PAGES
3 TAPES: 3 HOURS

OH 1301
FRANK NEWMAN INTERVIEW

Frank Newman explains: rural and community health care; the WAMI (Washington, Alaska, Montana, and Idaho) Physicians Education and Training Program and his involvement in it; recruitment of health care professionals to Montana's rural areas; WICHE (Western Interstate Commission for Higher Education) rural health delivery systems; HEALTHCON (the electronic information resource system for health professionals); his experiences as an instructor of microbiology at Montana State University in Bozeman; his employment as director of AHEC (Montana Area Health Education Center); the Medical Assistance Facilities Demonstration Project.
INTERVIEWED BY JOHN TERREO, NOVEMBER 21, 1989, MISSOULA.
TRANSCRIPT: 41 PAGES
2 TAPES: 1 HOUR, 20 MINUTES

OH 1302
JAN LEISHMAN INTERVIEW

Jan Leishman recounts: her nursing education and training at Montana State University in Bozeman from

1976 to 1981; her work in St. Ignatius and at St. James Hospital in Butte; her employment as a registered nurse/midwife in Bozeman; the effects of liability insurance on midwifery; discrimination in rural health care; nursing credentials.

INTERVIEWED BY JOHN TERREO, NOVEMBER, 21, 1989, BOZEMAN.

TRANSCRIPT: 54 PAGES

2 TAPES: 1 HOUR, 20 MINUTES

OH 1303
ANNA SHANON INTERVIEW

Anna Shanon (b. 1929) discusses: her childhood in Dillon; experiences as a student nurse at Missouri Baptist Hospital in St. Louis, Missouri; initial experiences in nursing; work as dean of the Montana State University School of Nursing in Bozeman; organizing the consortium of the Schools of Nursing in Montana; the economics and complexities of nursing and nursing education; the effects of legislative and political issues on nursing.

INTERVIEWED BY JOHN TERREO, NOVEMBER 22, 1989, BOZEMAN.

TRANSCRIPT: 46 PAGES

2 TAPES: 1 HOUR, 20 MINUTES

OH 1304
BERTHA KENISON INTERVIEW

Bertha Kenison (b. 1913) talks about: her childhood in Lima in the 1920s; her work as a nurse's aide at the Barrett Hospital in Dillon from 1959 to 1975; changes in health care; raising children in Dillon.

INTERVIEWED BY JOHN TERREO, DECEMBER 6, 1989, DILLON.

TRANSCRIPT: 13 PAGES

2 TAPES: 2 HOURS

OH 1305
CLARABEL BOGUT INTERVIEW

Montana nurse Clarabel Bogut (b. 1911) reviews: her childhood near Malta; disease and quarantines; her training at Deaconess Hospital in Great Falls; her 15-year career as a college nurse at Western Montana College in Dillon; her work as a Beaverhead County health nurse.

INTERVIEWED BY JOHN TERREO, DECEMBER 6, 1989, DILLON.

TRANSCRIPT: 40 PAGES

2 TAPES: 1 HOUR

OH 1306
JOHN C. SEIDENSTICKER INTERVIEW

John Seidensticker (b. 1915) describes: his childhood on a ranch; attending Twin Bridges schools; medical school;

his service in the U.S. Army in Europe during World War II; his work as a physician in Madison County, serving the state orphanage at Twin Bridges and hospitals at Sheridan and Dillon; medical care changes; his retirement.

INTERVIEWED BY JOHN TERREO, DECEMBER 7, 1989, DILLON.

TRANSCRIPT: 53 PAGES

3 TAPES: 3 HOURS

OH 1307
ALBERT JUERGENS INTERVIEW

Albert Juergens (b. 1918)—a Dillon physician—relates: his medical experiences with the U.S. Army in Europe during World War II; his residence in Salmon, Idaho, after the war; establishment of a medical practice in Dillon in 1950; Dillon-area medical care; federal regulations and programs; liability insurance.

INTERVIEWED BY JOHN TERREO, DECEMBER 7, 1989, DILLON.

SUMMARY: 12 PAGES

2 TAPES: 1 HOUR, 10 MINUTES

OH 1308
ANNA PEARL SHERRICK INTERVIEW

Anna Sherrick discusses: her childhood and education in Illinois; her teaching position at Deaconess Hospital in Great Falls; the Montana State University School of Nursing in Bozeman; the U.S. Cadet Nurse Corps during World War II; changes in training; her thoughts about modern medical care.

INTERVIEWED BY JOHN TERREO, DECEMBER 6, 1989, BOZEMAN.

SUMMARY: 8 PAGES

1 TAPE: 1 HOUR

OH 1309
WILMA CATRON INTERVIEW

Wilma Catron (b. 1944) tells about: her childhood and health care training in Glasgow; experiences as a nurse's aide at Trinity Hospital in Wolf Point and at Francis Mahon Deaconess Hospital in Glasgow; work as a hospice aide for St. Peter's Hospital in Helena.

INTERVIEWED BY JOHN TERREO, JANUARY 22, 1990, HELENA.

TRANSCRIPT: 52 PAGES

2 TAPES: 1 HOUR, 40 MINUTES

OH 1310
BONNIE ADEE INTERVIEW

Bonnie Adee (b. 1947)—a Helena resident—depicts: her involvement in the St. Peter's Hospital Hospice Program; the program's beginnings, its administration by Westmont Health Services, and its acquisition by St. Peter's in the early 1980s; the funding of hospice programs; the development of volunteer and professional hospice-care nurses, aides, and counselors; the effects of liability laws and state/federal legislation on hospices locally and nationally; the care of terminally ill people; philosophies of death.

INTERVIEWED BY JOHN TERREO, JANUARY 23, 1990, HELENA.

TRANSCRIPT: 39 PAGES

2 TAPES: 1 HOUR, 10 MINUTES

OH 1311
GRADY WALTON INTERVIEW

Grady Walton discusses: his tenure as administrator of the Deaconess Home in Helena from 1959 to 1962, including staff, children, and the facility; the mission of the home; the physical and emotional needs of the home's children; finances and fund-raising; relocation of the facility; initiation of the cottage system.

INTERVIEWED BY JOHN TERREO, NOVEMBER 30, 1989, HELENA.

SUMMARY: 4 PAGES

2 TAPES: 1 HOUR, 15 MINUTES

OH 1312
KEITH McCARTY INTERVIEW

Keith McCarty reviews: his academic background; his work as project director for the Medical Assistance Demonstration Project in Montana; systems for providing limited in-patient service in rural areas as an alternative to hospitals.

INTERVIEWED BY JOHN TERREO, JANUARY 29, 1990, HELENA.

SUMMARY: 8 PAGES

1 TAPE: 1 HOUR

OH 1313
MARGE VANDERHOOF INTERVIEW

Marge Vanderhoof (b. 1946) discusses: her education and training as a nursing student in Great Falls and at Montana State University in Bozeman, circa 1980–1986; her employment as a registered nurse at St. Peter's Hospital in Helena; her activities as treasurer of the Montana Nurses Association; assistance to nurses

recovering from drug and alcohol addictions; other related issues.

INTERVIEWED BY JOHN TERREO, JANUARY 29, 1990, HELENA.

TRANSCRIPT: 42 PAGES

2 TAPES: 1 HOUR, 20 MINUTES

OH 1314
HARRY S. ETTER INTERVIEW

Harry Etter (b. 1951) talks about: his youth as the son of a U.S. Navy physician in Bethesda, Maryland, and in other U.S. locations; his medical education at the University of Maryland; his internship in San Diego; his experiences as a physician in the U.S. Navy; his service in submarine squadrons; his arrival in Montana; his medical practice in Helena; the effects of a busy practice on his family life; medical ethics; the effects of technology on health care and on the practice of medicine; liability insurance; life and aging; Medicare and Medicaid; state and federal legislation affecting physicians; the recruitment of physicians for rural areas.

INTERVIEWED BY JOHN TERREO, FEBRUARY 6, 1990, HELENA.

TRANSCRIPT: 43 PAGES

2 TAPES: 2 HOURS

OH 1315
WILMA NICHOLSON INTERVIEW

Wilma Nicholson describes: her early life in Seattle, Washington; her education, training, and service as a nurse at Providence Hospital in Seattle; her work in the coronary care unit at St. James Hospital in Butte in the early 1960s; her experiences teaching in a vocational program for licensed practical nurses in Butte; her work as a nurse practitioner at the SOS clinic in Seeley Lake.

INTERVIEWED BY JOHN TERREO, FEBRUARY 8, 1990, SEELEY LAKE.

TRANSCRIPT: 31 PAGES

2 TAPES: 1 HOUR, 15 MINUTES

OH 1316
VIRGINIA KENYON INTERVIEW

Virginia Kenyon (b. circa 1915) discusses: her nursing education and training at Deaconess Hospital in Great Falls, beginning in 1932; her recollections of Anna Pearl Sherrick; her work as a public health nurse in Dawson and Fergus counties from the mid-1930s to 1942; her experiences as a U.S. Army nurse with the 81st General Hospital during World War II; her later nursing experiences; rural nursing.

INTERVIEWED BY JOHN TERREO, MARCH 23, 1990,
HELENA.
SUMMARY: 24 PAGES
2 TAPES: 1 HOUR, 20 MINUTES

OH 1317
MONA VANEK INTERVIEW

Mona Vanek—a resident of Noxon—discusses: health care and living conditions throughout her life; societal attitudes regarding health care; various home remedies; the effects of distance on medical care; area hospitals, clinics, and physicians; lice epidemics; childbirth and midwives; drugs; family health problems; dentists; the first physician's assistant in western Sanders County; Louie and Madge Post and developing the Western Sanders County Ambulance Service; increasing costs of medical insurance and health care; medical liability; her involvement with the local ambulance service; Montana's Good Samaritan Law.
INTERVIEWED BY JOHN TERREO, APRIL 2, 1990, NOXON.
TRANSCRIPT: 86 PAGES
3 TAPES: 2 HOURS, 40 MINUTES

OH 1318
MARIA SOLCE MYERS INTERVIEW

Heron resident Maria Myers (b. 1952) recounts: her work as an emergency medical technician for the Western Sanders County Ambulance Service from 1980 to 1990; the area in which the service operated; Montana's Good Samaritan Law; liability insurance; other issues related to emergency health care.
INTERVIEWED BY JOHN TERREO, APRIL 2, 1990, HERON.
TRANSCRIPT: 56 PAGES
2 TAPES: 1 HOUR, 20 MINUTES

OH 1319
JOYCE COUPAL INTERVIEW

Joyce Coupal (b. 1929) talks about: growing up as the daughter of missionaries in India; her work as a registered nurse in the maternity ward and clinic of the Murray Hospital in Butte; the emergency medical treatment of Butte miners; her experiences as a Noxon volunteer for the Western Sanders County Ambulance Service; her views on the quality of medical care in Sanders County.
INTERVIEWED BY JOHN TERREO, APRIL 3, 1990, NOXON.
TRANSCRIPT: 36 PAGES
2 TAPES: 1 HOUR, 15 MINUTES

OH 1320
ALICE DETTWILER INTERVIEW

Alice Dettwiler (b. 1927) depicts: her early life in Kalispell; health care in Kalispell during her childhood; her education, training, and nursing work in Minnesota; her return to Montana in 1954; her work as an office nurse in the Noxon clinic from 1962 to 1980; the Western Sanders County Ambulance Service; her work as a school nurse at Noxon High School; nursing in rural areas.
INTERVIEWED BY JOHN TERREO, APRIL 5, 1990, NOXON.
SUMMARY: 19 PAGES
2 TAPES: 1 HOUR, 40 MINUTES

OH 1321
DARRELL HALL AND SONYA HALL INTERVIEW

Noxon residents Darrell Hall and Sonya Hall describe: their involvement with the Western Sanders County Ambulance Service; the organization of the service; their emergency medical technician training; experiences as members of the ambulance crew; various aspects of health care in western Sanders County.
INTERVIEWED BY JOHN TERREO, APRIL 5, 1990, NOXON.
TRANSCRIPT: 52 PAGES
2 TAPES: 1 HOUR, 20 MINUTES

OH 1322
ANITA JOPLING INTERVIEW

Anita Jopling (b. 1913) discusses: her experiences as a nursing student at St. Mary's Hospital in Walla Walla, Washington, during the early 1930s; her work as a nurse with World War I veterans at the Veterans Hospital in Walla Walla; her relocation to Trout Creek in 1948; her work as a public health nurse in Sanders County from 1963 to 1973; the general health care situation in Sanders County; nursing and health care in extremely rural areas.
INTERVIEWED BY JOHN TERREO, APRIL 5, 1990, TROUT CREEK.
SUMMARY: 18 PAGES
2 TAPES: 2 HOURS

OH 1323
ELINOR "NAN" COMPTON INTERVIEW

Nan Compton (b. 1927) tells about: home health care during her childhood in Heron and Sandpoint, Idaho; her education and training in the U.S. Cadet Nurse Corps during World War II; her initial nursing experiences; her work as a nurse during the construction of the Noxon Dam; her experiences as an office nurse; her employment at Bonner Hospital in Sandpoint, Idaho; rural health

care and nursing in Sanders County.
INTERVIEWED BY JOHN TERREO, APRIL 5, 1990, HERON.
TRANSCRIPT: 72 PAGES
2 TAPES: 1 HOUR, 45 MINUTES

OH 1324
THOMAS L. LAWRENCE INTERVIEW

Thomas Lawrence (b. 1946) discusses: health care during his childhood in Kalispell; his medical training and education at the University of South Dakota and the University of Colorado; his 1972 summer internship in Lewistown; his general medical practice in Sandpoint, Idaho; life as a physician in a rural area; recruiting physicians and other health care professionals for rural communities; his role as supervisor of the ambulance service in western Sanders County; legal issues of state jurisdictions on emergency medical transportation; his views on medical liability insurance.
INTERVIEWED BY JOHN TERREO, APRIL 5, 1990, HERON.
TRANSCRIPT: 51 PAGES
2 TAPES: 1 HOUR, 20 MINUTES

OH 1325
ERABERT STOBIE AND ELDORA STOBIE INTERVIEW

Erabert Stobie (b. 1937) and Eldora Stobie (b. 1937) talk about: their role in the organization of the Western Sanders County Ambulance Service; personnel training; daily routine; liability insurance; accidents.
INTERVIEWED BY JOHN TERREO, APRIL 6, 1990, NOXON.
TRANSCRIPT: 44 PAGES
2 TAPES: 2 HOURS

OH 1326
JOHN C. HARKER INTERVIEW

Heron resident John Harker (b. 1918) discusses: health care in western Sanders County; the medical services provided by Drs. Jones and Osland during the 1920s and 1930s; his military service during World War II; logging; his Christmas tree business. *[See also Montanans at Work OH 659.]*
INTERVIEWED BY JOHN TERREO, APRIL 7, 1990, HERON.
SUMMARY: 15 PAGES
2 TAPES: 1 HOUR, 20 MINUTES

OH 1327
SHIRLEY McLINDEN INTERVIEW

Shirley McLinden, a resident of Trout Creek, relates: her experiences as a member of the Western Sanders County Ambulance Service; her emergency medical tech-

nician training; ambulance vehicles; the effects of weather and distance on service; the influx of senior citizens into the county; the history of the ambulance service; liability issues.
INTERVIEWED BY JOHN TERREO, MAY 31, 1990, TROUT CREEK.
TRANSCRIPT: 35 PAGES
2 TAPES: 1 HOUR, 10 MINUTES

OH 1328
PAUL SEIFERT INTERVIEW

Paul Seifert (b. 1918) discusses: his early life in Missoula and Deer Lodge; his medical education; his residency in Spokane, Washington; his U.S. Army service caring for German prisoners of war; his medical practice in Libby, 1947–1987; the effects of government regulations and programs; rural health care; recruiting physicians for rural areas; the use of aircraft in medical emergencies; liability insurance; the Libby Hospital.
INTERVIEWED BY JOHN TERREO, JUNE 3, 1990, BULL CREEK.
SUMMARY: 18 PAGES
2 TAPES: 1 HOUR, 45 MINUTES

OH 1329
DEANA ELDER INTERVIEW

Deana Elder (b. 1953) reviews: trout-farm operations in Noxon; her involvement with the Western Sanders County Ambulance Service; her training to become an emergency medical technician; her experiences as a trainer/instructor for the ambulance service; medical and legal issues associated with operating a volunteer, rural ambulance service; comparisons between the Western Sanders County Ambulance Service and the Libby Ambulance Service.
INTERVIEWED BY JOHN TERREO, JUNE 4, 1990, LIBBY.
TRANSCRIPT: 51 PAGES
2 TAPES: 1 HOUR, 20 MINUTES

OH 1330
LARRY ELDER INTERVIEW

Larry Elder (b. 1953) discusses: trout-farm operations in Noxon; his reasons for becoming involved with the Western Sanders County Ambulance Service; his training to become an emergency medical technician; various issues regarding rural emergency medical transportation; the effects of weather; health care in extremely rural areas.

INTERVIEWED BY JOHN TERREO, JUNE 4, 1990, LIBBY.
TRANSCRIPT: 72 PAGES
2 TAPES: 2 HOURS

OH 1331
JESSE BROWN INTERVIEW

Jesse Brown (b. 1951) tells of: his experiences in the U.S. Navy as a corpsman during the Vietnam conflict; his education and teaching in the Johns Hopkins University physician-associates program; his experiences in establishing one of Montana's first satellite clinics in Noxon; emergency medical transportation in western Sanders County; his involvement with the Western Sanders County Ambulance Service; recruiting health care professionals to rural areas of Montana; medical liability.

INTERVIEWED BY JOHN TERREO, JUNE 6, 1990, LIBBY.
TRANSCRIPT: 76 PAGES
2 TAPES: 1 HOUR, 40 MINUTES

OH 1332
JUDITH C. MACHLER INTERVIEW

Judith Machler (b. 1917) discusses: growing up on a homestead north of Lewistown; home medical remedies; the education and training of nurses at St. Joseph's Hospital in Lewistown; the 1930s Depression; working as a nurse at Deaconess Hospital in Great Falls and at the Valley Vista Nursing Home in Lewistown; liability insurance for nurses; changes in nursing; rural medical care.

INTERVIEWED BY JOHN TERREO, JUNE 16, 1990, BILLINGS.
TRANSCRIPT: 34 PAGES
2 TAPES: 1 HOUR, 20 MINUTES

OH 1333
ROBERTA TAYLOR PULLEN INTERVIEW

Lewistown resident Roberta Pullen (b. 1921) talks about: the osteopathic practice of her father, Dr. Fred Taylor; her mother's child-rearing techniques; the quarantine of persons with contagious diseases; the "pest house"; the training of nurses at Johns Hopkins University; her work at the Murray Clinic in Butte from 1914 until the 1970s.

INTERVIEWED BY JOHN TERREO, JUNE 19, 1990,
LEWISTOWN.
TRANSCRIPT: 61 PAGES
3 TAPES: 2 HOURS, 20 MINUTES

OH 1334
DONALD R. BROWNE INTERVIEW

Donald Browne (b. 1921)—a Lewistown resident and a member of the advisory boards of St. Joseph's Hospital and the Central Montana Medical Center—discusses: the reasons for the closing of St. Joseph's and for the formation of Central Montana Medical Facilities; nursing educations programs; the construction of the original St. Joseph's Hospital building and remodeling for subsequent use; the Daughters of Jesus; medical care; finances.

INTERVIEWED BY JOHN TERREO, JUNE 20, 1990,
LEWISTOWN.
SUMMARY: 11 PAGES
1 TAPE: 50 MINUTES

OH 1335
KEN BYERLY AND FRANCES "SCOTTIE" BYERLY INTERVIEW

Ken Byerly recounts: the history of Lewistown; the establishment of St. Joseph's Hospital by Catholic nuns; the 1918 Spanish influenza epidemic; the 1930s Depression; work as owner/editor of the local newspaper; fund-raising for the construction of the new Central Montana Hospital. Scottie Byerly (b. 1921) reviews: her life as the daughter of a U.S. Army physician in the Philippines, Panama, and Hawaii; her education at the University of North Carolina; her marriage to Ken Byerly and move to Lewistown; state/federal regulations; St. Joseph's Hospital and the county's acquisition of the old hospital; recruiting health care professionals; moving patients to the new facility during a blizzard; emergency medical transportation. *[See also Women as Community Builders OH 1024].*

INTERVIEWED BY JOHN TERREO, JUNE 20, 1990,
LEWISTOWN.
TRANSCRIPT: 35 PAGES
2 TAPES: 1 HOUR, 40 MINUTES

OH 1336
ELEANOR HELMER INTERVIEW

Eleanor Helmer (b. circa 1929) describes: her childhood health care in Fergus County; her training with the U.S. Cadet Nurse Corps in Seattle; her work as a nurse in San Diego during the late 1940s; her relocation to Lewistown in 1952; her experiences as an obstetrics and surgical nurse—and later director of nursing—at St. Joseph's Hospital in Lewistown; changes in nursing education, individual attitudes, and salaries since 1948; the management of hospital nurses and other personnel; liability insurance.

INTERVIEWED BY JOHN TERREO, JUNE 22, 1990,
LEWISTOWN.
TRANSCRIPT: 51 PAGES
2 TAPES: 1 HOUR, 35 MINUTES

OH 1337
EARL ECK INTERVIEW

Earl Eck (b. 1908) tells about: his pharmaceutical training at the University of Montana in Missoula; his early jobs as a pharmacist; pharmaceutical practices; the preparation and uses of drugs and narcotics; his relationships with local physicians.
INTERVIEWED BY JOHN TERREO, JUNE 23, 1990,
LEWISTOWN.
SUMMARY: 14 PAGES
1 TAPE: 1 HOUR

OH 1338
CORRINE DERIANA INTERVIEW

Corrine Deriana (b. 1924) discusses: her early life on the Fort Berthold Indian Reservation, North Dakota; Indian medicine and health care; family life on the reservation; the 1930s Depression and World War II; attending Indian boarding school in Chemwa, Oregon; her work as a nursing assistant in Portland, Oregon; her work as a tray girl and nursing assistant at Galen and Warm Springs state hospitals; her experiences with tuberculosis and silicosis patients; the treatment of mental patients; American Indian views on death and dying; working at St. James Hospital in Butte; becoming a licensed practical nurse (LPN); lobbying for LPNs in Montana; working conditions in nursing homes; education and credentials for nurses; differences between registered nurses and LPNs; the Green Thumb Program; the Helena Indian Alliance; changes in nursing and health care during her life.
INTERVIEWED BY JOHN TERREO, AUGUST 6, 1990, HELENA.
TRANSCRIPT: 48 PAGES
2 TAPES: 1 HOUR, 40 MINUTES

OH 1339
GLEN HALVER INTERVIEW

Glendive veterinarian Glen Halver (b. 1915) speaks of: Montana veterinary practices; his early interest in veterinary medicine; his education; his service on the Montana Livestock Sanitary Board; establishing a veterinary practice.

INTERVIEWED BY JOHN TERREO, OCTOBER 1, 1990,
HELENA.
SUMMARY: 3 PAGES
2 TAPES: 2 HOURS

OH 1340
NAOMI SUMMERS INTERVIEW

Naomi Summers (b. 1945) discusses: her childhood in Kalispell; home remedies and community health care; her licensed practical nurse (LPN) education and training in Butte under the Manpower Development Training Act; her work at the Warm Springs Psychiatric Hospital; the first Cardiac Care Unit at St. Patrick's Hospital, Missoula; her employment at the Kalispell Regional Hospital, including flying with patients on helicopters and working in the intensive care unit; government regulations regarding nursing; her service on the Montana State Board of Nursing; differences between registered nurses and LPNs; liability insurance; medical costs; the morale of health care workers; legislation addressing impaired nurses; volunteer emergency medical technicians and transportation; the Montana Licensed Practical Nurses Association; LPN credentials; the Montana Nurses Board.
INTERVIEWED BY JOHN TERREO, SEPTEMBER 26, 1990,
WHITEFISH.
TRANSCRIPT: 42 PAGES
2 TAPES: 1 HOUR, 40 MINUTES

OH 1341
RAYMOND READ AND ANGELINE READ
INTERVIEW

Raymond Read depicts: his early life in North Dakota; his veterinary training at Iowa State University; his veterinary practice at Ronan from 1941 to 1986; the National Bison Range at Moiese; his experiences as the personal veterinarian to the white buffalo "Big Medicine"; brucellosis vaccinations; his service on the Montana State Board of Veterinarians. Angeline Read relates: her experiences as office manager and bookkeeper for her husband's veterinary practice; the effects of government regulations and new technologies on veterinary medicine.
INTERVIEWED BY JOHN TERREO, SEPTEMBER 27, 1990,
RONAN.
SUMMARY: 11 PAGES
2 TAPES: 1 HOUR, 45 MINUTES

OH 1342
VERNIE BURNS INTERVIEW

Vernie Burns (b. 1912) talks about: her early life in Tweet and Polson; her education and training at Deaconess Hospital in Great Falls during the early 1930s; her recollections of Anna Pearl Sherrick; her employment at Deaconess; the uses of penicillin; the effects of World War II; pilots ferrying military aircraft to Alaska for eventual use by the Soviet Union; raising a family; working conditions for nurses; surgical and pediatric nursing; her work as a public health nurse in Lincoln and Augusta during the 1970s; Hutterites and health care; the clinic in Lincoln and its part-time physicians; the history of the clinic's emergency medical transportation; the Women and Infant Children Program (WIC).
INTERVIEWED BY JOHN TERREO, SEPTEMBER 19, 1990, LINCOLN.
TRANSCRIPT: 33 PAGES
1 TAPE: 1 HOUR

OH 1344
TRUDY MALONE INTERVIEW

Trudy Malone discusses: her early life in North Dakota; her nursing education and training at the Mayo Clinic in Minnesota; her work as a nurse; raising a family; her experiences as a U.S. Army nurse in Europe during World War II; her work as director of the Montana State Board of Nursing; the education and training of licensed practical nurses; liability insurance; changes in education and nurses' attitudes; her two terms as president of the Montana Nurses Association.
INTERVIEWED BY JOHN TERREO, SEPTEMBER 21, 1990, BIGFORK.
TRANSCRIPT: 51 PAGES
3 TAPES: 2 HOURS, 15 MINUTES

OH 1345
STEVEN ZWISLER INTERVIEW

Steven Zwisler (b. 1948) recounts: his childhood in Evanston, Illinois; his education at St. John's University (Minnesota) and the University of Utah; choosing a career in health care and relocating to Montana; his employment at Holy Cross Hospital in Salt Lake City as a kitchen worker and nurse's aide; his work as a nurse's aide at the Clark Fork Valley Hospital in Plains; his service with the U.S. Army; the Vietnam conflict; his nursing education at Montana State University in Bozeman; his early nursing and obstetric experiences; his views on midwifery; liability issues; his work as a staff nurse and discharge planner at North Valley Hospital in Whitefish;

Flathead Valley emergency medical transportation.
INTERVIEWED BY JOHN TERREO, OCTOBER 24, 1990, WHITEFISH.
TRANSCRIPT: 55 PAGES
2 TAPES: 1 HOUR, 40 MINUTES

OH 1346
JOHN TERREO INTERVIEW

John Terreo (b. 1954) chronicles: St. Peter's Hospital Hospice Program's purchase of the Covenant United Methodist Church parsonage in Helena; his involvement in this transaction as secretary of the church's administrative board. [See also 20th Century Montana Military Veterans OH 1195 and General Montana OH 1196.]
INTERVIEWED BY JANET SPERRY, JANUARY 24, 1990, HELENA.
SUMMARY: 4 PAGES
1 TAPE: 45 MINUTES

OH 1347
JAMES E. McGREEVEY INTERVIEW

James McGreevey (b. 1916) discusses: his early life and education in Iowa City, Iowa; his military service with the U.S. Army in Africa and Europe during World War II; his relocation to Montana; his experiences with the Murray Clinic in Butte.
INTERVIEWED BY JOHN TERREO, JANUARY 10, 1991, BUTTE.
TRANSCRIPT: 33 PAGES
2 TAPES: 2 HOURS

OH 1348
BRUCE McINTYRE INTERVIEW

Bruce McIntyre reviews: his family; his early life in St. John, Washington; his father's medical practice; his own medical education and internship; his medical practice in Whitefish; his work as a public health officer for Whitefish and for Flathead County; the 1964 flood; the operation of his satellite office in Eureka; family planning; illegal abortions; legislation affecting public health.
INTERVIEWED BY JOHN TERREO, FEBRUARY 27, 1991, LAKESIDE.
SUMMARY: 12 PAGES
2 TAPES: 1 HOUR, 35 MINUTES

OH 1349
MARY MUNGER INTERVIEW

Mary Munger (b. circa 1943) describes: her parents' immigration from Canada to Butte; life in Butte; home medical remedies; scarlet fever; her nursing training at St. James Hospital in Butte; working in the emergency room on injured miners; the training of psychiatric nurses at Warm Springs; the U.S. Cadet Nurse Corps during World War II; the Bolton bill and federal monies for nursing scholarships; the Montana State Department of Health in Helena; preventative medicine; the attitudes of physicians toward nurses; the Montana Nurses Association; credentials for registered nurses; certification for LPNs; her work as a Lake County public health nurse; public attitudes about health care professionals; Ethel Mitchell, Agnes Pauline, and Muriel Lewis; the Forand bill and national health insurance; salaries, work problems, and labor negotiations. [See also Medicine, Health Care, and Nursing OH 1511.]

INTERVIEWED BY JOHN TERREO, SEPTEMBER 23, 1991, HELENA.

TRANSCRIPT: 54 PAGES

2 TAPES: 1 HOUR, 50 MINUTES

OH 1350
DONALD L. GILLESPIE INTERVIEW

Donald Gillespie (b. 1907) speaks of: his family and early life in Minnesota; becoming a physician; his experiences as the first pediatrician in Butte; the Murray Clinic, the Silverbow County Hospital, and the Anaconda Copper Mining Company; house calls; infectious diseases; traveling clinics; medical care in Butte during World War II; liability insurance and health care costs.

INTERVIEWED BY JAMES E. MCGREEVY, FEBRUARY 5, 1991, BUTTE.

SUMMARY: 3 PAGES

1 TAPE: 1 HOUR

OH 1351
DOLLY BROWDER INTERVIEW

Dolly Browder, Missoula, recounts: her family's attitudes on health care; the distance to the nearest medical facility; early obstetrics; influences on her choice to become a midwife; rural medical care; emergency medical care; legalities associated with midwifery.

INTERVIEWED BY JOHN TERREO, SEPTEMBER 28, 1990, MISSOULA.

3 TAPES: 3 HOURS

OH 1352
STELLA "SUNNY" PETERS INTERVIEW

Lame Deer resident Sunny Peters discusses: her experiences as a nursing student in Miles City during the 1930s; her later work as a registered nurse on the Northern Cheyenne Indian Reservation. [See also Montanans at Work OH 495.]

INTERVIEWED BY JOHN TERREO, AUGUST 6, 1992, LAME DEER.

TRANSCRIPT: 63 PAGES

3 TAPES: 2 HOURS, 30 MINUTES

OH 1428
JIM OLIVERSON INTERVIEW

Jim Oliverson (b. 1938) describes: his decision to enter the health care profession; his work with the Red Cross in Minneapolis, Minnesota; relocating to Montana; his experiences as the hospital administrator for St. Luke's Community Hospital in Ronan; the difficulties that small rural hospitals encounter in conforming to government regulations; liability insurance; the Hill-Burton program, providing federal monies for the construction and remodeling of hospitals.

INTERVIEWED BY JOHN TERREO, SEPTEMBER 27, 1990, KALISPELL.

TRANSCRIPT: 28 PAGES

1 TAPE: 40 MINUTES

OH 1511
MARY MUNGER INTERVIEW

Mary Munger (b. circa 1943) talks about: technological changes in nursing that have affected the American Medical Association and various nursing organizations; labor contract negotiations and collective bargaining; the Northern Pacific Beneficial Association; her work as executive secretary of the Montana Nurses Association; professional standards; legislation; Medicaid and Medicare; the Montana Hospital Association; Charles Huppe, Allen Donahue, Lee Metcalf, Dorothy Bradley, and John Anderson; the American Nurses Association; illegal abortions; her work as a nursing instructor at Carroll College in Helena; her work as Montana chair of the International Women's Year committee. [See also Medicine, Health Care, and Nursing in Montana OH 1349.]

INTERVIEWED BY JOHN TERREO, MAY 13, 1992, HELENA.

TRANSCRIPT: 59 PAGES

2 TAPES: 1 HOUR, 25 MINUTES

Metals Manufacturing in Four Montana Communities Oral History Project

This project examined the metals manufacturing industry and the four Montana communities most directly affected by that industry: Anaconda, Black Eagle, Columbia Falls, and East Helena. Members of these communities share their experiences as merchants, bartenders, union organizers, and families of smelter workers living in towns dominated by metals manufacturing plants. The project was the first in a series designed to explore Montana's industrial heritage and the role of industry in shaping community identity.

OH 903
BRUCE BARRETT INTERVIEW

Bruce Barrett (b. 1951) describes: working for the Anaconda Mining Company's Great Falls Reduction Department from 1969 to 1980; trade union activities; the community of Black Eagle; the impact of that plant's closure on workers' and their families.
INTERVIEWED BY LAURIE MERCIER, FEBRUARY 27, 1986, GREAT FALLS.
SUMMARY: 4 PAGES
1 TAPE: 1 HOUR, 5 MINUTES

OH 904
WILLIAM A. TONKOVICH INTERVIEW

William Tonkovich (b. 1919) depicts: his work for the Anaconda Company's Great Falls Reduction Department from 1938 to 1941 and 1956 to 1980; the ethnic groups (especially the Croatians), neighborhoods, churches, and entertainment in Black Eagle, from 1918 to 1980.
INTERVIEWED BY LAURIE MERCIER, FEBRUARY 27, 1986, GREAT FALLS.
SUMMARY: 5 PAGES
1 TAPE: 1 HOUR

OH 905
LAWRENCE E. TESSMAN INTERVIEW

Lawrence Tessman (b. 1920) discusses: his work for the Anaconda Company's Great Falls Reduction Depart-ment from 1939 to 1980; operations, working conditions, safety, and management at the plant; his participation in the International Union of Mine, Mill and Smelter Work-ers (Mine-Mill); his youth in Great Falls as one of four-teen children; life in the community of Black Eagle.
INTERVIEWED BY LAURIE MERCIER, FEBRUARY 28, 1986, GREAT FALLS.
SUMMARY: 8 PAGES
2 TAPES: 2 HOURS

OH 906
JOHANNA MICHELETTI HAMER AND HOWARD HAMER INTERVIEW

Johanna Hamer (b. 1920) reviews: the Italian com-munity in Black Eagle from the 1920s to the 1980s. Howard Hamer (b. 1922) recounts: his work for the Ana-conda Company's Great Falls Reduction Department from 1950 to 1980; the effects of the plant's closure on workers and on the community.
INTERVIEWED BY LAURIE MERCIER, FEBRUARY 28, 1986, BLACK EAGLE.
SUMMARY: 4 PAGES
1 TAPE: 1 HOUR

OH 907
CLARENCE H. SILLOWAY INTERVIEW

Clarence Silloway (b. 1895) relates: his duties as a timekeeper for the Anaconda Company's Great Falls Reduction Department from 1916 to 1918; his work as

an engineer in the company's electrical shop from 1918 to 1961; innovations he implemented at the plant.
INTERVIEWED BY LAURIE MERCIER, FEBRUARY 15, 1986, GREAT FALLS.
SUMMARY: 8 PAGES
4 TAPES: 3 HOURS, 50 MINUTES

OH 908
MARGARET "PEGGY" CONDON TABARACCI INTERVIEW

Peggy Tabaracci (1922–1987) talks about: the effects of the 1980 Anaconda Company smelter shutdown on Black Eagle; 1981 efforts to obtain the former Anaconda Company clubhouse for the Black Eagle Civic Club; her work at Borrie's Restaurant from the 1950s to the 1970s.
INTERVIEWED BY LAURIE MERCIER, FEBRUARY 27, 1986, BLACK EAGLE.
SUMMARY: 5 PAGES
1 TAPE: 1 HOUR

OH 909
ZAIRA STEFANI LUKES INTERVIEW

Zaira Lukes (b. 1913) reviews: community life in Black Eagle from 1927 to 1986; her work at the local Miami Club; operating the Two Brothers Market.
INTERVIEWED BY LAURIE MERCIER, FEBRUARY 28, 1986, BLACK EAGLE.
SUMMARY: 6 PAGES
1 TAPE: 1 HOUR, 5 MINUTES

OH 910
EMELIA TABARACCI QUNELL INTERVIEW

Emelia Qunell (b. 1921) discusses: growing up in Black Eagle; neighborhood life; the Italian and Croatian communities in Black Eagle; the establishment of the Black Eagle Civic Club; the shutdown of the Anaconda Company's Great Falls Reduction Department; the removal of the company smokestack; the Catholic Church.
INTERVIEWED BY LAURIE MERCIER, FEBRUARY 6, 1986, BLACK EAGLE.
TRANSCRIPT: 19 PAGES
1 TAPE: 50 MINUTES

OH 911
MELVIN A. SHARP INTERVIEW

Melvin Sharp (b. 1933) speaks of: the management of the American Smelting and Refining Company (ASARCO) smelter in East Helena from 1982 to 1986; the plant's employee relations, ore supplies, and marketing; community relations; environmental concerns.

INTERVIEWED BY LAURIE MERCIER, MARCH 10, 1986, EAST HELENA.
SUMMARY: 7 PAGES
2 TAPES: 1 HOUR, 55 MINUTES

OH 912
KENNETH R. ST. CLAIR INTERVIEW

Kenneth St. Clair (b. 1925) describes: his work—as a relief foreman and as a foreman in the blast-furnace department—for the ASARCO smelter in East Helena from 1947 to 1985; his involvement with the East Helena Volunteer Fire Department; his service as mayor of East Helena.
INTERVIEWED BY LAURIE MERCIER, MARCH 5, 1986, EAST HELENA.
SUMMARY: 7 PAGES
2 TAPES: 1 HOUR, 50 MINUTES

OH 913
LYLE PELLETT INTERVIEW

Lyle Pellett (b. 1916) reviews: his work—as a stripper in the zinc plant from 1940 to 1955 and as a safety man in the first-aid department from 1955 to 1980—at the Anaconda Company's Great Falls Reduction Department; his participation in the Mine-Mill union.
INTERVIEWED BY LAURIE MERCIER, MARCH 13, 1986, GREAT FALLS.
SUMMARY: 5 PAGES
2 TAPES: 1 HOUR, 25 MINUTES

OH 914
AMELIA GUZOVICH POLICH INTERVIEW

Amelia Polich (b. 1904) comments on: her family's operation of the Chicago Mercantile in Black Eagle; Croatian traditions; Catholic Church activities; Anaconda Company relations with the Black Eagle community from 1910 to 1980.
INTERVIEWED BY LAURIE MERCIER, MARCH 13, 1986, BLACK EAGLE.
SUMMARY: 7 PAGES
2 TAPES: 1 HOUR, 35 MINUTES

OH 915
CHARLES MICHELETTI INTERVIEW

Charles Micheletti (1907–1987) recounts: his work—as a truck driver in the zinc plant and in the surface department—at the Anaconda Company's Great Falls Reduction Department from the 1920s to 1969; the operation's managers, ethnic groups and unions; the Italian community; Anaconda Company relations with the

community of Black Eagle.
INTERVIEWED BY LAURIE MERCIER, MARCH 13, 1986,
BLACK EAGLE.
SUMMARY: 6 PAGES
2 TAPES: 1 HOUR, 40 MINUTES

OH 916
LORADO MAFFIT INTERVIEW

Lorado Maffit (b. 1916) describes his work in the Anaconda Company's Great Falls Reduction Department from 1937 to 1977.
INTERVIEWED BY LAURIE MERCIER, MARCH 14, 1986,
GREAT FALLS.
SUMMARY: 4 PAGES
1 TAPE: 1 HOUR

OH 917
ERNIE GRASSESCHI INTERVIEW

Ernie Grasseschi (b. 1926) explains: his family's operation of Borrie's Restaurant in Black Eagle from 1938 until 1986; his involvement in the Black Eagle Civic Club; the club's acquisition of the former Anaconda Company clubhouse; the Anaconda Company's relations with the community of Black Eagle.
INTERVIEWED BY LAURIE MERCIER, MARCH 19, 1986,
BLACK EAGLE.
SUMMARY: 6 PAGES
2 TAPES: 1 HOUR, 25 MINUTES

OH 918
DAVID COPP INTERVIEW

David Copp talks about: the operation of the Black Eagle Community Center in Black Eagle from 1984 to 1986; the changes in the Black Eagle community since the shutdown of the Anaconda Company's operation in 1980.
INTERVIEWED BY LAURIE MERCIER, MARCH 19, 1986,
BLACK EAGLE.
SUMMARY: 3 PAGES
1 TAPE: 1 HOUR

OH 919
DAVID JOHN EVANKO INTERVIEW

David Evanko (b. 1945) speaks of: his work in the zinc plant and with a surface crew at the Anaconda Company's Great Falls Reduction Department from 1966 to 1980; strikes; United Steelworkers of America; the impact of the Anaconda Company refinery's closure on the workers; his search for employment after the shutdown.

INTERVIEWED BY LAURIE MERCIER, MARCH 20, 1986,
GREAT FALLS.
SUMMARY: 7 PAGES
2 TAPES: 1 HOUR, 35 MINUTES

OH 920
MYRTLE MOE FAGENSTROM INTERVIEW

Myrtle Fagenstrom (b. 1899) describes: community life in Black Eagle from 1910 to 1921, including among the Swedish and Norwegian communities; the Moe family; working at Matteucci's store from 1916 to 1921.
INTERVIEWED BY LAURIE MERCIER, MARCH 14, 1986,
BLACK EAGLE.
SUMMARY: 6 PAGES
2 TAPES: 1 HOUR, 35 MINUTES

OH 921
BERT KANE INTERVIEW

Bert Kane (b. 1906) reviews: his work as a chemist and a plant manager for the Anaconda Company zinc smelter at East Helena from 1935 to 1970; his work as a youth at the ASARCO smelter; his father's livery and coal businesses in East Helena; community life in East Helena; the Broadwater Natatorium.
INTERVIEWED BY LAURIE MERCIER, MAY 15, 1986, EAST
HELENA.
SUMMARY: 6 PAGES
2 TAPES: 1 HOUR, 50 MINUTES

OH 922
ANN WAGENBACH PETEK INTERVIEW

Ann Petek (b. 1905) summarizes: community life in East Helena from 1923 to the 1980s; relations between ASARCO and the town; her participation in activities at Saints Cyril and Methodius Catholic Church; her work at the East Helena Post Office.
INTERVIEWED BY LAURIE MERCIER, MAY 16, 1986, EAST
HELENA.
SUMMARY: 7 PAGES
2 TAPES: 1 HOUR, 40 MINUTES

OH 923
JEROLD M. HANSEN INTERVIEW

Jerold Hansen (b. 1930)—who worked in the ferromanganese and the masonry departments at the Anaconda Company smelter at Anaconda from 1949 to 1982—depicts: his employment at the smelter; United Steel Workers of America; the Mine-Mill union; management, accidents, strikes, and changes in operations from 1959 until the 1980 shutdown; Anaconda neighborhoods and eth-

nic groups; the Anaconda Historical Society and efforts to preserve historic structures and revitalize the local economy after the shutdown.
INTERVIEWED BY LAURIE MERCIER, MAY 27, 1986, ANACONDA.
SUMMARY: 19 PAGES
5 TAPES: 5 HOURS, 20 MINUTES

OH 924
TOM DICKSON INTERVIEW
Tom Dickson relates: his work at the Anaconda Company smelter in Anaconda from the 1940s to the 1970s; his involvement with the Mine-Mill union; labor-management negotiations; the 1934 and 1954 strikes; the United Steelworkers of America and their eventual takeover of Mine-Mill in 1968; the annual Smelterman's Day festivities; the influence of the Anaconda Company on unionism and on the community; his views on taxation. [See also Montanans at Work OH 216 and General Montana OH 1424.]
INTERVIEWED BY LAURIE MERCIER, MAY 30, 1986, ANACONDA.
SUMMARY: 18 PAGES
3 TAPES: 2 HOURS, 55 MINUTES

OH 925
BOB VINE INTERVIEW
Bob Vine (b. 1925) discusses: his work for the Anaconda Company—particularly as a personnel manager—in Anaconda from 1957 to 1983; United Steelworkers of America; reasons for the plant's closure in 1980; the effects of the closure on the town of Anaconda.
INTERVIEWED BY LAURIE MERCIER, MAY 27 AND 29, 1986, ANACONDA.
TRANSCRIPT: 74 PAGES
2 TAPES: 2 HOURS, 10 MINUTES

OH 926
DONALD H. NYQUIST, JR., INTERVIEW
Donald Nyquist, Jr. (b. 1951), comments on: growing up in Anaconda in the 1960s and early 1970s; his family history; his identification as a "hippie"; his work at the Anaconda Company smelter; relations between the company and the town; the impact of the 1980 shutdown on the community.
INTERVIEWED BY LAURIE MERCIER, MAY 27, 1986, ANACONDA.
SUMMARY: 8 PAGES
2 TAPES: 1 HOUR, 35 MINUTES

OH 927
WILLIAM PORTER INTERVIEW
William Porter (b. 1929) talks of: the history of the American Chemet Company; the move of that company to East Helena in 1946; the zinc-fuming operation; American Chemet's and the local Anaconda Company plant; the establishment of the Columbia Paint Company as a subsidiary; his role in American Chemet since 1957.
INTERVIEWED BY LAURIE MERCIER, JUNE 12, 1986, HELENA/EAST HELENA.
SUMMARY: 7 PAGES
1 TAPE: 1 HOUR, 5 MINUTES

OH 928
ANDREW MacKANICH INTERVIEW
Andrew MacKanich (b. 1907) reviews: community life in East Helena from 1910 to the 1940s; relations between the town and the ASARCO smelter; his employment at the smelter from 1924 to 1927; his career as a teacher in East Helena schools from 1935 to 1942; local baseball.
INTERVIEWED BY LAURIE MERCIER, JUNE 12, 1986, HELENA/EAST HELENA.
SUMMARY: 9 PAGES
2 TAPES: 1 HOUR, 25 MINUTES

OH 929
HERB CARVER INTERVIEW
Herb Carver (b. 1902) speaks of: the operation of the East Pacific Mine near Winston from 1935 to 1950; gold mining; the relationship between the mine and the ASARCO smelter in East Helena; the Mine-Mill union; the challenges facing small, independent miners—particularly regarding labor relations and government regulations.
INTERVIEWED BY LAURIE MERCIER, JUNE 11, 1986, WINSTON.
SUMMARY: 9 PAGES
2 TAPES: 1 HOUR, 25 MINUTES

OH 930
RUDOLPH "POTSY" ANDOLSEK INTERVIEW
Rudolph Andolsek (b. 1912) discusses: his life in East Helena; his work as a laborer, pipefitter, and foreman at the ASARCO smelter in East Helena from 1946 until 1972; United Steelworkers of America; the Mine-Mill union; his Slovene-American background.
INTERVIEWED BY LAURIE MERCIER, JUNE 17, 1986, EAST HELENA.

TRANSCRIPT: 73 PAGES
2 TAPES: 1 HOUR, 40 MINUTES

OH 931
PAUL KLEFFNER INTERVIEW

Paul Kleffner (b. 1916)—owner of the Kleffner Ranch near East Helena—discusses: swine breeding; relations between the ranch and the ASARCO smelter; his participation in East Helena clubs, in community activities, and in Saints Cyril and Methodius Catholic Church.
INTERVIEWED BY LAURIE MERCIER, JULY 10, 1986, EAST HELENA.
SUMMARY: 10 PAGES
2 TAPES: 1 HOUR, 55 MINUTES

OH 932
ANNE PREBIL INTERVIEW

Anne Prebil (b. 1908) reflects on: the Slovenian community and its traditions in East Helena; her work at the ASARCO plant during World War II.
INTERVIEWED BY LAURIE MERCIER, JULY 10, 1986, EAST HELENA.
SUMMARY: 6 PAGES
2 TAPES: 1 HOUR, 25 MINUTES

OH 933
WALTER VALACICH INTERVIEW

Walter Valacich (b. 1911) recounts: his youth in Black Eagle from 1915 to 1930; Croatian heritage and traditions; the influence of the Anaconda Company on Black Eagle and Great Falls; local politics; the Great Falls *Tribune*; the Mine-Mill union.
INTERVIEWED BY LAURIE MERCIER, JULY 17, 1986, GREAT FALLS.
SUMMARY: 12 PAGES
2 TAPES: 1 HOUR, 35 MINUTES

OH 934
EUGENE G. COX INTERVIEW

Eugene Cox depicts: his work as clerk and personnel manager for the Anaconda Company's Great Falls Reduction Department from 1926 to 1971; company managers and management-worker relations; the community of Black Eagle; the Depression; Great Falls politics; the Mine-Mill union; his African-American heritage.
INTERVIEWED BY LAURIE MERCIER, JULY 16, 1986, GREAT FALLS.
SUMMARY: 12 PAGES
2 TAPES: 2 HOURS, 5 MINUTES

OH 935
OLANDA RINARI VANGELISTI AND CLAIRE VANGELISTI DEL GUERRA INTERVIEW

Olanda Vangelisti (b. 1906) and Claire Del Guerra discuss: community life in Black Eagle from the 1920s to the 1980s; Italian heritage and traditions in Black Eagle; the Anaconda Company smelter's role in the community.
INTERVIEWED BY LAURIE MERCIER, JULY 16, 1986, BLACK EAGLE.
SUMMARY: 9 PAGES
2 TAPES: 1 HOUR, 55 MINUTES

OH 936
JOHN LUKE McKEON INTERVIEW

Attorney John McKeon (b. 1925) describes: neighborhoods, ethnic groups, the Catholic Church, and the Anaconda Company in Anaconda from 1930 to 1980; the Communist Party in Montana; his law practice's representation of workers and unions; the Mine-Mill union and the United Steelworkers of America; his terms in the Montana State Senate from 1961 to 1973; the effects of the Anaconda Company smelter's closure.
INTERVIEWED BY LAURIE MERCIER, JULY 29, 1986, ANACONDA.
SUMMARY: 16 PAGES
2 TAPES: 2 HOURS, 5 MINUTES

OH 937
SISTER GILMARY VAUGHAN INTERVIEW

Sister Vaughan (b. 1920) explains: the impact of the Anaconda Company smelter's shutdown on the town of Anaconda; efforts to provide social services in Anaconda; the Irish heritage and traditions of Anaconda; the role of the Catholic Church in the community; the Mine-Mill union.
INTERVIEWED BY LAURIE MERCIER, JULY 30, 1986, ANACONDA.
SUMMARY: 8 PAGES
2 TAPES: 1 HOUR, 30 MINUTES

OH 938
HOWARD ROSENLEAF INTERVIEW

Howard Rosenleaf (b. 1936) tells of: his work as a carpenter at the Anaconda Company smelter in Anaconda from 1955 until 1970; his job as the business agent for the carpenters union in Anaconda from the 1960s into the 1980s; growing up in the community during the 1940s and 1950s; changes in the labor movement after the plant's shutdown in 1980; the United Steelworkers of

America; the United Brotherhood of Carpenters and Joiners of America; the Hotel and Restaurant Employees and Bartenders International Union; his Swedish-American background; operating the King's X Bar from 1964 to 1974.

INTERVIEWED BY LAURIE MERCIER, JULY 29, 1986, ANACONDA.

SUMMARY: 13 PAGES

2 TAPES: 2 HOURS, 10 MINUTES

OH 939
RUDOLPH W. POLICH INTERVIEW

Rudolph Polich (b. 1913) reviews: social life and businesses in Black Eagle from the 1920s to the 1950s; Croatian customs in the community; relations between the Anaconda Company and the community; his participation in several labor strikes; the former company superintendent, Al Wiggin. *[See also Montanans at Work OH 467.]*

INTERVIEWED BY LAURIE MERCIER, FEBRUARY 6, 1986, BLACK EAGLE.

SUMMARY: 5 PAGES

2 TAPES: 1 HOUR, 20 MINUTES

OH 940
KATHRYN WETZEL NEWTON DEWING INTERVIEW

Kathryn Dewing (b. 1923) comments on: living in Anaconda from the 1940s to the 1980s; the Mine-Mill union; Hotel and Restaurant Employees and Bartenders International Union; her work at the Anaconda Company smelter during World War II; her 40-plus years working as a waitress at the Park Cafe.

INTERVIEWED BY LAURIE MERCIER, AUGUST 11, 1986, ANACONDA.

TRANSCRIPT: 64 PAGES

2 TAPES: 1 HOUR, 50 MINUTES

OH 941
RUTH PARRY MEIDL INTERVIEW

Ruth Meidl (b. 1925) depicts: growing up and living in Anaconda; owning and operating—with her husband, Mel Meidl—the Mill Bar in Anaconda from 1964 to 1986.

INTERVIEWED BY LAURIE MERCIER, AUGUST 11, 1986, ANACONDA.

SUMMARY: 4 PAGES

1 TAPE: 55 MINUTES

OH 942
JOSEPH H. SCHWARTZ INTERVIEW

Joseph Schwartz (b. 1899) describes: the operation of Schwartz's department store in Anaconda from 1912 to 1981; his participation in community activities; the changing business climate in Anaconda.

INTERVIEWED BY LAURIE MERCIER, AUGUST 12, 1986, ANACONDA.

SUMMARY: 10 PAGES

2 TAPES: 1 HOUR, 50 MINUTES

OH 943
JOSEPH BOLKOVATZ AND FRANCES BOLKOVATZ INTERVIEWS

Anaconda residents Joseph Bolkovatz (b. 1911) and Frances Bolkovatz (1915–1987) relate: various attitudes toward the Anaconda Company, the Mine-Mill union, leisure-time activities, neighborhoods, and religious life in Anaconda; their survival on a smelter worker's income; the Croatian-American community.

INTERVIEWED BY LAURIE MERCIER, AUGUST 12, 1986, ANACONDA.

SUMMARY: 13 PAGES

2 TAPES: 2 HOURS

OH 944
WALTER L. SCHMITZ INTERVIEW

Walter Schmitz (b. 1928) reflects on: his youth in Anaconda during the 1930s; his summer work for the ASARCO smelter in East Helena during the late 1940s; the work of his father, Walter S. Schmitz, for the Anaconda Company in East Helena.

INTERVIEWED BY LAURIE MERCIER, AUGUST 24, 1986, HELENA.

SUMMARY: 4 PAGES

1 TAPE: 50 MINUTES

OH 945
ROBERT J. KELLY INTERVIEW

Retired Anaconda Company employee Robert Kelly (b. 1919) discusses: his security work for the smelter in Anaconda from 1951 to 1980; his work as a Deer Lodge County deputy sheriff from 1951 to 1954; strikes; the United Steelworkers of America; the Mine-Mill union; law enforcement; community recreation and sports in Anaconda from the 1930s to the 1950s.

INTERVIEWED BY LAURIE MERCIER, OCTOBER 2, 1986, ANACONDA.

SUMMARY: 11 PAGES

2 TAPES: 2 HOURS, 10 MINUTES

OH 946
ERMA ROCKHILL BENNETT INTERVIEW

Erma Bennett (b. 1913) speaks of: her various work experiences in Anaconda from the 1930s to the 1960s; her job at the Anaconda Company smelter during World War II; her struggles as a widow to support her children during the 1940s.

INTERVIEWED BY LAURIE MERCIER, SEPTEMBER 30, 1986, ANACONDA.

TRANSCRIPT: 46 PAGES

2 TAPES: 1 HOUR, 45 MINUTES

OH 947
ARTHUR A. "TINY" LONGFELLOW INTERVIEW

Tiny Longfellow depicts: his operation of the Longfellow-Finnegan Funeral Home in Anaconda from 1933 to 1986; his service as Deer Lodge County coroner from the mid-1930s into the 1970s.

INTERVIEWED BY LAURIE MERCIER, OCTOBER 2, 1986, ANACONDA.

SUMMARY: 7 PAGES

1 TAPE: 1 HOUR, 5 MINUTES

OH 948
FLORA BEAL SULLIVAN INTERVIEW

Flora Sullivan (b. 1898) talks about: Beal family history; her work as a beauty operator in Anaconda from 1929 to 1941; her involvement with the Girl Scouts.

INTERVIEWED BY LAURIE MERCIER, OCTOBER 1, 1986, ANACONDA.

SUMMARY: 4 PAGES

1 TAPE: 1 HOUR, 5 MINUTES

OH 949
ISABEL TRACY McCARTHY INTERVIEW

Isabel McCarthy (b. 1918) describes: her childhood in Anaconda in the 1920s; neighborhoods in the community; St. Peter's Catholic Church; entertainment; raising 12 children in Anaconda; the role of the Anaconda Company smelter in providing employment for townspeople.

INTERVIEWED BY LAURIE MERCIER, OCTOBER 2, 1986, ANACONDA.

SUMMARY: 8 PAGES

2 TAPES: 2 HOURS, 10 MINUTES

OH 950
JOHN B. "JACK" HARRIS INTERVIEW

Jack Harris recounts: his work for the Anaconda Company and for the ASARCO smelters in East Helena from 1946 to 1983; his participation in the Mine-Mill union; his involvement as a union representative in local, state, and national negotiations; the United Steelworkers of America takeover of Mine-Mill (circa 1967); industrial safety; differences between the Anaconda Company and the ASARCO plants. *[General Montana OH 1410.]*

INTERVIEWED BY LAURIE MERCIER, OCTOBER 30, 1986, EAST HELENA.

SUMMARY: 18 PAGES

3 TAPES: 2 HOURS, 40 MINUTES

OH 951
CHARLES DONALD MANSFIELD INTERVIEW

Charles Mansfield (b. 1905) reviews: employment opportunities in the Columbia Falls area from 1920 to 1985; his work for the Great Northern Railway Company and the Plum Creek Lumber Company; the impact of the Anaconda Aluminum Company plant construction on the area's development and environment; his service on the Columbia Falls city council.

INTERVIEWED BY LAURIE MERCIER, NOVEMBER 6, 1986, COLUMBIA FALLS.

SUMMARY: 9 PAGES

2 TAPES: 1 HOUR, 55 MINUTES

OH 952
VICTOR E. CORDIER INTERVIEW

Victor Cordier discusses: his work as a potman, tapper, and truck driver at the Anaconda Aluminum Company plant in Columbia Falls from 1955 to 1985; aluminum-plant processes and safety; the Aluminum Workers Trades Council; local attitudes about the smelter.

INTERVIEWED BY LAURIE MERCIER, NOVEMBER 6, 1986, COLUMBIA FALLS.

SUMMARY: 10 PAGES

2 TAPES: 1 HOUR, 20 MINUTES

OH 953
JUDY BERARDI INTERVIEW

Columbia Falls resident Judy Berardi (b. 1955) relates: her involvement in the "Save the Plant" (or "People for Jobs") organization formed in 1985 to find a buyer for the ARCO aluminum smelter in Columbia Falls; organizing efforts, lobbying, and Bonneville Power Administration hearings; the aluminum plant purchaser, Brad Duker.

INTERVIEWED BY LAURIE MERCIER, NOVEMBER 7, 1987, COLUMBIA FALLS.

SUMMARY: 6 PAGES

1 TAPE: 50 MINUTES

OH 954
EDWARD GARDIPEE INTERVIEW

Edward Gardipee (b. 1937) talks about: the impact of the closure of the Anaconda Company's mining and smelter operations on the families, communities, and opportunities in Butte and Anaconda; working at the company smelter in Anaconda from 1969 to 1980; his involvement in the Anaconda Indian Alliance.

INTERVIEWED BY LAURIE MERCIER, NOVEMBER 20, 1986, BUTTE.

SUMMARY: 7 PAGES

1 TAPE: 1 HOUR, 5 MINUTES

OH 955
KLAAS DE WIT INTERVIEW

Klaas De Wit (b. 1909) talks of: his work as a warehouse manager at the Anaconda Aluminum Company plant in Columbia Falls from 1954 into the 1970s; the local Lions Club; relations between the Anaconda Company and the community of Columbia Falls.

INTERVIEWED BY LAURIE MERCIER, DECEMBER 3, 1986, COLUMBIA FALLS.

SUMMARY: 16 PAGES

1 TAPE: 1 HOUR

OH 956
DWIGHT "DOC" KIMZEY INTERVIEW

Dwight Kimzey of Columbia Falls describes: the construction and initial operation of the Anaconda Aluminum Company plant in 1954–1955; his work as superintendent of the casting plant until 1978; his participation in community activities; relations between the company and the community of Columbia Falls.

INTERVIEWED BY LAURIE MERCIER, DECEMBER 3, 1986, COLUMBIA FALLS.

SUMMARY: 5 PAGES

2 TAPES: 1 HOUR, 20 MINUTES

OH 957
WILLIAM J. DAKIN INTERVIEW

William Dakin (b. 1949) depicts: his life in Columbia Falls since the mid-1950s; the effects of the Anaconda Aluminum Company—later the ARCO—plant on the community.

INTERVIEWED BY LAURIE MERCIER, DECEMBER 4, 1986, CORAM.

TRANSCRIPT: 30 PAGES

2 TAPES: 1 HOUR, 35 MINUTES

OH 958
RUTH L. RENFROW INTERVIEW

Ruth Renfrow comments on: her move to Columbia Falls in 1954; the operation of Renfrow's Cabinet Shop; her participation in Church Women United and other community groups.

INTERVIEWED BY LAURIE MERCIER, DECEMBER 4, 1986, COLUMBIA FALLS.

SUMMARY: 4 PAGES

1 TAPE: 1 HOUR

OH 959
FAY LOVEALL AND BEULAH GRAHAM LOVEALL INTERVIEW

Fay Loveall (b. 1903) reviews: her work for various Columbia Falls businesses; her operation of Fay's Electric Shop from 1953 to 1960. Beulah Loveall (d. 1987) discusses: her work at the electric shop; teaching in Columbia Falls from 1923 to 1927. Together the two women talk about: community life; town personalities; the construction of the Hungry Horse Dam; family history.

INTERVIEWED BY LAURIE MERCIER, DECEMBER 4, 1986, COLUMBIA FALLS.

SUMMARY: 7 PAGES

2 TAPES: 2 HOURS, 10 MINUTES

OH 960
EDWIN O. WOSTER INTERVIEW

Edwin Woster tells of: the initial operations of the Anaconda Aluminum Company smelter in Columbia Falls from 1954 to 1955; aluminum-company management; his recollection of Ed Smith and H. G. Satterthaite; his work as potline superintendent; his employment as plant manager from 1966 to 1979; the company's impact on the community and the environment.

INTERVIEWED BY LAURIE MERCIER, OCTOBER 9, 1986, COLUMBIA FALLS.

SUMMARY: 6 PAGES

2 TAPES: 2 HOURS, 10 MINUTES

OH 961
LESTER A. MERGENTHALER AND JUNE MERGENTHALER INTERVIEW

Lester Mergenthaler (b. 1918) comments on: his work at the ASARCO lime quarry, south of East Helena, from 1944 to 1977; his father's garage business in East Helena; local employment opportunities in the 1930s. June Mergenthaler describes: social life in East Helena; the community's characteristics.

INTERVIEWED BY LAURIE MERCIER, DECEMBER 11, 1986, EAST HELENA.
SUMMARY: 3 PAGES
1 TAPE: 1 HOUR, 5 MINUTES

OH 962
DAVID FOSTER INTERVIEW

David Foster (b. 1936) reviews: the major issues that he faced as mayor of East Helena from 1961 to 1979; the effects of the ASARCO smelter on the community; East Helena's ethnic traditions; baseball and other community entertainments; Saints Cyril and Methodius Catholic Church.
INTERVIEWED BY LAURIE MERCIER, DECEMBER, 19, 1986, EAST HELENA.
SUMMARY: 8 PAGES
2 TAPES: 1 HOUR, 55 MINUTES

OH 963
ELLEN M. KLOKER INTERVIEW

Ellen Kloker (b. circa 1948) explains: her work as a secretary, switchboard operator, and supply clerk for the Anaconda Company smelter at Anaconda from 1967 to 1982; the impact of the smelter's shutdown on the community.
INTERVIEWED BY LAURIE MERCIER, FEBRUARY 28, 1987, ANACONDA.
SUMMARY: 9 PAGES
2 TAPES: 1 HOUR, 20 MINUTES

OH 964
PAUL L. LATRAY INTERVIEW

Paul Latray (b. 1917) discusses: his work as a crane operator at the Anaconda Company smelter in Anaconda from 1950 to 1981; participating in the Anaconda Indian Alliance from the 1960s through the 1980s.
INTERVIEWED BY LAURIE MERCIER, FEBRUARY 25, 1987, ANACONDA.
SUMMARY: 4 PAGES
1 TAPE: 1 HOUR, 5 MINUTES

OH 965
VIRGINIA SCHEET INTERVIEW

East Helena resident Virginia Scheet reviews: relations between the ASARCO smelter and the community from 1956 to 1986; her involvement with the East Helena Improvement Association; the local acceptance of smelter effluents.
INTERVIEWED BY LAURIE MERCIER, APRIL 21, 1987, EAST HELENA.

SUMMARY: 4 PAGES
1 TAPE: 45 MINUTES

OH 966
CAROLYN CRISLER INTERVIEW

Carolyn Crisler (b. 1950) speaks of: her operation of the Anaconda Indian Alliance from 1977 to 1986; specific alliance programs she promoted; her work as a secretary at the Anaconda Company smelter from 1974 to 1975.
INTERVIEWED BY LAURIE MERCIER, MARCH 16, 1987, ANACONDA.
SUMMARY: 5 PAGES
1 TAPE: 40 MINUTES

OH 967
JENNIE RANIERI SIGNORI INTERVIEW

Jennie Signori (b. 1897) recounts: her family's operation of Ranieri's General Mercantile store and boarding house in Black Eagle from 1909 to 1918; Italian traditions, foods, and fraternal lodges in Black Eagle.
INTERVIEWED BY LAURIE MERCIER, APRIL 23, 1987, SPOKANE.
SUMMARY: 7 PAGES
2 TAPES: 1 HOUR, 45 MINUTES

OH 968
MARIE "COOKIE" PALAGI GODLEWSKI INTERVIEW

Marie Godlewski (b. 1918) discusses community life, ethnic traditions, and church activities in Black Eagle from the 1920s to the 1950s.
INTERVIEWED BY LAURIE MERCIER, MAY 7, 1987, BLACK EAGLE.
SUMMARY: 4 PAGES
1 TAPE: 1 HOUR, 5 MINUTES

OH 969
ANN WASHATKO INTERVIEW

Ann Washatko speaks of: her life in Columbia Falls; her work for the "People for Jobs" organization, attempting to prevent the closure of the Anaconda Aluminum Company plant in the mid-1980s.
INTERVIEWED BY LAURIE MERCIER, JUNE 11, 1987, COLUMBIA FALLS.
SUMMARY: 3 PAGES
1 TAPE: 35 MINUTES

OH 970
CURTIS O. PETERSON INTERVIEW

Curtis Peterson tells about: his work for the Anaconda Aluminum Company plant in Columbia Falls from 1961 to 1986; his participation in the Aluminum, Brick, and Glass Workers' International Union and in the Aluminum Workers Trades Council; differences in management styles between the Anaconda Company and ARCO; the Columbia Falls Aluminum Company purchase of the aluminum plant in 1986.

INTERVIEWED BY LAURIE MERCIER, JUNE 11, 1987, COLUMBIA FALLS.

SUMMARY: 7 PAGES

1 TAPE: 1 HOUR, 5 MINUTES

OH 971
STANLEY M. LANE INTERVIEW

Stanley Lane depicts: his work as a metallurgist and plant superintendent for ASARCO smelter in East Helena from 1935 to 1978; technological changes in plant operations during that period; workers' priorities; labor-management negotiations; environmental concerns; Joe Roy; United Steelworkers of America; the Mine-Mill union.

INTERVIEWED BY LAURIE MERCIER, SEPTEMBER 22, 1987, HELENA.

SUMMARY: 8 PAGES

2 TAPES: 1 HOUR, 35 MINUTES

OH 972
WILLIAM P. HRELLA INTERVIEW

William Hrella discusses: the history and operation of Hrella's Grocery and Meat Market in East Helena from 1889 to 1987; his grocery-trade training; his participation in community activities; the character of the East Helena community; Croatian-American traditions.

INTERVIEWED BY LAURIE MERCIER, SEPTEMBER 24, 1987, EAST HELENA.

SUMMARY: 5 PAGES

1 TAPE: 45 MINUTES

OH 973
ETHEL HOGFOSS BYBERG INTERVIEW

Ethel Byberg reviews: community life in East Helena from the 1940s into the 1960s; her husband, Wesley Byberg; Norwegian-American traditions.

INTERVIEWED BY LAURIE MERCIER, DECEMBER 7, 1987, HELENA.

SUMMARY: 4 PAGES

1 TAPE: 45 MINUTES

OH 974
ANNA MAE NOVIS MILES INTERVIEW

Anna Miles (b. 1922) describes: her parents' immigration from Yugoslavia; growing up in Anaconda in the late 1920s and the 1930s; her work as a switchboard operator at the Anaconda Company smelter during World War II; Ann Lescantz Novis'(Anna's mother) work as a smelter worker during World War II.

INTERVIEWED BY LAURIE MERCIER, DECEMBER 7, 1987, ANACONDA.

TRANSCRIPT: 27 PAGES

1 TAPE: 45 MINUTES

OH 975
URSULA KABLIN JURICH INTERVIEW

Ursula Jurich (b. 1900) speaks of: family ownership and operation of Jurich's Grocery Store in Anaconda from 1926 to 1943; her work at the local Anaconda Company smelter during World War II and at Anaconda department stores.

INTERVIEWED BY LAURIE MERCIER, JANUARY 8, 1988, ANACONDA.

SUMMARY: 7 PAGES

2 TAPES: 2 HOURS, 15 MINUTES

OH 976
MARGARET ANDERSON INTERVIEW

Great Falls resident Margaret Anderson talks about: her Norwegian heritage; a neighborhood on the north side of Great Falls early in the twentieth century.

INTERVIEWED BY CLARA B. HEFFERN, SEPTEMBER 8, 1986, GREAT FALLS.

SUMMARY: 2 PAGES

2 TAPES: 1 HOUR, 20 MINUTES

OH 977
JOAN BROZICEVICH EARL INTERVIEW

Joan Earl (b. 1934) discusses: church activities and local businesses in Black Eagle during the 1940s and 1950s; women's work; ethnic traditions and various neighborhoods in the community.

INTERVIEWED BY LAURIE MERCIER, JANUARY 19, 1988, BLACK EAGLE.

SUMMARY: 5 PAGES

1 TAPE: 1 HOUR

OH 978
DOROTHY MORAN ANDERSON INTERVIEW

Dorothy Anderson (b. 1907) relates: her family history; growing up in Sun River circa 1910–1930; farm-

ing in Teton County in the 1930s; her work at the Anaconda Company's Great Falls Reduction Department during World War II.
INTERVIEWED BY LAURIE MERCIER, JANUARY 19, 1988, GREAT FALLS.
SUMMARY: 6 PAGES
2 TAPES: 1 HOUR, 55 MINUTES

OH 979
MURIEL VERRILL ROSSBERG INTERVIEW

Muriel Rossberg recounts her experiences as a mail carrier at the Anaconda Company's Great Falls Reduction Department during World War II.
INTERVIEWED BY LAURIE MERCIER, JANUARY 18, 1988, GREAT FALLS.
SUMMARY: 3 PAGES
1 TAPE: 35 MINUTES

OH 980
ROBERT ROSSBERG INTERVIEW

Robert Rossberg (b. 1923) talks about his work as a machinist at the Anaconda Company's Great Falls Reduction Department from 1942 to 1980; the International Association of Machinists and Aerospace Workers; trade unionism.
INTERVIEWED BY LAURIE MERCIER, JANUARY 18, 1988, GREAT FALLS.
SUMMARY: 6 PAGES
1 TAPE: 1 HOUR

OH 981
EARL L. LENCI AND CHARLENE KRAULICH LENCI INTERVIEW

Earl Lenci (b. 1933) and Charlene Lenci (b. 1935) comment on: their childhoods in Black Eagle during the 1940s; their operation of Earl's Bar in Black Eagle since 1958.
INTERVIEWED BY LAURIE MERCIER, JANUARY 19, 1988, GREAT FALLS.
TRANSCRIPT: 47 PAGES
2 TAPES: 1 HOUR, 15 MINUTES

OH 982
SAM RYAN INTERVIEW

Sam Ryan (b. 1916) tells of: his work at the Anaconda Company and the ASARCO smelters in East Helena from 1942 to 1972; his involvement in the Mine-Mill union; United Steelworkers of America; the union's statewide negotiations; local grievances; the declining influence of labor in Montana. *[See also General Mon-*

tana OH 1419.]
INTERVIEWED BY LAURIE MERCIER, DECEMBER 26, 1986, HELENA.
SUMMARY: 9 PAGES
2 TAPES: 2 HOURS, 10 MINUTES

OH 983
JAMES R. REARDON INTERVIEW

James Reardon (b. 1955)—a member and officer of the United Steelworkers of America, Local 72—reports on: his youth in East Helena during the 1960s; his work at the ASARCO smelter in East Helena from 1975 through 1988; strikes; his union participation, including various official positions held.
INTERVIEWED BY LAURIE MERCIER, JULY 29, 1988, EAST HELENA.
SUMMARY: 8 PAGES
2 TAPES: 2 HOURS

OH 984
LEAH LONA PLUMLEE ALBRIGHT INTERVIEW

Leah Albright (b. circa 1919) depicts her work as a chemist at the ASARCO smelter in East Helena from 1943 until her retirement in 1984.
INTERVIEWED BY LAURIE MERCIER, JULY 27, 1988, HELENA.
SUMMARY: 4 PAGES
1 TAPE: 1 HOUR

OH 985
ETHEL FLEURY SCHEET INTERVIEW

Ethel Scheet (b. 1944) discusses: living in East Helena from 1958 to 1988; her involvement with the East Helena School Board from 1976 to 1985; her work with the East Helena Historic Preservation Society in its attempt to save the Saints Cyril and Methodius Catholic Church.
INTERVIEWED BY LAURIE MERCIER, AUGUST 17, 1988, EAST HELENA.
SUMMARY: 5 PAGES
2 TAPES: 1 HOUR, 20 MINUTES

Montanans at Work Oral History Project

Statewide in scope, this oral history project was the first implemented by the Montana Historical Society. Nearly 400 interviews were conducted with Montanans who lived and worked in the state from 1910 to 1945. The project focused on three major occupational areas that dominated Montana's economy during this period: mining, agriculture, and forest products. Interviews conducted with people in auxiliary occupations—including merchants, logging camp cooks, teachers, cattle buyers, and railroad workers—augment the recollections of sheepherders, ranch wives, miners, and sawyers. This collection reveals the interplay between livelihood and family life, the formation of public and private identities, and the impact of occupation on definitions of community.

OH 183
KATE LADNER INTERVIEW

Kate Ladner (b. 1886) discusses: homesteading and sheep ranching in Teton County; German immigration to Montana in the 1890s; the processing and marketing of wool; her girlhood experiences on a sheep ranch near Choteau.
INTERVIEWED BY LAURIE MERCIER, AUGUST 6, 1981, POLSON.
SUMMARY: 2 PAGES
1 TAPE: 1 HOUR

OH 184
MAURICE CUSICK INTERVIEW

Maurice Cusick (b. 1909) depicts: logging and timber management in Flathead County; his job as a check-scaler for the Diamond Match Company; his work as a fire warden and a ranger for the U.S. Forest Service; the American Timber Company in Olney; his involvement with the Civilian Conservation Corps (CCC); lumber mills; Christmas tree production.
INTERVIEWED BY LAURIE MERCIER, AUGUST 7, 1981, WHITEFISH.
SUMMARY: 4 PAGES
2 TAPES: 1 HOUR, 45 MINUTES

OH 185
FRED METCALF INTERVIEW

Fred Metcalf (b. 1893) describes: working on, and supervising, logging and timber-scaling jobs in Flathead County for the Montana State Forester and for the U.S. Forest Service; his experiences with the CCC.
INTERVIEWED BY LAURIE MERCIER, AUGUST 8, 1981, KALISPELL.
SUMMARY: 6 PAGES
2 TAPES: 1 HOUR, 45 MINUTES

OH 186
CLINTON G. STRANAHAN INTERVIEW

Clinton Stranahan (b. 1896) discusses: his father Ferrand Stranahan's career as an attorney; life in Fort Benton; the impact of homesteading on the area; steamboating on the Missouri River; farming and livestock ranching; the Depression; the Milner Cattle Company; World War II.
INTERVIEWED BY LAURIE MERCIER, SEPTEMBER 1, 1981, FORT BENTON.
SUMMARY: 4 PAGES
3 TAPES: 2 HOURS, 25 MINUTES

OH 187
LURA GESSAMAN INTERVIEW

Lura Gessaman recalls: homesteading in the Egly area; teaching in rural schools; the destructive impact of insects on farming; agricultural methods employed by early farmers; the use of farm machinery.
INTERVIEWED BY LAURIE MERCIER, SEPTEMBER 1, 1981, FORT BENTON.

TRANSCRIPT: 6 PAGES
SUMMARY: 3 PAGES
2 TAPES: 1 HOUR, 40 MINUTES

OH 188
ZOYD MONEY INTERVIEW

Zoyd Money (b. 1890) speaks of: homesteading in the Geraldine area; his job as a drummer in various dance and circus bands; dry farming.

INTERVIEWED BY LAURIE MERCIER, SEPTEMBER 2, 1981, FORT BENTON.
SUMMARY: 4 PAGES
1 TAPE: 1 HOUR

OH 189
VINA STIRLING INTERVIEW

Vina Stirling (b. 1892) reflects on: her childhood on a farm near Havre, in Hill County; domestic jobs; homesteading; raising her family; ranching.

INTERVIEWED BY LAURIE MERCIER, SEPTEMBER 3, 1981, HAVRE.
SUMMARY: 3 PAGES
2 TAPES: 1 HOUR, 55 MINUTES

OH 190
STEVE BOYCE INTERVIEW

Havre resident Steve Boyce discusses: his experiences trapping wolves for the U.S. government; cattle ranching in Hill County; cowboys; roundups; trail-herding, shipping, and marketing cattle.

INTERVIEWED BY LAURIE MERCIER, SEPTEMBER 3, 1981, HAVRE.
SUMMARY: 4 PAGES
2 TAPES: 1 HOUR, 30 MINUTES

OH 191
STEVE V. FROHLICHER INTERVIEW

Steve Frohlicher (b. 1906) relates: his experiences of the lumber-industry operations in Flathead County; his work as a fire lookout for the U.S. Forest Service in the 1920s.

INTERVIEWED BY LAURIE MERCIER, SEPTEMBER 4, 1981, GREAT FALLS.
SUMMARY: 3 PAGES
2 TAPES: 1 HOUR, 40 MINUTES

OH 192
WILLIAM J. KILLORN AND NINA M. KILLORN INTERVIEW

William Killorn and Nina Killorn—residents of Livingston—remember: the farming and ranching backgrounds of their respective families; their automobile and tractor business in the 1940s.

INTERVIEWED BY LAURIE MERCIER, SEPTEMBER 18, 1981, LIVINGSTON.
SUMMARY: 4 PAGES
2 TAPES: 1 HOUR, 50 MINUTES

OH 193
OPAL G. MAXEY INTERVIEW

Opal Maxey (1886–1982) reviews: her childhood in Livingston; her courtship and marriage to Dave Maxey; the Maxey family coal mine in Park County; her years teaching school; ranching; farming; cooking for threshing crews and for government-sponsored school programs.

INTERVIEWED BY LAURIE MERCIER, SEPTEMBER 21, 1981, LIVINGSTON.
SUMMARY: 11 PAGES
2 TAPES: 2 HOURS

OH 194
AL OLSON INTERVIEW

Al Olson (b. 1885) talks about: Cokedale; the local coal mines; cattle ranching on his father's land; his job as a brakeman for the Northern Pacific Railroad.

INTERVIEWED BY LAURIE MERCIER, SEPTEMBER 21, 1981, LIVINGSTON.
TRANSCRIPT: 43 PAGES
3 TAPES: 2 HOURS, 20 MINUTES

OH 195
KRISTINA FALLAN INTERVIEW

Kristina Fallan (1890–1987) tells of: her emigration from Norway; acquiring a homestead at age 21; ranching; wheat and flax farming; marrying Ole Fallan; her feelings of patriotism.

INTERVIEWED BY LAURIE MERCIER, SEPTEMBER 22, 1981, LIVINGSTON.
SUMMARY: 7 PAGES
3 TAPES: 2 HOURS, 30 MINUTES

OH 196
HELEN SHUTE RAYMOND INTERVIEW

Helen Raymond (b. 1899) remembers: bootlegging in Butte during the 1920s; operating the Ruby Hotel and a chicken-dinner house in Sheridan in 1927; managing the Barkell Hot Springs in Silver Star in the early 1930s; running The Tavern and several mines in Virginia City from 1934 until 1946.

Interviewed by Laurie Mercier, October 9, 1981, Butte.
Summary: 4 pages
2 tapes: 1 hour, 45 minutes

OH 197
BRIAN O'CONNELL INTERVIEW

Brian O'Connell (1896–1983) describes: cattle and sheep buying; speculation in meat-packing plants; his cattle business based in Helena, in Lewis and Clark County; his involvement with the Montana Stockgrowers Association.
Interviewed by Laurie Mercier, January 26 and 28, 1981, Helena.
Transcript: 113 pages
4 tapes: 3 hours, 55 minutes

OH 198
TOM J. MacWILLIAMS INTERVIEW

Billings resident Tom MacWilliams (b. 1884) recalls: his boyhood experiences working on a ranch; his employment as a cowboy; the Swan Land Cattle Company; his career as a fireman and engineer with the Great Northern Railway.
Interviewed by Laurie Mercier, October 22, 1981, Billings.
Summary: 4 pages
2 tapes: 2 hours

OH 199
W. J. "RED" KILLEN INTERVIEW

Red Killen—a Miles City–area sheep rancher—discusses: his migration to Montana from Ireland, by way of Canada, in 1923; his sheep-ranching work, including herding, lambing, shearing, and selling wool; training sheep dogs.
Interviewed by Laurie Mercier, October 23, 1981, Miles City.
Summary: 5 pages
3 tapes: 2 hours, 50 minutes

OH 200
CHARLES MAHONEY INTERVIEW

Charles Mahoney (b. 1906) reviews: the history of Garfield County; homesteaders; ranchers and ranching; sheepherding; his political career as state representative (1937–1943) and state senator (1949–1959).
Interviewed by Laurie Mercier, October 24, 1981, Miles City.

Summary: 3 pages
2 tapes: 2 hours

OH 201
AUGUST SOBOTKA INTERVIEW

August Sobotka (b. 1911) speaks of: the history of several small towns in eastern Montana—including Burns, Savage, Crane, Fairview, Sidney, and Stipek; wheat farming; ranching; his family's coal mines; German immigration to the Yellowstone Valley; the impact of the Lower Yellowstone Irrigation Project on the area.
Interviewed by Laurie Mercier, October 24, 1981, Glendive.
Summary: 3 pages
2 tapes: 1 hour, 50 minutes

OH 202
JOE CRISAFULLI INTERVIEW

Joe Crisafulli recalls: his father's grocery store in Glendive; area farming; the local Italian community.
Interviewed by Laurie Mercier, October 24, 1981, Glendive.
Summary: 1 page
1 tape: 1 hour

OH 203
JOHN KUBESH INTERVIEW

Glendive resident John Kubesh (b. 1918) describes: homesteading; cattle and sheep ranching; the history of Glendive; his boyhood chores on the farm; schooling hardships; the 1930s Depression and its impact on dry land farmers.
Interviewed by Laurie Mercier, October 25, 1981, Glendive.
Summary: 3 pages
2 tapes: 1 hour, 20 minutes

OH 204
ANNA FLETCHER INTERVIEW

Anna Fletcher (b. 1911) reviews: growing up on a farm near Glendive; her education; teaching in rural schools in eastern Montana; her job in a Spokane, Washington, factory during World War II; her duties as county superintendent of schools; cattle ranching in Dawson County.
Interviewed by Laurie Mercier, October 26, 1981, Intake.
Summary: 7 pages
2 tapes: 1 hour, 30 minutes

OH 205
EDNA PATTERSON INTERVIEW

Edna Patterson (1901–1983) talks of: homesteading in Dawson County; teaching; working odd jobs; her marriage to Byard Patterson; her husband's auto-body shop; living in Intake; operating the first motel in Glendive.

INTERVIEWED BY LAURIE MERCIER, OCTOBER 26 AND 29, 1981, GLENDIVE.
SUMMARY: 9 PAGES
6 TAPES: 6 HOURS

OH 206
EZRA MILLER AND DAN MILLER INTERVIEW

Ezra Miller (b. 1904) and Dan Miller (b. 1903) reflect on: their arrival in the Bloomfield area; farming; ranching; relations with the general Dawson County community, 1910–1920; World War I experiences; changes in farming methods; attitudes of the community towards Mennonites.

INTERVIEWED BY LAURIE MERCIER, OCTOBER 27, 1981, BLOOMFIELD.
SUMMARY: 3 PAGES
2 TAPES: 1 HOUR, 50 MINUTES

OH 207
VERNA McKEAN CARLSON INTERVIEW

Verna Carlson (b. 1895) depicts: her childhood; moving with her family to McCone County; farming; ranching; her involvement with the Montana Farmers Union; the use of wind chargers before Rural Electrification Administration (REA) power arrived; the growth and development of McCone County.

INTERVIEWED BY LAURIE MERCIER, OCTOBER 27, 1981, CIRCLE.
SUMMARY: 7 PAGES
3 TAPES: 2 HOURS, 55 MINUTES

OH 208
HOBART McKEAN INTERVIEW

Hobart McKean (b. 1896) remembers: dry farming; horse ranching; teaching in rural schools in McCone County; the Socialist movement in the United States; the Industrial Workers of the World (IWW).

INTERVIEWED BY LAURIE MERCIER, OCTOBER 28, 1981, CIRCLE.
SUMMARY: 8 PAGES
2 TAPES: 2 HOURS

OH 209
MARY STEPHENSON INTERVIEW

Mary Stephenson (b. 1891) tells of: homesteading with her husband in McCone County in 1910; the history of Redwater; sheep ranching with her son Sowler Stephenson during the 1930s and 1940s.

INTERVIEWED BY LAURIE MERCIER, OCTOBER 29, 1981, CIRCLE.
TRANSCRIPT: 40 PAGES
2 TAPES: 2 HOURS

OH 210
VIRGINIA JOHNSON INTERVIEW

Virginia Johnson (b. 1910) comments on: logging operations in Missoula County; operation of the Double Arrow Dude Ranch near Seeley Lake.

INTERVIEWED BY LAURIE MERCIER, NOVEMBER 12, 1981, MISSOULA.
SUMMARY: 3 PAGES
2 TAPES: 1 HOUR, 30 MINUTES

OH 211
LORENZ WUSTNER INTERVIEW

Lorenz Wustner (b. 1904) portrays: the butcher trade; work in various butcher shops from Minnesota to Montana, including Glendive; kosher butchering and meat-cutting; the effects of farming trends on the butcher trade; the meat-cutting industry during the 1930s Depression and during World War II.

INTERVIEWED BY LAURIE MERCIER, NOVEMBER 12, 1981, MISSOULA.
SUMMARY: 3 PAGES
2 TAPES: 2 HOURS

OH 212
DON MacKENZIE INTERVIEW

Don MacKenzie (b. 1887) reviews: his work as supervisor of logging operations for the Anaconda Company in the Blackfoot River Valley of western Montana; the development of the logging industry in Montana; the effects on the industry brought by the 1930s Depression and by two world wars.

INTERVIEWED BY LAURIE MERCIER, NOVEMBER 13, 1981, MISSOULA.
TRANSCRIPT: 63 PAGES
2 TAPES: 2 HOURS

OH 213
BESSIE TOWEY MULHERN INTERVIEW

Bessie Mulhern (b. 1902) discusses: emigrating from

Ireland; managing the Towey Hotel in Butte; living in Butte during and after World War II.
INTERVIEWED BY LAURIE MERCIER, NOVEMBER 23, 1981, BUTTE.
SUMMARY: 3 PAGES
2 TAPES: 1 HOUR, 40 MINUTES

OH 214
JOHN PHILLIP INTERVIEW
John Phillip (b. 1910) speaks about: his work as a laborer and carpenter at the Anaconda Company's smelter in Anaconda from 1928 to 1972; union activity; job conditions; construction industry changes that affected the carpentry trade.
INTERVIEWED BY LAURIE MERCIER, NOVEMBER 24, 1981, ANACONDA.
TRANSCRIPT: 100 PAGES
2 TAPES: 2 HOURS

OH 215
ROY ROSENLEAF INTERVIEW
Roy Rosenleaf (b. 1908) talks of: his work as a carpenter for the Anaconda Company during the 1920s and 1930s; his involvement in the Carpenters Union; the construction industry.
INTERVIEWED BY LAURIE MERCIER, NOVEMBER 24, 1981, ANACONDA.
SUMMARY: 2 PAGES
2 TAPES: 1 HOUR, 20 MINUTES

OH 216
TOM DICKSON INTERVIEW
Tom Dickson (b. 1908) explains: his work as an Anaconda Company smelterman in Anaconda from the 1930s into the 1950s; his involvement in the Mine-Mill union; general union activity; the processing of ore. *[See also Metals Manufacturing in Four Montana Communities OH 924 and General Montana OH 1424.]*
INTERVIEWED BY LAURIE MERCIER, NOVEMBER 25, 1981, ANACONDA.
TRANSCRIPT: 56 PAGES
3 TAPES: 2 HOURS

OH 217
MORDY JOHNSON INTERVIEW
Kalispell resident Mordy Johnson (b. 1905) reflects on: his work as a cook at several Anaconda Company lumber operations in the 1920s and early 1930s; privately owned cafes; his own restaurant in Kalispell.

INTERVIEWED BY LAURIE MERCIER, DECEMBER 1, 1981, KALISPELL.
SUMMARY: 3 PAGES
2 TAPES: 1 HOUR, 45 MINUTES

OH 218
EDIE BENNETT INTERVIEW
Edie Bennett (b. 1899) discusses: her childhood in Somers; her 13-year employment as that town's postmistress; her observations of the Somers community.
INTERVIEWED BY LAURIE MERCIER, DECEMBER 2, 1981, SOMERS.
SUMMARY: 2 PAGES
2 TAPES: 1 HOUR, 20 MINUTES

OH 219
WILLIS MARCH INTERVIEW
Willis March (b. 1896) recalls: his involvement with the Enterprise Lumber Company, Flathead County, western Montana; his management of sawmills on the family's property south of Kila during the 1920s.
INTERVIEWED BY LAURIE MERCIER, DECEMBER 2, 1981, KALISPELL.
SUMMARY: 2 PAGES
2 TAPES: 1 HOUR, 55 MINUTES

OH 220
TOM BENNETT INTERVIEW
Tom Bennett (b. 1894)—a Somers resident—speaks of his work bucking ties at the Somers Tie Yard and treating ties at the Somers Tie Plant.
INTERVIEWED BY LAURIE MERCIER, DECEMBER 3, 1981, SOMERS.
SUMMARY: 2 PAGES
2 TAPES: 1 HOUR, 20 MINUTES

OH 221
HOKEN LINRUDE INTERVIEW
Hoken Linrude (b. 1895) tells of: his emigration from Norway, circa 1911; his acquisition and sale of a homestead near Dutton; the Somers Lumber, Kalispell Lumber, and Eureka Lumber companies; labor relations in the 1920s and 1930s.
INTERVIEWED BY LAURIE MERCIER, DECEMBER 4, 1981, KALISPELL.
SUMMARY: 3 PAGES
2 TAPES: 1 HOUR, 30 MINUTES

OH 222
WILLIAM TWEEDIE INTERVIEW
    Bill Tweedie (b. 1902) talks about: coal mining in Bearcreek and Stockett; his work as foreman at the Giffin Mine in Stockett; the Smith Mine disaster, 1943, and accidents at the Washoe Mine.
INTERVIEWED BY LAURIE MERCIER, DECEMBER 14, 1981, KALISPELL.
SUMMARY: 3 PAGES
2 TAPES: 2 HOURS

OH 223
ROSS J. MacDONALD INTERVIEW
    Ross MacDonald reviews: his experiences as a cowboy; homesteading and ranching in Teton County from 1910 until the 1950s; local ethnic communities; the town of Brady.
INTERVIEWED BY LAURIE MERCIER, DECEMBER 14, 1981, GREAT FALLS.
SUMMARY: 4 PAGES
3 TAPES: 2 HOURS

OH 224
JANE PHILLIPS INTERVIEW
    Jane Phillips (1888–1987) remembers: the history of Elkhorn; her emigration from England and her arrival in Helena; dressmaking; the creation and operation of Phillips Dairy.
INTERVIEWED BY LAURIE MERCIER, JANUARY 11, 1982, HELENA.
SUMMARY: 3 PAGES
2 TAPES: 2 HOURS

OH 225
HERBERT A. MICKELSON INTERVIEW
    Herbert Mickelson (b. 1912) relates: his work as a miner for the Anaconda Company in Butte; working conditions in the mines; his injury in a mine accident; obtaining compensation; the light work he performed after the accident.
INTERVIEWED BY LAURIE MERCIER, JANUARY 12, 1982, HELENA.
SUMMARY: 3 PAGES
2 TAPES: 1 HOUR, 30 MINUTES

OH 226
JULIAN TERRETT INTERVIEW
    Julian Terrett (b. 1921) discusses: his family's cattle-ranching operations in the Tongue River Valley, Custer County; the arrival of homesteaders; the Montana Stockgrowers Association; the Taylor Grazing Act; the cattle business.
INTERVIEWED BY LAURIE MERCIER, JANUARY 14, 1982, HELENA.
SUMMARY: 3 PAGES
2 TAPES: 2 HOURS

OH 227
MABEL TAYLOR BALLANTYNE INTERVIEW
    Mabel Ballantyne (1880–1983) reflects on: her arrival in Montana; settling on a homestead near Rudyard in Hill County; the family's move to a ranch near Bozeman in Gallatin County.
INTERVIEWED BY LAURIE MERCIER, JANUARY 18, 1982, HELENA.
SUMMARY: 3 PAGES
1 TAPE: 1 HOUR

OH 228
KARL WESTERMARK INTERVIEW
    Karl Westermark (b. 1890) recounts: his childhood in Sweden; his immigration to Parshall, North Dakota; his arrival in the Oilmont/Kevin area during the 1920s; acquiring his farm south of Shelby, in Toole County, in the 1940s; his work as a machinist.
INTERVIEWED BY VICTORIA WESTERMARK (KARL WESTERMARK'S GRANDDAUGHTER), NOVEMBER 25-26, 1981, SHELBY.
TRANSCRIPT: 47 PAGES
2 TAPES: 3 HOURS

OH 229
FAYE ANDERSON INTERVIEW
    Faye Anderson (b. 1904) recalls: her education and teaching experiences in Bearcreek and Billings; the effects of severe economic times on children.
INTERVIEWED BY MARY MELCHER, JANUARY 5, 1982, BOZEMAN.
SUMMARY: 5 PAGES
2 TAPES: 1 HOUR, 30 MINUTES

OH 230
RITA LaVOIE INTERVIEW
    Rita LaVoie (b. 1905) tells of: her childhood in Milltown, circa 1910–1920; her work as a young housewife and mother in the 1920s; the ethnic groups in Milltown; the impact of national social movements and world events on that community.
INTERVIEWED BY MARY MELCHER, DECEMBER 19, 1981, MISSOULA.

SUMMARY: 5 PAGES

2 TAPES: 1 HOUR, 45 MINUTES

OH 231
REVEREND MARY WESSEL INTERVIEW

The Rev. Mary Wessel (b. 1882) discusses: her marriage to Louie Wessel; her husband's job mapping the Belt and Castle mountains for the U.S. Forest Service; her organization of Unity Church ministries in Butte, Bozeman, Billings, and Livingston.

INTERVIEWED BY MARY MELCHER, JANUARY 5, 1982, BOZEMAN.

SUMMARY: 5 PAGES

2 TAPES: 1 HOUR, 15 MINUTES

OH 232
ANNE NEEDHAM INTERVIEW

Anne Needham (b. 1902) details: her education in Missoula and Winnett schools; her work as a journalist; her college and teaching experiences; organizing the Parent-Teachers Association (PTA) in Great Falls; her husband's job as a safety inspector for the Anaconda Company.

INTERVIEWED BY MARY MELCHER, DECEMBER 1, 1981, ANACONDA.

SUMMARY: 4 PAGES

2 TAPES: 1 HOUR, 20 MINUTES

OH 233
LYLE HAIGHT INTERVIEW

Lyle Haight (b. 1914) describes: his childhood years on a homestead between Suffolk and Winifred; his work as a U.S. Weather Bureau employee throughout Montana during the early 1940s.

INTERVIEWED BY LAURIE MERCIER, JANUARY 29, 1982, HELENA.

SUMMARY: 3 PAGES

2 TAPES: 1 HOUR, 50 MINUTES

OH 234
HARRY LAUBACH INTERVIEW

Harry Laubach (b. 1900) depicts: his parents' experiences homesteading near Dutton in 1914; wheat-farming techniques from 1914 through the 1930s Depression; wheat marketing.

INTERVIEWED BY LAURIE MERCIER, FEBRUARY 5, 1982, GREAT FALLS.

SUMMARY: 3 PAGES

2 TAPES: 2 HOURS

OH 235
HARRIETT OLSON HARRIS INTERVIEW

Harriett Harris (1895–1984) comments on: her homestead experiences near Winifred circa 1910–1920; teaching school in Cut Bank; life in Great Falls during the 1930s Depression and during World War II; her work in Shandeling's Dress Store.

INTERVIEWED BY LAURIE MERCIER, FEBRUARY 3, 1982, GREAT FALLS.

TRANSCRIPT: 38 PAGES

2 TAPES: 2 HOURS

OH 236
MARK SHERMAN INTERVIEW

Mark Sherman (b. 1903) discusses: his work as a blacksmith and a miner in Unionville; various gold mines in the area, including the Spring Hill Mine.

INTERVIEWED BY LAURIE MERCIER, FEBRUARY 23, 1982, UNIONVILLE.

SUMMARY: 2 PAGES

2 TAPES: 1 HOUR, 20 MINUTES

OH 237
CHRISTINA HABEL MULLINS INTERVIEW

Christina Mullins (b. 1887) reflects on: the early history of Marysville and her childhood there; her father's mining work; Thomas Cruse and his daughter Mamie.

INTERVIEWED BY LAURIE MERCIER, FEBRUARY 19, 1982, HELENA.

SUMMARY: 2 PAGES

2 TAPES: 1 HOUR, 30 MINUTES

OH 238
ELBERT "BUCK" JONES INTERVIEW

Buck Jones (b. 1904) describes: his work in Butte area mines; placer gold mining with his parents; his work with Montana Power Company.

INTERVIEWED BY LAURIE MERCIER, FEBRUARY 25, 1982, BUTTE.

SUMMARY: 2 PAGES

1 TAPE: 1 HOUR

OH 239
GORDON ORD INTERVIEW

Butte resident Gordon Ord (b. 1902) remembers: "bumming" to find work; difficulties faced as a single man looking for work in Butte; various jobs working in Butte mines, 1920s–1930s.

INTERVIEWED BY LAURIE MERCIER, FEBRUARY 26, 1982, BUTTE.

SUMMARY: 1 PAGE
1 TAPE: 50 MINUTES

OH 240
HERBERT CARLISLE INTERVIEW

Herb Carlisle (b. 1907) speaks of working in Butte mines, 1928–1969, for the Anaconda Copper Mining Company; unions; benefits; safety on the job.
INTERVIEWED BY LAURIE MERCIER, FEBRUARY 26, 1982, BUTTE.
SUMMARY: 2 PAGES
2 TAPES: 1 HOUR, 10 MINUTES

OH 241
MADOLYN BALLANTYNE LANGE LOVE INTERVIEW

Madolyn Love (b. 1902) talks about: her childhood in Bozeman; education; her marriage to Herbert Lange; work with her husband, an insurance underwriter; travel; her work at Shodair Hospital in Helena.
INTERVIEWED BY LAURIE MERCIER, FEBRUARY 24, 1982, BUTTE.
SUMMARY: 4 PAGES
2 TAPES: 2 HOURS

OH 242
HEDLEY "HAP" HOLLOWAY INTERVIEW

Hap Holloway (b. 1891) remembers: his arrival in Montana after the turn of the century; his work in various jobs; his employment as a timekeeper for the Anaconda Company in Butte.
INTERVIEWED BY LAURIE MERCIER, MARCH 9, 1982, BUTTE.
SUMMARY: 2 PAGES
2 TAPES: 1 HOUR, 30 MINUTES

OH 243
EDWARD P. SULLIVAN INTERVIEW

Edward Sullivan (b. 1898) tells of: his childhood in Butte; his position in the Anaconda Company's mines office; Butte's Chinatown; activities of the IWW; Irish traditions in Butte.
INTERVIEWED BY LAURIE MERCIER, FEBRUARY 25 AND MARCH 10, 1982, BUTTE.
SUMMARY: 1 PAGE
1 TAPE: 55 MINUTES

OH 244
GRACE CUNNINGHAM INTERVIEW

Grace Cunningham (b. 1902) comments on her work as a silent-film piano accompanist in Butte theaters during the late 1920s. Also included is a brief segment of the piano theme for the film *What Price Glory.*
INTERVIEWED BY LAURIE MERCIER, MARCH 11, 1982, BUTTE.
SUMMARY: 3 PAGES
2 TAPES: 1 HOUR, 38 MINUTES

OH 245
WILLIAM MAKI INTERVIEW

William Maki (b. 1913) considers: his work as a station-tender and blacksmith for the Anaconda Company in Butte; working conditions; union activity; learning the blacksmith trade.
INTERVIEWED BY LAURIE MERCIER, MARCH 11, 1982, BUTTE.
TRANSCRIPT: 39 PAGES
2 TAPES: 2 HOURS

OH 246
TED WORRALL INTERVIEW

Ted Worrall (b. 1913) depicts: wheat farming near Fort Benton, Chouteau County; his years in the U.S. Navy; the development and operation of farm machinery; the shortcomings of federal farm programs.
INTERVIEWED BY LAURIE MERCIER, FEBRUARY 4, 1982, LOMA.
SUMMARY: 2 PAGES
2 TAPES: 1 HOUR, 45 MINUTES

OH 247
FRED BLYTH INTERVIEW

Fred Blyth describes: the communities of Geraldine and Belt; dry farming and ranching; raising horses; Work Projects Administration (WPA) activities; farm machinery; developments in farm technology.
INTERVIEWED BY LAURIE MERCIER, MARCH 16, 1982, GERALDINE.
SUMMARY: 4 PAGES
3 TAPES: 2 HOURS, 45 MINUTES

OH 248
ISABELLA MOGSTAD INTERVIEW

Isabella Mogstad (b. 1886) details: homesteading near Fort Benton, circa 1910–1930; her family's move to Geraldine; life on the farm; her work as a wife and mother of five children.
INTERVIEWED BY LAURIE MERCIER, MARCH 17, 1982, GERALDINE.

SUMMARY: 3 PAGES
2 TAPES: 1 HOUR, 30 MINUTES

OH 249
ART OLSON INTERVIEW

Art Olson (b. 1895) examines: homesteading in Golden Valley County; his WPA experiences; trucking; ranching; his involvement with the Montana Farmers Union in Judith Basin County.
INTERVIEWED BY LAURIE MERCIER, MARCH 17, 1982, STANFORD.
SUMMARY: 3 PAGES
2 TAPES: 2 HOURS

OH 250
VERLE QUIGLEY INTERVIEW

Verle Quigley speaks of: homesteading in the Geraldine area, circa 1910–1920; his banking career in Geraldine.
INTERVIEWED BY LAURIE MERCIER, MARCH 18, 1982, GERALDINE.
SUMMARY: 1 PAGE
1 TAPE: 1 HOUR

OH 251
SAIMA KOSKI MYLLYMAKI INTERVIEW

Saima Myllymaki discusses: her childhood; the Finnish community; her husband Ted Myllymaki's work in Judith Basin and Stanford.
INTERVIEWED BY LAURIE MERCIER, MARCH 19, 1982, STANFORD.
SUMMARY: 3 PAGES
2 TAPES: 2 HOURS

OH 252
FAYE HOVEN INTERVIEW

Faye Hoven (b. 1894) describes: her parents' homestead south of Winnett before 1920; farming and ranching at Hobson from the 1920s into the 1950s; family and ranch life.
INTERVIEWED BY LAURIE MERCIER, MARCH 30, 1982, HOBSON.
SUMMARY: 3 PAGES
2 TAPES: 1 HOUR, 50 MINUTES

OH 253
CLYDE GORE INTERVIEW

Clyde Gore (1905–1987) discusses: farming south of Hobson, Fergus County, circa 1910–1930; his work as a hired hand on various area ranches; his work in a gyp-

sum plant; owning a Chrysler garage and dealership in Hobson from the 1950s on.
INTERVIEWED BY LAURIE MERCIER, MARCH 30, 1982, HOBSON.
SUMMARY: 1 PAGE
1 TAPE: 1 HOUR

OH 254
ELWOOD PITTENGER INTERVIEW

Elwood Pittenger (b. 1897) recalls: farming and ranching in the Hobson area; life in the Hobson community.
INTERVIEWED BY LAURIE MERCIER, MARCH 31, 1982, HOBSON.
SUMMARY: 2 PAGES
2 TAPES: 1 HOUR, 20 MINUTES

OH 255
LYDIA KEATING INTERVIEW

Lydia Keating (b. 1899) portrays: her childhood on a homestead near Utica in the early 1900s; homesteading with her husband near Stanford through the 1940s.
INTERVIEWED BY LAURIE MERCIER, MARCH 31, 1982, UTICA.
SUMMARY: 3 PAGES
2 TAPES: 1 HOUR, 50 MINUTES

OH 256
ROLAND MATTHEWS INTERVIEW

Roland Matthews (1886–1987) recounts: his work as a cowboy near Malta, Phillips County, circa 1910–1930; ranching along the Missouri River.
INTERVIEWED BY LAURIE MERCIER, APRIL 1, 1982, LEWISTOWN.
TRANSCRIPT: 35 PAGES
2 TAPES: 1 HOUR, 40 MINUTES

OH 257
THEODORE W. OLSEN AND JOE J. HOLLAND INTERVIEW

Theodore Olsen and Joe Holland describe: farm and ranch work in the Utica area, circa 1910–1930; the communities of Lehigh and Utica; trapping; WPA jobs during the 1930s.
INTERVIEWED BY LAURIE MERCIER, APRIL 1, 1982, UTICA.
SUMMARY: 4 PAGES
2 TAPES: 2 HOURS

OH 258
C. ALBERT TONEY INTERVIEW

Albert Toney (1885–1982) reports on: his arrival in Lewistown in 1907; homesteading on Hamilton Coulee; ranching in Fergus County.
INTERVIEWED BY LAURIE MERCIER, APRIL 2, 1982, LEWISTOWN.
SUMMARY: 3 PAGES
2 TAPES: 1 HOUR, 30 MINUTES

OH 259
ANDREW GRANDE INTERVIEW

Andrew Grande (b. 1913) reviews: sheep ranching and cattle ranching near Lennep, Meagher County, 1920s–1970s; the differences between raising sheep and raising cattle; changes in the livestock industry; his involvement with the Montana Woolgrowers Association; the Montana Department of State Lands and Investments.
INTERVIEWED BY LAURIE MERCIER, APRIL 14, 1982, WHITE SULPHUR SPRINGS.
SUMMARY: 4 PAGES
2 TAPES: 2 HOURS

OH 260
ELMER D. HANSON INTERVIEW

Elmer Hanson (b. 1923)—owner of a cattle ranch west of White Sulphur Springs, Meagher County—speaks about: ranch operations from the 1930s to the 1950s; his participation in the Montana Stockgrowers Association.
INTERVIEWED BY LAURIE MERCIER, APRIL 13, 1982, WHITE SULPHUR SPRINGS.
SUMMARY: 2 PAGES
2 TAPES: 2 HOURS

OH 261
OAKLEY R. JACKSON INTERVIEW

Oakley Jackson (1886–1983) remembers: the steam-plowing business, 1910–1920; homesteading; cattle raising and haying on his ranch near White Sulphur Springs, Meagher County, 1910–1960.
INTERVIEWED BY LAURIE MERCIER, APRIL 13, 1982, WHITE SULPHUR SPRINGS.
SUMMARY: 2 PAGES
2 TAPES: 2 HOURS

OH 262
CHARLES McDONALD INTERVIEW

Charles McDonald (b. 1897) reflects on: his childhood on the Flathead Indian Reservation; defending Indian rights; the Wheeler-Howard Indian Rights Act; the CCC; his work as a packer and a scaler for the Bureau of Indian Affairs (BIA), Forestry Branch, and the U.S. Forest Service.
INTERVIEWED BY LAURIE MERCIER, APRIL 20 AND 23, 1982, ST. IGNATIUS.
SUMMARY: 5 PAGES
3 TAPES: 3 HOURS

OH 263
A. L. "SAM" CLAIRMONT INTERVIEW

Sam Clairmont (b. 1908) recalls: his work with the BIA, Forestry Branch; the CCC; logging projects; real-estate contracts.
INTERVIEWED BY LAURIE MERCIER, APRIL 21, 1982, POLSON.
SUMMARY: 3 PAGES
2 TAPES: 1 HOUR, 45 MINUTES

OH 264
HARVEY COLE INTERVIEW

Harvey Cole (b. 1899) discusses: his work as a teamster, loader, and hoist operator for Polleys Lumber Company in the Big Blackfoot River Valley of western Montana; life in Ronan on the Flathead Indian Reservation; the family farm south of Ronan.
INTERVIEWED BY LAURIE MERCIER, APRIL 21, 1982, POLSON.
SUMMARY: 3 PAGES
2 TAPES: 1 HOUR, 20 MINUTES

OH 265
FLORENCE McDONALD SMITH INTERVIEW

Florence Smith (b. 1895) talks about: life on the Flathead Indian Reservation in western Montana; cooking for restaurants and for the CCC during the 1930s; her marriage to Howard Smith; changes on the reservation in the 1920s and 1930s.
INTERVIEWED BY LAURIE MERCIER, APRIL 22, 1982, RONAN.
SUMMARY: 3 PAGES
2 TAPES: 1 HOUR, 35 MINUTES

OH 266
CHARLES KENNEDY INTERVIEW

Charles Kennedy (b. 1896) depicts: his work as a logger and teamster in Bonner and Milltown from 1908 into the 1930s; his work sheepherding, shearing, and lambing from the 1930s until World War II; his postwar return to logging; his involvement in the IWW; work for the Anaconda Copper Mining Company.

INTERVIEWED BY LAURIE MERCIER, APRIL 23, 1982, DIXON.
TRANSCRIPT: 81 PAGES
3 TAPES: 3 HOURS

OH 267
RUBY GREENWELL INTERVIEW

Ruby Greenwell (b. 1902) tells of: cattle ranching; wheat farming; WPA assistance; hardships of the 1930s Depression in Chouteau County; insect infestation.
INTERVIEWED BY LAURIE MERCIER, APRIL 2, 1982, GERALDINE.
SUMMARY: 3 PAGES
2 TAPES: 1 HOUR, 40 MINUTES

OH 268
ELIZABETH BIRKELAND INTERVIEW

Fort Benton resident Elizabeth Birkeland (b. 1896) addresses farming and ranching in the Fort Benton, Chouteau County, area from circa 1910 into the 1950s.
INTERVIEWED BY LAURIE MERCIER, APRIL 27, 1982, FORT BENTON.
SUMMARY: 2 PAGES
2 TAPES: 1 HOUR, 25 MINUTES

OH 269
HELEN VICKROY SERIGHT INTERVIEW

Helen Seright (b. 1901) details: the family farm near Moore, Chouteau County; wheat farming with her husband in Montague; local activities of the WPA during the 1930s.
INTERVIEWED BY LAURIE MERCIER, APRIL 27, 1982, FORT BENTON.
SUMMARY: 3 PAGES
2 TAPES: 2 HOURS

OH 270
SELMER HELLAND INTERVIEW

Selmer Helland (b. 1888) summarizes: homesteading in the Galata area, Chouteau County; dryland wheat farming near Galata, outside Belt, and on the Highwood Bench; farming during the 1930s Depression; effects of the introduction of machinery on farming.
INTERVIEWED BY LAURIE MERCIER, APRIL 30, 1982, FORT BENTON.
SUMMARY: 4 PAGES
2 TAPES: 1 HOUR, 50 MINUTES

OH 271
AGNES JELINEK INTERVIEW

Agnes Jelinek (b. 1901) reviews: her family's migration from Europe to Coffee Creek, Chouteau County, in 1906; her Czechoslovakian background; her homesteading and farming experiences.
INTERVIEWED BY LAURIE MERCIER, APRIL 30, 1982, COFFEE CREEK.
SUMMARY: 2 PAGES
2 TAPES: 1 HOUR, 20 MINUTES

OH 272
JOEL OVERHOLSER INTERVIEW

Joel Overholser (b. 1911)—longtime publisher and editor of the weekly Fort Benton *River Press*—reports on: his boyhood introduction to newspaper work; learning the newspaper trade; Montana journalism; the *River Press*'s involvement with the Chouteau County agricultural community.
INTERVIEWED BY LAURIE MERCIER, APRIL 29, 1982, FORT BENTON.
SUMMARY: 2 PAGES
1 TAPE: 1 HOUR

OH 273
IDONIEA GOLDING DUNTLEY INTERVIEW

Idoniea Duntley (b. 1889) recalls: homesteading near Fort Benton, Chouteau County; her restaurant work in Geraldine and Great Falls; her duties as a matron and a cook at the Geraldine High School dormitory.
INTERVIEWED BY LAURIE MERCIER, APRIL 28, 1982, FORT BENTON.
SUMMARY: 2 PAGES
2 TAPES: 1 HOUR, 25 MINUTES

OH 274
MARY ZANTO INTERVIEW

Mary Zanto (b. 1894) reflects on: her childhood in the Stockett-Eden area; her work as a farm wife in the Highwood-Shonkin area.
INTERVIEWED BY LAURIE MERCIER, APRIL 28, 1982, FORT BENTON.
TRANSCRIPT: 50 PAGES
2 TAPES: 2 HOURS

OH 275
JOSEPH S. SMITH INTERVIEW

Joseph Smith (b. 1901) remembers dryland wheat farming on the Highwood Bench and in surrounding areas from 1917 to the 1940s.

INTERVIEWED BY LAURIE MERCIER, APRIL 29, 1982, FORT BENTON.
SUMMARY: 3 PAGES
2 TAPES: 1 HOUR, 30 MINUTES

OH 276
ROSE LARSON INTERVIEW
Rose Larson (1908–1983) discusses: operating a small coal mine with her husband near Roundup in the late 1920s; specific tasks in the mine; first-aid and massage work; her job cooking at the Vienna Cafe in Roundup.
INTERVIEWED BY LAURIE MERCIER, MAY 10, 1982, ROUNDUP.
SUMMARY: 3 PAGES
2 TAPES: 2 HOURS

OH 277
ANDREW WICKLAND INTERVIEW
Andrew Wickland (b. 1903) recounts his work as a nipper, a muleskinner, and a miner at the Roundup Coal Company's Number Three Mine, west of Roundup; the Williams Coal Company in Roundup.
INTERVIEWED BY LAURIE MERCIER, MAY 11, 1982, ROUNDUP.
SUMMARY: 1 PAGE
1 TAPE: 45 MINUTES

OH 278
DELBERT WALKER INTERVIEW
Delbert Walker (b. 1889) describes: homesteading near Flatwillow from 1912 to 1927; his work as a mortician in Roundup.
INTERVIEWED BY LAURIE MERCIER, MAY 11, 1982, ROUNDUP.
SUMMARY: 3 PAGES
2 TAPES: 2 HOURS

OH 279
CHARLES FIRM INTERVIEW
Charles Firm (b. 1902) reviews: his family's involvement in mining, primarily with the Klein Mine and Republic Coal Company near Roundup; his own work as a machinist for this mine from the 1930s to the 1950s.
INTERVIEWED BY LAURIE MERCIER, MAY 12, 1982, ROUNDUP.
SUMMARY: 4 PAGES
3 TAPES: 3 HOURS, 30 MINUTES

OH 280
MARK LACEY INTERVIEW
Mark Lacey (b. 1903) recounts: his work as a coal miner in the Klein Mine and Republic Coal Company Mine from 1919 to 1957; social and community life in Klein and nearby Roundup.
INTERVIEWED BY LAURIE MERCIER, MAY 13, 1982, ROUNDUP.
SUMMARY: 3 PAGES
3 TAPES: 2 HOURS, 40 MINUTES

OH 281
PAUL SMITH INTERVIEW
Paul Smith (b. 1908) discusses: his work in Roundup coal mines from 1928 to 1956; the effects of mechanization in the mines; industrial safety; accidents; "black lung" disease; the United Mine Workers of America (UMW).
INTERVIEWED BY LAURIE MERCIER, MAY 13, 1982, ROUNDUP.
SUMMARY: 3 PAGES
2 TAPES: 2 HOURS

OH 282
HENRY BUJOK INTERVIEW
Henry Bujok (b. 1908) talks about: his work as a miner at the Roundup Coal Company's Number Three Mine, west of Roundup, from 1928 to 1963; the UMW.
INTERVIEWED BY LAURIE MERCIER, MAY 13, 1982, ROUNDUP.
SUMMARY: 3 PAGES
2 TAPES: 1 HOUR, 58 MINUTES

OH 283
AGNES STEFOVICH NESHEIM INTERVIEW
Agnes Nesheim (b. 1908) details: growing up on a farm west of Roundup during the 1920s; her husband's work in the Roundup coal mines; her work in the local telephone company office.
INTERVIEWED BY LAURIE MERCIER, MAY 14, 1982, ROUNDUP.
SUMMARY: 2 PAGES
1 TAPE: 1 HOUR

OH 284
J. H. "TED" McINTYRE INTERVIEW
Ted McIntyre describes: homesteading; cattle, horse, and sheep ranching in Valley County, 1930s–1950s; work as a cowboy; his work in taverns as a bartender during construction of the Fort Peck Dam in the mid-1930s.

INTERVIEWED BY LAURIE MERCIER, MAY 20, 1982, GLASGOW.
SUMMARY: 5 PAGES
3 TAPES: 3 HOURS

OH 285
THELMA MARIE DOBSON CZYZESKI INTERVIEW

Thelma Czyzeski (b. 1906) depicts: the Dobson family; ranching along the Musselshell River near Cat Creek; ranch experiences in Phillips County; nursing in Independence, Missouri, and in Malta and Zortman, Montana; the hardships and struggles of supporting a family from the 1930s into the 1960s. [An excerpt from this interview appears in: Montana Historical Society, *The Last Best Place* (Helena: Montana Historical Society; 1988).]
INTERVIEWED BY LAURIE MERCIER, MAY 21, 1982, GLASGOW.
TRANSCRIPT: 88 PAGES
3 TAPES: 3 HOURS

OH 286
PAULINE DeBRAY AND LEO DeBRAY INTERVIEW

Pauline DeBray and Leo DeBray describe: the DeBray and Lenz families; cooking for threshing crews; ranch life; sheepherding and sheep ranching; Valley County; experiences during the World War I era; work on the Fort Peck Dam.
INTERVIEWED BY LAURIE MERCIER, MAY 23, 1982, GLASGOW.
SUMMARY: 7 PAGES
5 TAPES: 5 HOURS

OH 287
IRMA McINERNY INTERVIEW

Irma McInerny comments on: life on her parents' homestead north of Nashua, from 1915 to 1932; teaching in rural schools in Valley County during the 1930s; her work as deputy superintendent of Valley County schools from the 1940s into the 1950s.
INTERVIEWED BY LAURIE MERCIER, MAY 24, 1982, GLASGOW.
SUMMARY: 4 PAGES
2 TAPES: 2 HOURS

OH 288
CHRISTIAN O. CHRISTIANSON INTERVIEW

Christian Christianson (b. 1889) discusses: his home-steading experiences near Saco; his relinquishment of the homestead; his work on the Fort Peck Dam from 1933 to 1953.
INTERVIEWED BY LAURIE MERCIER, MAY 25, 1982, GLASGOW.
SUMMARY: 2 PAGES
1 TAPE: 1 HOUR

OH 289
CHARLES BROCKSMITH INTERVIEW

Glasgow resident Charles Brocksmith (b. 1902) remembers: his banking career in Valley County; working for the First National Bank in Nashua, 1920–1936, the Federal Land Bank, 1936–1940s, and the First Security Bank in Glasgow, 1940s–1982; working on the Brocksmith family ranch, north of Nashua, 1910–1920.
INTERVIEWED BY LAURIE MERCIER, MAY 25 AND 27, 1982, GLASGOW.
SUMMARY: 3 PAGES
2 TAPES: 2 HOURS

OH 290
MARTIN CAPDEVILLE INTERVIEW

Martin Capdeville (b. 1896) speaks about: his migration to the United States from France; sheepherding; owning his own sheep ranch near Opheim.
INTERVIEWED BY LAURIE MERCIER, MAY 26, 1982, OPHEIM.
SUMMARY: 3 PAGES
3 TAPES: 2 HOURS, 50 MINUTES

OH 291
MARY GOFORTH REDFIELD INTERVIEW

Mary Redfield (b. 1888) remembers: teaching in Opheim; homesteading and farming in Valley County.
INTERVIEWED BY LAURIE MERCIER, MAY 26, 1982, OPHEIM.
SUMMARY: 3 PAGES
2 TAPES: 1 HOUR, 50 MINUTES

OH 292
NATHAN GOODRICH INTERVIEW

Nathan Goodrich (b. 1906) talks about: his parents' homestead southwest of Glendive; his work on the Fort Peck Dam and on other power plants; his employment with the U.S. Army Corps of Engineers and with the U.S. Bureau of Reclamation.
INTERVIEWED BY LAURIE MERCIER, MAY 27, 1982, GLASGOW.

SUMMARY: 4 PAGES
2 TAPES: 1 HOUR, 37 MINUTES

OH 293
FERN HARSHMAN INTERVIEW
Fern Harshman (b. 1891) discusses: her career as an Avon cosmetics dealer in the Chinook area from the early 1930s into the 1980s; changes in the Chinook community during that time.
INTERVIEWED BY LAURIE MERCIER, JUNE 7, 1982, CHINOOK.
SUMMARY: 4 PAGES
2 TAPES: 1 HOUR, 40 MINUTES

OH 294
BILL ROSS INTERVIEW
Bill Ross (b. 1905) tells of: his father's ranch and homestead in Blaine County in 1887; his own work as a vocational-agriculture teacher in Conrad; his work as a county agent in several Montana counties, including Stillwater, 1930s–1940s; cattle ranching in the Bears Paw Mountains, south of Chinook, through the 1960s.
INTERVIEWED BY LAURIE MERCIER, JUNE 8, 1982, CHINOOK.
SUMMARY: 5 PAGES
2 TAPES: 2 HOURS

OH 295
HAZEL ANDERSON KLOTZBUECHER INTERVIEW
Hazel Klotzbuecher (1885–1982)—a Chinook resident—describes: her teaching career in Montana and Canada from the 1920s into the 1930s; homesteading in northern Blaine County, circa 1910–1920; working in a salmon cannery in Alaska.
INTERVIEWED BY LAURIE MERCIER, JUNE 9, 1982, CHINOOK.
SUMMARY: 5 PAGES
2 TAPES: 1 HOUR, 50 MINUTES

OH 296
TOM STAFF INTERVIEW
Tom Staff (b. 1899) recalls: ranching near Chinook; hay farming and irrigation; his road work in Blaine County in the 1920s; his service in the U.S. Air Force during World War II; his involvement with the Montana Farmers Union and with the Triangle Telephone Company.
INTERVIEWED BY LAURIE MERCIER, JUNE 9, 1982, CHINOOK.

SUMMARY: 4 PAGES
2 TAPES: 2 HOURS

OH 297
HERMAN FRIEDE INTERVIEW
Herman Friede (b. 1905) remembers: homesteading in Blaine County; working as a sugar beet farmer; moving to the Paradise Valley; his participation in WPA activities; his involvement with the Montana Farmers Union.
INTERVIEWED BY LAURIE MERCIER, JUNE 10, 1982, CHINOOK.
SUMMARY: 8 PAGES
2 TAPES: 2 HOURS

OH 298
PEARL RESER REEVES INTERVIEW
Pearl Reeves (b. 1892) discusses: homesteading north of Chinook circa 1910–1930; her work as the Chinook postmistress; dairy farming during the 1930s. *[See also Small Town Montana OH 792.]*
INTERVIEWED BY LAURIE MERCIER, JUNE 10, 1982, CHINOOK.
SUMMARY: 4 PAGES
2 TAPES: 1 HOUR, 25 MINUTES

OH 299
SEVERIN SIVERTSON INTERVIEW
Severin Sivertson (b. 1881) details sheepherding and sheep ranching in the Bears Paw Mountains of Blaine County from 1900 into the 1940s.
INTERVIEWED BY LAURIE MERCIER, JUNE 10, 1982, CHINOOK.
SUMMARY: 2 PAGES
2 TAPES: 1 HOUR, 20 MINUTES

OH 300
FRANK DEVILLE INTERVIEW
Frank Deville (b. 1912) discusses: his work in the Bearcreek coal mines; the 1943 Smith Mine disaster, focusing on the rescue efforts and the disaster's effect on the mining industry; the Foster and Brophy mines.
INTERVIEWED BY LAURIE MERCIER, JUNE 21, 1982, BEARCREEK.
SUMMARY: 5 PAGES
2 TAPES: 1 HOUR, 45 MINUTES

OH 301
LESLIE LYONS INTERVIEW
Leslie Lyons (b. 1892) describes: his work in the Red

Lodge coal mines; his employment as a mine electrician; operating the Red Lodge Electric Shop; the creation and operation of the See 'Em Alive Zoo in Red Lodge.

INTERVIEWED BY LAURIE MERCIER, JUNE 23, 1982, RED LODGE.

SUMMARY: 5 PAGES

2 TAPES: 1 HOUR, 45 MINUTES

OH 302
OLLIE ANDERSON INTERVIEW

Ollie Anderson (b. 1895) depicts: his work as a miner in the Red Lodge and Bearcreek coal mines; the Finnish community in Red Lodge; the 1943 Smith Mine disaster; the UMW.

INTERVIEWED BY LAURIE MERCIER, JUNE 23, 1982, RED LODGE.

TRANSCRIPT: 26 PAGES

2 TAPES: 1 HOUR, 40 MINUTES

OH 303
LILLIAN HELENA MATTSON LAMPI INTERVIEW

Lillian Lampi (b. circa 1900) describes: the Finnish community in Red Lodge; her work in the Pollard Hotel dining room; her jobs with Bloom and Company in Red Lodge.

INTERVIEWED BY LAURIE MERCIER, JUNE 23, 1982, RED LODGE.

TRANSCRIPT: 33 PAGES

2 TAPES: 1 HOUR, 30 MINUTES

OH 304
LEO MICHELCIC INTERVIEW

Leo Michelcic (b. 1912) remembers: his employment in the Bearcreek and Washoe coal mines, near Red Lodge, from 1929 to 1958; the Foster and Brophy mines; particulars about the work of a nipper, a joy loader, a boxcar loader, and a cutting machine operator; his work as a sanitation engineer in Yellowstone National Park, 1958 to 1976.

INTERVIEWED BY LAURIE MERCIER, JUNE 25, 1982, RED LODGE.

SUMMARY: 2 PAGES

1 TAPE: 1 HOUR

OH 305
TONY PERSHA INTERVIEW

Tony Persha (b. 1908) comments on: his work in the Red Lodge and Bearcreek coal mines from 1926 into the 1940s; the 1943 Smith Mine disaster; his duties as president of the local UMW chapter.

INTERVIEWED BY LAURIE MERCIER, JUNE 25, 1982, RED LODGE.

SUMMARY: 3 PAGES

2 TAPES: 2 HOURS

OH 306
MORRIS STEWART INTERVIEW

Morris Stewart (b. 1894) recounts: homesteading near Carter; the management of wheat crops and cattle; the 1919 drought; the 1930s Depression.

INTERVIEWED BY LAURIE MERCIER, JULY 13, 1982, GREAT FALLS.

SUMMARY: 4 PAGES

2 TAPES: 1 HOUR, 50 MINUTES

OH 307
MARY FONTANA TANNER INTERVIEW

Mary Tanner (b. 1903) reflects on: homesteading with her parents near Round Butte, circa 1910–1920; homesteading and ranching with her husband, John Tanner, near Square Butte, 1920s–1960s; Quincy Granite Company; Chouteau County agriculture.

INTERVIEWED BY LAURIE MERCIER, JULY 14, 1982, SQUARE BUTTE.

SUMMARY: 2 PAGES

1 TAPE: 1 HOUR

OH 308
ARTHUR MOE INTERVIEW

Arthur Moe (b. 1899) talks about: his work as a projectionist in Butte and Great Falls movie theaters during the 1920s and 1930s; his employment in the Anaconda Company's Great Falls Reduction Department from the 1920s on; his other jobs around Montana.

INTERVIEWED BY LAURIE MERCIER, JULY 14, 1982, GREAT FALLS.

SUMMARY: 3 PAGES

2 TAPES: 1 HOUR, 25 MINUTES

OH 309
LUCILLE WEBSTER BRIDGES INTERVIEW

Lucille Bridges (b. 1898) reports on: her jobs as a child on her father's cattle ranch near Shawmut; working the same ranch as an adult, with her husband, Joe Bridges; the nearby Winnecook Ranch.

INTERVIEWED BY LAURIE MERCIER, JULY 15, 1982, WHITE SULPHUR SPRINGS.

SUMMARY: 4 PAGES

2 TAPES: 1 HOUR, 50 MINUTES

OH 310
CHARLES BANDEROB INTERVIEW
Ballantine resident Charles Banderob (b. 1905) describes: the history of farming in the Huntley Project area; farmers' struggles during droughts and during the 1930s Depression; his involvement with the Farmers Union.
INTERVIEWED BY LAURIE MERCIER, JULY 19, 1982, BALLANTINE.
SUMMARY: 4 PAGES
3 TAPES: 2 HOURS, 30 MINUTES

OH 311
GEORGE WILLIAM SHAWVER INTERVIEW
George Shawver (1894–1982) reviews: homesteading in the Missouri Breaks region of Garfield County, circa 1910–1960; raising horses and cattle in the Breaks.
INTERVIEWED BY LAURIE MERCIER, JULY 20, 1982, BILLINGS.
SUMMARY: 3 PAGES
2 TAPES: 1 HOUR, 55 MINUTES

OH 312
BILL KORELL AND RUTH GARDNER KORELL INTERVIEW
Bill Korell (b. 1906) and Ruth Korell speak of: their grocery business in Utica; the Korell Guest Ranch in the Judith Basin. Bill Korell also tells of his childhood in Utica circa 1910–1920. Ruth Korell discusses her childhood in the community of Straw.
INTERVIEWED BY LAURIE MERCIER, JULY 20, 1982, BILLINGS.
SUMMARY: 3 PAGES
2 TAPES: 1 HOUR, 30 MINUTES

OH 313
TYLER REYNOLDS INTERVIEW
Tyler Reynolds (b. circa 1910) describes: his work at Ryan's Grocery in Billings; his employment as a salesman on the HI-LINE during the 1930s; changes in the grocery business, 1919–1980.
INTERVIEWED BY LAURIE MERCIER, JULY 21, 1982, BILLINGS.
SUMMARY: 4 PAGES
2 TAPES: 2 HOURS

OH 314
GLADYS KNOWLES INTERVIEW
Gladys Knowles (b. circa 1895) discusses: ranching in Big Horn County; the Republican Party and cattle ranching.

INTERVIEWED BY LAURIE MERCIER, JULY 21, 1982, BILLINGS.
SUMMARY: 2 PAGES
1 TAPE: 45 MINUTES

OH 315
ART WATSON INTERVIEW
Art Watson (d. 1983) details: cattle ranching in the Smith River Valley of Meagher County; his work as a cattle buyer; his involvement in the organization of the Montana Cattlemen's Association as an alternative to the Montana Stockgrowers Association; his 1930s legislative career; his involvement with "county-buster" Dan McKay.
INTERVIEWED BY LAURIE MERCIER, JULY 22, 1982, WHITE SULPHUR SPRINGS.
TRANSCRIPT: 61 PAGES
3 TAPES: 2 HOURS, 40 MINUTES

OH 316
GERALD BYBEE INTERVIEW
Gerald Bybee (b. 1923) summarizes: logging in western Montana during the 1940s; the Thompson Falls Lumber Company and other sawmill operations; the Lumber and Sawmill Workers Union and trade unionism; his work as a head filer.
INTERVIEWED BY LAURIE MERCIER, JULY 28, 1982, THOMPSON FALLS.
SUMMARY: 5 PAGES
3 TAPES: 2 HOURS, 50 MINUTES

OH 317
ANNE SLOAN INTERVIEW
Anne Sloan (b. 1911) speaks of: her childhood in Butte; her marriage to Verne Sloan; her husband's operation of sawmills in the Thompson Falls area.
INTERVIEWED BY LAURIE MERCIER, JULY 28, 1982, THOMPSON FALLS.
SUMMARY: 2 PAGES
1 TAPE: 1 HOUR

OH 318
ETHEL WIDNER INTERVIEW
Ethel Widner (b. 1923) reviews: her childhood; her marriage to Bill Widner, a truck driver for several logging companies; her life in Thompson Falls.
INTERVIEWED BY LAURIE MERCIER, JULY 29, 1982, THOMPSON FALLS.
SUMMARY: 2 PAGES
1 TAPE: 55 MINUTES

OH 319
LILLIAN BEAMISH INTERVIEW
Thompson Falls resident Lillian Beamish (b. 1903) reports on: her childhood in Granite and Sanders counties; farming with her husband near Plains; working at the post office and at the general store in Paradise.
INTERVIEWED BY LAURIE MERCIER, JULY 29, 1982, THOMPSON FALLS.
SUMMARY: 3 PAGES
2 TAPES: 1 HOUR, 40 MINUTES

OH 320
THOMAS R. GARRISON INTERVIEW
Thomas Garrison (b. 1900) remembers: his work as a logger and a teamster for the Montana Logging Company in Sanders County, circa 1910–1930; the International Brotherhood of Electrical Workers and trade unionism; his employment with the Montana Power Company in Thompson Falls.
INTERVIEWED BY LAURIE MERCIER, JULY 28, 1982, THOMPSON FALLS.
SUMMARY: 3 PAGES
2 TAPES: 1 HOUR, 40 MINUTES

OH 321
CLIFFORD MILLER INTERVIEW
Clifford Miller (b. 1902) relates: his work in a sawmill at Kalispell; his management-level position at the Kalispell Lumber Company; changes in the lumber industry.
INTERVIEWED BY LAURIE MERCIER, AUGUST 31, 1982, KALISPELL.
SUMMARY: 3 PAGES
2 TAPES: 1 HOUR, 50 MINUTES

OH 322
PERRY S. MELTON INTERVIEW
Perry Melton (b. 1907) reflects on: his life in Kalispell; his work as a labor-union organizer in Flathead County from 1938 to 1951; his involvement with the Kalispell Trades and Labor Council; the *Treasure State Labor Journal*; dealings on the state level with the American Federation of Labor–Congress of Industrial Organizations (AFL-CIO); his role in publishing the *Flathead Labor Journal*; the IWW.
INTERVIEWED BY LAURIE MERCIER, AUGUST 26, 1982, KALISPELL.
TRANSCRIPT: 44 PAGES
3 TAPES: 2 HOURS, 45 MINUTES

OH 323
GLEN E. MONTGOMERY INTERVIEW
Glen Montgomery (b. 1907) recounts: his jobs as flunky and cook at U.S. Forest Service and National Park Service stations in Lincoln and Flathead counties during the 1920s and 1930s; the WPA; the CCC; his work as a blacksmith and a welder in Montgomery's Blacksmith Shop in Kalispell.
INTERVIEWED BY LAURIE MERCIER, AUGUST 25, 1982, KALISPELL.
SUMMARY: 5 PAGES
3 TAPES: 2 HOURS, 40 MINUTES

OH 324
RAMONA ROE JELLISON INTERVIEW
Ramona Jellison (b. 1902)—a Lakeside resident—discusses: life in Flathead County from the 1920s to the 1950s; farming with her husband near LaSalle; teaching at Echo Lake; her community-service work in Kalispell.
INTERVIEWED BY LAURIE MERCIER, AUGUST 25, 1982, LAKESIDE.
SUMMARY: 4 PAGES
3 TAPES: 1 HOUR, 50 MINUTES

OH 325
JIM DREW INTERVIEW
Jim Drew (b. 1920) recalls his work at the Somers Lumber Company in Somers from 1938 to 1941.
INTERVIEWED BY LAURIE MERCIER, SEPTEMBER 31, 1982, SOMERS.
SUMMARY: 1 PAGE
1 TAPE: 25 MINUTES

OH 326
RACHEL CORAM PATERSON INTERVIEW
Rachel Paterson (b. 1895) portrays: her childhood on Flathead Lake and in Kalispell; her marriage to Archie Paterson; her husband's work at the Kalispell Mercantile Company; Coram.
INTERVIEWED BY LAURIE MERCIER, AUGUST 30, 1982, KALISPELL.
SUMMARY: 2 PAGES
1 TAPE: 1 HOUR

OH 327
JAMES KEHOE INTERVIEW
James Kehoe (b. 1907) explains: his father's operation of the Flathead Lake steamboat *Helena* out of the port of Bigfork, circa 1910–1930; his personal involvement with this freight-hauling business.

INTERVIEWED BY LAURIE MERCIER, AUGUST 29, 1982, BIGFORK.
TRANSCRIPT: 69 PAGES
2 TAPES: 1 HOUR, 45 MINUTES

OH 328
GLADYS PHILBRICK LITTLE INTERVIEW

Gladys Little (b. 1891) examines: life in the community of Castle during the early 1900s; the town of Martinsdale from 1910 to 1914; her work on a Meagher County sheep ranch; her employment at the Kalispell Mercantile; community activities in Kalispell from 1928 to 1945.
INTERVIEWED BY LAURIE MERCIER, SEPTEMBER 1, 1982, POLSON.
SUMMARY: 3 PAGES
2 TAPES: 2 HOURS

OH 329
LORNE H. MacDONELL INTERVIEW

Lorne MacDonell (b. 1903) comments on: his childhood in Somers; his work for the Somers Lumber Company from the 1920s into the 1930s; his jobs in Missoula and Superior; additional work in Washington and Idaho; steamboats; the IWW.
INTERVIEWED BY LAURIE MERCIER, AUGUST 31 AND SEPTEMBER 1, 1982, SOMERS.
SUMMARY: 5 PAGES
4 TAPES: 4 HOURS

OH 330
GULNARE LUTTS INTERVIEW

Gulnare Lutts considers: homesteading near Ollie, in Fallon County, circa 1910–1930s; farmers' hardships; community life in Ollie.
INTERVIEWED BY JULIE FOSTER, AUGUST 7, 1982, BAKER.
SUMMARY: 1 PAGE
1 TAPE: 50 MINUTES

OH 331
MARION HANSON INTERVIEW

Marion Hanson (b. 1917) describes: homesteading near Willard; grain farming; development of the Willard community; social events in Baker and in Fallon County.
INTERVIEWED BY JULIE FOSTER, AUGUST 6, 1982, BAKER.
SUMMARY: 1 PAGE
1 TAPE: 1 HOUR

OH 332
GEORGE GRIFFITH INTERVIEW

George Griffith depicts homesteading and cattle ranching in Fallon County.
INTERVIEWED BY JULIE FOSTER, AUGUST 8, 1982, BAKER.
SUMMARY: 1 PAGE
1 TAPE: 50 MINUTES

OH 333
JESS HICKEY INTERVIEW

Jess Hickey (b. 1909) describes his work as a cowboy in Fallon County in the 1920s.
INTERVIEWED BY JULIE FOSTER, AUGUST 11, 1982, BAKER.
SUMMARY: 6 PAGES
1 TAPE: 1 HOUR

OH 334
LORENE KIRSCHTEN INTERVIEW

Lorene Kirschten (b. 1895) details: homesteading east of Baker; her work as a school librarian in Baker.
INTERVIEWED BY JULIE FOSTER, AUGUST 1, 1982, BAKER.
SUMMARY: 2 PAGES
1 TAPE: 1 HOUR

OH 335
ED HERBST INTERVIEW

Ed Herbst speaks of: homesteading near Baker, Fallon County, circa 1910–1920; sheep ranching; his work as a barber in Baker.
INTERVIEWED BY JULIE FOSTER, AUGUST 10, 1982, BAKER.
SUMMARY: 3 PAGES
1 TAPE: 1 HOUR

OH 336
J. R. "BOB" KINSEY INTERVIEW

Bob Kinsey tells about: his work in Fallon County from the 1920s to the 1970s; writing poetry; cowboys; trapping; herding sheep; ranching; training horses; trading horses; busting broncs.
INTERVIEWED BY JULIE FOSTER, AUGUST 13, 1982, BAKER.
SUMMARY: 3 PAGES
1 TAPE: 1 HOUR

OH 337
CHARLES H. ABRAMS INTERVIEW

Charles Abrams discusses operating his ranch in Fallon County from the 1920s to the 1940s.
INTERVIEWED BY JULIE FOSTER, AUGUST 13, 1982, BAKER.
SUMMARY: 2 PAGES
1 TAPE: 55 MINUTES

OH 338
ARCHIE GROVER INTERVIEW
Archie Grover (b. 1906) talks of: his work as a miner, trapper, and lumberjack while living in Butte; his labor-union activities; community life in Butte; the Campbell Farming Corporation.
INTERVIEWED BY JULIE FOSTER, AUGUST 20, 1982, HARDIN.
SUMMARY: 2 PAGES
1 TAPE: 1 HOUR

OH 339
CAROLYN REYNOLDS RIEBETH INTERVIEW
Carolyn Riebeth (b. 1898)—a Hardin resident—recalls: life with her father on the Crow Agency; Samuel Reynolds's work as the agent for the Crow Tribe; the Crow community.
INTERVIEWED BY JULIE FOSTER, AUGUST 19, 1982, HARDIN.
SUMMARY: 2 PAGES
3 TAPES: 2 HOURS, 15 MINUTES

OH 340
NELLIE AGNSTROM OLSON INTERVIEW
Nellie Olson (b. 1900) remembers: migrating from Canada to Montana; her early life in Cut Bank and Valier; living and working in Hardin and on the Crow Indian Reservation.
INTERVIEWED BY JULIE FOSTER, AUGUST 20, 1982, HARDIN.
SUMMARY: 1 PAGE
1 TAPE: 40 MINUTES

OH 341
FLORENCE MILLER WELLS INTERVIEW
Florence Wells reflects on: cattle ranching in Big Horn County; teaching in Lodge Grass.
INTERVIEWED BY JULIE FOSTER, AUGUST 21, 1982, HARDIN.
SUMMARY: 3 PAGES
1 TAPE: 1 HOUR, 45 MINUTES

OH 342
LEONE DYGERT INTERVIEW
Leone Dygert relates his experiences cattle ranching on the Crow Indian Reservation.
INTERVIEWED BY JULIE FOSTER, AUGUST 21, 1982, HARDIN.
SUMMARY: 3 PAGES
2 TAPES: 1 HOUR, 30 MINUTES

OH 343
RUSSELL L. DANIELSON INTERVIEW
Hardin resident Russell Danielson (b. 1906) reports on: farming and ranching in Big Horn County from 1910 to 1950; local cowboys.
INTERVIEWED BY JULIE FOSTER, AUGUST 22, 1982, HARDIN.
SUMMARY: 3 PAGES
2 TAPES: 1 HOUR, 15 MINUTES

OH 344
EARLE MARSH INTERVIEW
Earle Marsh recounts: his work as a cowboy on various ranches in the Hardin area; his employment with the Campbell Farming Corporation.
INTERVIEWED BY JULIE FOSTER, AUGUST 23, 1982, HARDIN.
SUMMARY: 2 PAGES
1 TAPE: 1 HOUR

OH 345
MINNIE KEILCHER LANDON INTERVIEW
Minnie Landon (b. 1894) recalls: her early life near Roundup; the community of Sarpy; ranching and farming with her husband near the Crow Agency.
INTERVIEWED BY JULIE FOSTER, AUGUST 24, 1982, HARDIN.
SUMMARY: 2 PAGES
1 TAPE: 1 HOUR

OH 346
LEE TURLEY INTERVIEW
Lee Turley (b. 1899) explains his work as a cowboy and a sheepherder in Big Horn County.
INTERVIEWED BY JULIE FOSTER, AUGUST 25, 1982, HARDIN.
SUMMARY: 2 PAGES
2 TAPES: 1 HOUR, 25 MINUTES

OH 347
DORIS VICKERS NOVARK INTERVIEW
Doris Novark (b. 1911) examines: community life in Hardin from 1913 to 1980; various local organizations; Hardin businesses and industries; her work as a housewife.
INTERVIEWED BY JULIE FOSTER, AUGUST 25, 1982, HARDIN.
SUMMARY: 2 PAGES
1 TAPE: 45 MINUTES

OH 348
ELEANOR SULLIVAN STARINA INTERVIEW
   Eleanor Starina (b. 1903) tells about: ranch life near Kirby, Big Horn County; her work as a schoolteacher; her duties as superintendent of Big Horn County schools.
INTERVIEWED BY JULIE FOSTER, AUGUST 25, 1982, HARDIN.
SUMMARY: 2 PAGES
1 TAPE: 1 HOUR

OH 349
NILS E. TORSKE AND LOIS TORSKE INTERVIEW
   Nils Torske and Lois Torske discuss dryland farming in Big Horn County from the 1920s to 1980.
INTERVIEWED BY JULIE FOSTER, AUGUST 26, 1982, CROW AGENCY.
SUMMARY: 2 PAGES
1 TAPE: 45 MINUTES

OH 350
DOROTHY CARTWRIGHT JOHNSTON INTERVIEW
   Dorothy Johnston (b. 1887) remembers: her experiences on a ranch in Meagher County from 1894 to 1932; her work as the city clerk of White Sulphur Springs from 1932 to 1957; the 1930s Depression; her jobs as a waitress, cook, and musician at the Rainbow Cafe and Bar in White Sulphur Springs.
INTERVIEWED BY LAURIE MERCIER, MAY 3, 1983, TOWNSEND.
SUMMARY: 3 PAGES
3 TAPES: 2 HOUR, 10 MINUTES

OH 351
BERNICE JOHNSON KINGSBURY INTERVIEW
   Bernice Kingsbury (1910–1982) comments on: growing up near Dupuyer; sheep ranching in Pondera County; operating a beauty shop in Valier; serving as a Democratic Party committeewoman; running as a legislative candidate in the 1940s.
INTERVIEWED BY LAURIE MERCIER, SEPTEMBER 17, 1982, HELENA.
TRANSCRIPT: 57 PAGES
3 TAPES: 2 HOURS, 10 MINUTES

OH 352
BLANCHE McMANUS INTERVIEW
   Blanche McManus chronicles: teaching in rural schools in Lincoln County; teaching in Harlem and Sunburst; her work in logging camps.

INTERVIEWED BY REX C. MYERS, SEPTEMBER 14, 1982, DILLON.
SUMMARY: 1 PAGE
1 TAPE: 1 HOUR

OH 353
D. WAYNE MYERS INTERVIEW
   Wayne Myers (b. 1896) details his work in creameries in Miles City, Billings, Missoula, and Dillon.
INTERVIEWED BY REX C. MYERS, SEPTEMBER 14, 1982, DILLON.
SUMMARY: 1 PAGE
2 TAPES: 2 HOURS

OH 354
GEORGIANNA CROUSE ANDERSEN INTERVIEW
   Georgianna Andersen (b. 1913) relates: her life as a sheep rancher's wife in Beaverhead County; cooking for ranch hands and for sheep-shearing crews; the Ames Ranch, Beaverhead County. [See also General Montana OH 576.]
INTERVIEWED BY REX C. MYERS, SEPTEMBER 19, 1982, DILLON.
SUMMARY: 1 PAGE
2 TAPES: 1 HOUR, 30 MINUTES

OH 355
WILLIS F. KOENEKE INTERVIEW
   Willis Koeneke (b. 1911) remembers: operating jewelry stores in North Dakota and in Dillon, Montana; community activities in Dillon; A. J. Oliver and Company.
INTERVIEWED BY REX C. MYERS, SEPTEMBER 20, 1982, DILLON.
SUMMARY: 1 PAGE
2 TAPES: 1 HOUR, 20 MINUTES

OH 356
DANIEL M. McDONALD INTERVIEW
   Daniel McDonald (b. 1910) reports on: his work as a coal miner in Bearcreek and Washoe from 1925 to 1967; the 1943 Smith Mine disaster; life in the communities of Bearcreek, Washoe, and Red Lodge; the UMW and trade unionism.
INTERVIEWED BY LAURIE MERCIER, SEPTEMBER 21, 1982, RED LODGE.
SUMMARY: 3 PAGES
2 TAPES: 1 HOUR, 45 MINUTES

OH 357
SENIA KALLIO INTERVIEW

Senia Kallio (b. 1908) reviews: her work experiences in Red Lodge from 1920 to 1968—particularly at the Kallio Sauna and Bathhouse, at the Red Lodge Cannery, and at the Variety Store; the Finnish community in Red Lodge.

INTERVIEWED BY LAURIE MERCIER, SEPTEMBER 22, 1982, RED LODGE.

TRANSCRIPT: 38 PAGES

2 TAPES: 1 HOUR, 40 MINUTES

OH 358
"MONTANA VERA" LAY BUENING INTERVIEW

"Montana Vera" Buening (b. 1909)—a Red Lodge resident—speaks of: working on ranches and in households in Carbon County from 1928 to 1935; her performing career as Montana Vera; the community of Red Lodge from 1935 to 1945.

INTERVIEWED BY LAURIE MERCIER, SEPTEMBER 22, 1982, RED LODGE.

SUMMARY: 3 PAGES

2 TAPES: 1 HOUR, 35 MINUTES

OH 359
WALPAS A. KOSKI INTERVIEW

Walpas Koski (b. 1907) reflects on: the Finnish community in Red Lodge; his work in the Red Lodge Drug Store from 1927 through the 1930s; his work at the Olcott Funeral Home from the 1930s through the 1950s; the 1943 Smith Mine disaster; working as a musician in a Red Lodge swing band; Prohibition.

INTERVIEWED BY LAURIE MERCIER, SEPTEMBER 23, 1982, RED LODGE.

TRANSCRIPT: 71 PAGES

3 TAPES: 2 HOURS, 40 MINUTES

OH 360
NAZZARENO GOLFI AND ADELE GOLFI INTERVIEW

Nazzareno Golfi (b. 1891) recounts his work as a coal miner in Red Lodge and Bearcreek from 1917 to the 1940s. Adele Golfi (b. 1897) discusses her work at Natali's Imperio Mercantile in Bearcreek during the 1930s; the Italian American community; the 1943 Smith Mine disaster.

INTERVIEWED BY LAURIE MERCIER, SEPTEMBER 23, 1982, RED LODGE.

SUMMARY: 2 PAGES

1 TAPE: 1 HOUR

OH 361
J. H. "PAT" PATTEN INTERVIEW

Pat Patten (b. 1905) recalls his work for the Northern Pacific Railroad Company in Red Lodge from 1928 to 1971.

INTERVIEWED BY LAURIE MERCIER, SEPTEMBER 23, 1982, RED LODGE.

SUMMARY: 2 PAGES

2 TAPES: 1 HOUR, 30 MINUTES

OH 362
CLIFFORD W. HELT INTERVIEW

Clifford Helt (b. 1901) portrays: his work for the Anaconda Copper Mining Company in Anaconda during the 1920s; his employment with the Ohio Oil Company in Bridger from 1930 to 1945; his experiences farming near Bridger; farm workers; his duties as mayor of Bridger and as Carbon County commissioner.

INTERVIEWED BY LAURIE MERCIER, SEPTEMBER 24, 1982, RED LODGE.

SUMMARY: 2 PAGES

2 TAPES: 1 HOUR, 30 MINUTES

OH 363
LILLIAN JARUSSI AND LORETTA JARUSSI INTERVIEW

Lillian Jarussi and Loretta Jarussi talks about: their teaching experiences in rural schools in Stillwater and Valley counties; the Italian community in Red Lodge; the impacts of the Depression and World War II on the area; Spanish Influenza epidemics and lice infestation. [See also General Montana OH 1487.]

INTERVIEWED BY LAURIE MERCIER, SEPTEMBER 24, 1982, RED LODGE.

SUMMARY: 4 PAGES

3 TAPES: 2 HOURS, 20 MINUTES

OH 364
BURTON C. NIMOCHS INTERVIEW

Burton Nimochs (b. 1916) tells of his work at the Anaconda Company sawmill in Bonner, 1934–1970s; the Champion International Corporation; the Lumber and Sawmill Workers Union.

INTERVIEWED BY MATTHEW HANSEN, SEPTEMBER 13, 1982, MILLTOWN.

SUMMARY: 2 PAGES

1 TAPE: 45 MINUTES

OH 365
EARL KOLPPA INTERVIEW
     Earl Kolppa (b. 1909) summarizes: his work for the Anaconda Company sawmill in Bonner, 1926–1970s; the organization of the Lumber and Sawmill Workers Union in the 1940s; the Finnish community in Milltown.
INTERVIEWED BY MATTHEW HANSEN, SEPTEMBER 15, 1982, MILLTOWN.
SUMMARY: 3 PAGES
2 TAPES: 1 HOUR, 15 MINUTES

OH 366
CHARLES E. GENDROW INTERVIEW
     Charles Gendrow (b. 1910) addresses: his work as a band-saw fitter and engineer for the Anaconda Company sawmill in Bonner and for the Western Lumber Company in Milltown into the 1930s; the Lumber and Sawmill Workers Union; trade unionism; his firefighting with the U.S. Forest Service; community life in Milltown, 1920s–1970s.
INTERVIEWED BY MATTHEW HANSEN, SEPTEMBER 15, 1982, MILLTOWN.
SUMMARY: 2 PAGES
1 TAPE: 1 HOUR

OH 367
PATRICK THIBODEAU INTERVIEW
     Patrick Thibodeau chronicles: his work for the Anaconda Company sawmill in Bonner; his involvement with the Lumber and Sawmill Workers Union; the communities of Bonner and Milltown; the Champion International Corporation.
INTERVIEWED BY MATTHEW HANSEN, SEPTEMBER 16, 1982, MISSOULA.
SUMMARY: 3 PAGES
2 TAPES: 1 HOUR, 40 MINUTES

OH 368
ELMER B. KING INTERVIEW
     Columbus resident Elmer King (b. 1889) comments on: his work as a fur trapper and a game warden in south central and southeastern Montana, beginning in 1912; his farming experiences; World War I, including the 1918 Spanish influenza epidemic and anti-German sentiment.
INTERVIEWED BY JULIE FOSTER, SEPTEMBER 2, 1982, COLUMBUS.
SUMMARY: 2 PAGES
1 TAPE: 50 MINUTES

OH 369
FRED WOLTERMAN INTERVIEW
     Fred Wolterman (b. 1888) depicts: homesteading and farming in Stillwater County from 1909 to 1949; his involvement on the local and state levels of the Montana Farmers Union.
INTERVIEWED BY JULIE FOSTER, SEPTEMBER 2, 1982, COLUMBUS.
SUMMARY: 2 PAGES
2 TAPES: 1 HOUR, 15 MINUTES

OH 370
MATTIE LATHAM SCOTT INTERVIEW
     Mattie Scott (b. 1897) describes: living on a ranch and teaching at rural schools in Stillwater County, circa 1910–1920; the community of Columbus from 1920 to 1960; her work in the Stillwater County abstract office.
INTERVIEWED BY JULIE FOSTER, SEPTEMBER 2, 1982, COLUMBUS.
SUMMARY: 3 PAGES
2 TAPES: 1 HOUR, 40 MINUTES

OH 371
GRACE THOMPSON BRICKER INTERVIEW
     Grace Bricker (b. 1908)—an Absarokee resident—details: ranch life in Stillwater County, circa 1910–1930; the important roles played by rural schools, churches, and community organizations in rural settlements.
INTERVIEWED BY JULIE FOSTER, SEPTEMBER 7, 1982, ABSAROKEE.
SUMMARY: 2 PAGES
1 TAPE: 1 HOUR

OH 372
LOTTIE HUFFORD PRICE INTERVIEW
     Lottie Price (b. 1894) discusses sheep raising and ranch life in Stillwater County, circa 1910–1930.
INTERVIEWED BY JULIE FOSTER, SEPTEMBER 8, 1982, ABSAROKEE.
SUMMARY: 2 PAGES
1 TAPE: 40 MINUTES

OH 373
AKLEEN KIRCHMAN KENNEDY INTERVIEW
     Akleen Kennedy (b. 1899) examines: business, ranch, and community life in the Fishtail area from about 1910 into the 1940s; flour mills; the operation of the Kennedy family's dry-goods store in Fishtail.
INTERVIEWED BY JULIE FOSTER, SEPTEMBER 8, 1982,

ABSAROKEE.
SUMMARY: 2 PAGES
1 TAPE: 50 MINUTES

OH 374
EDNA HUDSON LANNEN INTERVIEW
Edna Lannen (b. 1897) surveys: her experiences ranching in Stillwater County from about 1910 into the 1940s; the impact of the 1930s Depression on the ranch.
INTERVIEWED BY JULIE FOSTER, SEPTEMBER 9, 1982, ABSAROKEE.
SUMMARY: 2 PAGES
1 TAPE: 1 HOUR

OH 375
ALICE SCHWENGER KIRCH INTERVIEW
Alice Kirch (b. 1894) summarizes: life on her parents' ranch in Carbon County, circa 1910–1920; ranching with her husband near Absarokee from the 1920s into the 1940s.
INTERVIEWED BY JULIE FOSTER, SEPTEMBER 8, 1982, ABSAROKEE.
SUMMARY: 2 PAGES
1 TAPE: 45 MINUTES

OH 376
ELMEN H. TORGRIMSON AND LEONE TORGRIMSON INTERVIEW
Elmen Torgrimson and Leone Torgrimson review their operation of a grocery store and a movie theater in Absarokee from 1923 to 1940.
INTERVIEWED BY JULIE FOSTER, SEPTEMBER 10, 1982, ABSAROKEE.
SUMMARY: 2 PAGES
1 TAPE: 50 MINUTES

OH 377
HOBART SADLER INTERVIEW
Hobart Sadler speaks of his work as a cowboy on the Spear Ranch and on other cattle ranches in Stillwater County, from the 1920s into the 1950s.
INTERVIEWED BY JULIE FOSTER, SEPTEMBER 10, 1982, FISHTAIL.
SUMMARY: 2 PAGES
2 TAPES: 1 HOUR, 20 MINUTES

OH 378
DONALD McGANN INTERVIEW
Donald McGann (b. 1906) reports on: his work as a miner in Coeur d'Alene, Idaho, and in Stillwater and Park counties, Montana; mining in Jardine from 1924 to 1941; his involvement in the Mine-Mill union.
INTERVIEWED BY JULIE FOSTER, SEPTEMBER 10, 1982, COLUMBUS.
SUMMARY: 2 PAGES
2 TAPES: 1 HOUR, 10 MINUTES

OH 379
HENRY BEDFORD INTERVIEW
Henry Bedford (b. 1908) remembers his work as a watchman at the Columbus chromium mines from 1957 to 1963.
INTERVIEWED BY JULIE FOSTER, SEPTEMBER 12, 1982, FISHTAIL.
SUMMARY: 1 PAGE
1 TAPE: 25 MINUTES

OH 380
HENRY ESP INTERVIEW
Henry Esp (b. 1900) relates his experiences as a sheep rancher near Big Timber, in Sweetgrass County—including breeding, shearing, and tending sheep.
INTERVIEWED BY LAURIE MERCIER, SEPTEMBER 11, 1982, FISHTAIL.
SUMMARY: 2 PAGES
2 TAPES: 1 HOUR, 15 MINUTES

OH 381
SAM W. MALONEY INTERVIEW
Sam Maloney reflects on: work on his sheep ranch near Alder, Madison County, from 1932 to 1945; the marketing and shipping of lambs and wool; lambing; problems associated with sheep raising; changes that have occurred in the livestock business, 1920s–1970s.
INTERVIEWED BY JULIE FOSTER, SEPTEMBER 15, 1982, ALDER.
SUMMARY: 2 PAGES
1 TAPE: 50 MINUTES

OH 382
TORREY JOHNSON INTERVIEW
Busby resident Torrey Johnson (b. 1916) recounts: his family's ranching history; the Spear family; cattle ranching in Big Horn County on Northern Cheyenne Indian Reservation land; cattle ranching in general.
INTERVIEWED BY GILLIAN MALONE, JUNE 12, 1982, BUSBY.
SUMMARY: 3 PAGES
2 TAPES: 2 HOURS

OH 383
EDMOND "NED" RANDOLPH INTERVIEW
Ned Randolph (b. 1903)—a Sheridan, Wyoming, resident—recalls: his first ranching experiences; his career as an author of books on western life and on cattle ranching in Rosebud County; the Brown-Randolph Cattle Company.
INTERVIEWED BY GILLIAN MALONE, JUNE 21, 1982, SHERIDAN, WY.
SUMMARY: 1 PAGE
1 TAPE: 1 HOUR

OH 384
WILLIAM J. B. GRAHAM INTERVIEW
William Graham (b. 1896) speaks of: homesteading near Jordan, Garfield County, circa 1910–1920; ranching from the 1920s into the 1950s; family life; the Crow Indian Reservation.
INTERVIEWED BY GILLIAN MALONE, SEPTEMBER 1, 1982, BIG HORN, WY.
SUMMARY: 3 PAGES
3 TAPES: 2 HOURS, 30 MINUTES

OH 385
JUDY HOLMES INTERVIEW
Sheridan, Wyoming, resident Judy Holmes (b. 1894) discusses: cattle ranching near Decker; English traditions; ranch life.
INTERVIEWED BY GILLIAN MALONE, JULY 28, 1982, SHERIDAN, WY.
SUMMARY: 3 PAGES
2 TAPES: 2 HOURS

OH 386
CECIL CHANNEL INTERVIEW
Cecil Channel (b. 1894) talks about: his childhood in Busby, on the Northern Cheyenne Indian Reservation; his work as a section hand for the Union Pacific Railroad; lumber-mill work; coal mining on the reservation.
INTERVIEWED BY GILLIAN MALONE, JULY 31, 1982, SHERIDAN, WY.
SUMMARY: 2 PAGES
2 TAPES: 2 HOURS

OH 387
HANS C. ANDERSEN INTERVIEW
Hans Andersen (b. 1906) comments on sheep ranching in Beaverhead County, from 1917 to 1973. *[See also General Montana OH 1500.]*

INTERVIEWED BY REX C. MYERS, SEPTEMBER 30, 1982, SHERIDAN, WY.
SUMMARY: 1 PAGE
2 TAPES: 1 HOUR, 28 MINUTES

OH 388
LENORE T. McCOLLUM INTERVIEW
Lenore McCollum (b. 1890?) considers: her childhood in Twin Bridges; the lumberyards at Twin Bridges; teaching school in Dillon; her grandfather J. F. Bishop's sheep ranch in Beaverhead County. *[See also General Montana OH 571.]*
INTERVIEWED BY REX C. MYERS, SEPTEMBER 27, 1982, DILLON.
SUMMARY: 1 PAGE
2 TAPES: 1 HOUR, 35 MINUTES

OH 389
ANNA FRIELUCH JUVAN INTERVIEW
Anna Juvan (b. 1906) describes: her childhood on the family farm in Park County; working and living in the Red Lodge area during the 1920s; her marriage; operating a ranch and a dairy in Park County from 1930 to 1964; her Yugoslavian ancestry.
INTERVIEWED BY LAURIE MERCIER, SEPTEMBER 28, 1982, LIVINGSTON.
SUMMARY: 5 PAGES
2 TAPES: 2 HOURS

OH 390
ELSIE BRAWNER EYMAN INTERVIEW
Elsie Eyman (b. 1893) reflects on: her work as a teacher in Park County during the 1920s; her experiences as a ranch wife from 1927 into the 1950s; her father Robert Brawner's dairy business in Yellowstone National Park.
INTERVIEWED BY LAURIE MERCIER, SEPTEMBER 28, 1982, LIVINGSTON.
SUMMARY: 4 PAGES
3 TAPES: 2 HOURS, 30 MINUTES

OH 391
JOHN A. McCLELLEN AND GENEVIEVE LaFORGE McCLELLEN INTERVIEW
John McClellen and his wife, Genevieve McClellen (b. 1913), recall: local businesses, neighborhoods, social life, and customs in Bonner from the 1920s through the 1960s; his work as an accountant for the Anaconda Company's lumber operation in Bonner; the Blackfoot Fire Protection Association.

INTERVIEWED BY MATTHEW HANSEN, SEPTEMBER 23, 1982,
BONNER.
SUMMARY: 3 PAGES
2 TAPES: 1 HOUR, 55 MINUTES

OH 392
HAZEL BEADLE KARKANEN INTERVIEW

Hazel Karkanen (b. 1900) describes: community life
in Milltown from 1910 to 1950; her work as a teacher
and a librarian in Milltown; the history of the Karkanen
Milltown Library.
INTERVIEWED BY MATTHEW HANSEN, SEPTEMBER 14, 1982,
MILLTOWN.
SUMMARY: 2 PAGES
2 TAPES: 1 HOUR, 20 MINUTES

OH 393
MILDRED MILLER DUFRESNE INTERVIEW

Mildred Dufresne (b. 1910) portrays: her work as a
teacher in Missoula County and in Milltown, from the
1930s into the 1940s; the community of Milltown from
1935 into the 1950s; how Milltown has changed since
the 1970s.
INTERVIEWED BY MATTHEW HANSEN, SEPTEMBER 23, 1982,
MILLTOWN.
SUMMARY: 3 PAGES
1 TAPE: 50 MINUTES

OH 394
DOROTHY BENBOW RAGSDALE INTERVIEW

Dorothy Ragsdale discusses: the life of her inventor-
miner father, Thomas C. Benbow; the Benbow chromium
mine on Rock Creek near Columbus, in Stillwater
County.
INTERVIEWED BY DONNA FREY, JUNE 14, 1982, COLUMBUS.
SUMMARY: 2 PAGES
1 TAPE: 45 MINUTES

OH 395
SANDY MALCOLM INTERVIEW

Sandy Malcolm (b. 1900) discourses on: his childhood in the Paradise Valley, Park County; wildlife; his
leasing of Chico Hot Springs from Dr. George A.
Townsend during the 1920s; the acquisition of his own
ranch in the 1930s; raising seed peas; running whiskey
during Prohibition.
INTERVIEWED BY DONNA GRAY, FEBRUARY 5 AND 25, AND
MAY 26, 1982, PRAY.
SUMMARY: 6 PAGES
4 TAPES: 4 HOURS

OH 396
ARTHUR LEHTI INTERVIEW

Arthur Lehti (b. 1911) describes: his work for William A. Clark at the copper magnate's Western Lumber
Company sawmill in Milltown; his employment as care-
taker of Clark's Salmon Lake cabins during the 1920s;
local businesses and entertainment in Milltown during
the 1920s and 1930s; Prohibition.
INTERVIEWED BY MATTHEW HANSEN, SEPTEMBER 15, 1982,
MILLTOWN.
SUMMARY: 2 PAGES
1 TAPE: 1 HOUR

OH 397
DONALD L. SKILLICORN INTERVIEW

Donald Skillicorn tells about: his work as a flunky,
cook, swamper, and scaler for the Anaconda Company's
Lumber Department in the Big Blackfoot River area of
western Montana from 1935 to 1959; the struggles of
the Skillicorn family to survive on a small Blackfoot
River Valley ranch during the 1930s Depression.
INTERVIEWED BY MATTHEW HANSEN, SEPTEMBER 20, 1982,
GREENOUGH.
SUMMARY: 2 PAGES
2 TAPES: 1 HOUR, 20 MINUTES

OH 398
EARL E. COOLEY INTERVIEW

Earl Cooley portrays his work as a smoke jumper and
a foreman with the U.S. Forest Service in the Bitterroot
Valley and in Missoula from 1940 to 1946.
INTERVIEWED BY MATTHEW HANSEN, SEPTEMBER 21, 1982,
MISSOULA.
SUMMARY: 3 PAGES
2 TAPES: 1 HOUR, 30 MINUTES

OH 399
ROSS LEAVITT INTERVIEW

Ross Leavitt (b. 1906)—a resident of Missoula—depicts: his career with the U.S. Forest Service in Idaho
and Montana from 1929 to 1970; the 1924 and 1926
political campaigns of his father, U.S. Congressman Scott
Leavitt; the Blackfoot Fire Protection Association.
INTERVIEWED BY MATTHEW HANSEN, SEPTEMBER 21, 1982,
MISSOULA.
SUMMARY: 2 PAGES
1 TAPE: 1 HOUR

OH 400
TONY BENGOCHEA AND CONCEPCION BENGOCHEA INTERVIEW

Nashua residents Tony Bengochea and Concepcion Bengochea (b. 1908) report on: their work herding sheep and cooking for crews at the Etchart Ranch in Valley County from the 1920s to 1947; their purchase and operation of a sheep ranch north of Nashua; experiences of Basques in northeastern Montana.
INTERVIEWED BY LAURIE MERCIER, OCTOBER 19, 1982, NASHUA.
SUMMARY: 3 PAGES
2 TAPES: 2 HOURS

OH 401
CLARENCE M. ONSTAD INTERVIEW

Clarence Onstad (b. 1903) discusses: farming; his involvement in the oil business in Sheridan County, circa 1910–1980; the town of Coalridge; area coal-mining operations.
INTERVIEWED BY LAURIE MERCIER, OCTOBER 20, 1982, PLENTYWOOD.
SUMMARY: 3 PAGES
2 TAPES: 1 HOUR, 50 MINUTES

OH 402
CHARLES CARBONE INTERVIEW

Charles Carbone (b. 1893)—a Plentywood resident—discusses his work as a laborer and a section-gang foreman for the Great Northern Railway on the Redstone and Plentywood lines from 1921 until 1945; Italian Americans; Japanese Americans.
INTERVIEWED BY LAURIE MERCIER, OCTOBER 21, 1982, PLENTYWOOD.
SUMMARY: 2 PAGES
2 TAPES: 1 HOUR, 35 MINUTES

OH 403
EARL HOLJE INTERVIEW

Earl Holje (b. 1916) speaks of: his father's hardware store in Reserve; the mechanization of farming during the 1920s; the impact of the 1930s Depression on Sheridan County; the effects of the Depression on the Holje brothers' implement business in Plentywood into the 1970s.
INTERVIEWED BY LAURIE MERCIER, OCTOBER 21, 1982, PLENTYWOOD.
SUMMARY: 3 PAGES
2 TAPES: 1 HOUR, 30 MINUTES

OH 404
ANDREW L. MICHELS INTERVIEW

Andrew Michels (b. 1911) surveys: his family's homesteading experiences near Archer, circa 1910–1930; operating a coal-hauling business in the 1930s; managing a garage during the 1940s; returning to farming in the 1960s.
INTERVIEWED BY LAURIE MERCIER, OCTOBER 21, 1982, PLENTYWOOD.
SUMMARY: 2 PAGES
2 TAPES: 1 HOUR, 30 MINUTES

OH 405
WALTER YEAGER AND LEONA PARKHURST YEAGER

Walter Yeager (b. 1891) talks about: his homesteading experiences in the Plentywood area, circa 1910–1920; operating a coal mine during the 1930s. Leona Yeager discusses her teaching experiences on the Fort Peck Indian Reservation during the 1920s; the WPA and the Depression.
INTERVIEWED BY LAURIE MERCIER, OCTOBER 22, 1982, PLENTYWOOD.
SUMMARY: 3 PAGES
2 TAPES: 1 HOUR, 25 MINUTES

OH 406
ANNA BOE DAHL INTERVIEW

Anna Dahl (d. 1987) chronicles: her husband Andrew Dahl's efforts to organize REA associations in northeastern Montana; his REA involvement on local, state, and national levels; his experiences and work with the Montana Farmers Union from the 1920s into the 1940s.
INTERVIEWED BY LAURIE MERCIER, OCTOBER 20 AND 22, 1982, PLENTYWOOD.
SUMMARY: 4 PAGES
3 TAPES: 2 HOURS, 15 MINUTES

OH 407
MINNIE SAMPSON CHRISTENSEN INTERVIEW

Minnie Christensen (1899–1987) tells of: her work as a cook, waitress, maid, and farm wife in Sheridan County, circa 1910–1950; the Danish population in northeastern Montana; the communities of Reserve and Dagmar.
INTERVIEWED BY LAURIE MERCIER, OCTOBER 23, 1982, PLENTYWOOD.
SUMMARY: 3 PAGES
2 TAPES: 1 HOUR, 35 MINUTES

OH 408
ROY RUE AND HELEN DAHL RUE INTERVIEW

Roy Rue (b. 1916) and Helen Rue discuss: Plentywood from the 1930s into the 1940s; area businesses; Communist activities in northeastern Montana. Roy comments on operations of the Sheridan Milling Company and the Reba Lumber Company. Helen talks of her work for the Plentywood *Herald* during the 1940s.

INTERVIEWED BY LAURIE MERCIER, OCTOBER 23, 1982, PLENTYWOOD.

SUMMARY: 3 PAGES
2 TAPES: 2 HOURS

OH 409
LILLIAN NELSON KITZENBERG INTERVIEW

Lillian Kitzenberg (b. 1899) portrays: the operation of Kitzenberg's Store in Plentywood from 1921 to 1980; her work at her father Ted Nelson's racket (five-and-dime) store in Dooley, circa 1910–1920; the impact of the 1930s Depression on the area.

INTERVIEWED BY LAURIE MERCIER, OCTOBER 24, 1982, PLENTYWOOD.

SUMMARY: 5 PAGES
3 TAPES: 2 HOURS, 50 MINUTES

OH 410
PIERRE TAYLOR INTERVIEW

Pierre Taylor (b. 1904) recalls: his work as a teacher and an organizer of schools in the Fort Peck area during the construction of the Fort Peck Dam in the 1930s; his career as a salesman for the Northern School Supply Company of Great Falls from 1938 to 1980.

INTERVIEWED BY LAURIE MERCIER, NOVEMBER 4, 1982, SPOKANE, WA.

SUMMARY: 7 PAGES
3 TAPES: 2 HOURS, 55 MINUTES

OH 411
FRANK ZOGARTS INTERVIEW

Frank Zogarts (b. 1899) recounts his work as a foreman for various operations at the Anaconda Company's smelter in Anaconda, from the 1920s into the 1950s.

INTERVIEWED BY LAURIE MERCIER, NOVEMBER 18, 1982, ANACONDA.

SUMMARY: 4 PAGES
2 TAPES: 1 HOUR, 45 MINUTES

OH 412
ALBERT J. CLARK INTERVIEW

Albert Clark (b. 1912) reflects on: welding and his other jobs at the Anaconda Company's smelter in Anaconda, from 1928 to the 1950s; his work on an Opportunity-area ranch; the 1930s Depression; his participation in the Mine-Mill union.

INTERVIEWED BY LAURIE MERCIER, NOVEMBER 19, 1982, ANACONDA.

SUMMARY: 5 PAGES
3 TAPES: 2 HOURS, 40 MINUTES

OH 413
FLORENCE L. "PEGGY" MESSNER INTERVIEW

Peggy Messner (b. 1899) discusses: businesses in Anaconda, circa 1910–1930; the Anaconda Company smelter in Anaconda; her work as a reporter for the Anaconda *Standard* during the 1920s.

INTERVIEWED BY LAURIE MERCIER, NOVEMBER 20, 1982, ANACONDA.

SUMMARY: 3 PAGES
2 TAPES: 1 HOUR, 30 MINUTES

OH 414
MIKE McNELIS INTERVIEW

Mike McNelis (b. 1906) describes: his work at the Anaconda Company smelter in Anaconda; his subsequent job as a clerk for the company; community life in Anaconda and Butte.

INTERVIEWED BY LAURIE MERCIER, NOVEMBER 22, 1982, ANACONDA.

TRANSCRIPT: 119 PAGES
3 TAPES: 2 HOURS, 40 MINUTES

OH 415
MARY KANDUCH INTERVIEW

Mary Kanduch (b. 1889) remembers: her emigration from Austria in 1913; her work as a cook for several Anaconda Company logging camps in Deer Lodge County from 1914 to 1925; her husband Joe Kanduch's sawmill, which operated west of Anaconda until 1971.

INTERVIEWED BY LAURIE MERCIER, NOVEMBER 23, 1982, ANACONDA.

SUMMARY: 2 PAGES
2 TAPES: 2 HOURS

OH 416
LEO "SKIPPER" KELLY INTERVIEW

Skipper Kelly (b. 1915)—retired from serving as a Butte, Anaconda, and Pacific Railroad (BAP) accountant then president—reviews: community life in Anaconda; his career with the BAP, 1939–1970.

INTERVIEWED BY LAURIE MERCIER, NOVEMBER 23, 1983, ANACONDA.
SUMMARY: 2 PAGES
2 TAPES: 1 HOUR, 40 MINUTES

OH 417
HUGO KENCK AND MARGARET McMANN KENCK INTERVIEW

Hugo Kenck (b. 1892) and Margaret Kenck (b. 1907) speak of: music teachers, musical groups, and performers in Butte from 1900 to 1940; Butte's ethnic groups and neighborhoods; the city's German clubs; the California Brewery; the Miner's Bank. Kenck may have been the first man to sing over the radio in Montana, 1915.
INTERVIEWED BY LAURIE MERCIER, DECEMBER 8, 1982, BUTTE.
SUMMARY: 3 PAGES
3 TAPES: 2 HOURS, 10 MINUTES

OH 418
JOHN CONNORS INTERVIEW

John Connors (b. 1916) summarizes his work as a miner in the Anaconda Company mines in Butte from the 1930s into the 1950s.
INTERVIEWED BY LAURIE MERCIER, DECEMBER 9, 1982, BUTTE.
SUMMARY: 3 PAGES
2 TAPES: 2 HOURS

OH 419
GLADYS OLSON ANDERSEN INTERVIEW

Gladys Andersen (1900–1983) speaks of: farming with her husband, A. P. Andersen, near Ulm, Cascade County, circa 1910–1950; the community of Ulm.
INTERVIEWED BY LAURIE MERCIER, DECEMBER 16, 1982, GREAT FALLS.
SUMMARY: 2 PAGES
2 TAPES: 1 HOUR, 40 MINUTES

OH 420
WILLIAM F. COUTURE INTERVIEW

William Couture examines: his experiences training and racing horses in the Bitterroot Valley of western Montana; his youth spent on the Flathead Indian Reservation.
INTERVIEWED BY MATTHEW HANSEN, SEPTEMBER 28, 1982, HAMILTON.
SUMMARY: 2 PAGES
2 TAPES: 1 HOUR, 20 MINUTES

OH 421
SAMUEL J. BILLINGS INTERVIEW

Hamilton resident Samuel Billings discusses: his career with the U.S. Forest Service in western Montana; specific aspects of his work as a ranger in the Bitterroot and Kootenai national forests from the 1920s into the 1960s.
INTERVIEWED BY MATTHEW HANSEN, OCTOBER 4, 1982, HAMILTON.
SUMMARY: 4 PAGES
3 TAPES: 2 HOURS, 30 MINUTES

OH 422
RUTH GRAY ROMNEY INTERVIEW

Ruth Romney describes: her life in the Bitterroot Valley of western Montana; the Ravalli County fruit-orchard boom, circa 1910–1920; her husband Miles Romney's operation of the (Hamilton) *Western News*.
INTERVIEWED BY MATTHEW HANSEN, OCTOBER 5, 1982, HAMILTON.
SUMMARY: 2 PAGES
1 TAPE: 1 HOUR, 10 MINUTES

OH 423
ALBERT E. "KELLY" ROBBINS INTERVIEW

Kelly Robbins (b. 1893) describes his work logging and farming in the Bitterroot Valley of western Montana, circa 1910–1950.
INTERVIEWED BY MATTHEW HANSEN, OCTOBER 5, 1982, HAMILTON.
SUMMARY: 2 PAGES
1 TAPE: 50 MINUTES

OH 424
AGNES E. HANNON COOPER INTERVIEW

Agnes Cooper (b. 1907) depicts: teaching in Ravalli County schools; her duties as Ravalli County superintendent of schools from 1948 to 1958; communities in the Bitterroot Valley.
INTERVIEWED BY MATTHEW HANSEN, OCTOBER 5, 1982, DARBY.
SUMMARY: 2 PAGES
1 TAPE: 1 HOUR, 10 MINUTES

OH 425
BESSIE KERLEE MONROE INTERVIEW

Bessie Monroe (b. 1888) delineates: the history of the Bitterroot Valley; her work as a journalist on several area newspapers, including the *Western News* and the

Ravalli *Republic*; her struggles as a widow raising six children.
INTERVIEWED BY MATTHEW HANSEN, SEPTEMBER 29, 1982, HAMILTON.
SUMMARY: 2 PAGES
1 TAPE: 1 HOUR

OH 426
FRED WILKERSON INTERVIEW
Fred Wilkerson (b. 1896) considers: his work as a sawyer for Harper's logging outfit of Darby, Ravalli County, 1930s–1950s; his logging work for the Anaconda Company in the Bitterroot Valley, circa 1910–1940; construction work.
INTERVIEWED BY MATTHEW HANSEN, OCTOBER 7, 1982, HAMILTON.
SUMMARY: 2 PAGES
1 TAPE: 1 HOUR

OH 427
JOHN E. HAWKER INTERVIEW
John Hawker (b. 1892) comments on: his work logging and farming in Ravalli County, in the Bitterroot Valley; agricultural laborers; sugar beets. *[See also General Montana 1444.]*
INTERVIEWED BY MATTHEW HANSEN, SEPTEMBER 29, 1982, CORVALLIS.
SUMMARY: 2 PAGES
2 TAPES: 1 HOUR, 25 MINUTES

OH 428
KENNETH TROWBRIDGE INTERVIEW
Kenneth Trowbridge chronicles: his work as a cowboy in the Lemhi Valley of Idaho from the 1920s into the 1940s; his logging and sawmill work in Ravalli County, near Darby.
INTERVIEWED BY MATTHEW HANSEN, OCTOBER 6, 1982, DARBY.
SUMMARY: 3 PAGES
2 TAPES: 1 HOUR, 50 MINUTES

OH 429
FRED THORNING INTERVIEW
Fred Thorning talks about: his experiences farming in Ravalli County, in the Bitterroot Valley, 1920s–1950s; his work at area sawmills; the impact of agriculture and of the lumber industry on the Bitterroot Valley's economy.
INTERVIEWED BY MATTHEW HANSEN, OCTOBER 6, 1982, DARBY.

SUMMARY: 2 PAGES
2 TAPES: 1 HOUR, 30 MINUTES

OH 430
GARD LOCKWOOD INTERVIEW
Hamilton resident Gard Lockwood speaks of: farming in Ravalli County from the 1920s into the 1940s; the impacts of the sugar beet and apple industries on the local economy.
INTERVIEWED BY MATTHEW HANSEN, SEPTEMBER 28, 1982, HAMILTON.
SUMMARY: 2 PAGES
2 TAPES: 1 HOUR, 20 MINUTES

OH 431
RUSSELL CORN INTERVIEW
Russell Corn (b. 1907) discusses: gold drift mining and placer mining in Mineral County from the 1920s into the 1940s; his work for the U.S. Forest Service as a fire lookout; his jobs involving trail and road construction.
INTERVIEWED BY MATTHEW HANSEN, JANUARY 3, 1983, SUPERIOR.
SUMMARY: 2 PAGES
1 TAPE: 1 HOUR

OH 432
ARTHUR JENSEN AND HAZEL JENSEN INTERVIEW
Arthur Jensen tells about: his work as a signal operator for the Northern Pacific Railroad in eastern Montana, circa 1910–1930; his job as a theater operator in Superior during the 1930s; the roles of local industry and the Democratic Party in Mineral County. Hazel Jensen discusses: irrigated agriculture in Treasure County, circa 1910–1940; her work as a schoolteacher; Hispanic Americans; sugar beets.
INTERVIEWED BY MATTHEW HANSEN, OCTOBER 19, 1982, SUPERIOR.
SUMMARY: 3 PAGES
2 TAPES: 1 HOUR, 30 MINUTES

OH 433
WALTER R. HAHN INTERVIEW
Superior resident Walter Hahn discusses: his work for the U.S. Forest Service in the Lolo National Forest during the 1930s; wildlife and trapping in the Bob Marshall Wilderness Area; his CCC work; the Mineral County economy.

INTERVIEWED BY MATTHEW HANSEN, OCTOBER 20, 1982, SUPERIOR.
SUMMARY: 2 PAGES
2 TAPES: 1 HOUR, 30 MINUTES

OH 434
DON HELLINGER INTERVIEW
Don Hellinger (b. 1902) portrays farming operations and agriculture in Toole County from about 1910 into the 1940s.
INTERVIEWED BY MATTHEW HANSEN, DECEMBER 9, 1982, SHELBY.
SUMMARY: 2 PAGES
1 TAPE: 55 MINUTES

OH 435
CARL J. IVERSON INTERVIEW
Carl Iverson (b. 1915) recalls: his involvement in the oil-and-gas industry in Toole County during the 1940s and 1950s; wheat farming in the Sweet Grass Hills.
INTERVIEWED BY MATTHEW HANSEN, DECEMBER 9, 1982, SHELBY.
SUMMARY: 2 PAGES
1 TAPE: 1 HOUR

OH 436
EARL DOUGHTY INTERVIEW
Earl Doughty recounts: his work in the oil industry in Kevin, Cut Bank, and Sunburst; his experiences in oil camps; life in Oilmont.
INTERVIEWED BY MATTHEW HANSEN, DECEMBER 13, 1982, OILMONT.
TRANSCRIPT: 34 PAGES
1 TAPE: 1 HOUR

OH 437
MILDRED FREED HUMES INTERVIEW
Mildred Humes (b. 1900) considers: her homesteading and farming experiences north of Cut Bank, circa 1910–1960; the community of Cut Bank.
INTERVIEWED BY MATTHEW HANSEN, DECEMBER 14, 1982, CUT BANK.
SUMMARY: 2 PAGES
2 TAPES: 1 HOUR, 30 MINUTES

OH 438
J. R. "ED" RAMBO INTERVIEW
Ed Rambo (b. 1897) reflects on: his work for the Northern Pacific Railroad in Missoula from the 1920s through the 1950s; transportation businesses in Missoula;

the lumber industry in western Montana.
INTERVIEWED BY MATTHEW HANSEN, NOVEMBER 8, 1982, MISSOULA.
SUMMARY: 2 PAGES
1 TAPE: 1 HOUR

OH 439
MABEL R. ANDERSON SMITH INTERVIEW
Mabel Smith (b. 1900) relates: the reasons that her parents moved from Wisconsin to Montana; her experiences living and teaching school in Mineral County, circa 1910–1940.
INTERVIEWED BY MATTHEW HANSEN, NOVEMBER 8, 1982, MISSOULA.
SUMMARY: 2 PAGES
1 TAPE: 1 HOUR

OH 440
NITA DANIELS OLSON AND ANDREW OLSON INTERVIEW
Nita Olson (b. 1930) recalls living in Superior and Mineral County from the 1930s into the 1950s; the Diamond Match Company. Andrew Olson discusses working in Mineral County gold mines and sawmills.
INTERVIEWED BY MATTHEW HANSEN, DECEMBER 19, 1982, SUPERIOR.
SUMMARY: 2 PAGES
1 TAPE: 1 HOUR

OH 441
HAROLD B. COLE INTERVIEW
Harold Cole (b. 1915) reports on: his work for the Chicago, Milwaukee, St. Paul and Pacific Railroad (Milwaukee Road); life in the town of Alberton from the 1920s to the 1950s.
INTERVIEWED BY MATTHEW HANSEN, NOVEMBER 9, 1982, ALBERTON.
SUMMARY: 2 PAGES
1 TAPE: 1 HOUR

OH 442
ELMER L. CYR INTERVIEW
Elmer Cyr (b. 1907) reviews: employment, industries, and transportation in Mineral County, 1920s–1970s; his work for the U.S. Forest Service in western Montana; his jobs with the Northern Pacific Railroad in Alberton.
INTERVIEWED BY MATTHEW HANSEN, NOVEMBER 10, 1982, ALBERTON.
SUMMARY: 2 PAGES
1 TAPE: 1 HOUR

OH 443
GEORGE M. GILDERSLEEVE INTERVIEW
George Gildersleeve (b. 1903) discusses: his work as a gold miner in Mineral County, circa 1910–1950; the Amadir Mine; conditions in logging camps, circa 1910–1920; the IWW in western Montana; bootlegging; CCC camps in Mineral County; the Depression.
INTERVIEWED BY MATTHEW HANSEN, OCTOBER 20, 1982, SUPERIOR.
SUMMARY: 3 PAGES
2 TAPES: 2 HOURS

OH 444
OLIVE M. AHOLA KIELTY AND CHARLES NELSON INTERVIEW
Olive Kielty (b. 1908) surveys: the town of St. Regis from the 1920s into the 1950s; the local economy during that period. Her cousin Charles Nelson discusses: life in St. Regis, circa 1910–1920; the local lumber industry; his work in Mineral County, especially in Butte during the 1930s.
INTERVIEWED BY MATTHEW HANSEN, NOVEMBER 9, 1982, ST. REGIS.
SUMMARY: 3 PAGES
2 TAPES: 1 HOUR, 50 MINUTES

OH 445
NED APPLEBURY INTERVIEW
Ned Applebury talks about: his work at the Agricultural Experiment Station in Ravalli County during the 1930s; fruit and vegetable farming in the Bitterroot Valley.
INTERVIEWED BY MATTHEW HANSEN, OCTOBER 2, 1982, HAMILTON.
SUMMARY: 2 PAGES
1 TAPE: 40 MINUTES

OH 446
CECIL B. ALSUP INTERVIEW
Shelby resident Cecil Alsup (b. 1903) portrays: his work as the sheriff of Toole County, 1930s–1940s; his family's homestead near Galata; his work on oil rigs in Toole County.
INTERVIEWED BY MATTHEW HANSEN, DECEMBER 10, 1982, SHELBY.
SUMMARY: 3 PAGES
2 TAPES: 1 HOUR, 25 MINUTES

OH 447
JOHN H. AGEN INTERVIEW
John Agen (b. 1900) describes his career in the oil-drilling business in Casper, Wyoming, and Shelby, Montana, from 1917 to 1982.
INTERVIEWED BY MATTHEW HANSEN, DECEMBER 9, 1982, SHELBY.
SUMMARY: 2 PAGES
1 TAPE: 1 HOUR

OH 448
GLADYS MILLER HAGLUND INTERVIEW
Gladys Haglund (b. 1905) discusses: her father James Miller's sheep-ranching operation east of Cut Bank, circa 1910–1920; her experiences farming with her husband, Serem Haglund, during the 1940s.
INTERVIEWED BY MATTHEW HANSEN, DECEMBER 15, 1982, CUT BANK.
SUMMARY: 1 PAGE
1 TAPE: 45 MINUTES

OH 449
FLORENCE SULLIVAN HOFLAND INTERVIEW
Florence Hofland (b. 1899) examines: her father Florence Aloysius Sullivan's operation of the Marias Slope Ranch, circa 1910–1920; her cattle-ranching experiences from the 1920s into the 1950s; the impact of the petroleum industry on Toole County.
INTERVIEWED BY MATTHEW HANSEN, DECEMBER 16, 1982, CUT BANK.
SUMMARY: 3 PAGES
2 TAPES: 1 HOUR, 30 MINUTES

OH 450
RICHARD A. KULLBERG INTERVIEW
Cut Bank resident Richard Kullberg discusses: his career in the oil-and-gas business—particularly with the Ohio Oil Company of Toole County from the 1920s to the 1950s; the Kevin Sunburst Oil Field.
INTERVIEWED BY MATTHEW HANSEN, DECEMBER 16, 1982, CUT BANK.
SUMMARY: 3 PAGES
1 TAPE: 55 MINUTES

OH 451
JAMES H. McCOURT INTERVIEW
James McCourt depicts: his work as a geologist for the Union Oil Company in Cut Bank from the 1930s through the 1950s; the oil industry in Glacier and Toole counties.

INTERVIEWED BY MATTHEW HANSEN, DECEMBER 16, 1982, CUT BANK.
SUMMARY: 3 PAGES
1 TAPE: 50 MINUTES

OH 452
MILDRED BEAUDOIN INTERVIEW

Mildred Beaudoin comments on: her career as a rural schoolteacher in Madison and Toole counties, 1920s–1950s; the Liberty Mine.
INTERVIEWED BY MATTHEW HANSEN, DECEMBER 10, 1982, SHELBY.
SUMMARY: 2 PAGES
1 TAPE: 1 HOUR

OH 453
FRANK GORSICH INTERVIEW

Frank Gorsich (b. 1889) considers: his emigration from Yugoslavia; his butcher shops in East Helena and Roundup; his operation of the Casino Bar in East Helena.
INTERVIEWED BY LAURIE MERCIER, JANUARY 17, 1983, HELENA.
SUMMARY: 2 PAGES
2 TAPES: 1 HOUR, 40 MINUTES

OH 454
MINNIE PIAZZOLA INTERVIEW

Minnie Piazzola (1907–1984) talks about: her work as a cook in Meaderville; social life in Meaderville's Italian community during the 1920s and 1930s.
INTERVIEWED BY LAURIE MERCIER, MARCH 11, 1982, BUTTE.
SUMMARY: 1 PAGE
1 TAPE: 30 MINUTES

OH 455
EDWARD J. VOLLMER INTERVIEW

Edward Vollmer (b. 1910) tells of: his family's ranching operations south of East Helena, in Lewis and Clark County, from 1916 to 1933; his career with the Montana Highway Department from 1932 to 1969.
INTERVIEWED BY LAURIE MERCIER, JANUARY 20, 1983, HELENA.
SUMMARY: 3 PAGES
2 TAPES: 2 HOURS

OH 456
JOHN SCRENAR AND AGNES RICHARDSON SCRENAR INTERVIEW

John Screnar and Agnes Screnar (1903–1988) describe: community life and businesses in East Helena, circa 1910–1950, especially Richardson's Drug Store. John recalls: his work at the ASARCO smelter in East Helena from 1925 to 1972; industrial safety; the effects of the smelter on the local economy.
INTERVIEWED BY LAURIE MERCIER, JANUARY 24, 1983, EAST HELENA.
TRANSCRIPT: 36 PAGES
2 TAPES: 2 HOURS

OH 457
MARY ANN SMITH AND FRANCES SMITH RIGLER INTERVIEW

Mary Ann Smith (b. 1903) and Frances Rigler (b. 1902) discuss the businesses, ethnic groups, and community life of East Helena from 1910 to 1945. Mary Ann Smith reflects on her work at Smith's Bar from 1919 into the 1970s. Frances Rigler describes her work cleaning offices at the ASARCO smelter complex in East Helena.
INTERVIEWED BY LAURIE MERCIER, JUNE 13, 1984, EAST HELENA.
TRANSCRIPT: 68 PAGES
2 TAPES: 1 HOUR, 40 MINUTES

OH 458
GUSTAF M. CARLSON INTERVIEW

Gustaf Carlson surveys: the operation of the Spring Hill Mine near Helena during the 1930s; other Carlson mining interests in the area.
INTERVIEWED BY LAURIE MERCIER, FEBRUARY 28, 1983, HELENA.
SUMMARY: 3 PAGES
2 TAPES: 2 HOURS

OH 459
G. B. "GUS" COOLIDGE INTERVIEW

Gus Coolidge talks of his career in the petroleum industry in the Kevin Sunburst Oil Field and other areas of Toole County, 1930s–1970s.
INTERVIEWED BY MATTHEW HANSEN, DECEMBER 9, 1982, SHELBY.
SUMMARY: 2 PAGES
1 TAPE: 55 MINUTES

OH 460
JAMES PATTEN AND PHYLLIS McLEOD PATTEN
INTERVIEW

James Patten (b. 1888) recalls: his work as a miner in Philipsburg and Butte from 1907 through the 1950s; the workings of several Philipsburg-area silver, copper, and manganese mines. Phyllis Patten describes the community of Philipsburg, circa 1910–1920. *[See also Small Town Montana OH 741.]*

INTERVIEWED BY LAURIE MERCIER, FEBRUARY 9, 1983, PHILIPSBURG.

SUMMARY: 4 PAGES

3 TAPES: 2 HOURS, 30 MINUTES

OH 461
FRANK J. FITZGERALD INTERVIEW

Frank Fitzgerald (b. 1912) describes: the community of Garnet, circa 1910–1940; his efforts to renovate a family cabin located in Garnet.

INTERVIEWED BY LAURIE MERCIER, FEBRUARY 9, 1983, DRUMMOND.

SUMMARY: 1 PAGE

1 TAPE: 1 HOUR

OH 462
ROSE WEAVER LORENSEN INTERVIEW

Rose Lorensen (b. 1898) recalls: her work as a farm wife in Powell and Granite counties from the 1920s into the 1960s; Drummond and other communities in the area during the early 1900s.

INTERVIEWED BY LAURIE MERCIER, FEBRUARY 8, 1983, DRUMMOND.

SUMMARY: 2 PAGES

2 TAPES: 1 HOUR, 55 MINUTES

OH 463
NEVIN W. MORSE INTERVIEW

Nevin Morse (b. 1911) surveys: operating Morse's Grocery in Hall and Drummond, circa 1910–1930 and 1934–1941; his work as a stull (timber mine-support) contractor for the Anaconda Company in Granite County; the operation of the Standard Oil Company bulk plant in Drummond; life in Drummond, circa 1910–1970.

INTERVIEWED BY LAURIE MERCIER, FEBRUARY 10, 1983, DRUMMOND.

SUMMARY: 2 PAGES

2 TAPES: 2 HOURS

OH 464
EVELYN RUTHERFORD MARKS INTERVIEW

Evelyn Marks (b. 1901) comments on: life in Clancy from 1924 to 1982; ranching near Clancy; her experiences teaching school in Garfield County and in Clancy.

INTERVIEWED BY LAURIE MERCIER, FEBRUARY 2, 1983, CLANCY.

SUMMARY: 2 PAGES

2 TAPES: 1 HOUR, 45 MINUTES

OH 465
ERIC WHITE INTERVIEW

Eric White (1896–1992) depicts: his career as a U.S. Forest Service ranger in the Absaroka, Gallatin, Deer Lodge, and Helena national forests from 1921 to 1957; his service with the U.S. Army in France during World War I; the CCC; the Mann Gulch fire; life in Anaconda.

INTERVIEWED BY LAURIE MERCIER, FEBRUARY 2 AND 3, 1983, HELENA.

TRANSCRIPT: 117 PAGES

6 TAPES: 5 HOURS, 10 MINUTES

OH 466
EDITH HALLIDAY HAMMERSTROM INTERVIEW

East Helena resident Edith Hammerstrom (b. 1898) describes: East Helena, 1905–1970s; her involvement with the East Helena Women's Club; teaching in Rosebud during the 1920s; community life in Helena, circa 1910–1930s.

INTERVIEWED BY LAURIE MERCIER, FEBRUARY 1, 1983, EAST HELENA.

SUMMARY: 3 PAGES

3 TAPES: 2 HOURS, 30 MINUTES

OH 467
RUDOLPH W. POLICH INTERVIEW

Rudolph Polich (b. 1913) details: life in Black Eagle; his work in the brickyard and the smelter of the Anaconda Company's Great Falls Reduction Department from 1934 to 1978. *[See also Metals Manufacturing in Four Montana Communities OH 939.]*

INTERVIEWED BY LAURIE MERCIER, FEBRUARY 15, 1983, GREAT FALLS.

TRANSCRIPT: 71 PAGES

2 TAPES: 2 HOURS, 5 MINUTES

OH 468
GEORGE TESINSKI AND SOPHIE KAPSTAFER
TESINSKI INTERVIEW

George Tesinski (b. 1902) and Sophie Tesinski recall

Stockett from 1910 to the 1950s. George Tesinski discusses: his work as a coal miner for the Cottonwood Coal Company during the 1930s and 1940s; his Czechoslovakian ancestry; the UMW and trade unionism.
INTERVIEWED BY LAURIE MERCIER, FEBRUARY 16, 1983, STOCKETT.
SUMMARY: 3 PAGES
3 TAPES: 2 HOURS, 30 MINUTES

OH 469
MARY SEKNYAK SURMI INTERVIEW
Mary Surmi (b. 1899) reflects on: life in Sand Coulee; her experiences as a coal miner's wife from the 1920s into the 1940s; her emigration from Czechoslovakia; Czechoslovakian traditions in Montana.
INTERVIEWED BY LAURIE MERCIER, FEBRUARY 15, 1983, SAND COULEE.
SUMMARY: 2 PAGES
2 TAPES: 1 HOUR, 35 MINUTES

OH 470
NELL O'BRIEN O'MALLEY INTERVIEW
Nell O'Malley (b. 1892) talks about: the community of Big Sandy; her work on the McNamara Ranch; operating a beauty shop in Big Sandy.
INTERVIEWED BY LAURIE MERCIER, FEBRUARY 16, 1983, GREAT FALLS.
SUMMARY: 2 PAGES
2 TAPES: 1 HOUR, 40 MINUTES

OH 471
RICHARD SETTERSTROM INTERVIEW
Butte resident Richard Setterstrom portrays: his work for the Westinghouse Corporation during the early 1930s; his move to Butte in 1932; his career with the Montana Power Company (MPC) in Butte, 1940–1970s; promoting electric power use and industrial development; his involvement with the Montana Planning Board and the Rural Area Development (RAD) committee.
INTERVIEWED BY LAURIE MERCIER, MARCH 1, 1983, BUTTE.
SUMMARY: 7 PAGES
3 TAPES: 3 HOURS, 10 MINUTES

OH 472
WILLIAM BARTHOLOMEW INTERVIEW
William Bartholomew (b. 1909) recalls: his work as a contract miner in the Leonard Mine at Butte from 1941 to 1954; his haying and road-construction jobs near

Helmville from 1920 into the 1930s; the Western Federation of Miners; strikes.
INTERVIEWED BY LAURIE MERCIER, MARCH 2, 1983, BUTTE.
SUMMARY: 5 PAGES
3 TAPES: 3 HOURS

OH 473
SILVIO SCIUCHETTI INTERVIEW
Silvio Sciuchetti (b. 1921) reflects on his work as a miner in Butte from 1937 to 1946.
INTERVIEWED BY LAURIE MERCIER, MARCH 2, 1983, BUTTE.
SUMMARY: 2 PAGES
2 TAPES: 1 HOUR, 5 MINUTES

OH 474
MAY BELL POWELL APPLEGATE INTERVIEW
May Bell Applegate (b. 1909) recalls: the mining town of Emory, in Powell County; ranch life near Deer Lodge.
INTERVIEWED BY LAURIE MERCIER, MARCH 7, 1983, DEER LODGE.
SUMMARY: 2 PAGES
2 TAPES: 1 HOUR, 30 MINUTES

OH 475
LOUIS E. PETERSON INTERVIEW
Louis Peterson (b. 1898) remembers: the community of Racetrack, located near Deer Lodge; his experiences running small farms in Deer Lodge and Powell counties from 1925 through the 1970s; jobs growing potatoes, raising poultry, and running dairy cattle. [Included with these tapes is a recording that Louis Peterson made to augment the information initially provided to Laurie Mercier.]
INTERVIEWED BY LAURIE MERCIER, MARCH 8, 1983, DEER LODGE.
SUMMARY: 3 PAGES
3 TAPES: 3 HOURS

OH 476
WILLIAM HENRY GUSTAFSON INTERVIEW
William Gustafson (b. 1894) relates: his work at the Anaconda Company smelter in Anaconda and at the Southern Cross Mine near Georgetown Lake from 1916 into the 1950s; his service in the U.S. Army during World War I; the community of Anaconda during the early 1900s.
INTERVIEWED BY LAURIE MERCIER, MARCH 10, 1983, ANACONDA.

SUMMARY: 6 PAGES
3 TAPES: 3 HOURS, 10 MINUTES

OH 477
CARL SWANSON INTERVIEW

Carl Swanson (1903–1983) reports on: his work in the freight office of the Butte, Anaconda and Pacific Railroad (BAP) in Anaconda from 1922 to 1970; community life in Anaconda from 1910 to 1950; Swedish Americans.

INTERVIEWED BY LAURIE MERCIER, MARCH 10, 1983, ANACONDA.

SUMMARY: 2 PAGES
1 TAPE: 1 HOUR

OH 478
WILLIAM R. LINTZ INTERVIEW

William Lintz (b. 1914) reviews: his work as a fireman and an engineer for the Milwaukee Road in Deer Lodge from 1936 to 1974; his involvement with the Brotherhood of Locomotive Firemen and Enginemen (BLFE).

INTERVIEWED BY LAURIE MERCIER, MARCH 11, 1983, DEER LODGE.

SUMMARY: 2 PAGES
2 TAPES: 2 HOURS

OH 479
ROBERT L. INMAN INTERVIEW

Deer Lodge resident Robert Inman discusses his work as a fireman and an engineer on the Alberton-to-Avery line of the Milwaukee Road from the late 1940s to the early 1970s.

INTERVIEWED BY LAURIE MERCIER, MARCH 11, 1983, MISSOULA.

SUMMARY: 2 PAGES
2 TAPES: 1 HOUR, 30 MINUTES

OH 480
VERN F. JENKS INTERVIEW

Vern Jenks (b. 1918) speaks of his career as a Milwaukee Road clerk at Harlowton, Great Falls, and Deer Lodge from 1936 through the 1970s.

INTERVIEWED BY LAURIE MERCIER, MARCH 21, 1983, DEER LODGE.

SUMMARY: 2 PAGES
2 TAPES: 2 HOURS

OH 481
RALPH G. DAVIS INTERVIEW

Deer Lodge resident Ralph Davis (b. 1902) summarizes his work as a brakeman and a conductor for the Milwaukee Road on the Three Forks–to–Butte line from 1922 into the 1960s.

INTERVIEWED BY LAURIE MERCIER, MARCH 21, 1983, DEER LODGE.

SUMMARY: 2 PAGES
2 TAPES: 2 HOURS

OH 482
SAMUEL B. McDONALD INTERVIEW

Samuel McDonald (b. 1895) describes: his work as a machinist for the Butte, Anaconda and Pacific Railroad (BAP) in Anaconda from 1914 to 1919; similar work for the Milwaukee Road in Deer Lodge from 1920 to 1960; the International Association of Machinists and Aerospace Workers; trade unions.

INTERVIEWED BY LAURIE MERCIER, MARCH 23, 1983, DEER LODGE.

SUMMARY: 3 PAGES
2 TAPES: 1 HOUR, 40 MINUTES

OH 483
WALTER DUNCAN, PERDITA DUNCAN, ELMO FORTUNE, AND WILLIAM FENTER INTERVIEW

Walter Duncan, Perdita Duncan (d. 1985), Elmo Fortune (b. 1909), and William Fenter survey: the African-American community in Butte from about 1910 into the 1940s; African-American employment, social life, churches, and clubs in Butte; the Silver City Club; physicians; prevalent white attitudes towards African Americans.

INTERVIEWED BY LAURIE MERCIER, MARCH 24, 1983, BUTTE.

SUMMARY: 4 PAGES
3 TAPES: 2 HOURS, 35 MINUTES

OH 484
PERLE WATTERS INTERVIEW

Perle Watters (b. 1909) talks about: his work as a miner in various Butte mines from 1940 to 1972; the Anaconda Copper Mining Company.

INTERVIEWED BY LAURIE MERCIER, MARCH 25, 1983, BUTTE.

SUMMARY: 4 PAGES
3 TAPES: 2 HOURS, 25 MINUTES

OH 485
JOE NAVARRO INTERVIEW
Joe Navarro (b. 1923) examines: his work as a miner in Butte from 1941 through the 1970s; Hispanic Americans; the Anaconda Copper Mining Company.
INTERVIEWED BY LAURIE MERCIER, MARCH 25, 1983, BUTTE.
SUMMARY: 3 PAGES
3 TAPES: 2 HOURS, 20 MINUTES

OH 486
JOSEPHINE WEISS CASEY INTERVIEW
Anaconda resident Josephine Casey (b. 1910) talks about: her family; the 1918 Spanish influenza epidemic; the 1930s polio epidemic; Christmas toys; early grocers in Anaconda; the history and operation of the Weiss Grocery in Anaconda.
INTERVIEWED BY LAURIE MERCIER, MARCH 23, 1983, ANACONDA.
SUMMARY: 3 PAGES
2 TAPES: 1 HOUR, 30 MINUTES

OH 487
DONALD R. CONNER AND LEE GRANT INTERVIEW
Donald Conner and Lee Grant reflect on: their careers as brakemen and conductors for the Great Northern Railway, stationed in Havre from the 1930s into the 1960s; the Order of Railway Conductors and Brakemen; the Brotherhood of Railroad Trainsmen.
INTERVIEWED BY LAURIE MERCIER, APRIL 7, 1983, HAVRE.
SUMMARY: 5 PAGES
5 TAPES: 5 HOURS

OH 488
PEARL METROVICH INTERVIEW
Pearl Metrovich (b. 1898) recounts: childhood experiences on her parents' Arrow Creek Bench homestead in Fergus County from 1900 to 1917; ranch life during the 1920s and 1930s.
INTERVIEWED BY KATHLEEN TURECK, SEPTEMBER 15, 1982, STANFORD.
SUMMARY: 3 PAGES
2 TAPES: 1 HOUR, 30 MINUTES

OH 489
EMMA L. ROGERS INTERVIEW
Emma Rogers (b. 1916) comments on: the mining community of Lehigh from 1917 to 1926; her farming experiences near Windham between 1937 and 1947; the Depression; Austrian Americans.
INTERVIEWED BY KATHLEEN TURECK, SEPTEMBER 15, 1982, STANFORD.
SUMMARY: 2 PAGES
1 TAPE: 1 HOUR

OH 490
GUSTAF KOSKI INTERVIEW
Gustaf Koski (b. 1902) recalls: his work on ranches and farms in Judith Basin County during the 1920s and 1930s; mining in Butte; fur-trapping in central Montana during the 1940s.
INTERVIEWED BY KATHLEEN TURECK, MARCH 20, 1983, GEYSER.
SUMMARY: 2 PAGES
1 TAPE: 1 HOUR

OH 491
LIANE R. McGUIRE INTERVIEW
Liane McGuire portrays: her childhood experiences on her parents' homestead near Moore, circa 1910–1920; her work with her husband, Robert McGuire, teaching in the Fort Kipp School on the Fort Peck Indian Reservation during the 1930s.
INTERVIEWED BY KATHLEEN TURECK, SEPTEMBER 26, 1982, STANFORD.
SUMMARY: 2 PAGES
2 TAPES: 1 HOUR, 35 MINUTES

OH 492
KATIE M. ADAMS INTERVIEW
Katie Adams (b. 1888) recalls homesteading and farming in northern Hill County, near the Canada–U.S. boundary, from 1912 into the 1950s.
INTERVIEWED BY LAURIE MERCIER, APRIL 5, 1983, HAVRE.
SUMMARY: 3 PAGES
2 TAPES: 1 HOUR, 30 MINUTES

OH 493
GORDON C. SANDS INTERVIEW
Gordon Sands (b. 1900) considers: farming in Hill County, near Havre, from the 1920s into the 1950s; the aerial crop-spraying business; his work for the Federal Land Bank and for the H. Earl Clack Oil Company.
INTERVIEWED BY LAURIE MERCIER, APRIL 6, 1983, HAVRE.
SUMMARY: 4 PAGES
3 TAPES: 2 HOURS, 30 MINUTES

OH 494
GINA HOUGE LIPPARD AND CHARLES W.
LIPPARD INTERVIEW

Gina Lippard (b. 1893) briefly talks about her home-steading experiences in Choteau County, near Malta. Charles Lippard (b. 1903) depicts cattle and sheep ranching northeast of Fort Benton, circa 1910 into the 1950s.
INTERVIEWED BY LAURIE MERCIER, APRIL 7, 1983, HAVRE.
SUMMARY: 4 PAGES
2 TAPES: 2 HOURS, 5 MINUTES

OH 495
STELLA "SUNNY" PETERS INTERVIEW

Sunny Peters discusses: her work as a nurse for the Northern Cheyenne Indian Health Service during the 1940s; health care and living conditions on the Northern Cheyenne Indian Reservation. [See also Medicine, Health Care, and Nursing in Montana OH 1352.]
INTERVIEWED BY BEVERLY BADHORSE, MARCH 4, 1983, LAME DEER.
SUMMARY: 10 PAGES
2 TAPES: 1 HOUR, 30 MINUTES

OH 496
DOUGLAS GLENMORE AND JOSEPHINE
GLENMORE INTERVIEW

Douglas Glenmore and Josephine Glenmore describe: life on the Northern Cheyenne Indian Reservation from the 1920s to the 1940s; domestic crafts. Douglas Glenmore discusses his work as a cowboy.
INTERVIEWED BY BEVERLY BADHORSE, MARCH 15, 1983, BUSBY.
SUMMARY: 1 PAGE
2 TAPES: 1 HOUR, 50 MINUTES

OH 497
ALICE KINZEL INTERVIEW

Lame Deer resident Alice Kinzel reviews: ranch life on the Northern Cheyenne Indian Reservation from 1900 to 1950; her life as the wife of a trail driver from Texas.
INTERVIEWED BY BEVERLY BADHORSE, MARCH 12, 1983, LAME DEER.
SUMMARY: 1 PAGE
1 TAPE: 50 MINUTES

OH 498
TED RISINGSUN INTERVIEW

Ted Risingsun speaks of education and tribal government on the Northern Cheyenne Indian Reservation from the 1920s through the 1960s; the BIA; the U.S. Indian Reorganization Act.
INTERVIEWED BY BEVERLY BADHORSE, MARCH 28, 1983, BUSBY.
TRANSCRIPT: 15 PAGES
2 TAPES: 1 HOUR, 15 MINUTES

OH 499
EDWARD E. THATE INTERVIEW

Edward Thate (b. 1895) summarizes his work for the Ideal Cement Company in Trident from the 1930s into the 1950s.
INTERVIEWED BY PENELOPE LOUCAS, APRIL 12, 1983, THREE FORKS.
SUMMARY: 3 PAGES
2 TAPES: 1 HOUR, 30 MINUTES

OH 500
JOE ANDRIOLO AND JENNIE ANDRIOLO
INTERVIEW

Joe Andriolo (b. 1915) tells about: his work at the Ideal Cement Company plant in Trident from 1939 into the 1960s; the history and operations of the plant; 1946 union-organizing efforts; the United Cement, Lime, Gypsum and Allied Workers International Union. Jennie Andriolo discusses: the town of Trident; labor-management relations at the Ideal Cement Company; the Trident school; life in Gallatin County.
INTERVIEWED BY PENELOPE H. LOUCAS, APRIL 11, 1983, THREE FORKS.
SUMMARY: 6 PAGES
3 TAPES: 2 HOURS, 40 MINUTES

OH 501
HAROLD LEHFELDT AND ANNA SOPER
LEHFELDT INTERVIEW

Harold Lehfeldt (b. 1899) and Anna Lehfeldt (b. 1906) explain: their sheep-ranching operation in Golden County, near Lavina, from 1919 into the 1980s; local sheepherders; sheep-shearing techniques; marketing wool.
INTERVIEWED BY LAURIE MERCIER, APRIL 18, 1983, LAVINA.
SUMMARY: 3 PAGES
3 TAPES: 2 HOURS, 25 MINUTES

OH 502
HOWARD BILLING AND TERESA HAUGHIAN
BILLING INTERVIEW

Howard Billing (b. 1908) reports on his work as a

sheepshearer and a sheep rancher from the 1920s into the 1950s. Teresa Billing depicts: her teaching experiences near Brockway; sheep ranching with her husband, Howard; agricultural life in Rosebud, Garfield, and Custer counties.
INTERVIEWED BY LAURIE MERCIER, MARCH 19, 1983, MILES CITY.
SUMMARY: 5 PAGES
3 TAPES: 2 HOURS, 40 MINUTES

OH 503
BETTY WILSON VIMONT CARTER AND HARVEY CARTER INTERVIEW

Betty Carter discusses: farm life; her involvement with 4-H and with Home Demonstration clubs; operating the Fair Price Grocery Store in Miles City; working as a cook. Harvey Carter (b. 1893) discusses farming in Custer and Rosebud counties.
INTERVIEWED BY LAURIE MERCIER, MARCH 20, 1983, MILES CITY.
SUMMARY: 4 PAGES
2 TAPES: 2 HOURS, 5 MINUTES

OH 504
HAROLD WATTS INTERVIEW

Harold Watts (b. 1915) describes: the Kinsey Irrigation Project, in Custer County, downriver from Miles City; irrigated farming and sugar beet production; his involvement with the American Beetgrowers Association; negotiations with the Holly Sugar Company.
INTERVIEWED BY LAURIE MERCIER, APRIL 21, 1983, MILES CITY.
SUMMARY: 4 PAGES
2 TAPES: 1 HOUR, 45 MINUTES

OH 505
JESSE TRAFTON INTERVIEW

Jesse Trafton (b. 1890) portrays: working on the Manus sheep ranch in Prairie County, near Fallon, 1905–1906; his jobs as a piledriver, a pipefitter, and a construction crewman for the Milwaukee Road in Miles City from 1906 into the 1950s; his recollections of Evelyn Cameron and of the Terry area.
INTERVIEWED BY LAURIE MERCIER, APRIL 21, 1983, MILES CITY.
SUMMARY: 4 PAGES
3 TAPES: 3 HOURS

OH 506
MATHIAS "MIKE" MARTINZ INTERVIEW

Mike Martinz (1889–1988) remembers: sheep ranching in Phillips County during the 1920s and the 1930s; his operation of the Montana Hotel in Malta; his work as a miner in Butte for a few years during the 1920s.
INTERVIEWED BY LAURIE MERCIER, APRIL 27, 1983, MALTA.
SUMMARY: 4 PAGES
2 TAPES: 2 HOURS

OH 507
ALICE SALVESON FJELL INTERVIEW

Alice Fjell (b. 1916) summarizes ranching in the Tongue River Valley, Rosebud County, from the 1920s into the 1940s; Norwegian Americans.
INTERVIEWED BY MARGOT LIBERTY, APRIL 13, 1983, BIRNEY.
SUMMARY: 1 PAGE
1 TAPE: 1 HOUR

OH 508
BURTON B. BREWSTER INTERVIEW

Burton Brewster (b. 1902) recalls cattle drives and cowboys associated with the Quarter Circle U Ranch, in Rosebud County, near Birney.
INTERVIEWED BY MARGOT LIBERTY, APRIL 13. 1983, BIRNEY.
SUMMARY: 1 PAGE
1 TAPE: 1 HOUR

OH 509
NATHALIE PENSON INTERVIEW

Nathalie Penson describes ranching in Big Horn County, near Decker, from the 1920s through the 1940s.
INTERVIEWED BY MARGOT LIBERTY, APRIL 15, 1983, KIRBY.
SUMMARY: 2 PAGES
1 TAPE: 55 MINUTES

OH 510
ELMER "DEKE" REISCH INTERVIEW

Deke Reisch (b. 1910) reviews his work as a cowboy in Rosebud County, near Birney, from the 1920s through the 1940s.
INTERVIEWED BY MARGOT LIBERTY, APRIL 17, 1983, SHERIDAN, WY.
SUMMARY: 2 PAGES
1 TAPE: 1 HOUR

OH 511

HELEN HOBBS BUCKLEY INTERVIEW

Helen Buckley examines teaching in the Decker area during the 1930s and 1940s.

INTERVIEWED BY SHARON THORNBURG, APRIL 12, 1983, SHERIDAN, WY.

SUMMARY: 1 PAGES

1 TAPE: 1 HOUR

OH 512

RUSSELL M. "BUD" STADALMAN INTERVIEW

Bud Stadalman reflects on: his experiences in the CCC near Alder during the 1930s; working for the Northern Pacific Railroad in Laurel. *[See also New Deal in Montana OH 1104.]*

INTERVIEWED BY SHARON THORNBURG, MARCH 15, 1983, LAUREL.

SUMMARY: 1 PAGE

1 TAPE: 1 HOUR

OH 513

JOHN A. MESSER INTERVIEW

John Messer surveys: working in the sugar beet industry in Carbon County during the 1930s; his military service in Italy during World War II.

INTERVIEWED BY SHARON THORNBURG, MARCH 13-14, 1983, BILLINGS.

SUMMARY: 1 PAGE

1 TAPE: 1 HOUR

OH 514

WILLIAM T. SHAW INTERVIEW

William Shaw tells of coal mining and the early history of the Lodge Grass area in southeast Montana.

INTERVIEWED BY SHARON THORNBURG, MARCH 28, 1983, LODGE GRASS.

SUMMARY: 1 PAGE

1 TAPE: 1 HOUR

OH 515

LEONARD LUTGEN INTERVIEW

Leonard Lutgen recalls: farming in Stillwater County, circa 1910–1940s; the community of Wheat Basin.

INTERVIEWED BY SHARON THORNBURG, MARCH 14, 1983, RAPELJE.

SUMMARY: 1 PAGE

1 TAPE: 1 HOUR

OH 516

WILLIAM GLANCY INTERVIEW

William Glancy (1899–1985) chronicles: the 1943 Smith Mine disaster in Bearcreek; his participation in the Smith Mine rescue operations; coal mining in the Roundup area, including the Roundup Coal Mining Company and the Bair-Collins Coal Company; his involvement in the UMW; chromium mines.

INTERVIEWED BY KEN KARSMIZKI, SEPTEMBER 28, 1983, ROUNDUP.

TRANSCRIPT: 71 PAGES

2 TAPES: 1 HOUR, 40 MINUTES

OH 517

ELSA SPEAR BYRON INTERVIEW

Elsa Byron discusses the Spear Brothers (Willis and Benton) Ranch in Big Horn County from 1890 to 1920.

INTERVIEWED BY MARGOT LIBERTY, MARCH 10, 1983, SHERIDAN, WY.

SUMMARY: 1 PAGE

1 TAPE: 50 MINUTES

OH 518

WILLIAM J. COTTER INTERVIEW

William Cotter (b. 1904) discusses: his ranching operation in Phillips County; the Phillips Development Company; the impact of the Taylor Grazing Act; participating in the Malta Homesteads Project on the Milk River from the 1920s into the 1950s.

INTERVIEWED BY LAURIE MERCIER, APRIL 27, 1983, MALTA.

SUMMARY: 3 PAGES

2 TAPES: 1 HOUR, 15 MINUTES

OH 519

SUSIE CLARKE HUSTON INTERVIEW

Susie Huston (1890–1985) recalls her experiences homesteading, teaching, and sheep ranching in northern Garfield County from 1914 into the 1960s.

INTERVIEWED BY LAURIE MERCIER, APRIL 23, 1983, JORDAN.

SUMMARY: 4 PAGES

2 TAPES: 1 HOUR, 58 MINUTES

OH 520

DR. B. C. FARRAND INTERVIEW

B. C. Farrand (b. 1900?) describes: his medical internship at the Miles City hospital in 1924; his career as the lone physician in Jordan and Garfield counties from

1925 until 1980; his work to establish a blood bank and hospital at Jordan.
INTERVIEWED BY LAURIE MERCIER, APRIL 23, 1983, JORDAN.
SUMMARY: 4 PAGES
2 TAPES: 2 HOURS, 5 MINUTES

OH 521
STEPHEN WEBER INTERVIEW
Stephen Weber (b. 1890) remembers: homesteading north of Nashua, circa 1910–1920s; his work as Valley County treasurer during the 1930s; his involvement with the Montana Farmers Union; his duties on the Glasgow school board.
INTERVIEWED BY LAURIE MERCIER, APRIL 25, 1983, GLASGOW.
SUMMARY: 4 PAGES
3 TAPES: 2 HOURS, 40 MINUTES

OH 522
FRED S. ARMSTRONG INTERVIEW
Fred Armstrong (b. 1909) reflects on: Fort Peck; his work as a brakeman for the Great Northern Railway on the Glasgow-to-Whitefish line from 1929 into the 1970s.
INTERVIEWED BY LAURIE MERCIER, APRIL 26, 1983, FORT PECK.
SUMMARY: 3 PAGES
2 TAPES: 1 HOUR, 40 MINUTES

OH 523
PERLE W. BAILEY INTERVIEW
Glasgow resident Perle Bailey (b. 1907) discusses his work as a laborer and a conductor for the Great Northern Railway on the Williston (North Dakota)-to-Glasgow line, 1926–1969.
INTERVIEWED BY LAURIE MERCIER, APRIL 26, 1983, GLASGOW.
SUMMARY: 2 PAGES
2 TAPES: 2 HOURS

OH 524
MYRTLE MILLS ROUNDTREE INTERVIEW
Myrtle Roundtree (b. 1905) recalls: her work sewing sacks at the Ideal Cement Company plant in Trident during World War II; family life; her disillusionment with farming; raising turkeys.
INTERVIEWED BY PENELOPE LOUCAS, MAY 2, 1983, MANHATTAN.
SUMMARY: 4 PAGES
2 TAPES: 1 HOUR, 40 MINUTES

OH 525
RALPH K. CARROLL INTERVIEW
Ralph Carroll (b. 1910) portrays: his work as a repairman, a miller, and a laboratory analyst for the Ideal Cement Company in Trident from the 1930s into the 1970s; plant operations; industrial safety conditions; personalities; the United Cement, Lime, Gypsum, and Allied Workers International Union.
INTERVIEWED BY PENELOPE LOUCAS, MARCH 28, 1983, MANHATTAN.
SUMMARY: 4 PAGES
3 TAPES: 2 HOURS, 35 MINUTES

OH 526
GEORGE EVERETT OYLER AND HELEN OYLER INTERVIEW
George Oyler (b. 1910) recounts: his work as a quarry-based shovel operator for the Ideal Cement Company in Trident; plant operations and management; the United Cement, Lime, Gypsum, and Allied Workers International Union. Helen Oyler discusses the community of Trident.
INTERVIEWED BY PENELOPE LOUCAS, APRIL 29, 1983, MANHATTAN.
SUMMARY: 6 PAGES
3 TAPES: 2 HOURS, 25 MINUTES

OH 527
SIMON "SAM" JOHNSON INTERVIEW
Sam Johnson (b. 1884) relates: his work for the Ideal Cement Company in Trident from the 1920s to the 1960s; the United Cement, Lime, Gypsum and Allied Workers International Union; farming in Gallatin County from 1919 into the 1930s; the communities of Logan and Trident.
INTERVIEWED BY PENELOPE LOUCAS, MAY 4, 1983, MANHATTAN.
SUMMARY: 8 PAGES
4 TAPES: 3 HOURS, 55 MINUTES

OH 528
MINDA P. BROWNELL McANNALLY INTERVIEW
Glendive resident Minda McAnnally (b. 1898) reports on: her work as a telegraph operator for the Northern Pacific Railroad in eastern Montana and in Richardson, North Dakota, from 1917 to 1920; the lives of women operators during World War I.
INTERVIEWED BY LAURIE MERCIER, APRIL 24, 1983, GLENDIVE.
SUMMARY: 2 PAGES
2 TAPES: 1 HOUR, 40 MINUTES

OH 529
BIRDIE LOWER INTERVIEW
Birdie Lower (b. 1919) speaks of: her work as an oiler in the cooler of the Ideal Cement Plant in Trident during World War II; her childhood in Willow Creek during the 1930s.
INTERVIEWED BY PENELOPE LOUCAS, MAY 11, 1983, WILLOW CREEK.
SUMMARY: 6 PAGES
2 TAPES: 2 HOURS

OH 530
JOHN TINJUM INTERVIEW
John Tinjum (b. 1913) describes: his duties with the CCC during the 1930s; his work for the Ideal Cement Company in Trident from 1935 to 1975; the United Cement, Lime, Gypsum, and Allied Workers International Union.
INTERVIEWED BY PENELOPE LOUCAS, MAY 12, 1983, THREE FORKS.
SUMMARY: 6 PAGES
3 TAPES: 2 HOURS, 10 MINUTES

OH 531
GEORGIE OLSEN WELLHOUSER INTERVIEW
Georgie Wellhouser (b. 1916) recalls: her experiences growing up in the Logan area; Trident from 1925 to 1940—particularly its neighborhoods and personalities; Japanese Americans; the Ideal Cement Company in Trident.
INTERVIEWED BY PENELOPE LOUCAS, MAY 12, 1983, MANHATTAN.
SUMMARY: 3 PAGES
2 TAPES: 1 HOUR, 20 MINUTES

OH 532
EDNA M. OLSEN GILLESPIE INTERVIEW
Edna Gillespie (b. 1908) discusses: operating a Trident hotel and boarding house with her mother, Eva Lena Burrell Olsen, during the 1920s; the towns of Trident and Logan from the 1920s to the 1940s; the Ideal Cement Company
INTERVIEWED BY PENELOPE LOUCAS, MAY 12, 1983, THREE FORKS.
SUMMARY: 5 PAGES
2 TAPES: 1 HOUR, 50 MINUTES

OH 533
PEARL D. JOHNSON INTERVIEW
Pearl Johnson relates her experiences farming and

ranching north of Frazer from 1910 to 1947.
INTERVIEWED BY DIANE SANDS, JUNE 9, 1982, FRAZER.
SUMMARY: 2 PAGES
1 TAPE: 1 HOUR

OH 534
NOLA B. HOLTBERG INTERVIEW
Nola Holtberg describes: her work at the Frazer Hotel during the 1920s; housework; her involvement in the Frazer community from the 1920s into the 1940s.
INTERVIEWED BY DIANE SANDS, JUNE 9, 1983, GLASGOW.
SUMMARY: 1 PAGE
1 TAPE: 1 HOUR

OH 535
JOE DOBRAVEC INTERVIEW
Joe Dobravec (b. 1913) talks about: his work as a logger in Sanders County from the 1920s into the 1940s; his duties for the CCC during the 1930s; his work as a small rancher in northwestern Montana.
INTERVIEWED BY DIANE SANDS, MAY 31, 1983, NOXON.
SUMMARY: 3 PAGES
2 TAPES: 1 HOUR, 35 MINUTES

OH 536
NINA ARMSTRONG BURKETT INTERVIEW
Nina Burkett (b. 1893) discourses on: her husband, A. P. Burkett, and his work as a chemist for the Ideal Cement Company in Trident from 1917 to 1957; the town of Trident; the role of the cement company in the community; labor-management relationships; Italian Americans.
INTERVIEWED BY PENELOPE LOUCAS, MAY 20, 1983, TRIDENT.
SUMMARY: 9 PAGES
4 TAPES: 3 HOURS, 45 MINUTES

OH 537
CARROLL O. WATSON INTERVIEW
Carroll Watson (b. 1902) tells of: homesteading and farming near Cardwell from 1915 through the 1950s; technological developments in farm machinery; the 1930s Depression; raising and breaking horses.
INTERVIEWED BY PENELOPE LOUCAS, MAY 25, 1983, CARDWELL.
SUMMARY: 8 PAGES
3 TAPES: 2 HOURS, 40 MINUTES

OH 538
JAMES NELSON, JR., INTERVIEW
James Nelson, Jr., details: his work as a mechanic for the Ideal Cement Company in Trident during the 1940s; his father James Nelson's work for the company; the community of Trident; Japanese Americans in the community.
INTERVIEWED BY PENELOPE LOUCAS, MAY 24, 1983, HELENA.
SUMMARY: 4 PAGES
2 TAPES: 1 HOUR, 35 MINUTES

OH 539
EDWIN G. BELLACH INTERVIEW
Edwin Bellach (b. 1910) discusses: his dynamite-drilling work at the Ideal Cement Company's quarry in Trident during the 1920s; the plumbing business; bootlegging; the IWW; bridge-construction work; other jobs he held in the Logan–Three Forks–Trident area.
INTERVIEWED BY PENELOPE LOUCAS, MAY 27, 1983, THREE FORKS.
SUMMARY: 9 PAGES
3 TAPES: 2 HOURS, 40 MINUTES

OH 540
BILL BLAKELY INTERVIEW
Bill Blakely (b. 1912) depicts: his work as a chemist in the Ideal Cement Company laboratory at Trident from the 1940s into the 1960s; his involvement in the United Cement, Lime, Gypsum, and Allied Workers International Union; his early work as a ranch hand.
INTERVIEWED BY PENELOPE LOUCAS, MAY 27, 1983, THREE FORKS.
SUMMARY: 6 PAGES
3 TAPES: 2 HOURS, 10 MINUTES

OH 541
FOUR SOULS INTERVIEW
Four Souls (1907–1984), an American Indian of the Cree tribe, describes: his experiences as the son of Little Bear and grandson of Big Bear; his life on the Rocky Boy's Indian Reservation from 1915 to 1939; his trip to Rapid City, South Dakota, to attend the Northwest Plains Conference in 1934.
INTERVIEWED BY ANGELA THOMPSON, APRIL 20 AND MAY 3, 1983, BOX ELDER.
SUMMARY: 3 PAGES
2 TAPES: 1 HOUR, 15 MINUTES

OH 542
JAMES GOPHER INTERVIEW
James Gopher (b. 1902) characterizes: his life as a Cree Indian living and working in northern Montana; the efforts of Cree tribal members to establish a reservation. [The interview is conducted in the Cree language.]
INTERVIEWED BY NADINE MORSETTE, MAY 25, 1983, BOX ELDER.
SUMMARY: 5 PAGES
3 TAPES: 30 MINUTES

OH 543
WILLIAM DENNY, SR., INTERVIEW
William Denny, Sr. (b. 1910), describes: the establishment of the Rocky Boy's Indian Reservation; educational and work opportunities for Cree Indians from 1920 to 1950. [This interview is conducted in the Cree language.]
INTERVIEWED BY NADINE MORSETTE, MARCH 14, 1983, BOX ELDER.
SUMMARY: 4 PAGES
1 TAPE: 30 MINUTES

OH 544
REVEREND SCHUYLER DelCAMP INTERVIEW
Reverend Schuyler DelCamp (b. 1900) comments on: his work as a field foreman near Hardin, from 1929 to 1941; Tom Campbell; the farm corporation's operations.
INTERVIEWED BY LAURIE MERCIER, JUNE 7, 1983, CUSTER.
SUMMARY: 4 PAGES
2 TAPES: 1 HOUR, 45 MINUTES

OH 545
LOUIS LAROCHE INTERVIEW
Louis LaRoche (b. 1906) describes: his work as deputy treasurer of Daniels and Dawson counties during the 1930s; his abstract business in Malta from 1940 to 1965; his French-Canadian ancestry.
INTERVIEWED BY LAURIE MERCIER, JUNE 8, 1983, BILLINGS.
SUMMARY: 2 PAGES
1 TAPE: 1 HOUR, 5 MINUTES

OH 546
J. N. "BUCK" CORNELIO INTERVIEW
Buck Cornelio (b. 1904) describes: Red Lodge from 1900 to 1933; his work in the family's bootlegging business; the Iris Theatre from 1919 to 1933; his job driving a bus in Yellowstone National Park during the 1930s; his Italian-American ancestry.

INTERVIEWED BY LAURIE MERCIER, JUNE 9, 1983,
BILLINGS.
SUMMARY: 3 PAGES
2 TAPES: 2 HOURS, 5 MINUTES

OH 547
KENNETH DAVIS INTERVIEW

Kenneth Davis (b. 1909) chronicles: the Kevin Sunburst petroleum boom during the 1920s; the establishment and operation of his Cut Bank oil refinery during the 1930s; his work for the Husky Oil Company; the Dempsey-Gibbons fight in Shelby in 1923.
INTERVIEWED BY LAURIE MERCIER, JUNE 9, 1983,
BILLINGS.
SUMMARY: 3 PAGES
2 TAPES: 2 HOURS

OH 548
ANITA STEWART WATSON AND MARSHALL WATSON INTERVIEW

Anita Watson (b. 1908) talks about her youth in Butte during the 1920s. Marshall Watson (b. 1910) tells of: his work on ranches in Blaine County and in Idaho; his duties as a ditch rider on the Milk River Irrigation Project during the 1930s.
INTERVIEWED BY LAURIE MERCIER, JUNE 21, 1983,
CORVALLIS.
SUMMARY: 3 PAGES
1 TAPE: 1 HOUR, 5 MINUTES

OH 549
MAX McKEE INTERVIEW

Max McKee (b. 1905) discusses: his work as a bacteriologist at the Rocky Mountain Laboratory in Hamilton from 1932 to 1964; his logging-camp jobs in northern Idaho during the 1920s; the National Institute of Allergy and Infectious Diseases; Rocky Mountain spotted fever.
INTERVIEWED BY LAURIE MERCIER, JUNE 21, 1983,
CORVALLIS.
SUMMARY: 4 PAGES
3 TAPES: 2 HOURS, 35 MINUTES

OH 650
WILLIAM R. "BUD" MOORE INTERVIEW

Bud Moore (b. 1917) speaks of: his work for the U.S. Forest Service as a Powell District ranger in Idaho; fire-control duties for the Forest Service; trapping in the northern Bitterroot Mountains during the 1920s and 1930s; logging work for the Anaconda Company; the Selway-Bitterroot Wilderness.

INTERVIEWED BY LAURIE MERCIER, JUNE 23, 1983,
CONDON.
SUMMARY: 6 PAGES
3 TAPES: 2 HOURS, 50 MINUTES

OH 651
RICHARD ROSSIGNOL INTERVIEW

Richard Rossignol (b. 1904) reviews: logging in Montana and Idaho from the 1920s into the 1960s; his father Paul Rossignol's lumber mill near Lolo.
INTERVIEWED BY LAURIE MERCIER, JUNE 24, 1983, LOLO.
SUMMARY: 2 PAGES
2 TAPES: 1 HOUR, 10 MINUTES

OH 652
H. LEE HAMES INTERVIEW

Lee Hames reports on: his work as a lumberjack in Missoula County during the 1930s and 1940s; Anaconda Company logging camps; the life of a lumberjack; his work in the Blackfoot River Valley; horse-logging teams; his experiences trucking for rodeo tours during the 1950s. *[See also General Montana OH 1447.]*
INTERVIEWED BY LAURIE MERCIER, JUNE 21, 1983, LOLO.
SUMMARY: 5 PAGES
3 TAPES: 2 HOURS, 5 MINUTES

OH 653
LISLE SCANLAND INTERVIEW

Lisle Scanland (b. 1903) remembers: his work as a miner in Butte during the 1920s; his jobs with Hansen's Packing Company in Butte during the early 1930s; raising fruit and livestock near Corvallis from 1935 into the 1960s.
INTERVIEWED BY LAURIE MERCIER, JUNE 22, 1983,
CORVALLIS.
SUMMARY: 6 PAGES
4 TAPES: 3 HOURS, 45 MINUTES

OH 654
WILBUR "MAC" McKINNEY INTERVIEW

Mac McKinney (b. 1908) describes: his work for the U.S. Weather Bureau in Great Falls, Kalispell, and Helena from 1940 to 1968; the bureau's relationship with farmers; the impact of World War II on the Weather Service; problems involved with predicting weather in Montana.
INTERVIEWED BY LAURIE MERCIER, FEBRUARY 25, 1983,
HELENA.
SUMMARY: 3 PAGES
2 TAPES: 2 HOURS

OH 655
EDNA G. COX McCANN INTERVIEW
Edna McCann (b. 1902) reflects on: her family's homestead near Trout Creek; trapping; childhood chores; the forest fires of 1910; berry picking; volunteer work during World War I; prospecting.
INTERVIEWED BY DIANE SANDS, MAY 5, 1983, TROUT CREEK.
TRANSCRIPT: 46 PAGES
2 TAPES: 2 HOURS

OH 656
JOE GARRISON INTERVIEW
Joe Garrison (1887–1983) talks about: raising horses, ranching, and logging in Sanders County from 1910 to 1940; prostitution; the IWW.
INTERVIEWED BY DIANE SANDS, MAY 30, 1983, PLAINS.
SUMMARY: 1 PAGE
1 TAPE: 1 HOUR

OH 657
ROBERT "SPARKY" HILEMAN INTERVIEW
Sparky Hileman recalls: his career as a professional forester with the J. Neils Lumber Company from 1939 to 1970; logging operations in northwestern Montana from the 1940s into the 1960s; specific forest policies; typical logging camps in Lincoln County.
INTERVIEWED BY DIANE SANDS, JUNE 6, 1983, LIBBY.
SUMMARY: 3 PAGES
2 TAPES: 1 HOUR, 35 MINUTES

OH 658
MELVIN HOY INTERVIEW
Melvin Hoy portrays: the organization of the Lumber and Sawmill Workers Union in Sanders County; his work as a union official during the 1940s; his duties as a trimmer at the Brown Brothers sawmill in Thompson Falls.
INTERVIEWED BY DIANE SANDS, MAY 7, 1983, LIBBY.
SUMMARY: 2 PAGES
2 TAPES: 1 HOUR, 30 MINUTES

OH 659
JOHN C. HARKER INTERVIEW
John Harker tells about: ranch work in Sanders County in the 1920s; dam construction jobs on the Clark Fork River during the 1950s; his work in a Heron sawmill during the 1950s and 1960s. *[See also Medicine, Health Care, and Nursing in Montana OH 1326.]*

INTERVIEWED BY DIANE SANDS, JUNE 6, 1983, HERON.
SUMMARY: 2 PAGES
2 TAPES: 1 HOUR, 20 MINUTES

OH 660
WILBERT J. "WIB" HARRER INTERVIEW
Wib Harrer (1901–1986?)—known popularly in Montana as "Mr. Angus"—talks of: his career ranching and promoting Angus cattle from 1923 to 1978; his involvement with the Montana Dairyman's Association and with the Montana Angus Association; his efforts to improve purebred Angus herds in Montana; annual cattle sales at the Green Meadow Ranch in the Prickly Pear (Helena) Valley.
INTERVIEWED BY LAURIE MERCIER, JULY 12 AND 19, 1983, HELENA.
SUMMARY: 6 PAGES
3 TAPES: 2 HOURS, 50 MINUTES

OH 661
JACK PARRISH INTERVIEW
Jack Parrish (b. 1923) surveys: his logging work in the Rexford division of the J. Neils Lumber Company from 1948 through the 1970s; his duties as mayor of Rexford; his opposition to the construction of the Libby Dam; forest fires.
INTERVIEWED BY LAURIE MERCIER, AUGUST 4, 1983, REXFORD.
SUMMARY: 6 PAGES
3 TAPES: 3 HOURS, 10 MINUTES

OH 662
BERT WILKE INTERVIEW
Bert Wilke (1893–1984) reviews: logging work in Lincoln County from 1910 into the 1940s; horse packing and firefighting for the U.S. Forest Service from 1910 to 1958; the last river log-drives during the early 1920s; the Baker Brothers Logging Company; his involvement with the IWW; World War I peace movements. *[See also General Montana OH 695.]*
INTERVIEWED BY LAURIE MERCIER, AUGUST 26, 1983, FORTINE.
SUMMARY: 7 PAGES
4 TAPES: 3 HOURS, 10 MINUTES

OH 663
WALTER E. SCHURCH INTERVIEW
Walter Schurch (b. 1894) comments on his operation of a dairy farm in Powell County, near Deer Lodge, from 1910 to 1945.

INTERVIEWED BY LOIS MCDONALD, AUGUST 23, 1983, DEER LODGE.
SUMMARY: 3 PAGES
2 TAPES: 1 HOUR, 20 MINUTES

OH 664
ALBERT S. HENDRICKSON INTERVIEW

Albert Hendrickson (b. 1912) considers: his family's Finnish background; his childhood and early life in Southern Cross, near Georgetown Lake; gold and manganese mining activities at Granite, Southern Cross, and Norris.
INTERVIEWED BY LAURIE MERCIER, SEPTEMBER 15, 1983, HELENA.
SUMMARY: 4 PAGES
2 TAPES: 2 HOURS, 10 MINUTES

OH 665
NOLA PAYNE SLOAN INTERVIEW

Nola Sloan (b. 1893) describes: her childhood and young adulthood in Troy from 1901 to 1923; teaching school in Lincoln County during the early 1920s; her participation in community activities and local organizations since the 1940s.
INTERVIEWED BY LAURIE MERCIER, SEPTEMBER 20, 1983, TROY.
SUMMARY: 3 PAGES
2 TAPES: 1 HOUR, 35 MINUTES

OH 666
LEONARD "SLIM" SHEFFIELD INTERVIEW

Leonard Sheffield (1899–1984) examines: his post–World War I work for the J. Neils Company sawmill in Libby; his work as a carpenter; the organization of the local carpenters' union; the IWW; illegal trapping activities in Lincoln County forests.
INTERVIEWED BY LAURIE MERCIER, SEPTEMBER 20, 1983, LIBBY.
SUMMARY: 3 PAGES
2 TAPES: 1 HOUR, 55 MINUTES

OH 667
MARK BUCKLEY AND PETRENA DRAGSETH BUCKLEY INTERVIEW

Mark Buckley (b. 1903) and Petrena Buckley (b. 1905) discuss: ranching and teaching in Prairie County, on the Dragseth Ranch, circa 1910–1930s; the Conrad Lumber Mill; operating a store/post office/dancehall in Marion, 1940s–1950s.

INTERVIEWED BY LAURIE MERCIER, OCTOBER 17, 1983, KALISPELL.
SUMMARY: 4 PAGES
2 TAPES: 2 HOURS, 10 MINUTES

OH 668
JOHN GEORGE MITTAL INTERVIEW

John Mittal (b. 1907) discusses: his work as a miner for several coal companies in Cascade County, 1928–1950s; the operation of local mines; the community of Sand Coulee; his work with the local UMW chapter; the Cottonwood Coal Company; his Slovene-American ancestry.
INTERVIEWED BY LAURIE MERCIER, OCTOBER 20, 1983, SAND COULEE.
SUMMARY: 5 PAGES
3 TAPES: 2 HOURS, 40 MINUTES

OH 669
DANIEL HILGER, BRYAN HILGER, AND AMELIA F. "BABE" HILGER INTERVIEW

Daniel Hilger (b. 1908), Bryan Hilger (b. 1913), and Amelia Hilger (b. 1918) speak of: the history and operation of the Hilger Ranch north of Helena; the introduction of purebred Hereford cattle to their herd; the evolution of haying techniques and irrigation methods.
INTERVIEWED BY LAURIE MERCIER, NOVEMBER 8, 1983, HELENA.
SUMMARY: 5 PAGES
3 TAPES: 2 HOURS, 35 MINUTES

OH 670
MAURICE PALMER INTERVIEW

Maurice Palmer (b. 1904) details: the operation of the Palmer sawmill, west of Eureka, in Lincoln County, from 1913 through the 1950s; the Eureka Lumber Company mill during the 1920s; the activities of local IWW members.
INTERVIEWED BY LAURIE MERCIER, NOVEMBER 14, 1983, TREGO.
SUMMARY: 4 PAGES
2 TAPES: 1 HOUR, 50 MINUTES

OH 671
ALBERT SCHLICHTIG INTERVIEW

Albert Schlichtig (b. 1899) describes his work on Northern Pacific Railroad section crews in Harrison from the 1920s into the 1960s.
INTERVIEWED BY LAURIE MERCIER, FEBRUARY 7, 1984, HARRISON.

SUMMARY: 2 PAGES
1 TAPE: 45 MINUTES

OH 672
OLIVE NIELAND HELLICKSON INTERVIEW

Olive Hellickson (b. 1910) depicts: her work as a teacher in North Dakota in the 1930s and in St. Regis in the 1960s; ranching in Daniels County from 1939 to 1960. INTERVIEWED BY LAURIE MERCIER, FEBRUARY 28, 1984, CHOTEAU.
SUMMARY: 2 PAGES
1 TAPE: 55 MINUTES

OH 673
DOROTHY BRUNER FLOERCHINGER
INTERVIEW

Dorothy Floerchinger (b. 1901) characterizes: farming in Ponderay County from 1913 into the 1950s; her participation in the Montana Farmers Union; the role of women in developing communities; the importance of such organizations as Home Demonstration clubs, the Conrad Women's Club, and the Montana Farmers Union cooperatives; the Montana Study. INTERVIEWED BY LAURIE MERCIER, APRIL 10, 1984, CONRAD.
SUMMARY: 5 PAGES
3 TAPES: 2 HOURS, 40 MINUTES

OH 674
ROBERT P. CORBETT INTERVIEW

Robert Corbett (b. 1918) portrays: the Anaconda Company's mining operations in Butte; his work as an engineer, 1940–1978; the evolution of open-pit mining in Butte; the 1977 ARCO purchase of Anaconda Company properties; labor relations—including the 1934, the 1946, and the 1967 strikes. INTERVIEWED BY LAURIE MERCIER, APRIL 17, 1984, BUTTE.
SUMMARY: 5 PAGES
2 TAPES: 2 HOURS, 10 MINUTES

OH 675
JESSIE WILHOIT MOLA INTERVIEW

Jessie Mola (b. 1908) recalls: the mining town of Marysville from 1917 to 1945; her work as the Marysville postmistress from 1931 to 1944; her experiences as a telephone operator in Helena during the 1920s. INTERVIEWED BY LAURIE MERCIER, APRIL 25, 1984, HELENA.

OH 676
ROSALIND REYNOLDS HARPER INTERVIEW

Rosalind Harper (b. 1902) tells of: operating, with her husband, Leland Harper, the Harper Logging Company of Missoula, from 1921 to 1958; specific logging contracts; camp life; cooking for lumberjacks; the effects of mechanization on the industry. INTERVIEWED BY LAURIE MERCIER, JUNE 1, 1984, BILLINGS.
SUMMARY: 3 PAGES
2 TAPES: 1 HOUR, 25 MINUTES

OH 677
ARTHUR WHITNEY INTERVIEW

Arthur Whitney (b. 1911) reports on: his work as a U.S. Forest Service ranger in the Flathead National Forest of western Montana from 1931 through the 1960s; the community of Bigfork; Flathead Lake steamboats; the local forest-products industry. INTERVIEWED BY LAURIE MERCIER, AUGUST 31, 1984, BIGFORK.
SUMMARY: 7 PAGES
3 TAPES: 3 HOURS, 5 MINUTES

OH 678
ABIGAIL MITTON INTERVIEW

Abigail Mitton (b. 1889) recalls: her experiences in the Flathead Valley from 1900 to 1922; working for the J. C. Penney store in Kalispell, circa 1910–1920. INTERVIEWED BY LAURIE MERCIER, SEPTEMBER 5, 1984, KALISPELL.
SUMMARY: 4 PAGES
2 TAPES: 2 HOURS, 10 MINUTES

OH 679
OLIVER NELSON INTERVIEW

Oliver Nelson (b. 1914) chronicles his years logging for various lumber companies in western Montana and in Salmon, Idaho, from the 1930s into the 1960s. INTERVIEWED BY LAURIE MERCIER, SEPTEMBER 5, 1985, MISSOULA.
SUMMARY: 4 PAGES
2 TAPES: 1 HOUR, 30 MINUTES

OH 680

MARGARET E. GEE INTERVIEW

Margaret Gee (b. 1900) comments on: her youth on a Gallatin County farm from 1905 until 1920; family relations; schooling; farm work; the 1918 Spanish influenza epidemic.

INTERVIEWED BY JACKIE DAY, AUGUST 2, 1984, BELGRADE.

SUMMARY: 4 PAGES

2 TAPES: 1 HOUR, 45 MINUTES

OH 681

BOB COONEY INTERVIEW

Bob Cooney (b. 1909) depicts: growing up on a ranch subsequently flooded by the Canyon Ferry Reservoir, east of Helena; his artist mother, Fanny Young Cory Cooney; his years working in the recreation and parks division of the Montana Department of Fish and Game.

INTERVIEWED BY PATRICIA BORNEMAN, JUNE 24, 1986, HELENA.

SUMMARY: 8 PAGES

2 TAPES: 2 HOURS

OH 726

CECELIA LYONAIS BARNHART AND FLOYD BARNHART INTERVIEW

Cecelia Barnhart and Floyd Barnhart describe the community of Columbia Falls since 1947. Floyd discusses his work at the Plum Creek Lumber Company in Columbia Falls. Cecelia considers her work with a local 4-H club and with St. Richard's Catholic Church.

INTERVIEWED BY LAURIE MERCIER, NOVEMBER 18, 1983, JORDAN.

SUMMARY: 3 PAGES

2 TAPES: 1 HOUR, 35 MINUTES

Native American Educators Oral History Project

Cosponsored by the Office of Public Instruction and the Montana Advisory Council on Indian Education, this project recorded the reminiscences of those active in Native American education, both on and off the reservations, from the early twentieth century through the 1980s. Interviewees discuss the boarding school system, the challenges of higher education, theories of teaching, and the development of Native American educational programs across the state.

OH 1226
JOSEPH MEDICINE CROW INTERVIEW

Joe Medicine Crow (b. 1913) tells about: his education at the Lodge Grass School on the Crow Indian Reservation; his years at an Oklahoma boarding school and at college; relations with non-Indians; difficulties finding employment; his experiences teaching; his directorship of Crow Central Education; the establishment of Little Big Horn College at Crow Agency.
INTERVIEWED BY BILL LAFORGE, JANUARY 30, 1989, LODGE GRASS.
TRANSCRIPT: 24 PAGES
1 TAPE: 1 HOUR

OH 1227
JOSEPHINE PEASE RUSSELL INTERVIEW

Josephine Russell (b. 1914) speaks of: her childhood on the Crow Indian Reservation during the 1920s; her education at Lodge Grass School; attending college in Oregon; teaching at Crow Agency; the Head Start program.
INTERVIEWED BY BILL LAFORGE, FEBRUARY 24 AND 25, 1989, LODGE GRASS.
TRANSCRIPT: 24 PAGES
1 TAPE: 1 HOUR

OH 1228
BENJAMIN PEASE, JR., INTERVIEW

Benjamin Pease, Jr. (b. 1923), recalls: growing up at Crow Agency; attending schools in Lodge Grass and Hardin; his education at Carlisle, Pennsylvania, and at Linfield, Oregon; earning a college degree from Rocky Mountain College in Billings; receiving punishment for

speaking the Crow Language in schools as a child; bilingualism; Joe Medicine Crow; the Baptist missionary educator W. A. Petzoldt; Crow Indian culture; discrimination; athletics and academics; teaching and coaching sports in Nespelem and Wilbur, Washington; his return to Montana; education in general.
INTERVIEWED BY BILL LAFORGE, FEBRUARY 24 AND 25, 1989, BILLINGS.
TRANSCRIPT: 35 PAGES
1 TAPE: 1 HOUR

OH 1229
FRANK SHONE INTERVIEW

Frank Shone (b. 1946) talks about: his parents; his early life in Meaderville; his education at Montana State University in Bozeman; his employment as minority coordinator for Helena's Model Cities Program; his work with urban Native American students; discrimination against American Indians; his tenure as Youth Director at the Helena Indian Alliance; biculturalism; differences between urban and rural Native Americans; parental and community involvement in Native American education.
INTERVIEWED BY JOHN TERREO, APRIL 3, 1989, HELENA.
TRANSCRIPT: 35 PAGES
2 TAPES: 1 HOUR, 10 MINUTES

OH 1230
MURTON McCLUSKEY INTERVIEW

Murton McCluskey (b. 1936) recalls: his childhood and the death of his parents; attending boarding school, where he endured physical and mental abuse; life with his grandparents; his service with the U.S. Navy; the 1950s federal-government relocation program for Indi-

ans; his college education; his experiences as a teacher. *[See also Native American Educators OH 1467.]*
INTERVIEWED BY LAURIE MERCIER, APRIL 4, 1984, GREAT FALLS.
SUMMARY: 5 PAGES
2 TAPES: 1 HOUR, 20 MINUTES

OH 1231
REBECCA ROBERTS INTERVIEW
Great Falls resident Rebecca Roberts (b. 1946) remembers: her childhood on the Blackfeet Indian Reservation; her education at a boarding school in Babb; attending Northern Montana College in Havre; teaching jobs in California and in Hays and Great Falls; the Educational Talent Search Program.
INTERVIEWED BY JOHN TERREO, MAY 15, 1989, GREAT FALLS.
TRANSCRIPT: 50 PAGES
2 TAPES: 2 HOURS

OH 1232
CARLENE OLD ELK INTERVIEW
Carlene Old Elk (b. 1943) reflects on: her childhood and education in South Carolina; her VISTA (Volunteers in Service to America) work for the Head Start program on the Crow Indian Reservation; her marriage into the Crow tribe; bilingual education; teaching at Little Big Horn College in Crow Agency; voting rights; discrimination.
INTERVIEWED BY JOHN TERREO, MAY 31, 1989, LITTLE BIG HORN COLLEGE, CROW AGENCY.
TRANSCRIPT: 47 PAGES
2 TAPES: 2 HOURS

OH 1233
ELMER MAIN INTERVIEW
Elmer Main describes: his birth and family; growing up in a traditional Indian culture; his college education; his work as superintendent of schools in Dodson, just off the Fort Belknap Indian Reservation; his employment at Lodge Grass School; the impact of federal legislation on Native American education; American Indian culture.
INTERVIEWED BY MINERVA ALLEN, MAY 16, 1989, HAYS.
SUMMARY: 4 PAGES
1 TAPE: 1 HOUR

OH 1234
MINERVA ALLEN INTERVIEW
Minerva Allen (b. 1936)—a Hays resident—recalls: her childhood on the Fort Belknap Indian Reservation;

teaching school at Lodgepole; living conditions on the reservation; her training for the Head Start program; her directorship of that program; bilingual programs; the role of women.
INTERVIEWED BY JOHN TERREO, JUNE 7, 1989, HAYS.
TRANSCRIPT: 65 PAGES
3 TAPES: 2 HOURS, 30 MINUTES

OH 1235
GEORGE SHIELDS, SR., INTERVIEW
George Shields, Sr., a member of the Assiniboine tribe, discusses: his Indian name, *Yam Ma Pa* (Three Strike); his education and life on the Fort Belknap Indian Reservation; boarding schools; discipline he received for speaking his native language; the 1930s Depression; raising cattle on the reservation; Native American health; tribal council meetings; the 1936 forest fire that destroyed a vast area of the Little Rockies; his family.
INTERVIEWED BY MINERVA ALLEN, JUNE 15, 1989, HARLEM.
SUMMARY: 3 PAGES
1 TAPE: 40 MINUTES

OH 1236
VERNIE CHOPWOOD BELL INTERVIEW
Vernie Bell discusses: her childhood on the Fort Belknap Indian Reservation; her Native American name, *Cha Knock Ba* (Sweet Balm); her Assiniboine–Gros Ventre heritage; her education; Fort Belknap Indian College; her work with the Head Start program in Lodgepole; the impacts of the Johnson-O'Malley Act and Title IV on Native American education; her work with senior citizens at the Lodgepole Senior Center.
INTERVIEWED BY MINERVA ALLEN, JUNE 12, 1989, DODSON.
SUMMARY: 2 PAGES
1 TAPE: 30 MINUTES

OH 1237
DR. HENRIETTA WHITEMAN INTERVIEW
Missoula resident Dr. Henrietta Whiteman recalls: her childhood in Oklahoma; her family's strong support for education; learning the Cheyenne language; accusations that she wanted to be white because she did not live in an Indian camp; the impact of World War II on her father; Indian boarding schools; her education; teaching in the Native American Studies program at the University of Montana in Missoula; her work as the first female director

of the BIA Office of Indian Education; discrimination in schools.

INTERVIEWED BY KARL EDWARDS, JULY 10, 1989, MISSOULA.

SUMMARY: 4 PAGES
2 TAPES: 2 HOURS

OH 1238
ERNESTINE SINE CORNELIUS AND CARMEN CORNELIUS TAYLOR INTERVIEW

Ernestine Cornelius (b. 1919) discusses: her family; her early life on the Flathead Indian Reservation; attending various boarding schools; subsequent educational experiences. Her daughter Carmen Taylor (b. 1949) depicts: her family; discrimination against Native Americans in education; her employment with the BIA; legislation affecting Native American education.

INTERVIEWED BY KAREN CORNELIUS FENTON, JULY 21, 1989, ALBUQUERQUE, NM.

SUMMARY: 6 PAGES
2 TAPES: 2 HOURS

OH 1239
ELMER "SONNY" MORIGEAU INTERVIEW

Sonny Morigeau (b. 1929) describes: his childhood in St. Ignatius; his father's work with the BIA; discrimination in reservation schools; the Two-Eagle River School in Pablo; the Salish-Kootenai Community College in Pablo; joining the U.S. Navy; serving for 23 years on the tribal council of the Confederated Salish-Kootenai Tribes; his experiences as chief of police; police corruption; water rights and irrigation battles on the reservation.

INTERVIEWED BY KAREN CORNELIUS FENTON, JULY 31, 1989, DIXON.

SUMMARY: 2 PAGES
1 TAPE: 50 MINUTES

OH 1240
JOSEPH McDONALD INTERVIEW

Joseph McDonald (b. 1933) comments on: his early life and education in Post Creek and Dixon; his work in sawmills and as a smoke jumper to finance his education; attending Western Montana College in Dillon; Louie Nine Pipe; powwows; promoting Native American culture as principal of Ronan High School; teaching and coaching at Oilmont, at the State Industrial School for Boys in Miles City, and at Northern Montana College in Havre; biculturalism and vocational education; the 1972 Indian Education Act; difficulties electing Indians to the

Polson school board; the 1921 Johnson-O'Malley Act; the development of the Two-Eagle River School in Pablo; school financing and certification; the Salish-Kootenai Community College in Pablo.

INTERVIEWED BY KAREN CORNELIUS FENTON, JULY 28, 1989, PABLO.

SUMMARY: 19 PAGES
2 TAPES: 1 HOUR, 45 MINUTES

OH 1286
RACHEL BOWERS INTERVIEW

Rachel Bowers reports on: her family; her early life in Charlo and Arlee; her education and experiences in public schools; her employment with the Community Action Program; difficulties with state and federal agencies; Native American religious customs; attitudes concerning Native American studies programs; federal legislation affecting Native American education; her part-time work as a bartender; her work with youth; alternative schools; Native American medicine.

INTERVIEWED BY LAURIE MERCIER, JUNE 25, 1988, ARLEE.

SUMMARY: 14 PAGES
2 TAPES: 1 HOUR, 20 MINUTES

OH 1287
BOB McANALLY INTERVIEW

Bob McAnally discusses: his family; his early life on the Fort Peck Reservation; the Assiniboine culture; his grandmother's experiences at boarding schools; his recollections of the Indian Health Service; some effects of the 1960s civil-rights movement on Native Americans; his military service; hostile attitudes toward Native Americans; legislation and other issues affecting Native American education.

INTERVIEWED BY LAURIE MERCIER, JUNE, 26, 1988, MISSOULA.

SUMMARY: 21 PAGES
3 TAPES: 2 HOURS, 5 MINUTES

OH 1467
MURTON McCLUSKEY INTERVIEW

Murton McCluskey (b. 1936) recalls: his experiences as a teacher at Rocky Boy School, Rocky Boy; his work as Director of Indian Studies at Great Falls Community College; issues affecting Native Americans. [See also Native American Educators OH 1230.]

INTERVIEWED BY JOHN TERREO, MAY 15, 1989, GREAT FALLS.

TRANSCRIPT: 49 PAGES
2 TAPES: 1 HOUR, 35 MINUTES

New Deal in Montana/Fort Peck Dam Oral History Project

This oral history project documented the economic recovery programs initiated by President Franklin D. Roosevelt in the 1930s and 1940s. These Depression-era programs—including the Work Projects Administration (WPA), Civilian Conservation Corps (CCC), and the Resettlement Administration—played a significant economic role in the state of Montana, which was listed as second in per capita receipt of New Deal dollars during the Depression. A large portion of the interviews focused on the lives of the workers involved in the Fort Peck Dam project, including cultural and social life in the area. The interviewees include people involved in agricultural programs, commerce, cultural development, Native American culture, labor, work projects, or state and county government.

OH 1051
MADELIA JONES, DOROTHA DEWEY SMITH, AND DORIS JEFFRIES INTERVIEW

Madelia Jones (b. 1905), Dorotha Smith (b. 1926), and Doris Jeffries—all of whom lived in the Fort Peck area during the construction of the Fort Peck Dam in the late 1930s—comment on: their work in the hospital at Wheeler; their childhoods; a tick fever epidemic; their parents' work.
INTERVIEWED BY LAURIE MERCIER, AUGUST 1, 1987, FORT PECK.
SUMMARY: 5 PAGES
1 TAPE: 1 HOUR

OH 1052
KENNETH D. TURNER, MARJORIE PEARSON TURNER, AND BARBARA PEARSON KAISER INTERVIEW

Kenneth Turner, his wife, Marjorie Turner, and her sister Barbara Kaiser—all residents of the Fort Peck area during the construction of the Fort Peck Dam in the late 1930s—discuss: the operation of Hotel Wheeler; their work in the project barracks and the mess hall; recreation.
INTERVIEWED BY LAURIE MERCIER, AUGUST 1, 1987, FORT PECK.
SUMMARY: 4 PAGES
1 TAPE: 50 MINUTES

OH 1053
WALTER INLOW INTERVIEW

Walter Inlow (b. 1913), who lived in Fort Peck during construction of the Fort Peck Dam, from 1936 to 1939, describes: dredge work on the dam; general working conditions; hardships of the times; recreation.
INTERVIEWED BY LAURIE MERCIER, AUGUST 1, 1987, FORT PECK.
SUMMARY: 4 PAGES
1 TAPE: 40 MINUTES

OH 1054
CARTER V. JOHNSON INTERVIEW

A Fort Peck resident during the late 1930s, Carter Johnson considers: the overall construction of the Fort Peck Dam; his work as an electrician on the project; recreation; living quarters; construction safety; general working conditions.
INTERVIEWED BY LAURIE MERCIER, AUGUST 1, 1987, FORT PECK.
SUMMARY: 5 PAGES
1 TAPE: 45 MINUTES

OH 1055
PETER PENNER INTERVIEW

Peter Penner (b. 1892)—a resident of Fort Peck during the construction of the Fort Peck Dam in the late

1930s—discusses: his work as a laborer; his work on dredging crews and sawmill teams; life at Park Grove; the slide disaster of 1938.

INTERVIEWED BY LAURIE MERCIER, AUGUST 1, 1987, FORT PECK.

SUMMARY: 4 PAGES

1 TAPE: 45 MINUTES

OH 1056
WILLARD C. "CRAIG" SAXTON INTERVIEW

Craig Saxton (b. 1914), who lived in the Fort Peck area during the late 1930s, converses on: his work on the Fort Peck Dam; hazards; methods of tunnel construction; his interest in the Fort Peck area's paleontology; recreation; the secrets of dancehall girls; the nature of work crews; living quarters.

INTERVIEWED BY LAURIE MERCIER, JULY 31, 1987, FORT PECK.

SUMMARY: 12 PAGES

3 TAPES: 2 HOURS, 25 MINUTES

OH 1057
VERNON AND GUSTAV EMANUELSON INTERVIEW

Vern Emanuelson and his brother Gus Emanuelson (b. 1909)—both of whom lived in Fort Peck during the construction of the Fort Peck Dam in the late 1930s—describe: living conditions; area recreation. Gus Emanuelson discusses: his work in the tunnels; road building for the WPA.

INTERVIEWED BY LAURIE MERCIER, JULY 28, 1987, SACO.

SUMMARY: 4 PAGES

1 TAPE: 45 MINUTES

OH 1058
IVER MARTIN INTERVIEW

A Fort Peck resident during the late 1930s, Iver Martin (b. 1913) describes: driving trucks and buses on the Fort Peck Dam project; the slide disaster of 1938; his work at a CCC camp in Troy; wages; a visit to Fort Peck by President Franklin D. Roosevelt.

INTERVIEWED BY LAURIE MERCIER, JULY 27, 1987, FORT PECK.

SUMMARY: 7 PAGES

2 TAPES: 1 HOUR, 30 MINUTES

OH 1059
ROY DEDOBBELEER INTERVIEW

Roy DeDobbeleer (b. 1907), who lived in Fort Peck during the construction of the Fort Peck Dam in the late

1930s, depicts: his work as a laborer and a pneumatic-drill operator; living conditions; farming; his employment in other states and in Costa Rica.

INTERVIEWED BY LAURIE MERCIER, JULY 27, 1987, FORT PECK.

SUMMARY: 5 PAGES

2 TAPES: 1 HOUR, 50 MINUTES

OH 1060
JACK SCHYE INTERVIEW

Jack Schye (b. 1913)—a resident of the Fort Peck area during construction of Fort Peck Dam from 1936 to 1939—discusses: the towns of Park Grove and Wheeler; working in the shafts; recreation.

INTERVIEWED BY LAURIE MERCIER, JULY 27, 1987, FORT PECK.

SUMMARY: 3 PAGES

1 TAPE: 1 HOUR

OH 1061
LLOYD LARSON INTERVIEW

A resident of the Fort Peck area during construction of the Fort Peck Dam in the late 1930s, Lloyd Larson (b. 1908) describes: his work as a saw operator; the slide disaster of 1938; construction accidents; his work for the Bowen Equipment rock-hauling operation at Fort Peck; living in Glasgow and Wheeler.

INTERVIEWED BY LAURIE MERCIER, JULY 26, 1987, FORT PECK.

SUMMARY: 7 PAGES

2 TAPES: 1 HOUR, 25 MINUTES

OH 1062
NORENE ROMIG BROWN INTERVIEW

Norene Brown (b. 1917), who lived in Fort Peck during the construction of the Fort Peck Dam in the late 1930s, details: her work at Vornholt's Drug Store in Fort Peck; recreation; dances; living quarters; the slide disaster of 1938; living in Glasgow; her husband's work on the dam.

INTERVIEWED BY LAURIE MERCIER, JULY 26, 1987, FORT PECK.

SUMMARY: 7 PAGES

1 TAPE: 1 HOUR, 30 MINUTES

OH 1063
CARL H. PLUMLEE INTERVIEW

Carl Plumlee (b. 1909)—a resident of the Fort Peck area during the construction of Fort Peck Dam in the late 1930s—discusses: his schooling at Bozeman; his

work for the Montana Power Company; surveying; construction problems; building dredges; living conditions.
INTERVIEWED BY LAURIE MERCIER, JULY 31, 1987, FORT PECK.
SUMMARY: 8 PAGES
2 TAPES: 2 HOURS

OH 1064
LEONARD BOWSER INTERVIEW
A Fort Peck resident during the 1930s, Leonard Bowser (b. 1911) speaks of: his work mapping the Fort Peck Dam site; living conditions for workers and their families; the slide disaster of 1938; surveying tunnels.
INTERVIEWED BY LAURIE MERCIER, JULY 31, 1987, FORT PECK.
SUMMARY: 3 PAGES
1 TAPE: 1 HOUR

OH 1065
THELMA STEARNS BONDY INTERVIEW
Thelma Bondy (b. 1914) discusses: life in Fort Peck during construction of the Fort Peck Dam in the 1930s; the nearby town of Martinville; her work at a hotel, a store, and a cafe in Fort Peck; the slide disaster of 1938; the flood of 1935.
INTERVIEWED BY LAURIE MERCIER, JULY 31, 1987, FORT PECK.
TRANSCRIPT: 21 PAGES
1 TAPE: 55 MINUTES

OH 1066
OLAF H. "OLE" GILBERTSON INTERVIEW
Ole Gilbertson (b. 1919), a resident of Fort Peck during construction of the Fort Peck Dam in the late 1930s, discusses: living conditions; area towns; recreation; the slide disaster of 1938; conducting soil samples; truck driving.
INTERVIEWED BY LAURIE MERCIER, JULY 30, 1987, FORT PECK.
SUMMARY: 4 PAGES
1 TAPE: 1 HOUR

OH 1067
ROBERT TAYLOR AND STELLA CLARK TAYLOR INTERVIEW
Robert Taylor (b. 1920) and his wife, Stella Taylor—both residents of the Fort Peck area during construction of the Fort Peck Dam in the late 1930s—portray: his work as a surveyor and an engineering technician; community

life in Park Grove; living conditions in the Fort Peck area.
INTERVIEWED BY LAURIE MERCIER, JULY 26, 1987, FORT PECK.
SUMMARY: 4 PAGES
1 TAPE: 1 HOUR

OH 1068
ERICK OLSON INTERVIEW
A Fort Peck area resident during the construction of the Fort Peck Dam in the late 1930s, Erick Olson (b. 1907) recalls: his work as a tractor operator building pipeline; life in the barracks; recreation; wages; hours; an injury to his leg.
INTERVIEWED BY LAURIE MERCIER, JULY 28, 1987, FORT PECK.
SUMMARY: 9 PAGES
2 TAPES: 2 HOURS

OH 1069
WILBUR BRYSON INTERVIEW
Wilbur Bryson (b. 1918), who lived in Fort Peck during construction of the Fort Peck Dam in the late 1930s, reflects on: life in the barracks; work hours; recreation; work on the spillway gates and on the cut-off wall.
INTERVIEWED BY LAURIE MERCIER, JULY 28, 1987, FORT PECK.
SUMMARY: 4 PAGES
1 TAPE: 1 HOUR

OH 1070
MELVIN L. HANSON INTERVIEW
Melvin Hanson (b. 1918)—a resident of Fort Peck during construction of the Fort Peck Dam in the late 1930s—recounts: his work on the Fort Peck project as a railroad fireman and an engineer on the Saco branch line; quarry work at Snake Butte; recreation; living conditions.
INTERVIEWED BY LAURIE MERCIER, JULY 28, 1987, FORT PECK.
TRANSCRIPT: 24 PAGES
1 TAPE: 55 MINUTES

OH 1071
RUTH SHANAHAN VAN FAASEN
Ruth Van Faasen (b. 1913), who lived in the Fort Peck area during construction of the Fort Peck Dam in the late 1930s, recalls: her work as a secretary in the project's accounting office; living in a hotel; recreation.
INTERVIEWED BY MARY MURPHY, AUGUST 3, 1987, FORT PECK.

SUMMARY: 2 PAGES
1 TAPE: 35 MINUTES

OH 1072
ROBERT RHODES INTERVIEW

A Fort Peck resident during the late 1930s, Robert Rhodes (b. 1903) describes: his work on a dredge crew; his fellow workers; the slide disaster of 1938.
INTERVIEWED BY MARY MURPHY, AUGUST 2, 1987, FORT PECK.
SUMMARY: 3 PAGES
1 TAPE: 1 HOUR

OH 1073
CHARLES "CHUCK" JOHNSTON INTERVIEW

Chuck Johnston (b. 1915), who lived in the Fort Peck area during the construction of the Fort Peck Dam from 1936 to 1939, remembers: dredge work on the dam; photography; the Fort Peck Flying Service; area towns; recreation; living conditions; his subsequent U.S. Navy career as a pilot.
INTERVIEWED BY MARY MURPHY, AUGUST 2, 1987, FORT PECK.
SUMMARY: 4 PAGES
1 TAPE: 1 HOUR

OH 1074
KERMIT BAECKER INTERVIEW

A Fort Peck resident during construction of the Fort Peck Dam in the late 1930s, Kermit Baecker (b. 1909) discusses: his work as a deckhand on several Missouri River boats; moving floating equipment on the Missouri River; wages; living in Wheeler; recreation; the slide disaster of 1938.
INTERVIEWED BY MARY MURPHY, JULY 31, 1987, FORT PECK.
SUMMARY: 6 PAGES
2 TAPES: 1 HOUR, 40 MINUTES

OH 1075
DAVID GREGG, WILLIAM WHISENHAND, AND LYLE NELSON INTERVIEW

David Gregg (b. 1918), William Whisenhand (b. 1916), and Lyle Nelson—all residents of Fort Peck during construction of the Fort Peck Dam—report on: the New Deal era (1933–1942); raising vegetables; the slide disaster of 1938; living conditions; recreation; work on the dam.
INTERVIEWED BY MARY MURPHY, AUGUST 1, 1987, FORT PECK.

SUMMARY: 7 PAGES
2 TAPES: 1 HOUR, 15 MINUTES

OH 1076
LLOYD CARLSON INTERVIEW

Lloyd Carlson, a Fort Peck resident during construction of the Fort Peck Dam, reviews: his work in the tunnels; his duties as a truck driver; working conditions; recreation; his career as a civil servant.
INTERVIEWED BY MARY MURPHY, SEPTEMBER 2, 1987, FORT PECK.
SUMMARY: 4 PAGES
1 TAPE: 1 HOUR

OH 1077
JOHN MAXNESS AND LEILA McPHERSON MAXNESS INTERVIEW

John Maxness and his wife, Leila Maxness, who lived in the Fort Peck area during construction of the Fort Peck Dam, speak of: living in McCone City; Leila's work running a tavern with her first husband, Tom McPherson; recreation; John's employment clearing brush.
INTERVIEWED BY MARY MURPHY, AUGUST 1, 1987, FORT PECK.
SUMMARY: 3 PAGES
1 TAPE: 55 MINUTES

OH 1078
ORVILLE SHEFELBINE INTERVIEW

A Fort Peck area resident during construction of the Fort Peck Dam in the late 1930s, Orville Shefelbine (b. 1914) surveys: his employment clearing brush; working on the construction of the spillway; CCC camps; living conditions; recreation; the town of New Deal.
INTERVIEWED BY MARY MURPHY, AUGUST 1, 1987, FORT PECK.
SUMMARY: 3 PAGES
1 TAPE: 1 HOUR

OH 1079
JAMES WISEMAN AND FLORENCE WISEMAN INTERVIEW

James Wiseman (b. 1906) and his wife, Florence Wiseman—both residents of the Fort Peck area during the construction of the Fort Peck Dam—summarize: James's work on the railroad, on the spillway, and on the rigger; Florence's duties in a local laundry; general living conditions; recreation.
INTERVIEWED BY MARY MURPHY, AUGUST 1, 1987, FORT PECK.

Summary: 3 pages
1 tape: 1 hour

OH 1080
LINDA KUEBLER SKINNER INTERVIEW
Linda Skinner (b. 1908), who lived in the Fort Peck area during construction of the Fort Peck Dam, surveys: her work in a New Deal meat market; living conditions; recreation; the slide disaster of 1938; her duties in the U.S. Army Corps of Engineers information booth at the dam site.
Interviewed by Mary Murphy, July 31, 1987, Fort Peck.
Summary: 5 pages
2 tapes: 1 hour, 5 minutes

OH 1081
EDI G. MASSA SERNEL INTERVIEW
Edi Sernel, a resident of the Fort Peck area during construction of the Fort Peck Dam from 1936 to 1939, talks about: her childhood in Red Lodge; her work as a telephone operator for the project; general living conditions; recreation.
Interviewed by Mary Murphy, July 31, 1987, Fort Peck.
Summary: 4 pages
1 tape: 40 minutes

OH 1082
WILLIAM FLY INTERVIEW
William Fly (b. 1914)—a Fort Peck resident during the construction of the Fort Peck Dam—discusses: his childhood in Laurel; his clerical work on the dam project; life in the barracks; recreation; the slide disaster of 1938.
Interviewed by Mary Murphy, July 31, 1987, Fort Peck.
Transcript: 15 pages
2 tapes: 1 hour, 30 minutes

OH 1083
ETHELYN "BROWNIE" MASON INTERVIEW
A Fort Peck area resident during construction of Fort Peck Dam from 1936 to 1939, Brownie Mason tells of: her secretarial work for the project; local recreation.
Interviewed by Mary Murphy, July 31, 1987, Fort Peck.
Summary: 2 pages
1 tape: 45 minutes

OH 1084
ALDEN CANTERBURY INTERVIEW
Alden Canterbury (b. 1909), who lived in Fort Peck during the construction of the Fort Peck Dam in the late 1930s, talks about: his work on the dredge crew; his tugboat duties; overall living conditions.
Interviewed by Mary Murphy, July 30, 1987, Fort Peck.
Summary: 4 pages
1 tape: 55 minutes

OH 1085
OWEN WILLIAMS INTERVIEW
Owen Williams (b. 1915), a resident of the Fort Peck area during construction of the Fort Peck Dam, discusses: area recreation; life in the barracks; his work on the dam; his Crow Indian heritage.
Interviewed by Rick Duncan, August 1, 1987, Fort Peck.
Summary: 5 pages
2 tapes: 1 hour, 30 minutes

OH 1086
PHILIP GANNON INTERVIEW
Philip Gannon (b. 1916), a resident of Fort Peck during construction of Fort Peck Dam, discusses: his work as an engineer; the slide disaster of 1938; recreation in the area.
Interviewed by Rick Duncan, August 2, 1987, Fort Peck.
Summary: 3 pages
1 tape: 45 minutes

OH 1087
JEROLD VAN FAASEN INTERVIEW
Jerold Van Faasen (b. 1913), who resided in the Fort Peck area during construction of the Fort Peck Dam, discourses on: both survey and concrete work; living conditions; recreation; his employment as an engineer.
Interviewed by Rick Duncan, August 3, 1987, Fort Peck.
Summary: 5 pages
1 tape: 1 hour, 10 minutes

OH 1088
FRED MICHELS INTERVIEW
Fred Michels (b. 1914)—a resident of the Fort Peck area during construction of Fort Peck Dam—recalls: his employment at a Buttrey's store; recreation; wages.

INTERVIEWED BY RICK DUNCAN, AUGUST 2, 1987, FORT PECK.
SUMMARY: 3 PAGES
1 TAPE: 45 MINUTES

OH 1089
CLARENCE CRANE INTERVIEW
A Fort Peck resident during construction of Fort Peck Dam, Clarence Crane (b. 1910) discusses: his stripping work on the dam; living conditions.
INTERVIEWED BY RICK DUNCAN, AUGUST 1, 1987, FORT PECK.
SUMMARY: 3 PAGES
1 TAPE: 35 MINUTES

OH 1090
JAMES MONTFORT INTERVIEW
James Montfort (b. 1914), who lived in the Fort Peck area during construction of Fort Peck Dam, speaks of: his stripping work at the dam; truck driving; living in the community of Wilson; recreation.
INTERVIEWED BY RICK DUNCAN, AUGUST 1, 1987, FORT PECK.
SUMMARY: 3 PAGES
1 TAPE: 45 MINUTES

OH 1091
HAROLD BRYANT INTERVIEW
Harold Bryant (b. 1920), a Fort Peck resident during construction of Fort Peck Dam, details: quarry work; living in Park Grove; the slide disaster of 1938; recreation in and around Fort Peck.
INTERVIEWED BY RICK DUNCAN, JULY 31, 1987, FORT PECK.
SUMMARY: 3 PAGES
1 TAPE: 45 MINUTES

OH 1092
JOHN PORTEEN INTERVIEW
John Porteen (b. 1903), who resided in the Fort Peck area during construction of Fort Peck Dam, recalls: his work on the dam following the slide disaster of 1938; living conditions; recreation.
INTERVIEWED BY RICK DUNCAN, AUGUST 1, 1987, FORT PECK.
SUMMARY: 3 PAGES
1 TAPE: 55 MINUTES

OH 1093
PETER FRIESEN INTERVIEW
Peter Friesen (b. 1912)—an inhabitant of Fort Peck during construction of Fort Peck Dam—describes: his concrete work; training as a welder; recreation; the local scarlet fever epidemic of 1935.
INTERVIEWED BY RICK DUNCAN, JULY 31, 1987, FORT PECK.
SUMMARY: 4 PAGES
2 TAPES: 1 HOUR, 10 MINUTES

OH 1094
MYRON F. "BARNEY" BAKER INTERVIEW
A Fort Peck resident during construction of Fort Peck Dam, Barney Baker recalls: driving a truck; living in Wheeler; recreation; the slide disaster of 1938; his work in Glasgow.
INTERVIEWED BY RICK DUNCAN, JULY 29, 1987, FORT PECK.
SUMMARY: 4 PAGES
2 TAPES: 1 HOUR, 40 MINUTES

OH 1095
WALTER LUSE INTERVIEW
Walter Luse (b. 1907), who lived in the Fort Peck area during construction of Fort Peck Dam, depicts: his work clearing brush; his other jobs; the drilling business; the slide disaster of 1938.
INTERVIEWED BY RICK DUNCAN, JULY 30, 1987, FORT PECK.
SUMMARY: 3 PAGES
1 TAPE: 1 HOUR

OH 1096
TOM MULLEN INTERVIEW
Tom Mullen (b. 1903), a resident of the Fort Peck area during construction of Fort Peck Dam, reflects on: his work in tunnels and on pipelines; his job on a derrick boat; the slide disaster of 1938; working conditions; recreation.
INTERVIEWED BY RICK DUNCAN, JULY 30, 1987, FORT PECK.
SUMMARY: 5 PAGES
2 TAPES: 1 HOUR, 25 MINUTES

OH 1097
EMIL KRAVIK INTERVIEW
Emil Kravik (b. 1919), who resided in the Fort Peck area during construction of Fort Peck Dam, describes: his work on dredges and on pipelines; truck driving; rec-

reation; working conditions.

INTERVIEWED BY RICK DUNCAN, JULY 30, 1987, FORT PECK.

SUMMARY: 4 PAGES

2 TAPES: 1 HOUR, 20 MINUTES

OH 1098
JIM WARDLOW INTERVIEW

Jim Wardlow (b. 1906), a Fort Peck area inhabitant during the construction of Fort Peck Dam, relates: living on a houseboat; his work on a drilling crew; his experiences flying; recreation.

INTERVIEWED BY RICK DUNCAN, JULY 31, 1987, FORT PECK.

SUMMARY: 2 PAGES

1 TAPE: 55 MINUTES

OH 1099
GEORGE LARSON INTERVIEW

George Larson (b. 1920), a resident of the Fort Peck area during construction of Fort Peck Dam, recalls: his pipeline work; recreation; the slide disaster of 1938; working conditions.

INTERVIEWED BY DIANE SANDS, AUGUST 1, 1987, FORT PECK.

SUMMARY: 3 PAGES

1 TAPE: 35 MINUTES

OH 1100
RAYMOND HOLDERMAN INTERVIEW

Raymond Holderman (b. 1919)—a resident of Fort Peck during construction of Fort Peck Dam—remembers: his father's work in the state-owned liquor store; recreation; wages; his duties in the quarry; the slide disaster of 1938.

INTERVIEWED BY DIANE SANDS, AUGUST 1, 1987, FORT PECK.

SUMMARY: 5 PAGES

2 TAPES: 1 HOUR, 22 MINUTES

OH 1101
MARGE FITZSIMMONS INTERVIEW

Marge Fitzsimmons (b. 1917), who was a resident of Fort Peck during construction of Fort Peck Dam, briefly converses about: her childhood; working in Flaten's dress shop in Glasgow; her employment at the Fort Peck Buttrey's store; recreation in the Fort Peck area.

INTERVIEWED BY DIANE SANDS, AUGUST 1, 1987, FORT PECK.

SUMMARY: 1 PAGE

1 TAPE: 15 MINUTES

OH 1102
RUBY MORTON MARTIN INTERVIEW

Ruby Martin (b. 1911), who lived in the Fort Peck area during construction of Fort Peck Dam, reports on: her training and work as a nurse; health care facilities at the dam; residing in a hotel; recreation; living conditions.

INTERVIEWED BY DIANE SANDS, JULY 31, 1987, FORT PECK.

SUMMARY: 7 PAGES

2 TAPES: 1 HOUR, 35 MINUTES

OH 1103
ANTONE GORENC INTERVIEW

Antone Gorenc (b. 1915), a resident of Fort Peck during construction of Fort Peck Dam, recalls: his construction work on the Beartooth Highway; his duties on sawmill and cement crews at the dam; conducting soil tests; living conditions.

INTERVIEWED BY DIANE SANDS, AUGUST 2, 1987, FORT PECK.

SUMMARY: 4 PAGES

2 TAPES: 1 HOUR, 25 MINUTES

OH 1104
RUSSELL M. "BUD" STADALMAN INTERVIEW

Bud Stadalman (b. 1915) briefly discusses: his experiences with the CCC in the Alder and Olney areas; winter working conditions; construction of a giant water trough; firefighting activities near Elk Lake; such recreational activities as boxing and fishing. [See also Montanans at Work OH 512.]

INTERVIEWED BY MIKE KORN, JULY, 9, 1988, DILLON.

SUMMARY: 4 PAGES

1 TAPE: 15 MINUTES

OH 1105
FRED FROEBEL INTERVIEW

Fred Froebel (b. circa 1920) comments on: his experiences in the CCC; his job as a canteen steward; recreation and life in Winifred and Lewistown; wages.

INTERVIEWED BY DONI PHILLIPS, JULY 9, 1988, DILLON.

SUMMARY: 7 PAGES

1 TAPE: 1 HOUR

OH 1106
SIDNEY D. KEIL INTERVIEW

A North Dakota native, Sidney Keil (b. 1917) reviews:

joining the CCC in 1935; his CCC camp duties, living conditions, and experiences in North Dakota, Washington, and Minnesota; enlisting in the U.S. Army in 1941.
INTERVIEWED BY DONI M. PHILLIPS, JULY 9, 1988, DILLON.
SUMMARY: 8 PAGES
1 TAPE: 1 HOUR

OH 1107
HERBERT JACOBSON INTERVIEW

Herbert Jacobson (b. 1913) discusses: growing up in Fairview, North Dakota, and in Lambert, Montana; the loss of the family homestead during the 1930s Depression; his work with the CCC—particularly camp organization, discipline, carpentry in Alder, Paradise, and Thompson Falls areas, firefighting at Elk Lake, and his jobs building roads and trails; the impact of Fort Peck Dam; his education at Montana State University, Bozeman; serving in the U.S. Navy during World War II; wildlife control; health care; his views on Franklin D. Roosevelt, Adolph Hitler, Joseph Stalin, Communism, and the Anaconda Company.
INTERVIEWED BY DONI PHILLIPS, JULY 9, 1988, DILLON.
TRANSCRIPT: 28 PAGES
1 TAPE: 45 MINUTES

OH 1108
JOE KNUTSON INTERVIEW

Joe Knutson, who was a CCC worker in West Yellowstone in the late 1930s, chronicles: building roads; camp life; social activities; equipment used.
INTERVIEWED BY DONI PHILLIPS, JULY 9, 1988, DILLON.
SUMMARY: 4 PAGES
1 TAPE: 1 HOUR

OH 1109
EDMOND B. CHERRY, JR., INTERVIEW

Edmond Cherry, Jr. (b. 1916)—a CCC worker in Montana in the 1930s—speaks of: traveling during the 1930s Depression; life in CCC camps; fighting fires; social activities in Dillon; camp leaders.
INTERVIEWED BY DONI PHILLIPS, JULY 9-10, 1988, DILLON.
SUMMARY: 6 PAGES
2 TAPES: 2 HOURS

OH 1110
MILTON RITTER INTERVIEW

Milton Ritter, a Civilian Conservation Corpsman in Glacier National Park during the 1930s, recalls: general conditions during the 1930s Depression; building campgrounds; surveying for a telephone line; fighting forest fires; camp life; a visit to Glacier Park by President Franklin D. Roosevelt; his military service.
INTERVIEWED BY DONI PHILLIPS, JULY 9, 1988, DILLON.
SUMMARY: 17 PAGES
1 TAPE: 2 HOURS

OH 1111
HAROLD SHREWSBERRY INTERVIEW

Harold Shrewsberry (b. 1918), who served in the CCC in the Libby area during the 1930s, summarizes: camp life; his duties as a camp cook; wages; equipment; social activities.
INTERVIEWED BY LAURIE MERCIER, JULY 9, 1988, DILLON.
SUMMARY: 3 PAGES
1 TAPE: 40 MINUTES

OH 1112
GLEN MOORE INTERVIEW

Glen Moore (b. 1912), a member of the CCC during the late 1930s, talks of: his duties on the Kerr Dam project; construction work on the St. Regis road; camp life; his jobs on a Utah bird refuge.
INTERVIEWED BY LAURIE MERCIER, JULY 9, 1988, DILLON.
SUMMARY: 4 PAGES
1 TAPE: 50 MINUTES

OH 1113
LARRY NORRIS INTERVIEW

Larry Norris (b. 1914)—a Civilian Conservation Corpsman in California and in Paradise and Moiese, Montana, during the 1930s—surveys: firefighting; his duties as a camp clerk; morale in the camps.
INTERVIEWED BY LAURIE MERCIER, JULY 9, 1988, DILLON.
SUMMARY: 2 PAGES
1 TAPE: 30 MINUTES

OH 1114
KNUTE KAMPEN INTERVIEW

Knute Kampen (b. 1916), who served in the CCC at Medicine Lake, Squaw Creek, and Thompson Falls from 1937 to 1938, addresses: his jobs at a bird refuge; his work on a rock crew; building trails; camp life.
INTERVIEWED BY LAURIE MERCIER, JULY 9, 1988, DILLON.
SUMMARY: 3 PAGES
1 TAPE: 45 MINUTES

OH 1115
ROBERT HALLIDAY INTERVIEW

Robert Halliday, a CCC worker in the Crow Creek Valley and Birch Creek camps during the 1930s, tells of:

conditions in the 1930s Depression; a CCC camp strike; recreation; relations with Dillon townspeople; his duties as the head of a maintenance crew; wages. *[See also General Montana OH 1626.]*
INTERVIEWED BY LAURIE MERCIER, JULY 9, 1988, DILLON.
SUMMARY: 4 PAGES
1 TAPE: 1 HOUR

OH 1116
KENNETH GILLESPIE INTERVIEW
Kenneth Gillespie, who served in the CCC in Havre and at Fort Missoula during the 1930s, discusses: creating the post-exchange system for the Fort Missoula district; his military career.
INTERVIEWED BY LAURIE MERCIER, JULY 26, 1988, DILLON.
SUMMARY: 2 PAGES
1 TAPE: 25 MINUTES

OH 1117
JESS STOVALL INTERVIEW
Jess Stovall (b. 1910), a female employee of the CCC in Yellowstone National Park during the 1930s, recalls: Depression conditions; camp life; social activities; men in the camp.
INTERVIEWED BY LAURIE MERCIER, JULY 9, 1988, DILLON.
SUMMARY: 7 PAGES
1 TAPE: 1 HOUR

OH 1118
RALPH BOATMAN INTERVIEW
A Civilian Conservation Corpsman in Utah and Idaho during the 1930s, Ralph Boatman (b. 1914) recalls: road construction; life in several camps; work accidents.
INTERVIEWED BY MICHAEL KORN, JULY 9, 1988, DILLON.
SUMMARY: 5 PAGES
1 TAPE: 1 HOUR

OH 1119
ALBERT TONG INTERVIEW
Albert Tong (b. 1915) surveys: his early childhood in Montana; his experiences in the CCC camps at Nine Mile, Goat Creek, and Belton; daily life at the camps; his motorcycle. *[See also General Montana OH 1639.]*
INTERVIEWED BY LAURIE MERCIER, JULY 9, 1988, DILLON.
SUMMARY: 11 PAGES
1 TAPE: 1 HOUR

OH 1120
HAROLD DUCELLO INTERVIEW
Harold Ducello (b. circa 1918) reflects on his experiences in the CCC near Ekalaka and Augusta.
INTERVIEWED BY LAURIE MERCIER, JULY 9, 1988, DILLON.
SUMMARY: 12 PAGES
1 TAPE: 50 MINUTES

OH 1121
STUART MARKLE INTERVIEW
Stuart Markle (b. 1916) relates: his experiences in the CCC at Slam Lake near Glidden, Wisconsin; his World War II service on a U.S. Navy seaplane-bomber operating in Ecuador and the Galapagos Islands.
INTERVIEWED BY MIKE KORN, JULY 9, 1988, DILLON.
SUMMARY: 6 PAGES
1 TAPE: 25 MINUTES

OH 1122
ARTHUR MORANG INTERVIEW
Arthur Morang remembers: his experiences with the CCC at Nine Mile, Montana, and at Moab, Utah; his later life.
INTERVIEWED BY MIKE KORN, JULY 9, 1988, DILLON.
SUMMARY: 2 PAGES
1 TAPE: 35 MINUTES

OH 1123
ARTHUR CHARKOFF INTERVIEW
Arthur Charkoff (b. circa 1917) reports on: his parents' emigration from Russia and their settlement in Montana; his service in the CCC at Camp FS76 near Libby; various reactions of the local people to CCC workers; his duties in the camp infirmary; his service in the U.S. Army Air Force in Europe during World War II; his college education; his employment following his military service.
INTERVIEWED BY MIKE KORN, JULY 9, 1988, DILLON.
SUMMARY: 7 PAGES
1 TAPE: 35 MINUTES

OH 1124
TOM COLLERAN INTERVIEW
Tom Colleran (b. circa 1900), who served as a Montana Relief Commission worker in Jordan and Baker from 1934 to 1948, reviews: his job as a caseworker: the process of applying for relief; various clients; types of relief; the Depression.
INTERVIEWED BY DONI PHILLIPS, JULY 23, 1988, MILES CITY.

SUMMARY: 3 PAGES
1 TAPE: 1 HOUR

OH 1125
MARY BRADY INTERVIEW

A Miles City resident, Mary Brady summarizes: her work in the Miles City WPA office from 1935 to 1938; the Depression; her brief employment with the U.S. Civil Works Administration (CWA).

INTERVIEWED BY DONI PHILLIPS, JULY 19, 1988, MILES CITY.

SUMMARY: 15 PAGES
1 TAPE: 55 MINUTES

OH 1126
JOE W. LOVEC INTERVIEW

Joe Lovec (b. 1915) speaks of: his early life on a homestead near Baker; his experiences in CCC camps at Whitetail and Volborg in 1934 and 1935; camp construction; camp life; recreation; discipline; his opinions of the New Deal; life in eastern Montana during the 1930s Depression; sheep and cattle ranching in Fallon and Custer counties.

INTERVIEWED BY DONI PHILLIPS, JULY 21, 1988, MILES CITY.

SUMMARY: 20 PAGES
1 TAPE: 1 HOUR

OH 1127
JEAN STANLEY INTERVIEW

Jean Stanley briefly details: growing up near Ismay; working in a WPA sewing room; her father's WPA work; living conditions during the 1930s Depression; the New Deal.

INTERVIEWED BY DONI PHILLIPS, JULY 20, 1988, MILES CITY.

SUMMARY: 4 PAGES
1 TAPE: 15 MINUTES

OH 1128
ELLIOT AND ELLA MILLER INTERVIEW

Elliot Miller describes: his parents' covered-wagon journey from South Dakota to Montana in 1914; home-steading; his experiences with the National Youth Administration (NYA) at Fort Keogh—including horse-breeding and frozen-semen studies conducted by Dr. Stuart McKenzie; his education at Montana State University, Bozeman; ranching; poetry. Ella Miller discusses: her parents' emigration from Ireland; her mother's death; her marriage to Elliot; raising a family; her expe-riences with the NYA; athletics; coping with insects; ranching.

INTERVIEWED BY DONI PHILLIPS, JULY 22, 1988, MILES CITY.

SUMMARY: 14 PAGES
2 TAPES: 1 HOUR, 50 MINUTES

OH 1129
DAVID RIVENES INTERVIEW

David Rivenes—a Miles City resident—depicts: his work with the U.S. Department of Agriculture during the 1930s Depression; the government's Land Utiliza-tion program (LU); the Soil Conservation Service (SCS); agricultural practices; drought; dryland-farming tech-niques; grazing districts; the operation of his Miles City television station (KATL); amateur athletics, including tae kwon do and sumo wrestling.

INTERVIEWED BY DONI PHILLIPS, JULY 20, 1988, MILES CITY.

SUMMARY: 9 PAGES
2 TAPES: 1 HOUR, 50 MINUTES

OH 1130
C. MAX HUGHES INTERVIEW

Max Hughes describes: his parents' homestead in the Roundup area; his college education; the Kinsey Farms Resettlement Project; the WPA; the Land Utilization Project (LU); dam construction in eastern Montana; the Soil Conservation Service (SCS); the 1930s Depression.

INTERVIEWED BY DONI PHILLIPS, JULY 21, 1988, MILES CITY.

SUMMARY: 7 PAGES
1 TAPE: 55 MINUTES

OH 1131
JEROME COOKSEY INTERVIEW

Jerome Cooksey delineates: his work with the fed-eral Agriculture Survey in Custer County during the 1930s; various New Deal programs; the 1930s Depres-sion; his experiences at the CCC camp near Ashland; his employment with the local cannery; working for the Montana-Dakota Utilities Company (MDU).

INTERVIEWED BY DONI PHILLIPS, AUGUST 5, 1988, MILES CITY.

SUMMARY: 13 PAGES
2 TAPES: 1 HOUR, 50 MINUTES

OH 1132
JOSEPH W. DENT INTERVIEW

Joseph Dent (b. 1902) talks about: his duties with the

WPA in Broadus, Lame Deer, and Forsyth as a foreman and a finance officer in construction, timbering, surveying, and road work; his involvement in community activities.

INTERVIEWED BY DONI PHILLIPS, AUGUST 6, 1988, BROADUS.

SUMMARY: 14 PAGES

3 TAPES: 2 HOURS, 20 MINUTES

OH 1133
CECIL E. WYNES INTERVIEW

Cecil Wynes (b. 1910) converses on: his parents' homestead outside Miles City; his experiences during the 1930s Depression; working with the WPA in the Miles City and Glendive areas; his military service; his employment as an automobile mechanic; his retirement.

INTERVIEWED BY DONI PHILLIPS, AUGUST 8, 1988, MILES CITY.

SUMMARY: 9 PAGES

2 TAPES: 45 MINUTES

OH 1134
GEORGE GRAY INTERVIEW

George Gray—a Civilian Conservation Corpsman at Camp 967 in Glacier National Park during the 1930s—considers: the camp's organization; its entertainment activities; the camp's U.S. Army administrators; winter living conditions; deserters; the installation of telephone cable under Going-to-the-Sun Highway; his later life.

INTERVIEWED BY DONI PHILLIPS, AUGUST 8, 1988, MILES CITY.

SUMMARY: 11 PAGES

2 TAPES: 1 HOUR, 35 MINUTES

OH 1135
DONALD MORROW AND AGNES WAGNER MORROW INTERVIEW

Donald Morrow (b. 1916) comments on: growing up in Mildred and Glasgow; his marriage to Agnes; his family's work during construction of Fort Peck Dam in the late 1930s; President Franklin D. Roosevelt's visit to the dam in 1937; his memories of the community of Wheeler; his relocation to the town of Harlem; his experiences during construction of the Snake Butte Dam; health care. Agnes Morrow speaks of: the construction of the Fort Peck Dam; the 1930s Depression; women's employment in the Fort Peck area; family life.

INTERVIEWED BY LAURIE MERCIER, AUGUST 15, 1988, HELENA.

SUMMARY: 17 PAGES

2 TAPES: 1 HOUR, 35 MINUTES

OH 1136
JOHN MORRISON, SR., INTERVIEW

Helena resident John Morrison (b. 1902) chronicles: his childhood in England; his immigration to Montana in 1922; his work on the Bozeman Hill Road and the Mosby Bridge; conditions during the 1930s Depression; the WPA; his work as a Montana Highway Department engineer; highway construction standards and materials.

INTERVIEWED BY JOHN TERREO, NOVEMBER 7, 1988, HELENA.

TRANSCRIPT: 38 PAGES

3 TAPES: 3 HOURS

OH 1137
ETHEL E. GEORGE INTERVIEW

Ethel George (b. 1903) describes: her childhood in the Midwest; raising a family in Montana during the 1930s Depression; family life and health care; farming and ranching in the Miles City area; her relocation to the town of Kinsey as part of the Kinsey Farms Resettlement Project; the 1943 flood in the lower Yellowstone Valley.

INTERVIEWED BY JOHN TERREO, NOVEMBER 18, 1988, KINSEY.

SUMMARY: 4 PAGES

1 TAPE: 45 MINUTES

OH 1138
MADELINE O'NEILL INTERVIEW

Madeline O'Neill (1912–1990) addresses: her work as a nurse in Bozeman and in Helena from the 1930s to the 1960s; various diseases; the lack of antibiotics; nurses' relationships with physicians.

INTERVIEWED BY JOHN TERREO, NOVEMBER 11, 1988, BOZEMAN.

SUMMARY: 3 PAGES

1 TAPE: 1 HOUR

OH 1139
CHARLOTTE EDWARDS INTERVIEW

Charlotte Edwards (b. 1913) discusses: her youth and schooling in Custer and Powder River counties; working with the federal Agricultural Adjustment Administration (AAA) in Powder River County; conditions during the 1930s Depression; her work in the Custer County treasurer's office.

INTERVIEWED BY JOHN TERREO, NOVEMBER 14, 1988, HELENA.
TRANSCRIPT: 30 PAGES
2 TAPES: 2 HOURS

OH 1140
ELIZABETH PHELPS INTERVIEW

Sidney resident Elizabeth Phelps (b. 1923) recalls: her childhood during the 1930s; the 1930s Depression; her mother's employment at a WPA nursery school; social activities in Sidney; living conditions; farm activities; NYA projects.
INTERVIEWED BY JOHN TERREO, NOVEMBER 16, 1988, SIDNEY.
TRANSCRIPT: 36 PAGES
2 TAPES: 2 HOURS

OH 1141
HELEN MATHIASON AND RENA ESKRO INTERVIEW

Helen Mathiason (b. 1921) and Rena Eskro (b. 1912)—both residents of Mildred—recount: their work with the NYA during the 1930s; WPA developments; the 1930s Depression; their relatives' work for the Milwaukee Road.
INTERVIEWED BY JOHN TERREO, NOVEMBER 17, 1988, MILDRED.
SUMMARY: 4 PAGES
1 TAPE: 1 HOUR

OH 1142
KENTON STICKNEY INTERVIEW

Kenton Stickney (b. 1911) discusses: the 1930s Depression in the Ismay area; ranching; social activities; WPA matters.
INTERVIEWED BY JOHN TERREO, NOVEMBER 17, 1988, ISMAY.
SUMMARY: 3 PAGES
1 TAPE: 1 HOUR

OH 1143
MARY A. BALLENTINE INTERVIEW

Mary Ballentine (b. 1901), a Miles City resident, discusses: growing up in Idaho and Montana; her schooling; social activities in Miles City; her marriage and family; her husband's jobs with the WPA as a welding instructor; conditions during the 1930s Depression.
INTERVIEWED BY JOHN TERREO, NOVEMBER 17, 1988, MILES CITY.

SUMMARY: 4 PAGES
2 TAPES: 2 HOURS

OH 1144
FRED L. CAMPBELL, SR., INTERVIEW

Fred Campbell (1912–1989), a Kinsey resident, examines: his schooling; Depression conditions of the 1930s; working for the WPA building dams, surveying, farming; and social activities.
INTERVIEWED BY JOHN TERREO, NOVEMBER 18, 1988, KINSEY.
SUMMARY: 4 PAGES
1 TAPE: 1 HOUR

OH 1145
HENRY CHRISTMAN AND LYDIA CHRISTMAN INTERVIEW

Plevna residents Henry Christman (b. 1911) and his wife, Lydia Christman, discuss: conditions during the 1930s Depression; working for the WPA moving buildings; social activities; their children.
INTERVIEWED BY JOHN TERREO, NOVEMBER 18, 1988, PLEVNA.
SUMMARY: 3 PAGES
1 TAPE: 1 HOUR

OH 1146
BERDETTE ASKIN INTERVIEW

Berdette Askin (b. 1907), who lived in Ismay and Terry, tells about: his schooling; his work digging wells; his duties with the WPA in the Kinsey area; general conditions during the 1930s Depression.
INTERVIEWED BY JOHN TERREO, NOVEMBER 17, 1988, ISMAY.
SUMMARY: 2 PAGES
1 TAPE: 25 MINUTES

OH 1147
JOHN WILLMAN AND MONTE RENE WILLMAN INTERVIEW

John Willman and his wife, Monte Willman, recall: their childhoods; conditions during the 1930s Depression; their duties with the WPA and with the NYA; social activities in Plevna; members of the Northern Cheyenne tribe in the Lame Deer area.
INTERVIEWED BY JOHN TERREO, NOVEMBER 17, 1988, PLEVNA.
SUMMARY: 8 PAGES
1 TAPE: 1 HOUR

OH 1148
FRED ROSLER AND MARTHA ROSLER
INTERVIEW

Plevna residents Fred Rosler and his wife, Martha Rosler (b. 1899), briefly portray: conditions during the 1930s Depression; his jobs with the WPA; farm life; drought.

INTERVIEWED BY JOHN TERREO, NOVEMBER 17, 1988, PLEVNA.

SUMMARY: 2 PAGES
1 TAPE: 20 MINUTES

OH 1149
LAWRENCE HAMAN AND LILY HAMAN
INTERVIEW

Lawrence Haman and his wife, Lily Haman, survey: conditions during the 1930s Depression; their employment by the WPA; ranching; droughts; social activities in Miles City.

INTERVIEWED BY JOHN TERREO, NOVEMBER 18, 1988, MILES CITY.

SUMMARY: 7 PAGES
1 TAPE: 45 MINUTES

OH 1150
J. KENNETH TURNER INTERVIEW

Kenneth Turner (b. 1914) recalls: growing up on a homestead near Great Falls; the 1930s Depression; his work in gold mines and coal mines; the REA; the Resettlement Administration (RA); the Farmers Home Administration (FHA); the CCC; the WPA; bootlegging.

INTERVIEWED BY JOHN TERREO, NOVEMBER 22, 1988, KREMLIN.

SUMMARY: 12 PAGES
2 TAPES: 1 HOUR, 25 MINUTES

OH 1151
LEO REMSH INTERVIEW

Leo Remsh (b. 1914) summarizes: his childhood and education in Great Falls; his experiences during the 1930s Depression; his work with the CCC during the 1930s in Glacier National Park, and in Moab, Utah; life in Great Falls.

INTERVIEWED BY JOHN TERREO, DECEMBER 1, 1988, GREAT FALLS.

SUMMARY: 12 PAGES
2 TAPES: 1 HOUR, 20 MINUTES

OH 1152
JULIA JUNE CHITWOOD TREES INTERVIEW

Fishtail resident Julia Trees (b. 1920) recounts: growing up in Carbon County during the 1930s Depression; her mother's duties in a WPA sewing room; her own experiences with the NYA; her career as a teacher.

INTERVIEWED BY JOHN TERREO, DECEMBER 13, 1988, FISHTAIL.

TRANSCRIPT: 58 PAGES
2 TAPES: 1 HOUR, 50 MINUTES

OH 1153
HENRY JORGENSEN INTERVIEW

Henry Jorgensen (b. 1912) speaks of: his family's homestead near Dagmar; business and agriculture in Sheridan County; the formation of Sheridan County; the 1930s Depression; construction of Fort Peck Dam; his experiences with the WPA Historical Records Survey; his duties as principal at Central High School in Helena; his memories of C. R. Anderson; teaching; public education.

INTERVIEWED BY JOHN TERREO, JANUARY 31, 1989, HELENA.

TRANSCRIPT: 33 PAGES
2 TAPES: 1 HOUR, 25 MINUTES

OH 1154
BESSIE HEJLESEN INTERVIEW

Bessie Hejlesen reflects on: her early life; the family's relocation to Montana in a covered wagon; the family homestead; raising her own family; the 1930s Depression.

INTERVIEWED BY JOHN TERREO, FEBRUARY 15, 1989, HELENA.

SUMMARY: 6 PAGES
1 TAPE: 1 HOUR

OH 1155
GRANT MEYERS INTERVIEW

Helena resident Grant Meyers reviews: 1930s road-construction projects, including MacDonald Pass and ones at Lolo Hot Springs, Libby, Elliston, and Helena; types of horse-drawn equipment; paving materials; general living and working conditions for construction gangs and survey crews.

INTERVIEWED BY JOHN TERREO, FEBRUARY 15, 1989, HELENA.

TRANSCRIPT: 34 PAGES
2 TAPES: 1 HOUR, 15 MINUTES

OH 1156
GEORGE BROOKS AND NEVA BROOKS
INTERVIEW

George Brooks (1902–1990) recalls: growing up in Livingston; his work as a printer for the Livingston *Enterprise* and the Helena *Independent-Record*; the 1930s Depression. Neva Brooks (b. 1908) recalls: her early life and family; attitudes toward women during the 1920s and 1930s; her employment as a telephone operator; the 1930s Depression; her duties with the Montana legislature during the 1950s; her retirement.

INTERVIEWED BY JOHN TERREO, FEBRUARY 16, 1989, HELENA.

TRANSCRIPT: 28 PAGES

2 TAPES: 1 HOUR, 10 MINUTES

OH 1157
DORIS GRIBBLE INTERVIEW

Doris Gribble (1908–1992) remembers: her early childhood in Alysworth, Oklahoma; her family's relocation to Montana in 1916; attending school in Lewistown; raising a family in Great Falls during the 1930s Depression; her husband's experiences with the WPA; her work as a licensed practical nurse (LPN) in Great Falls and Townsend; the licensing of LPNs in Montana; changes in nursing since the late 1940s.

INTERVIEWED BY JOHN TERREO, FEBRUARY 28, 1989, HELENA.

TRANSCRIPT: 36 PAGES

2 TAPES: 1 HOUR, 10 MINUTES

OH 1158
CLARICE THOMAS INTERVIEW

Clarice Thomas discusses: her children and family; her experiences as a Montana ranch wife before and during the 1930s Depression; President Franklin D. Roosevelt's welfare programs, including the WPA, the CCC, and the Production Credit Association (PCA); her home in the town of Shawmut, making and selling applebox furniture; social activities; the role of women in health care; living without electricity; drought; welfare dependency; Christianity.

INTERVIEWED BY JOHN TERREO, MARCH 14, 1989, TOWNSEND.

SUMMARY: 4 PAGES

2 TAPES: 1 HOUR, 45 MINUTES

OH 1159
MARGARET DAVIS INTERVIEW

Margaret Davis (b. 1889), a Helena resident, ad-dresses: her childhood; her parents' homestead near Blossburg; her own homestead; starting a family; the 1930s Depression; seeing her first airplane; getting electricity; the importance of road construction; the 1935 earthquakes in Helena; relocating to Helena; World War I; World War II; health care in rural areas.

INTERVIEWED BY JOHN TERREO, APRIL 19, 1989, HELENA.

SUMMARY: 14 PAGES

2 TAPES: 1 HOUR, 30 MINUTES

OH 1160
MARK LaROWE INTERVIEW

Mark LaRowe (b. 1915) discusses: his work with the CCC in California and in Haugan during the late 1930s; living conditions and social activities in the CCC camps; his work as camp cook; his service with the U.S. Navy in the Pacific theater during World War II; operating a motel in Circle.

INTERVIEWED BY JOHN TERREO, MAY 19, 1989, ROBERTS.

TRANSCRIPT: 51 PAGES

2 TAPES: 2 HOURS

OH 1161
MARY LaROWE INTERVIEW

Mary LaRowe (b. 1918) tells about: her parents; growing up on a homestead near Glendive; her marriage and family; New Deal programs; the Depression.

INTERVIEWED BY JOHN TERREO, MAY 19, 1989, ROBERTS.

SUMMARY: 10 PAGES

1 TAPE: 1 HOUR

OH 1162
MAE TAKES GUN CHILDS INTERVIEW

Crow Agency resident Mae Takes Gun Childs (b. 1892), mother of Dessie Bad Bear, discusses: the differences between the Crow Agency superintendents C. A. Asbury and Robert (Robbie) Yellowtail; the return of the Sun Dance to the Crow Reservation; Crow Fair celebrations; attending St. Xavier Mission school, run by the Ursuline Sisters; peyote and the police; CCC camps; the Crow language.

INTERVIEWED BY CARSON WALKS OVER ICE, MAY 10, 1989, CROW AGENCY.

SUMMARY: 13 PAGES

1 TAPE: 1 HOUR

OH 1163
EFFIE HOGAN INTERVIEW

Effie Hogan (b. 1905) shares: her recollections of C. A. Asbury, the superintendent on the Crow Reservation; her husband, Superintendent Robert (Robbie) Yellowtail; the Shoshone Sun Dance; the Sun Dancers Caleb Bull Shows, William Big Day, Camel Big Hail, and Henry Big Day; Crow Fair celebrations; the construction of roundhalls; the Crow language.

INTERVIEWED BY CARSON WALKS OVER ICE, MAY 22, 1989, LITTLE BIGHORN NATIONAL BATTLEFIELD, CROW AGENCY.

TRANSCRIPT: 10 PAGES

1 TAPE: 1 HOUR

OH 1164
THOMAS BULL-OVER-HILL INTERVIEW

Thomas Bull-Over-Hill depicts: the Crow Reservation superintendents C. A. Asbury and Robert (Robbie) Yellowtail; the district boss farmers at Crow Agency; the first celebration of the Shoshone Sun Dance at Crow Agency in 1941; Crow Fair celebrations, including the Crow Fair rodeo; the rodeo participants Carl Leider, George Shaver, Jimmy Cooper, Joe Littlebird, and Anos High Eagle; building roundhalls; peyote use and conflicts with police; his work with the CCC and WPA; herding buffalo; the Crow language.

INTERVIEWED BY CARSON WALKS OVER ICE, MAY 27, 1987, CROW AGENCY.

TRANSCRIPT: 9 PAGES

1 TAPE: 45 MINUTES

OH 1165
JOHN BULLTAIL INTERVIEW

John Bulltail (b. circa 1916), an elder in the Crow Tribe, discusses: the Sun Dance on the Crow Reservation; the origins of the Crow Fair celebrations; Fourth of July celebrations in Lodge Grass; the Indian Self-Determination Act; CCC projects; the BIA cabin near Indian Creek; the Crow language. [See also 20th Century Montana Military Veterans OH 1535.]

INTERVIEWED BY CARSON WALKS OVER ICE, JUNE 13, 1989, HARDIN.

TRANSCRIPT: 14 PAGES

1 TAPE: 1 HOUR

OH 1166
GEORGE TAKES THE GUN INTERVIEW

George Takes The Gun (1909–1993), a member of the Crow Tribe, talks about: the differences between Crow Agency superintendents C. A. Asbury and Robert (Robbie) Yellowtail; the boss farmer program; the history of the Crow Fair; various Crow Fair celebrations; the Sun Dance; his work caring for a buffalo herd in the

1940s; going to school in Lodge Grass; building roundhalls; WPA programs; peyote; his experiences in road construction; life on the Crow Indian Reservation and the Crow language.

INTERVIEWED BY CARSON WALKS OVER ICE, JUNE 8, 1989, HARDIN.

TRANSCRIPT: 17 PAGES

1 TAPE: 1 HOUR

OH 1167
GERARD PESMAN INTERVIEW

Gerard Pesman (b. 1906) considers: his father's work on the irrigation projects at Huntley and Hysham, beginning in 1909; his own work driving tour buses in Yellowstone National Park from 1926 to 1941; the CCC; his childhood; the community of Ballantine.

INTERVIEWED BY JOHN TERREO, JUNE 19, 1989, BOZEMAN.

TRANSCRIPT: 57 PAGES

3 TAPES: 2 HOURS, 45 MINUTES

OH 1168
RAY J. QUIST INTERVIEW

Ray Quist (b. 1916) reviews: his childhood in Forsyth; his family's relocation to Bozeman in 1925; his experiences as a mechanic and a tour-bus driver in Yellowstone National Park from 1935 to 1939; his World War II service as an aircraft mechanic, working on B-17 bombers; his experiences in the farm-machinery business.

INTERVIEWED BY JOHN TERREO, JUNE 19, 1989, BOZEMAN.

SUMMARY: 13 PAGES

1 TAPE: 1 HOUR

OH 1169
BUD POSTEMA INTERVIEW

Bud Postema (b. 1911) comments on: his parents; homesteading in the Manhattan area; his early life and education; his family's grocery business; the 1930s Depression; the CCC; the Yellowstone Park Transportation Company (YPTC); his experiences and recollections as a tour-bus driver; Yellowstone National Park visitors; his relationships with other drivers and with various YPTC employees; his retirement.

INTERVIEWED BY JOHN TERREO, JUNE 20, 1989, BOZEMAN.

TRANSCRIPT: 56 PAGES

2 TAPES: 2 HOURS

OH 1170
DONALD STEELE INTERVIEW

Billings resident Donald Steele (b. 1912) remembers: his childhood in Billings; his father's work as chief of

the Billings Fire Department; his own experiences as a
tour-bus driver in Yellowstone National Park from 1935
to 1941.

INTERVIEWED BY JOHN TERREO, JUNE 22, 1989, BILLINGS.
SUMMARY: 21 PAGES
2 TAPES: 1 HOUR, 35 MINUTES

OH 1202
EUGENE A. DUNLOP INTERVIEW

Eugene Dunlop chronicles: his work as a mechanic
and a dispatcher for the Yellowstone Park Transportation Company (YPTC); various models of tour buses used
in Yellowstone Park.

INTERVIEWED BY JOHN TERREO, JUNE 26, 1989, HELENA.
SUMMARY: 4 PAGES
2 TAPES: 1 HOUR, 20 MINUTES

Small Town Montana Oral History Project

This project explored the history and development of 12 Montana communities: Broadus, Chinook, Choteau, Columbia Falls, Cut Bank, Eureka, Forsyth, Philipsburg, Plains, Plentywood, Roundup, and Sidney. Ranging in population from 800 to 4,500, these towns reflect the diversity of Montana's smaller communities and the people and industries that help them thrive. Topics discussed include the role of local institutions, industry, community development programs, celebrations, education, religion, and health care in small town life.

OH 701
FRANCIS M. SHENEFELT INTERVIEW
Francis Shenefelt (1896–1987) addresses: his work for the local logger Columbus Clark and for other logging outfits in the Eureka area; his duties as foreman for a slash-disposal crew in the Stillwater State Forest.
INTERVIEWED BY LAURIE MERCIER, AUGUST 3, 1983, EUREKA.
SUMMARY: 2 PAGES
2 TAPES: 1 HOUR, 20 MINUTES

OH 702
MAYE BUTLER ALVERSON INTERVIEW
Eureka resident Maye Alverson (b. 1897) treats: the early logging and ranching economies of Eureka and Lincoln County; her work for Whithicomb's Drug Store in Eureka in the 1930s; Eureka churches, lodges, businesses, and neighborhoods from 1907 to 1983.
INTERVIEWED BY LAURIE MERCIER, AUGUST 5, 1983, EUREKA.
SUMMARY: 3 PAGES
2 TAPES: 2 HOURS, 10 MINUTES

OH 703
JULIA WEST VANLEISHOUT INTERVIEW
Julia Vanleishout (b. 1901) characterizes: farm life in the Tobacco Valley from 1910 to 1960; events in Eureka between 1910 and 1960; her family's role in the town; her involvement with the local Grange and the Methodist Church.
INTERVIEWED BY LAURIE MERCIER, AUGUST 23, 1983, EUREKA.

SUMMARY: 2 PAGES
1 TAPE: 1 HOUR, 5 MINUTES

OH 704
CLARA ENDEN BROCK FEWKES INTERVIEW
Clara Fewkes (b. 1900) tells about: working as a practical nurse at the Eureka hospital from 1919 to 1923; health care in Eureka; living in the West Kootenai neighborhood from the late 1920s into the 1940s; her involvement in various community organizations, including the Help Each Other Club. *[See also General Montana OH 160.]*
INTERVIEWED BY LAURIE MERCIER, AUGUST 24, 1983, REXFORD.
SUMMARY: 3 PAGES
2 TAPES: 2 HOURS, 10 MINUTES

OH 705
HELEN T. SCHAGEL INTERVIEW
Helen Schagel (b. 1910) chronicles: Eureka from about 1910 into the 1980s; her work for the county/state Department of Public Welfare; the Majestic Theatre in Eureka; her involvement with community organizations, including the Junior Women's Club.
INTERVIEWED BY LAURIE MERCIER, AUGUST 24, 1983, EUREKA.
SUMMARY: 6 PAGES
4 TAPES: 4 HOURS, 15 MINUTES

OH 706
JOHN W. VUKONICH INTERVIEW
John Vukonich (b. 1908) talks of: his work for the

U.S. Forest Service as a fire lookout and trail-maintenance crewman at Fortine from 1924 to 1965; his employment at the A. J. Thomas Christmas tree farm in Eureka; his impressions of Eureka; the Industrial Workers of the World (IWW).
INTERVIEWED BY LAURIE MERCIER, AUGUST 26, 1983, FORTINE.
SUMMARY: 3 PAGES
2 TAPES: 1 HOUR, 50 MINUTES

OH 707
CLARENCE "SONNY" HOYT INTERVIEW

Sonny Hoyt (b. 1929) of Eureka comments on: his work logging and operating heavy equipment for logging operators—particularly Fred King—in the Tobacco Valley; the timber industry in the Eureka area from the 1940s to the 1980s; efforts to establish a bus line that would serve Eureka; local merchants and their involvement in town activities.
INTERVIEWED BY LAURIE MERCIER, AUGUST 27, 1983, EUREKA.
SUMMARY: 5 PAGES
3 TAPES: 2 HOURS, 35 MINUTES

OH 708
DONALD R. BOSLAUGH INTERVIEW

Eureka resident Donald Boslaugh (b. 1909) surveys: his activities as principal of Lincoln County High School in Libby from 1946 to 1959; the operation of the Ksanka Lumber Company from the 1950s to 1968; the lumber industry in the Eureka area; his teaching experiences in Flaxville and Colstrip during the 1930s and 1940s.
INTERVIEWED BY LAURIE MERCIER, AUGUST 23, 1983, EUREKA.
SUMMARY: 3 PAGES
2 TAPES: 2 HOURS, 5 MINUTES

OH 709
HELEN MOSES BOLEN INTERVIEW

Helen Bolen (b. 1913) considers: the community of Eureka from the 1920s into the 1980s; her participation in such community groups as the Eureka Hospital Association, the Eureka Cemetery Association, and the Tobacco Valley Improvement Association; teaching in the Tobacco Valley during the 1930s.
INTERVIEWED BY LAURIE MERCIER, AUGUST 29, 1983, EUREKA.
SUMMARY: 3 PAGES
2 TAPES: 2 HOURS, 10 MINUTES

OH 710
WILLIAM L. FEWKES INTERVIEW

William Fewkes (b. 1903) summarizes: his operation of the Fewkes General Store in Rexford from the 1920s into the 1960s; his participation in the Tobacco Valley Improvement Association, in the local Red Cross chapter, and in the Eureka Cemetery Association. [See also General Montana OH 160.]
INTERVIEWED BY LAURIE MERCIER, AUGUST 30, 1983, REXFORD.
SUMMARY: 2 PAGES
1 TAPE: 1 HOUR, 5 MINUTES

OH 711
WINTON WEYDEMEYER INTERVIEW

Winton Weydemeyer (b. 1903) converses on: the operation of the Weydemeyer Ranch near Fortine from the 1920s into the 1970s; the local Grange; the Montana Conservation Council; local Christmas tree production; the Little Theater Club; the Lincoln County Fair Board. [See also General Montana OH 161.]
INTERVIEWED BY LAURIE MERCIER, AUGUST 30, 1983, FORTINE.
SUMMARY: 3 PAGES
2 TAPES: 2 HOURS

OH 712
FRED KING INTERVIEW

Fred King (b. 1920)—a resident of Eureka—speaks of: his operation of a contract logging business in the Eureka area from 1944 into the 1980s; innovations in logging and in road-building work during the late 1940s; the J. Neils Lumber Company.
INTERVIEWED BY LAURIE MERCIER, SEPTEMBER 21, 1983, EUREKA.
SUMMARY: 2 PAGES
1 TAPE: 1 HOUR

OH 713
BURGESS DRAKE AND FRANCES KOPP DRAKE INTERVIEW

Burgess Drake (b. 1899) and Frances Drake discuss: their experiences living and working on farms in the Tobacco Valley of northwestern Montana; their affiliation with such Eureka community groups as the Baptist Church, the local Grange, and Lincoln County High School. Burgess also discusses his work at local lumber mills.
INTERVIEWED BY LAURIE MERCIER, SEPTEMBER 21, 1983, EUREKA.

SUMMARY: 3 PAGES
2 TAPES: 1 HOUR, 40 MINUTES

OH 714
VICTOR PELTIER AND MARIE SHEA PELTIER INTERVIEW

Victor Peltier (b. 1913) and Marie Peltier (b. 1915) review their operation of a creamery, a laundry, and a meat-locker business in Eureka from the 1930s into the 1960s.

INTERVIEWED BY LAURIE MERCIER, SEPTEMBER 22, 1983, EUREKA.

SUMMARY: 2 PAGES
1 TAPE: 45 MINUTES

OH 715
ALBINA PELTIER JOHNSON INTERVIEW

Albina Johnson (b. 1906) discusses: the community of Eureka; her work for the Peltier Creamery from 1945 to 1953; her involvement with the Lincoln County Rural Electrification Association (REA) from 1952 to 1970.

INTERVIEWED BY LAURIE MERCIER, SEPTEMBER 22, 1983, EUREKA.

SUMMARY: 2 PAGES
1 TAPE: 1 HOUR

OH 716
WYLIE OSLER INTERVIEW

Wylie Osler (b. 1923) recalls: the history and operation of the Osler Lumber Mill in Fortine, from the 1940s into the 1960s; the relationship of the mill with the U.S. Forest Service; competition among area mills; his association with the Eureka Lions Club and with the Flathead Lumbermen Who-Who Club.

INTERVIEWED BY LAURIE MERCIER, SEPTEMBER 23, 1983, FORTINE.

SUMMARY: 3 PAGES
2 TAPES: 1 HOUR, 30 MINUTES

OH 717
CLARA MENTZER FLEMING INTERVIEW

Clara Fleming depicts: community life in Eureka; her participation in several area clubs and organizations, including the Garden Club, the Little Theatre Club, the Study Club, and the Tobacco Valley Improvement Association; the formation of local Girl Scout troops; her teaching experiences in Lincoln County; her views on local education.

INTERVIEWED BY LAURIE MERCIER, AUGUST 23, 1983, EUREKA.

SUMMARY: 3 PAGES
2 TAPES: 2 HOURS, 10 MINUTES

OH 718
HANK LEONARD INTERVIEW

Hank Leonard (b. 1904) talks about: his work for the Brooks-Scanlon Company lumber mill in Eureka from 1916 to 1917; his involvement with the radical IWW; operating a barber shop in Eureka, 1937–1974.

INTERVIEWED BY LAURIE MERCIER, AUGUST 3, 1983, EUREKA.

SUMMARY: 2 PAGES
2 TAPES: 1 HOUR, 10 MINUTES

OH 719
ELIZABETH GREGORY GREENE INTERVIEW

Elizabeth Greene (b. 1895) discusses: community life in Columbia Falls, from 1916 into the 1950s; local women's groups; chautauquas; area churches; health care; various neighborhoods in Columbia Falls.

INTERVIEWED BY LAURIE MERCIER, OCTOBER 18, 1983, COLUMBIA FALLS.

SUMMARY: 2 PAGES
2 TAPES: 1 HOUR, 35 MINUTES

OH 720
DOROTHY JORDAN BRADING AND MARGARET JORDAN WALKER INTERVIEW

Longtime Columbia Falls residents, Dorothy Brading (b. 1907) and Margaret Walker (b. 1909) remember: community life from 1915 to 1940; the A. L. Jordan Lumber Company; local businesses; town celebrations; area churches; women's groups. [See also General Montana OH 559.]

INTERVIEWED BY LAURIE MERCIER, OCTOBER 19, 1983, JORDAN.

SUMMARY: 3 PAGES
2 TAPES: 1 HOUR, 55 MINUTES

OH 721
ORLA E. KIMZEY INTERVIEW

Orla Kimzey describes: social life in Columbia Falls from 1954 to 1983; local government; area churches; community organizations; her teaching experiences at the Columbia Falls grade school from 1955 to 1978.

INTERVIEWED BY LAURIE MERCIER, NOVEMBER 15, 1983, COLUMBIA FALLS.

SUMMARY: 3 PAGES
2 TAPES: 1 HOUR, 45 MINUTES

OH 722
EDWARD HULA INTERVIEW

Edward Hula (b. 1921) describes: the community of Columbia Falls from 1930 to 1983; his work on the Hungry Horse Dam construction project in 1947; his employment at the nearby Anaconda Aluminum Company (AAC) plant from 1953 to 1977; his duties as a Columbia Falls policeman, water supervisor, road superintendent, and volunteer fireman; the Aluminum, Brick, and Glass Workers' International Union.

INTERVIEWED BY LAURIE MERCIER, NOVEMBER 16, 1983, COLUMBIA FALLS.

TRANSCRIPT: 78 PAGES

2 TAPES: 2 HOURS, 10 MINUTES

OH 723
ESTELLA LOVEALL MATEKA INTERVIEW

Estella Mateka (b. 1891) discourses on: the community of Columbia Falls from 1900 to 1950; local businesses; fraternal lodges; area churches; transportation; community celebrations; health care; town law enforcement; her operation of the Mateka (People's) Meat Market from 1925 to 1952.

INTERVIEWED BY LAURIE MERCIER, NOVEMBER 17, 1983, COLUMBIA FALLS.

SUMMARY: 4 PAGES

2 TAPES: 2 HOURS

OH 724
JOE T. OPALKA INTERVIEW

Joe Opalka (b. 1902) reflects on: his work in the Columbia Falls area from the 1920s into the 1970s in sawmills, as chief of police, and in positions on the road and water commissions; the IWW; the Silver Basin Mine; his duties as a state liquor store employee; his employment in Glacier National Park; his involvement in various community organizations, particularly the Columbia Falls Volunteer Fire Department.

INTERVIEWED BY LAURIE MERCIER, NOVEMBER 17, 1983, COLUMBIA FALLS.

TRANSCRIPT: 78 PAGES

2 TAPES: 2 HOURS, 10 MINUTES

OH 725
J. TED ROGERS AND LULU LEOFFLER ROGERS INTERVIEW

Columbia Falls residents Ted Rogers (b. 1910) and Lulu Rogers (b. 1921) discourse on: their farming experiences in Flathead County, just east of Columbia Falls. Ted Rogers also discusses running his local milk route from 1917 until 1942. Lulu Rogers discusses her work as a telephone switchboard operator during the 1930s.

INTERVIEWED BY LAURIE MERCIER, NOVEMBER 18, 1983, COLUMBIA FALLS.

SUMMARY: 4 PAGES

2 TAPES: 2 HOURS

OH 726
CECELIA LYONAIS BARNHART AND FLOYD BARNHART INTERVIEW

Cecelia Barnhart and Floyd Barnhart reflect on community life in Columbia Falls from 1947 to 1983. Floyd Barnhart discusses his work for the Plum Creek Lumber Company. Cecelia Barnhart talks of her involvement with the local 4-H club and with St. Richard's Catholic Church.

INTERVIEWED BY LAURIE MERCIER, NOVEMBER 18, 1983, JORDAN.

SUMMARY: 3 PAGES

2 TAPES: 1 HOUR, 35 MINUTES

OH 727
FLOYD DARLING AND VERA GREENE DARLING INTERVIEW

Floyd Darling (1914–1986) and Vera Darling (b. 1921) describe: life in Columbia Falls from the 1920s into the 1960s; the Depression; his work for the U.S. Forest Service; her job at the Bank of Columbia Falls from 1960 to 1979.

INTERVIEWED BY LAURIE MERCIER, NOVEMBER 28, 1983, COLUMBIA FALLS.

SUMMARY: 4 PAGES

2 TAPES: 2 HOURS

OH 728
CALVIN CROUCH INTERVIEW

Calvin Crouch (b. 1924) talks of: his operation of Crouch's Jewelry Store in Columbia Falls from 1947 into the 1980s; community life in Columbia Falls; his involvement in such local groups as the city council and the chamber of commerce.

INTERVIEWED BY LAURIE MERCIER, NOVEMBER 29, 1983, BIGFORK.

SUMMARY: 5 PAGES

2 TAPES: 2 HOURS

OH 729
CLARENCE SAUREY INTERVIEW
Clarence Saurey (b. 1893) recalls: his work for the Stoltze Lumber Company in Columbia Falls from 1942 to 1953; his other timber-industry work; the IWW; the community development of Columbia Falls.
INTERVIEWED BY LAURIE MERCIER, NOVEMBER 29, 1983, KALISPELL.
SUMMARY: 4 PAGES
2 TAPES: 1 HOUR, 40 MINUTES

OH 730
TEDDY R. ANDREW INTERVIEW
Teddy Andrew recalls: his 34-year career at the U.S. Post Office in Columbia Falls, from 1949 into the 1980s; his duties as postmaster; his involvement with various civic groups; his time on the local school board.
INTERVIEWED BY LAURIE MERCIER, NOVEMBER 30, 1983, COLUMBIA FALLS.
SUMMARY: 3 PAGES
1 TAPE: 1 HOUR, 5 MINUTES

OH 731
MEL RUDER INTERVIEW
Mel Ruder (b. 1914)—retired editor and publisher of the Columbia Falls Hungry Horse News—discusses: his newspaper career from 1946 to 1978; his receipt of the Pulitzer Prize in 1965; his work with the Columbia Falls Chamber of Commerce; the impacts of Hungry Horse Dam and the Anaconda Aluminum Company plant on the community.
INTERVIEWED BY LAURIE MERCIER, NOVEMBER 30, 1983, COLUMBIA FALLS.
SUMMARY: 4 PAGES
2 TAPES: 1 HOUR, 55 MINUTES

OH 732
ROBERT WALTMIRE INTERVIEW
Robert Waltmire discusses: life in Columbia Falls; his work on the Columbia Falls city council during the 1970s.
INTERVIEWED BY LAURIE MERCIER, DECEMBER 1, 1983, COLUMBIA FALLS.
SUMMARY: 2 PAGES
1 TAPE: 1 HOUR, 5 MINUTES

OH 733
M. COLLEEN McCARTNEY ALLISON INTERVIEW
Colleen Allison remembers: her experiences as a member of the Columbia Falls city council from 1972 to 1978; her subsequent work as mayor and as executive secretary of the local school board.
INTERVIEWED BY LAURIE MERCIER, DECEMBER 1, 1983, COLUMBIA FALLS.
SUMMARY: 2 PAGES
1 TAPE: 1 HOUR

OH 734
ROBERT SNEDDON INTERVIEW
Robert Sneddon addresses: the establishment of the Anaconda Aluminum Company (AAC) plant in Columbia Falls in the early 1950s; his career as an AAC maintenance inspector and plant manager from 1954 into the 1980s.
INTERVIEWED BY LAURIE MERCIER, DECEMBER 1, 1983, COLUMBIA FALLS.
SUMMARY: 2 PAGES
1 TAPE: 1 HOUR

OH 735
GLADYS VAN SHAY INTERVIEW
Gladys Van Shay (b. 1928) chronicles: community life in Columbia Falls; the town's development; her career with the weekly Hungry Horse News from 1946 to 1976; her various part-time jobs in the area; her involvement with several community organizations and youth groups.
INTERVIEWED BY LAURIE MERCIER, DECEMBER 1, 1983, COLUMBIA FALLS.
SUMMARY: 4 PAGES
2 TAPES: 2 HOURS, 5 MINUTES

OH 736
LELAND H. PAGE, SR., INTERVIEW
Leland Page (b. 1911) talks about: neighborhoods, entertainment, mines, and mills in Philipsburg; manganese mines; local businesses, including the Antler Bar, the Masonic Lodge, and the Philipsburg Grocery.
INTERVIEWED BY LAURIE MERCIER, FEBRUARY 22, 1984, PHILIPSBURG.
SUMMARY: 5 PAGES
3 TAPES: 3 HOURS, 10 MINUTES

OH 737
HAROLD B. KAISER INTERVIEW
A Philipsburg resident, Harold Kaiser (b. 1907) discusses: the Kaiser family; his work in manganese and gold mines near Philipsburg; road work; the World War I economic boom; operating a candy shop; neighborhoods

and businesses in Philipsburg; his work for the Anaconda Company in Anaconda and Butte.
INTERVIEWED BY LAURIE MERCIER, JANUARY 25, 1984, PHILIPSBURG.
SUMMARY: 4 PAGES
3 TAPES: 2 HOURS, 50 MINUTES

OH 738
AGNES L. McGARVEY KEARNS INTERVIEW

Agnes Kearns (b. 1904) depicts: her childhood on the family ranch in Granite County, circa 1910–1920; her career at the Philipsburg State Bank and at the Flint Creek Valley Bank from 1919 to 1969.
INTERVIEWED BY LAURIE MERCIER, JANUARY 25, 1984, PHILIPSBURG.
SUMMARY: 5 PAGES
2 TAPES: 2 HOURS, 10 MINUTES

OH 739
AGNES MAEHL McDONALD INTERVIEW

Agnes McDonald (b. 1905) describes: churches, clubs, and schools in Philipsburg from the 1920s into the 1970s; her work as Granite County clerk and recorder during the 1950s; her operation of a local ranch; her participation in local agricultural organizations.
INTERVIEWED BY LAURIE MERCIER, JANUARY 26, 1984, PHILIPSBURG.
SUMMARY: 4 PAGES
2 TAPES: 1 HOUR, 55 MINUTES

OH 740
DORA HUFFMAN PENINGTON AND FLORENCE HUFFMAN NEAL INTERVIEW

Dora Penington (b. 1904) and Florence Neal (b. 1905) discourse on: the history and operation of Huffman's Grocery Store in Philipsburg; their work as teachers in Philipsburg schools; the community's businesses, clubs, and social life.
INTERVIEWED BY LAURIE MERCIER, JANUARY 27, 1984, PHILIPSBURG.
SUMMARY: 4 PAGES
2 TAPES: 2 HOURS, 5 MINUTES

OH 741
JAMES PATTEN AND PHYLLIS McLEOD PATTEN INTERVIEW

James Patten (b. 1888) and Phyllis Patten examine: community life in Philipsburg; World War I protests; local manganese mining and milling; the establishment of the Philipsburg public library; the publication of *Small*

Town Stuff, a controversial book based on life in Philipsburg. *[See also Montanans at Work OH 460.]*
INTERVIEWED BY LAURIE MERCIER, JANUARY 27, 1984, PHILIPSBURG.
TRANSCRIPT: 68 PAGES
2 TAPES: 2 HOURS, 10 MINUTES

OH 742
EDWARD R. "HEINE" WINNINGHOFF INTERVIEW

Heine Winninghoff (b. 1906) discusses: his ownership and operation of Winninghoff Motors in Philipsburg; the town's neighborhoods; his involvement with the local Rotary Club; the blacksmith shop owned by his father, Francis X. Winninghoff.
INTERVIEWED BY LAURIE MERCIER, FEBRUARY 8, 1984, PHILIPSBURG.
SUMMARY: 3 PAGES
2 TAPES: 1 HOUR, 45 MINUTES

OH 743
BETTY GROVES HORRIGAN CHRISTENSON INTERVIEW

Betty Christenson (b. 1908) recalls: her ownership and operation of the Granada Theatre in Philipsburg from 1935 to 1981; community life in Philipsburg; her participation in local clubs and civic organizations.
INTERVIEWED BY LAURIE MERCIER, FEBRUARY 9, 1984, PHILIPSBURG.
SUMMARY: 4 PAGES
3 TAPES: 2 HOURS, 30 MINUTES

OH 744
JENNY KAISER SAURER INTERVIEW

Jenny Saurer (b. 1898) recalls: various neighborhoods in Philipsburg; the Kaiser family; her work at the local Golden Rule Store; lodges and clubs in Philipsburg; community life; her German-American ancestry.
INTERVIEWED BY LAURIE MERCIER, FEBRUARY 9, 1984, PHILIPSBURG.
SUMMARY: 2 PAGES
1 TAPE: 1 HOUR, 5 MINUTES

OH 745
WILLARD E. BRUNS, SR., AND WILLMA M. APPLEGATE BRUNS INTERVIEW

Willard Bruns (b. 1900) and Willma Bruns (b. 1900) were longtime Philipsburg residents. Willard reflects on: his duties with the U.S. Forest Service at the Rock Creek Station in Granite County during the 1930s; his work

with the Mine-Mill union. Willma discusses: living at Rock Creek; community life in Philipsburg.
INTERVIEWED BY LAURIE MERCIER, FEBRUARY 9, 1984, PHILIPSBURG.
SUMMARY: 3 PAGES
2 TAPES: 1 HOUR, 30 MINUTES

OH 746
DOROTHY "DOLLY" MAY EMERSON PAGE INTERVIEW
Dolly Page (b. 1915) describes: businesses she operated in Philipsburg from the 1930s into the 1980s; community activities; local politics; the Junior Women's Club; the hospital auxiliary; her early years in Butte; recollections of Leland Page.
INTERVIEWED BY LAURIE MERCIER, FEBRUARY 10 AND APRIL 18, 1984, PHILIPSBURG.
SUMMARY: 11 PAGES
6 TAPES: 5 HOURS, 25 MINUTES

OH 747
LOUIS E. CROWLEY INTERVIEW
Louis Crowley (b. 1906) remembers: various mining companies and their proprietors in Granite and Philipsburg; his work as a teamster for the Trout Mining Company from 1931 to 1942.
INTERVIEWED BY LAURIE MERCIER, FEBRUARY 10, 1984, PHILIPSBURG.
SUMMARY: 4 PAGES
2 TAPES: 2 HOURS, 10 MINUTES

OH 748
PERCY ROBINSON INTERVIEW
Percy Robinson (b. 1911) speaks of: the history of the Robinson Ranch, south of Choteau; the development of its sheep and cattle operations from 1919 to 1950.
INTERVIEWED BY LAURIE MERCIER, MARCH 1, 1984, CHOTEAU.
SUMMARY: 3 PAGES
1 TAPE: 1 HOUR, 5 MINUTES

OH 749
ALVA LARSON ARMSTRONG INTERVIEW
Alva Armstrong (b. 1904) surveys: education, commerce, and entertainment in Choteau from 1910 to 1931; the involvement of her father, Thomas O. Larson, in Choteau business and politics.
INTERVIEWED BY LAURIE MERCIER, MARCH 1, 1984, CHOTEAU.

SUMMARY: 3 PAGES
1 TAPE: 1 HOUR, 5 MINUTES

OH 750
MYLES L. STANDISH INTERVIEW
Myles Standish (b. 1908) tells about: his schooling in Choteau during the 1920s; farming in Teton County from 1927 to 1969; the town of Choteau and its residents' relationships with local farmers from the 1930s into the 1980s.
INTERVIEWED BY LAURIE MERCIER, MARCH 1, 1984, CHOTEAU.
SUMMARY: 4 PAGES
2 TAPES: 1 HOUR, 50 MINUTES

OH 751
BETTY KRABER WHITE INTERVIEW
Betty White (b. 1903) discusses: community life in Choteau; the Beaupre Hotel, owned and operated by her mother, Emma Thompson.
INTERVIEWED BY LAURIE MERCIER, FEBRUARY 29, 1984, CHOTEAU.
SUMMARY: 2 PAGES
1 TAPE: 45 MINUTES

OH 752
BUD TAYLOR INTERVIEW
Bud Taylor (b. 1915) talks of: operating the Taylor Garage in Choteau from the 1920s into the 1950s; his involvement in community activities.
INTERVIEWED BY LAURIE MERCIER, FEBRUARY 24, 1984, CHOTEAU.
SUMMARY: 2 PAGES
1 TAPE: 1 HOUR

OH 753
JOEL OTNESS INTERVIEW
Joel Otness (b. 1900) describes: his family's homestead near Farmington; rural life in Teton County from 1910 into the 1940s; the town of Choteau; his Norwegian-American heritage.
INTERVIEWED BY LAURIE MERCIER, FEBRUARY 29, 1984, CHOTEAU.
SUMMARY: 2 PAGES
1 TAPE: 1 HOUR

OH 754
EMILY STURGEON CRARY INTERVIEW
Emily Crary (b. 1886) reviews: her operation of the Royal Theatre in Choteau from 1913 to 1946; her in-

volvement in the Women's Club; her participation in other community activities.
INTERVIEWED BY LAURIE MERCIER, FEBRUARY 29, 1984, CHOTEAU.
SUMMARY: 4 PAGES
2 TAPES: 1 HOUR, 55 MINUTES

OH 755
JESSE MALONE AND NORA LEMON MALONE INTERVIEW

Jesse Malone and Nora Malone remember: cattle ranching at the Flying U Ranch, north of Choteau, from 1940 into the 1970s; the development of their Simmental herd; their participation in various Choteau community and medical care organizations, including the hospital auxiliary, 4-H, and the Teton County Oldest Settlers Club.
INTERVIEWED BY LAURIE MERCIER, FEBRUARY 28, 1984, CHOTEAU.
SUMMARY: 5 PAGES
2 TAPES: 2 HOURS, 5 MINUTES

OH 756
CLYDE J. NEU INTERVIEW

Clyde Neu (b. 1903) reviews: his operation of the Neu's Family Store, a clothing business in Philipsburg, from 1948 to 1965; his work as Granite County treasurer from 1932 to 1937; his duties as a Granite County commissioner from 1955 to 1965; area mines; businesses, entertainment, sports, and ethnic groups in Philipsburg; the Fort Missoula alien detention center during World War II.
INTERVIEWED BY LAURIE MERCIER, MARCH 9, 1984, PHILIPSBURG.
SUMMARY: 5 PAGES
3 TAPES: 3 HOURS, 10 MINUTES

OH 757
MYRTLE BUSHMAN REARDON INTERVIEW

Myrtle Reardon (b. 1911) recounts: businesses and entertainment in Choteau from the 1920s into the 1940s; Indian-white relations in the area. *[See also General Montana OH 1655.]*
INTERVIEWED BY LAURIE MERCIER, MARCH 1, 1984, CHOTEAU.
SUMMARY: 2 PAGES
1 TAPE: 1 HOUR, 5 MINUTES

OH 758
OLGA WAGNILD MONKMAN INTERVIEW

Olga Monkman (b. 1895) recalls her life on a homestead north of Choteau, from 1900 to 1940.
INTERVIEWED BY LAURIE MERCIER, FEBRUARY 29, 1984, CHOTEAU.
SUMMARY: 4 PAGES
1 TAPE: 40 MINUTES

OH 759
GRACE HOMAN DUFFEY INTERVIEW

Choteau resident Grace Duffey (b. 1900) discusses: her family background; her work with her aunt, Mrs. Beaupre, operating the Beaupre Hotel in Choteau; her experiences as a teacher and as a singer; her involvement with St. Joseph's Catholic Church in Choteau.
INTERVIEWED BY LAURIE MERCIER, MARCH 19, 1984, CHOTEAU.
2 TAPES: 1 HOUR, 35 MINUTES

OH 760
MARY LEMMON SCHOONMAKER INTERVIEW

Mary Schoonmaker (b. 1910) remembers her ownership and operation of the Cornell Hotel in Choteau from 1951 to 1978.
INTERVIEWED BY LAURIE MERCIER, MARCH 20, 1984, CHOTEAU.
SUMMARY: 2 PAGES
1 TAPE: 1 HOUR, 5 MINUTES

OH 761
LEON M. GOLLEHON INTERVIEW

Leon Gollehon (b. 1914) discusses: his experiences as a city policeman and as the chief of police in Choteau from 1957 to 1977; his construction and ranch work in Chouteau and Teton counties.
INTERVIEWED BY LAURIE MERCIER, MARCH 19, 1984, CHOTEAU.
SUMMARY: 3 PAGES
2 TAPES: 1 HOUR, 20 MINUTES

OH 762
JESSE C. BLEECKER AND JEAN K. LASSALE BLEECKER INTERVIEW

Jesse Bleecker (b. 1913) and Jean Bleecker describe community life in Choteau from the 1930s into the 1960s. Jesse Bleecker talks of his work as a carpenter and a stonemason. Jean Bleecker discusses her experiences as a nurse in local hospitals.

INTERVIEWED BY LAURIE MERCIER, MARCH 21, 1984, CHOTEAU.
SUMMARY: 4 PAGES
2 TAPES: 2 HOURS, 5 MINUTES

OH 763
AFTON CAUFIELD SCOTT INTERVIEW

Afton Scott (b. 1916) converses about: community life in Choteau; her work for Dr. Ernest B. Maynard from 1934 to 1938; her 25-year career as a nurse in the Teton County Nursing Home in Choteau.
INTERVIEWED BY LAURIE MERCIER, MARCH 21, 1984, CHOTEAU.
SUMMARY: 2 PAGES
1 TAPE: 40 MINUTES

OH 764
ISABELLE LEMMON TRUCHOT INTERVIEW

Isabelle Truchot (b. 1913) comments on: her employment with the Ed Hirshberg family in Choteau from 1926 to 1935; ranch life in northern Teton County from the 1930s into the 1940s; her involvement in various community groups; her Scottish-American background.
INTERVIEWED BY LAURIE MERCIER, APRIL 10, 1984, CHOTEAU.
SUMMARY: 2 PAGES
1 TAPE: 1 HOUR, 5 MINUTES

OH 765
GUS THOMPSON INTERVIEW

Gus Thompson (b. 1900) discusses his work as the Choteau city engineer from the 1930s through the 1960s.
INTERVIEWED BY LAURIE MERCIER, MARCH 19, 1984, CHOTEAU.
SUMMARY: 3 PAGES
2 TAPES: 1 HOUR, 25 MINUTES

OH 766
IRENE JONES DAUWALDER McMANUS INTERVIEW

Irene McManus (b. 1899) describes: Bole from 1914 to 1939; community life in Choteau from 1939 into the 1980s; her involvement in several clubs, including the Home Demonstration Club, the Bole Women's Club, the Choteau Women's Club, the Rebekahs, the Dorcas Society, and 4-H.
INTERVIEWED BY LAURIE MERCIER, MARCH 20, 1984, CHOTEAU.
SUMMARY: 4 PAGES
2 TAPES: 2 HOURS, 10 MINUTES

OH 767
JAMES DELLWO AND JAMES HAMILTON INTERVIEW

James Dellwo and James Hamilton portray: their respective jobs as city manager and as mayor of Choteau during the 1970s and 1980s; major issues facing the town; difficulties involved with managing city services; dealing with federal regulations; high operating costs.
INTERVIEWED BY LAURIE MERCIER, APRIL 11, 1984, CHOTEAU.
SUMMARY: 2 PAGES
1 TAPE: 1 HOUR, 5 MINUTES

OH 768
IONA DAVIDSON ZGODA INTERVIEW

Iona Zgoda (b. 1908) recounts: her childhood and education; her work in the county extension service agent's office in Choteau from 1927 to 1948; her marriage to Frank Zgoda; the innovative agricultural and community programs developed by the county agent Robert Clarkson; Teton County's own chautauqua; the effects of the 1930s Depression; the Teton County Planning Board; cultural and social activities in the area.
INTERVIEWED BY LAURIE MERCIER, APRIL 11, 1984, CHOTEAU.
SUMMARY: 3 PAGES
2 TAPES: 1 HOUR, 35 MINUTES

OH 769
DOROTHY HOLMES O'NEIL INTERVIEW

Dorothy O'Neil (b. circa 1915) recalls: her work at the Citizen's State Bank in Choteau from 1937 through the 1960s; her involvement in several community-service organizations; the Freemen Ranch.
INTERVIEWED BY LAURIE MERCIER, APRIL 10, 1984, CHOTEAU.
SUMMARY: 2 PAGES
1 TAPE: 1 HOUR, 5 MINUTES

OH 770
DOROTHY ARENSMEYER COOK INTERVIEW

Dorothy Cook (b. 1916) describes: her youth in the Farmington area in the 1920s; life in Choteau from the 1930s into the 1970s; her work at the Parkway Cafe and at the U.S. Post Office in Choteau; her involvement with various community organizations.
INTERVIEWED BY LAURIE MERCIER, APRIL 11, 1984, CHOTEAU.
SUMMARY: 5 PAGES
2 TAPES: 1 HOUR, 50 MINUTES

OH 771
AUSTIN CAMPBELL INTERVIEW
Choteau resident Austin Campbell reflects on: his memories of the community from the 1920s through the 1940s; his work on area sheep ranches; his friendships with local cowboys.
INTERVIEWED BY LAURIE MERCIER, APRIL 9, 1984, CHOTEAU.
SUMMARY: 4 PAGES
2 TAPES: 1 HOUR, 40 MINUTES

OH 772
DOROTHY JACKSON ARMSTRONG INTERVIEW
Dorothy Armstrong (b. 1924) reports on: community life in Choteau; her work at the Teton Steam Laundry, at the J. C. Penney store, at the Citizen's State Bank, and at the Teton County Courthouse; her activities as a volunteer for the local chapter of the Red Cross; her father, John G. Jackson, and his participation in Choteau community affairs.
INTERVIEWED BY LAURIE MERCIER, APRIL 9, 1984, CHOTEAU.
SUMMARY: 3 PAGES
2 TAPES: 1 HOUR, 50 MINUTES

OH 773
ALBERT T. TESCH INTERVIEW
Albert Tesch remembers: operating the Tesch Farm Implement Company in Choteau from 1946 to 1955; running a heating and plumbing business in the same community from 1946 into the 1980s; the importance of agriculture to the local economy; his participation in community organizations; his experiences on the Choteau city council during the 1970s.
INTERVIEWED BY LAURIE MERCIER, APRIL 16, 1984, CHOTEAU.
SUMMARY: 2 PAGES
2 TAPES: 1 HOUR, 20 MINUTES

OH 774
HILDEGARDE E. McDOUGAL INTERVIEW
Philipsburg resident Hildegarde McDougal (1896–1984) reviews: her work as the clerk and recorder for Granite County from 1936 to 1962; community life in Philipsburg from 1919 into the 1960s.
INTERVIEWED BY LAURIE MERCIER, APRIL 18, 1984, PHILIPSBURG.
SUMMARY: 2 PAGES
1 TAPE: 1 HOUR

OH 775
MAURINE THOMAS SMITH INTERVIEW
Maurine Smith (b. 1909) discusses: her childhood in Eureka; community events, businesses, and townspeople; her teaching career in the area; local Christmas celebrations.
INTERVIEWED BY CATHRYN SCHROEDER, APRIL 14, 1984, EUREKA.
SUMMARY: 6 PAGES
2 TAPES: 1 HOUR, 30 MINUTES

OH 776
BYRON "BARNEY" OLSON INTERVIEW
Barney Olson (b. 1912) talks of: his childhood in Eureka; life in the community—including businesses, townspeople, schools, sawmills, the ice house, and the fish hatchery; his mother's operation of a maternity home and an emergency medical station in their residence; his work as a soda jerk in Sayling's Rexall Drugstore; his duties as a bull cook.
INTERVIEWED BY CATHRYN SCHROEDER, JANUARY 21, 1984, EUREKA.
SUMMARY: 4 PAGES
2 TAPES: 2 HOURS, 5 MINUTES

OH 777
WILLIAM CURTIS BALL INTERVIEW
William Ball (b. 1908) speaks of: the history and operation of the Valley Hotel in Sidney; business and industry in the community from about 1910 into the 1980s; his three terms as mayor of Sidney during the 1950s.
INTERVIEWED BY LAURIE MERCIER, MAY 26, 1984, SIDNEY.
SUMMARY: 3 PAGES
2 TAPES: 1 HOUR, 25 MINUTES

OH 778
HAROLD MERCER INTERVIEW
Harold Mercer (b. 1919) talks about: his work as mayor and as the director of public works in Sidney from the 1940s into the 1980s; the vagaries of community politics; the effects of post–World War II oil development on Sidney.
INTERVIEWED BY LAURIE MERCIER, MAY 28, 1984, SIDNEY.
SUMMARY: 3 PAGES
2 TAPES: 1 HOUR, 40 MINUTES

OH 779
JOHN A. KNOOP INTERVIEW
Sidney businessman John Knoop (b. 1924) surveys: his operation of the Sidney Drug Store from the 1930s

into the 1980s; the impact of the post–World War II oil boom on Sidney.
INTERVIEWED BY LAURIE MERCIER, MAY 26, 1984, SIDNEY.
SUMMARY: 3 PAGES
1 TAPE: 1 HOUR

OH 780
ANNA JENSEN GABRIELSON INTERVIEW
Anna Gabrielson (b. 1890) recalls: her experiences homesteading north of Sidney; her work as a nurse in the Sidney Community Memorial Hospital from 1939 to 1956.
INTERVIEWED BY LAURIE MERCIER, MAY 25, 1984, SIDNEY.
SUMMARY: 2 PAGES
1 TAPE: 55 MINUTES

OH 781
SANTOS CARRANZA INTERVIEW
Santos Carranza (b. 1912) tells of: his employment as a field hand and as a labor supervisor for the Holly Sugar Company in Sidney from 1943 to 1977; his experiences as a beet worker and as a beet farmer from 1925 into the 1940s; his time as a city councilman in Sidney during the 1980s.
INTERVIEWED BY LAURIE MERCIER, MAY 24, 1984, SIDNEY.
SUMMARY: 6 PAGES
3 TAPES: 2 HOURS, 55 MINUTES

OH 782
RUSSELL G. MERCER INTERVIEW
Sidney resident Russell Mercer (b. 1915) talks of: his work at the Holly Sugar Company plant in Sidney from 1935 to 1942; cattle ranching in Richland County; his role in organizing the area Montana Farm Bureau group; his participation on the local water, school, and library boards.
INTERVIEWED BY LAURIE MERCIER, MAY 28, 1984, SIDNEY.
SUMMARY: 5 PAGES
3 TAPES: 2 HOURS, 40 MINUTES

OH 783
GLADYS LINK ATKINSON INTERVIEW
Gladys Atkinson (b. 1909) recalls: the operation of the Lone Tree Inn in Sidney from 1929 to 1964; other local cafes and bars.
INTERVIEWED BY LAURIE MERCIER, MAY 29, 1984, SIDNEY.
SUMMARY: 3 PAGES
2 TAPES: 1 HOUR, 25 MINUTES

OH 784
ELDON F. KEMMIS INTERVIEW
Eldon Kemmis (b. 1934)—a Sidney businessman—discusses: his operation of The Toggery clothing business from 1974 to 1984; the impact of the 1970s oil boom on Sidney; his involvement with the Sidney Chamber of Commerce and with the local Kiwanis Club; his service on the city council.
INTERVIEWED BY LAURIE MERCIER, MAY 29, 1984, SIDNEY.
SUMMARY: 4 PAGES
2 TAPES: 2 HOURS, 10 MINUTES

OH 785
DONALD W. REES INTERVIEW
Donald Rees (b. 1925) discourses on: his work as manager of the Sidney airport from 1965 through 1984; his efforts to bring and to keep air transportation in Sidney; his involvement with the local Jaycees, with the city council, and with the Richland County Fair Board; the significance of the sugar beet and oil industries in the area's economy.
INTERVIEWED BY LAURIE MERCIER, MAY 29, 1984, SIDNEY.
SUMMARY: 3 PAGES
2 TAPES: 1 HOUR, 35 MINUTES

OH 786
GERALDINE ATWATER AND GEORGE J. ATWATER III, INTERVIEW
Geraldine Atwater and George Atwater detail: life in Sidney; the impact of the oil industry on the area; their participation in community activities from 1980 to 1984; Geraldine Atwater's high school teaching career.
INTERVIEWED BY LAURIE MERCIER, MAY 30, 1984, SIDNEY.
SUMMARY: 2 PAGES
1 TAPE: 45 MINUTES

OH 787
INGVARD SVARRE INTERVIEW
Ingvard Svarre (1902–1984) discusses: sugar beet farming in the Sidney area; his operation of the S & H Cattle Company, a livestock auction market in Sidney from 1929 to 1969.
INTERVIEWED BY LAURIE MERCIER, MAY 30, 1984, SIDNEY.
SUMMARY: 2 PAGES
1 TAPE: 50 MINUTES

OH 788
WALTER JENSEN AND MARY MICHELETTO JENSEN INTERVIEW
Walter Jensen (b. 1919) and Mary Jensen (b. 1918)

discuss: their operation of a dairy and a milk-route business in Sidney during the 1920s and 1930s; area agriculture; their participation in the Montana Farmers Union local; their involvement in the Sidney Catholic Church; the John Birch Society; various town controversies.
INTERVIEWED BY LAURIE MERCIER, MAY 31, 1984, SIDNEY.
SUMMARY: 8 PAGES
2 TAPES: 1 HOUR, 50 MINUTES

OH 789
MARY ALICE REHBEIN INTERVIEW
Mary Rehbein describes: her work as a Richland County public health nurse; health care and health programs in Sidney since 1950.
INTERVIEWED BY LAURIE MERCIER, MAY 31, 1984, SIDNEY.
SUMMARY: 3 PAGES
1 TAPE: 1 HOUR, 5 MINUTES

OH 790
MARGARET J. SEITZ INTERVIEW
Margaret Seitz (b. 1932) discusses: her work as a teacher in Sidney during the 1950s; her service on the Sidney school board from 1973 to 1983; local education issues.
INTERVIEWED BY LAURIE MERCIER, MAY 31, 1984, SIDNEY.
SUMMARY: 4 PAGES
2 TAPES: 2 HOURS, 10 MINUTES

OH 791
SYNOVE BRATBERG LALONDE INTERVIEW
Sidney resident Synove Lalonde speaks of: her work as a nurse for a local physician and in the Sidney hospital during the 1930s; the history of health care in the community; social life and entertainment; Lalonde family business enterprises; the effects of the sugar beet and the oil industries on the area's economy.
INTERVIEWED BY LAURIE MERCIER, MAY 25, 1984, SIDNEY.
SUMMARY: 3 PAGES
2 TAPES: 2 HOURS, 5 MINUTES

OH 792
BEN McKINNIE, LAURA McKINNIE PALM, AND PEARL RESER REEVES INTERVIEW
Ben McKinnie (b. 1911), Laura Palm (b. 1910), and Pearl Reeves—all three Chinook residents—consider: their individual family histories; community businesses, social life, customs, and physical changes from 1910 to 1980. [See also Montanans at Work OH 298.]
INTERVIEWED BY LAURIE MERCIER, JUNE 29, 1984, CHINOOK.

SUMMARY: 3 PAGES
2 TAPES: 2 HOURS, 10 MINUTES

OH 793
PAULINE BILGER DOUGHTEN INTERVIEW
Pauline Doughten (b. 1918) converses about: businesses, entertainment, civic organizations, and influential individuals in Chinook from the 1920s into the 1980s; O'Hanlon Company sugar beet farming in the Paradise Valley; the impacts of agriculture on Chinook businesses.
INTERVIEWED BY LAURIE MERCIER, JUNE 28, 1984, CHINOOK.
SUMMARY: 4 PAGES
2 TAPES: 1 HOUR, 50 MINUTES

OH 794
GEORGE C. MUNDT INTERVIEW
George Mundt (b. 1894) describes: Chinook businesses that catered to area ranchers, sheepherders, and cowboys; community festivities on the Fourth of July; ranching in Blaine County, south of Chinook, from 1900 into the 1960s; his German-American heritage.
INTERVIEWED BY LAURIE MERCIER, JUNE 28, 1984, CHINOOK.
SUMMARY: 3 PAGES
1 TAPE: 1 HOUR, 5 MINUTES

OH 795
ROBERT J. DOLAN INTERVIEW
Chinook resident Robert Dolan (b. 1919) comments on: his 33-year employment with the Chinook Production Credit Association; the role of agriculture in the community; working for the local Utah-Idaho Sugar Company factory in the 1930s; his participation in various civic activities.
INTERVIEWED BY LAURIE MERCIER, JUNE 27, 1984, CHINOOK.
SUMMARY: 3 PAGES
1 TAPE: 1 HOUR, 5 MINUTES

OH 796
GEORGE VANDE VEN INTERVIEW
George Vande Ven (b. 1913) addresses: the community of Hollandville, from 1913 to 1952; his work in the Hollandville coal mine; his saloon business in Chinook from 1947 to 1967; the impact of area agriculture on Chinook.
INTERVIEWED BY LAURIE MERCIER, JULY 23, 1984, CHINOOK.

SUMMARY: 4 PAGES
2 TAPES: 2 HOURS, 5 MINUTES

OH 797
ISABEL GRIFFIN BONIFAS INTERVIEW

Isabel Bonifas (b. 1913) discusses: her operation of several movie theaters in Chinook from the 1920s to 1970; other Bonifas family business enterprises; neighborhoods and community activities in Chinook, including the Blaine County Museum.
INTERVIEWED BY LAURIE MERCIER, JULY 11, 1984, CHINOOK.
SUMMARY: 5 PAGES
3 TAPES: 2 HOURS, 20 MINUTES

OH 798
DR. ROBERT H. LEEDS AND LUCIA TIMMONS LEEDS INTERVIEW

Robert Leeds (b. 1915) discusses: his work as a physician in Chinook from 1941 to 1978; his duties as Blaine County Health Officer; the nature of health care and specific health problems in Chinook; health care debates in the community. Lucia Leeds treats: her work teaching piano and vocal music in Chinook from the 1940s into the 1980s; musical opportunities in the area.
INTERVIEWED BY LAURIE MERCIER, JULY 11, 1984, CHINOOK.
SUMMARY: 3 PAGES
2 TAPES: 1 HOUR, 35 MINUTES

OH 799
THELMA ABEL JOHNSON INTERVIEW

Chinook resident Thelma Johnson (b. 1904) talks about: the operation of the weekly *Chinook Opinion* from 1936 to 1984; her specific duties with the newspaper.
INTERVIEWED BY LAURIE MERCIER, JULY 12, 1984, CHINOOK.
SUMMARY: 2 PAGES
1 TAPE: 1 HOUR, 5 MINUTES

OH 800
MADELINE MacARTHUR MARSONETTE INTERVIEW

Madeline Marsonette (b. 1924) tells of: the neighborhoods, churches, and businesses of Chinook; the Blaine County Museum; the local Hispanic-American community; her work for the Utah-Idaho Sugar Company's sugar beet plant during the 1940s.
INTERVIEWED BY LAURIE MERCIER, JULY 10, 1994, CHINOOK.

SUMMARY: 4 PAGES
2 TAPES: 1 HOUR, 50 MINUTES

OH 801
KATHRYN VARKO SMITH INTERVIEW

Kathryn Smith (b. 1909) recalls: her father, Charles Earl Varko; the family's operation of the Yellowstone Mercantile Company in Sidney from 1906 into the 1970s; the development of the Sidney community from 1910 to 1930.
INTERVIEWED BY LAURIE MERCIER, JUNE 25, 1985, MISSOULA.
SUMMARY: 3 PAGES
2 TAPES: 1 HOUR, 15 MINUTES

OH 802
BEULAH G. HAMES INTERVIEW

Beulah Hames talks of: life in Philipsburg from 1917 to 1922; Carmichael's Livery Stable.
INTERVIEWED BY LAURIE MERCIER, JULY 27, 1984, MISSOULA.
SUMMARY: 1 PAGE
1 TAPE: 45 MINUTES

OH 803
BOYNTON G. PAIGE INTERVIEW

B. G. Paige (b. 1905) reviews: his management of the Flint Creek Valley Bank in Philipsburg from 1940 to 1983; the role of the bank in town affairs and in Granite County matters.
INTERVIEWED BY LAURIE MERCIER, JULY 26, 1984, PHILIPSBURG.
SUMMARY: 3 PAGES
1 TAPE: 1 HOUR

OH 804
WALTER N. "PETE" SCOTT INTERVIEW

Walter Scott (b. 1938) speaks of: his work as superintendent of schools in Chinook from 1976 to 1984; the operation of specific District 1 school programs; relations among the local schools, the community, and the school board; his involvement in the Chinook Lions Club and in particular club activities.
INTERVIEWED BY LAURIE MERCIER, AUGUST 28, 1984, CHINOOK.
SUMMARY: 3 PAGES
1 TAPE: 55 MINUTES

OH 805
KAREN CHAPMAN INTERVIEW

Karen Chapman (b. 1966) reports: her experiences as a teenager in Chinook from 1979 to 1984; the high school curriculum; community activities, entertainment, and work opportunities for young people.
INTERVIEWED BY LAURIE MERCIER, AUGUST 29, 1984, CHINOOK.
SUMMARY: 3 PAGES
1 TAPE: 1 HOUR, 5 MINUTES

OH 806
MARGARET CAMPFIELD PERRY INTERVIEW

Margaret Perry (b. 1916) recalls: Campfield's Cash and Carry, the grocery store her father, William Campfield, operated in Chinook from 1919 to 1943; her childhood; her teaching experiences in Blaine County; community activities in Chinook.
INTERVIEWED BY LAURIE MERCIER, AUGUST 29, 1984, CHINOOK.
SUMMARY: 4 PAGES
2 TAPES: 1 HOUR, 25 MINUTES

OH 807
BERNARD THOMAS AND ELISE WIPF THOMAS INTERVIEW

Bernard Thomas recalls: his career as an attorney in Chinook; his service as city attorney and as district judge. Elise Thomas (b. 1917) discusses her work as the Blaine County home demonstration agent during the 1940s.
INTERVIEWED BY LAURIE MERCIER, AUGUST 29, 1984, CHINOOK.
SUMMARY: 5 PAGES
2 TAPES: 2 HOURS

OH 808
DORIS MARTIN FIEVET INTERVIEW

Doris Fievet (b. 1907) discusses: her work for the local telephone company in Roundup from the 1920s into the 1950s; Roundup businesses, neighborhoods, and entertainment; her French-American heritage.
INTERVIEWED BY LAURIE MERCIER, OCTOBER 10, 1984, ROUNDUP.
SUMMARY: 5 PAGES
2 TAPES: 2 HOURS, 10 MINUTES

OH 809
HAZEL BIRTHWRAITE WILSON INTERVIEW

Hazel Wilson (b. 1899) recounts: teaching in Roundup and in Musselshell County from the 1920s through the 1960s; Roundup lodges, clubs, and entertainment; Japanese laborers; area coal mines.
INTERVIEWED BY LAURIE MERCIER, OCTOBER 10, 1984, ROUNDUP.
SUMMARY: 4 PAGES
2 TAPES: 2 HOURS, 10 MINUTES

OH 810
TONY PRESHERN INTERVIEW

Tony Preshern (b. 1906) reflects on: his operation of Preshern's Bar, west of Roundup, from the 1920s into the 1980s; the Roundup Coal Company's Number Three Mine camp; the local Slovenian community; Prohibition.
INTERVIEWED BY LAURIE MERCIER, OCTOBER 11, 1984, ROUNDUP.
SUMMARY: 4 PAGES
2 TAPES: 1 HOUR, 35 MINUTES

OH 811
AGNES KUBE SIMKINS INTERVIEW

Agnes Simkins (b. 1904) portrays: her operation of the Maverick Bar in Roundup from 1939 to 1984; the 1930s Depression; local entertainment; other Roundup businesses.
INTERVIEWED BY LAURIE MERCIER, OCTOBER 12, 1984, ROUNDUP.
SUMMARY: 2 PAGES
1 TAPE: 1 HOUR

OH 812
LOUISE G. EISELEIN RASMUSSEN INTERVIEW

Louise Rasmussen (b. 1914) recalls: the operation of the Roundup weekly *Record-Tribune* from the 1940s to the 1980s; community life in Roundup during the 1920s and 1930s; the Ku Klux Klan; local coal mining.
INTERVIEWED BY LAURIE MERCIER, OCTOBER 11, 1984, ROUNDUP.
SUMMARY: 4 PAGES
2 TAPES: 1 HOUR, 50 MINUTES

OH 813
JOE VICARS INTERVIEW

Joe Vicars (b. 1912) discusses: Ku Klux Klan activities in Roundup during the 1920s; his operation of Vicars' Drug Store in Roundup from the 1940s into the 1980s; the administration of the local hospital by his mother, Frances Barnard Vicars; the Roundup Coal Company Number Three Mine camp; the impacts of coal mining on the community; his participation in local government.

INTERVIEWED BY LAURIE MERCIER, NOVEMBER 2, 1984, ROUNDUP.
SUMMARY: 4 PAGES
2 TAPES: 1 HOUR, 35 MINUTES

OH 814
JENNY RACKI LIND INTERVIEW

Jenny Lind (b. 1912) discusses: operating a dairy and a milk-route business in Roundup from the 1930s into the 1950s; the Roundup Coal Company's Number Three Mine camp; local entertainment; her Yugoslav-American heritage.
INTERVIEWED BY LAURIE MERCIER, OCTOBER 24, 1984, ROUNDUP.
SUMMARY: 3 PAGES
1 TAPE: 1 HOUR, 5 MINUTES

OH 815
ANNIE EVANS LARSEN INTERVIEW

Annie Larsen (b. 1913) describes: businesses, community activities, churches, schools, hospitals, and clubs in Roundup from the 1920s into the 1980s; teaching journalism at Roundup High School in the 1940s.
INTERVIEWED BY LAURIE MERCIER, OCTOBER 24, 1984, ROUNDUP.
SUMMARY: 4 PAGES
2 TAPES: 1 HOUR, 35 MINUTES

OH 816
BETTY SMITH TUCKER INTERVIEW

Betty Tucker (b. 1908) reviews: living near the Roundup Coal Company's Number Three Mine near Roundup from the 1920s into the 1950s; coal-mining operations; housing, entertainment, and ethnic groups in the area; the impact of coal mining on the community; local businesses, doctors, and churches.
INTERVIEWED BY LAURIE MERCIER, OCTOBER 24, 1984, ROUNDUP.
SUMMARY: 4 PAGES
2 TAPES: 1 HOUR, 45 MINUTES

OH 817
CHARLES CAIN INTERVIEW

Charles Cain (b. 1903) considers: his work in various coal mines near Roundup from 1925 to 1971; Roundup's businesses and its ethnic population; the leisure activities of miners.
INTERVIEWED BY LAURIE MERCIER, OCTOBER 24, 1984, ROUNDUP.

SUMMARY: 5 PAGES
2 TAPES: 2 HOURS, 5 MINUTES

OH 818
NINA CROUSE ROGERSON INTERVIEW

Nina Rogerson (b. 1918) reports on: community life in Roundup from 1918 into the 1980s; the town's neighborhoods, businesses, schools, hospital, entertainment, and lodges; her involvement with the Roundup Women's Club.
INTERVIEWED BY LAURIE MERCIER, OCTOBER 24, 1984, ROUNDUP.
SUMMARY: 4 PAGES
2 TAPES: 1 HOUR, 35 MINUTES

OH 819
LILLIAN ROGERS KIRKPATRICK INTERVIEW

Lillian Kirkpatrick (b. 1903) examines: her work for and her management of the Bair-Collins Coal Company of Roundup during the 1950s; the impact of coal mining on the town; her work as mayor of Roundup in the 1950s; the establishment of the local hospital; the UMW president W. A. "Tony" Boyle's association with the Roundup mines.
INTERVIEWED BY LAURIE MERCIER, OCTOBER 31, 1984, HELENA.
SUMMARY: 3 PAGES
2 TAPES: 1 HOUR, 35 MINUTES

OH 820
JOE MEAGHER INTERVIEW

Joe Meagher (b. 1914) talks about: his work as mayor of Cut Bank from 1971 to 1984; town controversies; the local economy; relations between the white community and the Blackfeet Indian Reservation.
INTERVIEWED BY JACKIE DAY, OCTOBER 30, 1984, CUT BANK.
SUMMARY: 2 PAGES
1 TAPE: 40 MINUTES

OH 821
JAMES R. BROWN INTERVIEW

James Brown (b. 1913)—a Cut Bank resident—details: his work for the Great Northern Railway Company; his involvement with the Freemasons.
INTERVIEWED BY JACKIE DAY, OCTOBER 31, 1984, CUT BANK.
SUMMARY: 4 PAGES
2 TAPES: 1 HOUR, 35 MINUTES

OH 822
CATHERINE M. BROWN INTERVIEW
Catherine Brown surveys: health care in Cut Bank from 1945 to 1984; public nursing; local physicians; the community hospital; the Hutterite community.
INTERVIEWED BY LAURIE MERCIER, OCTOBER 21, 1984, CUT BANK.
SUMMARY: 4 PAGES
1 TAPE: 1 HOUR

OH 823
MARJORIE HARTMANN INTERVIEW
Marjorie Hartmann (b. 1918)—a teacher and principal in the Cut Bank schools from the 1940s into the 1960s—discusses: her work in the school system; her experiences teaching in rural schools.
INTERVIEWED BY JACKIE DAY, NOVEMBER 1, 1984, CUT BANK.
SUMMARY: 3 PAGES
1 TAPE: 55 MINUTES

OH 824
SELDON FRISBEE INTERVIEW
Cut Bank resident Seldon Frisbee (b. 1915) chronicles: Cut Bank businesses, particularly banking; the area oil industry; health care; labor unions; Glacier County politics; social life and entertainment in Cut Bank; local clubs and organizations; the role of the Great Northern Railway Company in the town's social and economic fabric; Prohibition; post–World War II changes in the community; Blackfeet tribal land litigations; Indian-white relations; the restaurant workers strike during the 1950s; physical improvements in Cut Bank.
INTERVIEWED BY JACKIE DAY, NOVEMBER 1 AND 27, 1984, CUT BANK.
SUMMARY: 13 PAGES
4 TAPES: 3 HOURS, 35 MINUTES

OH 825
FRED H. INGRAM INTERVIEW
Fred Ingram (b. 1902) recalls: his work for the Great Northern Railway Company in Cut Bank during the 1920s and 1930s; his experiences as deputy sheriff and as police judge in Cut Bank during the 1960s; labor, law enforcement and the economy in Glacier County.
INTERVIEWED BY JACKIE DAY, NOVEMBER 1, 1984, CUT BANK.
SUMMARY: 3 PAGES
1 TAPE: 1 HOUR, 5 MINUTES

OH 826
RAY MAIER INTERVIEW
Cut Bank resident Ray Maier (b. 1939) describes: the role of the school system in the community; local employment opportunities for young people; public support for education; his philosophy regarding teaching and the humanities.
INTERVIEWED BY JACKIE DAY, NOVEMBER 1, 1984, CUT BANK.
SUMMARY: 3 PAGES
1 TAPE: 50 MINUTES

OH 827
JEWELL PETERSON WOLK INTERVIEW
Jewell Wolk (b. 1924) remembers: growing up on the family homestead near Cut Bank; her social activities; community development during the 1930s and 1940s; the effects of oil-and-gas development on the area; the contributions of community women; contraception, unwanted pregnancy, and abortion.
INTERVIEWED BY JACKIE DAY, NOVEMBER 29, 1984, CUT BANK.
TRANSCRIPT: 63 PAGES
2 TAPES: 2 HOURS

OH 828
LOIS W. NELSON INTERVIEW
Lois Nelson (b. 1919) comments on her participation in various women's organizations in Cut Bank from the 1950s into the 1980s, including Women's Homemakers, Soroptimists, Toastmistresses, and the Cut Bank Women's Club.
INTERVIEWED BY JACKIE DAY, NOVEMBER 29, 1984, CUT BANK.
SUMMARY: 3 PAGES
1 TAPE: 50 MINUTES

OH 829
LUCILLE L. DUROCHER INTERVIEW
Cut Bank resident Lucille Durocher describes: her involvement in the local Catholic church from 1947 into the 1980s; changes in Catholic religious practices since the 1960s; the relationships among the various churches in Cut Bank.
INTERVIEWED BY JACKIE DAY, NOVEMBER 27, 1984, CUT BANK.
SUMMARY: 2 PAGES
1 TAPE: 50 MINUTES

OH 830
WILLIAM S. CROFT INTERVIEW

William Croft speaks of: the oil-and-gas industry in the Cut Bank area from 1946 to 1984; the Croft Petroleum operations; the impact of the petroleum industry on the area's economy; specific individuals associated with the oil-and-gas industry.

INTERVIEWED BY JACKIE DAY, NOVEMBER 27, 1984, CUT BANK.

SUMMARY: 3 PAGES

1 TAPE: 1 HOUR

OH 831
MARJORY O'DAY INTERVIEW

Marjory O'Day details: her management of the Cut Bank weekly *Western Breeze* from 1955 to 1984; the participation of women in local businesses.

INTERVIEWED BY JACKIE DAY, NOVEMBER 28, 1984, CUT BANK.

SUMMARY: 2 PAGES

1 TAPE: 35 MINUTES

OH 832
WILLIAM NANINI INTERVIEW

William Nanini (b. 1927) addresses: community life in Cut Bank from the 1930s into the 1950s; the local Italian community; employment opportunities and entertainment in Cut Bank.

INTERVIEWED BY JACKIE DAY, NOVEMBER 29, 1984, CUT BANK.

SUMMARY: 3 PAGES

1 TAPE: 1 HOUR, 5 MINUTES

OH 833
ROBERT "BOB" DAVENPORT INTERVIEW

Bob Davenport comments on: his operation of the Davenport and McAlpine Hardware Hank Store in Cut Bank from 1954 to 1984; his "Hardware Hank" franchise beginning in 1980; general commercial activity in the area.

INTERVIEWED BY JACKIE DAY, NOVEMBER 29, 1984, CUT BANK.

SUMMARY: 2 PAGES

1 TAPE: 30 MINUTES

OH 834
WILBUR WERNER INTERVIEW

Attorney Wilbur Werner (b. 1913) describes: relations between the white community in Cut Bank and the Blackfeet Indian Reservation from the 1930s into the 1980s; local entertainment; town controversies and politics; the Catholic Church; the local Elks Lodge. *[See also General Montana OH 91.]*

INTERVIEWED BY JACKIE DAY, NOVEMBER 29, 1984, CUT BANK.

SUMMARY: 4 PAGES

2 TAPES: 1 HOUR, 25 MINUTES

OH 835
PRUDENCE HOLLENBECK GARLAND INTERVIEW

Prudence Garland (b. 1917) describes: her life in Forsyth during the 1930s; her grandfather, Thomas Alexander, one of the town's founding fathers.

INTERVIEWED BY JACKIE DAY, JANUARY 15, 1985, FORSYTH.

SUMMARY: 2 PAGES

1 TAPE: 1 HOUR, 15 MINUTES

OH 836
ROBERT "SHORTY" MEREDITH INTERVIEW

Shorty Meredith (b. 1892) discourses on the Northern Pacific Railroad Company's influence on the character and the local businesses of Forsyth from 1915 into the 1930s.

INTERVIEWED BY JACKIE DAY, JANUARY 16, 1985, FORSYTH.

SUMMARY: 2 PAGES

1 TAPE: 1 HOUR

OH 837
ART W. KAMHOOT INTERVIEW

Forsyth resident Art Kamhoot discusses: the issues and controversies he faced as a Rosebud County commissioner from 1975 to 1981; Forsyth businesses; the local Lions Club; the county's tax structure; commerce and industry in Forsyth.

INTERVIEWED BY JACKIE DAY, JANUARY 16, 1985, FORSYTH.

SUMMARY: 4 PAGES

2 TAPES: 1 HOUR, 35 MINUTES

OH 838
KATHERINE ERPELDING INTERVIEW

Katherine Erpelding (b. 1899) recalls: her life on a dryland farm near Forsyth from 1915 to 1935; the relationship between local ranchers and farmers; the role played by the homestead movement in area development.

INTERVIEWED BY JACKIE DAY, JANUARY 16, 1985, FORSYTH.

SUMMARY: 2 PAGES
1 TAPE: 50 MINUTES

OH 839
ROBERT P. THIESEN INTERVIEW
Forsyth resident Robert Thiesen (b. circa 1920) discusses: the operation of the First Bank of Forsyth, formerly called the Forsyth State Bank; changes in banking practices since 1957; the impact of the Colstrip coal development on Forsyth; local businesses and issues; his participation in community activities.
INTERVIEWED BY JACKIE DAY, JANUARY 17, 1985, FORSYTH.
SUMMARY: 3 PAGES
1 TAPE: 1 HOUR, 5 MINUTES

OH 840
J. R. "TOPPY" LEE INTERVIEW
Toppy Lee remembers: ranching near Forsyth; agricultural developments in Rosebud County from 1950 to 1985; relations between local ranchers and the Forsyth community.
INTERVIEWED BY JACKIE DAY, JANUARY 17, 1985, FORSYTH.
SUMMARY: 2 PAGES
1 TAPE: 1 HOUR, 5 MINUTES

OH 841
MORRIS COLE AND LAURAINE CRANDELL COLE INTERVIEW
Morris Cole (b. 1907) and Lauraine Cole—Forsyth residents—review: the impacts of Colstrip coal development on the town of Forsyth; population changes in the area; the growth of Forsyth businesses and employment; community groups; local agriculture.
INTERVIEWED BY JACKIE DAY, JANUARY 17, 1985, FORSYTH.
SUMMARY: 2 PAGES
1 TAPE: 1 HOUR, 5 MINUTES

OH 842
JOHN HENRY SMITH INTERVIEW
John Smith surveys his operation of the Joseph Cafe in Forsyth from 1948 to 1975.
INTERVIEWED BY JACKIE DAY, FEBRUARY 12, 1985, FORSYTH.
SUMMARY: 2 PAGES
1 TAPE: 45 MINUTES

OH 843
ESTHER NELSTEAD DEAN INTERVIEW
Esther Dean (b. 1918) treats: the impact of the Northern Pacific Railroad Company on the overall character of Forsyth; her experiences in the Forsyth Women's Club; her husband, Walter Dean; their operation of the Howdy Hotel, formerly called the Hotel Commercial.
INTERVIEWED BY JACKIE DAY, FEBRUARY 12, 1985, FORSYTH.
SUMMARY: 2 PAGES
1 TAPE: 1 HOUR, 5 MINUTES

OH 844
MAX BLAKESLEY INTERVIEW
Max Blakesley (b. 1909) tells about: his family's longtime operation of Blakesley's Cigar Store in Forsyth; community life in Forsyth during the 1920s and the 1930s; the Depression.
INTERVIEWED BY JACKIE DAY, FEBRUARY 12, 1985, FORSYTH.
SUMMARY: 1 PAGE
2 TAPES: 1 HOUR, 10 MINUTES

OH 845
DOROTHY R. GREGORY INTERVIEW
Dorothy Gregory describes: her work as a registered nurse at the Rosebud County Community Hospital in Forsyth from 1949 to 1985; health care in the community.
INTERVIEWED BY JACKIE DAY, FEBRUARY 13, 1985, FORSYTH.
SUMMARY: 2 PAGES
1 TAPE: 45 MINUTES

OH 846
EDITH JACKSON FINCH INTERVIEW
Forsyth resident Edith Finch (b. 1890) discusses: the hardships of the ranching profession; the various jobs she held during the 1930s Depression.
INTERVIEWED BY JACKIE DAY, FEBRUARY 13, 1985, FORSYTH.
SUMMARY: 2 PAGES
1 TAPE: 30 MINUTES

OH 847
WILLIAM F. SCHWARZKOPH INTERVIEW
Forsyth resident William Schwarzkoph discusses: his work for the Western Energy Company from 1980 to 1985; the impact of coal development on Forsyth, Colstrip, and other communities in southeastern Mon-

tana; his participation on the Rosebud County Planning Board; attitudes among area residents regarding community development.

INTERVIEWED BY JACKIE DAY, FEBRUARY 13, 1985, FORSYTH.

TRANSCRIPT: 50 PAGES

2 TAPES: 1 HOUR, 25 MINUTES

OH 848
NELLIE SCHMIDT WEIPERT INTERVIEW

Nellie Weipert (b. 1903)—a Forsyth resident—recalls: her work for the Rosebud County welfare department, primarily on the Northern Cheyenne Indian Reservation, during the 1950s and 1960s; social life in Forsyth; her career teaching in rural schools.

INTERVIEWED BY JACKIE DAY, FEBRUARY 14, 1985, FORSYTH.

SUMMARY: 3 PAGES

1 TAPE: 1 HOUR, 5 MINUTES

OH 849
FAYE BURRINGTON BERES INTERVIEW

Faye Beres (b. 1904) discusses: social life and entertainment in Forsyth from 1914 into the 1960s; her husband, Max Beres; her husband's work as a mayor of Forsyth and as a Northern Pacific Railroad Company employee.

INTERVIEWED BY JACKIE DAY, FEBRUARY 14, 1985, FORSYTH.

SUMMARY: 2 PAGES

1 TAPE: 1 HOUR, 5 MINUTES

OH 850
JACK CREECY INTERVIEW

Jack Creecy (b. 1901) examines: his work for the Northern Pacific Railroad Company based in Forsyth from 1923 to 1955; the railroad's influence on the character of the town; McGowan's Commercial Company.

INTERVIEWED BY JACKIE DAY, FEBRUARY 15, 1985, LAUREL.

SUMMARY: 2 PAGES

1 TAPE: 1 HOUR, 5 MINUTES

OH 851
WENDELL STEPHENS INTERVIEW

Wendell Stephens (b. 1912) discusses: community life in Plains from the 1920s into the 1970s; changes in the town's business enterprises, social life, and character; logging and agriculture in the area.

INTERVIEWED BY JACKIE DAY, MARCH 20, 1985, PARADISE.

SUMMARY: 4 PAGES

2 TAPES: 1 HOUR, 20 MINUTES

OH 852
CARL RICHARDSON INTERVIEW

Carl Richardson (b. 1918) depicts: logging in the Plains area from 1910 to 1985; operation of the Flodine Lumber Mill; the Anaconda Copper Mining Company; small logging operators in the area; the town of Plains; early logging celebrations; the Plains Land Development Project; the importance of Native American trade to the town.

INTERVIEWED BY JACKIE DAY, MARCH 19, 1985, PLAINS.

SUMMARY: 4 PAGES

2 TAPES: 1 HOUR, 45 MINUTES

OH 853
MILFORD MYERS INTERVIEW

Plains resident Milford Myers (b. 1911) converses about: the lumber industry in the area from the 1930s into the 1980s; local natural disasters; the Flodine Lumber Mill; religious life in the community.

INTERVIEWED BY JACKIE DAY, MARCH 20, 1985, PLAINS.

SUMMARY: 2 PAGES

1 TAPE: 1 HOUR, 5 MINUTES

OH 854
LAVENIA GAGNON CLARK INTERVIEW

Lavenia Clark (b. 1910) chronicles: life in Plains from the 1920s into the 1940s; her operation of a service station in town; McGowan's Commercial Company.

INTERVIEWED BY JACKIE DAY, MARCH 21, 1985, PLAINS.

SUMMARY: 2 PAGES

1 TAPE: 1 HOUR

OH 855
FLORENCE HOWES SMITH INTERVIEW

Florence Smith (b. 1908) talks about: teaching school in Plains during the 1950s; local education, sports, and entertainment; women's clubs; businesses in Plains; population changes in the area.

INTERVIEWED BY JACKIE DAY, MARCH 21, 1985, PLAINS.

SUMMARY: 2 PAGES

1 TAPE: 1 HOUR

OH 856
MAUDE WEBBER JOHNSON INTERVIEW

Maude Johnson (b. 1903) considers: her work teaching in Plains schools from the 1920s into the mid-1980s; the changing relationships between teachers and the com-

munity; management of the Plains bank; the history of the local women's club.
INTERVIEWED BY JACKIE DAY, MARCH 21, 1985, PLAINS.
SUMMARY: 3 PAGES
1 TAPE: 1 HOUR, 5 MINUTES

OH 857
WESLEY W. STEARNS INTERVIEW

Wesley Stearns delineates: local government in Plains and Sanders County from the 1960s into the 1980s; the timber industry in the area since the 1940s; the Diehl Lumber Company; Champion International; prominent figures in Plains history; local hospital and school issues.
INTERVIEWED BY JACKIE DAY, MARCH 21, 1985, PLAINS.
SUMMARY: 4 PAGES
2 TAPES: 1 HOUR, 40 MINUTES

OH 858
WESLEY W. "MIKE" SCOTT INTERVIEW

Mike Scott (b. 1907) details: community life in Plains during the 1930s and 1940s; his operation of the *Plainsman* weekly newspaper from 1938 to 1942; his participation in the town's volunteer fire department.
INTERVIEWED BY JACKIE DAY, MAY 16, 1985, PLAINS.
SUMMARY: 2 PAGES
1 TAPE: 45 MINUTES

OH 859
C. G. "BILL" JOHNSON INTERVIEW

Plains resident Bill Johnson (b. 1911) describes: the history and operation of the First National Bank of Plains; the banking business in Plains from about 1910 into the 1980s; the area's economy; the impact of the 1930s Depression on the community; local issues.
INTERVIEWED BY JACKIE DAY, APRIL 16, 1985, PLAINS.
SUMMARY: 3 PAGES
1 TAPE: 1 HOUR

OH 860
JACOB "JACK" LULACK INTERVIEW

Jack Lulack discusses: controversies surrounding the establishment of the Clark Fork Valley Hospital in Plains during the early 1970s; the problems inherent in practicing rural medicine; the demands placed on rural physicians.
INTERVIEWED BY JACKIE DAY, APRIL 17, 1985, PLAINS.
SUMMARY: 3 PAGES
1 TAPE: 1 HOUR, 5 MINUTES

OH 861
BRUCE SWANSON INTERVIEW

Bruce Swanson discusses: the operation of the First National Bank of Plains; the role of the bank in the community; the history of McGowan's Commercial Company; the population of Plains; the future of the community.
INTERVIEWED BY JACKIE DAY, APRIL 17, 1985, PLAINS.
SUMMARY: 2 PAGES
1 TAPE: 55 MINUTES

OH 862
MILLAR T. BRYCE INTERVIEW

Millar Bryce (1920)—a Plains resident—discusses: the operation of the Flodine Lumber Mill in Plains from the 1940s into the 1980s; her participation on the local school board during the 1960s; the role of schools in rural life; her involvement in locating a new local hospital.
INTERVIEWED BY JACKIE DAY, APRIL 17, 1985, PLAINS.
SUMMARY: 3 PAGES
2 TAPES: 1 HOUR, 15 MINUTES

OH 863
BLANCHE BRACKETT RICHARDSON INTERVIEW

Blanche Richardson (b. 1920) recounts: teaching home economics in the Plains school system from 1942 until 1979; the relationship of the U.S. Forest Service to the community; how some local families coped with poverty.
INTERVIEWED BY JACKIE DAY, APRIL 17, 1985, PLAINS.
SUMMARY: 2 PAGES
1 TAPE: 1 HOUR

OH 864
DONALD R. COE INTERVIEW

Plains resident Donald Coe remembers: his work as the editor of the weekly *Plainsman* newspaper from 1948 to 1985; the role of the community newspaper in a small town; local businesses; town controversies; rivalries among towns in Sanders County.
INTERVIEWED BY JACKIE DAY, APRIL 18, 1985, PLAINS.
SUMMARY: 3 PAGES
1 TAPE: 1 HOUR, 5 MINUTES

OH 865
DORREEN HAMPTON WOLFE INTERVIEW

Dorreen Wolfe (b. 1916) reviews: her work for the McGowan's Commercial Company store in Plains during the 1950s and 1960s; the store's relationship to the

community; U.S. Forest Service operations in the area.
INTERVIEWED BY JACKIE DAY, APRIL 18, 1985, PLAINS.
SUMMARY: 2 PAGES
1 TAPE: 55 MINUTES

OH 866
DOUGLAS SHANER INTERVIEW

Douglas Shaner surveys: his career as a forester in the Plains area from the 1960s into the 1980s; forest-management practices; data collection in the timber industry; firewood; hunting; roads; timber harvesting; outfitters; the U.S. Forest Service.
INTERVIEWED BY JACKIE DAY, APRIL 1985, PLAINS.
SUMMARY: 7 PAGES
1 TAPE: 1 HOUR

OH 867
EINAR KLOFSTAD INTERVIEW

Einar Klofstad (b. 1911) treats: his work at Woodward's general store in Plentywood from 1944 into the 1960s; his service on the local school board; the local economy; the Socialist Party.
INTERVIEWED BY JACKIE DAY, MAY 13, 1985, PLENTYWOOD.
SUMMARY: 2 PAGES
1 TAPE: 55 MINUTES

OH 868
PAULINE BLUE DEEM INTERVIEW

Pauline Deem (b. 1916)—a Plentywood resident—discusses: her work with various homemaker clubs for the Sheridan County Agricultural Extension Service in Plentywood during the 1950s; the life of rural women; Scandinavian traditions in the area; changes in the Plentywood community since the 1950s; her Norwegian-American ancestry.
INTERVIEWED BY JACKIE DAY, MAY 14, 1985, PLENTYWOOD.
SUMMARY: 2 PAGES
2 TAPES: 1 HOUR, 15 MINUTES

OH 869
ARTHUR GABRIELSON INTERVIEW

Arthur Gabrielson (b. 1907) describes his struggles as a farmer near Plentywood during the 1930s Depression.
INTERVIEWED BY JACKIE DAY, MAY 17, 1985, PLENTYWOOD.
SUMMARY: 2 PAGES
1 TAPE: 1 HOUR

OH 870
FAY CHANDLER AND VIOLET CYBULSKI CHANDLER INTERVIEW

Fay Chandler (b. 1918) depicts: his father's operation of poolhalls and bootleg parlors in Sheridan County during Prohibition; hardships encountered during the 1930s Depression; leftist groups in Plentywood during the 1920s and 1930s, including Socialists and Communists. Violet Chandler discusses her childhood on a farm near Plentywood.
INTERVIEWED BY JACKIE DAY, MAY 15, 1985, PLENTYWOOD.
SUMMARY: 3 PAGES
1 TAPE: 1 HOUR, 5 MINUTES

OH 871
BERNADINE PRADER LOGAN INTERVIEW

Bernadine Logan (b. 1906) details: her work teaching in Plentywood during the 1930s; the local leftist political groups of the time, including Socialists and Communists.
INTERVIEWED BY JACKIE DAY, MAY 14, 1985, PLENTYWOOD.
SUMMARY: 2 PAGES
1 TAPE: 45 MINUTES

OH 872
MAE MARSH HARK INTERVIEW

Mae Hark (b. 1924) delineates: her work for the telephone company in Plentywood from 1948 to 1964; her employment at the local J.C. Penney's store from the 1960s to 1985; the impact of World War II on the community; local employment opportunities for women; entertainment patterns in Plentywood; rural-town differences.
INTERVIEWED BY JACKIE DAY, MAY 16, 1985, PLENTYWOOD.
SUMMARY: 2 PAGES
1 TAPE: 1 HOUR

OH 873
LOUISE KAVON INTERVIEW

Plentywood resident Louise Kavon (b. 1893) describes: the operation of Plentywood Motor Sales, a Ford automobile dealership, circa 1910 through the 1920s; area farm problems—including drought and depression—from 1915 into the 1930s; the establishment of the first hospital in Plentywood; the local bootlegging business during Prohibition.

INTERVIEWED BY JACKIE DAY, MAY 16, 1985,
PLENTYWOOD.
SUMMARY: 2 PAGES
1 TAPE: 1 HOUR, 5 MINUTES

OH 874
NANCY MARRON INTERVIEW

Nancy Marron (b. 1905) recalls: operating a ranch near Plentywood from 1933 to 1976; her successful efforts to save the ranch during the 1930s Depression.
INTERVIEWED BY JACKIE DAY, MAY 16, 1985,
PLENTYWOOD.
SUMMARY: 2 PAGES
1 TAPE: 55 MINUTES

OH 875
CHESTER "CHET" HOLJE INTERVIEW

Chet Holje discourses on: changes in the community of Plentywood from the 1930s to the 1980s; the 1930s Depression; the local effects of World War II; the area oil booms during the 1950s and the 1970s; agricultural practices; transportation patterns; government programs.
INTERVIEWED BY JACKIE DAY, MAY 16, 1985,
PLENTYWOOD.
SUMMARY: 3 PAGES
1 TAPE: 1 HOUR

OH 876
CLIFFORD PETERSON INTERVIEW

Clifford Peterson (b. 1910) converses on: his operation of Peterson's Ready-to-Wear clothing store in Plentywood from the 1930s into the 1980s; his work as city mayor and city councilman during the 1950s; local businesses and politics; the Lions Club; the 1930s Depression; the Socialist Party; the oil industry's impact on the area's economy.
INTERVIEWED BY JACKIE DAY, MAY 13, 1985,
PLENTYWOOD.
SUMMARY: 4 PAGES
2 TAPES: 1 HOUR, 15 MINUTES

OH 877
LOREN O'TOOLE INTERVIEW

Plentywood resident Loren O'Toole (b. 1930) examines: the development of the oil industry in the Plentywood area since the 1950s; the impact of the industry on the local economy, agriculture, and government; the role of religion in Plentywood.
INTERVIEWED BY JACKIE DAY, MAY 17, 1985,
PLENTYWOOD.

SUMMARY: 3 PAGES
1 TAPE: 1 HOUR, 5 MINUTES

OH 878
WILLARD "WOODY" MICHELS INTERVIEW

Woody Michels (b. 1942) considers: the operation of his real estate and insurance business in Plentywood during the 1970s and early 1980s; area churches; local agriculture; social life and politics in Plentywood.
INTERVIEWED BY JACKIE DAY, MAY 14, 1985,
PLENTYWOOD.
SUMMARY: 3 PAGES
1 TAPE: 1 HOUR

OH 879
IRVIN "SHORTY" TIMMERMAN INTERVIEW

Shorty Timmerman (b. 1918) addresses: community life in Plentywood during the 1920s and 1930s; his term as city mayor from 1959 to 1962; the Box Elder Dam project; the radical newspaperman Charlie Taylor; socialism; local government.
INTERVIEWED BY JACKIE DAY, MAY 17 1985,
PLENTYWOOD.
SUMMARY: 3 PAGES
2 TAPES: 1 HOUR, 10 MINUTES

OH 880
MORRIS NELSON AND MARY LOU MATKIN
NELSON INTERVIEW

Plentywood residents Morris Nelson and Mary Lou Nelson comment on: the establishment and operation of Plentywood's first FM radio station (KPWD) from 1962 to 1968; community clubs and women's organizations; Mary Lou Nelson's operation of The Vogue—a women's clothing store—from 1968 to 1984.
INTERVIEWED BY JACKIE DAY, MAY 15, 1985,
PLENTYWOOD.
SUMMARY: 3 PAGES
1 TAPE: 1 HOUR, 5 MINUTES

OH 881
HAROLD DeSILVA INTERVIEW

Harold DeSilva (b. 1918) discusses: music, celebrations, aviation, buildings, entertainment, and politics in Plentywood from the 1920s into the 1950s; Communism; his operation of the Wildwood Beverages bottling plant from 1946 to 1972; the establishment of Wildwood Park and the Plentywood City Band by his father, Harry DeSilva.

Interviewed by Jackie Day, May 15, 1985,
Plentywood.
Summary: 5 pages
2 tapes: 1 hour, 35 minutes

OH 882
HERB KNUTSEN INTERVIEW

Herb Knutsen (b. circa 1940) chronicles: his experiences as a Lutheran minister in Plentywood during the 1970s; the problems and values associated with small town life; social relations among Plentywood churches; difficulties faced by farm families.
Interviewed by Jackie Day, May 23, 1985, Belgrade.
Summary: 3 pages
1 tape: 1 hour, 5 minutes

OH 883
MARY POMEROY INTERVIEW

Broadus resident Mary Pomeroy (b. circa 1960) discusses: her work as a county extension service agent in Powder River County during 1984 and 1985; local 4-H Club projects; the importance of agriculture to the Broadus economy; rural-town relationships.
Interviewed by Laurie Mercier, June 4, 1985, Broadus.
Summary: 3 pages
1 tape: 1 hour, 5 minutes

OH 884
JEAN CATHEY HOUGH INTERVIEW

Jean Hough (b. 1929) characterizes: her operation of the C-Bar-J Motel in Broadus from 1956 into the mid-1980s; her participation in the community hospital planning committee, on the school board, and in other organizations; the local economy; rural-town relations.
Interviewed by Laurie Mercier, June 4, 1985, Broadus.
Summary: 5 pages
2 tapes: 1 hour, 50 minutes

OH 885
ROBERT D. McCURDY, JR., INTERVIEW

Bob McCurdy (b. 1921) discusses: his operation of a service station in Broadus beginning in the late 1930s; his automobile dealership and his farm-implement business from the late 1940s into the 1980s; his involvement in such community groups as the Commercial Club, the Masonic Lodge, and the Highway 212 Association; various efforts to promote tourism in southeastern Montana.

Interviewed by Laurie Mercier, June 1, 1985, Broadus.
Summary: 5 pages
2 tapes: 2 hours

OH 886
ROBERT "MAC" McCURDY, SR., INTERVIEW

Mac McCurdy (1889–1986) addresses: his development of the rock, mineral, and shell collections at Mac's Museum in Broadus during the 1960s; his work as a Watkins' soap products salesman, circa 1910–1920; his experiences as the Powder River County clerk and recorder from 1930 to 1957.
Interviewed by Laurie Mercier, June 2, 1985, Broadus.
Summary: 2 pages
1 tape: 1 hour, 5 minutes

OH 887
TOM WILLIAMS INTERVIEW

Broadus resident Tom Williams (b. 1907) treats: his experiences on ranches during the 1920s; his road-construction and road-maintenance work from the 1930s into the 1950s; his service as Powder River County sheriff during the 1950s; community life in Broadus.
Interviewed by Laurie Mercier, May 31, 1985, Broadus.
Summary: 4 pages
2 tapes: 1 hour, 35 minutes

OH 888
EVA CRANE SULLIVAN INTERVIEW

Eva Sullivan (b. 1901) tells about: teaching in rural schools near Broadus during the 1920s; her operation of the Broadus Mercantile from 1951 to 1969; community activities.
Interviewed by Laurie Mercier, May 30, 1985, Broadus.
Summary: 5 pages
2 tapes: 1 hour, 50 minutes

OH 889
DON HEIDEL INTERVIEW

Don Heidel (b. 1923) talks of: the history of the Powder River Bank in Broadus; small town banking in general; the religious, cultural, and social life of Broadus from the 1930s into the 1980s.
Interviewed by Laurie Mercier, June 3, 1985, Broadus.

SUMMARY: 9 PAGES
3 TAPES: 2 HOURS, 50 MINUTES

OH 890
MIKE COPPS INTERVIEW

Mike Copps surveys: his operation of the True Value Hardware store in Broadus from 1981 to 1985; the importance of agriculture to the local economy; his participation in such community groups as the Commercial Club and the Volunteer Fire Department.
INTERVIEWED BY LAURIE MERCIER, JUNE 4, 1985, BROADUS.
SUMMARY: 3 PAGES
1 TAPE: 50 MINUTES

OH 891
MARIE MILLER TRAUB INTERVIEW

Marie Traub (b. 1917) summarizes: the operation of the Miller Hospital in Broadus by her mother, Marie M. Miller; the management of the Broadus Flour Mill by her father, John P. Miller; local health care; entertainment; the Catholic Church; her participation in such community groups as 4-H and the Community Church.
INTERVIEWED BY LAURIE MERCIER, MAY 31, 1985, BROADUS.
SUMMARY: 5 PAGES
2 TAPES: 1 HOUR, 45 MINUTES

OH 892
FORRA FLOYD "BUNK" HUCKINS INTERVIEW

Bunk Huckins (b. 1912)—a Broadus resident—speaks of: his terms as Powder River County commissioner from 1956 into the 1960s, and from 1980 to 1985; issues facing local government; cattle ranch operations; the impacts of oil and coal development on the area; rural-town relationships.
INTERVIEWED BY LAURIE MERCIER, JUNE 3, 1985, BROADUS.
SUMMARY: 5 PAGES
2 TAPES: 1 HOUR, 30 MINUTES

OH 893
FRANK McLAIN AND EDITH BOYES McLAIN INTERVIEW

Frank McLain (b. 1906) reviews: his operation of a mail route between Broadus and Arvada from 1924 to 1985; playing baseball in Broadus from the 1920s into the 1950s. Edith McLain (b. 1905) discusses: her involvement in local politics; her service as Powder River County superintendent of schools, as county treasurer, as clerk of the district court, and as Broadus town treasurer; her participation in the Community Club; the impact of the 1930s Depression on the community; relationships between the town and the county.
INTERVIEWED BY LAURIE MERCIER, JUNE 3, 1985, BROADUS.
SUMMARY: 6 PAGES
2 TAPES: 1 HOUR, 35 MINUTES

OH 894
RUTH HARRINGTON NEWMILLER INTERVIEW

Ruth Newmiller (b. 1902) recalls: her teaching career in Broadus and in Powder River County; the plumbing business of her husband, Carl Newmiller.
INTERVIEWED BY LAURIE MERCIER, JUNE 3, 1985, BROADUS.
SUMMARY: 4 PAGES
2 TAPES: 1 HOUR, 35 MINUTES

OH 895
THOMAS J. DAILY AND ELLEN DAILY INTERVIEWS

Broadus residents Thomas Daily (b. 1899) and Ellen Daily report on: their work for McMann and Burton groceries from 1933 to 1958; the operation of their own grocery in Broadus from 1958 to 1966; local government; small town business practices.
INTERVIEWED BY LAURIE MERCIER, MAY 31, 1985, BROADUS.
SUMMARY: 2 PAGES
1 TAPE: 1 HOUR, 5 MINUTES

OH 896
ED LARKIN INTERVIEW

Ed Larkin (b. 1892) remembers: his operation of the Pasttime Bar in Chinook prior to World War I; running a nonalcoholic Pasttime during Prohibition; his work as a Blaine County deputy sheriff during the 1930s.
INTERVIEWED BY LAURIE MERCIER, JULY 10-11, 1984, CHINOOK.
SUMMARY: 1 PAGE
1 TAPE: 30 MINUTES

OH 897
OLIVE SATTLEEN INTERVIEW

Olive Sattleen (b. 1891) describes: her childhood in Yantic (later Lohman) in the early 1900s; homesteading and sheep ranching in the Milk River Valley; her children; community life in Chinook.

INTERVIEWED BY ANN CARMERSON, DECEMBER 21, 1984, CHINOOK.
SUMMARY: 3 PAGES
2 TAPES: 2 HOURS

OH 898
ROBERT J. BROOKS INTERVIEW

Broadus resident Robert Brooks relates: his work as city attorney for Broadus and as county attorney for Powder River County from 1960 to 1984; the impact of the Belle Creek oil boom on the area; his term as mayor of Broadus from 1970 to 1971; the character of the Broadus community.
INTERVIEWED BY LAURIE MERCIER, AUGUST 6, 1985, BROADUS.
SUMMARY: 4 PAGES
2 TAPES: 1 HOUR, 30 MINUTES

OH 899
THEODORE DOZOIS INTERVIEW

Theodore Dozois (b. 1902) reflects on: community life in Roundup during the 1920s; his father's operation of Conden's Department Store in Roundup.
INTERVIEWED BY LAURIE MERCIER, OCTOBER 8, 1985, ROUNDUP.
SUMMARY: 3 PAGES
1 TAPE: 50 MINUTES

OH 900
WILBUR WOOD INTERVIEW

Wilbur Wood (b. 1942) recounts: life in Roundup from the 1950s into the 1970s; the impact of coal-mine closures on the town's character and economy; the growth of subdivisions in Musselshell County; the Bull Mountains Landowner Association's fight against local strip mining; the possibilities for small-scale industry in the economic revitalization of Roundup.
INTERVIEWED BY LAURIE MERCIER, MARCH 28, 1986, ROUNDUP.
SUMMARY: 7 PAGES
2 TAPES: 1 HOUR, 50 MINUTES

OH 1194
PHYLLIS KNOTT MOEN

Phyllis Moen (b. 1917) recalls: her family and life in Eureka; area health care and physicians; her father's photography business in Eureka; the poet Jim Whilt; residents, buildings, and businesses in Eureka; social events and holidays in the community.

INTERVIEWED BY CATHRYN SCHROEDER, DECEMBER 15, 1992, EUREKA.
TRANSCRIPT: 13 PAGES
1 TAPE: 1 HOUR, 30 MINUTES

OH 1385
FRANKLIN LONG AND GEORGE LONG INTERVIEW

Franklin Long (b. 1913) and George Long (b. 1910) discuss: their parents; growing up in the Eureka area; their father's local medical practice; their mother's activities as chair of the local school board; health care and area physicians; businesses, buildings, and people in Eureka.
INTERVIEWED BY CATHRYN SCHROEDER, SEPTEMBER 29, 1992, EUREKA.
TRANSCRIPT: 12 PAGES
1 TAPE: 1 HOUR

OH 1386
LUCILLE HOLDER BURCH PAYNE INTERVIEW

Lucille Payne (b. 1908) recalls: her family and life in Eureka; businesses, buildings, and people in the community; local forest fires; social activities and politics in Eureka.
INTERVIEWED BY CATHRYN SCHROEDER, JULY 29, 1992, EUREKA.
TRANSCRIPT: 10 PAGES
1 TAPE: 1 HOUR

20th Century Montana Military Veterans Oral History Project

From World War I through the Persian Gulf War, Montana has ranked in the highest percentile nationally in the number of its citizens serving as military personnel. These numbers include nearly 5,000 women since 1940 and a majority of male Montanan tribal members. Montana played a significant role in American military strategies during the Cold War, due to the presence of Malmstrom Air Force Base and its numerous missile silos. This project records the experiences of Montana's veterans, with discussions of families, precombat training, service on the home front and overseas, returning to civilian life, career military life, and feelings about military conflicts.

OH 1195
JOHN TERREO INTERVIEW

John Terreo (b. 1954) addresses: his work as a civilian employee with the U.S. Navy during the early 1970s; the "20th Century Montana Military Veterans Oral History Project"; uses of oral history in documenting recent historical events. [See also Medicine, Health Care, and Nursing OH 1346 and General Montana OH 1196.]
INTERVIEWED BY ROY CALDWELL, APRIL 14, 1993, HELENA.
TRANSCRIPT: 50 PAGES
2 TAPES: 2 HOURS

OH 1197
DAVID C. THOMAS INTERVIEW

David Thomas chronicles his experiences during Operation Desert Shield/Storm (the Persian Gulf War) as a member of the Montana National Guard's 103rd Public Affairs Detachment attached to the 3rd Armored Cavalry Regiment.
INTERVIEWED BY JOHN TERREO, MARCH 19, 1993, FORT HARRISON.
TRANSCRIPT: 39 PAGES
2 TAPES: 2 HOURS

OH 1198
NEELIAN NELSON AND MARGARET NELSON INTERVIEW

Neelian Nelson (b. 1915) talks about: his early life in Wisconsin; his experiences as a U.S. Army officer as-signed to the Camp Rimini Dog Reception and Training Center in Rimini during World War II; his other military assignments. Margaret Nelson discusses: her family; growing up in Wisconsin; her experience as an army officer's wife at Camp Rimini.
INTERVIEWED BY JOHN TERREO, FEBRUARY 2, 1993, MISSOULA.
SUMMARY: 4 PAGES
2 TAPES: 1 HOUR, 25 MINUTES

OH 1199
SUSAN GIBB INTERVIEW

Missoula resident Susan Gibb (b. 1946) comments on: her family; growing up in Hysham; her education; her employment as a schoolteacher in Washington state; her enlistment and career in the U.S. Air Force. [See also 20th Century Montana Military Veterans OH 1455.]
INTERVIEWED BY JOHN TERREO, FEBRUARY 2, 1993, MISSOULA.
SUMMARY: 4 PAGES
2 TAPES: 1 HOUR, 25 MINUTES

OH 1200
EMIL CHRISTIANSEN INTERVIEW

Emil Christiansen—a Billings resident—converses about: his experiences with the Montana Army National Guard on the Mexican border in 1916; his service with a U.S. Army medical company in France during World

War I; post–World War I activities with the Montana National Guard.

INTERVIEWED BY PHIL CURRY, DECEMBER 12, 1987, FORT HARRISON.

SUMMARY: 2 PAGES

1 TAPE: 40 MINUTES

OH 1208
JOHN C. HARRISON INTERVIEW

John Harrison (b. 1913) considers: his early life in the Judith Basin; the communities of Harlowton, Judith Gap, Martinsdale, and Twodot; small town medical care; his work as a Boy Scout master during the late 1920s; Prohibition; the 1930s Depression; his undergraduate education at Montana State College in Bozeman during the early 1930s; his legal education at Montana State University in Missoula during the mid-1930s; his campaigns for elective office during the 1950s and 1960s; McCarthyism; communism; state and national politics; U.S. Senator Burton K. Wheeler; drug enforcement; his career as a justice on the Montana Supreme Court. *[See also 20th Century Montana Military Veterans OH 1453.]*

INTERVIEWED BY MARIE DEEGAN, FEBRUARY 19, 1990, HELENA.

TRANSCRIPT: 59 PAGES

2 TAPES: 1 HOUR, 40 MINUTES

OH 1219
DAVID SAYRE INTERVIEW

Great Falls resident David Sayre (b. 1948) talks about: the Montana Army National Guard 103rd Public Affairs Detachment's mobilization and departure for Operation Desert Shield/Storm (the Persian Gulf War); his responsibilities and the unit's mission; his service with the U.S. Marine Corps during the Vietnam War; nuclear, chemical, biological warfare training; his work with the Great Falls *Tribune*; his views on the Iraqi invasion of Kuwait and on the U.S. response to that invasion. *[See also 20th Century Montana Military Veterans OH 1457-58.]*

INTERVIEWED BY JOHN TERREO, DECEMBER 9, 1990, FORT HARRISON.

TRANSCRIPT: 19 PAGES

1 TAPE: 35 MINUTES

OH 1220
PATRICK MOHAN INTERVIEW

Patrick Mohan (b. 1948) recalls: his service with the Montana Army National Guard 103rd Public Affairs Detachment; his position, duties, and responsibilities within that unit; his concerns about operating sensitive video equipment in a desert environment; his civilian employment as a special-education teacher; his reactions to being mobilized for Operation Desert Shield/Storm (the Persian Gulf War); his experiences interacting with a very different society; rules imposed on U.S. military personnel by the Saudi Arabian government; reasons for the U.S. military presence in the Middle East. *[See also 20th Century Montana Military Veterans OH 1459.]*

INTERVIEWED BY JOHN TERREO, DECEMBER 9, 1990, FORT HARRISON.

TRANSCRIPT: 14 PAGES

1 TAPE: 25 MINUTES

OH 1221
ROY CALDWELL INTERVIEW

Roy Caldwell (b. 1953) describes: his reasons for joining the Montana Army National Guard; his military service with the U.S. Air Force and with the Montana Air National Guard; his duties and responsibilities in the 103rd Public Affairs Detachment; his impressions of the mobilization for Operation Desert Shield/Storm (the Persian Gulf War); concerns about the operation of a darkroom in a desert environment; rules of conduct for U.S. military personnel in Saudi Arabia; the reasons for U.S. military response to crisis situations; the cooperation of his civilian employer. *[See also 20th Century Montana Military Veterans OH 1564-66.]*

INTERVIEWED BY JOHN TERREO, DECEMBER 9, 1990, FORT HARRISON.

TRANSCRIPT: 16 PAGES

1 TAPE: 40 MINUTES

OH 1222
KAREENE OSTERMILLER

Kareene Ostermiller (b. 1957)—a Shepard resident—discusses: the U.S. Army; the mobilization of the Montana Army National Guard 103rd Public Affairs Detachment for Operation Desert Shield/Storm (the Persian Gulf War); the unit's mission; the invasion of Kuwait by Iraq; her experiences with the Montana Air National Guard; her position as the first female aide-de-camp in the Montana Army National Guard's state headquarters; sexual discrimination against women in the military; her concerns about her family and the different environment; her perceptions of an unfamiliar culture, particularly its treatment of women. *[See also 20th Century Montana Military Veterans OH 1463.]*

INTERVIEWED BY JOHN TERREO, DECEMBER 9, 1990, FORT
HARRISON.

TRANSCRIPT: 21 PAGES

1 TAPE: 35 MINUTES

OH 1223
TERRANCE M. YOUNG INTERVIEW

Terrance Young (b. 1942) describes: his service with
the U.S. Navy (Naval Reserve) during the 1960s; his reasons for joining the Montana National Guard; his experiences serving with a tank unit in Shelby; his assignment to the 103rd Public Affairs Detachment; his duties
and responsibilities within that unit; his civilian occupation; the effects of the Middle East crisis on his employer
and on his family; the primary mission of the 103rd Detachment; his views regarding U.S. involvement in the
Persian Gulf War. *[See also 20th Century Montana Military Veterans OH 1464.]*

INTERVIEWED BY JOHN TERREO, DECEMBER 9, 1990, FORT
HARRISON.

TRANSCRIPT: 17 PAGES

1 TAPE: 25 MINUTES

OH 1224
CHARLES "MILO" McLEOD INTERVIEW

Milo McLeod (b. 1947) discourses on: his service in
the U.S. Army's 173rd Airborne Brigade in Vietnam during 1969; joining the Montana Army National Guard in
1976; the mobilization of the 103rd Public Affairs Detachment for Operation Desert Shield/Storm (the Persian Gulf War); the U.S. response to the invasion of Kuwait by Iraq; the "Total Force" concept; his employment
by the U.S. Forest Service and its cooperation with the
National Guard; family concerns; differences between
the Persian Gulf War and the Vietnam War. *[See also
20th Century Montana Military Veterans OH 1465.]*

INTERVIEWED BY JOHN TERREO, DECEMBER 9, 1990, FORT
HARRISON.

TRANSCRIPT: 15 PAGES

1 TAPE: 30 MINUTES

OH 1225
TODD BUHMILLER INTERVIEW

Todd Buhmiller (b. 1963) discusses: joining the Montana Army National Guard; the mobilization of the 103rd
Public Affairs Detachment for Operation Desert Shield/
Storm (the Persian Gulf War); how the unit functioned;
his personal responsibilities within the unit; the cooperation shown by his employer, Montana State University, regarding his activation; his training in Nuclear/

Biological/Chemical (NBC) warfare; the U.S. response
to Iraq's invasion of Kuwait. *[See also 20th Century Montana Military Veterans OH 1466.]*

INTERVIEWED BY JOHN TERREO, DECEMBER 9, 1990, FORT
HARRISON.

TRANSCRIPT: 18 PAGES

1 TAPE: 25 MINUTES

OH 1241
GREG FOX INTERVIEW

Greg Fox (b. 1953) discusses: why he enlisted in the
Montana Army National Guard; his posting to the 103rd
Public Affairs Detachment in 1985; the unit's responsibilities and operation; the mobilization of the unit for
Operation Desert Shield/Storm (the Persian Gulf War);
his civilian employment; his concerns about the unit's
equipment in a desert environment; specific rules that
the Saudi Arabian government imposed on U.S. military
forces; the role played by the petroleum industry in the
Gulf situation; family matters. *[See also 20th Century
Montana Military Veterans OH 1468.]*

INTERVIEWED BY JOHN TERREO, DECEMBER 9, 1990, FORT
HARRISON.

TRANSCRIPT: 15 PAGES

1 TAPE: 25 MINUTES

OH 1242
PATRICK HERMANSON INTERVIEW

Billings resident Patrick Hermanson (b. 1951) discusses: his service with the U.S. Army, 656th Air Defense Artillery Battalion and with the 7th Infantry Division during the 1970s; joining the Montana Army
National Guard; taking command of the 103rd Public
Affairs Detachment in 1987; the mobilization of his unit
for Operation Desert Shield/Storm (the Persian Gulf
War); his civilian employment; the U.S. response to the
invasion of Kuwait by Iraq; the mission of the 103rd
Detachment; his concerns as a commanding officer; family members. *[See also 20th Century Montana Military
Veterans OH 1469.]*

INTERVIEWED BY JOHN TERREO, DECEMBER 10, 1990, FORT
HARRISON.

TRANSCRIPT: 14 PAGES

1 TAPE: 20 MINUTES

OH 1243
JODIE YELTON INTERVIEW

Jodie Yelton (b. 1944) briefly speaks of: his reasons
for joining the Montana Army National Guard; his posting to the 103rd Public Affairs Detachment in 1980; the

mobilization of his unit for Operation Desert Shield/Storm (the Persian Gulf War); his experiences dealing with another culture; the U.S. military presence in Saudi Arabia; the responsibilities and operation of the 103rd Detachment. *[See also 20th Century Montana Military Veterans OH 1470.]*

INTERVIEWED BY JOHN TERREO, DECEMBER 10, 1990, FORT HARRISON.

TRANSCRIPT: 9 PAGES

1 TAPE: 15 MINUTES

OH 1244
ANDY LEE JOHNSON INTERVIEW

Andy Johnson (b. 1968) recalls: the mobilization of the Montana Army National Guard's 103rd Public Affairs Detachment from Fort Harrison for Operation Desert Shield/Storm (the Persian Gulf War); the unit's mission; his particular job assignment; his observations regarding the U.S. response to the invasion of Kuwait by Iraq. *[See also 20th Century Montana Military Veterans OH 1471.]*

INTERVIEWED BY JOHN TERREO, DECEMBER 10, 1990, FORT HARRISON.

TRANSCRIPT: 9 PAGES

1 TAPE: 20 MINUTES

OH 1246
DUANE LONGFELLOW INTERVIEW

Duane Longfellow (b. 1971) talks about: his early life in Helena; his basic-training experiences as a U.S. Air Force recruit in Lackland, Texas; his special training as an Air Force Security Specialist; his training in Air Base Ground Defense; the possibility of his assignment to the Middle East for Operation Desert Shield/Storm (the Persian Gulf War); his personal feelings regarding the U.S. presence in the Gulf.

INTERVIEWED BY JOHN TERREO, JANUARY 17, 1991, HELENA.

TRANSCRIPT: 40 PAGES

2 TAPES: 1 HOUR, 15 MINUTES

OH 1250
MARY FELDER INTERVIEW

Mary Felder (b. 1918) recalls: her early life in Savannah, Georgia, and in Butte; her uncle, Pat Felder, who began the *Postal Telegraph* in Helena at the turn of the century; her nurse's education and training; her work as a private-duty nurse in Townsend and in Helena in soldiers' homes; her experiences as one of the first stewardesses employed by Western Airlines during the late

1930s; her service aboard the hospital ship U.S.S. *Bountiful* during World War II; her employment with the Navy Relief Society; her work as a real-estate agent in Helena during the 1970s. *[See also 20th Century Montana Military Veterans OH 1472.]*

INTERVIEWED BY JOHN TERREO, MARCH 3, 1991, COLUMBIA FALLS.

TRANSCRIPT: 60 PAGES

2 TAPES: 1 HOUR, 45 MINUTES

OH 1251
LARRY LONGFELLOW INTERVIEW

Larry Longfellow (b. 1945) portrays: growing up in Helena; his enlistment in the United States Navy in 1960s; basic training in San Diego; his experiences as a helmsman on the cruiser U.S.S. *Galveston* (CG-1); fire-support missions along the Vietnam coast during the mid-1960s; his adventures rescuing downed pilots; various ports of call; Captain (later Rear Admiral) Arthur Goodfellow of the *Galveston*; his comparison of the Vietnam War to Operation Desert Shield/Storm (Persian Gulf War).

INTERVIEWED BY JOHN TERREO, MARCH 22, 1991, HELENA.

TRANSCRIPT: 36 PAGES

2 TAPES: 1 HOUR, 10 MINUTES

OH 1252
JUANITA COOKE INTERVIEW

Juanita Cooke (b. circa 1920)—a Helena resident—reflects on: her early flying experiences in California; her acquisition of a pilot's license in the late 1930s; the Japanese attack on Pearl Harbor in 1941; government restrictions placed on nonmilitary flights after Pearl Harbor; her service in the Women's Air Force Service Pilots (WASPS) in the U.S. Army Air Forces, from 1942 to 1944; primary, basic, and advanced flight training at Avenger Field, in Sweetwater, Texas; living conditions at Avenger; various aircraft that she flew; women air pilots' experiences ferrying fighter aircraft to various bases in the United States, including Great Falls. *[See also 20th Century Montana Military Veterans OH 1473.]*

INTERVIEWED BY JOHN TERREO, MARCH 27, 1991, HELENA.

TRANSCRIPT: 21 PAGES

1 TAPE: 1 HOUR

OH 1253
ERNEST FACHNER INTERVIEW

Ernest Fachner (b. 1925) recounts: his experiences

as an infantry soldier with the 24th U.S. Army Division in New Guinea and in the Philippine Islands during World War II; wartime living conditions; combat conditions; his basic training at Camp Roberts, California.
INTERVIEWED BY JOHN TERREO, APRIL 7, 1991, LEWISTOWN.
TRANSCRIPT: 25 PAGES
1 TAPE: 1 HOUR

OH 1254
TERRANCE E. PERRY INTERVIEW
Terrance Perry remembers: his service with the U.S. Marine Corps from 1942 to 1946; his basic-training experiences; medical air-evacuation missions in the central Pacific; his service with the U.S. Air Force at Malmstrom Air Force Base in Great Falls from 1947 to 1949; his duties with the Marine Corps Reserves from 1950 to 1958; his work in the Montana Air National Guard from 1963 to 1966; his responsibilities as a recruiter for the U.S. Naval Reserve from 1967 to 1976; retirement; his views on the Persian Gulf War.
INTERVIEWED BY JOHN TERREO, MARCH 2, 1991, COLUMBIA FALLS.
TRANSCRIPT: 18 PAGES
1 TAPE: 45 MINUTES

OH 1255
HUGH CLIFFORD CUMMING INTERVIEW
Hugh Cumming (b. 1926) talks about: growing up in Philipsburg; his early education; his service with the U.S. Marine Corps during World War II; basic training in San Diego; Browning Automatic Rifle Training at Camp Elliot, California; life aboard troop ships; his experiences as part of a Marine Division mortar squad on Guam and on Iwo Jima; earning the Bronze Star; the American Legion; veterans and veterans' benefits; military conflicts following World War II.
INTERVIEWED BY JOHN TERREO, JUNE 26, 1991, HELENA.
TRANSCRIPT: 43 PAGES
2 TAPES: 1 HOUR, 15 MINUTES

OH 1256
ORVILLE QUICK INTERVIEW
Orville Quick (b. 1922) reviews: growing up in Nebraska and moving to Montana in 1930; joining the U.S. Army 29th Engineers, Construction Battalions in 1940; the military induction process; his basic training at Oceanside, California; his service in Hawaii; the Japanese attack on Pearl Harbor; amphibious landings, combat, and airfield construction on the Pacific islands Baker,

Makin, and Saipan; the destruction of Japanese aircraft by U.S. P-61 night-fighters; living conditions on Pacific islands; the mass burial of Japanese soldiers; the capture of Japanese civilians; encounters with U.S. Navy Construction Battalions; troop transports; his views on U.S. military conflicts, including World War II and after.
INTERVIEWED BY JOHN TERREO, JUNE 20, 1991, CIRCLE.
TRANSCRIPT: 53 PAGES
2 TAPES: 2 HOURS

OH 1257
LARRY KILMER INTERVIEW
Larry Kilmer (b. 1952) summarizes: growing up in Helena; his enlistment in the U.S. Coast Guard; his training experiences; his duty assignments in Alaska and Washington state; his adventures in the federal drug war, while serving aboard the Coast Guard cutters U.S.S. *Lipan* and U.S.S. *Confidence*; the role played by the Coast Guard in Operation Desert Shield/Storm (the Persian Gulf War).
INTERVIEWED BY JOHN TERREO, JULY 10, 1991, HELENA.
TRANSCRIPT: 53 PAGES
2 TAPES: 2 HOURS

OH 1258
KERMIT EDMONDS INTERVIEW
Kermit Edmonds (b. 1938)—a Missoula resident—recalls: his experiences in the Montana Army National Guard from 1959 to 1966; his return to the guard in 1976; his participation in Operation Desert Shield/Storm (the Persian Gulf War) as a member of the Montana Guard's 103rd Public Affairs Detachment; general views on war.
INTERVIEWED BY JOHN TERREO, FEBRUARY 13, 1992, MISSOULA.
TRANSCRIPT: 70 PAGES
3 TAPES: 2 HOURS, 30 MINUTES

OH 1259
FRANK LAWLOR INTERVIEW
Frank Lawlor briefly speaks of: his service in the U.S. Air Force; his employment by the U.S. Department of Agriculture; community life in Kalispell; the Montana Soldiers' Home in Columbia Falls.
INTERVIEWED BY RAELYN OLSEN, MAY 23, 1991, COLUMBIA FALLS.
SUMMARY: 1 PAGE
1 TAPE: 20 MINUTES

OH 1260
GERALD R. BENTLEY INTERVIEW
Gerald Bentley (b. 1930) very briefly surveys his two years of service in the U.S. Army.
INTERVIEWED BY SHANE BIDWELL, MAY 9, 1991, COLUMBIA FALLS.
SUMMARY: 1 PAGE
1 TAPE: 10 MINUTES

OH 1261
LEE J. CORWIN INTERVIEW
Lee Corwin briefly tells of: his service with the U.S. Air Force; his duties guarding military aircraft in the Vietnam War; his subsequent assignments in the Philippines and Guam; his retirement; his move to the Montana Soldiers' Home in Columbia Falls.
INTERVIEWED BY CHUCK PETERSON, MAY 10, 1991, COLUMBIA FALLS.
SUMMARY: 1 PAGE
1 TAPE: 20 MINUTES

OH 1262
ROY HOELKE INTERVIEW
Roy Hoelke (b. 1918) talks about: his family and childhood in Wisconsin; his education at the University of Idaho in Moscow; his visits to Sanders County; his service in the Reserve Officer Training Cadet (ROTC) program during World War II; his experiences with the U.S. Army Air Force 389th Heavy Bombardment Group over Europe during World War II, as a bombardier on a B-24 heavy bomber; heavy-bomber strategy and tactics; military training at the San Antonio, Texas, Aviation Cadet Center; his postmilitary life.
INTERVIEWED BY JOHN TERREO, JULY 22, 1992, HELENA.
TRANSCRIPT: 58 PAGES
2 TAPES: 2 HOURS

OH 1263
HENRY ZIMMERMAN INTERVIEW
Henry Zimmerman—born in Great Falls—talks about: his university education in agriculture economics; his service in the U.S. Air Force and in the Montana National Guard; his father's work on a cattle ranch and as a bookkeeper at Malmstrom Air Force Base in Great Falls.
INTERVIEWED BY LAVON HABETS, JUNE 6, 1991, COLUMBIA FALLS.
SUMMARY: 1 PAGE
1 TAPE: 20 MINUTES

OH 1264
JAMES E. HARPER INTERVIEW
James Harper discusses: his service with the U.S. Army during World War II; his experiences with medics, artillery, and tank destroyers.
INTERVIEWED BY ALICIA HUFF, JUNE 6, 1991, COLUMBIA FALLS.
SUMMARY: 1 PAGE
1 TAPE: 20 MINUTES

OH 1265
PHILIP SMITH INTERVIEW
Philip Smith (b. 1908) discusses: his service with the U.S. Navy Construction Battalions during World War II; community life in Kalispell following World War II.
INTERVIEWED BY JILL DAUGHERTY, MAY 16, 1991, COLUMBIA FALLS.
SUMMARY: 2 PAGES
1 TAPE: 30 MINUTES

OH 1266
CARSON WALKS OVER ICE INTERVIEW
Carson Walks Over Ice—a resident of Crow Agency—speaks of: the warrior traditions of the Crow tribe; his enlistment in the U.S. Army; basic and airborne training; his combat experiences in the Vietnam War as a U.S. Army Ranger; the efficiency of the North Vietnamese Army; his homecoming.
INTERVIEWED BY JOHN TERREO, AUGUST 5, 1992, CROW AGENCY.
TRANSCRIPT: 51 PAGES
2 TAPES: 2 HOURS

OH 1270
MICHAEL A. SANDERS INTERVIEW
Michael Sanders (b. 1971) interprets his experiences as an infantry soldier during Operation Desert Shield/Storm (the Persian Gulf War).
INTERVIEWED BY NESTOR AURITA, MARCH 24, 1992, MISSOULA.
SUMMARY: 4 PAGES
1 TAPE: 45 MINUTES

OH 1271
DOROTHY ANNE DAVIS FORRESTER INTERVIEW
Dorothy Forrester (b. 1919) examines: her family; growing up in Dillon; her education; her home front work with the American Red Cross during World War II; women and war.

INTERVIEWED BY LEE GRAVES, APRIL 15, 1992, DILLON.
TRANSCRIPT: 47 PAGES
2 TAPES: 1 HOUR, 10 MINUTES

OH 1272
ROY WILLIAM FORRESTER INTERVIEW

Roy Forrester (b. 1919) portrays: his family; growing up in Dillon; his service with the U.S. Army during World War II; the Saipan Island campaign of 1944.
INTERVIEWED BY LEE GRAVES, APRIL 15, 1992, DILLON.
TRANSCRIPT: 48 PAGES
2 TAPES: 1 HOUR, 15 MINUTES

OH 1273
CARL M. DAVIS INTERVIEW

Carl Davis (b. 1922)—a resident of Dillon—discourses on: his family; his early life in Dillon; his education; his service with the U.S. Navy during World War II and during the Korean War; his experiences fighting in the Pacific.
INTERVIEWED BY LEE GRAVES, APRIL 25, 1992, DILLON.
TRANSCRIPT: 42 PAGES
2 TAPES: 1 HOUR, 20 MINUTES

OH 1274
ROBERT D. ANDERSON INTERVIEW

Robert Anderson (b. 1945) recalls: his family; growing up in Baldwin, Wisconsin; his education; his enlistment during the Vietnam War; his service with the U.S. Army in Vietnam; General William Westmoreland; drug use among U.S. troops; the Vietnamese people; his postmilitary life.
INTERVIEWED BY LEE GRAVES, APRIL 9, 1992, HELENA.
TRANSCRIPT: 70 PAGES
3 TAPES: 2 HOURS, 15 MINUTES

OH 1275
RAY FITCHETT INTERVIEW

Heron resident Ray Fitchett (b. 1931) describes: his early life; his enlistment in the U.S. Marine Corps in 1951; basic training; his service in the Marine Guard aboard the heavy cruiser U.S.S. *Helena* during the Korean War; his experiences as a Marine raider and as a spotter for warship gunfire support; his combat wounds; meeting and guarding President Dwight D. Eisenhower; flying from Long Beach, California, to Montana with Governor John Bonner and J. R. Wine, the mayor of Helena; his postmilitary life.
INTERVIEWED BY SARA LOU SPRINGER, MAY 14, 1992, HERON.

TRANSCRIPT: 23 PAGES
1 TAPE: 45 MINUTES

OH 1276
DORIS BRANDER INTERVIEW

Doris Brander (b. 1921) recounts: her service in the U.S. Navy's Women Accepted for Volunteer Emergency Service (WAVES) program during World War II; her reasons for joining the WAVES; her wartime duties; life on the home front in Montana and in Washington state; United Service Organizations (USO) shows; Eleanor Roosevelt; minority women in military service; the 1930s Depression; women and war; the women's military memorial in Washington, D.C.; her postmilitary life.
INTERVIEWED BY ROSETTA KAMLOWSKY, JUNE 11, 1992, HELENA.
SUMMARY: 3 PAGES
2 TAPES: 1 HOUR, 20 MINUTES

OH 1277
HELEN DAWSON INTERVIEW

Helen Dawson details: her experiences with the U.S. WAVES during World War II; serving as a U.S. Navy storekeeper; her duty at the Naval Air Station in Alameda, California, and in Honolulu; women and war; postmilitary life.
INTERVIEWED BY ROSETTA KAMLOWSKY, JUNE 11, 1992, HELENA.
Transcript: 32 pages
1 TAPE: 1 HOUR

OH 1278
GENEVIEVE SQUIRES ADAIR INTERVIEW

Genevieve Adair (b. 1911) reflects on: her family; her earliest years in Plainview, Nebraska; relocating to Butte in 1916; attending the Normal School (later Western Montana College) in Dillon; her enlistment in the Women's Auxiliary Army Corps (WAAC); officers' training; her work classifying female recruits at the Fort Des Moines WAAC training center in Iowa; her transfer to Fort Meade, Maryland; African-American military personnel; the military pay scales; nursing; her postmilitary life.
INTERVIEWED BY ROSETTA KAMLOWSKY, JULY 29, 1992, HELENA.
SUMMARY: 3 PAGES
1 TAPE: 50 MINUTES

OH 1279
ELDORA McBRIDE INTERVIEW

Helena resident Eldora McBride (b. 1923) describes: her childhood; her education at Northern Montana College in Havre; medical-secretary training; her enlistment in the U.S. Navy in 1944; military training at Hunter College in New York City; racial discrimination; women and promotions in the military; uniforms; living conditions; her transfer to the Medical Center in Bethesda, Maryland; her subsequent move to the naval facility at Corvallis, Oregon; the nature of war; her transfer to the Naval Air Base in Seattle, Washington; the educational benefits of the GI Bill (Veterans Benefit Act, 1944); her postmilitary life.

INTERVIEWED BY ROSETTA KAMLOWSKY, MAY 28, 1992, HELENA.

SUMMARY: 3 PAGES

1 TAPE: 1 HOUR

OH 1280
HERBERT GOODWIN INTERVIEW

Herbert Goodwin (b. 1919) relates: growing up in Canada; his service with the Canadian Army; his experiences with the combined Canadian/American First Special Service Force during World War II; training at Fort William Henry Harrison near Helena; the Kiska Island landing; various European operations; his recollections of General Robert T. Frederick, commander of the First Special Service Force.

INTERVIEWED BY JOHN TERREO, JUNE 17, 1992, HELENA.

TRANSCRIPT: 40 PAGES

2 TAPES: 1 HOUR, 40 MINUTES

OH 1376
MABEL HAYNES INTERVIEW

Mabel Haynes depicts: her family; her early life in Judith Gap; her father's ownership and operation—with C. R. Stone—of the First National Bank in Judith Gap; the Hayes Store; the Stone Gaugler Ranch; her education; her enlistment and service in the U.S. Marine Corps as an aircraft control-tower operator during World War II; women in the military.

INTERVIEWED BY JENNIFER PETERSON, DECEMBER 1, 1991, JUDITH GAP.

SUMMARY: 6 PAGES

1 TAPE: 45 MINUTES

OH 1378
WILLIAM NIELSEN INTERVIEW

William Nielsen (b. 1939)—a Stanford resident—re-

members: his family; growing up in Lewistown; his enlistment in the U.S. Navy; his service aboard surface ships and submarines; his involvement in the Vietnam War; his participation in the rescue of downed U.S. pilots and air crewmen; his post-Vietnam military service; his retirement; his views on the Vietnam War and on Operation Desert Shield/Storm (the Persian Gulf War).

INTERVIEWED BY SHANNON PLOVANIC, DECEMBER 1, 1991, STANFORD.

SUMMARY: 5 PAGES

1 TAPE: 25 MINUTES

OH 1381
JEANNE LeCLAIR ROBINETTE INTERVIEW

Jeanne Robinette (b. 1920) delineates: her family; growing up in Delphia; her education; her work at the Boeing aircraft plant in Seattle during World War II; her return to Montana after the war; her nursing career; her retirement.

INTERVIEWED BY MONICA BREWINGTON, DECEMBER 6, 1991, BALLANTINE.

SUMMARY: 3 PAGES

1 TAPE: 30 MINUTES

OH 1391
GERALD McFADDEN INTERVIEW

Gerald McFadden reports on: his experiences as a soldier in the Canadian Army and in the First Special Service Force during World War II; special training at Fort William Henry Harrison, near Helena; the Anzio campaign.

INTERVIEWED BY JOHN TERREO, AUGUST 19, 1992, HELENA.

TRANSCRIPT: 10 PAGES

1 TAPE: 20 MINUTES

OH 1453
JOHN C. HARRISON INTERVIEW

Montana Supreme Court Justice John Harrison (b. 1913) discusses: his service with the U.S. Army prior to and during World War II; his experiences as a staff officer with the army's VII Corps; preparations for D day; his involvement in investigations of atrocities against U.S. military personnel perpetrated by German military forces and civilians, including the Malemedy massacre; the liberation of German concentration camps at Nordhausen and Torgau; preparations for the invasion of Japan. *[See also 20th Century Montana Military Veterans OH 1208.]*

INTERVIEWED BY JOHN TERREO, JANUARY 29, 1992, HELENA.

TRANSCRIPT: 46 PAGES

2 TAPES: 1 HOUR, 50 MINUTES

OH 1455
SUSAN GIBB INTERVIEW

Susan Gibb (b. 1946), a resident of Missoula, discusses: personal theories and philosophies of military leadership; returning home to Hysham following her retirement from the military. *[See also 20th Century Montana Military Veterans OH 1199.]*

INTERVIEWED BY JOHN TERREO, APRIL 20, 1993, HELENA.

SUMMARY: 2 PAGES

1 TAPE: 40 MINUTES

OH 1457
DAVID SAYRE INTERVIEW

David Sayre (b. 1948) converses on: his experiences as a member of the Montana Army National Guard's 103rd Public Affairs Detachment during Operation Desert Shield/Storm (the Persian Gulf War); the division of the unit into two cells; the 3rd Armored Cavalry Regiment; his duties as a first sergeant; living and working conditions in the Middle East; complementary military issues. *[See also 20th Century Montana Military Veterans OH 1219 and OH 1458.]*

INTERVIEWED BY JOHN TERREO, JUNE 1, 1991, FORT HARRISON.

TRANSCRIPT: 46 PAGES

2 TAPES: 1 HOUR, 25 MINUTES

OH 1458
DAVID SAYRE INTERVIEW

David Sayre (b. 1948) reviews: growing up in Glasgow; joining the U.S. Marine Corps; his experiences with the special Montana Training Platoon; Marine boot camp; his infantry training; his experiences with the 26th Marine Regiment in Vietnam; the Siege of Que Son; U.S. military involvement in Southeast Asia. *[See also 20th Century Montana Military Veterans OH 1219 and OH 1457.]*

INTERVIEWED BY JOHN TERREO, MARCH 3, 1992, GREAT FALLS.

TRANSCRIPT: 36 PAGES

2 TAPES: 2 HOURS

OH 1459
PATRICK MOHAN INTERVIEW

Patrick Mohan (b. 1948) considers: his experiences as a member of the Montana Army National Guard's 103rd Public Affairs Detachment during Operation Desert Shield/Storm (the Persian Gulf War); division of the unit into two cells; his experiences with 3rd Armored Cavalry Regiment; his responsibilities as a cell officer; living and working conditions in the Middle East; his return to Montana after the Persian Gulf crisis. *[See also 20th Century Montana Military Veterans OH 1220.]*

INTERVIEWED BY JOHN TERREO, AUGUST 1991, FORT HARRISON.

TRANSCRIPT: 48 PAGES

2 TAPES: 1 HOUR, 25 MINUTES

OH 1463
KAREENE OSTERMILLER INTERVIEW

Kareene Ostermiller speaks of: her experiences as the only female member of the Montana Army National Guard's 103rd Public Affairs Detachment in Operation Desert Shield/Storm (the Persian Gulf War); women in military service; the different roles played by women in American and Arabian cultures; females as leaders; gender issues; racial and sexual harassment; desert life; daily activities; her return to Montana. *[See also 20th Century Montana Military Veterans OH 1222.]*

INTERVIEWED BY JOHN TERREO, AUGUST 4, 1992, SHEPARD.

TRANSCRIPT: 120 PAGES

5 TAPES: 4 HOURS, 30 MINUTES

OH 1464
TERRANCE YOUNG INTERVIEW

Terrance Young discusses: his experiences as a member of the Montana Army National Guard's 103rd Public Affairs Detachment, assigned to the 18th Airborne Corps Artillery; his refresher training at Fort Lewis, Washington; his arrival in Saudi Arabia; life in the "Cement City," located outside Dhahran, Saudia Arabia; living conditions in the Middle East; his unit's work during Operation Desert Shield/Storm (the Persian Gulf War); technology; his return to Montana. *[See also 20th Century Montana Military Veterans OH 1223.]*

INTERVIEWED BY JOHN TERREO, NOVEMBER 18, 1992, HELENA.

TRANSCRIPT: 44 PAGES

2 TAPES: 1 HOUR, 30 MINUTES

OH 1465
CHARLES "MILO" McLEOD INTERVIEW

Milo McLeod (b. 1947) discusses: his experiences as a member of the Montana Army National Guard's 103rd Public Affairs Detachment during Operation Desert

Shield/Storm (the Persian Gulf War); the unit's division into two cells; the 3rd Armored Cavalry Regiment; living and working conditions in a desert environment; military food, especially MREs (Meals Ready to Eat); working with the civilian media; his readjustment to civilian life. *[See also 20th Century Montana Military Veterans OH 1224.]*
INTERVIEWED BY JOHN TERREO, JUNE 1, 1991, HELENA.
TRANSCRIPT: 38 PAGES
2 TAPES: 1 HOUR, 15 MINUTES

OH 1466
TODD BUHMILLER INTERVIEW

Todd Buhmiller (b. 1963) summarizes his experiences with the Montana Army National Guard's 103rd Public Affairs Detachment in the Middle East during Operation Desert Shield/Storm (the Persian Gulf War). *[See also 20th Century Montana Military Veterans OH 1225.]*
INTERVIEWED BY JOHN TERREO, DECEMBER 11, 1992, HELENA.
4 TAPES: 4 HOURS

OH 1468
GREG FOX INTERVIEW

Greg Fox (b. 1953) chronicles: his work with the Montana Army National Guard's 103rd Public Affairs Detachment in Operation Desert Shield/Storm (the Persian Gulf War); his assignment to the 3rd Armored Cavalry Regiment; his refresher training at Fort Lewis, Washington; the unit's arrival at "Cement City," located outside Dhahran, Saudia Arabia; the unit's division into two cells; attitudes among regular-army personnel regarding military and civilian media; the unit's activities and operations; serving as an escort for the civilian media; desert living conditions; his return to Montana; his general opinions about the conflict. *[See also 20th Century Montana Military Veterans OH 1241.]*
INTERVIEWED BY JOHN TERREO, FEBRUARY 11, 1992, SUPERIOR.
TRANSCRIPT: 34 PAGES
1 TAPE: 1 HOUR, 10 MINUTES

OH 1469
PATRICK HERMANSON INTERVIEW

Patrick Hermanson—a Billings resident—comments on his experiences as the commanding officer of the Montana Army National Guard's 103rd Public Affairs Detachment during Operation Desert Shield/Storm (the Persian Gulf War). *[See also 20th Century Montana Military Veterans OH 1242.]*

INTERVIEWED BY JOHN TERREO, AUGUST 3, 1993, BILLINGS.
TRANSCRIPT: 45 PAGES
2 TAPES: 2 HOURS

OH 1470
JODIE YELTON INTERVIEW

Jodie Yelton (b. 1948) surveys: his experiences as a member of the Montana Army National Guard's 103rd Public Affairs Detachment in Operation Desert Shield/Storm (the Persian Gulf War); the unit's division into two cells; living and working conditions in the desert; his assignment as his cell's first sergeant; the duties and responsibilities of that position; his experiences with the 18th Airborne Corps Artillery; his readjustment to civilian life; his personal opinions concerning the conflict. *[See also 20th Century Montana Military Veterans OH 1243.]*
INTERVIEWED BY JOHN TERREO, JUNE 1991, FORT HARRISON.
TRANSCRIPT: 82 PAGES
3 TAPES: 2 HOURS, 20 MINUTES

OH 1471
ANDY LEE JOHNSON INTERVIEW

Andy Johnson (b. 1948) characterizes: his experiences as a member of the Montana Army National Guard's 103rd Public Affairs Detachment during Operation Desert Shield/Storm (the Persian Gulf War); his unit's arrival at "Cement City," outside Dhahran, Saudia Arabia; serving as a media escort for the Columbia Broadcasting System (CBS) television correspondent Bob Martin; living and working conditions in the desert; military food, especially MREs (Meals Ready to Eat); the role of the military media. *[See also 20th Century Montana Military Veterans OH 1244.]*
INTERVIEWED BY JOHN TERREO, JUNE 1, 1991, FORT HARRISON.
TRANSCRIPT: 32 PAGES
1 TAPE: 1 HOUR

OH 1472
MARY FELDER INTERVIEW

Mary Felder (b. 1918) briefly talks of: her service in the U.S. Navy Hospital Corps; her life at the Montana Veterans Home in Columbia Falls. *[See also 20th Century Montana Military Veterans OH 1250.]*
INTERVIEWED BY KARI NELSON, MAY, 23, 1990, COLUMBIA FALLS.

SUMMARY: 1 PAGE

1 TAPE: 20 MINUTES

OH 1473
JUANITA W. COOKE INTERVIEW

Helena resident Juanita Cooke addresses: her early flying lessons; landing a malfunctioning P-40 fighter plane at the Billings airport; the rules and regulations for military ferry flights; her experiences as a Women's Air Force Service Pilots (WASP) Squadron Commander; difficulties she encountered while flying a B-25 medium bomber and while instrument-flying a C-47 transport plane; aircraft instrument panels; WASP uniforms; de-activation of the WASPs in December 1944; her post–World War II life. *[See also 20th Century Montana Military Veterans OH 1252.]*

INTERVIEWED BY JOHN TERREO, MAY 8, 1991, HELENA.

TRANSCRIPT: 19 PAGES

1 TAPE: 45 MINUTES

OH 1521
FRANK BACKBONE INTERVIEW

Crow tribal member Frank Backbone (b. 1917) discusses: his service with the U.S. Army during World War II; his posting to the 91st Infantry Division; combat near Rome and in the Po Valley, Italy, and at Boulogne, France; being wounded; life after his honorable discharge.

INTERVIEWED BY CARSON WALKS OVER ICE, MARCH 1, 1991, CROW AGENCY.

SUMMARY: 2 PAGES

2 TAPES: 1 HOUR, 17 MINUTES

OH 1522
CHARLES BROWN, JR., INTERVIEW

Charles Brown, Jr. (b. 1921), of Crow Agency describes: his service with the U.S. Army 127th Infantry Division during World War II; his basic training at Fort Ord, California; meeting other Crow Indians while at Fort Ord; fighting the Japanese in New Guinea; being wounded; life after his honorable discharge.

INTERVIEWED BY CARSON WALKS OVER ICE, JUNE 18, 1990, CROW AGENCY.

SUMMARY: 2 PAGES

1 TAPE: 45 MINUTES

OH 1523
BARNEY OLD COYOTE, JR., INTERVIEW

Barney Old Coyote, Jr. (b. 1923), surveys: his service with the U.S. Army Air Force during World War II;

basic training; his assignment, with his brother Henry, to the 48th Bomb Group in Africa; his service with the Royal Navy; sinking a German submarine (U-boat); his duties with the 47th Bomb Group on raids in occupied Europe; his honorable discharge; life after military service.

INTERVIEWED BY CARSON WALKS OVER ICE, MARCH 14, 1991, CROW AGENCY.

SUMMARY: 2 PAGES

2 TAPES: 1 HOUR, 30 MINUTES

OH 1524
HUBERT DAWES, SR., INTERVIEW

Hubert Dawes, Sr. (b. 1928), delineates: his service with the U.S. Navy prior to and during the Korean War; his basic training; service aboard the U.S.S. *Current* (ARS-22) and the U.S.S. *Hitchiti* (ATF-103) off the Korean Coast; patrol missions and salvage missions; his discharge.

INTERVIEWED BY CARSON WALKS OVER ICE, MARCH 28, 1991, CROW AGENCY.

SUMMARY: 1 PAGE

1 TAPE: 40 MINUTES

OH 1525
JOHN W. PEASE, SR., INTERVIEW

Crow tribal member John Pease, Sr. (b. 1924), summarizes: his service with the U.S. Army Air Force during World War II; his basic training; electronics training; his service with the 1309th Army Air Force Unit in India; flying supply missions as a radio operator on various aircraft; life after his military discharge.

INTERVIEWED BY CARSON WALKS OVER ICE, MARCH 27, 1991, CROW AGENCY.

SUMMARY: 2 PAGES

1 TAPE: 55 MINUTES

OH 1526
FRANK IRON, SR., INTERVIEW

Frank Iron, Sr. (b. 1917)—a resident of Crow Agency—depicts: his duties with the Oklahoma National Guard prior to World War II; his posting to, and service with, the U.S. Army 158th Infantry Division; his combat experiences in the South Pacific and in the Philippine Islands; being wounded; life after his military discharge.

INTERVIEWED BY CARSON WALKS OVER ICE, MARCH 29, 1991, CROW AGENCY.

SUMMARY: 1 PAGE

1 TAPE: 35 MINUTES

OH 1527
GILBERT W. SCOTT, JR., INTERVIEW
Gilbert Scott, Jr. (b. 1937), recalls: his enlistment in the U.S. Marine Corps; basic training; his service with the 9th Marine Division in Japan; his assignments aboard various ships; life after his military discharge from the Marines.
INTERVIEWED BY CARSON WALKS OVER ICE, MARCH 29, 1991, CROW AGENCY.
SUMMARY: 2 PAGES
1 TAPE: 35 MINUTES

OH 1528
ISAAC SHANE, SR., INTERVIEW
Crow tribesman Isaac Shane, Sr. (b. 1921), considers: his service with the U.S. Army during World War II; his postings to various military units; assignments in the Pacific theater; his spinal injury; life after his military discharge.
INTERVIEWED BY CARSON WALKS OVER ICE, MARCH 28, 1991, CROW AGENCY.
SUMMARY: 2 PAGES
1 TAPE: 35 MINUTES

OH 1529
WILLIAM MEDICINE TAIL INTERVIEW
William Medicine Tail (b. 1932) relates: his assignments with the U.S. Navy during the Korean War; service aboard the destroyers U.S.S. *Bausell* and U.S.S. *Anderson* as a gunner; life after his military discharge.
INTERVIEWED BY CARSON WALKS OVER ICE, MARCH 29, 1991, CROW AGENCY.
SUMMARY: 1 PAGE
1 TAPE: 35 MINUTES

OH 1530
FREDERICK TURNS BACK INTERVIEW
Crow Agency resident Frederick Turns Back treats: his service with the U.S. Army; basic training; his duties with the 40th Infantry Division and with the 24th Signal Company in Korea; his return to the United States on rotation; his military discharge.
INTERVIEWED BY CARSON WALKS OVER ICE, MARCH 1, 1991, CROW AGENCY.
SUMMARY: 1 PAGE
1 TAPE: 50 MINUTES

OH 1531
GEORGE PEASE INTERVIEW
George Pease (b. 1898) briefly examines: his military service with the U.S. Navy; duty aboard the U.S.S. *Minneapolis* and other ships; the Brooklyn Naval Yard, New York; life after his military discharge.
INTERVIEWED BY CARSON WALKS OVER ICE, JUNE 5, 1990, CROW AGENCY.
SUMMARY: 1 PAGE
1 TAPE: 11 MINUTES

OH 1532
DAVID J. STEWART INTERVIEW
David Stewart (b. 1929), of Crow Agency comments on: his service with U.S. Army during the Korean War; specific training; his assignment to the 955th Field Artillery Battalion; his participation in major battles; life after his military discharge.
INTERVIEWED BY CARSON WALKS OVER ICE, JUNE 12, 1990, CROW AGENCY.
SUMMARY: 1 PAGE

OH 1533
COLLENA L. CAPLETT INTERVIEW
Collena Caplett (b. 1952) speaks of: her service in the U.S. Army; basic training; file-clerk training; her duty assignments; life after her military discharge.
INTERVIEWED BY CARSON WALKS OVER ICE, JUNE 27, 1990, CROW AGENCY.
SUMMARY: 2 PAGES
1 TAPE: 1 HOUR

OH 1534
CHRISTINE STOPS HILL INTERVIEW
Christine Stops Hill (b. 1957) addresses: her reasons for enlisting in the U.S. Air Force; her basic training; special training; her duties with the 321st Security Police Squadron as a security specialist; her military discharge; her subsequent work in law enforcement; difficulties in working with men.
INTERVIEWED BY CARSON WALKS OVER ICE, MARCH 26, 1991, CROW AGENCY.
SUMMARY: 2 PAGES

OH 1535
JOHN BULLTAIL INTERVIEW
Crow tribesman John Bulltail (b. 1922) relates: the reasons he was not accepted into the military service during World War II; his acceptance into the U.S. Army in 1951; basic training; his military-police training; duties with the 45th Infantry Division during Korean War; his combat experiences; being wounded on Bloody Ridge in Korea; his recovery; service with 123rd Infantry Di-

vision; his military discharge. *[See also New Deal in Montana OH 1165.]*

INTERVIEWED BY CARSON WALKS OVER ICE, OCTOBER 26, 1990, CROW AGENCY.

SUMMARY: 2 PAGES

OH 1564
ROY CALDWELL INTERVIEW

Roy Caldwell (b. 1953) treats: his experiences as a member of the Montana Army National Guard's 103rd Public Affairs Detachment during Operation Desert Shield/Storm (the Persian Gulf War); refresher training and last-minute preparations at Fort Lewis, Washington; his unit's flight to Saudi Arabia and arrival at Dhahran; a temporary stay at "Cement City," outside Dhahran; serving as a media escort for the Columbia Broadcasting System (CBS) television correspondent Bob Martin, the Detroit *Free Press* reporter Frank Bruni, and the Washington *Post* photographer Lucian Perkins; attitudes of regular-army personnel toward the civilian and military news media; his unit's activities; living conditions; equipment acquisitions; changing morale of the unit; MREs (Meals Ready to Eat); equipment acquisitions; opinions concerning the 3rd Armored Cavalry Regiment's troops and its officers; the theoretical and the actual functioning of the military's Joint Information Bureau (JIB); the nature of the air war; the ground war; future concerns for military media. *[See also 20th Century Montana Military Veterans OH 1221 and OH 1565-66.]*

INTERVIEWED BY JOHN TERREO, JUNE 24, 1991, HELENA.

TRANSCRIPT: 47 PAGES

2 TAPES: 1 HOUR, 50 MINUTES

OH 1565
ROY CALDWELL INTERVIEW

Helena resident Roy Caldwell (b. 1953) briefly tells about: the 103rd Public Affairs Detachment's drill weekend that immediately followed the Iraqi invasion of Kuwait (August 2, 1990); views disclosed upon the first anniversary of the invasion. *[See also 20th Century Montana Military Veterans OH 1221, OH 1564, and OH 1566.]*

INTERVIEWED BY JOHN TERREO, AUGUST 2, 1991, HELENA.

TRANSCRIPT: 13 PAGES

1 TAPE: 30 MINUTES

OH 1566
ROY CALDWELL INTERVIEW

Roy Caldwell (b. 1953) examines: his experiences as a member of the Montana Army National Guard's 103rd Public Affairs Detachment, attached to the 3rd Armored

Cavalry Regiment; the attitudes of regular-army personnel toward civilian and military media; escorting civilian media; obtaining transportation supplies; military suppression of the civilian media; restrictions imposed by the Saudi Arabian government. *[See also 20th Century Montana Military Veterans OH 1221 and OH 1564-65.]*

INTERVIEWED BY JOHN TERREO, MARCH 18, 1992, HELENA.

TRANSCRIPT: 45 PAGES

2 TAPES: 2 HOURS

OH 1587
MICHAEL FITZPATRICK INTERVIEW

Crow Indian Reservation resident Michael Fitzpatrick (b. 1911) discusses: his service with the U.S. Army during World War II; his posting to the 66th Quartermaster Regiment, which remained stateside; his hip injury; life after his military discharge.

INTERVIEWED BY CARSON WALKS OVER ICE, FEBRUARY 28, 1991, CROW AGENCY.

SUMMARY: 1 PAGE

1 TAPE: 35 MINUTES

OH 1599
RON DAVIS INTERVIEW

Ron Davis (b. 1947) discusses: being drafted into the U.S. Army during the Vietnam War; basic training at Fort Lewis, Washington; his Advanced Infantry Training in jungle warfare; stateside instruction programs; his views concerning soldiers on both sides of the Vietnam War; U.S. goals in Southeast Asia; morale; politics on the home front; lingering effects of the Vietnam War; stereotypes of Vietnam veterans; "the Wall"; his work as a Disabled American Veterans (DAV) representative.

INTERVIEWED BY AMY MCKINNEY, SEPTEMBER 29, 1994, HELENA.

2 TAPES: 1 HOUR, 20 MINUTES

OH 1644
CHRISTIAN HANSEN INTERVIEW

Christian Hansen describes: his experiences with the Montana National Guard, as a reservist in Sidney and with the 163rd Infantry during World War II; his childhood in Sidney; the 1930s Depression; early training in Sidney (two hours once a week in the American Legion Hall); Fort Lewis training; activation and going overseas; returning home.

INTERVIEWED BY JODIE FOLEY, SEPTEMBER 9, 1995, BOZEMAN.
1 TAPE: 45 MINUTES

OH 1645
PAUL E. TIMM INTERVIEW

Paul Timm portrays: his experiences with the Montana National Guard, as a reservist in Glendive and with the 163rd Infantry during World War II; the day his unit was activated; anecdotes about training and service; Fort Peck work; Fort Lewis training; going overseas; his military career.
INTERVIEWED BY JODIE FOLEY, SEPTEMBER 9, 1995, BOZEMAN.
1 TAPE: 55 MINUTES

OH 1646
HAROLD "DOC" SHAMLEY INTERVIEW

Doc Shamley discusses: his experiences with the Montana National Guard, as a reservist in Wolf Point and with the 163rd during World War II; entering the guard in high school to help the family; CCC work; Fort Lewis training; activation and going overseas; returning home.
INTERVIEWED BY JODIE FOLEY, SEPTEMBER 9, 1995, BOZEMAN.
1 TAPE: 40 MINUTES

OH 1647
ADAM PETROVICH INTERVIEW

Adam Petrovich discusses: his experiences with the 163rd Infantry during World War II; being drafted into service from Michigan; preparing the Queen Elizabeth II for war duty; his work with B Company (primarily comprised of Sioux Indians); going overseas to Australia; overall service experience; returning home.
INTERVIEWED BY JODIE FOLEY, SEPTEMBER 9, 1995, BOZEMAN.
1 TAPE: 45 MINUTES

OH 1648
HOWARD McKINNEY INTERVIEW

Howard McKinney describes: his experiences with the National Guard in Culbertson as a high school student and with the 163rd Infantry during World War II; growing up in Lanark; life during the 1930s Depression; training in the Legion Hall in Culbertson; Fort Lewis training; going overseas; his family's activities during the war; returning home.
INTERVIEWED BY JODIE FOLEY, SEPTEMBER 9, 1995,

BOZEMAN.
1 TAPE: 45 MINUTES

OH 1649
ROBERT PARKER INTERVIEW

Robert Parker discusses: his experiences with the National Guard in Iowa; being inducted into the 163rd Infantry during World War II; basic training; transfer to Fort Ord, California; going overseas; occupation of Japan; returning home; veteran's organizations.
INTERVIEWED BY JODIE FOLEY, SEPTEMBER 9, 1995, BOZEMAN.
1 TAPE: 30 MINUTES

OH 1650
OTTO DAEMS INTERVIEW

Otto Daems describes: his experiences with the Montana National Guard as a reservist in Bozeman and with the 163rd Infantry during World War II; his family's early history in Alder Gulch with the vigilantes; getting into the National Guard in Butte as a high school student; the 1930s Depression; feelings at being activated in 1940; training at Fort Lewis; going overseas; army service after World War II; feelings about the 163rd association.
INTERVIEWED BY JODIE FOLEY, SEPTEMBER 9, 1995, BOZEMAN.
1 TAPE: 30 MINUTES

Women as Community Builders Oral History Project

A group of Montana women historians conducted interviews discussing the development and impact of women's organizations in Montana. Women's groups often established a community's first library, school, museum, symphony, or recreational park, so their stories are of vital interest to anyone studying the development of a given town. Interviewees discuss the importance of lodges, church groups, professional associations, and ethnic clubs in fostering women's involvement in community building. They also discuss the reasons groups flourished at certain times and floundered at others; the differences among autonomous, auxiliary, and coed organizations; and specific goals, issues, and projects tackled by various women's groups.

OH 1001
MARIAN SCHAPIRO CANAVAN INTERVIEW

Butte resident Marian Canavan (b. 1905) discusses: the history of the community's Marian White Arts and Craft Club, organized in 1905; her 40-year membership in the club; the Westside Shakespeare Club; the Toastmistress Club; other social activities in Butte from 1927 to 1987.
INTERVIEWED BY MARY MURPHY, MAY 20, 1987, BUTTE.
TRANSCRIPT: 32 PAGES
1 TAPE: 1 HOUR

OH 1002
GWEN MITCHELL INTERVIEW

Gwen Mitchell (b. 1909) discusses: growing up in Butte, circa 1910–1930; her 44 years as a teacher at Franklin Elementary School and at East Junior High in Butte; after-school and social activities; her duties in the Butte Business and Professional Women's Club; her involvement in other civic organizations.
INTERVIEWED BY MARY MURPHY, MAY 24, 1987, BUTTE.
SUMMARY: 11 PAGES
2 TAPES: 1 HOUR, 30 MINUTES

OH 1003
SHEILA CONNORS INTERVIEW

Sheila Connors discusses: her childhood in Chicago, Illinois; her involvement in several volunteer organizations; her relocation to Montana in 1983; her work as the executive director of the Young Women's Christian

Association (YWCA) in Great Falls; issues confronting the YWCA; concerns of young women during the 1970s and 1980s; the Women's Lobbyist Fund.
INTERVIEWED BY DIANE SANDS, MAY 20, 1987, GREAT FALLS.
SUMMARY: 12 PAGES
2 TAPES: 1 HOUR, 35 MINUTES

OH 1004
GERRY JENNINGS INTERVIEW

Gerry Jennings (b. 1941) talks of: her move from New York state to Great Falls in 1975; her work experiences; her involvement with the Junior League in Great Falls; her service with the YWCA from 1976 to 1987.
INTERVIEWED BY DIANE SANDS, MAY 20, 1987, GREAT FALLS.
SUMMARY: 11 PAGES
2 TAPES: 1 HOUR, 55 MINUTES

OH 1005
PAULA PETRIK AND KATHY A. VAN HOOK INTERVIEW

Paula Petrik and Kathy Van Hook examine: their involvement in the Women's Lobbyist Fund; the Montana Alliance for Progressive Policy; the Montana Committee for an Effective Legislature (MontCEL); issues constituting the feminist movement.
INTERVIEWED BY DIANE SANDS, NOVEMBER 7, 1987, HELENA.

SUMMARY: 8 PAGES
2 TAPES: 1 HOUR, 30 MINUTES

OH 1006
VIVIAN BROOKE INTERVIEW

Vivian Brooke—a resident of Missoula—discusses: her childhood; her membership in Girl Scouts and other youth groups; her college education; church activities; the church nursery; religion and the role of women in society; community work; the Catholic Church; her involvement with the League of Women Voters of Montana (LWV).

INTERVIEWED BY DIANE SANDS, MAY 4, 1987, MISSOULA.
SUMMARY: 5 PAGES
2 TAPES: 2 HOURS, 5 MINUTES

OH 1007
MARGARET LAUGHLIN KELLY INTERVIEW

Margaret Kelly discourses on: her involvement in the Anaconda Veterans of Foreign Wars (VFW) Auxiliary; her membership in the Isabellas and other community organizations; local social activities; her Irish ethnic background.

INTERVIEWED BY ALICE FINNEGAN, JULY 7, 1987, ANACONDA.
SUMMARY: 5 PAGES
2 TAPES: 1 HOUR, 50 MINUTES

OH 1008
MILDRED GOLLICK INTERVIEW

Mildred Gollick (b. 1903) describes: her parents; growing up in England; immigrating to Montana in 1917; her nursing training at St. James Hospital in Butte; her employment at St. Ann's Hospital in Anaconda; her work as a private-duty nurse; her membership in the Order of the Eastern Star; her involvement in other organizations; her retirement.

INTERVIEWED BY ALICE FINNEGAN, JULY 3, 1987, ANACONDA.
SUMMARY: 5 PAGES
3 TAPES: 2 HOURS, 15 MINUTES

OH 1009
ALICE SHEPKA INTERVIEW

Alice Shepka (b. 1925) talks of: her early family life in Deer Lodge; her education at schools and colleges in Anaconda and Butte; her mother's civic and volunteer activities; her involvement in the (National Youth Administration) NYA; labor unions; her volunteer activities.

INTERVIEWED BY ALICE FINNEGAN, JUNE 17, 1987, ANACONDA.
SUMMARY: 12 PAGES
2 TAPES: 2 HOURS

OH 1010
ALENE STONER INTERVIEW

Alene Stoner (b. 1938) describes: her family; her childhood and adolescence in Great Falls; marriage and raising a family; her volunteer work with the Girl Scouts, with the Rainbow Girls, and with other youth groups; the Montana Extension Homemakers Clubs; the West Helena Valley Volunteer Fire Department.

INTERVIEWED BY LAURIE MERCIER, JULY 23, 1987, HELENA.
SUMMARY: 14 PAGES
2 TAPES: 2 HOURS

OH 1011
SHERRY WULF INTERVIEW

Kalispell resident Sherry Wulf (b. 1949) discusses: her parents; her early life in the Flathead Valley; her volunteer activities in college; her involvement with various Kalispell community organizations, including the Kalispell Women's Center, the local Human Resources Development Council, the United Way, and the Child Abuse Prevention Council; the differences between women volunteers and men volunteers.

INTERVIEWED BY DIANE SANDS, JUNE 10, 1987, KALISPELL.
SUMMARY: 10 PAGES
2 TAPES: 1 HOUR, 45 MINUTES

OH 1012
KATHERINE G. McDONNELL INTERVIEW

Katherine McDonnell (b. 1896) talks of: her youth in Anaconda; her parents' backgrounds; her family life; her education at the University of Wisconsin; her experiences in journalism; her employment as a schoolteacher; community work; the Federation of Women's Clubs; religion; the Equal Rights Amendment (ERA); her travels in pre–World War I Africa; marriage; child-rearing; the 1930s Depression; the Republican Party; the National Organization for Women (NOW); the American Association of University Women (AAUW); personal perceptions of women and men; discrimination against women in employment situations.

INTERVIEWED BY DIANE SANDS, JUNE 9, 1987, SOMERS.
SUMMARY: 15 PAGES
2 TAPES: 1 HOUR, 50 MINUTES

OH 1013
MARY GIBSON INTERVIEW

Mary Gibson (b. 1931) delineates: her childhood and family background; work as a camp counselor in Colorado during the 1940s; her college education; marriage; child-rearing; her involvement with the AAUW chapter in Kalispell from the 1960s to the 1980s; other volunteer organizations.

INTERVIEWED BY DIANE SANDS, JUNE 9, 1987, KALISPELL.
SUMMARY: 15 PAGES
2 TAPES: 2 HOURS

OH 1014
GEORGIA MALLAS INTERVIEW

Georgia Mallas converses on: her Greek-immigrant parents; growing up in Great Falls; the role and influence of the Greek Orthodox Church; her involvement in church affairs; her experiences as a choir director; cultural and ethnic aspects of a close-knit Greek community; her membership in the Daughters of Penelope; extended-family life; her long-term employment with an insurance company.

INTERVIEWED BY DIANE SANDS, AUGUST 5, 1987, GREAT FALLS.
SUMMARY: 10 PAGES
2 TAPES: 2 HOURS

OH 1015
ALICE FINNEGAN INTERVIEW

Alice Finnegan (b. 1940) talks about: her family; life in Anaconda; her religious views; the Catholic Church; Catholic politics and administration; Anaconda's Catholic community; Bishop Raymond Hunthausen and other clergy members; the field of historic preservation; Anaconda's Chinese community; labor unions; local economic development efforts; the local historical society.

INTERVIEWED BY LAURIE MERCIER, AUGUST 13, 1987, ANACONDA.
TRANSCRIPT: 142 PAGES
4 TAPES: 4 HOURS, 30 MINUTES

OH 1016
SISTER KATHLEEN O'SULLIVAN

Sister Kathleen O'Sullivan considers: her parents' emigration from Ireland to the United States; the Catholic Church; the Sisters of Charity of the Blessed Virgin Mary; her relocation to Butte; her activities with the Butte Community Union; teaching.

INTERVIEWED BY LAURIE MERCIER, AUGUST 13, 1987, BUTTE.

SUMMARY: 5 PAGES
2 TAPES: 1 HOUR, 40 MINUTES

OH 1017
LULA MARTINEZ INTERVIEW

Lula Martinez (b. 1922) comments on: her childhood; her early family life in Butte; education; her involvement with migrant workers in Oregon and Idaho; her work in health clinics in Idaho; Hispanic traditions; her volunteer activities with the Butte Community Union and with other groups; her personal outlook on life and volunteer work.

INTERVIEWED BY LAURIE MERCIER, SEPTEMBER 1987, PORTLAND, OR.
TRANSCRIPT: 53 PAGES
2 TAPES: 1 HOUR, 35 MINUTES

OH 1018
MARY SMITH INTERVIEW

Anaconda resident Mary Smith reviews: her involvement in the community; the Rotana Club; the community hospital; the Elks Does; the Daughters of Isabella.

INTERVIEWED BY ALICE FINNEGAN, AUGUST 6, 1987, ANACONDA.
2 TAPES: 1 HOUR, 40 MINUTES

OH 1019
PHYLLIS LEWIS INTERVIEW

Phyllis Lewis—a Belgrade resident—discusses: her work as Gallatin County extension homemaker; her involvement in local volunteer groups; her service to the Belgrade Public Library.

INTERVIEWED BY DIANE SANDS, JULY 27, 1987, BELGRADE.
2 TAPES: 1 HOUR, 50 MINUTES

OH 1020
GLADYS GORMAN INTERVIEW

Gladys Gorman chronicles: her 24-year service as an administrative aide for the Montana State University nursing program in Bozeman; her views on women.

INTERVIEWED BY DIANE SANDS, JULY 28, 1987, BOZEMAN.
2 TAPES: 2 HOURS

OH 1021
NORMA HOUSON INTERVIEW

Big Timber resident Norma Houson discusses: her involvement in the Montana CowBelles organization from 1961 to 1986; her service in the Montana Farm Bureau from 1962 to 1976; her participation in the local Lutheran Church; her interest in mental-health care programs; her reception of the Jefferson Award for Outstanding Public Service.

INTERVIEWED BY DIANE SANDS, JULY 28, 1987, MISSOULA.

2 TAPES: 1 HOUR, 50 MINUTES

OH 1022
JUDY HELIN MATHRE INTERVIEW

Judy Mathre (b. 1937), a resident of Bozeman, addresses: her childhood in Oklahoma City, Oklahoma; her parents' Presbyterian Church activities; her community service while in a college sorority; the AAUW; her work as the Hunger Action Enabler for the Yellowstone Presbyter; her membership in the LWV; the United Presbyterian Women; Bozeman politics; her campaign and election as mayor of Bozeman in 1979; her duties as mayor; the Bozeman Public Library; the Retired Seniors Volunteer Program (RSVP); relations between the city of Bozeman and Montana State University; volunteerism; state politics; feminism.

INTERVIEWED BY DIANE SANDS, JULY 28, 1987, BOZEMAN.

SUMMARY: 13 PAGES

2 TAPES: 1 HOUR, 45 MINUTES

OH 1023
KATHLEEN QUAM INTERVIEW

Frazer resident Kathleen Quam treats: her early days in the Lutheran Church; intercultural relations within white and Indian communities; her work as a supporter and pianist for the Dakota Indian Presbyterian Church in Frazer; her employment as a substitute teacher; tutoring a paralyzed Indian student, Mitchell Todd.

INTERVIEWED BY DIANE SANDS, AUGUST 2, 1987, MISSOULA.

1 TAPE: 55 MINUTES

OH 1024
FRANCES "SCOTTIE" BYERLY INTERVIEW

Scottie Byerly of Lewistown surveys: her relocation to Lewistown from North Carolina in 1971; her membership on the Central Montana Hospital Board; difficulties in recruiting health care professionals to the area; issues surrounding the construction of a new hospital; her volunteer work. [See also Helena Business History OH 1335.]

INTERVIEWED BY DIANE SANDS, AUGUST 4, 1987, LEWISTOWN.

SUMMARY: 6 PAGES

1 TAPE: 1 HOUR

OH 1025
SHEILA RICE INTERVIEW

Sheila Rice (b. 1947) summarizes: her work as a program planner for Community Coordinated Childcare in Great Falls; her duties as vice-president of marketing for the Great Falls Gas Company; her volunteer work for various social-service agencies, including the Great Falls Children's Receiving Home, the Junior League, the Human Resources Development Council, the Community Action Program, and the United Way; fund-raising; women in the work force.

INTERVIEWED BY DIANE SANDS, AUGUST 5, 1987, GREAT FALLS.

SUMMARY: 17 PAGES

2 TAPES: 1 HOUR, 55 MINUTES

OH 1026
JEANICE FEE INTERVIEW

Jeanice Fee—a Fairfield resident—speaks of: her work as state director of the Junior Women's League; her service as a 4-H leader; her involvement with the Lutheran Church Women.

INTERVIEWED BY DIANE SANDS, AUGUST 5, 1987, MISSOULA.

1 TAPE: 1 HOUR

OH 1027
ESTHER MACE STAHL INTERVIEW

Esther Stahl (b. circa 1900) discusses: her life in Great Falls; her work as a high school and college speech, English, Latin, and physical education teacher; her involvement with the AAUW.

INTERVIEWED BY DIANE SANDS, AUGUST 1987, GREAT FALLS.

2 TAPES: 2 HOURS

OH 1028
BERNICE KNIERNIM INTERVIEW

Bernice Kniernim (b. 1910) remembers: her childhood in Butte; earning her teacher's certification at Western Montana College in Dillon; teaching school in Glasgow during the 1930s; drought; construction of the Fort Peck Dam; the 1930s Depression; the measles epidemic of the mid-1930s; business and social activities in Glasgow; her marriage and family life; her volunteer activities with St. Matthew's Episcopal Church in Glasgow; her involvement with the local hospital guild from 1936 to 1987; changing attitudes about volunteerism.

Interviewed by Diane Sands, August 5, 1987,
Missoula.
Summary: 10 pages
2 tapes: 2 hours

OH 1029
PHYLLIS BAIRD INTERVIEW

Lewistown resident Phyllis Baird reports on: her association with the Zion Lutheran Church; her involvement with the local Parent-Teachers Association (PTA); her membership in the rural Health-Home Demonstration Club from the age of 19; the local Soroptimists.
Interviewed by Diane Sands, August 4, 1987,
Missoula.
2 tapes: 1 hour, 45 minutes

OH 1030
JO ANN FORSNESS INTERVIEW

Jo Ann Forsness—a resident of Wolf Point—reflects on: her membership in Women Involved in Farm Economics (WIFE); her volunteer work at the Faith Lutheran Retirement Home in Wolf Point; her experiences as a longtime farmer/rancher; her involvement with the Roosevelt County Historical Society.
Interviewed by Diane Sands, August 2, 1987,
Missoula.
Summary: 6 pages
2 tapes: 2 hours

OH 1031
MARGE STERNHAGEN ULRICH INTERVIEW

Marge Ulrich (b. 1920) relates: her experiences in women's clubs in Hamilton, Bridger, and Lewistown; her involvement with the AAUW; the General Federation of Women's Clubs; specific women's issues.
Interviewed by Diane Sands, August 5, 1987,
Lewistown.
Summary: 8 pages
2 tapes: 1 hour, 20 minutes

OH 1032
JESSE UDIN INTERVIEW

Fairfield resident Jesse Udin talks about: her relocation to Fairfield in 1939; her work with the local senior citizens drop-in center since 1972; her participation in the Teton County Council on Aging; her involvement in the local Lutheran Church; her acceptance of the Senior Citizen Auxiliary Award; her volunteer work with the American Cancer Society.

Interviewed by Diane Sands, August 6, 1987,
Fairfield.
1 tape: 50 minutes

OH 1033
FLORENCE BALDWIN INTERVIEW

Florence Baldwin—a resident of Stevensville—recalls: her membership in the Stevensville Women's Club; activities of the Stevensville Garden Club; her terms on the Stevensville library board; her involvement with the local Methodist Church; her life as a retired teacher.
Interviewed by Diane Sands, August 29, 1987,
Stevensville.
2 tapes: 1 hour, 50 minutes

OH 1034
LILLIAN FELLOWS KIRKEMO INTERVIEW

Lillian Kirkemo portrays: her family's move from South Dakota to Montana; following mining employment to Butte, to Deer Lodge, and then into Idaho; her church activities in Plains, including temperance work; politics and social activities in western Montana; her work with the Red Cross in Montana.
Interviewed by Diane Sands, August 31, 1987,
Missoula.
3 tapes: 2 hours, 20 minutes

OH 1035
MARY JO HOPWOOD INTERVIEW

Mary Jo Hopwood discusses: her military service in the WAVES from 1943 to 1946; her relocation to Darby in 1955; her membership in the local American Legion and in the American Legion Auxiliary; her participation in the Darby Women's Club; activities of the local museum and the public library; her involvement in the Darby Garden Club; her work with the community's PTA; her views on volunteerism; different perceptions of volunteerism by men and by women.
Interviewed by Diane Sands, September 4, 1987,
Darby.
Summary: 11 pages
2 tapes: 1 hour, 55 minutes

OH 1036
HARRIETT C. MELOY INTERVIEW

Harriett Meloy (b. 1916) addresses: her childhood in Inkster, Pennsylvania; moving to Helena; her father's work with Intermountain College in Helena; the 1930s Depression; her life in Helena; her involvement in local organizations, including the Helena Women's Club, the

AAUW, the LWV, and the Helena PTA; her membership on the State Board of Education; McCarthyism; women's issues; the Equal Rights Amendment; her employment at the Montana Historical Society; the Helena school superintendent C. R. Anderson. [See also General Montana OH 24.]
INTERVIEWED BY LAURIE MERCIER, SEPTEMBER 15, 1987, HELENA.
TRANSCRIPT: 51 PAGES
2 TAPES: 1 HOUR, 45 MINUTES

OH 1037
GEORGIA WHIPPS INTERVIEW

Georgia Whipps (b. 1885) tells about: her early life in Montana; the formation of the Helena chapter of the AAUW; Belle Winestine; Dorothy Atwater.
INTERVIEWED BY LAURIE MERCIER, SUE NEAR, AND MARGE MERRILL, DECEMBER 10, 1986, HELENA.
TRANSCRIPT: 25 PAGES
1 TAPE: 45 MINUTES

OH 1038
NORMA PILLING GRONFEIN INTERVIEW

Butte resident Norma Gronfein (b. 1922) talks of: her involvement in local civic and volunteer organizations, including the AAUW, the Homer Club, the Campfire Girls, B'Nai Israel, the Butte Garden Club, the Butte Bridge Club, the PTA, and the Young Men's Christian Association (YMCA); issues related to volunteerism.
INTERVIEWED BY MARY MURPHY, OCTOBER 9, 1987, BUTTE.
TRANSCRIPT: 56 PAGES
2 TAPES: 1 HOUR, 40 MINUTES

OH 1039
MARJORIE KNOYLE DUNSTAN INTERVIEW

Marjorie Dunstan (b. 1924)—a Butte resident—surveys: her membership in the Daughters of Norway; her work developing the Daughters' scholarship fund; her participation in the Eastern Star chapter; her involvement in the Butte Toastmistress Club; the social aspects of different organizations.
INTERVIEWED BY MARY MURPHY, OCTOBER 2, 1987, BUTTE.
2 TAPES: 2 HOURS

OH 1040
MILLICENT INEZ HODGE SHIFTY INTERVIEW

Butte resident Millicent Shifty (b. 1913) comments on: her 1923 trip from her native England to Butte; Butte's Cornish community; Mountain View Methodist Church and other community churches; working at the telephone company cafeteria; food; the Rocky Mountain Garden Council; the Webster-Garfield Garden Club; the Sons of Saint George; the Marian White Arts and Crafts Club.
INTERVIEWED BY MARY MURPHY, OCTOBER 14, 1987, BUTTE.
TRANSCRIPT: 41 PAGES
2 TAPES: 2 HOURS

OH 1041
AILEEN DAVIS INTERVIEW

Butte resident Aileen Davis (b. 1906) discusses: growing up in Butte; her education at Western Montana College in Dillon; her life in Butte as a retired schoolteacher; her involvement in the Butte Orchestra Guild; her volunteer activities at the World Museum of Mining in Butte.
INTERVIEWED BY MARY MURPHY, NOVEMBER 11, 1987, BUTTE.
2 TAPES: 1 HOUR, 45 MINUTES

OH 1042
MARY TRBOVICH INTERVIEW

Mary Trbovich (b. 1912) discusses: her early childhood; her relocation to Butte; family life; her involvement in Serbian organizations and church groups; comparative characteristics of the community's ethnic groups; the impact of religion on her and on the Butte community; her work with senior citizens.
INTERVIEWED BY MARY MURPHY, NOVEMBER 4, 1987, BUTTE.
SUMMARY: 10 PAGES
2 TAPES: 1 HOUR, 40 MINUTES

OH 1043
ELSIE FOX INTERVIEW

Elsie Fox—a resident of Miles City—discusses: growing up in the Powder River Valley; the 1920s and 1930s depression; her relocations throughout the West; her retirement in 1972; her activities on the Montana Senior Citizens Association Board of Directors;
INTERVIEWED BY MARY MURPHY, OCTOBER 10, 1987, MILES CITY.
2 TAPES: 2 HOURS

OH 1044
LENA SLAUSEN INTERVIEW

Miles City resident Lena Slausen (b. 1917) assesses: African-American life in Butte; discrimination; her in-

volvement in the Butte Women's Club; her membership in the Pearl Club.
INTERVIEWED BY MARY MURPHY, DECEMBER 2, 1987, MILES CITY.
2 TAPES: 1 HOUR, 35 MINUTES

OH 1045
VIRGINIA WALTON INTERVIEW

Helena resident Virginia Walton (1908–1992) describes: her experiences as a librarian in Columbus; her work at the Montana Historical Society from 1953 to 1959; various library positions she held outside of Montana during the 1960s and the 1970s; her return to Helena; her retirement; her involvement in the Helena chapter of the AAUW; activities of the local Audubon Society.
[See also General Montana OH 624.]
INTERVIEWED BY LAURIE MERCIER, FEBRUARY 23, 1988, HELENA.
TRANSCRIPT: 47 PAGES
2 TAPES: 1 HOUR, 30 MINUTES

OH 1545
MOLDERS AND SHAPERS: MONTANA WOMEN AS COMMUNITY BUILDERS CONFERENCE

The Molders and Shapers Conference convened in Helena in 1987. It focused on: the impact of Montana women and of other western women on the development of western communities; institutions founded by women; the role of women as agents of change; the special roles of club women, ethnic women, and church women.
PRESENTATIONS AND DISCUSSIONS TAPED NOVEMBER 13-14, 1987, HELENA.
SUMMARY: 3 PAGES
15 TAPES: 14 HOURS

Non-Project Collections

General Montana History Collection

This section consists of oral histories and historic recordings that were conducted outside the parameters of a specific project or that were donated to the Montana Historical Society by other institutions or individuals. The interviewers include Montana Historical Society staff, professional historians, genealogists, and history buffs. The interviews range in scope from life histories to community histories, from one tape to thirty. Historic recordings include speeches, conference proceedings, and musical performances. The common theme is life in Montana and the West.

OH 1
OLE BERGE INTERVIEW

Ole Berge—a logger, sawyer, and lumber worker in the Hamilton area of the Bitterroot Valley—addresses: logging practices; logging-camp life; labor conditions; Industrial Workers of the World (IWW) activities; mill development in Ravalli County from 1919 to 1949.
INTERVIEWED BY AN UNIDENTIFIED MONTANA HISTORICAL SOCIETY STAFF MEMBER, JANUARY 20, 1970, HAMILTON.
2 TAPES: 1 HOUR, 10 MINUTES

OH 2
CHAMP HANNON INTERVIEW

A retired U.S. Forest Service employee, Champ Hannon (b. 1899) talks of the arrival of his father, Thomas Benton Hannon, to the Bitterroot River Valley during the 1800s; early forestry methods; the development of Ravalli County mills; trends in the logging industry; conservation practices.
INTERVIEWED BY JOHN R. COLEMAN, JANUARY 21, 1970, HELENA.
TRANSCRIPT: 12 PAGES
1 TAPE: 50 MINUTES

OH 3
EDWARD MacKAY INTERVIEW

Edward MacKay (b. 1893) reports on: his career as a U.S. Forest Service ranger in the Bitterroot Valley, Ravalli County; railroad and mill development in the area; logging practices; conservation; timber management from 1903 to 1970.

INTERVIEWED BY JOHN R. COLEMAN, JANUARY 21, 1970, HELENA.
1 TAPE: 50 MINUTES

OH 4
CHARLES HASKIN McDONALD INTERVIEW

Charles McDonald (b. 1900) comments on: his career as a U.S. Forest Service ranger in Utah, Idaho, and Montana from 1919 to the early 1960s; forestry practices; conservation; wilderness areas; the traits of Montana loggers; the Montana Study (1944–1946); the lumberman Lee Bass; the history of the Stevensville community.
INTERVIEWED BY JOHN R. COLEMAN, JANUARY 22, 1970, HELENA.
1 TAPE: 50 MINUTES

OH 5
GURNIE MAVER MOSS INTERVIEW

Gurnie Moss (b. 1884) addresses: his careers as a Montana legislator, educator, and publisher of the Whitefish *Pilot* newspaper; life in Whitefish, Ravalli County; his editorial philosophy.
INTERVIEWED BY SAM GILLULY, MAY 13, 1970, HELENA.
1 TAPE: 34 MINUTES

OH 6
LYDIA SLAYTON HOGAN INTERVIEW

Lydia Hogan (b. 1889)—the daughter of Daniel Webster Slayton, a sheep rancher and politician who settled near Lavina in the mid-1880s—tells about her

father's life in the Lavina area from 1884 to 1917. *[For related materials, see also the D. W. Slayton letters and diaries, MC 178.]*
INTERVIEWED BY JOHN R. COLEMAN, JANUARY 28, 1971, JOLIET.

1 TAPE: 60 MINUTES

OH 7
ELLA LAMPORT LEAVENS INTERVIEW

Ella Leavens, the widow of the cowboy Robert Leavens, talks of: the early communities of Bearcreek and Billings; area pioneers; Calamity Jane stories; various Billings residents.
INTERVIEWED BY AN UNIDENTIFIED MONTANA HISTORICAL SOCIETY STAFF MEMBER, APRIL 22, 1971, BILLINGS.

1 TAPE: 60 MINUTES

OH 8
FRED WRIGHT INTERVIEW

Fred Wright (b. 1875) of Red Lodge—a cowboy, stage-line operator, engineer, and politician who arrived in Montana from Pennsylvania and Illinois in 1893—explains myriad aspects of early Montana cattle ranching, from breaking saddle horses to shipping cattle to market. He also recalls Charlie Russell.
INTERVIEWED BY JOHN R. COLEMAN, APRIL 23, 1971, HELENA.

1 TAPE: 60 MINUTES

OH 9
BURTON KENDALL WHEELER INTERVIEW

U.S. Senator Burton Wheeler (1882–1975) summarizes: his early career in Butte as a private attorney; his work as a U.S. District Attorney in Montana; his unsuccessful campaign for the Montana governorship in 1920; his Senate career from 1923 to 1946; his association with the Democratic Party. *[See also General Montana OH 1547.]*
INTERVIEWED BY JOHN M. PAXON, FEBRUARY 7, 1972, WASHINGTON, D.C.

PARTIAL TRANSCRIPT: 15 PAGES
3 TAPES: 2 HOURS, 15 MINUTES

OH 10
PEARL BESSIE CONNER INTERVIEW

Pearl Conner discusses her homesteading experiences in the Camp Creek area north of Bozeman from about 1900 to 1905.
INTERVIEWED BY STUART W. CONNER, SEPTEMBER 6, 1970, BILLINGS.

TRANSCRIPT: 21 PAGES
1 TAPE: 60 MINUTES

OH 11
CARTER V. RUBOTTOM REMINISCENCE

The retired Townsend cattle rancher Carter Rubottom (b. 1890) assesses: his boyhood in Great Falls; his ranching experiences; early automobile travel; mining activities; the cowboy artist Charles M. Russell; other early Montana settlers.
RECORDED BY CARTER V. RUBOTTOM, CIRCA JUNE 10, 1971, TOWNSEND.

PARTIAL TRANSCRIPT: 6 PAGES
6 TAPES: 6 HOURS

OH 12
NORMAN B. HOLTER INTERVIEW

Norman Holter (1868–1957)—the son of the Helena pioneer businessman and hardware merchant Anton M. Holter—describes: early community life in Helena; his father's career; the "Capital Fight" of 1894; local hydroelectric power development on the Missouri River; the Chinese community in Helena; the cowboy artist Charles M. Russell. *[See also General Montana OH 14.]*
INTERVIEWED BY HOLTER FAMILY, CIRCA 1955, HELENA.

2 TAPES: 2 HOURS

OH 13
RALPH MIRACLE INTERVIEW

The retired rancher Ralph Miracle (b. 1904) chronicles: his work on the Montana Livestock Commission; his duties as executive secretary of the Montana Stockgrowers Association; the general development of Montana's cattle industry during this century—including geographical differences, transportation, marketing, government involvement, and state politics. *[See also Non-taped Interviews SC 1521.]*
INTERVIEWED BY JEFF SAFFORD, NOVEMBER 6, 1972, HELENA.

TRANSCRIPT: 43 PAGES
2 TAPES: 2 HOURS

OH 14
NORMAN B. HOLTER INTERVIEW

Norman Holter (1868–1957)—the son of the Helena pioneer businessman and hardware merchant Anton M. Holter—comments on various topics in the context of a Montana Institute of the Arts Festival presentation: his father's career; his own early experiences in Helena and Virginia City; the state's fledgling mining and lumber

industries. *[See also General Montana OH 12.]* Other participants in the session include: Robert Fletcher; K. Ross Toole; Merrill G. Burlingame; Norman Winestine.
RECORDED BY THE THIRD ANNUAL MONTANA INSTITUTE OF THE ARTS FESTIVAL, JUNE 10, 1951, VIRGINIA CITY.
1 TAPE: 50 MINUTES

OH 15
ETHNIC HISTORY SYMPOSIUM, BUTTE

The Ethnic History Symposium, convened in Butte on April 19, 1975, was one of five related conferences held throughout the state. Tapes from the symposium feature the reminiscences of longtime Butte residents of Irish, Italian, Cornish, Finnish, Serbian, and Asian descent.
RECORDED BY THE ETHNIC HISTORY SYMPOSIUM, APRIL 19, 1974, BUTTE.
4 TAPES: 3 HOURS, 35 MINUTES

OH 16
ETHNIC HISTORY SYMPOSIUM, GLENDIVE

The Ethnic History Symposium convened in Glendive on April 22, 1974, was one of five related conferences held throughout the state. Tapes from the symposium address: the settlement of eastern Montana; the influence of ethnic immigrants during the 1900–1925 homestead period; the activities of such diverse ethnic groups as the Danes, Amish, Italians, German-Russian Mennonites, Poles, Irish, and Scots. Also included is a talk by Professor Philip Tideman, of St. Cloud State University in Minnesota, entitled "Frontier Images on the Northern Plains."
RECORDED BY THE ETHNIC HISTORY SYMPOSIUM, APRIL 22, 1974, GLENDIVE.
5 TAPES: 4 HOURS, 20 MINUTES

OH 17
MONTANA HISTORY CONFERENCE PROCEEDINGS, 1974

At the First Montana History Conference, held in Helena from October 31 to November 2, 1974, a five-member panel considered political and economic developments in Montana since World War II. Panelists involved were: Richard Roeder, Montana State University; Harry Billings, Helena; Bill Mackay, Helena; Tom Payne, University of Montana; K. Ross Toole, University of Montana. Within this general topic, subjects include: strip mining coal; the political influence of the Montana Power Company; the attitudes of Montana cattlemen toward pertinent issues.

RECORDED BY THE MONTANA HISTORICAL SOCIETY, NOVEMBER 1, 1974, HELENA.
1 TAPE: 55 MINUTES

OH 18
REVEREND FRANCIS PAUL PRUCHA, S.J., SPEECH

Francis Prucha—a Jesuit priest, a professor of history at Marquette University in Milwaukee, Wisconsin, and an authority on the American Indian—delivers a speech entitled "The Political Status of the American Indian: An Historical Observation of Problems" in Helena on November 1, 1974. The talk is a component of the First Annual Montana History Conference. Introductory remarks are made by H. Duane Hampton, professor of history at the University of Montana in Missoula.
RECORDED BY THE MONTANA HISTORICAL SOCIETY, NOVEMBER 1, 1974, HELENA.
1 TAPE: 35 MINUTES

OH 19
ROBERT G. ATHEARN SPEECH

Robert Athearn—a professor of history at the University of Colorado in Boulder, Colorado—speaks at the First Montana History Conference, held in Helena from October 31 to November 2, 1974. His talk is entitled "Historical Parallels between Colorado and Montana, 1860 to 1974." Introductory comments are made by Vivian Paladin, editor of *Montana The Magazine of Western History*.
RECORDED BY THE MONTANA HISTORICAL SOCIETY, NOVEMBER 1, 1974, HELENA.
2 TAPES: 1 HOUR

OH 20
W. EUGENE HOLLON SPEECH

Eugene Hollon—a professor of history at the University of Toledo, in Toledo, Ohio—delivers a speech at the First Montana History Conference, held from October 31 to November 2, 1974, in Helena. The talk is entitled "The Changes and Exploitation of the Rocky Mountain States during the 1960s and 1970s." Topics include water pollution and Big Sky of Montana, Inc. Introductory comments are made by Robert Smith, a professor of history at Eastern Montana College in Billings.
RECORDED BY THE MONTANA HISTORY CONFERENCE, NOVEMBER 1, 1974, HELENA.
TRANSCRIPT: 20 PAGES
1 TAPE: 55 MINUTES

OH 21
ROBERT F. MORGAN LECTURE
Bob Morgan—an artist and a former curator with the Montana Historical Society Museum in Helena—speaks to a group of docents at the society on January 7, 1974. He discusses: the cowboy artist Charles M. Russell; Russell's art; Russell works in the Historical Society's collection.
RECORDED BY THE MONTANA HISTORICAL SOCIETY, JANUARY 7, 1974, HELENA.
TRANSCRIPT: 5 PAGES
1 TAPE: 30 MINUTES

OH 22
RICHARD B. BERG AND S. B. MacDUFFIE LECTURES
Richard Berg—a professor of geology at the Montana College of Mineral Science and Technology in Butte and a U.S. Bureau of Mines and Geology economic geologist—speaks to a gathering of Montana Historical Society docents in Helena on January 7, 1974, regarding western mining methods. S. B. MacDuffie, a Helena-based authority on gold, talks about the historical importance of gold and gold mining in Montana and in the West.
RECORDED BY THE MONTANA HISTORICAL SOCIETY, JANUARY 7, 1974, HELENA.
2 TAPES: 1 HOUR, 30 MINUTES

OH 23
ROBERT W. PARSLEY LECTURE
Robert Parsley—Indian Education Supervisor for the Montana Office of Public Instruction in Helena—delivers a speech entitled "Indians in Montana: A Contemporary View of Education and Socio-Economic Problems." The talk, given on January 7, 1974, before a group of docents at the Montana Historical Society in Helena, focuses on Indian education programs and problems encountered by Indians in Montana schools during the early 1970s.
RECORDED BY THE MONTANA HISTORICAL SOCIETY, JANUARY 7, 1974, HELENA.
1 TAPE: 45 MINUTES

OH 24
HARRIETT C. MELOY LECTURE
Harriett Meloy—the head librarian at the Montana Historical Society in Helena during the 1970s—speaks to a group of docents about the society's library and archives programs. She concludes with a slide show addressing the history of such Helena-area mining towns as Marysville, Diamond City, Montana City, Wickes, Elkhorn, and Corbin. [See also Women as Community Builders OH 1036.]
RECORDED BY THE MONTANA HISTORICAL SOCIETY, JANUARY 7, 1974, HELENA.
1 TAPE: 60 MINUTES

OH 25
ARTHUR T. "PUNK" WARD INTERVIEW
Arthur Ward (1884–1975) appears before a group of docents at the Montana Historical Society in Helena on January 7, 1974, and he converses about: living in Helena, from the 1890s into the 1930s; a story about the cowboy artist Charles M. Russell's wife, Nancy.
RECORDED BY THE MONTANA HISTORICAL SOCIETY, JANUARY 7, 1974, HELENA.
1 TAPE: 45 MINUTES

OH 26
JOHN TOWN INTERVIEW
John Town recalls: his life in Malta and in Phillips County; stories told to him by early immigrants to Montana.
INTERVIEWED BY EDWIN JOHNSTON, JULY 12 AND 16, 1962, BRIDGER.
3 TAPES: 2 HOURS, 20 MINUTES

OH 27
MICHAEL P. MALONE AND RICHARD B. ROEDER LECTURE
Michael Malone and Richard Roeder—two professors of history from Montana State University in Bozeman—discuss: Montana territorial politics from 1864 to 1889; Thomas Francis Meagher; Sidney Edgerton; the statehood movement during the 1880s; the Montana constitutional conventions of 1884 and 1889. This October 18, 1973, presentation in Helena was the first in a series of five talks on Montana history sponsored by the National Endowment for the Humanities (NEH). [See also General Montana OH 1589.]
RECORDED BY THE MONTANA HISTORICAL SOCIETY, OCTOBER 18, 1973, HELENA.
2 TAPES: 1 HOUR, 45 MINUTES

OH 28
EDWARD J. BYRNE INTERVIEW
Edward Byrne (1886–1972)—a Shelby rancher, state representative, and member of the Montana State Board of Equalization—describes: Montana politics and legis-

lative actions during the 1930s; his recollections of Frank Cooney and Edward Byrne; the Montana Power Company's opposition to the Havre-Shelby power lines constructed by the U.S. Reclamation Service in the 1930s.
INTERVIEWED BY FRANK W. WILEY, JUNE 19, 1969, SHELBY.
3 TAPES: 2 HOURS, 30 MINUTES

OH 29
HOWARD SCHUYLER INTERVIEW

Howard Schuyler, an officer of the Union Bank and Trust Company of Helena, depicts: the history of Helena's banks and related businesses from 1887 to 1911; George L. Ramsay's innovations as president of the Union Bank and Trust Company from 1904 to 1911.
INTERVIEWED BY HARRIETT C. MELOY, SPRING 1973, HELENA.
1 TAPE: 25 MINUTES

OH 30
JOHN "JACK" L. MALONEY INTERVIEW

Jack Maloney (b. 1885)—a longtime resident of Missoula and Helena—describes his business experiences in Missoula from 1900 to 1920.
INTERVIEWED BY FRANK W. WILEY, MAY 6, 1969, HELENA.
2 TAPES: 1 HOUR, 15 MINUTES

OH 31
PAUL ROSSI LECTURE

Paul Rossi—a western artist and a former director of the Gilcrease Institute in Tulsa, Oklahoma—presents a slide lecture at the Second Annual Rendezvous of Western Art, conducted by the Montana Historical Society in Helena in September 1973. His topic is the history and the development of western art. Introductory remarks are delivered by the society director, Sam Gilluly.
RECORDED AT THE SECOND ANNUAL RENDEZVOUS OF WESTERN ART, SEPTEMBER 15, 1973, HELENA.
2 TAPES: 1 HOUR, 35 MINUTES

OH 32
EVERETT E. "BOO" MacGILVRA INTERVIEW

E. E. MacGilvra (1893–1980)—a former Montana Historical Society Board of Trustees member and a Montana Power Company employee—describes: his experiences as a miner in the Zortman area from 1900 to the 1930s; many of the characters then living in the Little Rockies Mountains, including Harvey Logan, Jake Meyers, and the Hole in the Wall Gang. The interview

was conducted in a car traveling through the Zortman/Landusky country. [See also General Montana OH 109, OH 628-29, and OH 1546.]
INTERVIEWED BY ROBERT F. MORGAN AND VIVIAN A. PALADIN, AUGUST 13, 1974, ON THE ROAD.
2 TAPES: 1 HOUR, 55 MINUTES

OH 33
CHARLES DIGGS GREENFIELD, JR., INTERVIEW

The Helena newspaper reporter, writer, and publicist Charles Greenfield, Jr. (1885–1975), examines: Montana journalism; Montana political personalities Joseph M. Dixon, Thomas J. Walsh, and Thomas H. Carter; the history of Helena; his family life from the 1890s to the 1930s.
INTERVIEWED BY FRANK W. WILEY, MAY 14, 19, AND 28, 1970, AND BY SAM GILLULY, JANUARY 4 AND FEBRUARY 3, 1971, HELENA.
5 TAPES: 3 HOURS, 45 MINUTES

OH 34
ELISE MUNSER BECK WILSON INTERVIEW

Elise Wilson (b. 1881) briefly describes the early history of Basin, including its buildings and local personalities.
INTERVIEWED BY FRANK W. WILEY AND HARRIETT C. MELOY, AUGUST 17, 1967, BASIN.
1 TAPE: 15 MINUTES

OH 35
LUCILLE DYAS TOPPING INTERVIEW

A Helena resident, Lucille Topping discourses on: her father, Ralph Dyas; her grandfather, William F. Wheeler; her life in Helena with her husband Thomas Topping, a local realtor.
INTERVIEWED BY FRANK W. WILEY, CIRCA FEBRUARY 20, 1968, HELENA.
TRANSCRIPT: 20 PAGES
1 TAPE: 40 MINUTES

OH 36
FANNY SPERRY STEELE INTERVIEW

Fanny Steele (1887–1974) discusses: cattle ranching near Helena from 1912 to 1930; her career as a rodeo rough-stock rider; a wild-horse roundup near Helena (date unknown); the planned donation of her saddles to the Montana Historical Society Museum in Helena.
INTERVIEWED BY JOHN R. COLEMAN AND ROBERT GANT, MAY 18, 1970, HELENA.
1 TAPE: 25 MINUTES

OH 37
RUSS SHEEN INTERVIEW

Russ Sheen—the director of audio-visual education for the Montana Office of Public Instruction in Helena—briefly discusses: a Blackfeet Indian legend about Scarface; K. W. Bergan's making of a film; a religious ceremony performed at Heart Butte in 1956 by Maggie Swims Under of Browning—who had vowed to perform the ceremony if her grandson recovered from polio.
INTERVIEWED BY SAM GILLULY, MAY 9, 1968.
TRANSCRIPT: 5 PAGES
1 TAPE: 10 MINUTES

OH 38
MERYL ERWIN INTERVIEW

Meryl Erwin (b. 1883) recalls: her life in Dillon; her association with specific community residents; her work as a secretary for Governor Edwin L. Norris; her employment with several Beaverhead County attorneys; the Indian Queen Mine; early days in Bannack.
INTERVIEWED BY FRANK W. WILEY, JANUARY 14, 1969, DILLON.
2 TAPES: 2 HOURS, 30 MINUTES

OH 39
ARTHUR R. DESCHAMPS INTERVIEW

Arthur Deschamps (b. 1886)—a Missoula area rancher and agricultural implement dealer—portrays: his father, Gaspart Deschamps, an early Missoula County cattleman; Missoula businesses; Louis La Pierre; Missoula's agricultural history from the 1870s into the 1930s.
INTERVIEWED BY FRANK W. WILEY, MARCH 7, 1969, MISSOULA.
1 TAPE: 50 MINUTES

OH 40
JAMES TURNER FARRIS BIOGRAPHY

This recording presents James Farris (1865–1914): his experiences as the publisher of several Montana newspapers, including the (Glasgow) *Valley County Independent*; his final position as editor of the *Lincoln County Herald* in Libby. This recording is a narrated biography, delivered by his son John Mark Farris of Portland, Oregon.
RECORDED BY JOHN M. FARRIS, JULY, 1968, PORTLAND, OR.
1 TAPE: 30 MINUTES

OH 41
GEORGE S. McCONE BIOGRAPHY

George McCone (1854–1929)—the Dawson County rancher and Republican state legislator for whom McCone County was named—is the subject of this narrated biography, based primarily on newspaper clippings. The narrator is McCone's son-in-law John Mark Farris of Portland, Oregon.
RECORDED BY JOHN MARK FARRIS, SEPTEMBER 8, 1969, PORTLAND, OR.
2 TAPES: 1 HOUR, 40 MINUTES

OH 42
TOM H. MARKLE INTERVIEW

Tom Markle (1880–1972)—a Glasgow resident—recalls: early law enforcement in northeastern Montana; local agricultural practices; operating a hardware store and a fuel business in Glasgow; his service on the Glasgow City Council.
INTERVIEWED BY SAM GILLULY, MAY 29, 1968, GLASGOW.
TRANSCRIPT: 17 PAGES
1 TAPE: 40 MINUTES

OH 43
THOMAS JOSEPH HOCKING INTERVIEW

A Glasgow resident, Thomas Hocking recounts: his work as owner and publisher of the Glasgow *Courier* from 1913 to 1958; his newspaper experiences in northeastern Montana; community life in Glasgow; the Jess Arnot murder investigation in the 1930s.
INTERVIEWED BY SAM GILLULY, MAY 30, 1968, GLASGOW.
TRANSCRIPT: 21 PAGES
2 TAPES: 2 HOURS

OH 44
CHARLES A. "SONNY O'DAY" GEORGE INTERVIEW

Charles George (b. 1915)—a Butte boxer who fought under the name Sonny O'Day—reflects on: owning the Sonny O'Day Bar and Restaurant in Laurel; the sport of boxing in Montana from the 1920s into the 1960s; his own boxing career. The interview was conducted as George walked through the bar and discussed the scores of boxing photographs that cover the walls.
INTERVIEWED BY SAM GILLULY, JUNE 18, 1972, LAUREL.
1 TAPE: 55 MINUTES

OH 45
KENNETH ROSS TOOLE INTERVIEW

K. Ross Toole—author, former director of the Montana Historical Society in Helena, and professor of history at the University of Montana in Missoula—appears on the Art Linkletter television show "Life with Linkletter" in the spring of 1970. He discusses: his magazine article "An Angry Man Speaks Out"; college campus demonstrations; student attitudes of the late 1960s; the Kent State University incident of 1970. David Rudnick, a physicist from the University of California, Los Angeles (UCLA), speaks in opposition to Toole. *[See also General Montana OH 86.]*

RECORDED BY "LIFE WITH LINKLETTER," SPRING, 1970, LOS ANGELES.
TRANSCRIPT: 12 PAGES
1 TAPE: 25 MINUTES

OH 46
MAE REED PORTER SPEECH
Mae Porter—a Kansas City, Missouri, historical researcher and author—delivers a speech in Anaconda on August 3, 1953, recorded by KANA radio in Anaconda. She reports on: her purchase of 1,000 Alfred Jacob Miller sketches; her search in Scotland for artifacts of the early adventurer George Ruxton.

RECORDED BY KANA RADIO, AUGUST 3, 1953, ANACONDA.
1 TAPE: 25 MINUTES

OH 47
EDWARD B. SKEELS INTERVIEW
Edward Skeels describes: his work as a draftsman for the Gilmore and Pittsburgh Railroad, running out of Armstead into Idaho; a railroad-survey race between the Union Pacific Railroad and the Gilmore and Pittsburgh along the Lemhi and Salmon rivers of Idaho in 1909 and 1910.

RECORDED BY EDWARD B. SKEELS, AUGUST, 1969, AUBURN, CA.
SUMMARY: 6 PAGES
1 TAPE: 30 MINUTES

OH 48
ROLAND H. WILLCOMB INTERVIEW
The retired engineer and amateur anthropologist Roland Willcomb narrates Blackfeet Indian legends as told to him by tribal members, including tales of White Quiver and Three Calves. *[A transcript is available in the Roland H. Willcomb Papers, SC 332.]*

RECORDED BY ROLAND H. WILLCOMB, NOVEMBER AND DECEMBER, 1968, SILVERDALE, WA.
7 TAPES: 7 HOURS, 45 MINUTES

OH 49
J. K. RALSTON INTERVIEW
J. K. Ralston (b. 1896)—a Billings artist and cattleman—reviews: his experiences as a rancher in northeastern Montana from the early 1900s through the 1930s; the homestead boom after 1910; the effects of the 1910 forest fires on eastern Montana.

INTERVIEWED BY SUE GILLULY AND AN UNIDENTIFIED MALE, 1967, BILLINGS.
1 TAPE: 1 HOUR

OH 50
JOSEPH MONTGOMERY INTERVIEW
Joseph Montgomery (b. 1874)—in 1968, Montana's last surviving soldier of the Spanish-American War—speaks of: his life in Lewistown; his service in the Spanish-American War; the hotel owner Daniel "Pickhandle" Burke; the cowboy-artist Charles M. Russell's early romance in Utica.

INTERVIEWED BY FRANK W. WILEY AND AN UNIDENTIFIED MALE, SEPTEMBER 20, 1968, LEWISTOWN.
SUMMARY: 4 PAGES
1 TAPE: 55 MINUTES

OH 51
JOSEPH MONTGOMERY SPEECH
A Lewistown resident, Joseph Montgomery (b. 1874) delivers a speech in Helena on June 8, 1970, at a luncheon ceremony to terminate the Montana Spanish-American War unit. Several other speakers present tributes to Montgomery.

RECORDED BY THE MONTANA HISTORICAL SOCIETY, JUNE 8, 1970, HELENA.
1 TAPE: 45 MINUTES

OH 52
FRED BARTON INTERVIEW
Fred Barton—a Miles City horse wrangler—summarizes: working on horse ranches in the Miles City area; his experiences raising horses in Siberian Russia in 1911 and 1912; his work as a horseman in China from 1917 to 1937.

INTERVIEWED BY K. ROSS TOOLE, MICHAEL S. KENNEDY, AND SAM SOLBERG, AUGUST 30, 1955, HELENA.
TRANSCRIPT: 26 PAGES
2 TAPES: 1 HOUR

OH 53
NATIONAL LIBRARY WEEK SPEECHES
This National Library Week radio promotion presents

an April 22, 1966, discussion between Richard Bartlett—a history professor at Florida State University in Tallahassee, Florida—and Louis Shores—dean of the Library at Florida State—regarding their use of libraries for independent study. Introductory remarks by Mary K. Dempsey—head librarian at the Montana Historical Society in Helena—focus on the services and holdings of the society library. *[See also General Montana OH 54, OH 57, OH 78, and OH 144.]*
RECORDED BY THE MONTANA LIBRARY ASSOCIATION, APRIL 22, 1966, TALLAHASSEE, FL, AND HELENA.
1 TAPE: 20 MINUTES

OH 54
NATIONAL LIBRARY WEEK PANEL
This National Library Week radio promotion presents a 1967 discussion—by three members of the National Broadcasting Company (NBC) "Project Twenty" production team who worked on the historical documentary "End of the Trail"—about the cooperation they received from the Library staff at the Montana Historical Society in Helena. Introductory remarks by Mary K. Dempsey, head librarian at the society library, address the importance of photographs in historical research. *[See also General Montana OH 53, OH 57, OH 78, and OH 144.]*
RECORDED BY THE MONTANA LIBRARY ASSOCIATION, 1967, NEW YORK AND HELENA.
1 TAPE: 8 MINUTES

OH 55
NATIONAL LIBRARY WEEK INTERVIEWS
This National Library Week radio promotion combines April 1968 telephone interviews by the Intermountain News Service (INS) reporter Bill Yaeger with three Montana historians: Rex C. Myers, a graduate student at the University of Montana in Missoula; Thomas Clinch, a professor of history at Carroll College in Helena; J. Leonard Bates, a history professor at the University of Illinois in Champaign, Illinois. The interviewees talk about the importance of the city directory and newspaper collections held by the Montana Historical Society Library in Helena to their historical research.
RECORDED BY THE INTERMOUNTAIN NEWS SERVICE, APRIL, 1968, HELENA.
1 TAPE: 14 MINUTES

OH 56
NATIONAL LIBRARY WEEK INTERVIEWS
This National Library Week radio promotion includes May 19, 1969, telephone interviews by the Intermoun-

tain News Service (INS) reporter Bill Yaeger with two historians: Stan Davison, history professor at Western Montana College in Dillon; Robert G. Athearn, professor of history at the University of Colorado in Boulder. The academicians tell of their use of the Montana Historical Society Library in their western history research.
RECORDED BY THE INTERMOUNTAIN NEWS SERVICE, MAY 19, 1969, HELENA.
1 TAPE: 7 MINUTES

OH 57
KBLL RADIO PANEL DISCUSSION
This National Library Week radio promotion presents a March 15, 1967, panel discussion staged at the Helena radio station KBLL and moderated by the Intermountain News Service (INS) reporter Bill Yaeger. The panel comprises three members of the National Broadcasting Company (NBC) "Project Twenty" production team who worked on the television documentary "End of the Trail." The interviewees comment on the invaluable help provided by the Montana Historical Society librarian Mary K. Dempsey. *[See also General Montana OH 53, OH 54, OH 78, and OH 144.]*
RECORDED BY THE INTERMOUNTAIN NEWS SERVICE, MARCH 15, 1967, HELENA.
1 TAPE: 21 MINUTES

OH 58
MONTANA CRIMINAL CODE OF 1973 SEMINAR
In 1973 the Montana Legislature revised the Montana Criminal Code. As a result, six seminars were held across Montana to acquaint the legal community and the general public with the changes. Speakers at this seminar—held in Helena on November 15, 1974—include: the Montana Supreme Court Associate Justice Wesley Castles; the University of Montana Law School professors Larry Elison and William F. Crowley; the Criminal Law Revision Commission staff attorney Terrence Cosgrove.
RECORDED BY THE MONTANA BAR ASSOCIATION, NOVEMBER 15, 1974, HELENA.
5 TAPES: 4 HOURS, 45 MINUTES

OH 59
MARY ELLEN RAGEN INTERVIEW
A Broadwater County ranch wife, Mary Ellen Ragen (1867–1961) briefly speaks of: her early life in the Townsend area; her husband, Edward Ragen; her parents' overland journey from Omaha, Nebraska, to Virginia City, Montana Territory, in 1864.

INTERVIEWED BY AN UNIDENTIFIED MALE AND AN UNIDENTIFIED FEMALE, CIRCA 1960, TOWNSEND.
1 TAPE: 13 MINUTES

OH 60
W. A. SHERLOCK AND MARY SHERLOCK INTERVIEWS

W. A. Sherlock discusses: his parents' cattle and sheep ranch in Broadwater County; the Huntley and Clark Horse Ranch outside Townsend. Mary Sherlock discusses the establishment of the Crow Creek community.
INTERVIEWED BY AN UNIDENTIFIED FEMALE, CIRCA 1960, TOWNSEND.
SUMMARY: 2 PAGES
1 TAPE: 25 MINUTES

OH 61
IDA LOVELL BRUCE AND EMMA KEENE LOURIE INTERVIEW

Ida Bruce and Emma Lourie discuss their lives as ranch wives in Broadwater County from the 1880s into the 1930s. Ida Bruce also describes: her childhood in Diamond City; the history of Confederate Gulch. Emma Lourie also portrays: growing up as the daughter of the pioneer rancher Flavins J. Keene; her life with the Sheep Creek rancher Joseph H. Lourie; her family.
INTERVIEWED BY CORA POOLE AND HARRIET AVERILL, CIRCA 1960, TOWNSEND.
SUMMARY: 3 PAGES
1 TAPE: 20 MINUTES

OH 62
NICHE MORAN INTERVIEW

Niche Moran (b. 1868) talks of: his experiences as a cowhand in eastern Montana prior to the turn of the century; his life in Broadwater County from 1900 into the 1920s.
INTERVIEWED BY CORA POOLE, CIRCA 1960, TOWNSEND.
1 TAPE: 30 MINUTES

OH 63
DELLA JOHNSON WILLIAMS INTERVIEW

Della Williams—the mother of the actress Myrna Loy—discusses: her life in Radersburg and the Crow Creek Valley from the 1880s into the 1920s; her children, David and Myrna; Reverend William Van Orsdel.
INTERVIEWED BY CORA POOLE, CIRCA 1960, RADERSBURG.
SUMMARY: 2 PAGES
1 TAPE: 30 MINUTES

OH 64
TOM WILLIAMS INTERVIEW

Tom Williams briefly recalls: his arrival in Radersburg in 1889; community life in Radersburg; some of the town's more peculiar residents during the 1890s.
INTERVIEWED BY AN UNIDENTIFIED BROADWATER COUNTY EXTENSION SERVICE AGENT, CIRCA 1960, RADERSBURG.
TRANSCRIPT: 7 PAGES
1 TAPE: 15 MINUTES

OH 65
FREDERIC G. RENNER AND GINGER K. RENNER LECTURES

Fred and Ginger Renner—both experts on western art and particularly on the works of the cowboy-artist Charles M. Russell—deliver talks at the Third Annual Rendezvous of Western Art in Helena on September 7, 1974. Fred Renner recounts: the life of Russell from the 1880s into the 1920s; various myths that have developed concerning Russell. Ginger Renner, also the owner of a western-art studio, presents a slide show addressing the importance of contemporary western art.
RECORDED BY THE MONTANA HISTORICAL SOCIETY, SEPTEMBER 7, 1974, HELENA.
1 TAPE: 25 MINUTES

OH 66
MARY STUART ABBOTT AND OSCAR O. MUELLER LECTURES

In a single session, two speakers address a gathering sponsored by the Montana Institute of the Arts, in Lewistown on June 21, 1958. Mary Stuart Abbott—the wife of the cattleman and author "Teddy Blue" Abbott and the daughter of the Montana pioneer Granville Stuart—details: her childhood on the DHS/Pioneer Cattle Company ranch near Lewistown; stories told by her father, dating from the 1880s to 1929. Oscar Mueller—a Lewistown lawyer, local historian, and archaeologist—reflects on his research of the central Montana vigilante raids of 1884.
RECORDED BY MONTANA INSTITUTE OF THE ARTS, JUNE 21, 1958, LEWISTOWN.
1 TAPE: 1 HOUR, 10 MINUTES

OH 67
DEMOCRATIC PARTY STATE CONVENTION

This collection consists of the proceedings of the Montana Democratic Party's state convention, held in Helena on November 16, 1974. The activities involve: delegate selection; the Democratic charter convention;

eastern district proceedings; western district proceedings; balloting for delegates to represent Montana at the Democratic mini-convention in Kansas City, Missouri, December 6-8, 1974.

RECORDED BY THE MONTANA STATE DEMOCRATIC PARTY, NOVEMBER 16, 1974, HELENA.
SUMMARY: 4 PAGES
2 TAPES: 2 HOURS, 45 MINUTES

OH 68
MERLE JORDAN MOORE INTERVIEW

A Seattle, Washington, resident, Merle Moore—daughter of the Montana minister of the Christian Churches Walter M. Jordan—briefly describes: her childhood in Cascade and Helena; her mother's acquaintance with the cowboy-artist Charles M. Russell.

INTERVIEWED BY MICHAEL S. KENNEDY, CIRCA 1964, HELENA.
1 TAPE: 15 MINUTES

OH 69
WESTERN HISTORY ASSOCIATION CONFERENCE

The Western History Association's annual conference—held in Helena on October 14, 1965—featured a session addressing aviation on the frontier. Participants include: the history professor Howard Lee Scamehorn of the University of Colorado in Boulder, who presents a paper entitled "Air Transportation in the Mountain West [1925–1965]"; Frank W. Wiley, director of the Montana Aeronautics Commission in Helena, who comments on his book *Montana and the Sky,* about early Montana balloonists, and pioneer pilots.

RECORDED BY THE MONTANA HISTORICAL SOCIETY, OCTOBER 14, 1965, HELENA.
2 TAPES: 1 HOUR

OH 70
WESTERN HISTORY ASSOCIATION CONFERENCE

The Western History Association's annual conference—held in Helena on October 14, 1965—included a session concerning "Exploration in the West." Participants include: Professor John Duffy of the University of California–Davis, who presents a paper entitled "Medical Practices of the Western Indians"; Professor Morgan Sherwood of Tulane University in New Orleans, Louisiana, who gives a paper entitled "Science in Russian America to 1865"; Professor T. H. McDonald of Florida State University in Tallahassee, who speaks on "Sir

Alexander McKenzie's Exploration of the Canadian Northwest, 1789."

RECORDED BY THE MONTANA HISTORICAL SOCIETY, OCTOBER 14, 1965, HELENA.
1 TAPE: 1 HOUR, 45 MINUTES

OH 71
LESLIE A. FIEDLER SPEECH

Leslie Fiedler, Professor of English at the State University of New York–Buffalo, presents a talk at the Western History Association annual conference, held in Helena on October 14, 1974, entitled "The Literary Uses of Lewis and Clark." Topics include Sacajawea and Edgar Allen Poe. Dr. Fiedler is introduced by Professor Oscar O. Winther of Indiana University in Bloomington.

RECORDED BY THE MONTANA HISTORICAL SOCIETY, OCTOBER 14, 1974, HELENA.
1 TAPE: 50 MINUTES

OH 72
ALEXANDER W. BOTKIN AND FRANK N. CHESSMAN INTERVIEW

Alexander Botkin—the son of the Helena lawyer and Montana lieutenant governor (1893–1897) Alexander C. Botkin—accompanied by the Helena physician Dr. Frank Chessman—son of William A. Chessman, a Helena businessman and a 1889 Montana Constitutional Convention delegate—report on their respective childhoods in Helena and recall local personalities from the 1890s into the 1920s.

INTERVIEWED BY VIRGINIA WALTON, STAN DAVISON, ET AL., JULY, 1957, HELENA.
1 TAPE: 1 HOUR

OH 73
WILLIAM FLOYD HARDIN INTERVIEW

William Hardin (1890–1974), a rancher and businessman in the Malta area, recalls: the writing and publication of his book, *Campfires and Cowchips* (1972); general information about cattle raising on the Bloom Cattle Company's Circle Diamond Ranch near Malta. *[See also General Montana OH 131.]*

INTERVIEWED BY MICHAEL S. KENNEDY, 1971, HELENA.
2 TAPES: 1 HOUR, 50 MINUTES

OH 74
MAY G. FLANAGAN SPEECH

May Flanagan (1874–1958)—a Great Falls elementary school principal and the daughter of the Fort Benton druggist and postmaster Michael A. Flanagan—depicts:

Montana's fur-trade era; the history of Fort Benton; notable town residents from 1819 into the 1920s.
INTERVIEWED BY UNIDENTIFIED GROUP, CIRCA 1955, GREAT FALLS.
2 TAPES: 50 MINUTES

OH 75
CHET HUNTLEY PRESS CONFERENCE

The Montana native and television newscaster Chet Huntley—in his role as president of the board of directors of Big Sky of Montana, a Gallatin Canyon ski resort—announces the formation of Big Sky and then answers reporters' questions. Persons making complementary statements include Governor Forrest Anderson and Edwin M. Homer, president of the Chrysler Realty Corporation. Speakers are introduced by Bill Merrick, a reporter from KRBM radio in Bozeman. *[See also General Montana OH 90.]*
RECORDED BY KRBM RADIO, FEBRUARY 16, 1970, HELENA.
TRANSCRIPT: 8 PAGES
1 TAPE: 40 MINUTES

OH 76
JULIA SCHULTZ AND PETER LONG HORSE INTERVIEW

Julia Schultz and Peter Long Horse, two members of the Gros Ventre tribe of Montana, describe: Gros Ventre lifestyles; tribal customs; traditional stories. [Portions of this interview are in the Gros Ventre language.]
INTERVIEWED BY HOMER LOUCKS, APRIL 21, 1961, DODSON.
1 TAPE: 2 HOURS

OH 77
CHARLES M. RUSSELL STATUE COMPETITION DELIBERATIONS

On July 14, 1957, in Helena a panel of experts judged a competition to produce a sculpture of Charles M. Russell. In this instance, the judges first meet with the contestant H. M. Hazzard to hear his objections to the competition's format; they conclude with a closed discussion regarding selection of the winning artist. The judges include Alex J. Ettl, president of Sculpture House in New York City, John K. Sherman, arts editor of the Minneapolis *Tribune*, and Charles Beil, a sculptor from Banff, Alberta, Canada.
RECORDED BY THE MONTANA HISTORICAL SOCIETY, JULY 14, 1957, HELENA.
1 TAPE: 25 MINUTES

OH 78
MARY K. DEMPSEY INTERVIEW

Mary Dempsey—a librarian at the Montana Historical Society in Helena and formerly the head librarian at Marquette University in Milwaukee, Wisconsin—delineates: the Historical Society's holdings; the institution's services to the public. The KBLL radio executive Ron Davidson produced this interview as part of his Helena-based series, "Your State Government." *[See also General Montana OH 53-54 and OH 57.]*
INTERVIEWED BY KBLL RADIO, MARCH 15, 1968, HELENA.
1 TAPE: 15 MINUTES

OH 79
KSEN RADIO BROADCASTS

This composite of 1964 broadcasts covers the Montana flood of June 8-11, 1964, in Glacier, Pondera, and Toole counties. Commentary is provided by the KSEN radio news director Bob Norris, based in Shelby.
RECORDED BY KSEN RADIO, JUNE, 1964, SHELBY.
1 TAPE: 25 MINUTES

OH 80
GOVERNOR'S INDUSTRIAL DEVELOPMENT CONFERENCE

The Governor's Industrial Development Conference convened in Great Falls on April 19, 1968. Moderated by Sam Chapman, the conference addresses economic problems faced by the state during the 1960s, possible solutions to those problems, and Montana's industrial potential in the 1970s. Various speakers include: Governor Tim Babcock; Arthur E. Stauber; Donald L. Green; Kenneth A. Blevins. [Tape exists in a reel-to-reel format only.]
RECORDED BY THE STATE OF MONTANA, PLANNING AND ECONOMIC BUREAU, APRIL 19, 1968, GREAT FALLS.
1 TAPE: 7 HOURS, 5 MINUTES

OH 81
MONTANA PRESS ASSOCIATION PANEL

This panel discussion, held in Great Falls on April 16, 1975, considers the topic of journalism and its role in Montana politics since World War II. Six panel members consider: the sale of the Anaconda Company's newspaper chain to Lee Enterprises in 1959; the gubernatorial election of 1944; the senatorial primary of 1946; general changes made by daily and weekly newspapers in their reporting of politics. The Montana Press Association sponsored the session.

RECORDED BY THE MONTANA PRESS ASSOCIATION, APRIL 16, 1975, GREAT FALLS.
PARTIAL TRANSCRIPT: 11 PAGES
1 TAPE: 2 HOURS, 20 MINUTES

OH 82
THOMAS A. ROSS INTERVIEWS

A Blaine County rancher, Tom Ross reviews: ranching in the Bears Paw Mountains during the late 1800s and the early 1900s; the effects of drought and depression on area ranching; government farm programs; his service in the Montana Legislature; his terms as an officer of the Montana Stockgrowers Association.
INTERVIEWED BY JEFF SAFFORD AND MICHAEL MALONE, JUNE 2 AND DECEMBER 8, 1973, MAY 24, 1974, BOZEMAN.
TRANSCRIPT: 71 PAGES
3 TAPES: 2 HOURS

OH 83
ARNOLD RIEDER INTERVIEW

Arnold Rieder (b. 1906)—a Jefferson County rancher—discusses: the formation and aims of the Montana Cattlemen's Association in the early 1950s; his philosophy and views on ranching; his service in the Montana Legislature; his duties as a Montana Fish and Game Commissioner.
INTERVIEWED BY JEFF SAFFORD AND BILL LANG, OCTOBER 24, 1974, BOULDER.
TRANSCRIPT: 27 PAGES
2 TAPES: 2 HOURS

OH 84
ROBERT MOSHER INTERVIEW

Robert Mosher speaks of: the development of the Tee Bar Ranch near Augusta; his experiences breeding cattle, particularly Simmentals; the use of artificial insemination in a cattle-breeding program.
INTERVIEWED BY BILL LANG, JANUARY 14, 1975, AUGUSTA.
TRANSCRIPT: 24 PAGES
2 TAPES: 2 HOURS

OH 85
HARRY L. BILLINGS INTERVIEW

The longtime editor of *People's Voice* and the education/research director of the Montana State American Federation of Labor–Congress of Industrial Organizations (AFL-CIO), Harry Billings converses on: the relationship of Montana's livestock industry to issues viewed as critical by *People's Voice*; the political role played by the Montana Stockgrowers Association.
INTERVIEWED BY JEFF SAFFORD, JUNE 9, 1975, THOMPSON FALLS.
TRANSCRIPT: 30 PAGES
1 TAPE: 1 HOUR

OH 86
KENNETH ROSS TOOLE TESTIMONY

In 1975 K. Ross Toole—a Montana historian and University of Montana history professor—briefly discusses HB 656 before the 44th Montana Legislature's House Education Committee. He addresses: the value of student involvement in University of Montana faculty committees; his recommendation that the committee permit students to participate in the Board of Regents. [Tape separated from the records of the 44th Montana Legislative Assembly.] *[See also General Montana OH 45.]*
RECORDED BY THE MONTANA STATE LEGISLATURE, 1975, HELENA.
SUMMARY: 1 PAGE
1 TAPE: 7 MINUTES

OH 87
BELLE FLIGELMAN WINESTINE INTERVIEW

In a reminiscence entitled, "Belle Winestine: Feminist and Suffragette," Belle Winestine (1891–1985) discusses: her work as an aide to the Montana Congresswoman Jeannette Rankin during her 1917–1918 term; her observations of Rankin; the woman-suffrage movement; the Equal Rights Amendment; women as legislators and as professionals; women's roles in the international peace movement. *[See also General Montana OH 630.]*
INTERVIEWED BY GEORGE COLE, CIRCA 1976, HELENA.
SUMMARY: 3 PAGES
1 TAPE: 40 MINUTES

OH 88
HILL COUNTY INTERVIEW

This composite consists of interviews with several people in the Chinook and Rocky Boy's Reservation areas of Montana concerning local history during the 1930s.
INTERVIEWED BY AL LUCKE, APRIL 24, 1976, HILL COUNTY.
SUMMARY: 1 PAGE

1 TAPE: 20 MINUTES

OH 89
BEAVERHEAD ROCK COURT-HEARING RECORDS

This collection consists of questions and testimony—recorded during the 1974 Beaverhead County court hearing—regarding the State of Montana's purchase of Beaverhead Rock to establish a historical landmark. The pertinent issues include the appropriateness of the purchase and the difficulties involved in setting a price. E. E. "Boo" MacGilvra played an important role in the price negotiations [although the tape ends before the cross-examination of MacGilvra.] The Montana Department of Fish and Game assumed the lead role in the purchase transaction.

RECORDED BY E. E. MACGILVRA, 1974, DILLON.
SUMMARY: 4 PAGES
2 TAPES: 1 HOUR, 20 MINUTES

OH 90
CHET HUNTLEY INTERVIEW

The Montana native and network television news broadcaster Chet Huntley comments on: political party conventions; race relations; Presidential power; Congressional largess; bureaucratic waste, special-interest groups; public apathy; related national issues. *[See also General Montana OH 75.]*

INTERVIEWED BY GEORGE COLE, 1975, BIG SKY.
SUMMARY: 4 PAGES
1 TAPE: 1 HOUR

OH 91
WILBUR WERNER SPEECH

Wilbur Werner—a former president of the Lewis and Clark Trail Heritage Foundation and a longtime Cut Bank attorney—briefly introduces a slide show that addresses: the Lewis and Clark expedition; the Two Medicine Fight site; Camp Disappointment. KUFM public radio from Missoula recorded this segment on October 18, 1975. *[See also Small Town Montana OH 834.]*

RECORDED BY KUFM PUBLIC RADIO, OCTOBER 18, 1975, GREAT FALLS.
SUMMARY: 1 PAGE
1 TAPE: 10 MINUTES

OH 92
VIVIAN PALADIN SPEECH

Vivian Paladin, venerable editor of *Montana The Magazine of Western History*, spoke in Great Falls on October 18, 1975. She surveys: the role of Sacajawea in the Lewis and Clark expedition; Sacajawea's detractors; disputes over the spelling of her name; her tribal affiliation; the possible date and place of her death.

RECORDED BY KUFM PUBLIC RADIO, OCTOBER 18, 1975, GREAT FALLS.
SUMMARY: 2 PAGES
1 TAPE: 25 MINUTES

OH 93
VERA HANSCEN READING

Vera Hanscen reads "Indian Summer," her account of the enjoyable and educational summer of 1944, when she served as secretary to the Tribal Council of the Salish and Kootenai Tribes in Dixon. She also chronicles: her duties as the Associated Press reporter assigned to the Montana Indian Conference at Blue Bay; Salish cultural information on food, the seasons, and clothing.

RECORDED BY VERA HANSCEN, 1975, WOLF CREEK.
SUMMARY: 3 PAGES
1 TAPE: 30 MINUTES

OH 94
NATIONAL PUBLIC RADIO BROADCAST

This 1976 National Public Radio (NPR) documentary addresses the overall history of Montana and discusses specifically: the Lewis and Clark expedition; gold mining; the cattle industry; homesteading; the copper-mining and coal-mining industries; the Progressive movement; native-white warfare; the writing of the second Montana constitution in the early 1970s; the struggle to protect the state's environment and lifestyle. This segment is narrated by Roger Johnson as part of NPR's Bicentennial series entitled "The States of the Union."

RECORDED BY KUFM PUBLIC RADIO, 1976, MISSOULA.
SUMMARY: 3 PAGES
1 TAPE: 55 MINUTES

OH 95
MAIDA McCARTNEY INTERVIEW

The Chinook radio personality Maida McCartney talks about: her long-running program "Chinook Hour"; the philosophy of the show; her early years in broadcasting. Additional editorial comments are written by the co-owner of KOJM radio on the occasion of McCartney's retirement. *[Transcript is also included in SC 1586.]*

INTERVIEWED BY NORMA ASHBY, NOVEMBER 23, 1975, GREAT FALLS.
TRANSCRIPT: 16 PAGES
1 TAPE: 30 MINUTES

OH 96
GRANITE COUNTY STUDY COMMISSION
DISCUSSION

This composite includes 1975–1976 hearings conducted by the Granite County Study Commission, under a Montana law requiring periodic evaluation of local government. The commission characterizes: law enforcement; local, state, and federal authority; redistricting; various forms of county government; potential budget reductions; personnel needs; the Montana Board of Crime Control; and Citizens for Constitutional Government.
RECORDED BY CAP GORMAN, VARIOUS DATES IN 1975 AND 1976, PHILIPSBURG.
SUMMARY: 8 PAGES
5 TAPES: 4 HOURS, 20 MINUTES

OH 97
BLACKFEET INDIAN SONGS

This collection of various Blackfeet songs—with accompanying explanations/interpretations by Mrs. James A. Watters—includes: "Love Song"; "Grass Dance"; "Squaw Dance"; "Medicine Lodge"; "Victory Song"; "Good Luck Song"; "Handgame Song"; "Crazy Dog Society Song"; "Crow Beaver Society Song"; "Owl Song"; "Blacktail Song"; "Giveaway Song." [Originally these songs were recorded on a wire machine.]
INTERVIEWED BY RALPH MCFADDEN, N.D., BROWNING.
1 TAPE: 40 MINUTES

OH 98
HARRY REIDINGER INTERVIEW

An Austrian native, Harry Reidinger tells about: his life in Butte from 1913 to 1952; his employers; his residences; his tailoring business; the history of Butte; Butte's Jewish community.
INTERVIEWED BY RONALD SPECTOR, NOVEMBER 25, 1973, NEW YORK, NY.
1 TAPE: 1 HOUR

OH 99
FORT PECK AGENCY BROADCAST

KLTZ radio in Glasgow aired this program on the centennial of the Battle of the Little Bighorn (June 25, 1976). The format includes: a brief history and description of Old Fort Peck; a short summary of the Battle of the Little Bighorn; readings of correspondence between the Fort Peck Indian Agent Thomas J. Mitchell and Commissioner of Indian Affairs J. Q. Smith concerning the attitudes and movements of various native bands following the defeat of George Armstrong Custer.
RECORDED BY KLTZ RADIO, JUNE 25, 1976, GLASGOW.
1 TAPE: 20 MINUTES

OH 100
HILL COUNTY AND HAVRE LOCAL-
GOVERNMENT STUDY COMMISSION
INTERVIEW

KOJM radio in Havre produced this 1976 program of interviews with representatives of the Hill County Local-Government Study Commission and with the Havre Local-Government Study Commission—two bodies established under the 1972 Montana Constitution. The comments generally reflect the commissioners' deliberative processes and their concerns about proposed alternative forms of government.
INTERVIEWED BY KOJM RADIO, JANUARY 21, 1976, HAVRE.
1 TAPE: 45 MINUTES

OH 101
MORRIS LINDSEY INTERVIEW

Morris Lindsey (b. 1909), a Minnesota native, assesses: his work as a barnstorming pilot in the Billings area during the 1920s; his subsequent employment as a private and a commercial pilot; serving as a flight instructor during World War II and the Korean War; his work as a flight engineer in Panama; his duties as maintenance supervisor at Malmstrom Air Force Base in Great Falls; the history of Montana aviation.
INTERVIEWED BY FRANK WILEY, 1971, HELENA.
1 TAPE: 50 MINUTES

OH 102
DEER LODGE CITY LOCAL-GOVERNMENT
STUDY COMMISSION

In this 1975 composite, members of the Deer Lodge City Local-Government Study Commission interview four members of the Deer Lodge City Council concerning: specific problems faced by the community; the relationship between those problems and the current system of city government. Additional material consists of radio spots informing the public about the government-review process, prescribed by the 1972 Montana Constitution.
INTERVIEWED BY STEVE OWEN, APRIL-NOVEMBER, 1975, DEER LODGE.
4 TAPES: 6 HOURS, 45 MINUTES

OH 103
AMERICAN ASSOCIATION OF UNIVERSITY
WOMEN INTERVIEWS

This collection comprises interviews with four female children of pioneer families in the Dillon and the Centennial Valley areas: Florence Backus; Thelma Bean; Jane Buck; Elizabeth Davis. Each woman addresses local personalities and social and economic conditions in the region from 1885 to 1920. These discussions are part of a project called "Women Pioneer Interviews," produced by the Dillon chapter of the AAUW. [A printed biographical sketch that portrays each interviewee is also available.]

INTERVIEWED BY DILLON CHAPTER, AAUW, 1976, DILLON.
SUMMARY: 10 PAGES
4 TAPES: 2 HOURS, 20 MINUTES

OH 104
PIONEER MONTANA AVIATORS INTERVIEWS

This collection comprises interviews with three pioneer Montana aviators: Perry Moore, W. H. Minnerly, and Robert R. Johnson. Also included is a narrative identification of the photo albums of Robert R. Johnson and Johnson's Flying Service and Penn Stohr. [Separated from RS 77.]

INTERVIEWED BY FRANK WILEY, 1962 AND 1963, TWODOT AND MISSOULA.
2 TAPES: 1 HOUR, 50 MINUTES

OH 105
EDMUND B. CRANEY SPEECH COLLECTION

Ed Craney—a pioneer of Montana radio broadcasting—created this collection of speeches (1938–1952) by transferring selections from phonograph records. The series includes speeches made by 52 Montana candidates for county, state, and national office, including: James E. Murray; Burton K. Wheeler; Jacob O'Connell; Arthur Lamey; Roy Ayers; T. J. Collins; Frank Walker; E. C. Gene Burris; J. Hugo Aronson. Additional speakers include Franklin Delano Roosevelt and Adolf Hitler. [Tapes exist in reel-to-reel format only.]

RECORDED BY EDMUND B. CRANEY, 1938–1952, BUTTE.
SUMMARY: 24 PAGES
12 TAPES: 24 HOURS

OH 106
HUNTLEY IRRIGATION PROJECT INTERVIEWS

Several of the original homesteaders of the Huntley Irrigation Project—located just east of Billings on the Yellowstone River—treat: individual homesteading experiences on the project; social and economic developments in the project community from 1907 to 1920. The interviewees include: A. J. Bowman; M. C. Smith; R. B. Stout; J. H. Hancock; J. W. Fitzgerald; C. Reed; W. Barkemeyer; J. Graham; M. Waterman; Vaclav "Jim" Kratochuil; Agnes Kratochuil; George Kratochuil; and Thelma Kratochuil.

INTERVIEWED BY RHODA DAWES SEAMANS, 1968 AND 1969, BALLANTINE.
SUMMARY: 7 PAGES
2 TAPES: 2 HOURS

OH 107
SWANSON SISTERS INTERVIEW

The three Swanson sisters—Myrtle Swanson Tepling, Ruby Swanson, and Florence Swanson—discuss: the story of Swanson's Lodge in Troy built by their father, Frank Swanson, about 1900; the history of their family; the interior decoration of the lodge; plans for the future use of the complex. *[See also General Montana OH 155.]*

INTERVIEWED BY UNIDENTIFIED PERSON, FEBRUARY, 1976, TROY.
SUMMARY: 2 PAGES
1 TAPE: 20 MINUTES

OH 108
MONTANA FARMERS UNION INTERVIEWS

Each of 50 interviewees—either Montana homesteaders or the children of Montana homesteaders—describes: his ancestry; early agricultural life; the advantages of the rural lifestyle; various difficulties facing modern farmers; the political and social attitudes of rural Montanans in the second half of the twentieth century.

INTERVIEWED BY PUBLIC-SCHOOL STUDENTS, 1979, VARIOUS LOCATIONS IN MONTANA.
TRANSCRIPTS AND SUMMARIES: 120 PAGES
11 TAPES: 13 HOURS

OH 109
EVERETT E. "BOO" MacGILVRA SPEECH

E. E. MacGilvra (1893–1980), a longtime member of the Lewis and Clark Trail Heritage Foundation, addresses the major developments of the Lewis and Clark expedition. He delivers this talk in support of the U.S. Bureau of Outdoor Recreation's "Plan 4" to preserve the Lewis and Clark Trail in Montana. *[See also General Montana OH 32, OH 628-29, and OH 1546.]*

RECORDED BY E. E. MacGILVRA, CIRCA 1973, BUTTE.
1 TAPE: 50 MINUTES

OH 110
MONTANA LAND-USE CONFERENCE

The Montana Land-Use Conference convened in Great Falls on November 21-23, 1974, and focused on issues, attitudes, and controversies surrounding land-use planning. The conference participants include state and federal officials, special-interest representatives, and citizens.

RECORDED BY THE MONTANA DEPARTMENT OF COMMUNITY AFFAIRS, NOVEMBER 21-23, 1974, GREAT FALLS.
SUMMARY: 14 PAGES
15 TAPES: 13 HOURS

OH 111
WESTERN MONTANA COLLEGE, LOCAL-HISTORY INTERVIEWS

Four students from Dr. Rex C. Myers's Methods of Local History class at Western Montana College in Dillon interview area residents regarding specific topics: Donald C. Scott on the operation of the Gilmore and Pittsburgh Railroad during the 1930s; Elizabeth Turner on conditions at the Dillon Public Library during the 1950s; Hal Amundson on his lifetime of fiddling; Mamie Case on the families and the conditions in the Centennial Valley during the 1920s and the 1930s.

INTERVIEWED BY VARIOUS STUDENTS, 1979–1980, DILLON.
4 TRANSCRIPTS: 19 PAGES
4 TAPES: 1 HOUR, 15 MINUTES

OH 112
MONTANA HISTORY CONFERENCE PROCEEDINGS, 1980

This composite of speeches, sessions, and papers from the Seventh Annual Montana History Conference—held in Billings on October 23-25, 1980—includes: Spike Van Cleve's introductory remarks on dude ranching; a panel discussion on the historical and cultural significance of the Battle of the Little Bighorn; a speech by Norman Maclean, quoting from his book *A River Runs through It*; Ivan Doig's explanation of the genesis of his book *This House of Sky*; a panel discussion regarding the effects of Montana on its authors.

RECORDED BY THE MONTANA HISTORICAL SOCIETY, OCTOBER 23-25, 1980, BILLINGS.
5 TAPES: 4 HOURS

OH 113
ETCHART FAMILY NARRATIVE

This composite includes Kurt Peters reading his romanticized short story, entitled "An American Story,"

based on the Etchart family. An additional narrative, intended for radio, includes: a discussion of John Etchart's Basque heritage; his formative years; Etchart's return to the United States; his purchase of a ranch south of Glasgow; sheep ranching.

INTERVIEWED BY WARREN HALL, 1979, GLASGOW.
1 TAPE: 15 MINUTES

OH 114
MONTANA HISTORY CONFERENCE PROCEEDINGS, 1975

This compilation derives from the Second Annual Montana History Conference, held in Helena on October 23-25, 1975. Panel discussions address: Montana agrarian radicalism; the role of women in politics; Senator Burton K. Wheeler; Indian-reservation history; political changes in Montana since World War II; western literature; the writing of local history. The speakers include: Professor Richard Ruetten; the author A. B. Guthrie; Governor Ted Schwinden; the legislator Francis Bardanouve; Professor Richard Etulain.

RECORDED BY THE MONTANA HISTORICAL SOCIETY, OCTOBER 23-25, 1975, HELENA.
SUMMARY: 18 PAGES
15 TAPES: 13 HOURS

OH 115
DOROTHY BRADLEY INTERVIEW

Dorothy Bradley—a Bozeman legislator from 1971 until 1979—recalls: environmental politics during the 1970s; women's political activities in Montana during the same decade; Toni Rosell; Francis Bardanouve; Thomas Judge; the Montana Environmental Policy Act; the Major Facilities Siting Act; the Constitutional Convention of 1972; the League of Women Voters (LWV).

INTERVIEWED BY JEFF SAFFORD, NOVEMBER 11, 1978, BUTTE.
TRANSCRIPT: 20 PAGES
2 TAPES: 2 HOURS

OH 116
JACK BRENNER INTERVIEW

Jack Brenner—a former Montana state legislator and the owner of the Lazy E4 Ranch in Beaverhead County—reflects on: cattle ranching in southwestern Montana from 1920 to 1960; his legislative career from 1948 to 1965; the Lazy E4 Ranch; the Brenner Livestock Company; his recollections of John Alonson, James E. Murray, Ted Schwinden, Wesley D'Ewart and Tim Babcock.

INTERVIEWED BY JEFF SAFFORD, SEPTEMBER 11 AND
OCTOBER 7, 1976, HORSE PRAIRIE.
TRANSCRIPT: 89 PAGES
5 TAPES: 7 HOURS

OH 117
BILL CHRISTIANSEN INTERVIEW

A Montana Democratic legislator (1964–1972) and
lieutenant governor (1972–1976), Bill Christiansen recounts: significant legislative developments in Montana
during the 1960s and 1970s; the internal operations of
the legislature and the lieutenant-governor's office; the
relationship between those two political entities; the func-
tions of political operatives on the county level.
INTERVIEWED BY JEFF SAFFORD, SEPTEMBER 15, 1978,
BOZEMAN.
TRANSCRIPT: 43 PAGES
2 TAPES: 2 HOURS

OH 118
WILLIAM GROFF INTERVIEW

William Groff (b. 1920), a native of Victor, recalls:
his experiences as a state legislator from 1954 to 1978;
his duties as director of the Montana Department of Rev-
enue; Montana politics in general; specific legislative
actions; Republican Party unity; the role of lobbyists;
various landmark legislation during the 1960s and the
1970s.
INTERVIEWED BY BILL LANG, SEPTEMBER 20, 1978,
VICTOR.
TRANSCRIPT: 50 PAGES
3 TAPES: 3 HOURS

OH 119
CLYDE HAWKS INTERVIEW

Clyde Hawks (b. 1918)—a Big Horn County businessman, rancher, and state legislator—relates: his service as House majority leader in the 1961 Montana Legislative Assembly; his recollections of John Aronson, Tim
Babcock, Roland Rene, Donald Nutter, Charles
Mahoney; the state legislative process; prominent legislators; Montana politics in general; agriculture and ranching; the John Birch Society.
INTERVIEWED BY JEFF SAFFORD, JULY 6, 1978, BILLINGS.
TRANSCRIPT: 49 PAGES
4 TAPES: 2 HOURS

OH 120
TED SCHWINDEN INTERVIEW

A Montana rancher, state legislator, commissioner of

state lands, lieutenant governor, and governor, Ted
Schwinden talks of: significant political developments
in Montana during the 1960s and the 1970s; his recollections of Donald Nutter, Thomas Judge, Hugo Aronson,
Forrest Anderson, Tim Babcock; the effectiveness of the
state's executive branch during his tenure as lieutenant
governor (1977–1981).
INTERVIEWED BY JEFF SAFFORD, DECEMBER 12, 1978,
HELENA.
TRANSCRIPT: 43 PAGES
2 TAPES: 1 HOUR, 30 MINUTES

OH 121
GEORGE M. GOSMAN INTERVIEW

The Dillon pharmacist George Gosman (b. 1893) reports on: his family history; his military service in France
during World War I; his several terms as a Montana state
senator (1944–1952); his duties as lieutenant governor
(1952–1956); Burton K. Wheeler, Wellington Rankin,
and Roy Ayers; serving as a member of the State Board
of Education, the State Board of Pharmacy, and the Montana Highway Commission.
INTERVIEWED BY JEFF SAFFORD, NOVEMBER 12, 1979, AND
FEBRUARY 27, 1980, MISSOULA.
TRANSCRIPT: 50 PAGES

OH 122
WILLIAM R. MACKAY, SR., INTERVIEW

Bill Mackay (b. 1911)—a retired Roscoe rancher and
a state legislator (1951–1971)—speaks of: the 80-year
history of the Mackay Ranch; his legislative experiences;
the Rosebud Land and Cattle Company; Roland Renne,
Wellington Rankin, Donald Nutter, John Aronson, Tim
Babcock; his parents, Malcolm S. and Mary Raynor
Mackay; his parents' friendship with the artist Charles
M. Russell.
INTERVIEWED BY JEFF SAFFORD, SEPTEMBER 9-10, 1978,
ROSCO.
TRANSCRIPT: 81 PAGES
3 TAPES: 5 HOURS

OH 123
MONTANA HISTORY CONFERENCE
PROCEEDINGS, 1977

The Fourth Annual Montana History Conference, held
in Helena on November 3-5, 1977, includes two key presentations: John T. Schlebecker's discussion of the purposes, values, and practices involved in the collection of
artifacts; Joan Hoff Wilson's interpretation of how
Jeannette Rankin's personality affected her views on

American foreign policy.
RECORDED BY THE MONTANA HISTORICAL SOCIETY,
NOVEMBER 3-5, 1977, HELENA.
2 TAPES: 2 HOURS

OH 124
MONTANA HISTORY CONFERENCE
PROCEEDINGS, 1976

The Third Annual Montana History Conference, held in Helena on November 5-7, 1976, includes presentations addressing: Northern Pacific Railroad land grants; Montana reactions to ethnic groups; Indian water rights; water-management issues; K. Ross Toole's views on state-history and local-history education; genealogical research; the operation of local museums and historical societies. *[A transcript for tapes 6-7 can be found in SC 1432.]*
RECORDED BY THE MONTANA HISTORICAL SOCIETY,
NOVEMBER 5-7, 1976, HELENA.
SUMMARY: 16 PAGES
13 TAPES: 10 HOURS, 30 MINUTES

OH 125
MONTANA HISTORY CONFERENCE
PROCEEDINGS, 1978

This composite of presentations—delivered at the Fifth Annual Montana History Conference, held in Butte on October 26-28, 1978—includes: H. Duane Hampton on opposition to the establishment of national parks; Dorothy Johnson on her short story and movie "The Hanging Tree"; Hans Walker on Indian treaties; Michael P. Malone on William A. Clark.
RECORDED BY THE MONTANA HISTORICAL SOCIETY,
OCTOBER 26-28, 1978, BUTTE.
4 TAPES: 2 HOURS, 30 MINUTES

OH 126
MONTANA HISTORY CONFERENCE
PROCEEDINGS, 1979

The Sixth Annual Montana History Conference, held in Helena on October 11-13, 1979, incorporates: Bob Morgan's talk on western art; Robert Utley's description of the cavalry trooper on the frontier; Father Peter Powell's lecture on Cheyenne ledger art; Richard Roeder's analysis of Joseph K. Howard's attitudes; Jerry Rodger's comments on historic preservation in Montana.
RECORDED BY THE MONTANA HISTORICAL SOCIETY,
OCTOBER 11-13, 1979, HELENA.
SUMMARY: 10 PAGES
6 TAPES: 5 HOURS, 30 MINUTES

OH 127
JOSEPH DIXON CEREMONY

This collection consists of the proceedings accompanying the unveiling of the bust of Joseph M. Dixon in the Montana State Capitol rotunda in Helena on November 17, 1972, and includes three primary speakers: the historian John Toole; Governor Forrest Anderson; the Montana politician Burton K. Wheeler.
RECORDED BY THE MONTANA HISTORICAL SOCIETY,
NOVEMBER 17, 1972, HELENA.
1 TAPE: 45 MINUTES

OH 128
MONTANA HISTORICAL SOCIETY-
ADMINISTRATION LECTURES

This collection consists of two lectures addressing historical-society administration: Willa K. Baum on the procedures, practices, and historical value of oral history; Robert A. Weinstein on photography in history and on some of the problems confronting photo archivists.
RECORDED BY THE AMERICAN ASSOCIATION FOR STATE AND LOCAL HISTORY, 1969 AND 1972, NASHVILLE, TN.
1 TAPE: 1 HOUR, 45 MINUTES

OH 129
LANNY ROSS RECORDING

The Great Falls singer and songwriter Lanny Ross is the focus of this September 27, 1968, promotional piece for his record album "Silver Dollar Country," including: portions of songs from the album; a brief explanation of the origin of the album; the research basic to the song writing. Many of the lyrics reflect the artist's attitudes about the West and about Montana history.
INTERVIEWED BY JULIUS PETERS, SEPTEMBER 27, 1968, GREAT FALLS.
1 TAPE: 15 MINUTES

OH 130
TRI-STATE TV REPEATER ASSOCIATION
REPORT

Jim Barr, an official with Rattlesnake Free TV of Missoula, reports to Jim Beamer of the Tri-State TV Repeater Association concerning harassment he encountered when he tried to establish a TV booster station in the Rattlesnake Valley near Missoula. [Separated from the Edmund B. Craney Papers, MC 122.]
INTERVIEWED BY JIM BARR, CIRCA JUNE 10, 1959, MISSOULA.
1 TAPE: 30 MINUTES

OH 131
WILLIAM FLOYD HARDIN READING

William Hardin (1890–1974)—a rancher, business-man, and writer from the Malta area—reads brief excerpts from the work "A Quiet Night in a Roundup Camp," included in his book *Campfires and Cowchips.* In the work, Hardin relies on his involvement with the Bloom Cattle Company and with the Circle Diamond Ranch to describe open-range procedures. *[See also General Montana OH 73.]*
INTERVIEWED BY MICHAEL S. KENNEDY, 1971, HELENA.
SUMMARY: 1 PAGE
1 TAPE: 10 MINUTES

OH 132
JOE E. HOWARD CONCERT

The singer, songwriter, and entertainer Joe Howard performs in concert at the Helena Civic Center on June 20, 1957. The performance consists of numerous songs popular during the 1900–1925 period, including Montana's official state song, "Montana," written in 1910 by Howard and Charles A. Cohan of Butte.
RECORDED BY JEAN BAUCUS, JUNE 20, 1957, HELENA.
SUMMARY: 1 PAGE
1 TAPE: 30 MINUTES

OH 133
JOSEPH KINSEY HOWARD SPEECH

Joseph Kinsey Howard (1906–1951), a Great Falls author, newspaperman, and historian, delivered a Charter Day address at the University of Montana in Missoula on March 11, 1948. He emphasizes the importance of legislative funding of the university system.
RECORDED BY THE UNIVERSITY OF MONTANA, MARCH 11, 1948, MISSOULA.
SUMMARY: 2 PAGES
1 TAPE: 45 MINUTES

OH 134
MID-AMERICA COUNCIL OF OUTDOOR RECREATION PROCEEDINGS

Proceedings of a planning committee of the Mid-America Council of Outdoor Recreation that met in Salt Lake City, Utah, in August, 1974, to address: finances; election of a vice-chairman; type and location of regional and central meetings; the structure, use, and worth of research reports; multiagency cooperation in matters concerning recreation and the environment.
RECORDED BY THE MONTANA DEPARTMENT OF FISH, WILDLIFE AND PARKS, AUGUST, 1974, SALT LAKE CITY, UT.
SUMMARY: 2 PAGES
2 TAPES: 2 HOURS

OH 135
JUDITH BASIN NARRATIVE

This narrative contains readings from an 1883 diary kept by an unidentified person and from 1884 editions of the (Maiden/Lewistown) *Fergus County Argus* that identify some of the contemporary residents, the activities, and the geographic characteristics of the Judith Basin area of central Montana.
RECORDED BY THE CENTRAL MONTANA HISTORICAL ASSOCIATION, N.D., LEWISTOWN.
SUMMARY: 1 PAGE
1 TAPE: 15 MINUTES

OH 136
MONTANA HISTORICAL SOCIETY ADVERTISEMENT

This brief radio advertisement, produced by the Montana Historical Society, promotes: the society's new book *Calamity Jane* by Roberta B. Sollid; subscriptions to the quarterly *Montana The Magazine of Western History*; the society's new museum exhibits; its C. M. Russell Art Gallery.
RECORDED BY THE MONTANA HISTORICAL SOCIETY, CIRCA 1958, HELENA.
SUMMARY: 1 PAGE
1 TAPE: 15 MINUTES

OH 137
MONTANA HISTORICAL SOCIETY RADIO PROGRAM

The Montana Historical Society assistant archivist Jeff Cuniff appears on KBLL radio in Helena to explain the society's efforts to collect and to preserve documents reflecting Montana's past and to answer call-in questions about Helena history.
RECORDED BY KBLL RADIO, OCTOBER 30, 1972, HELENA.
SUMMARY: 2 PAGES
1 TAPE: 30 MINUTES

OH 138
MONTANA PRESS ASSOCIATION PANEL

This panel discussion—sponsored by the Montana Press Association at its annual convention held in Helena on August 15-17, 1974—addresses the controversial issue of the public's right to know versus the individual's right to privacy. Panelists include: representatives of the press; a Common Cause spokesperson; a Montana state legislator; an academic humanist. The discussion is followed by questions from the floor.

RECORDED BY SAM GILLULY, AUGUST 16, 1974, HELENA.

SUMMARY: 4 PAGES

2 TAPES: 2 HOURS

OH 139
ROBERT H. FLETCHER SONGS

This composite embraces the work of Robert Fletcher—a Montana author, songwriter, composer, historian, and the creator of the Montana Highway Department's distinctive historical roadside signs. Included are: renditions of various songs written by Fletcher, including "Don't Fence Me In"; Fletcher's explanation of the controversy surrounding Cole Porter and the royalties for "Don't Fence Me In."

INTERVIEWED BY LEON PEARSON, 1954, RADIO CITY, NY, AND HELENA.

SUMMARY: 2 PAGES

2 TAPES: 2 HOURS

OH 140
MONTANA HISTORICAL SOCIETY CEREMONY

This 1956 ceremony marks the dedication of a historical telephone-office diorama—sponsored by the Mountain States Telephone and Telegraph Company—in the Formal Museum of the Montana Historical Society. Speakers include: Governor J. Hugo Aronson; the society director, K. Ross Toole; the society staff member Michael Kennedy; the artist Robert Morgan; several telephone-company officials.

RECORDED BY THE MONTANA HISTORICAL SOCIETY, 1956, HELENA.

SUMMARY: 2 PAGES

1 TAPE: 15 MINUTES

OH 141
MAMIE COX INTERVIEW

A Lame Deer resident, Mamie Cox (b. 1880) reviews: her arrival in Montana in 1886; her experiences operating the Three Circle Ranch with her husband.

INTERVIEWED BY UNIDENTIFIED MALE, CIRCA 1974, LAME DEER.

SUMMARY: 2 PAGES

1 TAPE: 45 MINUTES

OH 142
MONTANA HISTORICAL SOCIETY BOARD OF TRUSTEES MEETING

At this meeting of the Board of Trustees of the Montana Historical Society, held in Helena on January 20, 1978, members consider: state-records preservation; the use of public buildings for private purposes; an Earle Erik Heikka lawsuit; the ghost town of Garnet; support for local historical societies.

RECORDED BY THE MONTANA HISTORICAL SOCIETY, JANUARY 20, 1978, HELENA.

SUMMARY: 2 PAGES

1 TAPE: 1 HOUR, 30 MINUTES

OH 143
SOCIETY OF AMERICAN ARCHIVISTS WORKSHOP

This Society of American Archivists workshop, held in Columbus, Ohio, on November 3, 1976, includes a discussion on the techniques of still photography.

RECORDED BY THE WISCONSIN HISTORICAL SOCIETY, NOVEMBER 3, 1976, COLUMBUS, OH.

SUMMARY: 1 PAGE

1 TAPE: 30 MINUTES

OH 144
MONTANA LIBRARY ASSOCIATION BROADCAST

The Montana Library Association sponsored this February 17, 1966, radio broadcast, which features two speakers: Dr. Louis Shores, dean of the Florida State University Library School in Tallahassee, Florida; Mary K. Dempsey, librarian at the Montana Historical Society in Helena. Shores addresses different types of libraries, independent-study programs, and the future of the profession. Dempsey describes the holdings of the Montana Historical Society Library. *[See also General Montana OH 53, OH 54, OH 57, and OH 78.]*

RECORDED BY THE MONTANA HISTORICAL SOCIETY, FEBRUARY 17, 1966, HELENA.

SUMMARY: 2 PAGES

1 TAPE: 45 MINUTES

OH 145
MONTANA TERRITORIAL CENTENNIAL BROADCAST

This brief radio broadcast of a celebration preceding the Tournament of Roses Parade unofficially begins Montana's Territorial Centennial year and includes: Governor Tim Babcock; Senator Mike Mansfield; music by the Montana Centennial Band.

RECORDED BY NBC RADIO, JANUARY 1, 1964, PASADENA, CA.

SUMMARY: 1 PAGE

1 TAPE: 10 MINUTES

OH 146
MONTANA HISTORICAL SOCIETY BOARD OF TRUSTEES MEETING

Members of the Board of Trustees of the Montana Historical Society meet in Helena on February 19, 1966, and address: Director Michael Kennedy's difficulties with society staff, especially with the business manager, Dick Duffy; sick leave for the librarian, Mary K. Dempsey; the reconstitution of the executive board; a conflict between two staff members.

RECORDED BY THE MONTANA HISTORICAL SOCIETY, FEBRUARY 19, 1966, HELENA.

SUMMARY: 4 PAGES

2 TAPES: 1 HOUR, 30 MINUTES

OH 147
ELFREDA WOODSIDE INTERVIEW

A Dillon resident and president of the Beaverhead County Museum Association, Elfreda Woodside surveys her 1950s work with Charles Bovey to restore and to gain a state park designation for the Bannack ghost town site. *[See also General Montana OH 553 and OH 573.]*

INTERVIEWED BY DONNA DYRDAHL, APRIL 28, 1981, DILLON.

TRANSCRIPT: 14 PAGES

1 TAPE: 1 HOUR

OH 148
MONTANA HISTORICAL SOCIETY NARRATIVE

This composite of scripts, numbered 1 through 18, provides narration for displays in the Montana Historical Society's Frontier Museum designed with the assistance of the Smithsonian Institution in Washington, D.C.

RECORDED BY THE MONTANA HISTORICAL SOCIETY, CIRCA 1960, HELENA.

1 TAPE: 30 MINUTES

OH 149
HARRY SNYDER INTERVIEW

The explorer and adventurer Harry Snyder (b. 1882) summarizes: his friendship with the artist Charles M. Russell; his experiences as a railroad crew timekeeper in Mexico.

INTERVIEWED BY FRANK WILEY, JULY 24, 1967, TUCSON, AZ.

TRANSCRIPT: 3 PAGES

1 PHONO RECORD

OH 150
BILL STEARNS RECORDING

This record includes two narrations by Bill Stearns concerning: the songwriter and composer Joe Howard, the writer of Montana's official state song, "Montana" (1910); the industrialist and entrepreneur Henry Ford.

RECORDED BY MARY H. KIRSCHNER, 1971, VERO BEACH, FL.

1 PHONO RECORD

OH 151
MONTANA HISTORICAL SOCIETY SYMPOSIUM

This symposium—held in conjunction with the opening of the Nicolai Fechin Centennial Exhibition at the Montana Historical Society in Helena on June 15, 1981—considers: the life of this Russian-American artist; the breadth of his work; a series of photographs depicting Fechin's use of color and texture. Speakers include: Robert Archibald; Rick Newby; Fechin's biographer, Mary Balcomb; the artist's daughter Eya Branham.

RECORDED BY THE MONTANA HISTORICAL SOCIETY, JUNE 15, 1981, HELENA.

SUMMARY: 2 PAGES

1 TAPE: 40 MINUTES

OH 152
BOB HERRIG AND INEZ HERRIG INTERVIEW

Libby residents Bob Herrig (b. 1906) and Inez Herrig (b. 1910) tell of: their ancestries; childhood memories; social activities; rural education; professional employment; the lumber trade; their attitudes regarding late-twentieth-century social and economic changes in the Libby area.

INTERVIEWED BY JENNIFER THOMPSON AND VICTOR BJORNBERG, APRIL 24, 1980, LIBBY.

TRANSCRIPT: 40 PAGES

3 TAPES: 2 HOURS, 20 MINUTES

OH 153
MARVIN GREEN AND ENID GREEN INTERVIEW

Marvin Green and his wife, Enid Green, talk about: his employment as a railroadman; his duties as a fire-tower lookout; his work as a lumber-camp cook and a sawmill setter; his experiences as a musician traveling throughout northwestern Montana; recreational and com-

mercial use of the Kootenai River.
INTERVIEWED BY VICTOR BJORNBERG, MAY 10 AND JULY 27, 1980, LIBBY.
TRANSCRIPT: 52 PAGES
3 TAPES: 2 HOURS, 20 MINUTES

OH 154
GEORGE NEILS INTERVIEW

The Libby resident George Neils details: the logging operations of the J. Neils Lumber Company in Cass Lake, Minnesota, at the turn of the century; similar operations in the Libby and Columbia Falls areas early in the twentieth century; logging equipment and techniques; changing personnel policies; community relations; specific forest-management practices; the Kootenai National Forest.
INTERVIEWED BY INEZ HERRIG, APRIL 22, 1976, LIBBY.
TRANSCRIPT: 62 PAGES

OH 155
RUBY SWANSON INTERVIEW

Ruby Swanson—a longtime Troy resident—discusses: the history of her family; her father's employment in the Flathead Valley; early residents of Troy; social life; education; her work as manager of the Congressional Club in Washington, D.C.; environmental questions relating to Libby Dam and to other Kootenai River projects. [See also General Montana OH 107.]
INTERVIEWED BY JENNIFER THOMPSON AND INEZ HERRIG, NOVEMBER 26, 1979, TROY.
TRANSCRIPT: 23 PAGES
1 TAPE: 1 HOUR

OH 156
HILMAR HANSEN INTERVIEW

Hilmar Hansen (b. 1916), a Somers resident, discusses: his childhood in Fortine and Kalispell; the logging industry in northwestern Montana; his employment with the Great Northern Railway Company; his work for the J. Neils Lumber Company; environmental questions concerning Libby Dam and other Kootenai River projects; politics in general.
INTERVIEWED BY VICTOR BJORNBERG, JUNE 26, 1981, LIBBY.
TRANSCRIPT: 35 PAGES
2 TAPES: 2 HOURS

OH 157
HARRY SMITH INTERVIEW

Harry Smith (b. 1920) of Troy examines: the manual harvesting of cedar logs at the B. J. Carney Pole, Coke, and Coal Company near St. Mary; logging practices used in northwestern Montana forests during the 1940s and the 1950s.
INTERVIEWED BY VICTOR BJORNBERG, JULY 16, 1980, TROY.
TRANSCRIPT: 22 PAGES
2 TAPES: 1 HOUR, 30 MINUTES

OH 158
VICTOR SATHER INTERVIEW

Victor Sather discourses on: his work as a telegraph operator and as a station agent for the Great Northern Railway Company at Troy from 1909 to 1966; the operation of the railroad; changes in Troy and in the surrounding area.
INTERVIEWED BY VICTOR BJORNBERG, APRIL 27, 1980, TROY.
TRANSCRIPT: 34 PAGES
2 TAPES: 2 HOURS

OH 159
PALMER KNUDSON INTERVIEW

Palmer Knudson, a native of Libby, talks of: the work of his father, John Knudson, for the J. Neils Lumber Company in Libby; his own employment by the same company; the company's name change to the St. Regis Lumber Company; differences between the town of Libby during his father's day and his own; community activities; the development and the use of natural resources.
INTERVIEWED BY VICTOR BJORNBERG, MARCH 27, 1980, LIBBY.
TRANSCRIPT: 25 PAGES
2 TAPES: 1 HOUR, 30 MINUTES

OH 160
BILL FEWKES AND CLARA BROCK FEWKES INTERVIEW

Bill Fewkes and Clara Fewkes detail: their families' backgrounds; history of the Tobacco Plains; their personal employment histories; community life in Libby; the impact of the Libby Dam on the community of Rexford. [See also Small Town Montana OH 704 and OH 710.]
INTERVIEWED BY INEZ HERRIG, OCTOBER 9, 1980, REXFORD.
TRANSCRIPT: 35 PAGES
2 TAPES: 1 HOUR, 30 MINUTES

OH 161
DON WEYDEMEYER AND WINTON
WEYDEMEYER INTERVIEW

The Fortine residents Don Weydemeyer and his brother Winton Weydemeyer disclose: their family background; the early economy of the Tobacco Valley area, particularly the lumber industry; the construction of Libby Dam; the impact of the dam on the area; the growth of the Christmas tree plantation business. *[See also Small Town Montana OH 711.]*
INTERVIEWED BY VICTOR BJORNBERG AND SPARKY HILEMAN, MAY 1980, FORTINE.
TRANSCRIPT: 17 PAGES
2 TAPES: 1 HOUR, 30 MINUTES

OH 162
GRACE A. KENELTY INTERVIEW

Grace Kenelty—a longtime Libby area resident—depicts: her family's filing on a homestead outside Libby in 1906; her experiences on the homestead; education; personalities in the Libby area; visits to Libby by President Herbert Hoover and by the author Edith Wharton; the forest fires of 1910. *[See also General Montana OH 1576.]*
INTERVIEWED BY INEZ HERRIG AND JENNIFER THOMPSON, JANUARY 16, 1981, LIBBY.
TRANSCRIPT: 33 PAGES
2 TAPES: 1 HOUR

OH 163
EARL LOVICK INTERVIEW

Earl Lovick (b. 1920) describes: his 32 years as an employee of the W. R. Grace/Zonolite Company in Libby; the mining, processing, marketing, and uses of vermiculite; the company's responses to environmental concerns; the firm's hiring practices.
INTERVIEWED BY VICTOR BJORNBERG, JUNE 1980, LIBBY.
TRANSCRIPT: 15 PAGES
1 TAPE: 1 HOUR

OH 164
BERT THOMAS INTERVIEW

Bert "Homestead" Thomas describes: his family background; his childhood in the Troy area; his work as a lumberjack for the J. Neils Lumber Company; logging camps; the U.S. Forest Service.
INTERVIEWED BY VICTOR BJORNBERG AND SPARKY HILEMAN, APRIL 11, 1980, TROY.
SUMMARY: 3 PAGES
2 TAPES: 1 HOUR, 40 MINUTES

OH 165
BEN BAENEN INTERVIEW

A Libby resident, Ben Baenen delineates: his personal and family backgrounds; his six years working for the Great Northern Railway Company; his duties during 30 years of employment with the U.S. Forest Service; his work as a self-employed guide and outfitter.
INTERVIEWED BY VICTOR BJORNBERG, JUNE, 1980, LIBBY.
TRANSCRIPT: 21 PAGES
1 TAPE: 1 HOUR

OH 166
PAULINE HARMON INTERVIEW

Pauline Harmon—a longtime resident of Libby—converses on: life in the area's mobile lumber camps during the early 1900s; her experiences homesteading on the plains near Malta.
INTERVIEWED BY SHERRY MCKEAN, JANUARY 12, 1978, LIBBY.
TRANSCRIPT: 11 PAGES
1 TAPE: 40 MINUTES

OH 167
F. W. McCORMICK INTERVIEW

F. W. McCormick considers: the experiences of his father, Jack McCormick, along the Yaak River in northwestern Montana at the turn of the century; growing up near the confluence of the Yaak and the Kootenai rivers; the community of Sylvanite; social, economic, and cultural life in the Troy area from 1910 to 1930.
INTERVIEWED BY VICTOR BJORNBERG, AUGUST, 1968, TROY.
TRANSCRIPT: 23 PAGES
1 TAPE: 1 HOUR

OH 168
BILL YOUNG INTERVIEW

Bill Young chronicles: his operation of the Kootenai River ferries at Ural and Warland from the 1930s into the 1950s; specifics concerning ferry construction and operation.
INTERVIEWED BY STEVE HICKMAN, JULY 7, 1977, EUREKA.
TRANSCRIPT: 15 PAGES
1 TAPE: 55 MINUTES

OH 169
JERRY FRITCH INTERVIEW

Jerry Fritch (b. 1888) comments on: his experiences in the Kootenai River Valley of Montana since 1904; his role in constructing and operating the river ferries at

Warland and Ural.
INTERVIEWED BY INEZ HERRIG, 1968, LIBBY.
SUMMARY: 2 PAGES
1 TAPE: 1 HOUR

OH 170
HARRY HUSON AND FRED HUSON INTERVIEW

Harry Huson and his brother Fred Huson assess: their arrival in the Libby area in 1919; their neighbors; education; area wildlife; unusual events in their lives.
INTERVIEWED BY INEZ HERRIG, 1968, LIBBY.
SUMMARY: 2 PAGES
1 TAPE: 40 MINUTES

OH 171
KATE PELOQUIN YOUNG AND JACK YOUNG INTERVIEW

Kate Young and her stepson Jack Young describe: her life in the Ural area; her childhood experiences on the Peloquin homestead in Lincoln County; log drives; her husband, Rufus Young. Jack Young discusses his experiences as the builder, maintainer, and operator of the Kootenai River ferry from 1930 into the 1950s.
INTERVIEWED BY INEZ HERRIG, OCTOBER 10, 1969, URAL.
SUMMARY: 2 PAGES
1 TAPE: 40 MINUTES

OH 175
HEDGE HAMMONS INTERVIEW

A Ural resident, Hedge Hammons addresses: filing on his homestead in the Ural area in 1923; his operation of the Ural ferry from 1938 to 1950; particulars about the construction and operation of the ferry; ferrymen; the area families who used the ferry.
INTERVIEWED BY INEZ HERRIG, 1978, LIBBY.
SUMMARY: 2 PAGES
1 TAPE: 20 MINUTES

OH 176
MARGARET GOMPF INTERVIEW

Margaret Gompf of Libby describes: the Gompf Funeral Home in Libby, owned by her father-in-law and managed by her mother-in-law, Lauradell Gompf; Lauradell Gompf's service as county coroner; family experiences both in Libby and across Montana.
INTERVIEWED BY JOY BANKS, 1978, LIBBY.
SUMMARY: 2 PAGES
1 TAPE: 55 MINUTES

OH 177
"PROBLEMS OF AGING" PROCEEDINGS

This public forum, entitled "The Problems of Aging," considers the various difficulties confronting the elderly. Social-service employees and state politicians provide introductory remarks. A summary of ideas expressed in small-group discussions—regarding taxes, housing, insurance, stereotyping, and political representation—concludes the program.
RECORDED BY THE LIBBY DAM BRANCH OF THE MONTANA HISTORICAL SOCIETY, SEPTEMBER 27, 1981, LIBBY.
TRANSCRIPT: 22 PAGES
2 TAPES: 1 HOUR, 30 MINUTES

OH 178
KOOTENAI SEMINAR: "WATERS OF WEALTH" PROCEEDINGS

This seminar, entitled "Waters of Wealth," was held in Libby on June 24-25, 1977, to examine the history of the Kootenai region of northwestern Montana and southern British Columbia. The proceedings consist of presentations by various professionals, including geologists, foresters, historians, engineers, linguists, and a physician.
RECORDED BY THE LIBBY DAM BRANCH OF THE MONTANA HISTORICAL SOCIETY, JUNE 24-25, 1977, LIBBY.
TRANSCRIPT: 237 PAGES
9 TAPES: 8 HOURS

OH 179
KOOTENAI SEMINAR: "THE SEARCH FOR THE KOOTENAI PAST" PROCEEDINGS

This seminar, designated "The Search for the Kootenai Past," was held in Libby on July 21-23, 1978, to explore the archaeological/historical issue of Kootenai Indian culture in the Kootenai River drainage of northwestern Montana and southern British Columbia. Speakers consider: archaeological investigations of Kootenai inhabitation in the area; links between the disciplines of history and archaeology (Harry Fritz); criticism of Anglo research and of Anglo interpretation of Kootenai archaeological findings (Kootenai tribal members); the American Bison.
RECORDED BY THE LIBBY DAM BRANCH OF THE MONTANA HISTORICAL SOCIETY, JULY 21-23, 1978, LIBBY.
TRANSCRIPT: 211 PAGES
9 TAPES: 8 HOURS

OH 180
KOOTENAI SEMINAR: "MINING IN THE KOOTENAI" PROCEEDINGS

This complementary seminar, entitled "Mining in the Kootenai," convened in Libby on August 3-4, 1979, to review the past, present, and future of the mining industry in the Kootenai region of northwestern Montana and southern British Columbia. Professional speakers treat: positive and negative ramifications of mining; various forms of mining legislation; the implementation of existing regulations governing mining.
RECORDED BY THE LIBBY DAM BRANCH OF THE MONTANA HISTORICAL SOCIETY, AUGUST 3-4, 1979, LIBBY.
TRANSCRIPT: 202 PAGES
9 TAPES: 8 HOURS

OH 181
A READERS' THEATER PLAY: "KOOTENAI LINEAGE"

"Kootenai Lineage"—a readers' theater presentation of the Libby Dam Branch of the Montana Historical Society and of the Lincoln County Heritage Museum—was produced in Libby in 1978. This compilation of interviews with longtime residents of the Kootenai River Valley of northwestern Montana is interspersed with narration; it presents an overview of the economic and social history of the valley and the origins of its early white settlers.
RECORDED BY THE LIBBY DAM BRANCH OF THE MONTANA HISTORICAL SOCIETY, 1978, LIBBY.
TRANSCRIPT: 55 PAGES

OH 182
CURLEY MEEK NARRATIVE

Curley Meek—who drilled the first oil well at Cat Creek, in 1920—describes a series of 1920 photographs taken by Herb Titters of the Corner Studio in Lewistown of the Cat Creek oil-field operations, identifying some individual workers. The photographs described are held by the Montana Historical Society Photo Archives.
PARTIAL TRANSCRIPT: 9 PAGES
1 TAPE: 1 HOUR

OH 550
DOMINICK BONTEMPS INTERVIEW

The Butte miner Dominick Bontemps tells of: his first underground job at age 16 in the Leonard Mine; the difficulties of getting to work; his subsequent employment in the Belmont, the Travonia, the Tramway, the Anselma, the Lexington, and the Mountain Con mines; mining techniques; specific mining terminology.
INTERVIEWED BY REX C. MYERS, 1982, BUTTE.
SUMMARY: 2 PAGES
1 TAPE: 20 MINUTES

OH 551
EMILY MAE SHERMAN INTERVIEW

Emily Sherman briefly recalls: her first two years of teaching at rural schools in Medicine Lodge and in Maudlow from 1929 to 1931; particulars of the physical facilities and functioning of those schools.
INTERVIEWED BY REX C. MYERS, NOVEMBER 19, 1982, BUTTE.
SUMMARY: 2 PAGES
1 TAPE: 13 MINUTES

OH 552
DELBERT HARTFORD INTERVIEW

Delbert Hartford, who served as the railroad station agent at Alder from 1950 to 1982, talks about: his move to Alder; the operation of the Alder station; the methods of ore shipment from Virginia City and from the Ruby Mountains; the shipment of cattle; the operation of the Northern Pacific Railroad (N.P.) versus the operation of the Burlington Northern Railroad (B.N.); the old N.P. depot versus the new B.N. depot.
INTERVIEWED BY ROSEANN TROYER, JULY 21, 1982, ALDER.
SUMMARY: 2 PAGES
1 TAPE: 50 MINUTES

OH 553
ELFREDA WOODSIDE INTERVIEW

Elfreda Woodside, the founder and the director of the Beaverhead County Museum in Dillon, talks about: the history of the museum; the challenges of operating a small town museum in Montana. [See also General Montana OH 147 and OH 573.]
INTERVIEWED BY REX C. MYERS, JULY 31, 1982, DILLON.
SUMMARY: 1 PAGE
1 TAPE: 33 MINUTES

OH 554
SAM DENNY INTERVIEW

Sam Denny—a trapper and a prospector in the Ruby Mountains of southwestern Montana—surveys: difficulties he encountered running trap lines in the heavy snows of 1931–1932; his experiences prospecting; his work for the CCC during the 1930s.
INTERVIEWED BY BRUCE ALLEN, JULY 1, 1982, BUTTE.

SUMMARY: 2 PAGES
1 TAPE: 30 MINUTES

OH 555
NELLIE TWEET INTERVIEW

A Butte resident, Nellie Tweet recalls: her childhood in Ireland; her journey alone to Butte in 1927; her work as a housemaid in the home of James Ryan Gaul on Butte's fashionable west side.

INTERVIEWED BY CLAUDIA CLAQUE TWEET, JULY 18, 1982, BUTTE.

SUMMARY: 4 PAGES
1 TAPE: 40 MINUTES

OH 556
MARY SHOBE FORD SPEECH

Mary Ford, wife of Governor Sam C. Ford (1941–1949), provides an anecdotal account of life in the Montana governor's mansion from the 1860s into the 1970s—focusing on the experiences of Mrs. Sidney Edgerton and on herself. *[See also General Montana OH 623.]*

RECORDED BY THE MONTANA HISTORICAL SOCIETY, 1978, HELENA.

SUMMARY: 1 PAGE
1 TAPE: 35 MINUTES

OH 557
AUGUSTA ELIASON TRASK INTERVIEW

Augusta Trask (b. 1862) discusses: her birth in a wagon, as her family moved to Utah; the family's migration to Idaho and then to Deer Lodge, Montana Territory; her mother's preparations for the rumored arrival of the retreating Nez Perces during the late summer of 1877; pioneer life in the Deer Lodge Valley during the 1870s.

INTERVIEWED BY THELMA SHAW, 1953, DEER LODGE.

SUMMARY: 2 PAGES
1 TAPE: 30 MINUTES

OH 558
WALTER JOHN POTTER INTERVIEW

Walter Potter recounts: growing up on a Minnesota farm; his military service at Fort Abraham Lincoln, North Dakota, and at Fort Keogh during the early 1890s; Indian customs; sports; the community of Miles City.

INTERVIEWED BY EDWARD BRADLEY, JUNE, 1961, SAN PABLO, CA.

SUMMARY: 1 PAGE
2 TAPES: 1 HOUR, 8 MINUTES

OH 559
DOROTHY BRADING AND MARGARET WALKER INTERVIEWS

Dorothy Brading and Margaret Walker—sisters who are longtime residents of Columbia Falls—speak of: their father, A. L. Jordan; the family's lumber business; their childhoods; their early work experiences; their educations at the University of Montana; social life in Columbia Falls during Prohibition and during the 1930s Depression. *[See also Small Town Montana OH 720.]*

INTERVIEWED BY MARY MURPHY, MARCH 14, 1982, COLUMBIA FALLS.

TRANSCRIPT: 50 PAGES
2 TAPES: 2 HOURS, 30 MINUTES

OH 560
TEDDY BURNS INTERVIEW

A Babb resident, Teddy Burns reflects on: his family's history in the St. Mary's area and in Glacier National Park; the liquor trade near the park; the problem of poaching in the park.

INTERVIEWED BY MARY MURPHY, APRIL 8, 1982, BABB.

TRANSCRIPT: 22 PAGES
1 TAPE: 1 HOUR

OH 561
LAURA MARBLE CUNNINGHAM INTERVIEW

Laura Cunningham reviews: growing up in North Dakota; her teaching experiences in Couer d'Alene, Idaho, and in Whitefish, Montana; working with her first husband, Ray Marble, to establish his photography business in the Flathead Valley; her employment as a switchboard operator at Apgar; her teaching job in West Glacier.

INTERVIEWED BY MARY MURPHY, JANUARY 29, 1982, WEST GLACIER.

TRANSCRIPT: 18 PAGES
1 TAPE: 1 HOUR

OH 562
HELENA DAWSON EDKINS INTERVIEW

Helena Edkins relates: the role of her father, Tom Dawson, in building Two Medicine Lodge in Glacier National Park; his construction of other buildings in the area; his experiences as a guide for hunting parties; her childhood on a dude ranch in East Glacier.

INTERVIEWED BY MARY MURPHY, APRIL 13, 1982, EAST GLACIER.

TRANSCRIPT: 12 PAGES
1 TAPE: 45 MINUTES

OH 563
ROBERT FRAUSON INTERVIEW

Robert Frauson recalls: his early career as a silversmith; his World War II service in the Mountain Division of the U.S. Army; his work at Rocky Mountain National Park in Colorado on ski patrol and as a mountain rescue ranger; his ranger career in Glacier National Park.

INTERVIEWED BY MARY MURPHY AND JERRY DESANTO, MARCH 30, 1982, ST. MARY.

TRANSCRIPT: 39 PAGES

2 TAPES: 3 HOURS

OH 564
DAN HUFFINE INTERVIEW

A Flathead Valley resident, Dan Huffine remembers: his work as a tour-bus driver and as a seasonal park ranger in Glacier National Park during the 1920s; owning and operating a tourist camp near Essex; managing the Kalispell bus depot during World War II.

INTERVIEWED BY MARY MURPHY, FEBRUARY 1, 1982, COLUMBIA FALLS.

TRANSCRIPT: 20 PAGES

1 TAPE: 1 HOUR, 30 MINUTES

OH 565
BEATRICE MACOMBER INTERVIEW

Beatrice Macomber reports on: her childhood on a Lake McDonald homestead, prior to the 1910 creation of Glacier National Park; life in Columbia Fall; the Lake McDonald boarding house and midwife businesses of her mother, Lydia Comeau; development around Lake McDonald during the twentieth century.

INTERVIEWED BY MARY MURPHY, FEBRUARY 12, 1982, KALISPELL.

TRANSCRIPT: 29 PAGES

1 TAPE: 1 HOUR, 30 MINUTES

OH 566
SELINA MONROE INTERVIEW

A Browning resident, Selina Monroe (b. 1895) discusses: her life in Browning as the daughter of a Blackfeet mother and an Irish father; relations between full-bloods and mixed-bloods on the Blackfeet Reservation; Native American ceremonies during the early 1900s; changes in area place-names. Selina Monroe's daughter, Babe Mutch, and her grandniece, Loretta Pepion, also participate in the interview.

INTERVIEWED BY MARY MURPHY, APRIL 6, 1982, BROWNING.

TRANSCRIPT: 37 PAGES

2 TAPES: 2 HOURS, 30 MINUTES

OH 567
EDWINA NOFFSINGER INTERVIEW

Edwina Noffsinger—the widow of the attorney and horse concessionaire George Noffsinger—addresses: growing up with the Charles E. Conrad family in Kalispell; teaching school in Puerto Rico; her work for her husband's Park Saddle Horse Company in Glacier National Park; unfair treatment of the horse concessionaire by the Great Northern Railway Company and by the National Park Service; dude ranches.

INTERVIEWED BY MARY MURPHY, APRIL 7, 1982, BABB.

TRANSCRIPT: 26 PAGES

2 TAPES: 2 HOURS

OH 568
PEGGY SARSFIELD INTERVIEW

Peggy Sarsfield—the daughter of Thomas Jefferson Davis, one of the founders of the Waterton-Glacier International Peace Park—describes: her father's early work for the YMCA; his long association with Rotary International, the sponsoring organization for the Peace Park.

INTERVIEWED BY MARY MURPHY, FEBRUARY 24, 1982, BUTTE.

TRANSCRIPT: 8 PAGES

1 TAPE: 30 MINUTES

OH 569
GERALD UNDERWOOD INTERVIEW

Gerald Underwood assesses: his work in the CCC, stationed in Glacier National Park from 1933 to 1935; his duties as a CCC camp commander from 1938 to 1941; the particulars of CCC camp administration; his employment as a procurement officer for the National Park Service in Glacier during the 1950s and the 1960s.

INTERVIEWED BY MARY MURPHY, FEBRUARY 23, 1982, MANHATTAN.

TRANSCRIPT: 25 PAGES

1 TAPE: 1 HOUR, 30 MINUTES

OH 570
JESS UNDERWOOD INTERVIEW

A Whitefish resident, Jess Underwood examines: his work as a fire lookout and as a timber cruiser during the 1930s; running trap lines; his duties at the Snow Laboratory at Summit; supervising logging at Hungry Horse Reservoir.

INTERVIEWED BY MARY MURPHY, MARCH 12, 1982,
WHITEFISH.
TRANSCRIPT: 30 PAGES
2 TAPES: 2 HOURS

OH 571
LENORE T. McCOLLUM INTERVIEW
Lenore McCollum characterizes: her childhood in
Twin Bridges; teaching high school math in Dillon; her
hobby of traveling to the headwaters of rivers around
the world. [See also Montanans at Work OH 388.]
INTERVIEWED BY KIM HOLLAND, JUNE 6, 1980, DILLON.
TRANSCRIPT: 11 PAGES
1 TAPE: 1 HOUR

OH 572
MAY TONREY INTERVIEW
May Tonrey—a longtime Dillon resident—discourses
on: growing up in Dillon and on a ranch outside of Dillon;
the types of entertainment available; playing in the
Tonrey-Baxter Orchestra with her husband, Francis
Tonrey, from 1914 to 1936.
INTERVIEWED BY KIM HOLLAND, MAY 21, 1980, DILLON.
TRANSCRIPT: 8 PAGES
1 TAPE: 45 MINUTES

OH 573
ELFREDA WOODSIDE INTERVIEW
Elfreda Woodside recalls: her childhood in Dillon;
Dillon's Chinese vegetable gardens; traveling circuses
that came to town; local political campaigns; her
husband's automobile dealership in Dillon; her husband's
interest in flying. [See also General Montana OH 147
and OH 553.]
INTERVIEWED BY KIM HOLLAND, JUNE 14, 1980, DILLON.
TRANSCRIPT: 7 PAGES
1 TAPE: 30 MINUTES

OH 574
JOHN SHAFFNER INTERVIEW
Dillon resident John Shaffner discloses: his work as
a telegrapher, as a railroad ticket agent, and as a freight
agent in Dillon; the expansion of his small homestead to
a 10,000-acre cattle ranch.
INTERVIEWED BY KIM HOLLAND, JUNE 13, 1980, DILLON.
TRANSCRIPT: 4 PAGES
1 TAPE: 20 MINUTES

OH 576
GEORGIANNA CROUSE ANDERSEN INTERVIEW
Georgianna Andersen comments on: farming on the
East Bench in Beaverhead County under difficult condi-
tions during the early 1900s; her married life on a sheep
ranch near Bannack; many of the old buildings in Dillon;
the locations of many former businesses in town. [See
also Montanans at Work OH 354.]
INTERVIEWED BY KIM HOLLAND, JUNE 21, 1980, DILLON.
TRANSCRIPT: 26 PAGES

OH 577
WINIFRED McMANNIS SCHWARTZ AND
RAYMOND M. SCHWARTZ INTERVIEW
Winifred Schwartz details: her childhood in Bannack
and in Argenta; her work as a telephone operator in
Dillon. Raymond Schwartz considers: his work as a
mortician; his duties as the Beaverhead County coroner;
his involvement in a posse that arrested the murderer
E. C. Davis in 1920.
INTERVIEWED BY KIM HOLLAND, JUNE 5, 1980, DILLON.
TRANSCRIPT: 16 PAGES

OH 578
J. E. SELWAY INTERVIEW
A Dillon inhabitant, J. E. Selway describes: his grandfather, James Selway, raising Percheron horses for use
in the Butte Fire Department; early Dillon rodeos; a trip
through Yellowstone National Park by wagon early in
the century; various types of buggies and wagons; home-
made skis; the creation of Selway Park, later renamed
Dilmont Park, in Dillon; the differences between lambing on early sheep ranches and on modern sheep ranches.
INTERVIEWED BY KIM HOLLAND, JUNE 14, 1980, DILLON.
TRANSCRIPT: 12 PAGES

OH 579
VICTOR GIUSEPPE SEGNA, SR., INTERVIEW
Victor Segna—a Tyrolean miner and musician in
Butte—converses on: his work in the Butte mines dur-
ing the 1920s; playing accordion at the Alley Bar in Finn
Town and in other bars around Butte. Louise Zanchi,
present during the taping, also contributes to this inter-
view. [See also General Montana OH 580.]
INTERVIEWED BY RUSS MAGNAGHI, MAY 3, 1983, BUTTE.
SUMMARY: 2 PAGES
1 TAPE: 30 MINUTES

OH 580
LOUISE ZANCHI INTERVIEW

A longtime Butte resident, Louise Zanchi depicts: the cultural/social/economic life of Italians in the Meaderville section of Butte. Victor Segna, present during the taping, also contributes to this interview. *[See also General Montana OH 579.]*
INTERVIEWED BY RUSS MAGNAGHI, MAY 3, 1983, BUTTE.
SUMMARY: 2 PAGES
2 TAPES: 50 MINUTES

OH 581
ANGELO PETRONI INTERVIEW

Angelo Petroni delineates: the activities, the goals, and the history of the Christoforo Columbo Lodge in Butte; the importance of the lodge to the Italian population of Butte; the community of Meaderville and its prominent institutions.
INTERVIEWED BY RUSS MAGNAGHI, MAY 4, 1983, BUTTE.
SUMMARY: 2 PAGES
1 TAPE: 50 MINUTES

OH 582
LUIGI PASINI AND NORMA PASINI INTERVIEW

Both Butte residents, Luigi Pasini and Norma Pasini discuss: their experiences as Italian immigrants living in Butte; the contrasts between the Italian communities in Butte and in Elkhorn; winemaking and food preparation; the Christoforo Columbo Lodge.
INTERVIEWED BY RUSS MAGNAGHI, MAY 4, 1983, BUTTE.
SUMMARY: 3 PAGES
1 TAPE: 1 HOUR

OH 583
CAMILLE MAFFEI AND LUCY MAFFEI INTERVIEW

Camille Maffei and her mother, Lucy Maffei, interpret the social life, the people, the businesses, and the churches of the Italian community of Meaderville, located adjacent to Butte.
INTERVIEWED BY RUSS MAGNAGHI, MAY 4, 1983, BUTTE.
SUMMARY: 3 PAGES
1 TAPE: 1 HOUR

OH 584
BILL FORREST INTERVIEW

Bill Forrest (1898–1984) of Helena discusses: his work in Montana stone quarries; the locations of various quarries; the evolution of tools and of techniques in stonemasonry during his career; projects he participated in.
INTERVIEWED BY PETER HELD, APRIL 1, 1980, HELENA.
SUMMARY: 2 PAGES
2 TAPES: 2 HOURS

OH 585
WILLIAM KELLER INTERVIEW

William Keller (b. 1929), an Opportunity stonemason, portrays: his apprenticeship with the stonemason Lewis H. Reid in Helena; specific techniques of stonemasonry; changes in the profession during his career; the tools of the trade.
INTERVIEWED BY PETER HELD, APRIL 10, 1980, OPPORTUNITY.
SUMMARY: 2 PAGES
1 TAPE: 45 MINUTES

OH 586
JOHN M. NICKEY INTERVIEW

The Bozeman stonemason John Nickey—author of *The Stoneworker's Bible* and *The Trowelworker's Bible*—addresses: stonemasonry; the advantages and disadvantages of different types of rock and different techniques; the history of stonemasonry; his philosophy about religion and politics.
INTERVIEWED BY PETER HELD, JUNE 7, 1980, BOZEMAN.
SUMMARY: 3 PAGES
2 TAPES: 2 HOURS

OH 587
CITIZENS' FORUM PROCEEDINGS, 1982

This Citizens' Forum convened in Helena on March 25-27, 1982, to observe the 10th anniversary of the 1972 Constitutional Convention. Speakers analyze the durability and the impact of the 1972 Montana Constitution. Sponsors include the Montana Constitutional Society of 1972 and the University of Montana's Bureau of Government Research; funding derived from the Montana Committee for the Humanities.
RECORDED BY THE MONTANA HISTORICAL SOCIETY, MARCH 25-27, 1982, HELENA.
SUMMARY: 2 PAGES
10 TAPES: 10 HOURS

OH 588
MONTANA HISTORY CONFERENCE PROCEEDINGS, 1981

The Eighth Annual Montana History Conference convened in Helena on October 1-3, 1981. The gathering includes panels on: the more colorful aspects of Butte; Senators James E. Murray, Mike Mansfield, and Lee

Metcalf; pioneer physicians; children on the frontier; the winners of "the five best books on Montana" contest (Harry Fritz).
RECORDED BY THE MONTANA HISTORICAL SOCIETY, OCTOBER 1-3, 1981, HELENA.
SUMMARY: 2 PAGES
9 TAPES: 9 HOURS

OH 589
WESTERN GOVERNORS' CONFERENCE ON AGRICULTURE

The Western Governors' Conference on Agriculture, hosted by Governor Tom Judge of Montana, met in Billings from March 31 to April 3, 1975. Participants discuss the relationship of western energy resources and western agriculture to the world food crisis. [Separated from the Governor Thomas Judge Records, RS 246.]
RECORDED BY THE MONTANA GOVERNOR'S OFFICE, MARCH 31–APRIL 3, 1975, BILLINGS.
SUMMARY: 3 PAGES
22 TAPES: 22 HOURS

OH 590
MOUNT HAGGIN WILDLIFE MANAGEMENT AREA CEREMONY

An official ceremony was held in 1976 to transfer William M. O'Neil's 53,000-acre Mount Haggin Ranch, located outside of Anaconda, to the Nature Conservancy, prior to the property becoming the Mount Haggin Wildlife Management Area. [Separated from the Governor Thomas Judge Papers, RS 246.]
RECORDED BY THE MONTANA GOVERNOR'S OFFICE, 1976, ANACONDA.
1 TAPE: 22 MINUTES

OH 591
THOMAS JUDGE SPEECHES

This composite of presentations made by Governor Thomas Judge (1973–1981) includes: his 1973 inauguration speech; 1976 and 1977 state of the state messages; a 1977 budget message; a 1975 speech to the Montana Farmers Union convention; several brief radio messages. [Separated from the Governor Thomas Judge Papers, RS 246.]
RECORDED BY OFFICE OF THE GOVERNOR, VARIOUS DATES, VARIOUS MONTANA LOCATIONS
SUMMARY: 2 PAGES
6 TAPES: 6 HOURS

OH 592
PAUL HARVEY RADIOCAST

Paul Harvey, a national radio news broadcaster, recounts: a day in 1976 in Cascade when he rode in the town's U.S. Bicentennial parade; the old-fashioned values and the lifestyle of the people of Cascade. [Separated from the Governor Tom Judge Papers, RS 246.]
RECORDED BY THE MONTANA GOVERNOR'S OFFICE, 1976, TAPED FROM A RADIO BROADCAST IN HELENA.
1 TAPE: 14 MINUTES

OH 593
ANNIE KIRCH BISBY INTERVIEW

Annie Bisby—a Winston resident—discusses: her parents, Lewis and Ann Kirch; the family's immigration to Montana from Austria; her childhood on a ranch near Winston during the late 1890s and the early 1900s; her adult life as a ranch wife.
INTERVIEWED BY THILDA NILSON WILLIAMS, JANUARY 20, 1983, LIVINGSTON.
SUMMARY: 2 PAGES
1 TAPE: 33 MINUTES

OH 594
MINNIE BOURBON BRUCE INTERVIEW

Minnie Bruce recalls: her childhood in the foothills of the Ozark Mountains of Missouri; her experiences teaching in one-room schools in Missouri and Wyoming; her homesteading, ranching, and oil-leasing interests in Wyoming and Montana.
INTERVIEWED BY THILDA NILSON WILLIAMS, MARCH 10, 1983, TOWNSEND.
SUMMARY: 2 PAGES
1 TAPE: 1 HOUR, 20 MINUTES

OH 595
JOHN MARTIN RALLS INTERVIEW

A Radersburg resident, John Ralls (b. 1909) discourses on: growing up in Cable Gulch near Radersburg; his father's operation of the local Keystone Mine; his education at the Montana College of Mines and Technology in Butte; his work in several assaying jobs; the 1948 establishment of his own company to supply iron ore to the Ideal Cement plant in Trident; life in and around Radersburg.
INTERVIEWED BY THILDA NILSON WILLIAMS, FEBRUARY 21, 1983, RADERSBURG.
SUMMARY: 2 PAGES
1 TAPE: 30 MINUTES

OH 596
MARY KEEGAN D'ARCY INTERVIEW

Mary D'Arcy, a resident of Townsend, discloses: her childhood in Ireland; problems with Irish landlords; her first husband, John Seery; her life on a ranch near Townsend, where she met her second husband, Will D'Arcy; living in the community of Townsend; her four children.

INTERVIEWED BY THILDA NILSON WILLIAMS, FEBRUARY 23, 1983, TOWNSEND.
SUMMARY: 2 PAGES
3 TAPES: 3 HOURS

OH 597
MILDRED FISHER HADCOCK INTERVIEW

Mildred Hadcock (b. 1897)—a lifelong resident of Broadwater County—reflects on: growing up on a ranch on Beaver Creek, in an area now covered by Canyon Ferry Lake; her later life on local ranches.

INTERVIEWED BY THILDA NILSON WILLIAMS, JANUARY, 1983, BROADWATER COUNTY REST HOME, TOWNSEND.
SUMMARY: 2 PAGES
1 TAPE: 45 MINUTES

OH 598
PEARL KITTO INTERVIEW

Pearl Kitto, a resident of the Crow Creek Valley near Radersburg, describes: her grandparents, who homesteaded in the area; her parents' experiences there; her life growing up in and around Radersburg.

INTERVIEWED BY THILDA NILSON WILLIAMS, MARCH 18, 1983, TOSTON.
SUMMARY: 1 PAGE
1 TAPE: 35 MINUTES

OH 599
OLIVE RYALL MIDDLETON INTERVIEW

A Townsend resident, Olive Middleton relates: growing up in North Dakota and in Brooks, Alberta, Canada, circa 1910–1920; her marriage to Lyall Middleton of Toston in 1924; her career as a telegraph operator for the Northern Pacific Railroad during World War II; early Toston businesses and residents.

INTERVIEWED BY THILDA NILSON WILLIAMS, MARCH 11, 1983, TOWNSEND.
SUMMARY: 1 PAGE
1 TAPE: 30 MINUTES

OH 600
ETTA GILL RILEY AND EDITH GILL ROOPE WALTER INTERVIEW

Two sisters from Broadwater County—Etta Riley and Edith Walter—describe: their childhood in the Canton area north of Townsend; their education at the Whaley School; their respective marriages, children, and grandchildren.

INTERVIEWED BY THILDA NILSON WILLIAMS, MARCH, 1983, TOWNSEND.
SUMMARY: 1 PAGE
1 TAPE: 37 MINUTES

OH 601
WALLACE TURMAN AND JUANITA TURMAN INTERVIEW

Wallace Turman remembers: his childhood in the Crow Creek Valley, west of Townsend; his schooling; working as a miner, horse breeder, and rancher. Juanita Turman depicts: growing up in Edgar; teaching school before her marriage to Wallace.

INTERVIEWED BY THILDA NILSON WILLIAMS, MARCH 11, 1983, TOSTON.
SUMMARY: 2 PAGES
2 TAPES: 1 HOUR, 30 MINUTES

OH 602
SUSAN DOCKETT RAGEN INTERVIEW

Susan Ragen (b. 1892), a lifelong resident of the Townsend area, reports on: growing up in the region; her early married years; working summers at her aunt Ida Lyng's boarding houses in Radersburg and in Hassel; her involvement in community theater.

INTERVIEWED BY THILDA NILSON WILLIAMS, FEBRUARY 2, 1983, TOWNSEND.
SUMMARY: 2 PAGES
1 TAPE: 1 HOUR

OH 603
HALE AVERILL SNYDER INTERVIEW

Hale Snyder (b. 1889) describes: her childhood in Townsend; teaching school in Hawaii; her life in Scarsdale, New York.

INTERVIEWED BY THILDA NILSON WILLIAMS, FEBRUARY 16, 1983, TOWNSEND.
1 TAPE: 1 HOUR

OH 604
OSCAR NILSON INTERVIEW

Oscar Nilson (d. 1977) recalls: his emigration from

Sweden; his work as a coal miner; his duties as a railroad employee; his arrival in Kalispell.

INTERVIEWED BY THILDA NILSON WILLIAMS, JULY, 1977, TOWNSEND.

TRANSCRIPT: 12 PAGES

2 TAPES: 2 HOURS

OH 605
JAMES FRANKLIN "MIKE" SITTON INTERVIEW

A Radersburg resident, Mike Sitton comments on: being crippled by polio as a child; growing up in Radersburg; driving buck rakes for grain harvests on local ranches; working as a bartender; his employment in the ASARCO smelter in East Helena; his work as a miner and a logger. The interview is replete with anecdotes.

INTERVIEWED BY THILDA NILSON WILLIAMS, APRIL 19, 1983, RADERSBURG.

SUMMARY: 2 PAGES

2 TAPES: 2 HOURS, 45 MINUTES

OH 606
JANE WILLIAMS BOTTLER INTERVIEW

A longtime resident of Radersburg, Jane Bottler (b. 1899) recalls her life and work on an area ranch, and relates her memories of local personalities.

INTERVIEWED BY THILDA NILSON WILLIAMS, MAY 16, 1983, RADERSBURG.

SUMMARY: 1 PAGE

1 TAPE: 21 MINUTES

OH 607
BILL KELLERMAN INTERVIEW

Bill Kellerman—who moved to the Zortman-Landusky area of Montana in 1894—discusses: the history of the region; local characters, including Pike Landusky, Harvey Logan ("Kid Curry"), and Tom Carter; rustling; train robberies; gambling; saloons; specific gunfights.

INTERVIEWED BY HOMER LOUCKS, DECEMBER 23, 1959, ZORTMAN.

TRANSCRIPT: 24 PAGES

2 TAPES: 1 HOUR, 40 MINUTES

OH 608
DON FOOTE AND STELLA A. FOOTE INTERVIEWS

In this combination of two interviews—taped in Billings in 1958 and in New York City in 1964—Don Foote and his mother, Stella Foote, consider: their ownership of the Treasures of the West collection, which

they eventually placed at the Buffalo Bill Museum in Cody, Wyoming; nickelodeons and other mechanical music-makers.

INTERVIEWED BY KGHL RADIO (BILLINGS), 1958 AND 1964, BILLINGS AND NEW YORK.

SUMMARY: 1 PAGE

1 TAPE: 20 MINUTES

OH 609
ANGELO D. MONACO INTERVIEW

Angelo Monaco—long an air-brake repairman for the Butte, Anaconda and Pacific Railway (BAP) in Anaconda—converses about: his arrival in the United States from Italy; his work for the Northern Pacific Railroad Company at Livingston; his duties in the car department of the BAP; the Italian community in Anaconda.

INTERVIEWED BY RUSS MAGNAGHI, AUGUST 10, 1983, ANACONDA.

SUMMARY: 2 PAGES

2 TAPES: 1 HOUR, 15 MINUTES

OH 610
EDITH M. EDDY INTERVIEW

Edith Eddy (b. 1881), the wife of the Northern Cheyenne Indian Reservation Superintendent John R. Eddy (1906–1914), chronicles life on the reservation from 1906 to 1914. She was 100 years old at the time of the interview.

INTERVIEWED BY IRA LAX, FEBRUARY 12, 1981, FARMINGTON HILLS, MI.

SUMMARY: 1 PAGE

1 TAPE: 1 HOUR, 20 MINUTES

OH 611
NORRIS HANFORD SPEECH

In a formal presentation before a Montana Grain Growers Association (MGGA) gathering at Fort Benton in 1975, Norris Hanford—a member of the board of directors of the MGGA—addresses: the history of the association; the history of its predecessor, the Montana Crop Improvement Association (MCIA); the future of the wheat industry in Montana.

RECORDED BY THE MONTANA GRAIN GROWERS ASSOCIATION, 1975, FORT BENTON.

TRANSCRIPT: 10 PAGES

OH 612
MONTANA HISTORICAL SOCIETY TEACHER-ADVISORY COMMITTEE PROCEEDINGS

The Montana Historical Society's Education Department established the Teacher Advisory Committee and organized a meeting held in Helena on June 18, 1983. At the gathering, participants discussed various ways in which the historical society could assist teachers of Montana history in public schools.

SUMMARY: 3 PAGES
4 TAPES: 4 HOURS
RECORDED BY MONTANA HISTORICAL SOCIETY, 1983, HELENA.

OH 613
BLACKFEET INDIAN SONGS PRESENTATION
The Blackfeet tribal members Wades-in-Water, his wife Julia Wades-in-Water, Chief Bull Head (Dick Sanderville), and Chief Eagle Calf sing traditional Blackfeet music and speak the Blackfeet language.

INTERVIEWED BY ROGER B. THOMPSON, CIRCA 1938, BROWNING.
SUMMARY: 2 PAGES
1 TAPE: 1 HOUR

OH 614
MONTANA HISTORICAL SOCIETY PROGRAM
The opening for the Rudy Autio Retrospective Show occurred at the Montana Historical Society, in Helena on June 18, 1983. Speakers include: the ceramic artist Rudy Autio; the society director, Robert Archibald; the Charles M. Russell Gallery director, Ray Steele. Autio assesses the history of the Archie Bray Foundation, and he answers general questions about his work.

RECORDED BY NORMAN AND BELLE WINESTINE, JUNE 18, 1983, HELENA.
SUMMARY: 1 PAGE
1 TAPE: 30 MINUTES

OH 615
FRIEDA FLIGELMAN INTERVIEW
Frieda Fligelman (1890–1978)—a linguistic sociologist and the daughter of Herman Fligelman, founder of the New York department store in Helena—reviews: her family's background in Romania; Herman Fligelman's immigration to the United States; her education at the University of Wisconsin and at Columbia University in New York City; the life of a cultured and intellectual Jewish family in Helena during the 1890s and the early 1900s.

INTERVIEWED BY KATHY WHITE, OCTOBER 22 AND NOVEMBER 11, 1976, HELENA.
SUMMARY: 3 PAGES
3 TAPES: 2 HOURS

OH 616
STUART MACE INTERVIEW
Stuart Mace—the commander of the U.S. Army Sled Dog Detachment at Rimini during World War II—discusses: the problems involved in procuring and training sled dogs and sled-dog drivers for use in search-and-rescue work in the Arctic; the history of the detachment from its inception at Camp Hale, Colorado, to its final days at Fort Robinson, Nebraska; administering the program; the project's difficulties, accomplishments, and failures.

INTERVIEWED BY KAREN FISCHER, JANUARY 8-10, 1982, TOKLAT LODGE.
TRANSCRIPT: 97 PAGES
5 TAPES: 4 HOURS, 30 MINUTES

OH 617
DAVID W. ARMSTRONG INTERVIEW
David Armstrong, who served with the U.S. Army Sled Dog Detachment at Rimini during World War II, speaks of: the overall project; methods of training the dogs; feeding and health problems encountered by the dogs; his service with the Arctic Search and Rescue Squadron in Newfoundland and Greenland.

INTERVIEWED BY KAREN FISCHER, JANUARY 8-10, 1982, TOKLAT LODGE.
TRANSCRIPT: 9 PAGES
1 TAPE: 35 MINUTES

OH 618
EDDIE BARBEAU INTERVIEW
The Helena resident Eddie Barbeau—who served as a purchasing agent at the Camp Rimini War Dog Reception and Training Center at Rimini during World War II—tells about: his prewar experiences with sled dogs; his work as a dog-purchasing agent during World War II; types of dogs and sleds.

INTERVIEWED BY KAREN FISCHER, JULY, 1982, HELENA.
TRANSCRIPT: 9 PAGES
1 TAPE: 35 MINUTES

OH 619
JOHN "JACK" ESLICK INTERVIEW
Jack Eslick—who was assigned to the Camp Rimini War Dog Reception and Training Center at Rimini during World War II—summarizes: his involvement with sled-dog rescue work in northern Canada; his duties in the Rimini operation; general dog-training problems; the idiosyncrasies of some specific sled dogs.

Interviewed by Karen Fischer, January 28, 1983, Helena.
Transcript: 49 pages
2 tapes: 1 hour, 30 minutes

OH 620
ALFRED CIPOLATO AND ANN D'ORAZI CIPOLATO INTERVIEW

Alfred Cipolato and Ann Cipolato, longtime owners of the Broadway Market in Missoula, recall: his trip to the United States in 1940; his internment at Fort Missoula as an enemy alien during World War II; operating his father's Italian grocery business.
Interviewed by Bill Lang, January 9, 1981, Missoula.
Summary: 2 pages
2 tapes: 1 hour, 15 minutes

OH 621
JOHN A. "RED" WOLRICH INTERVIEW

Red Wolrich, the owner of the Lazy B Ranch west of Helena, talks about: working on Henry Sieben's Adel Ranch, north of Helena, during the 1920s and the 1930s; his characterization of Sieben as "one of the best"—a man who really knew the cattle business. [Also present during the interview are Dick Pace and Margaret Sieben Hibbard.] See also Non-Taped Interviews SC 1493.]
Interviewed by Bill Lang, April 4, 1978, Helena.
Summary: 2 pages
2 tapes: 1 hour, 15 minutes

OH 622
PEARLE LEEDY RHEIN INTERVIEWS

Pearle Rhein discusses: her childhood in Helena during the early 1900s; her work with her husband, Leo Rhein, operating the Wolf Creek Hotel in Wolf Creek from 1927 to 1938; their duties managing the Lewis and Clark County Hospital from 1938 to 1957.
Interviewed by Bill Lang, October 20, 1982, Helena.
Summary: 2 pages
2 tapes: 1 hour, 30 minutes

OH 623
MARY SHOBE FORD INTERVIEW

Mary Ford, the wife of Governor Sam C. Ford (1941–1949), discusses: her childhood in Helena; her grandfather, Territorial Governor Preston H. Leslie (1887-1889); teaching piano in Marysville and in Helena; her marriage to Sam Ford; her life in the Montana governor's mansion in Helena during the 1940s. [See also General Montana OH 556.]

Interviewed by Bill Lang, August 6, 1980, Helena.
Summary: 2 pages
2 tapes: 1 hour, 15 minutes

OH 624
VIRGINIA WALTON AND RITA McDONALD INTERVIEW

Virginia Walton (d. 1992) and Rita McDonald address: their work as librarians at the Montana Historical Society Library in Helena during the 1950s; the move from the State Capitol basement to the new Veterans and Pioneers Building; the pivotal work of Elizabeth McDonald and Anne McDonnell in modernizing the operations of the library; K. Ross Toole's term as historical society director. [See also Women as Community Builders OH 1045.]
Interviewed by Bill Lang, August 14, 1980, Helena.
Summary: 2 pages
2 tapes: 1 hour

OH 625
NORMAN J. "JEFF" HOLTER INTERVIEW

Jeff Holter—a Helena hardware merchant, scientist, and artist—recalls: his youth in Helena circa 1910–1920; developing an interest in science; his work for the U.S. Navy both during World War II and during the Bikini Island atomic bomb tests; his development of the Holter Heart Monitor; his experiments with "Dynamite Art"; his irreverent attitude toward bureaucracy; his enthusiasm for scientific research; his opinions about changes in Helena over the years.
Interviewed by Bill Lang, December 13 and 20, 1982, and January 10, 1983, Helena.
Summary: 5 pages
6 tapes: 6 hours

OH 626
LEIF ERICKSON INTERVIEW

Leif Erickson, long an active member of the Democratic Party in Montana, examines: his duties as a Richland County attorney; his work as a Montana Supreme Court judge; his unsuccessfully campaigns for governor in 1944 and in 1950; his unsuccessful run for the U.S. Senate in 1946; various issues and personalities in Montana politics from the 1930s into the 1970s—including farm legislation, labor laws, the Missouri Valley Authority (MVA), the REA, the Anaconda Company's control of the press, the company's influence on the Montana legislature and U.S. Senator Burton K. Wheeler.
Interviewed by Bill Lang, June 26, 1982, Swan Lake.

SUMMARY: 4 PAGES
4 TAPES: 3 HOURS, 30 MINUTES

OH 627
BRANSON G. STEVENSON INTERVIEW

The artist Branson Stevenson (b. 1901) recalls: his early life in Central America; studying art at the Instituto Nacional de Panama under Roberto Luis; his work in Montana for the Sunburst Oil and Refining Company; his duties as Montana manager of the Mobile Oil Company; life in Great Falls; his study with the western artist Joe DeYong, a protégé of the cowboy-artist Charles M. Russell; his role in the establishment of the Archie Bray Foundation in Helena; his career as an innovator and an experimenter in artistic techniques, including stoneware, porcelain pottery, and the graphic arts. *[See also General Montana OH 1434.]*

INTERVIEWED BY JOHN C. BOARD, CIRCA 1969, GREAT FALLS.
TRANSCRIPT: 500 PAGES

OH 628
EVERETT E. "BOO" MacGILVRA INTERVIEW

E. E. MacGilvra (1893–1980) discourses on: his background in Baraboo, Wisconsin, and in Zortman, Montana; his move to Polson, where he operated a movie theater and raised cherries; his involvement with Montana politics and government as a legislator and as an assistant director of the Montana Relief Commission; his work for the Montana Power Company as a public relations officer. *[See also General Montana OH 32, OH 109, OH 629, and OH 1546.]*

INTERVIEWED BY BILL LANG, AUGUST 4, 1978, BUTTE.
SUMMARY: 2 PAGES
1 TAPE: 1 HOUR, 45 MINUTES

OH 629
EVERETT E. "BOO" MacGILVRA INTERVIEW

E. E. MacGilvra (1893–1980) recounts: his early travels with the Ringling Brothers Circus; his work as a miner, a homesteader, and a storekeeper in Zortman; the cowboy artist Charles M. Russell; William Wesley "Brother Van" Van Orsdel; his Shetland pony ranch near Butte; 24 years of work for the Montana Power Company as a public relations officer. *[See also General Montana OH 32, OH 109, OH 628, and OH 1546.]*

INTERVIEWED BY BILL LANG, CIRCA 1970, GREAT FALLS.
SUMMARY: 2 PAGES
2 TAPES: 1 HOUR, 45 MINUTES

OH 630
NORMAN WINESTINE AND BELLE FLIGELMAN WINESTINE INTERVIEW

Norman Winestine (1895–1986)—the owner of Fligelman's department store in Helena—and his wife, Belle Fligelman Winestine (1891–1985)—suffragist, newspaperwoman, and Congressional secretary—discuss: their early education and careers; the social and civic life of Helena from circa 1910 into the 1930s; the role of prominent Jewish families in community affairs; the newspaperman Will Campbell's influence; the effects of the 1930s Depression on Helena. *[See also General Montana OH 87.]*

INTERVIEWED BY BILL LANG, NOVEMBER 2, 1979, HELENA.
SUMMARY: 3 PAGES
2 TAPES: 1 HOUR, 30 MINUTES

OH 631
A. B. "BUDDY" COBB INTERVIEW

Buddy Cobb reflects on: the economics of cattle ranching; different types of cattle breeding; the marketing of bull meat; the inherently unfair system of grading meat used by the federal government.

INTERVIEWED BY BILL LANG, APRIL 2, 1975, AUGUSTA.
TRANSCRIPT: 35 PAGES
2 TAPES: 1 HOUR, 55 MINUTES

OH 632
SAMUEL STILLMAN BERRY INTERVIEW

Samuel Berry of Redlands, California, discusses: his father, Ralph Berry; the elder Berry's founding of the Winnecook Sheep Ranch on the Musselshell River; the stories that Charles W. Cook told him about the Cook-Folsom expedition to the upper Yellowstone River (later Yellowstone National Park) in 1869; his own infancy in Maine; his trip to Montana at the age of two.

INTERVIEWED BY BILL LANG, JULY 29, 1980, HARLOWTON.
SUMMARY: 2 PAGES
1 TAPE: 50 MINUTES

OH 633
DANISH ORAL HISTORY INTERVIEWS

This collection of 12 interviews includes individuals of Danish descent in Dagmar and Beaverhead County—specifically: Mette Petersen; Henry Crohn; Ingeborg Crohn; Leonora Johansen; Niels Nielsen; Virgil Andreasen; Ella Sundsted; Esther Christensen; Peter Lodahl; Otto Christensen; Axel Madsen; John Andersen, Jr. The Danes talk about: homesteading experiences;

sheep ranching; social life; Danish communities in Montana.

INTERVIEWED BY REX MYERS, MAY 28, 1984, PLENTYWOOD.

SUMMARY: 24 PAGES

19 TAPES: 19 HOURS

OH 634
MIGRANT-FARMWORKERS PROJECT INTERVIEWS

This composite consists of 28 interviews with Hispanic migrant farmworkers employed in Forsyth, Terry, Sidney, Hysham, Crane, Hardin, Fairview, and the Flathead Valley. The interviewees describe: working conditions; families; housing; education; various employers; wages; language difficulties; harvesting sugar beets, cherries, cucumbers, and other crops. [Rural Employment Opportunities, Inc., contracted this project. Some interviews are in Spanish, all transcripts are in English.]

INTERVIEWED BY PATRICIA NELSON, 1985, VARIOUS MONTANA LOCATIONS.

TRANSCRIPT: 461 PAGES

23 TAPES: 23 HOURS

OH 635
FRED HASTY INTERVIEW

The Glendive resident Fred Hasty remembers: his life in Glendive; family recollections of area events; local businesses and buildings; his work with Montana-Dakota Utilities.

INTERVIEWED BY MARK BORDSEN, JULY 24, 1987, GLENDIVE.

SUMMARY: 8 PAGES

4 TAPES: 4 HOURS

OH 636
HARRY BOSWELL INTERVIEW

Harry Boswell—a U.S. Border Patrol officer on the Montana Canadian border from the 1920s into the 1940s—describes: equipment; uniforms; his experiences in the Havre and Sweetgrass areas; promotions; specific incidents.

INTERVIEWED BY TERRIE CORNELL, MAY 26 AND JUNE 6, 1987, EL PASO, TX.

TRANSCRIPT: 21 PAGES

2 TAPES: 2 HOURS

OH 637
GREAT NORTH TRAIL ORAL HISTORIES

Dick Kenck, Philip "Bud" Bisnett, Adolph Dale, and Harold A. "Tot" Nett report on various aspects of the Great North Trail (also known as "the Old North Trail")—which ran just east of the Rocky Mountains, from northern Canada to Mexico—including: local Indian use of the trail; trapping along the trail; anthropology of the Montana-Alberta areas of the trail; mapping the trail. [See also General Montana OH 1653 and OH 1660.]

INTERVIEWED BY DAVID LOUTER, 1986–1987, VARIOUS LOCATIONS IN MONTANA.

SUMMARY: 14 PAGES

4 TAPES: 4 HOURS

OH 641
HENRY GARDINER INTERVIEW

Henry Gardiner (b. 1905) discusses: his childhood in Bozeman; his father's experiences as a farmer and as an employee of the Anaconda Copper Mining Company; his own education; the process of becoming an attorney; the Butte Miners' Union; working as a lawyer for the Anaconda Company; strikes in Butte; D. G. Stivers; the IWW; state political leaders, including Burton K. Wheeler; general Butte history.

INTERVIEWED BY BILL LANG AND MICHAEL MALONE, NOVEMBER 10, 1987, BOZEMAN.

TRANSCRIPT: 85 PAGES

3 TAPES: 3 HOURS

OH 642
CHARLES MARION RUSSELL COLLECTION

The Great Falls cowboy artist Charles M. Russell (b. 1864) is the subject of discussions with five Great Falls residents who recall Russell at Great Falls High School, at his studio, and at his funeral: George Houston; Inez Wilkinson; Sheridan Erickson; Elmer Eller; Ruth Hopkins.

INTERVIEWED BY RAPHAEL CRISTY, MARCH, 1986, GREAT FALLS.

6 TAPES: 6 HOURS

OH 644
NINA BLACK AND ELDON BLACK INTERVIEW

Nina Black (b. circa 1887–d. 1980) and her son Eldon Black (d. circa 1980) describe: life in Mammoth; mining in this Madison County region; the construction of a Montana Power Company line into the area; local social activities; two extant locust trees brought west in lard buckets in 1864 by Nina Black's grandfather, Jonas Butts, and planted at the old log cabin (Pioneer Cabin) in Last Chance Gulch in Helena.

INTERVIEWED BY BLANCHE UEHLING, SEPTEMBER 15, 1980, WHITEHALL.
PARTIAL TRANSCRIPT: 13 PAGES
2 TAPES: 2 HOURS

OH 645
FAYE MILLER LANDIS AND ROBERT BRUCE LANDIS INTERVIEW

Faye Landis and Robert Landis (b. 1902) recount: his work in the mines at Mammoth and Butte and in Arizona; living in Cardwell; adventures boarding school-children on their ranch; her experiences being transported to school for $3 a month by Elroy Shaw, who placed plank seats on each side of a truck and a canvas over the top.
INTERVIEWED BY BLANCHE UEHLING, OCTOBER 18, 1982, CARDWELL.
PARTIAL TRANSCRIPT: 7 PAGES
1 TAPE: 1 HOUR

OH 646
ROY WILKINSON INTERVIEW

A Cardwell resident, Roy Wilkinson (b. 1907) depicts: his childhood and schooling; selling milk in Harrison; fishing; his work on the road to the Mammoth Mine; powerline construction; his lodge work for the Masons; driving a school bus; running his Cardwell mercantile business; area recreation.
INTERVIEWED BY BLANCHE UEHLING, SEPTEMBER 29, 1982, CARDWELL.
1 TAPE: 1 HOUR

OH 647
KATHLEEN "TODDY" WINSLOW THOMPSON INTERVIEW

Toddy Thompson—a resident of Whitehall—talks of: her family; schooling; electrical and greenhouse businesses in Whitehall; parades; camping trips; social activities; area residents; senior citizens' activities; her cabin at Mammoth.
INTERVIEWED BY BLANCHE UEHLING, OCTOBER 1, 1982, WHITEHALL.
1 TAPE: 1 HOUR

OH 648
GEORGE HAKOLA INTERVIEW

George Hakola, a resident of both Whitehall and Boulder, delineates: his move to the Mammoth Mine during the 1930s; area activities and residents; mine operations; making cheese in the Whitehall Creamery; run-ning the Gambles hardware store in Boulder; the 1959 Hebgen Lake earthquake; fire in Whitehall.
INTERVIEWED BY BLANCHE UEHLING, AUGUST 13, 1980, WHITEHALL.
1 TAPE: 1 HOUR

OH 649
LAWRENCE TAYLOR INTERVIEW

Lawrence Taylor reviews: his family; horse and wagon travels; ranch work near Dillon; trapping; driving a bus; his service as a paratrooper in Australia and in the South Pacific during World War II; his work at the Children's Center (Montana Orphans' Home) in Twin Bridges; his marriage.
INTERVIEWED BY BLANCHE UEHLING, OCTOBER 18, 1980, MAMMOTH.
1 TAPE: 1 HOUR

OH 683
GENE GRUSH AND KEN BREITENSTEIN INTERVIEWS

Yaak residents Gene Grush and Ken Breitenstein converse about: local homestead sites and mining claims; Yaak-area personages; the work of the U.S. Forest Service in northwestern Montana. [Interview is part of the "Final Report of Cultural Resource Investigation Along Montana Forest Highway #62, Yaak," written by Powers Elevation of Denver, Colorado.]
INTERVIEWED BY POWERS ELEVATION, JUNE 23, 1982, YAAK.
TRANSCRIPT: 50 PAGES
3 TAPES: 3 HOURS

OH 684
EMMETT QUIRK INTERVIEW

Emmett Quirk (b. 1907) speaks of: his family's homesteading in the Eureka area; their subsequent ranch operation there; his childhood and schooling; the bootlegging of liquor during Prohibition; his marriage to Grace Downing; various farming practices; irrigation.
INTERVIEWED BY CATHRYN SCHROEDER, SEPTEMBER 7, 1984, EUREKA.
SUMMARY: 6 PAGES
1 TAPE: 1 HOUR, 15 MINUTES

OH 685
HAROLD MARION BROWN INTERVIEW

Harold Brown (b. 1902) considers: homesteading in the Big Sandy area; digging coal from local seams; teaching in Hopp; his confinement to the "pest house" at the

Lewis and Clark County Poor Farm in Helena during a smallpox epidemic, circa 1918.
INTERVIEWED BY JEFF CUNNIFF, OCTOBER 5, 1975, GREAT FALLS.
SUMMARY: 3 PAGES
1 TAPE: 58 MINUTES

OH 686
HOMER J. WELLMAN REMINISCENCE
Homer Wellman summarizes: the competition between Gilman and Augusta for the railroad and for other businesses; his work for the People's Bank of Augusta.
INTERVIEWED BY HOMER J. WELLMAN, CIRCA 1975, AUGUSTA.
SUMMARY: 3 PAGES
1 TAPE: 45 MINUTES

OH 687
PAUL HAZEL INTERVIEWS
Helena resident Paul Hazel comments on: his career with the U.S. Forest Service at various locations in Montana; fighting forest fires; managing wildlife; building trails in the Bob Marshall Wilderness Area; working with the Sun River elk herd.
INTERVIEWED BY ROBERT F. COONEY, FEBRUARY 1977–JUNE 1979, HELENA.
SUMMARY: 6 PAGES
11 TAPES: 11 HOURS

OH 688
LEONA LENARZ INTERVIEW
Leona Lenarz surveys: her childhood on a ranch near Eureka during the 1930s; her family; her marriage to Clarence Lenarz in 1938; her work as the librarian at the Eureka Public Library from 1955 to 1982.
INTERVIEWED BY CATHRYN SCHROEDER, OCTOBER 17, 1985, EUREKA.
SUMMARY: 1 PAGE
1 TAPE: 1 HOUR, 30 MINUTES

OH 689
WALTER JOSEPH GIBBONS INTERVIEW
Walter Gibbons (b. 1920) recalls: growing up in Eureka; operating a garage there.
INTERVIEWED BY CAROLYN SCHROEDER, OCTOBER 13, 1985, EUREKA.
SUMMARY: 1 PAGE
1 TAPE: 1 HOUR, 30 MINUTES

OH 690
PETER VIGO KLINKE, JR., INTERVIEW
Peter Klinke, Jr. (b. 1917), talks of: his father's operation of Klinke's Mercantile in Fortine from 1909 to 1931; his father's work in a local fish hatchery from 1931 to 1942; his own childhood in Fortine; his work in the mercantile business; his service in World War II; his operation of a Christmas tree farm near Eureka.
INTERVIEWED BY CATHRYN SCHROEDER, JANUARY 22, 1986, EUREKA.
SUMMARY: 3 PAGES
2 TAPES: 60 MINUTES

OH 691
M. LLOYD WEST INTERVIEW
Lloyd West (b. 1910) talks of: growing up in the Eureka area; attending the Glen Lake School outside Eureka; ranching; logging and the lumber industry in the Tobacco River Valley; efforts to designate the Ten Lakes Scenic Area as a wilderness area.
INTERVIEWED BY CATHRYN SCHROEDER, JANUARY 13, 1986, EUREKA.
SUMMARY: 3 PAGES
2 TAPES: 2 HOURS

OH 692
JAMES "BILL" STACY INTERVIEW
Bill Stacy (b. 1912) tells about: logging in the Eureka area; the general lumber industry in Lincoln County.
INTERVIEWED BY CATHRYN SCHROEDER, FEBRUARY 4, 1985, EUREKA.
SUMMARY: 2 PAGES
1 TAPE: 1 HOUR, 10 MINUTES

OH 693
ANDREW E. "GENE" McWHIRTER INTERVIEW
Gene McWhirter assesses: his business raising Christmas trees near Eureka; his work in the town's electrical plant before it was sold to the REA in 1953.
INTERVIEWED BY CATHRYN SCHROEDER, OCTOBER 23, 1985, EUREKA.
SUMMARY: 1 PAGE
1 TAPE: 1 HOUR, 30 MINUTES

OH 694
JOE STROZZI INTERVIEW
Whitehall resident Joe Strozzi (b. 1898) treats: his father Battista Strozzi's trip from Switzerland to the United States as a stowaway; his father's arrival in Butte; his own childhood, living on a dairy farm at Elk Park;

making and selling charcoal; the family's move to a ranch outside Whitehall in 1910; his marriage to Annie Harris in 1920; working at the Hanson Meat Packing Company in Butte.

INTERVIEWED BY DARCY STROZZI HALOIN, 1986, BOZEMAN.

SUMMARY: 7 PAGES

2 TAPES: 1 HOUR, 30 MINUTES

OH 695
BERT WILKE INTERVIEW

Bert Wilke (1893–1984) addresses: his career with the U.S. Forest Service from circa 1910 into the 1940s; planting trees, building roads, and fighting fires in the Fortine Ranger District (particularly the Ant Hill area) during that time; logging operations in northwestern Montana. [The U.S. Forest Service authorized this interview.] *[See also Montanans at Work OH 662.]*

INTERVIEWED BY ANNE HOFFMAN, 1983, FORTINE.

TRANSCRIPT: 120 PAGES

5 TAPES: 4 HOURS, 30 MINUTES

OH 696
MARGUERITE "TAD" SHANNON COLLINS AND RUTH "BABE" SHANNON MAYER INTERVIEW

The Shannon sisters—Marguerite Collins (b. 1896) and Ruth Mayer (b. 1900)—discuss: their parents, John C. and Angeline Hoyt Shannon; the family's arrival in Helena from Wisconsin in 1880; the family's move to a ranch near White Sulphur Springs; schooling; social life; homesteading.

INTERVIEWED BY CLARICE R. COX, SEPTEMBER 9, 1986, WHITE SULPHUR SPRINGS.

SUMMARY: 5 PAGES

2 TAPES: 2 HOURS

OH 697
RAY ROBBINS AND HELEN STAVES INTERVIEW

Flathead County residents Ray Robbins and Helen Staves talk about: their work in the cherry industry in the Flathead Lake area during the 1930s; the production, picking, and packing of cherries; variable weather; crop losses; the marketing, warehousing, and shipping of cherries; spraying cherry trees; experiences with migrant workers; the role of the Flathead Cherry Growers Association. [The U.S. Forest Service authorized this interview.]

INTERVIEWED BY GARY A. MCLEAN, 1983, POLSON.

SUMMARY: 6 PAGES

3 TAPES: 3 HOURS

OH 698
GRANT-KOHRS RANCH ORAL HISTORY COLLECTION

This 1980–1982 collection consists of interviews concerning: the Conrad Kohrs family; the Grant-Kohrs Ranch; social life in the area; homes on the ranch. Interviewees include: J. H. Gehrman, a nephew of Conrad Kohrs; Helen Prescott Dietrich, a friend of Augusta Kohrs; Betty Wingert Griffith, a niece of John and Anna Kohrs Boardman; Margaret Sieben Hibbard Warren Hershey, the wife of Robert Warren; Ann Warren Bache, a granddaughter of Conrad and Augusta Kohrs.

INTERVIEWED BY REX MYERS, 1980–1982, VARIOUS MONTANA LOCATIONS.

TRANSCRIPT: 463 PAGES

22 TAPES: 22 HOURS

OH 699
CLYDE AKIN INTERVIEW

Clyde Akin (b. 1901) speaks of: growing up in the Mammoth area; hauling ore to Cardwell by wagon; ranching near Boulder; delivering gas; managing the Standard Oil Company bulk plant in Whitehall.

INTERVIEWED BY BLANCHE UEHLING, 1980, WHITEHALL.

TRANSCRIPT: 26 PAGES

1 TAPE: 1 HOUR

OH 700
BARBARA HOLTER KIRKLAND INTERVIEW

Barbara Kirkland (b. 1924)—the granddaughter of the Helena hardware merchant Anton M. Holter—recalls: growing up in Helena during the 1930s; the 1935 Helena earthquakes; her schooling; her family.

INTERVIEWED BY LAURIE MERCIER, DECEMBER 1, 1987, HELENA.

TRANSCRIPT: 11 PAGES

1 TAPE: 1 HOUR, 10 MINUTES

OH 824
SELDON FRISBEE INTERVIEW

Seldon Frisbee (b. 1915), long a resident of Cut Bank, speaks about: Cut Bank businesses; area banking; the local oil industry; health care; labor unions; politics; the community's social life and entertainment; clubs; the Great Northern Railway Company; Prohibition; post–World War II changes in the area; Blackfeet tribal land litigations; Indian-white relations; the restaurant workers strike of the 1950s; physical improvements in Cut Bank.

INTERVIEWED BY JACKIE DAY, NOVEMBER 1 AND 27, 1984, CUT BANK.

SUMMARY: 15 PAGES

4 TAPES: 3 HOURS, 30 MINUTES

OH 840
J. R. "TOPPY" LEE INTERVIEW

Toppy Lee discourses on: ranching near Forsyth; agricultural developments in Rosebud County since 1950; relations between the area's ranching community and the residents of Forsyth.

INTERVIEWED BY JACKIE DAY, JANUARY 17, 1985, FORSYTH.

SUMMARY: 2 PAGES

1 TAPE: 1 HOUR, 4 MINUTES

OH 897
OLIVE SATTLEEN INTERVIEW

Chinook resident Olive Sattleen (b. 1891) discusses: her childhood at Yantic (Lohman) during the early 1900s; homesteading; sheep ranching in the Milk River Valley; her children; living in Chinook.

INTERVIEWED BY ANN CARMERSON, DECEMBER 21, 1984, CHINOOK.

SUMMARY: 3 PAGES

2 TAPES: 2 HOURS

OH 902
ALTA SANDERS INTERVIEW

Alta Sanders (1891–1987) details: growing up in Helena during the early 1900s; writing for the Helena *Treasure State* and *Montana Record-Herald* newspapers; her uncle Wilbur Fisk Sanders and other family members; the Chinese community in Helena; her work for the Montana Highway Commission; her move to Los Angeles; her work for the Los Angeles *Times*.

INTERVIEWED BY PATRICIA BORNEMAN, MARCH 27, 1982, HELENA.

SUMMARY: 9 PAGES

2 TAPES: 2 HOURS

OH 986
CHOUTEAU COUNTY ORAL-HISTORY PROJECT

This collection comprises interviews with 10 residents of the Brady (Pondera County) area: Fred Arnold; Bill Bandel; Martha Fornfiest Bandel; Tal Collins; Matilda Johnson; Ross MacDonald; Ray Woods; Marian Wagner Kovatch; Frank Merkling; Dorothy Floerchinger. The interviewees describe: Brady; the nearby towns of Genou and Ashmoor in Chouteau County; various area residents; homesteading experiences; recreation; raising crops; their families.

INTERVIEWED BY GARY GOLLEHON, 1986–1987, VARIOUS LOCATIONS IN PONDERA AND CHOUTEAU COUNTIES.

TRANSCRIPT: 98 PAGES

15 TAPES: 9 HOURS

OH 987
HATTIE OSTERBAUER INTERVIEW

Hattie Osterbauer (1886–1987) depicts: homesteading in Hill County in 1912, after her first husband's death; the hardships of life as a widow; her marriage to Lawrence Osterbauer in 1914; her involvement with the Gildford Ladies' Aid Society; other social activities. [The accompanying file includes a sketch and several photographs.]

INTERVIEWED BY MARGARET VANDE SANDT AND VIRGINIA JONES, 1986, GILDFORD.

4 TAPES: 5 HOURS

OH 988
GEORGE "RED" PETTIT INTERVIEW

Red Pettit—a resident of Dillon—describes: his family; his travels in Utah and Idaho; his work as a ranch and farm hand in the Dillon area; his experiences during the 1930s Depression; Dillon businesses and residents; his work as school custodian; retirement.

INTERVIEWED BY ROBERT K. MCDONALD, CIRCA 1972, DILLON.

SUMMARY: 4 PAGES

2 TAPES: 1 HOUR, 40 MINUTES

OH 989
MARGARET SIEBEN HIBBARD INTERVIEW

Helena resident Margaret Sieben Hibbard speaks of: her family; her experiences growing up; her schooling; Helena social life; friends; her volunteer work at St. Peter's Hospital in Helena; her father, Henry Sieben, a Helena Valley rancher; her husband, Alfred T. Hibbard, a banker. *[See also Non-Taped Interviews SC 1663.]*

INTERVIEWED BY BILL LANG, MAY 17, 1978, HELENA.

TRANSCRIPT: 54 PAGES

2 TAPES: 2 HOURS

OH 990
GOVERNOR'S ORIGINAL MANSION ORAL HISTORY PROJECT

This collection comprises a series of interviews with people involved in the original Montana governor's mansion in Helena including: Esther D. Brown (life in the mansion); Shirley Gannon (work as a tour guide); Edna Hinman (employment by Governor J. Hugo Aronson as a secretary); Elsie Jones (employment as a cook); Jim MacDonald (architectural study of the kitchen); Mary Pitch (restoration); Beryl Kaiserman and Joe Vantura (formation of the Governor's Original Mansion Restoration Board).

INTERVIEWED BY MARY HOFFSCHEWELLE, HARRIETT MELOY, AND CARLA CRONHOLM, 1982–1984, HELENA.
TRANSCRIPT: 198 PAGES
9 TAPES: 9 HOURS

OH 991
JACK GOE INTERVIEW

Jack Goe (b. 1915) converses about: his childhood in Anaconda; local social activities; his friends; school activities; summer jobs.
INTERVIEWED BY ALICE FINNEGAN, JUNE 10, 1987, ANACONDA.
SUMMARY: 4 PAGES
3 TAPES: 3 HOURS

OH 992
HUGH PEYTON ORAL REMINISCENCE

Hugh Peyton discusses his research on the controversy between Frederick A. Cook and the Montana guides Fred Printz and Ed Barrill over their attempted climb of Mount McKinley [Denali] in Alaska in 1906.
INTERVIEWED BY HUGH PEYTON, CIRCA JUNE, 1983, MEAD, WA.
SUMMARY: 2 PAGES
1 TAPE: 1 HOUR

OH 993
MABEL MANION AND PEARL ROGERS INTERVIEW

Mabel Manion and her sister Pearl Rogers comment on: growing up in Mammoth and Whitehall; their schooling; ranch chores; family members.
INTERVIEWED BY BLANCHE UEHLING, OCTOBER, 1984, CARDWELL.
SUMMARY: 5 PAGES
1 TAPE: 1 HOUR

OH 994
MIKE RICCI INTERVIEW

Livingston resident Mike Ricci (b. 1917) chronicles: his work with the CCC in Missoula, St. Regis, Haugen,

and Belton during the 1930s; his seasonal work driving a tour bus in Yellowstone National Park.
INTERVIEWED BY JOHN TERREO, NOVEMBER 18, 1989, LIVINGSTON.
SUMMARY: 4 PAGES
1 TAPE: 52 MINUTES

OH 995
MARGARET CLARK WUNSCH SONG

Margaret Wunsch sings "Montanaland," a song her father sang to her as a child.
RECORDED BY MARGARET CLARK WUNSCH, NOVEMBER, 1989, TWO RIVERS, WI.
1 TAPE: 10 MINUTES

OH 996
ROBERT ALLING INTERVIEW

Robert Alling—a resident of Helena—describes: his father, Ira Alling, who traveled to Montana Territory in 1882, hunted buffalo for the Northern Pacific Railroad, and ranched on the 4-Bar Ranch; his mother, Minnie Hearst, and her family; his own work for the Hearst family newspapers.
INTERVIEWED BY SARAH ALLING, 1975, HELENA.
1 TAPE: 1 HOUR

OH 997
MONTANA HISTORICAL SOCIETY PANEL

This panel discussion comprises a part of the opening of the museum exhibit "Women's Work: The Montana Women's Centennial Art Survey Exhibition, 1889–1989." Speakers include: Genny DeWeese; Frances Senska; Lela Autio. Topics addressed involve the nature of women's art and women artists reflected in the exhibit.
RECORDED BY THE MONTANA HISTORICAL SOCIETY, MARCH 7, 1990, HELENA.
1 TAPE: 1 HOUR

OH 998
WILLIAM JAMES JAMESON INTERVIEW AND SPEECH

This composite includes an interview of, and a speech by, William Jameson (b. 1898)—a Billings attorney and judge. Jameson assesses: his youth in Butte and Roundup; his law practice in Billings; the Montana Bar Association; specific cases and decisions that he encountered as a judge on the U.S. 9th Circuit Court. He delivered the speech, addressing his judicial career, on June 21, 1985, to a gathering of the Montana Bar Association in Billings.

INTERVIEWED BY U.S. 9TH JUDICIAL CIRCUIT HISTORICAL SOCIETY, JUNE 21, 1985, AND 1987, BILLINGS.
TRANSCRIPT: 81 PAGES

OH 999
AMY ROCKAFELLOW REMINISCENCE

Longtime resident of the Bitterroot Valley Amy Rockafellow addresses: her family life in the Hamilton area from 1927 to 1989; her employment with the U.S. Post Office Department; her husband, Lloyd Rockafellow; daughter, Amy Lee; grandchildren; her son-in-law, Everett Felix, who was taken hostage during the 1959 Montana State Prison riot in Deer Lodge; her activities in the Order of the Eastern Star, Montana Society, in the Rainbow Girls, in the Ancient, Free and Accepted Masons, and in the Golden Age Club; her retirement. *[See also General Montana OH 1449.]*
INTERVIEWED BY CLARENCE POPHAM, DECEMBER 10, 1989, CORVALLIS.
SUMMARY: 2 PAGES
1 TAPE: 25 MINUTES

OH 1046
JEANNETTE RANKIN INTERVIEW

Jeannette Rankin (1880–1973)—a Montana-born peace and social activist, a suffragist, the first woman elected to the U.S. Congress (1916), and a congresswoman who voted against U.S. involvement in both world wars (1917 and 1941)—speaks of: women's suffrage; her campaigns and elections; her role in Congress; the peace movement; Thomas J. Walsh; Wellington Rankin; World War I; World War II. *[See also General Montana OH 1288.]*
INTERVIEWED BY UNIDENTIFIED PERSON, AUGUST 29, 1963, GREAT FALLS.
SUMMARY: 2 PAGES
3 TAPES: 3 HOURS

OH 1047
MONTANA ANGLERS AND HUNTERS ORAL-HISTORY PROJECT

This collection comprises interviews with nine Montanans involved in fishing as a recreation and with fish-management as a profession: Joe Malaczweski; George Morrison; Emmett Colley; Ray Hurley; Arthur Whitney; George Holton; Jim Woodhull; Neil Travis; Don Williams. Topics include: the Yellowstone and Shields rivers; the Montana Department of Fish, Wildlife and Parks; fish populations; hatcheries; fisheries equipment and procedures; water conservation.

INTERVIEWED BY CHRISTOPHER CLANCY, 1984–1989, VARIOUS MONTANA LOCATIONS.
SUMMARIES: 18 PAGES
10 TAPES: 15 HOURS

OH 1048
FAY WHITE INTERVIEW

Fay White treats: her schooling; residents in the Pony area; local activities; her friends; her family.
INTERVIEWED BY BLANCHE UEHLING, OCTOBER 16, 1984, AVON.
SUMMARY: 7 PAGES
1 TAPE: 1 HOUR

OH 1049
WESLEY VAN GORDON AND VIRGINIA VAN GORDON INTERVIEW

Wesley Van Gordon and his wife, Virginia Van Gordon, talk about: life in Pony; their operation of the local Mammoth Mine during the 1940s; their ownership of a pottery shop in Cardwell; pottery making and equipment.
INTERVIEWED BY BLANCHE UEHLING, SEPTEMBER 18, 1984, PONY.
TRANSCRIPT: 13 PAGES
2 TAPES: 2 HOURS

OH 1050
BITTERROOT NATIONAL FOREST ORAL HISTORY PROJECT

The Bitterroot National Forest History Project comprises interviews with five Bitterroot Valley residents: Gilbert Lord; Juanita Lord; John McClintic; Fred Wetson; Edgar Wetson. The interviewees discuss: the community of Sula; various Bitterroot Valley residents; local social activities; trapping; forest fires; wildlife; home remedies; cattle ranching; sheep ranching; outfitting; homesteading; archaeological sites in the area.
INTERVIEWED BY DAVE FILIUS AND RICHARD WALKER, 1976–1977, VARIOUS BITTERROOT VALLEY LOCATIONS.
TRANSCRIPT: 106 PAGES

OH 1190
WALTER RANKIN INTERVIEW

Walter Rankin (1904–1983)—a Great Falls resident—summarizes: his childhood in Ohio; the family's move to Montana; his work with the CCC; his service in the Pacific theater during World War II; his involvement with the Montana state park system, including Lewis and Clark Caverns and Bannack; Rutledge Parker. [A report compiled by Rankin for this interview is also included.]

INTERVIEWED BY KEN KARSMIZKI, APRIL 10-11, 1983, BOZEMAN.
SUMMARY: 37 PAGES
7 TAPES: 7 HOURS

OH 1191
BILL L. HICKS INTERVIEW

Missoula resident and retired U.S. Forest Service geologist Bill Hicks speaks of: his training and work with the Forest Service, particularly in Region One; wilderness area and mineral legislation; other federal policies as they have affected the use of Forest Service lands from the early 1960s through the 1980s; some Forest Service colleagues; miners he has encountered. [The U.S. Forest Service authorized this interview.]
INTERVIEWED BY GERALD WILLIAMS, MAY 2, 1990, MISSOULA.
TRANSCRIPT: 27 PAGES
1 TAPE: 1 HOUR

OH 1192
ARNOLD W. BOLLE INTERVIEW

Arnold Bolle—the retired dean of the School of Forestry at the University of Montana in Missoula—reviews: his interest in forest policy and the relationship of that policy to the timber industry in the Bitterroot Valley of western Montana; spruce bark-beetle infestations; the development of local clear-cutting practices during the 1950s and the 1960s; U.S. Senator Lee Metcalf; Dale Burk of the *Missoulian*; the National Forest Management Act of 1976; the policy of "multiple use" of public lands; the activities of the Champion International and the Burlington Northern corporations; his involvement in the establishment of the Rattlesnake Recreation Area and Wilderness. [The U.S. Forest Service authorized this interview.]
INTERVIEWED BY GERALD WILLIAMS, MAY 1, 1990, MISSOULA.
TRANSCRIPT: 47 PAGES
2 TAPES: 2 HOURS

OH 1193
BERNIE ALT INTERVIEW

Bernie Alt—a Kalispell resident and a retired U.S. Forest Service grasslands expert—recalls: his career with the Forest Service in eastern Montana, from 1950 to 1990; his early work in the establishment of the National Grasslands program; grazing districts and fees; the agency's relations with ranchers; grass fires; trespass; Land Utilization (LU) lands and the Bureau of Land Management

(BLM); water; coyote control; eagles; his work, after retirement, with the Glacier Park Company in the Kalispell area. [The U.S. Forest Service authorized this interview.]
INTERVIEWED BY GERALD WILLIAMS, MAY 2, 1990, MISSOULA.
TRANSCRIPT: 47 PAGES
1 TAPE: 1 HOUR

OH 1196
JOHN TERREO INTERVIEW

The oral historian at the Montana Historical Society in Helena, John Terreo (b. 1954) reports on: his early interest in oral history; circumstances that led him to the Montana Historical Society; his philosophy of oral history. *[See also Medicine, Health Care, and Nursing OH 1346 and 20th Century Montana Military Veterans OH 1195.]*
INTERVIEWED BY JODIE FOLEY, APRIL 22, 1993, HELENA.
SUMMARY: 4 PAGES
2 TAPES: 1 HOUR, 30 MINUTES

OH 1201
ROGER STOPS INTERVIEW

Roger Stops, a member of the Crow tribe, remembers: the meaning of the Crow Indian Sun Dance ritual; music; prayer; visions; medicine bundles; tobacco; smudging; sweat baths; lodges.
INTERVIEWED BY STUART CONNER, OCTOBER 4, 1970, CROW AGENCY.
TRANSCRIPT: 60 PAGES
2 TAPES: 2 HOURS

OH 1203
JOHN MONTAGNE INTERVIEW

Bozeman resident John Montagne, Ph.D.—a longtime member and the first secretary/treasurer of the Montana Wilderness Association (MWA)—relates: the founding of The Wilderness Society (TWS) in the 1940s and the MWA in 1958; the Madison-Gallatin Alliance and its work in the Yellowstone National Park area; the Beartooth Range; the Madison Range; the Spanish Peaks Wilderness; Olaus J. Murie; Bob Cooney; John Craighead; Winton Weydemeyer; George Duvenback; Charles C. Bradley; changes in American wilderness activism from the 1960s to 1992; the development of that activism from a grassroots basis to a law-oriented basis.
INTERVIEWED BY ROLAND CHEEK, DECEMBER, 1992, BOZEMAN.

SUMMARY: 3 PAGES
1 TAPE: 32 MINUTES

OH 1205
ROXELLA WANDERS INTERVIEW

Roxella Wanders (b. 1896) reflects on: her family; her early life in Illinois; World War I; her husband; raising a family; her relocation to Montana; the 1930s Depression.
INTERVIEWED BY JOHN TERREO, SEPTEMBER 30, 1989, HELENA.
SUMMARY: 3 PAGES
2 TAPES: 1 HOUR, 5 MINUTES

OH 1206
ELIZABETH WHEELER COLMAN INTERVIEW

Elizabeth Colman (b. 1911) recounts: her childhood in Butte; her parents, Lula White Wheeler and U.S. Senator Burton K. Wheeler; her mother's role as the wife of a senator; social and political activities in Butte and in Washington, D.C.; the history of the Wheeler family; U.S. entry into World War II; Jeannette Rankin; Franklin D. Roosevelt.
INTERVIEWED BY JOHN TERREO, OCTOBER 17, 1989, HELENA.
TRANSCRIPT: 21 PAGES
1 TAPE: 45 MINUTES

OH 1207
RAY HOWARD INTERVIEW

Dillon resident Ray Howard (b. 1905) recalls: his parents' homesteads; growing up in Java and Mondak; working on riverboats and ferry boats; owning and operating a restaurant in McCone City during the construction of Fort Peck Dam in the 1930s; brothels in the Fort Peck area; living conditions during the 1930s Depression; his relocation to Dillon; his ownership and operation of various businesses.
INTERVIEWED BY JOHN TERREO, DECEMBER 5, 1989, DILLON.
TRANSCRIPT: 58 PAGES
3 TAPES: 2 HOURS, 17 MINUTES

OH 1209
MYRA WILSON INTERVIEW

Myra Wilson (b. 1904) portrays: her early childhood in Big Creek, Wisconsin; relocating to Montana in 1914; the family homestead near Franklin; the Spanish influenza epidemic of 1918; drought; her husband's work as a miner in Butte; relocating to Heron; railroad work; poor highway conditions; gardening; rural medical care; the 1930s Depression; the WPA.
INTERVIEWED BY JOHN TERREO, APRIL 3, 1990, HERON.
SUMMARY: 4 PAGES
2 TAPES: 2 HOURS

OH 1210
KARL DISSLY INTERVIEW

Karl Dissly discusses: his career as an attorney in Lewistown in 1940; his work as a Federal Bureau of Investigation (FBI) agent from 1941 to 1971; FBI assignments investigating Communists and German-American youth groups during World War II; civil-rights investigations in Tennessee and Mississippi; the criminal activities of the United Teamsters' Union president Jimmy Hoffa in Tennessee; the surveillance of the civil-rights leader Dr. Martin Luther King, Jr., during the mid-1960s.
[See also General Montana OH 1450.]
INTERVIEWED BY BILL LANG, MAY 4, 1989, EL PASO, TX.
TRANSCRIPT: 115 PAGES
4 TAPES: 3 HOURS, 45 MINUTES

OH 1211
BEN SIEGFORD AND DIANE SIEGFORD INTERVIEW

Ben Siegford and Diane Siegford discuss: Noxon; his work as a lineman for the Morgan Electric Company during the construction of the Noxon Rapids Dam; living accommodations; wildlife; their later life in Missoula.
INTERVIEWED BY MONA VANEK, MAY 16, 1990, MISSOULA.
TRANSCRIPT: 38 PAGES
1 TAPE: 1 HOUR

OH 1212
CATHERINE McDOWELL INTERVIEW

Catherine McDowell (b. 1906) speaks of: her father, Fabian J. Bissonet; her father's immigration to Montana from Canada; her childhood on a family ranch near Gold Creek; cooking for hay crews; her education in Catholic academies, including Sacred Heart School in Missoula; making quilts; childhood diseases; attending the normal school (Western Montana College) in Dillon; teaching; getting married and starting a family; relocating to the Noxon area; getting electricity for the first time; the 1930s Depression; relocating to Spokane, Washington; work as a chauffeur for the Naval Supply Base during World War II; duties as an accountant in Spokane; home medical remedies.

INTERVIEWED BY JOHN TERREO, MAY 30, 1990, NOXON.
SUMMARY: 4 PAGES
2 TAPES: 2 HOURS

OH 1213
HOWARD KELSEY INTERVIEW

Howard Kelsey (b. 1912) assesses: his childhood in Pine County, Minnesota; the family's relocation to Bozeman; his education at Montana State College in Bozeman; his work with the John Deere Company in 1936; World War II service with the U.S. Army in Europe; his acquisition and operation of the Nine Quarter-Circle Ranch in the Gallatin Canyon, south of Bozeman, for tourists and hunters; the history of the ranch, from 1892 to 1990; changing business procedures from the late 1940s to the late 1980s. [See also General Montana OH 1456.]
INTERVIEWED BY JACK BURRIS, FEBRUARY 22, 1990, BOZEMAN.
SUMMARY: 15 PAGES
1 TAPE: 1 HOUR

OH 1214
EDNA MAE SAINT CLAIRE INTERVIEW

Edna Saint Claire (b. 1914) comments on: her early life; her education; social and cultural activities in Woodhawk, north of Winifred; her parents' homestead there; the 1930s Depression; her service with the WPA; her employment with several Montana newspapers; her duties with the U.S. Navy; her work in various national parks; married life.
INTERVIEWED BY BETTY JONES, AUGUST 10, 1990, SEATTLE, WA.
TRANSCRIPT: 51 PAGES
2 TAPES: 1 HOUR, 30 MINUTES

OH 1215
DORIS PETERSON INTERVIEW

Helena resident Doris Peterson (b. 1928) discusses: her parents; the family ranch near Craig; area health care; her education in a one-room elementary school; her job as a long-distance telephone operator; life in Helena.
INTERVIEWED BY BETTY JONES, AUGUST 3, 1990, HELENA.
TRANSCRIPT: 43 PAGES
2 TAPES: 1 HOUR, 24 MINUTES

OH 1216
ELIZABETH EVANS STADLER INTERVIEW

Elizabeth Stadler (b. 1913) converses on: her family; her childhood in Butte; her father, Lewis Orvis Evans,

chief legal counsel for the Anaconda Copper Mining Company; Butte businesses, industries, and social life; the 1930s Depression; the activities of her mother, Martha Nicolls Evans, in state politics; the family summer home on Swan Lake; the writer Irvin S. Cobb; the cowboy-artist Charles M. Russell.
INTERVIEWED BY JOHN TERREO, SEPTEMBER 26, 1990, WHITEFISH.
TRANSCRIPT: 54 PAGES
2 TAPES: 2 HOURS

OH 1218
RUTH ARLENE NORA LENTZ INTERVIEW

Ruth Lentz (b. 1929) considers: her childhood in rural Wadena, Saskatchewan, Canada, during the 1930s; her family's move to Baker in 1943; nursing school in Minneapolis, Minnesota, from 1947 to 1951; her marriage; her relocation to Bozeman and then to Missoula; life in Missoula during the 1960s.
INTERVIEWED BY ELIZABETH TURNER, MARCH 13, 1990, MISSOULA.
TRANSCRIPT: 17 PAGES
1 TAPE: 1 HOUR, 10 MINUTES

OH 1245
WENDELL FOX INTERVIEW

Wendell Fox (b. 1911), a resident of Alder treats: his family; his early life in Nebraska; the 1930s Depression; his work as a cowboy on ranches in Montana, Idaho, Wyoming, South Dakota, Colorado, and Texas; his military service with the Wyoming National Guard and with the U.S. Army during World War II; relocating to Alder.
INTERVIEWED BY HAROLD M. PRICE, NOVEMBER 26 AND 27, 1990, ALDER.
SUMMARY: 10 PAGES
7 TAPES: 6 HOURS, 30 MINUTES

OH 1247
CLARENCE POPHAM SPEECH

Clarence Popham presents a speech at the 75th anniversary of the Western Agricultural Research Center in Corvallis and expands on his remarks in a lengthy interview.
INTERVIEWED BY PAT BIK, FEBRUARY 1-3, 1991, CORVALLIS.
9 TAPES: 9 HOURS

OH 1248
"CENTENNIAL MINUTE" RADIO PROGRAMS

"Centennial Minute" radio programs was a statehood

centennial project of the Montana Historical Society. The series consists of excerpts from oral histories recounting Montana pioneer experiences.

RECORDED BY LAURIE MERCIER, JANUARY-SEPTEMBER, 1988, VARIOUS MONTANA LOCATIONS.

TRANSCRIPT: 63 PAGES

8 TAPES: 8 HOURS

OH 1249
MONTANA HISTORY CONFERENCE PROCEEDINGS, 1990

The Seventeenth Annual Montana History Conference convened in Kalispell on October 25-27, 1990. Session topics include: fur trade and exploration; the 1910 and the 1988 forest fires; native-language projects; the Great Northern Railway; Glacier National Park.

RECORDED BY THE MONTANA HISTORICAL SOCIETY, OCTOBER 25-27, 1990, KALISPELL.

20 TAPES: 21 HOURS

OH 1267
TERRI ATWOOD INTERVIEW

Terri Atwood tells of: her service in the U.S. Air Force; her experiences in the Montana National Guard. [The Montana Department of Military Affairs, 103rd Public Affairs Detachment produced this interview.]

INTERVIEWED BY CHARLES MCLEOD, JANUARY 5, 1992, HELENA.

2 TAPES: 2 HOUR

OH 1268
JOSEPH W. UPSHAW INTERVIEW

Helena resident Joseph Upshaw talks about: the history of the Montana National Guard, including its activation during World War II; his career in the Montana Guard; Guard units in Chinook, Poplar, and other Montana communities; his World War II service in New Guinea; the postwar reorganization of the Montana Guard; the Vietnam War; draft dodgers. [The Montana Department of Military Affairs, 103rd Public Affairs Detachment produced this interview.]

INTERVIEWED BY CHARLES MCLEOD, JUNE 1, 1985, FORT HARRISON.

SUMMARY: 4 PAGES

1 TAPE: 33 MINUTES

OH 1269
WALTER GERTSON, EDWARD AZURE, AND ALBERT BRIERE INTERVIEW

Walter Gertson surveys: his service in the U.S. Army

Reserve and in the Alaska National Guard; the reorganization of the Montana National Guard in the late 1940s; his experiences with the Montana Guard; the Montana National Guard during the Vietnam conflict; morale levels of the Guard from the 1940s to the 1990s. Edward Azure and Albert Briere discuss: their World War II service in the Pacific theater; the reorganization of the Montana National Guard in the late 1940s; weekend training and drills; morale. [The Montana Department of Military Affairs, 103rd Public Affairs Detachment produced this interview.]

INTERVIEWED BY CHARLES MCLEOD, AUGUST 24, 1985, FORT HARRISON.

SUMMARY: 3 PAGES

1 TAPE: 1 HOUR

OH 1281
MARGARET S. DAVIS INTERVIEW

Margaret Davis (b. 1942) discusses: her parents; her childhood; her education; marriage to Gary Davis; her husband's military service in Germany; relocation to Helena; her involvement with the LWV and with the Montana Hunger Coalition. [See also Margaret S. Davis Papers, MC 233.]

INTERVIEWED BY JOHN TERREO, JUNE 11, 1992, HELENA.

TRANSCRIPT: 34 PAGES

2 TAPES: 1 HOUR, 15 MINUTES

OH 1282
MARY YOUNG INTERVIEW

Mary Young—a resident of Oilmont—speaks of: growing up in Toole County; ranching in the Sweetgrass Hills; her family's relocation to Kalispell; their subsequent move to Oilmont; Prohibition; her education; her experiences during the 1930s Depression.

INTERVIEWED BY MATT D. YOUNG, APRIL 18, 1992, OILMONT.

SUMMARY: 5 PAGES

1 TAPE: 50 MINUTES

OH 1283
DONALD G. LAMPHIER INTERVIEW

Donald Lamphier (b. 1917) reviews: growing up on homesteads in Terry and Glendive; his father's garbage-collection service in Glendive; his own work as a truck driver; employment with the WPA; the 1930s Depression; his work in highway construction; life during World War II.

INTERVIEWED BY JAMES LAMPHIER, III, JULY 23, 1987, BERWYN, IL.

SUMMARY: 1 PAGE
1 TAPE: 45 MINUTES

OH 1284
JAMES LAMPHIER INTERVIEW

James Lamphier (b. 1907) describes: his family; his early life in the Midwest; homesteading and ranching in eastern Montana; the relationship of transportation to rural health care; his family's relocation to Glendive; the family's garbage-collection service in Glendive.
RECORDED BY JAMES LAMPHIER, NOVEMBER 30, 1981.
SUMMARY: 3 PAGES
1 TAPE: 50 MINUTES

OH 1288
JEANNETTE RANKIN INTERVIEW

Jeannette Rankin (1880–1973)—a Montana-born peace and social activist, a suffragist, the first woman elected to the U.S. Congress (1916), and an opponent of U.S. involvement in both World War I (1917) and World War II (1941)—is interviewed as part of the University of California–Berkeley Suffragist Oral History Project in 1973. The interview is titled "Jeannette Rankin: Activist for World Peace, Women's Rights, and Democratic Government." Appended to the transcript are photographs and photocopies of clippings, magazine articles, and Rankin writings. *[See also General Montana OH 1046.]*
INTERVIEWED BY MALCA CHALL AND THE BERKELEY BANCROFT LIBRARY, JUNE-AUGUST 1972, CARMEL, CA.
TRANSCRIPT: 293 PAGES

OH 1289
HARRY BRAINARD INTERVIEW

Manhattan resident Harry Brainard (b. 1900) reports on: the history of the Sixteen Mile Creek area in Meagher and Gallatin counties; the communities of Sixteen, Maudlow, and Francis; the history of local families, individuals, and businesses; railroads, running from 1900 to 1952.
INTERVIEWED BY DAVID SCHWAB, AUGUST 24, 1990, MANHATTAN.
TRANSCRIPT: 18 PAGES
2 TAPES: 1 HOUR, 45 MINUTES

OH 1290
JOHN HOSSACK INTERVIEW

John Hossack remembers: his experiences as a fire lookout in the Flathead National Forest in Montana from 1943 to 1951; his duties as a dispatcher at the Nine Mile Ranger Station in the Lolo National Forest from 1951 to 1961; his work as a ranger in the Selway-Bitterroot Wilderness Area from 1962 to 1964 and in the Kootenai National Forest from 1965 to 1967; his responsibilities as a staff officer in the Clearwater National Forest from 1967 to 1971; his work as a district ranger in the Fernan District of the Couer d'Alene National Forest (Idaho) from 1972 to 1975; his duties as a deputy supervisor in the Bitterroot National Forest from 1976 to 1979; his assignment as supervisor of the Clearwater National Forest from 1980 to 1983. [The U.S. Forest Service authorized this interview.]
INTERVIEWED BY GERALD WILLIAMS, MAY 1, 1990, MISSOULA.
TRANSCRIPT: 37 PAGES
2 TAPES: 1 HOUR, 40 MINUTES

OH 1291
BESSIE REHM INTERVIEW

Bessie Rehm briefly reflects on: the Gallatin Canyon area during the 1950s; Pete Karst and the Karst Camp; Chet Huntley's Big Sky project; changes in the area caused by the development of Big Sky.
INTERVIEWED BY JACK BURRIS, DECEMBER 5, 1990, GALLATIN CANYON.
SUMMARY: 2 PAGES
1 TAPE: 18 MINUTES

OH 1293
MONTANA HISTORY CONFERENCE PROCEEDINGS, 1991

The Eighteenth Annual Montana History Conference convened in Helena on October 24-26, 1991, and focused on the theme "Times of Trouble: Conflict in the West." Presentations address: military medicine in Montana; effects of the European settlement of America; Indian perspectives on settlement; Native American personal thoughts and feelings regarding white participants in the 1870s Sioux wars; the Montana homefront during World War I—including the editor Will Campbell's contributions to war hysteria, the prosecution of Judge Charles L. Crum, and sedition legislation in Montana; Blackfeet and Crow warrior traditions; changing the name of the Custer Battlefield to the Little Bighorn Battlefield (presented by Robert M. Utley).
RECORDED BY THE MONTANA HISTORICAL SOCIETY, OCTOBER 24-26, 1991, HELENA.
SUMMARY: 5 PAGES
10 TAPES: 9 HOURS

OH 1296
CLIFFORD HARDLE INTERVIEW

Clifford Hardle reports on: his parents' emigration from Germany in 1900; his work as a miner in Butte; the Atlas Bar in Butte; Bannack; his service with the U.S. Navy during World War II.
INTERVIEWED BY JOHN TERREO, JUNE 18, 1991, BANNACK STATE PARK.
SUMMARY: 2 PAGES
1 TAPE: 45 MINUTES

OH 1297
HERB SILBERMAN INTERVIEW

Retired rancher and Montana native Herb Silberman reflects on: his German heritage; homesteading and ranching experiences in Teton County; his work to develop a water project for the Fairfield Bench area; his involvement in a number of community organizations in the Fairfield area, particularly 4-H.
INTERVIEWED BY JOHN TERREO, MAY 9, 1991, FAIRFIELD.
SUMMARY: 3 PAGES
3 TAPES: 3 HOURS

OH 1298
SPEECH: "WOMEN AVIATORS OF WORLD WAR II: THEIR PERSPECTIVE"

Montana Historical Society oral historian John Terreo—in a Brown Bag Lunch component of the Women's History Month lecture series—spoke at the Society in Helena on March 20, 1991. His talk describes the early days of the U.S. Army Air Force WASPS program during World War II.
RECORDED BY THE MONTANA HISTORICAL SOCIETY, MARCH 20, 1991, HELENA.
TRANSCRIPT: 17 PAGES
1 TAPE: 45 MINUTES

OH 1299
LLOYD CHRISTENSEN INTERVIEW

Lloyd Christensen (b. 1909)—a resident of Lakeside—recalls: his parents; his childhood in North Dakota; his ownership and operation of an auto-salvage yard in Dickinson; the 1930s Depression; his retirement in the Flathead Valley.
INTERVIEWED BY JOHN TERREO, FEBRUARY 27, 1991, LAKESIDE.
TRANSCRIPT: 24 PAGES
1 TAPE: 55 MINUTES

OH 1320
ALICE DETTWILER INTERVIEW

Noxon resident Alice Dettwiler (b. 1927) recalls: her early life in Kalispell; health care in Kalispell during the 1930s; her education, training, and nursing work in Minnesota; her return to Montana in 1954; her work as an office nurse in the Noxon clinic from 1962 to 1980; emergency medical transportation in western Sanders County; her duties as a school nurse at Noxon High School; nursing issues in rural areas.
INTERVIEWED BY JOHN TERREO, APRIL 5, 1990, NOXON.
SUMMARY: 19 PAGES
2 TAPES: 1 HOUR, 40 MINUTES

OH 1353
ALBERTA RAMSEY STONE INTERVIEW

Alberta Stone (b. 1918), a resident of Seattle, Washington, recalls: her experiences as the daughter of the railroad agent James Z. Ramsey; her father's work with the Chicago, Milwaukee, St. Paul and Pacific Railroad (Milwaukee Road), specifically on the Harlowton-to-Great Falls run; her family; her childhood in Denton; hobos; circus trains; her return to Denton as an adult.
INTERVIEWED BY ANNA ZELLICK, AUGUST 27, 1991, SEATTLE, WA.
TRANSCRIPT: 22 PAGES

OH 1354
ROBERT V. GORSUCH INTERVIEW

Robert Gorsuch (b. 1926) discusses: his childhood and family experiences in Idaho; World War II; attending the forest service school at the University of Idaho; starting a smoke-jumper unit in Yellowstone National Park; training at Ninemile Camp; work in the Kootenai National Forest, Flathead National Forest, Troy and Yaak, Montana district, and the Bungalow Ranger District, Clearwater Forest, Idaho; private forestry; changes in the forestry industry; and retirement.
INTERVIEWED BY DORIS B. GORSUCH, JUNE 21, 1992, BIGFORK.
TRANSCRIPT: 46 PAGES

OH 1374
GOVERNOR'S CONFERENCE ON TOURISM AND RECREATION

The Governor's Conference on Tourism and Recreation met in Helena on March 9, 1993. In this conference session, entitled, "Montana on Location," the speakers include: Lonie Stimac of Travel Montana's Film Office; Dennis Aig of KUSM public television in

Bozeman. The two men discuss Robert Redford's making of the motion picture *A River Runs Through It* in Montana. Aig also discusses his documentary entitled *Shadow Casting: The Making of "A River Runs Through It."*
RECORDED BY THE MONTANA DEPARTMENT OF COMMERCE, MARCH 9, 1993, HELENA.
1 TAPE: 15 MINUTES

OH 1375
FRED TICHBOURNE AND MARGARITE TICHBOURNE INTERVIEW

Fred Tichbourne (b. 1901) and Margarite Tichbourne (b. 1910) portray: their families; their early lives in Fortine and Kalispell respectively; the 1930s Depression; businesses, industries, and residents of Eureka.
INTERVIEWED BY CATHRYN SCHROEDER, FEBRUARY 2, 1993, EUREKA.
SUMMARY: 11 PAGES
1 TAPE: 1 HOUR

OH 1377
HAROLD OLSON INTERVIEW

Harold Olson (b. 1912), a resident of Judith Gap, discusses: his parents; his early life in Judith Gap; his employment with the Great Northern Railway Company; the 1930s Depression; the effects of World War II and the Vietnam War on railroads; his retirement.
INTERVIEWED BY KIRSTIN OLSON, DECEMBER 3, 1991, JUDITH GAP.
SUMMARY: 2 PAGES
1 TAPE: 20 MINUTES

OH 1379
CAROLYN DRYE INTERVIEW

Arlee resident Carolyn Drye (b. 1949) interprets: her career as a teacher; changes in the teaching profession during her career; the effects of technology and changing discipline on the classroom teacher.
INTERVIEWED BY LORI RAISLAND, NOVEMBER 30, 1991, ARLEE.
SUMMARY: 5 PAGES
1 TAPE: 20 MINUTES

OH 1380
TIM BUCKLEY INTERVIEW

Tim Buckley (b. 1954), a resident of Judith Gap, recalls: joining the Peace Corps; his experiences as a teacher in Botswana, Africa, from 1986 to 1989; differences between the American educational system and the one he encountered in Africa; cultural attitudes toward education; student life; educational facilities; sports and entertainment; student/teacher relationships; language differences; discipline of both teachers and students; his return to the United States; his employment as a teacher at Judith Gap High School.
INTERVIEWED BY GINA FINLEY, NOVEMBER 30, 1991, JUDITH GAP.
SUMMARY: 7 PAGES
1 TAPE: 1 HOUR, 10 MINUTES

OH 1382
MARVIN PELO REMINISCENCE

Marvin Pelo briefly describes his recollections of the 1943 Smith Mine disaster in Bearcreek.
TRANSCRIPT: 4 PAGES
1 TAPE: 18 MINUTES

OH 1383
BILL WORF INTERVIEW

Missoula resident Bill Worf (b. 1926) discusses: his family; his early life in Reed Point; his early experiences as a forest ranger; legislative issues concerning wilderness areas; the effects of logging and recreation on wilderness; his duties as the Bridger National Forest supervisor; wilderness management. [The U.S. Forest Service authorized this interview.]
INTERVIEWED BY GERALD WILLIAMS, MAY 1, 1990, MISSOULA.
TRANSCRIPT: 33 PAGES
1 TAPE: 30 MINUTES

OH 1384
NEWELL GOUGH, JR., INTERVIEW

Newell Gough, Jr. (b. 1913), speaks of: his family; the Missoula Mercantile Company; the Teton Land Company; his experiences with the Montana Stockgrowers Association; D. A. G. Floweree; E. A. Phillips; Ralph Miracle; Judge Charles Horsky; cattle and sheep ranching; cowboys; droughts; the 1930s Depression.
INTERVIEWED BY JOHN TERREO, NOVEMBER 18, 1992, HELENA.
TRANSCRIPT: 11 PAGES
1 TAPE: 40 MINUTES

OH 1388
MOTHER AMATA DUNNE INTERVIEW

Mother Dunne depicts: her life; her religion; experiences as a nun.

INTERVIEWED BY PATRICIA O'CONNELL, CIRCA 1968,
POLSON.
1 TAPE: 1 HOUR

OH 1389
MERRILL G. BURLINGAME INTERVIEW

Longtime history professor Merrill Burlingame (1901–1994) of Montana State University in Bozeman considers: his service on the Montana Historical Society's Board of Trustees; K. Ross Toole; Michael S. Kennedy; early Montana history; *Montana The Magazine of Western History*; the historical society's annual history conferences; the construction of the Veterans and Pioneers Memorial Building in Helena.
INTERVIEWED BY SUSAN M. GIBB, OCTOBER 17, 1992,
BOZEMAN.
TRANSCRIPT: 9 PAGES
1 TAPE: 45 MINUTES

OH 1390
BRUCE R. TOOLE INTERVIEW

Bruce Toole of Billings discusses: his brother Kenneth Ross Toole; the Montana Historical Society.
INTERVIEWED BY STEWART CONNER, AUGUST 21, 1992,
BILLINGS.
SUMMARY: 3 PAGES
1 TAPE: 50 MINUTES

OH 1393
WILLIAM TALL BULL LECTURE

William Tall Bull, a member of the Northern Cheyenne tribe, presented this lecture at the Montana Historical Society in Helena on October 20, 1987. In this talk he comments on: the plight of the Native Americans during the eighteenth and nineteenth centuries in comparison with the plight of the wolf and the grizzly bear of the twentieth century; the 1864 Sand Creek Massacre in Colorado; native tales of the wolf and the bear.
RECORDED BY THE MONTANA HISTORICAL SOCIETY,
OCTOBER 20, 1987, HELENA.
SUMMARY: 2 PAGES
1 TAPE: 27 MINUTES

OH 1394
LEROY "ANDY" ANDERSON LECTURE

In this lecture, given in Chinook on June 15, 1992, Andy Anderson chronicles: the activities of the Nez Perce Indians in the Cow Island/Bears Paw Battlefield area in 1877; travel on and the development of the Cow Island freighting road, running from the Cow Island Landing on the Missouri River to the Chinook vicinity.
RECORDED BY LEROY ANDERSON, JUNE 15, 1992,
CHINOOK.
SUMMARY: 6 PAGES
1 TAPE: 40 MINUTES

OH 1396
THOMAS TRACY LANKFORD INTERVIEW

Thomas Lankford (b. 1946) characterizes: his childhood on the Fort Belknap Indian Reservation; his grandparents' migration from Canada to the United States; life in Dodson; modern technology; his experiences in the U.S. Army during the 1970s; Martin Luther King, Jr.; civil-rights issues; prejudice against Native Americans.
INTERVIEWED BY GWEN LANKFORD, MARCH 29, 1992,
MISSOULA.
SUMMARY: 2 PAGES
1 TAPE: 1 HOUR

OH 1397
EUGENE MANLEY INTERVIEW

Eugene Manley, a resident of Hall, discusses: his family; irrigation; water rights and water use in the upper Clark Fork Basin; the Allendale Irrigation Company; the Rock Creek Flume and Ditch Company; litigation and legislation affecting water usage in the area.
INTERVIEWED BY JOHN TERREO, JULY 27, 1992,
DRUMMOND.
TRANSCRIPT: 89 PAGES
2 TAPES: 2 HOURS

OH 1398
HOWARD SCHENEFELT INTERVIEW

Eureka resident Howard Schenefelt addresses: his childhood; growing up on a homestead near Eureka; working as a logger in the Kootenai River drainage; life in logging camps; working for the J. Neils Lumber Company; hoboing; his career as a professional wrestler during the 1930s and the 1940s, under the professional name of "Bobby Burns"; changes since his childhood in the Tobacco Valley Plains area; Roscoe Combs; union organizing; the IWW; changes in the timber industry.
INTERVIEWED BY BARBARA SOMMER, OCTOBER 3, 1991,
EUREKA.
SUMMARY: 12 PAGES
2 TAPES: 1 HOUR, 30 MINUTES

OH 1399
YORK GULCH HISTORY INTERVIEWS

A group of residents discuss mining operations in the

York Gulch area of Lewis and Clark County: Betty Lou (Bickford) Christianson; Clinton Christianson; Bette K. Smith; Bennie G. Smith; Phyllis Warren Jakovac; Sydney Ann Hoy; Norma Byrd; Robert Elletson. They discuss: mines, including the Little Dandy, the Little Daisy, the Golden Messenger, and the Golden Charm; the Spratt Mining Company; Chinese laborers; the McEwen Ditch; local bars; Prohibition.

INTERVIEWED BY BARBARA SOMMER, SEPTEMBER 10, 1991, HELENA.

SUMMARY: 7 PAGES

1 TAPE: 1 HOUR

OH 1400
JAMES HAUGHEY INTERVIEW

James Haughey, an artist and a state senator from Yellowstone County, talks about: his education; his work with George Poindexter collecting modern art; specific artists and their work; his involvement in the Yellowstone Art Center in Billings; the future of the Poindexter Collection of Modern Art, housed in the Montana Historical Society in Helena.

INTERVIEWED BY MARCIA A. MORROW, JULY 19, 1993, BILLINGS.

TRANSCRIPT: 29 PAGES

2 TAPES: 1 HOUR, 20 MINUTES

OH 1401
TED TURNER SPEECH

Ted Turner, a television mogul and Montana rancher, delivered this speech at the annual meeting of the Montana Stockgrowers Association in Billings on December 10, 1993. Turner treats: the future of farming and ranching in Montana; the impacts of Montana's recent growth in population; the advantages of such organizations as the Nature Conservancy, working for conservation easements that will keep ranches from being subdivided and developed.

RECORDED BY THE MONTANA STOCKGROWERS ASSOCIATION, DECEMBER 10, 1993, BILLINGS.

1 TAPE: 35 MINUTES

OH 1402
ANN ZUPAN AND LUCAS F. ZUPAN INTERVIEW

Ann Zupan and Lucas Zupan—longtime residents of the Roundup area—discuss: their families, his Yugoslavian ancestry; living in Aldrich from 1905 to 1910; the closing of the local coal mine; coming to Roundup; the Slovenian community in Roundup; the Number Three Mine; Gibb Town; Farrow Town; Klein; his work as a

miner; ethnic fraternal activities and insurance services; wakes and burials; alcohol and Prohibition; St. Benedict's Catholic Church; local business, primarily saloons and grocers. *[See also General Montana OH 1403.]*

INTERVIEWED BY ANNA ZELLICK, JUNE 9, 1987, LEWISTOWN.

TRANSCRIPT: 46 PAGES

1 TAPE: 50 MINUTES

OH 1403
ANN ZUPAN AND LUCAS F. ZUPAN INTERVIEW

Ann Zupan and Lucas Zupan discuss: Yugoslavians in Roundup; their experiences in the community of Roundup. *[See also General Montana OH 1402.]*

INTERVIEWED BY ANNA ZELLICK, MARCH 4, 1988, ROUNDUP.

1 TAPE: 50 MINUTES

OH 1405
MRS. OSCAR BOEPPLE INTERVIEW

Mrs. Oscar Boepple, a native of Minnesota, briefly summarizes: her move to Libby; her education; her experiences as a teacher; family traditions.

INTERVIEWED BY SHERRY MCKEAN, CIRCA 1978, LIBBY.

SUMMARY: 1 PAGE

1 TAPE: 15 MINUTES

OH 1406
MRS. ARCHIE MINDE INTERVIEW

Norwegian immigrant Mrs. Archie Minde speaks of: her arrival in Libby in 1924; the town of Libby; the American Lutheran Church in town; Christmas festivities; education; various Libby residents.

INTERVIEWED BY SHERRY MCKEAN, CIRCA 1978, LIBBY.

SUMMARY: 1 PAGE

1 TAPE: 35 MINUTES

OH 1409
JAMES CURTIN INTERVIEW

James Curtin reviews: his parents' immigration from Ireland to the United States; his childhood in Butte; the bombing of the Miners' Union Hall in Butte in 1914; his father's work as a miner; his own education at the Butte Business College; his work for the Anaconda Copper Mining Company; the 1930s Depression; smoke pollution in Butte; the IWW; the 1933 strike; the reorganization of the Mine-Mill union workers in 1934; Communists in the Butte unions; the AFL-CIO; the merger of the Mine-Mill and the Smelter Workers unions; Anaconda Company informants; unions in the 1980s; his work on

the negotiating committee for better working conditions.
INTERVIEWED BY ARTHUR DAY, 1987, BUTTE.
SUMMARY: 3 PAGES
1 TAPE: 50 MINUTES

OH 1410
JOHN B. "JACK" HARRIS INTERVIEW

East Helena resident Jack Harris recalls: his family; his education; his experiences in the U.S. Army during World War II; beginning work at the ASARCO plant in East Helena in 1946; the Mine-Mill union; suspected Communists in the Montana unions; the AFL-CIO; the Anaconda Copper Mining Company; McCarthyism; the U.S. House Un-American Activities Committee (HUAC) hearings; the labor strikes of 1959 and 1967; local and national union leadership. [See also Metals Manufacturing in Four Montana Communities OH 950.]
INTERVIEWED BY ARTHUR DAY, SEPTEMBER 3, 1987, EAST HELENA.
SUMMARY: 3 PAGES
2 TAPES: 2 HOURS

OH 1411
ROBERT MELVIN INTERVIEW

Robert Melvin reports on: his parents' migration from Ireland to the United States; growing up in Butte; the 1930s Depression; the bombing of the Butte Miners' Union Hall in 1914; the murder of Frank Little, an IWW organizer in 1917; union organizing in Butte; the Mine-Mill union; Communists in the Butte unions; the AFL-CIO; strikes; his work for the Anaconda Copper Mining Company for 25 years; unions in the 1980s.
INTERVIEWED BY ARTHUR DAY, JUNE 6, 1988, BUTTE.
SUMMARY: 2 PAGES
1 TAPE: 1 HOUR, 20 MINUTES

OH 1412
LLOYD C. WENNER INTERVIEW

Lloyd Wenner remembers: his childhood in Minnesota; his parents' farm; the 1930s Depression; President Franklin D. Roosevelt; his move to Great Falls in 1937; his work at Columbus Hospital in Great Falls; his experiences as an apprentice for the Ironworkers and Structural Steel union; union leadership at the Great Falls smelter; the merger of the Mine-Mill union and the Smelter Workers union; negotiations for benefits; strikes.
INTERVIEWED BY ARTHUR DAY, SUMMER, 1987, CASCADE.
SUMMARY: 3 PAGES
2 TAPES: 1 HOUR, 25 MINUTES

OH 1413
THOMAS PARR, SR., INTERVIEW

Great Falls resident Thomas Parr relates: growing up in Whitehaven, England; his father's work as a coal miner; his own experiences as a miner in Britain and in the United States; unionism in the U.S. during the 1930s and the 1940s; the Progressives; Communism in Montana unions; the Steelworkers Union; the Mine-Mill union; his 45-year career working for the Anaconda Copper Mining Company.
INTERVIEWED BY ARTHUR DAY, SEPTEMBER 18, 1987, GREAT FALLS.
SUMMARY: 2 PAGES
1 TAPE: 1 HOUR, 5 MINUTES

OH 1414
OWEN P. McNALLY INTERVIEW

Owen McNally reflects on: growing up in Anaconda; ethnic clans; fraternal unions; his work for the Anaconda Copper Mining Company; local efforts to unionize the mills in the late 1930s; safety on the job; unionism during the 1940s; Communism; local strikes.
INTERVIEWED BY ARTHUR DAY, SUMMER, 1987, ANACONDA.
SUMMARY: 4 PAGES
2 TAPES: 1 HOUR, 35 MINUTES

OH 1415
PERRY SETON INTERVIEW

Perry Seton recounts: his family; growing up in North Platte, Nebraska; his father's work for the Northern Pacific Railroad; his father's experiences as a farmer; working as a cook at WPA camps in Oregon; his employment as a truck driver on various construction projects; his enlistment in the U.S. Navy; his experiences during World War II; his duties as a smelter worker; his union service negotiating contracts; the formation of the Mine-Mill union.
INTERVIEWED BY ARTHUR DAY, JULY 16, 1988, GREAT FALLS.
3 TAPES: 3 HOURS

OH 1416
REGINALD BEAVIS INTERVIEW

Walkerville resident Reginald Beavis recalls: his childhood in Butte; his father's work for the Mine-Mill union; the 1934 strike against the Anaconda Copper Mining Company; working conditions in the mines; his experiences in the Marines during World War II; improvements in benefits for mine workers after the war; Com-

munism in the Montana unions; the merger of the Mine-Mill union with the Smelter Workers union; the 1959 strike; his work on the history of the Butte unions.
INTERVIEWED BY ARTHUR DAY, JULY 7, 1987, WALKERVILLE.
SUMMARY: 3 PAGES
2 TAPES: 1 HOUR, 40 MINUTES

OH 1417
JAMES W. MURRAY INTERVIEW

James Murray portrays: growing up in Laurel; his father's work with the local chapter of the Oil, Chemical and Atomic Workers Union in Laurel; the development of labor unions in Montana; the Mine-Mill union; the United Steelworkers of America; union leadership; anti-Communist propaganda (e.g., *The Red Web over Montana*); civil rights; the Helena *People's Voice* weekly newspaper; the 1968–1969 strike against the Anaconda Copper Mining Company; the fight for workers' rights.
INTERVIEWED BY ARTHUR DAY, SEPTEMBER 26, 1987, HELENA.
SUMMARY: 3 PAGES
1 TAPE: 1 HOUR

OH 1418
MAX SALAZAR INTERVIEW

Max Salazar (b. 1929) interprets: his childhood in Wyoming and Utah; his father's work for the Kennecott Copper Mining Company in Utah; his enlistment in the U.S. Navy at the age of 14 in 1943; his discharge from the Navy in 1944; his work for the Anaconda Copper Mining Company in Butte; miners' unions; Communists in the Mine-Mill union; strikes; trials; the merger of the United Steelworkers of America with the Mine-Mill union; Fourth of July celebrations; union fights for better working conditions.
INTERVIEWED BY ARTHUR DAY, OCTOBER 1, 1987, BUTTE.
SUMMARY: 2 PAGES
1 TAPE: 1 HOUR, 5 MINUTES

OH 1419
SAM RYAN INTERVIEW

Sam Ryan (b. 1916), of Helena, indicates: his early life in Roundup; his experiences with the CCC; his employment with ASARCO in East Helena; union activities; the union official Bill Mason. *[See also Metals Manufacturing in Four Montana Communities OH 982.]*
INTERVIEWED BY ARTHUR DAY, SEPTEMBER 19, 1987, HELENA.

SUMMARY: 3 PAGES
2 TAPES: 45 MINUTES

OH 1420
BERNARD RASK INTERVIEW

Barney Rask (b. 1923) addresses: his Lebanese parents; his father's work as a teamster for the Pioneer Fuel and Brick Company in Butte; his graduation from high school; enlistment in the U.S. Navy; early involvement in union activities; repeated threats to his life for his union work; the advantages and the disadvantages of unionism.
INTERVIEWED BY ARTHUR DAY, JUNE 4, 1988, BUTTE.
TRANSCRIPT: 30 PAGES
2 TAPES: 3 HOURS

OH 1421
RAY RENIG INTERVIEW

Ray Renig (b. 1925) characterizes: his family; growing up in Helena; the family's ranch near the town of Dearborn; his experiences in the U.S. Navy; his work at the ASARCO smelter in East Helena, beginning in the 1950s; involvement in the Mine-Mill union; improvements in workers' conditions and benefits over time.
INTERVIEWED BY ARTHUR DAY, OCTOBER 14, 1987, HELENA.
2 TAPES: 2 HOURS

OH 1422
MAURICE "SUNNY" POWERS INTERVIEW

Sunny Powers (b. 1909) discusses: his Irish parents; growing up in Butte; the bombing of the Butte Miners' Union Hall in 1914; strikes; the hanging of Frank Little in 1917; the death of his father from injuries received during a union-related brawl; violence related to the Western Federation of Miners; working conditions in the mines; the organizing of mine workers in the 1930s; a non-Communist affidavit; union politics through the 1950s; his work with the state legislature to pass silicosis-related bills.
INTERVIEWED BY ARTHUR DAY, AUGUST 31, 1987, EAST HELENA.
TRANSCRIPT: 29 PAGES
4 TAPES: 4 HOURS

OH 1423
RAY GRAHAM INTERVIEW

Ray Graham (b. 1912) comments on: his childhood in Great Falls; the 1922 railroad strike; early labor history in Montana; his stepfather's work in the Anaconda

Company's Great Falls smelter; the 1930s Depression; the IWW; politics involved with local and national unions; his own career in the Great Falls smelter; union activities during strikes; worker efficiency and pride; the closing of the smelter in the 1980s; effects of the closure on Great Falls.

INTERVIEWED BY ARTHUR DAY, SEPTEMBER 17, 1987, GREAT FALLS.

2 TAPES: 2 HOURS

OH 1424
TOM DICKSON INTERVIEW

Tom Dickson speaks of: his early life in Anaconda; the use of troops to protect the strategic plants during World War I and World War II; early union leaders; Chase Powers; Bill Mason; the Mine-Mill union; Western Federation of Miners' activities; CCC work; union negotiations involving insurance, wage increases, and grievance procedures; the switch to a closed shop; claims of Communists in Montana unions; gains made as a result of strikes. [See also Metals Manufacturing in Four Montana Communities OH 924 and Montanans at Work OH 216.]

INTERVIEWED BY ARTHUR DAY, JULY 27, 1987, ANACONDA.

SUMMARY: 16 PAGES

2 TAPES: 3 HOURS

OH 1426
JAMES McKINNELL AND NAN McKINNELL INTERVIEW

Artists James McKinnell and Nan McKinnell converse about: their respective educations; their work in pottery and in ceramics; experiences with the Archie Bray Foundation in Helena.

INTERVIEWED BY MARTIN HOLT, JUNE 4, 1979, DENVER, CO.

SUMMARY: 3 PAGES

1 TAPE: 1 HOUR, 15 MINUTES

OH 1429
ARCHIE BRAY, JR., INTERVIEW

Archie Bray, Jr., considers: his family; his father's brickyard; brick production; clay digging; Norman "Jeff" Holter; pottery.

INTERVIEWED BY MARTIN HOLT, AUGUST 3, 1978, HELENA.

SUMMARY: 4 PAGES

1 TAPE: 45 MINUTES

OH 1430
JUDY CORNELL INTERVIEW

Judy Cornell delineates: her education; her marriage to David Cornell; experiences and activities involved with her role as associate director of the Archie Bray Foundation in Helena; teaching art; selling art; discrimination against women artists; gender roles in Montana; the Archie Bray Foundation; her relocation to San Francisco, California.

INTERVIEWED BY MARTIN HOLT, AUGUST 6, 1981, SAUSALITO, CA.

SUMMARY: 4 PAGES

1 TAPE: 1 HOUR, 30 MINUTES

OH 1431
DAVID CORNELL INTERVIEW

David Cornell recalls: his clay studies at Montana State University in Bozeman; his duties as director of the Archie Bray Foundation in Helena; art students; teaching.

INTERVIEWED BY MARTIN HOLT, AUGUST 8, 1978, TALENT, OR.

SUMMARY: 3 PAGES

1 TAPE: 1 HOUR, 15 MINUTES

OH 1432
HENRY "SKIP" LYMAN AND NINA LYMAN INTERVIEW

Skip Lyman describes: his early work in two-dimensional art; his change to ceramics; his study at the University of Montana in Bozeman under Rudy Autio; painting; his residency at the Archie Bray Foundation in Helena. Nina Lyman discusses: the interaction of artists and their families at the Archie Bray; special foods and events at the foundation.

INTERVIEWED BY MARTIN HOLT, AUGUST 13, 1978, CHENEY, WA.

SUMMARY: 5 PAGES

1 TAPE: 1 HOUR, 10 MINUTES

OH 1433
BILL SAGE INTERVIEW

Bill Sage depicts: his experiences at the Archie Bray Foundation in Helena; the evolution of his pottery.

INTERVIEWED BY MARTIN HOLT, AUGUST 2, 1978, CHENEY, WA.

SUMMARY: 5 PAGES

1 TAPE: 1 HOUR, 30 MINUTES

OH 1434
BRANSON STEVENSON INTERVIEW

Branson Stevenson discusses: Archie Bray, Sr.; Sister Trinitas; Peter Meloy; Peter Voulkos; Kelly Wong; other artists; bricklaying at the Archie Bray Foundation in Helena; developing glazes; clay pottery; ceramics. [See also General Montana OH 627.]

INTERVIEWED BY MARTIN HOLT, AUGUST 2, 1978, GREAT FALLS.
SUMMARY: 5 PAGES
1 TAPE: 45 MINUTES

OH 1435
PETER VOULKOS INTERVIEW

Peter Voulkos discusses: his education; pottery; his experiences at the Archie Bray Foundation in Helena.

INTERVIEWED BY MARTIN HOLT, AUGUST 7, 1978, OAKLAND, CA.
SUMMARY: 3 PAGES
1 TAPE: 1 HOUR

OH 1436
FRED WOLLSCHLAGER INTERVIEW

Fred Wollschlager discourses on: his education; his work in ceramics and pottery; his brief residency at the Archie Bray Foundation in Helena.

INTERVIEWED BY MARTIN HOLT, AUGUST 5, 1978, SAN FRANCISCO, CA.
SUMMARY: 2 PAGES
1 TAPE: 45 MINUTES

OH 1437
KELLY WONG INTERVIEW

Kelly Wong examines: his education at Montana State University in Bozeman; his relationships with Rudy Autio and Peter Voulkos; his early experiences with the Archie Bray Foundation in Helena, including work in the brickyard; a job teaching at Portland State University in Portland, Oregon, in 1951; teaching techniques; glaze experimentation; Archie Bray, Sr.; his artistic philosophy and beliefs; concerns regarding art students; the future of art.

INTERVIEWED BY MARTIN HOLT, AUGUST 10, 1978, PORTLAND, OR.
SUMMARY: 3 PAGES
1 TAPE: 40 MINUTES

OH 1438
KURT WEISNER INTERVIEW

Kurt Weisner details: his childhood; his education at the Kansas City Art Institute in Kansas City, Missouri; pottery and ceramic techniques.

INTERVIEWED BY MARTIN HOLT, OCTOBER 14, 1978.
SUMMARY: 6 PAGES
1 TAPE: 1 HOUR, 30 MINUTES

OH 1439
BOB DeWEESE AND GENNY DeWEESE INTERVIEW

Bob DeWeese and Genny DeWeese explain coming to Montana in 1949. Bob DeWeese discusses: teaching at Montana State University in Bozeman; Cubist ceramics; Archie Bray, Sr.; Peter Voulkos; other artists.

INTERVIEWED BY MARTIN HOLT, SEPTEMBER 19, 1979, BOZEMAN.
SUMMARY: 6 PAGES
1 TAPE: 35 MINUTES

OH 1440
KEN FERGUSON INTERVIEW

Ken Ferguson discusses: his education; pottery; experiences with the Archie Bray Foundation in Helena.

INTERVIEWED BY MARTIN HOLT, JULY 2, 1979, SHAWNEE MISSION, KS.
SUMMARY: 2 PAGES
1 TAPE: 35 MINUTES

OH 1441
FRANCES SENSKA AND JESSE WILBUR INTERVIEW

Frances Senska (b. 1914) and Jesse Wilbur discuss: ceramic art; their experiences at the Archie Bray Foundation in Helena; Peter Voulkos; Kelly Wong; Lillian Beauschar; Branson Stevenson. Frances Senska also talks about: her early life in Cameroon, West Africa; her education in industrial design.

INTERVIEWED BY MARTIN HOLT, JULY, 1979, BOZEMAN.
SUMMARY: 5 PAGES
1 TAPE: 1 HOUR, 10 MINUTES

OH 1442
WALLY BIVENS INTERVIEW

Helena resident Wally Bivens recalls: his interest in ceramics; his experiences with the Archie Bray Foundation in Helena.

INTERVIEWED BY MARTIN HOLT, OCTOBER 31, 1981, HELENA.
SUMMARY: 4 PAGES
1 TAPE: 45 MINUTES

OH 1443
PETER MELOY INTERVIEW

Peter Meloy—a Helena resident—portrays: his brother Hank Meloy, an artist; Archie Bray, Sr.; the development of the Archie Bray Foundation; Ken Ferguson; Frances Senska; Sue Bovey; other ceramic artists; his own work with high-fire ceramics during the late 1940s.
INTERVIEWED BY MARTIN HOLT, JUNE 19, 1977, HELENA.
SUMMARY: 6 PAGES
1 TAPE: 1 HOUR, 10 MINUTES

OH 1444
JOHN HAWKER INTERVIEW

John Hawker reflects on: living his entire life in the Bitterroot Valley of western Montana; his work logging and farming; clearing the land; building the community of Corvallis; his involvement with his church; the burdens placed on an owner/worker of prime farmland in light of suburban development. [See also Montanans at Work OH 427.]
INTERVIEWED BY CLARENCE POPHAM, JANUARY 4, 1989, CORVALLIS.
1 TAPE: 1 HOUR, 30 MINUTES

OH 1445
HAROLD WHITE AND ERNIE BUKER INTERVIEW

Harold White recounts: his birth and youth in Montana; his 12 years of service as a Ravalli County Commissioner; a lifetime of farming; his work building bridges; operation of the Victor Butcher Shop. Ernie Buker remembers: his birth and early years in Florence; his parents' homestead between Eight Mile and Dry Gulch early in the century; the difficulty of running cows without water on the homestead; being raised on canned milk.
INTERVIEWED BY CLARENCE POPHAM, FEBRUARY 27, 1989, VICTOR.
2 TAPES: 2 HOURS

OH 1447
H. LEE HAMES AND DAVE SCHROEDER INTERVIEW

Lee Hames describes: his birth in the upper Burnt Fork drainage of the Bitterroot Valley in western Montana; his grandfather, Sam Hames, who homesteaded the Vern Woolsey ranch in the Burnt Fork valley; his father, John Hames; the family's relocation to the Grist Mill Ranch; his friend, Nez Perce Chief Joseph's nephew; his experience as the water-rights holder of the oldest water

right recognized in the state of Montana. Dave Schroeder discusses: his youth in Lolo and Missoula; his grandfather, D. R. Maclay, one of the earliest white settlers in the lower Bitterroot Valley. [See also Montanans at Work OH 652.]
INTERVIEWED BY CLARENCE POPHAM, MARCH 7, 1989, STEVENSVILLE.
3 TAPES: 2 HOURS, 30 MINUTES

OH 1448
DOROTHEA BUCK SMOLA, WILLIAM HUNTER, DOROTHY WILLIAMS, AND HAROLD WHITESITT INTERVIEW

Dorothea Smola depicts: living in the house in Stevensville in which she was born; her grandfather, who built their home and had arrived in the Bitterroot Valley in the 1870s; her involvement, with her husband, in agriculture and business in the Stevensville area. William Hunter addresses: the arrival of his parents in Stevensville in 1888; the settlement of that community; his family. Dorothy Williams surveys: her family; their migration from the Nebraska "Dust Bowl" to Stevensville in 1938. Harold Whitesitt treats: his maternal grandparents' move from Canada to the Bitterroot Valley; his grandfather's first local job, planting 4,000 apple trees on the present-day Buffalo Ranch; his experiences starting a furniture store and a mortuary in Stevensville, businesses currently owned by the third generation of his family.
INTERVIEWED BY CLARENCE POPHAM, 1989, STEVENSVILLE.
1 TAPE: 1 HOUR, 30 MINUTES

OH 1449
AMY ROCKAFELLOW AND LLOYD ROCKAFELLOW INTERVIEW

Amy Rockafellow reports on: her maternal grandparents, who were among the earliest settlers of the Corvallis community; her work as the Corvallis postmistress from the 1930s until 1975. Lloyd Rockafellow addresses: his birth in Nebraska; his arrival in the Bitterroot Valley in 1902. [See also General Montana OH 999.]
INTERVIEWED BY CLARENCE POPHAM, JANUARY 9, 1990.
2 TAPES: 2 HOURS, 30 MINUTES

OH 1450
KARL DISSLY INTERVIEW

Karl Dissly reviews: his life in Lewistown; his parents' emigration from Switzerland; his father's life in central Montana; his father's First County Creamery in Lewistown. [See also General Montana OH 1210.]

INTERVIEWED BY BILL LANG, MAY 5, 1989, EL PASO, TX.
2 TAPES: 2 HOURS

OH 1456
HOWARD KELSEY INTERVIEW

Howard Kelsey (b. 1912) reveals: his involvement with the 1964 Montana Territorial Centennial Train; the train's initial concept; fund-raising; promotional activities; contributors; construction; the train's route; the disposition of some of the cars. *[See also General Montana OH 1213.]*

INTERVIEWED BY JACK BURRIS, JUNE 13, 1990, GALLATIN GATEWAY.
SUMMARY: 11 PAGES
1 TAPE: 1 HOUR

OH 1474
ROSE NAGLICH MacFARLAND INTERVIEW

Rose MacFarland (b. 1911) summarizes: her parents' emigration from Croatia to the United States in the early 1900s; her father's work in the mines at Bearcreek; life in Bearcreek, a largely immigrant community including Slovenians, Montenegrans, Serbs, and Croatians; the Catholic Church; local events and customs; her family.

INTERVIEWED BY ANNA ZELLICK, JUNE 6, 1991, RED LODGE.
TRANSCRIPT: 75 PAGES
3 TAPES: 2 HOURS, 30 MINUTES

OH 1475
REVEREND CHARLES STROM INTERVIEW

Father Charles Strom (b. 1914) speaks of: his family; his childhood in Whitefish; entering the priesthood of the Catholic Church; his experiences with the Libby and Columbia Falls parishes.

INTERVIEWED BY CHRIS LISS AND LINDA MOHAZAN, MAY 18, 1983, RONAN.
SUMMARY: 1 PAGE
1 TAPE: 1 HOUR

OH 1476
DANIEL W. DIMICH, WILLIAM M. DIMICH, DANNY DIMICH, AND WILLIAM N. DIMICH INTERVIEW

This interview involves two brothers—Daniel W. Dimich and William M. Dimich—as well as their respective sons—Danny Dimich and William N. Dimich. Daniel W. Dimich discusses: his father, Mike Dimich; his father's emigration from Yugoslavia to Montana in 1916; his own work in Great Falls for the Great Northern Rail-

way Company; his arranged marriage to Sophia Testlig; his relocation to Red Lodge; gaining U.S. citizenship; his attempt to start a modern grocery store in Red Lodge during the 1920s. Daniel W. Dimich joins the other three interviewees to talk about: life in Red Lodge; the family's wholesale business; Serbian foods and customs; fraternal organizations.

INTERVIEWED BY ANNA ZELLICK, JUNE 12, 1991, BILLINGS.
SUMMARY: 9 PAGES
2 TAPES: 1 HOUR, 5 MINUTES

OH 1477
WILLIAM A. ROMEK INTERVIEW

William Romek treats: his experiences working with Yugoslavian, Montenegran, Serbian, and Croatian miners in the Smith and Foster coal mines at Bearcreek from 1920 into the 1960s; Prohibition and bootlegging; local businesses, events, and personalities; gambling; other ethnic groups; the effects of the Northern Pacific Railroad on life in the Red Lodge area.

INTERVIEWED BY ANNA ZELLICK, MAY 9, 1991, BILLINGS.
TRANSCRIPT: 30 PAGES
2 TAPES: 1 HOUR, 40 MINUTES

OH 1478
JOHN KASTELITZ INTERVIEW

Red Lodge resident John Kastelitz tells of: his parents' emigration from Austria to the United States in 1906; his father's work in the Smith Mine at Bearcreek; the accident that killed his father; the 1943 Smith Mine disaster; growing up in Red Lodge; local businesses, events, and personalities; Catholicism; working in the mines; mine-related illnesses and injuries; the grocery trade; fraternal organizations, including Slavokska Narodna Podporna; burial benefits; union activities.

INTERVIEWED BY ANNA ZELLICK, JUNE 7, 1991, RED LODGE.
TRANSCRIPT: 24 PAGES
1 TAPE: 1 HOUR

OH 1479
TONY ZUPAN AND SHIRLEY ZUPAN INTERVIEW

Tony Zupan and Shirley Zupan detail: the emigration of Tony's father, Nick Zupan, from Yugoslavia to the United States; the arranged marriage of his parents; the family's relocation from Waterloo, Iowa, to Red Lodge in 1918; his father's work transporting coal cars from the mines to the Northern Pacific rail line; the United Mine Workers; the Croatian Fraternal Union; his mother's work in the home; Croatian, Finnish, Italian, Yugoslavian, Montenegran, and Serbian ethnic communities in the area; local events and people; the Festival of Nations. INTERVIEWED BY ANNA ZELLICK, JUNE 9, 1991, RED LODGE.

TRANSCRIPT: 58 PAGES

2 TAPES: 2 HOURS

OH 1480
MIKE J. BAROVICH INTERVIEW

Mike Barovich describes: the emigration of his parents, Sam and Mileva Barovich, from Niksich, Montenegro, to Bearcreek in 1921; his father's work in the local mines; fraternal organizations; his father's death in the Smith Mine disaster of 1943; Prohibition; his participation in high school sports; his service in the U.S. Navy during World War II.

INTERVIEWED BY ANNA ZELLICK, MAY 5, 1991, BILLINGS.

TRANSCRIPT: 22 PAGES

1 TAPE: 50 MINUTES

OH 1481
ALICE TRINAYSTICH MALLIN AND RICHARD MALLIN INTERVIEW

Alice Mallin discusses: her parents' immigration to the United States from Croatia in 1906; the family's relocation from Illinois to Red Lodge in 1911; her father's work in the local coal mines; the financial difficulties the family suffered after her father's accident in the mines; growing up in Red Lodge. Richard Mallin discusses: his work in the Carbon County mines; differences between mining techniques in his native Scotland and in Red Lodge; Prohibition; World War II; local athletes.

INTERVIEWED BY ANNA ZELLICK, JUNE 10, 1991, RED LODGE.

TRANSCRIPT: 32 PAGES

1 TAPE: 55 MINUTES

OH 1482
JOHN BAROVICH INTERVIEW

John Barovich (b. 1914) depicts: his family's emigration from Yugoslavia to Bearcreek in 1921; Ellis Island in the New York City harbor; growing up in Bearcreek; his father's death in the 1943 Smith Mine disaster; his participation in high school sports; his education at Montana State University in Bozeman; his experiences as a teacher in Columbus.

INTERVIEWED BY ANNA ZELLICK, MAY 24, 1991, BILLINGS.

TRANSCRIPT: 33 PAGES

2 TAPES: 1 HOUR, 20 MINUTES

OH 1483
MILDRED CHESAREK HARBOLT INTERVIEW

Mildred Harbolt (b. 1918) discourses on: her father's immigration to the United States in 1883; her mother's immigration to this country in 1903; the family's move to Bearcreek; her father's work operating the "First and Last Chance Saloon"; the role of the saloon in the Bearcreek community; relations between Slovenians and other ethnic groups; schools; special recipes; the Roman Catholic Church.

INTERVIEWED BY ANNA ZELLICK, APRIL 1 AND JULY 9, 1991, LEWISTOWN.

TRANSCRIPT: 36 PAGES

2 TAPES: 1 HOUR, 15 MINUTES

OH 1484
FATHER DUSAN KOPRIVICA AND WILLIAM G. PETROVICH INTERVIEW

Butte residents Father Dusan Koprivica, of the Serbian Orthodox Church, and William Petrovich, the Serbian Orthodox Church historian, discuss: the sect's first Montana church, in Butte; the church's first priests in the state; differences between the Roman Catholic and the Serbian Orthodox faiths; the followers of the Serbian Orthodox faith in Bearcreek.

INTERVIEWED BY ANNA ZELLICK, OCTOBER 9, 1991, BUTTE.

TRANSCRIPT: 15 PAGES

1 TAPE: 40 MINUTES

OH 1485
EDWARD BLAZINA INTERVIEW

Edward Blazina (b. 1910) examines: his father's immigration to the United States in 1899; the family's relocation to Red Lodge in 1904; his mother's experiences on Ellis Island in New York harbor; his father's work on a rescue crew during the Smith Mine disaster in 1943; growing up in Red Lodge; his education; local athletes; the Happy Brothers Campground; fraternal societies; his work as a dairy inspector; the political affiliations of local ethnic groups; World War II.

INTERVIEWED BY ANNA ZELLICK, MAY 7, 1991, BILLINGS.

TRANSCRIPT: 26 PAGES

2 TAPES: 1 HOUR, 30 MINUTES

OH 1486
ROSE JURKOVICH INTERVIEW

Rose Jurkovich (b. circa 1920), a resident of Red Lodge, describes: her parents' emigration from Niksich, Montenegro, to Edmonton, Alberta, Canada, in 1914; the family's relocation to Montana in 1922; prejudice against South Slavic immigrants in Red Lodge; visiting the Statue of Liberty as an adult; her education; her career working for the local phone company; caring for her mother and her brother.

INTERVIEWED BY ANNA ZELLICK, JUNE 8, 1991, RED LODGE.

TRANSCRIPT: 23 PAGES
2 TAPES: 1 HOUR, 10 MINUTES

OH 1487
LORETTA JARUSSI AND LILLIAN JARUSSI INTERVIEW

Two sisters, Loretta Jarussi and Lillian Jarussi, address: growing up in Red Lodge; their Italian heritage; their father's work as a cobbler; recollections of South Slavic children—first as fellow students, and later as teachers; Red Lodge's Festival of Nations; the rivalry between Red Lodge and Bearcreek; their respective college educations; their teaching jobs in Red Lodge; the original family homestead. *[See also Montanans at Work OH 363.]*

INTERVIEWED BY ANNA ZELLICK, JUNE 8, 1991, RED LODGE.

TRANSCRIPT: 19 PAGES
1 TAPE: 50 MINUTES

OH 1488
DAISY PEKICH LAZETICH INTERVIEW

Daisy Lazetich converses about: her parents' immigration to Bearcreek from Montenegro, Yugoslavia, in 1920; her father's partnership with her uncles in a combination grocery/bar; social and school activities in Bearcreek; local ethnic communities.

INTERVIEWED BY ANNA ZELLICK, MAY 6, 1991, BILLINGS.

TRANSCRIPT: 12 PAGES
1 TAPE: 45 MINUTES

OH 1489
VERA MARINCHEK NAGLICH INTERVIEW

Vera Naglich addresses: her family's emigration from Slovenia, Yugoslavia, to Wyoming; the family's relocation to Bearcreek to work in the coal mines in 1912; her father's life as a miner; her father's death in the 1943 Smith Mine disaster; social and school events in Bearcreek; alcohol and Prohibition; family traditions and holiday celebrations; the family of her husband, John Naglich. *[See also General Montana OH 1490.]*

INTERVIEWED BY ANNA ZELLICK, MAY 25, 1991, BILLINGS.

TRANSCRIPT: 39 PAGES
2 TAPES: 1 HOUR, 40 MINUTES

OH 1490
VERA MARINCHEK NAGLICH INTERVIEW

Vera Naglich considers prearranged marriages in her family and in the ethnic communities of Bearcreek and Red Lodge. *[See also General Montana OH 1489.]*

INTERVIEWED BY ANNA ZELLICK, JUNE 5, 1991, BILLINGS.

TRANSCRIPT: 14 PAGES
1 TAPE: 30 MINUTES

OH 1491
JOHN MICHUNOVICH INTERVIEW

John Michunovich discusses: his parents' immigration from Niksich, Montenegro; his father's World War I experiences in Yugoslavia; his father's work as a miner; home remedies practiced by his parents; relations between different ethnic groups in Bearcreek and Red Lodge; Catholicism and religious customs; food preservation and preparation; local fraternal organizations; and local social activities.

INTERVIEWED BY ANNA ZELLICK, JUNE 1991, LEWISTOWN.

TRANSCRIPT: 36 PAGES
2 TAPES: 1 HOUR, 25 MINUTES

OH 1492
ELIZABETH WINN INTERVIEW

Elizabeth Winn (b. 1904) comments on: her family; her early life in Hope, Idaho; her marriage; her relocation to Dillon; Bannack.

INTERVIEWED BY LEE GRAVES, JUNE 1, 1990, DILLON.

TRANSCRIPT: 8 PAGES
2 TAPES: 1 HOUR, 10 MINUTES

OH 1493
FRANK TURNER INTERVIEW

Frank Turner (b. 1920) characterizes: his early life in Melrose; his family's relocation to Bannack; his father's mining activities; Bannack residents and buildings; area mines and mills, including the Apex Mine; Prohibition.

INTERVIEWED BY LEE GRAVES, JULY 27, 1990, DEER LODGE.

TRANSCRIPT: 21 PAGES
2 TAPES: 1 HOUR, 24 MINUTES

OH 1494
LEO MUSBURGER INTERVIEW

Leo Musburger (b. 1908) recalls: his early life in Omemee, North Dakota, and in Lodge Grass, Montana;

his father's work in Yellowstone National Park; his job as an elementary school teacher in Bannack; Bannack residents and businesses; his life after leaving Bannack.
INTERVIEWED BY LEE GRAVES, AUGUST 24, 1990, DILLON.
TRANSCRIPT: 35 PAGES
2 TAPES: 1 HOUR, 19 MINUTES

OH 1495
EMERSON BROWN INTERVIEW

Emerson Brown (b. 1914) reports on: his childhood in Bannack; the town's buildings and their owners; his experiences working in a local mine.
INTERVIEWED BY LEE GRAVES, AUGUST 4, 1990, BANNACK.
TRANSCRIPT: 9 PAGES
1 TAPE: 35 MINUTES

OH 1496
EVELYN McMANNIS ORR DORAN INTERVIEW

Evelyn Doran (b. 1920) remembers: her family; her early life at Horse Prairie; the family's relocation to Bannack; the Bannack cemetery.
INTERVIEWED BY LEE GRAVES, AUGUST 9, 1990, DILLON.
TRANSCRIPT: 6 PAGES
1 TAPE: 22 MINUTES

OH 1497
H. E. "TOKE" CONTWAY INTERVIEW

Toke Contway (b. 1907) treats: his early life in Bannack; his family; Bannack businesses, buildings, and residents; local mines and mining; his duties with the WPA; the 1930s Depression; his life after leaving Bannack.
INTERVIEWED BY LEE GRAVES, AUGUST 24, 1990, DILLON.
TRANSCRIPT: 18 PAGES
2 TAPES: 1 HOUR, 35 MINUTES

OH 1498
WILLIAM DUNN INTERVIEW

William Dunn (b. 1905) recalls: growing up in Bannack; his father's work as a mining engineer at the Gold Leaf Mine and Mill; Bannack residents and buildings.
INTERVIEWED BY LEE GRAVES, JUNE 26, 1990, BANNACK.
TRANSCRIPT: 34 PAGES
1 TAPE: 40 MINUTES

OH 1499
ELVIN H. THOMPSON INTERVIEW

Elvin Thompson (b. 1922) reflects on: growing up in Bannack; the town's entertainment and social activities;

the Gold Leaf Mine and Mill; the Grater Mill; dredging operations; his employment at the local school. *[See also General Montana OH 1503.]*
INTERVIEWED BY LEE GRAVES, JUNE 28, 1990, DILLON.
TRANSCRIPT: 28 PAGES
1 TAPE: 45 MINUTES

OH 1500
HANS C. ANDERSEN INTERVIEW

Hans Anderson (b. 1906) describes: his parents' sheep ranch; attending school in Bannack; local businesses, buildings, and residents; the Retallack family; the local physician Robert Hood "Doc" Ryburn; the Gold Leaf Mine and Mill; dredging; mining operations; local social activities. *[See also Montanans at Work OH 387.]*
INTERVIEWED BY LEE GRAVES, JUNE 29, 1990, DILLON.
TRANSCRIPT: 17 PAGES
1 TAPE: 1 HOUR, 35 MINUTES

OH 1501
WILLIAM MURRAY HAND INTERVIEW

William Hand speaks of: his family; homesteading in the Argenta/Bannack area; the 1930s Depression; local gold mining; smelting and refining operations for various mineral ores; Bannack-area residents.
INTERVIEWED BY LEE GRAVES, JULY 24, 1990, DILLON.
TRANSCRIPT: 13 PAGES
1 TAPE: 1 HOUR, 10 MINUTES

OH 1502
JANE S. JOHNSON INTERVIEW

Jane Johnson (b. 1920) recalls: her family; the family's relocation to Bannack; local mining companies; Bannack businesses, residents, and buildings.
INTERVIEWED BY LEE GRAVES, AUGUST 30, 1990, DILLON.
TRANSCRIPT: 15 PAGES
1 TAPE: 45 MINUTES

OH 1503
ELVIN H. THOMPSON INTERVIEW

Elvin Thompson (b. 1922) addresses the buildings, businesses, and residents of Bannack. *[See also General Montana OH 1499.]*
INTERVIEWED BY LEE GRAVES, AUGUST 30, 1990, BANNACK.
TRANSCRIPT: 15 PAGES
1 TAPE: 55 MINUTES

OH 1504
ELLEN MURRELL INTERVIEW
Dillon resident Ellen Murrell (b. 1926) portrays: growing up in Dillon; her family; visiting Bannack in her youth; local schools; the uses of various buildings in Bannack; local activities and celebrations.
INTERVIEWED BY LILLIAN HEGSTEDT, JULY 23, 1992, DILLON.
1 TAPE: 50 MINUTES

OH 1505
JUNE UNDERWOOD ANDREASON INTERVIEW
June Andreason interprets: growing up in Bannack; local education; her various jobs as a young woman; local celebrations; Bannack personalities.
INTERVIEWED BY JOHN HOERNING, APRIL 20, 1993, SALMON, ID.
TRANSCRIPT: 14 PAGES
1 TAPE: 50 MINUTES

OH 1506
DODIE TURNER DAVIS INTERVIEW
Dodie Davis (b. 1918) reviews: growing up in Melrose and Millpoint; her relocation to Bannack in 1931; her education in Bannack; local mines; the Gold Leaf Mine and Mill; local merchants; Bannack's interaction with surrounding communities; changes in Bannack since she moved there; specific buildings in town.
INTERVIEWED BY KEVIN HEANEY, JUNE 11, 1993, DILLON.
TRANSCRIPT: 20 PAGES
3 TAPES: 2 HOURS, 40 MINUTES

OH 1507
ROY JACKSON INTERVIEW
Roy Jackson (b. 1912) speaks of: his early childhood in Dillon; his family's move to Bannack to open a boarding house; his work in the boarding house; jobs in local mines; specific Bannack miners; his relocation to Baker, Oregon, after the Excelsior Mine closed down in 1936; mining accidents; Bannack buildings and businesses.
INTERVIEWED BY KEVIN HEANEY, JUNE 25, 1993, DILLON.
1 TAPE: 35 MINUTES

OH 1508
GEORGIA PADDOCK DEPUTY INTERVIEW
Georgia Deputy (b. 1895), a resident of Dillon, summarizes: her family's moves from Redrock to Buffalo to Bannack; her early life and education in Bannack; local

businesses; fires; her brothers and sisters; and her mother's cooking.
INTERVIEWED BY LEE GRAVES, JUNE 29, 1990, DILLON.
TRANSCRIPT: 12 PAGES
1 TAPE: 55 MINUTES

OH 1509
OREN SASSMAN INTERVIEW
Oren Sassman describes: his work teaching in a one-room schoolhouse; various books about Montana history; his master's thesis on metals and mining in Montana, completed in 1939; the history of various mining camps, including Alhambra Hot Springs, Pioneer, Jahnke Mine, and Ruby Creek; the local history of Bannack; Bannack buildings and events; bootlegging; Fred Oliver; Robert "Doc" Ryburn.
INTERVIEWED BY LEE GRAVES, AUGUST 3, 1990, SALMON, ID.
TRANSCRIPT: 63 PAGES
2 TAPES: 1 HOUR, 45 MINUTES

OH 1510
HAROLD ENGLES INTERVIEW
Harold Engles (b. circa 1900) surveys: his career with the U.S. Forest Service; the installation of telephone lines in the national forests; his assistance to homesteaders during the early 1920s; changes in the Forest Service through the decades.
INTERVIEWED BY JOHN TERREO, JUNE 22, 1991, MISSOULA.
TRANSCRIPT: 11 PAGES
1 TAPE: 20 MINUTES

OH 1512
WILSON "BILL" A. BURLEY INTERVIEW
Wilson Burley talks about: the formation of Lake County in 1923; why Polson became the county seat; his work as a Lake County commissioner; the county's relationship with Native Americans.
INTERVIEWED BY MELISSA DENON, MAY 18, 1983, RONAN.
SUMMARY: 3 PAGES
1 TAPE: 48 MINUTES

OH 1514
EVELYN SLOAN WEBSTER INTERVIEW
Evelyn Webster (b. 1903) treats: growing up at Mud Creek Pass in the Flathead Valley; local economics; her father's operation of a ferry; her attendance at the Catholic boarding school in St. Ignatius.
INTERVIEWED BY DENISE GARDNER AND CHRIS BURLAND, APRIL 17, 1983, RONAN.

SUMMARY: 2 PAGES
1 TAPE: 26 MINUTES

OH 1515
JACK WELCH INTERVIEW

Jack Welch (b. 1892) tells about: moving from North Carolina to Glasgow in 1922; his family; breaking horses; his military service in Europe during World War I; owning and operating a saddle-making shop in Polson.
INTERVIEWED BY HAROLD SMITH, MAY 14, 1983, POLSON.
SUMMARY: 4 PAGES
1 TAPE: 1 HOUR, 25 MINUTES

OH 1516
HARRIET WHITWORTH INTERVIEW

Harriet Whitworth, a Salish Indian, briefly details: reservation life; her childhood; her education at St. Ignatius.
INTERVIEWED BY SHAWNA WHITWORTH, MAY 5, 1983, RONAN.
SUMMARY: 1 PAGE
1 TAPE: 20 MINUTES

OH 1517
ADELINE BEAVER INTERVIEW

Adeline Beaver discusses: her family; the family's relocation to Round Butte; her childhood; her education at Western Montana College in Dillon; her work as a teacher.
INTERVIEWED BY DAWNA RESNER, APRIL 14, 1983, ST. IGNATIUS.
SUMMARY: 2 PAGES
1 TAPE: 30 MINUTES

OH 1518
JOE McDONALD INTERVIEW

Joe McDonald discourses on: his work establishing a college for Native Americans at Pablo; early Indian schools in the area. [See also General Montana OH 1586.]
INTERVIEWED BY TONY PHILMAN, MAY 9, 1993, RONAN.
SUMMARY: 2 PAGES
1 TAPE: 30 MINUTES

OH 1519
ARTHUR GARBE AND MABLE GARBE INTERVIEW

Art Garbe and Mable Garbe examine: their family's relocation to Pablo in April 1918; farming; area businesses; childhood and education; local politics; the Kerr Dam on the Flathead Indian Reservation; the family's telephone company; the effects of World War I and World War II on the community; crop experiments in the area.
INTERVIEWED BY JOYCE G. DECKER, FEBRUARY 20, 1983, PABLO.
SUMMARY: 2 PAGES
1 TAPE: 50 MINUTES

OH 1520
INEZ M. SIEGRIST INTERVIEW

Polson resident Inez Siegrist (b. 1890) discusses: her family; proving up on a homestead alone in Montana; her work as a teacher; her employment with Marcus Daly III; photography; the WPA; forest fires; rattlesnakes; the Montana home front during World War I; women in the work force.
INTERVIEWED BY JOYCE G. DECKER, JULY 26, 1983, POLSON.
SUMMARY: 4 PAGES
2 TAPES: 1 HOUR, 30 MINUTES

OH 1536
ORVILLE G. CARPENTER AND RUTH PALMER RHODES CARPENTER INTERVIEW

Orville Carpenter (b. 1893) and Ruth Carpenter (b. 1896) talk about: their respective family histories; early Eureka, Hayden, and Gateway; the old Tobacco Plains School; the Iowa Flats School; area homesteaders; the Great Northern Railway; the Fewkes Store in Eureka.
INTERVIEWED BY CATHRYN W. SCHROEDER, NOVEMBER 30, 1988, EUREKA.
TRANSCRIPT: 14 PAGES
2 TAPES: 1 HOUR, 5 MINUTES

OH 1537
ROLENE TRIPP HABOUSH AND HELEN TRIPP UNKONICH INTERVIEW

Two sisters from Eureka—Rolene Haboush (b. 1908) and Helen Unkonich (b. 1913)—survey: their family; Eureka; friends; their schooling; the town of Warland; their father, Leland Edmund Tripp; local physicians; area entertainment.
INTERVIEWED BY CATHRYN SCHROEDER, AUGUST 13, 1988, EUREKA.
TRANSCRIPT: 15 PAGES
1 TAPE: 1 HOUR, 30 MINUTES

OH 1538
NORBERT SCHUCK AND MARY SCHUCK
INTERVIEWS

Norbert Schuck and Mary Schuck discuss: their respective families; social life in Eureka; World War II in the Pacific; the Eureka Rod and Gun Club.

INTERVIEWED BY CATHRYN SCHROEDER, JUNE 23, 1987, EUREKA.

SUMMARY: 4 PAGES
2 TAPES: 2 HOURS

OH 1539
JOE STOKEN AND HAZEL PORTER STOKEN
INTERVIEW

Fortine residents Joe Stoken (b. 1907) and Hazel Stoken converse on: their families; schooling; the Graves Creek area; logging; the U.S. Forest Service; the town of Fortine; WPA projects; raising Christmas trees.

INTERVIEWED BY CATHRYN SCHROEDER, JANUARY 12, 1988, FORTINE.

TRANSCRIPT: 8 PAGES
1 TAPE: 1 HOUR

OH 1542
IAN BRALEY INTERVIEW

Ian Braley portrays: the childhood in Butte of his father, the author Berton Braley; his father's work as a writer and poet; his father's freelance work with the noted news broadcaster Lowell Thomas; the Braley family's travels around the United States; family relationships; his mother Elliot Braley's ideals and contributions.

INTERVIEWED BY REX C. MYERS, JUNE 20, 29, 1984, FLAGSTAFF, AZ.

SUMMARY: 3 PAGES
4 TAPES: 4 HOURS

OH 1544
FRED L. ROBINSON BRIDGE DEDICATION
BROADCAST

This radio broadcast includes the dedication ceremony for the Fred L. Robinson Bridge over the Missouri River, held at the bridge site on August 16, 1959. Speakers include: James T. Harrison; Fred Quinnel; J. Hugo Aronson; Fred Robinson; J. T. Douglas. Several topics are discussed: the history of road construction in Montana, particularly the Dominion-Yellowstone Trail; the selection of the site for the bridge; Fred Robinson; the actual construction of the bridge.

RECORDED BY AN UNIDENTIFIED MONTANA RADIO STATION, AUGUST 16, 1959, CHOUTEAU COUNTY.

2 TAPES: 1 HOUR, 10 MINUTES

OH 1546
E. E. "BOO" MacGILVRA INTERVIEW

E. E. MacGilvra (1893–1980) reports on: his early travels with the Ringling Brothers' Circus; his years mining, homesteading, and storekeeping in Zortman; the cowboy-artist Charles M. Russell; his work at the Ruby Gulch Gold Mine. [See also General Montana OH 32, OH 109, OH 628, and OH 629.]

INTERVIEWED BY CHARLES C. PATTON, JULY 4, 1973, SHERIDAN.

TRANSCRIPT: 106 PAGES
2 TAPES: 2 HOURS

OH 1547
BURTON KENDALL WHEELER INTERVIEW

Burton K. Wheeler (1882–1975), U.S. senator from Montana (1929–1947), chronicles: his relationship with President Franklin D. Roosevelt; the monetization of silver; the Anaconda Copper Mining Company; his several political campaigns. [See also General Montana OH 9.]

INTERVIEWED BY PAUL HOPPER, MARCH 18, MARCH 22, MAY 1, 1968, AND MAY 27, 1969, WASHINGTON, D.C.

TRANSCRIPT: 153 PAGES

OH 1548
PACIFIC NORTHWEST HISTORY CONFERENCE

The joint meeting of the Pacific Northwest Historians, Northwest Oral History Association and Northwest Archivists convened in Helena on May 16-18, 1985. Events include: an address by Governor Ted Schwinden of Montana entitled, "Omnibus States and Centennial Celebrations"; a panel entitled "Oral History and Environmental History"; a discussion of Butte and Montana wilderness.

RECORDED BY THE MONTANA HISTORICAL SOCIETY, MAY 16-18, 1985, HELENA.

2 TAPES: 2 HOURS

OH 1549
MONTANA HISTORY CONFERENCE
PROCEEDINGS, 1982

The Ninth Annual Montana History Conference met in Great Falls on October 28-30, 1982. The proceedings include panels addressing: Waterton-Glacier International Peace Park; homesteading; Blackfeet Indians; Fort Benton; wagon freighting.

RECORDED BY THE MONTANA HISTORICAL SOCIETY,
OCTOBER 28-30, 1982, GREAT FALLS.
SUMMARY: 1 PAGE
15 TAPES: 15 HOURS

OH 1550
MONTANA HISTORY CONFERENCE
PROCEEDINGS, 1983
The Tenth Annual Montana History Conference convened in Helena on October 27-29, 1983. Its panels discuss: Helena's architecture; the Northern Pacific Railroad; World War II; sheep raising; western literature; natural resources; the Archie Bray Foundation; Blackfeet Indians; the Anaconda Copper Mining Company; wildlife; wilderness and forest management.
RECORDED BY THE MONTANA HISTORICAL SOCIETY,
OCTOBER 27-29, 1983, HELENA.
SUMMARY: 2 PAGES
13 TAPES: 13 HOURS

OH 1551
MONTANA HISTORY CONFERENCE
PROCEEDINGS, 1984
On October 25-27, 1984, the Eleventh Annual Montana History Conference assembled in Lewistown. It includes panels concerning: farming; homesteading; women; the Taylor Grazing Act; cowboys; ethnic groups—especially Danes, Hutterites, Germans, Croatians, and Métis.
RECORDED BY THE MONTANA HISTORICAL SOCIETY,
OCTOBER 25-27, 1984, LEWISTOWN.
SUMMARY: 1 PAGE
17 TAPES: 17 HOURS

OH 1552
MONTANA HISTORY CONFERENCE
PROCEEDINGS, 1985
The Twelfth Annual Montana History Conference met in Helena November 7-9, 1985. The various presentations emphasize interpreting heritage through ceremony and tradition—as shown in Native American cultures, in several ethnic groups, and in world's fairs. The panels encourage the use of photographs, historical sites, literature, and artifacts.
RECORDED BY THE MONTANA HISTORICAL SOCIETY,
NOVEMBER 7-9, 1985, HELENA.
SUMMARY: 1 PAGE
16 TAPES: 16 HOURS

OH 1553
MONTANA HISTORY CONFERENCE
PROCEEDINGS, 1986
The Thirteenth Annual Montana History Conference—held in Missoula on September 11-13, 1986—produced this composite. Panels address: post–World War II agriculture, economics, and culture; forest and wilderness management; the lumber industry; small town life; journalism; U.S. trade policy; Canadian relations; the Kerr Dam.
RECORDED BY THE MONTANA HISTORICAL SOCIETY,
SEPTEMBER 11-13, 1986, MISSOULA.
SUMMARY: 1 PAGE
15 TAPES: 15 HOURS

OH 1554
MONTANA HISTORY CONFERENCE
PROCEEDINGS, 1987
The Fourteenth Annual Montana History Conference, which convened in Helena on October 22-24, 1987, featured panels concerning: images of the West; women; roadways; underground mining; wolves; Native Americans; railroads; capitalists; and Going-to-the-Sun Road.
RECORDED BY THE MONTANA HISTORICAL SOCIETY,
OCTOBER 22-24, 1987, HELENA.
SUMMARY: 2 PAGES
21 TAPES: 20 HOURS

OH 1555
MONTANA HISTORY CONFERENCE
PROCEEDINGS, 1988
This collection offers presentations from the Fifteenth Annual Montana History Conference, held in Livingston on November 3-5, 1988. Panels discuss: Yellowstone County history, archaeology, travels, wolves, and military activities; Crow Indians; the Great Northern, the Chicago, Milwaukee, St. Paul and Pacific (Milwaukee Road), and the Northern Pacific railroads; Montana writers; Yellowstone National Park; the Yellowstone River; the Bozeman Trail; other trails; Frank J. Haynes; G. L. Henderson; the flight of the Nez Perces in 1877; missionaries.
RECORDED BY THE MONTANA HISTORICAL SOCIETY,
NOVEMBER 3-5, 1988, LIVINGSTON.
SUMMARY: 15 PAGES
17 TAPES: 17 HOURS

OH 1556
MONTANA HISTORY CONFERENCE PROCEEDINGS, 1989

The Sixteenth Annual Montana History Conference gathered in Helena on October 26-28, 1989. Presentations address: Billings; Helena; Missoula; the uses of oral history; "Jerks in Montana History"—including William A. Clark, Simon Pepin, A. J. Davis, and "Calamity Jane" Cannary; sacred Native American sites; Indian artifacts.

RECORDED BY THE MONTANA HISTORICAL SOCIETY, OCTOBER 26-28, 1989, HELENA.

SUMMARY: 1 PAGE

11 TAPES: 11 HOURS

OH 1557
VEVA MARKS SMITH INTERVIEW

Veva Smith (1878–1969)—the wife of Dr. Charles W. Smith and the daughter of the Townsend businessman James Rufus Marks—considers her childhood in Townsend from the 1880s to 1900.

INTERVIEWED BY CORA POOLE, CIRCA 1960, TOWNSEND.

1 TAPE: 27 MINUTES

OH 1558
WESTERN HISTORY ASSOCIATION CONFERENCE SESSION, 1965

The Western History Association conference that convened in Helena on October 14, 1965, included a session on religion and the West. W. L. Davis presents a paper entitled "On the Trail of Father Peter John DeSmet"; Leonard J. Arrington reads a paper on the "Secularization of Mormon History and Culture [in the 1900s]."

RECORDED BY THE MONTANA HISTORICAL SOCIETY, OCTOBER 14, 1965, HELENA.

2 TAPES: 1 HOUR, 30 MINUTES

OH 1559
ANTOINETTE "TONI" FRASER ROSELL INTERVIEW

Toni Rosell—a Billings educator and Republican legislator—speaks of: her political career in the Montana Legislative Assembly from 1956 until 1976; her unsuccessful campaigns for the U.S. Senate and for the Montana lieutenant governor's office; women's rights; the intricacies of the political and the legislative processes.

INTERVIEWED BY JEFF SAFFORD, NOVEMBER 24, 1978, BILLINGS.

TRANSCRIPT: 34 PAGES

2 TAPES: 1 HOUR, 30 MINUTES

OH 1560
CATHERINE FINNLAND INTERVIEW

Catherine Finnland remembers: childhood games; growing up in Libby; the community of Libby.

INTERVIEWED BY SHERRY MCKEAN, JANUARY 18, 1978, LIBBY.

TRANSCRIPT: 8 PAGES

1 TAPE: 30 MINUTES

OH 1561
MALCOLM STONE INTERVIEW

Malcolm Stone reflects on: the career of his father, A. L. Stone, as a banker in Dillon; his own reluctant entry into banking; the family's experiences during the Mexican Revolution of 1911; his performances as a member of the Tonrey-Baxter Band; moonshine liquor served at parties.

INTERVIEWED BY KIM HOLLAND, JUNE 5, 1980, DILLON.

TRANSCRIPT: 7 PAGES

1 TAPE: 35 MINUTES

OH 1562
WALTER BRUNDAGE INTERVIEW

Dillon resident Walter Brundage recalls: his position as a third-generation funeral-business owner in Dillon; changes in the business since his grandfather, Everett Hiram Brundage, started it in 1901.

INTERVIEWED BY KIM HOLLAND, JUNE 16, 1980, DILLON.

TRANSCRIPT: 6 PAGES

1 TAPE: 40 MINUTES

OH 1563
MONTANA HISTORY CONFERENCE PROCEEDINGS, 1993

The Twentieth Annual Montana History Conference—which met in Missoula on October 21-23, 1993—featured dual themes: "Higher Education in Montana" and "Native American Issues." Specific sessions include: a panel of university and college presidents on higher education; Governor Marc Racicot on school consolidation; K. Ross Toole; environmental issues on the Fort Belknap Indian Reservation, in the Mission Mountains, and in West Yellowstone; in loco parentis policies at Montana State University in Bozeman and at the University of Montana in Missoula; the Montana Study; rural communities in the West; hobos in Canada and in Montana; "Jerks in Montana History"—Butte police detective Edward Morrissey, the Anaconda Copper Mining Company v. ranchers in the Deer Lodge Valley, and the out-of-state "slob hunter" Sir St. George Gore; Na-

tive American history as literature; biographies of Wellington Rankin, Frank B. Linderman, and Norman Maclean; Native American storytelling traditions.
RECORDED BY THE MONTANA HISTORICAL SOCIETY, OCTOBER 21-23, 1993, MISSOULA.
SUMMARY: 6 PAGES
12 TAPES: 12 HOURS

OH 1567
WILFRED OTIS HALFMOON INTERVIEW
A Nez Perce, Wilfred Halfmoon (b. 1952) comments on: his family's religious beliefs v. old Indian traditions; his successful efforts to work for the U.S. National Park Service as an interpretive ranger; Crow history; alliances between the Crow tribe and the Nez Perces; the archaeological survey conducted at the Big Hole National Battlefield in 1991.
INTERVIEWED BY LEE GRAVES, MAY 12, 1993, BIG HOLE BATTLEFIELD NATIONAL MONUMENT.
TRANSCRIPT: 33 PAGES
1 TAPE: 1 HOUR

OH 1571
FRED BRIDENSTINE INTERVIEW
Fred Bridenstine, the owner of a Dillon western clothing store, briefly characterizes: his hobby/business of rodeo and aerial photography; climbing an unnamed peak in the Pioneer Range at the age of 77; naming that promontory Bridenstine Peak; his relationship with Christian students on the campus of Western Montana College in Dillon.
INTERVIEWED BY KIM HOLLAND, JUNE 18, 1980, DILLON.
TRANSCRIPT: 4 PAGES
1 TAPE: 15 MINUTES

OH 1572
EYRA SIEVERS AND MARGUERITE DAVIDSON INTERVIEW
Libby resident Eyra Sievers recalls: growing on a Minnesota farm in the early 1900s; Christmas festivities; forms of play on the family farm; teaching in rural schools near Billings and Dillon during the 1920s; her relocation to Libby in the 1940s. Marguerite Davidson discusses: a bisque doll owned by her sister in 1898; female social gatherings; Libby-area events, including Fourth of July activities, circus performances, and chautauqua weeks.
INTERVIEWED BY SHERRY MCKEAN, CIRCA 1978, LIBBY.
SUMMARY: 1 PAGE
1 TAPE: 20 MINUTES

OH 1573
VIRGINIA BEAULIEU INTERVIEW
Longtime Libby resident Virginia Beaulieu addresses the area's history.
INTERVIEWED BY JOY BANKS, CIRCA 1978, LIBBY.
SUMMARY: 1 PAGE
1 TAPE: 25 MINUTES

OH 1575
LUCY SAUER INTERVIEW
Lucy Sauer—a retired Lincoln County schoolteacher—describes: her family background; early residents of the county who came from Wisconsin. She also recites poetry that she used as part of her teaching curriculum.
INTERVIEWED BY SHERRY MCKEAN, JANUARY 13, 1978, LIBBY.
SUMMARY: 1 PAGE
1 TAPE: 20 MINUTES

OH 1576
GRACE A. KENELTY INTERVIEW
Grace Kenelty discusses: her family, who homesteaded near Libby in 1906; her childhood; her schooling; the economic poverty, but emotional warmth, of the family; the forest fires of 1910; her work teaching in Havre, Yaak, Stryker, and other northwestern Montana towns. [See also General Montana OH 162.]
INTERVIEWED BY SHERRY MCKEAN, 1978, LIBBY.
SUMMARY: 2 PAGES
1 TAPE: 20 MINUTES

OH 1578
EDNA TURNER MEAGHER INTERVIEW
Edna Meagher (b. 1908) discourses on: her family; businesses, residents, and buildings in Bannack; the Gold Bug Mine; health care; mining accidents; social activities and entertainment.
INTERVIEWED BY LEE GRAVES, JULY 27, 1990, DEER LODGE.
TRANSCRIPT: 23 PAGES
2 TAPES: 1 HOUR, 20 MINUTES

OH 1579
ALFRED B. NEWMAN INTERVIEW
Alfred Newman recalls: his early life in Bannack; his family; searching for work; his education as a mining engineer at the Montana College of Science and Technology (Montana Tech) in Butte; working in the mines; his difficulties with management.

INTERVIEWED BY LEE GRAVES, MAY 11, 1993, HELENA.
TRANSCRIPT: 22 PAGES
2 TAPES: 1 HOUR, 20 MINUTES

OH 1580
THOMAS MACKAY INTERVIEW

Thomas Mackay (b. 1919) speaks of: receiving his early education in Salmon, Idaho; summers spent in Bannack; staying with the Pond family in Bannack; local events and activities; changes in Bannack through a 50-year period; his family.

INTERVIEWED BY LEE GRAVES, JUNE 11, 1993, SALMON, ID.
TRANSCRIPT: 23 PAGES
1 TAPE: 45 MINUTES

OH 1581
MONTE DINGLEY AND SALLY GARRETT DINGLEY INTERVIEW

Monte Dingley (1915–1995) talks about: his early years in Dubois, Wyoming, and in Dillon, Montana; his work as a youth for the Dillon *Examiner*; the railroad in Beaverhead County. Sally Dingley discusses: her research into Dillon history; various books on the history of the Dillon area.

INTERVIEWED BY LEE GRAVES, JUNE 18, 1993, DILLON.
TRANSCRIPT: 28 PAGES
1 TAPE: 55 MINUTES

OH 1582
MONTANA HISTORY CONFERENCE PROCEEDINGS, 1992

The Nineteenth Annual Montana History Conference took place in Miles City on October 23-24, 1992. A combination of panels and speeches address: blacks in military service; the 1949 reorganization of the Montana Historical Society's Board of Trustees; the environmental effects of homesteading on eastern Montana; the fur trade.

RECORDED BY THE MONTANA HISTORICAL SOCIETY, OCTOBER 23-24, 1992, MILES CITY.
5 TAPES: 7 HOURS, 30 MINUTES

OH 1586
JOE McDONALD INTERVIEW

Joe McDonald discusses: activities at Fort Connah; the naming of Fort Connah; his great-grandfather Angus McDonald; his work with the Fort Connah Historical Association to restore buildings at the site; his family and their customs; burial sites for family members. *[See also General Montana OH 1518.]*

INTERVIEWED BY MIKE COLLINS AND DAVID DELAWENTI, MAY 9, 1983, RONAN.
SUMMARY: 2 PAGES
1 TAPE: 30 MINUTES

OH 1588
CENTENNIAL WEST: A CELEBRATION OF THE NORTHERN-TIER STATES' HERITAGE SYMPOSIUM

"The Centennial West: A Celebration of the Northern-Tier States' Heritage Symposium" convened in Billings on June 22-24, 1989, funded by the National Endowment for the Humanities (NEH). Topics addressed include: Norwegian immigrants to the region; Asian immigrants; ranching; logging; mining; libraries; regional culture; literature; Populism; teachers; railroads in the Northern Tier states; Walla Walla, Washington; Butte, Montana; Thomas C. Power; Prince Maximilian of Wied; Karl Bodmer.

RECORDED BY NATIONAL ENDOWMENT FOR THE HUMANITIES, JUNE 22-24, 1989, BILLINGS.
SUMMARY: 2 PAGES
22 TAPES: 22 HOURS

OH 1589
RICHARD B. ROEDER INTERVIEW

Montana historian Richard Roeder recalls: his education and training in American history; his early research in Montana history; work at Montana State University in Bozeman; his employment as the first researcher for the Montana Legislative Council; water-rights issues addressed by the 1972 Montana Constitutional Convention; changes in the establishment of water rights; the work of the Office of State Engineer to codify water codes; problems caused by the public's resistance to modernizing water-rights laws. *[See also General Montana OH 27.]*

INTERVIEWED BY JAMES E. SHEROW, AUGUST 16, 1994, HELENA.
1 TAPE: 55 MINUTES

OH 1590
EVERETT DARLINGTON INTERVIEW

Everett Darlington (b. 1918) portrays: his childhood; his early education; attending Montana State University in Bozeman; his early training as an engineer; his work as an engineer for the General Electric Corporation during the 1940s; his duties with the Montana State Planning Board as an industrial engineer; Montana Water

Board policies and politics; current trends in irrigation; dams on the Missouri River and its tributaries; general water-rights issues in Montana; his service as the last state engineer.

INTERVIEWED BY JAMES E. SHEROW, AUGUST 23, 1994, HELENA.

1 TAPE: 55 MINUTES

OH 1593
JOHN E. BENNETT INTERVIEW

Missoula resident John Bennett (b. 1926) recounts: his childhood in Anaconda; his education; his training to become a forester; his work for the U.S. Forest Service in the Deer Lodge district, in the Absaroka Primitive Area, in the West Yellowstone district, and in Alaska; his life after retirement.

INTERVIEWED BY RAYMOND KARR, APRIL 7, 1993, MISSOULA.

TRANSCRIPT: 77 PAGES

OH 1594
WILLIAM MAGNUSON INTERVIEW

William Magnuson reflects on: his childhood in Minneapolis, Minnesota; his education; his early career in forestry; working in the Nez Perce National Forest, Idaho.

INTERVIEWED BY JOHN EMERSON, AUGUST 24, 1993, ROLLINS.

TRANSCRIPT: 43 PAGES

OH 1595
DONALD PLUID INTERVIEW

Donald Pluid remembers: his childhood in Whitefish; his father's work logging in the Whitefish and the Eureka areas; his job running a local sawmill; early logging equipment; wildlife he encountered in the Kootenai National Forest; the impacts of certain logging techniques; the effects of the environmental movement on the timber industry in Montana.

INTERVIEWED BY CAROLYNNE MERRELL, AUGUST 25, 1992, LIBBY.

TRANSCRIPT: 36 PAGES

OH 1596
JOHN EMERSON INTERVIEW

John Emerson, a resident of Bigfork relates: his childhood in Missoula and in Mandan, North Dakota; his early experiences as a U.S. Forest Service employee in the Potlatch National Forest and in the Nez Perce National Forest of Idaho; his work at the Big Prairie Ranger Station in the Bob Marshall Wilderness; his wife's work as a camp cook; his work as supervisor of the Flathead National Forest.

INTERVIEWED BY DORIS GORSUCH, APRIL 17, 1993, BIGFORK.

TRANSCRIPT: 31 PAGES

OH 1597
CHARLES P. KERN INTERVIEW

Charles Kern recalls: his father's work as a local merchant who served Anaconda Copper Mining Company camps near Milltown; the local history of Milltown and Missoula; gambling on Salmon Lake; his early work with the U.S. Forest Service in the Superior Ranger District; his duties in various Montana locations, including the Pierce Ranger District and throughout the Gallatin National Forest.

INTERVIEWED BY JOHN EMERSON, MAY 14, 1993, MISSOULA.

TRANSCRIPT: 44 PAGES

OH 1598
LITTLE BIGHORN LEGACY SYMPOSIUM RECORDING

The Little Bighorn Legacy Symposium convened in Billings on August 3-6, 1994. The speakers address: federal Indian policy in the 1870s; Native American leadership during the Great Sioux War of the 1870s; archaeological techniques used at the Little Bighorn battle site; the myths of George Armstrong Custer in literature, in film, and in American culture; Lakota, Cheyenne, and Crow tribal interpretations of the campaigns; U.S. military perspectives on the Great Sioux War.

RECORDED BY THE MONTANA HISTORICAL SOCIETY, AUGUST 3-6, 1994, BILLINGS.

26 TAPES: 26 HOURS

OH 1600
MONTANA HISTORY CONFERENCE PROCEEDINGS, 1994

The Twenty-first Annual Montana History Conference met at the Rock Creek Lodge outside of Red Lodge on October 13-15, 1994. Sessions address various topics: the state of the Montana Historical Society; Pryor Mountains archaeology; cowboy recollections; Red Lodge history; homesteading women; Native American activities; area industry. *[See MM 7 for video recordings of presentations on tapes 4, 6, and 7.]*

RECORDED BY THE MONTANA HISTORICAL SOCIETY, OCTOBER 13-15, 1994, RED LODGE.

17 TAPES: 16 HOURS, 20 MINUTES

OH 1601
EINAR LARSON INTERVIEW

Longtime Helena resident Einar Larson reviews: Helena's Sixth Ward; the businesses and the personalities of that neighborhood; his father's business, the Montana Meat Company; his own historical research into this topic.

INTERVIEWED BY HARRIETT C. MELOY, JANUARY, 1994, HELENA.
SUMMARY: 4 PAGES
1 TAPE: 45 MINUTES

OH 1602
HOWARD CASHMORE INTERVIEW

Howard Cashmore discusses: his grandfather's migration from England to Butte; growing up in the Dillon area; attending mortician school in St. Louis, Missouri; the first crematoriums in Montana; his experiences as the Stillwater County coroner; changes in that job through the years; building a mortuary business in Laurel in 1960; a mortician's techniques and preparations.

INTERVIEWED BY HARRIETT C. MELOY, 1988, HELENA.
3 TAPES: 2 HOURS, 30 MINUTES

OH 1603
LOIS MUNNS TEAGUE INTERVIEW

Lois Teague speaks of: arriving in Montana in 1926, as a young woman, to teach; teaching jobs in Galata and Whitlash; life in the Sweetgrass Hills country; Prohibition; rum-running trucks; wild horses; Native American artifacts; Scandinavian settlers; blizzards; the local homestead boom of 1911; sheepshearers; other teaching experiences.

INTERVIEWED BY LAURIE MERCIER, AUGUST 27, 1994, SPOKANE, WA.
SUMMARY: 4 PAGES
2 TAPES: 1 HOUR, 40 MINUTES

OH 1604
AARON P. SMALL INTERVIEW

Billings resident Aaron Small, Ph.D., tells about: his arrival in Montana in 1955; the Jewish community in Billings; rabbis and rabbinical students who taught in the Billings Synagogue; the difficulties faced by Jewish people in rural Montana; the economic and social make-up of the Jewish community across Montana; the lack of full-time rabbis in the state; the political activism of Jewish people in Montana.

INTERVIEWED BY LAWRENCE SMALL, AUGUST 11, 1993, BILLINGS.
1 TAPE: 40 MINUTES

OH 1605
AUBREY HAINES INTERVIEW

The historian Aubrey Haines summarizes: his work in Yellowstone National Park, both before and after World War II; his education; his early military training; camp conditions; his military service overseas; his family; changes in Yellowstone Park from the 1930s to the present.

INTERVIEWED BY STUART W. CONNER, MARCH 16 AND 18, 1994, TUCSON, AZ.
TRANSCRIPT: 80 PAGES
4 TAPES: 3 HOURS, 45 MINUTES

OH 1606
ROBERT J. DOMROSE INTERVIEW

Robert Domrose surveys: his work as a fish biologist with the Fisheries Division of the Montana Department of Fish, Wildlife and Parks; his childhood in Wisconsin; fishing as a youngster; attending Montana State University in Bozeman; performing census work from a rubber raft; graduate work; his work at Fish, Wildlife and Parks beginning in 1963; life in Ovando; establishing the salmon-stocking program; the program's failure in some lakes due to trout competition; changes in the program to establish winter fishing; the expanding population of northern pike; problems in the Flathead River drainage; changes in the profession as a result of the increased use of Montana rivers and streams.

INTERVIEWED BY ART WHITNEY, APRIL 20, 1995, KALISPELL.
2 TAPES: 1 HOUR, 5 MINUTES

OH 1607
LANEY HANZEL INTERVIEW

Laney Hanzel talks of: growing up near Belt; his work as a high school student at the local fishery; his education in fish biology at Montana State University in Bozeman; the Marias River Rehabilitation Project; working with the Montana Department of Fish, Wildlife and Parks on Flathead Lake; developing fish-tagging and population-count techniques; working with boats on Flathead Lake; hydro-acoustic equipment developments; problems created by silt accumulation.

INTERVIEWED BY ART WHITNEY, MARCH 20, 1995, KALISPELL.
1 TAPE: 40 MINUTES

OH 1608
BRUCE MAY INTERVIEW

Kalispell resident Bruce May treats: growing up in Ohio; his education at Ohio State University in Columbus, Ohio, in biology; his first job in Dillon; his work on the Libby Dam Project, studying resident fish populations and migration plans; the Kootenai Project; the development of spawning runs; gas supersaturation at Whitefish Dam; the dangers of his work; computers and data collections; the effects of water-level fluctuations on fish.

INTERVIEWED BY ART WHITNEY, MARCH 21, 1995, KALISPELL.
1 TAPE: 25 MINUTES

OH 1609
JOE HUSTON INTERVIEW

Joe Huston discusses: growing up in Colorado; fishing as a child; his education in fish biology; his duties as the Missoula Project biologist; his work on the Thompson Falls, Hungry Horse, and Libby reservoirs; large-river sampling techniques performed by boat at night; navigating boats at night; fisheries work during the winter months; developing the modified "wolf trap" for netting; shrimp; changes in Montana fisheries since the 1940s.

INTERVIEWED BY ART WHITNEY, MARCH 21, 1995, KALISPELL.
1 TAPE: 25 MINUTES

OH 1610
ROBERT MITCHELL INTERVIEW

Robert Mitchell recalls: growing up in Paradise; his education at the University of Montana in Missoula; his work at the Anaconda Fish Hatchery; the rift between older, traditional employees and newer college-educated biologists; funding changes for various fisheries programs; pioneering the use of the airplane in mountain-lake fish surveys; changes in technology.

INTERVIEWED BY ART WHITNEY, NOVEMBER 11, 1993, KALISPELL.
1 TAPE: 30 MINUTES

OH 1611
EMMETT J. COLLEY INTERVIEW

Emmett Colley speaks of: growing up at the Emigrant fish hatchery; his father's work for the Montana Department of Fish, Wildlife and Parks; his first job at the Great Falls hatchery; World War II; his job in Lewistown at the Blue Water Fish Hatchery; his promo-

tion to the office of bureau chief in Helena; fish traps on the South Fork of the Madison River.

INTERVIEWED BY ART WHITNEY, APRIL 19, 1994, HELENA.
1 TAPE: 20 MINUTES

OH 1612
ROBERT SCHUMAKER INTERVIEW

Robert Schumaker discourses on: growing up in Minnesota; his education; his early fisheries work in Minnesota; World War II; working in fish-disease programs; relocating to Montana; crew research programs for cold water; reorganizing research-survey programs for the Montana Department of Fish, Wildlife and Parks (FWP); the department's early attempts at long-range planning; redesigning fish-stocking programs; developing the "boom-shocker" for use in fish surveys; the helicopter stocking of mountain lakes; creating working relationship between FWP and U.S. National Forest administrators to mitigate clear-cut and road-building damage to fish habitats; securing federal research money to study the impacts of mining and forest-products development on Montana streams and lakes.

INTERVIEWED BY ART WHITNEY, NOVEMBER 11, 1993, KALISPELL.
1 TAPE: 45 MINUTES

OH 1613
CLINT BISHOP INTERVIEW

Helena resident Clint Bishop details: his childhood in Shelby; his family ties to Fort Benton and Havre; his education at the Ursuline Academy in Great Falls and at Mount St. Charles (Carroll) College; earning a B.S. degree in forestry at Iowa State University in Ames, Iowa; his service in World War II; returning to Helena to work as a fish biologist for the Montana Department of Fish, Wildlife and Parks; setting up baseline files on all of the state's waterways; placing fisheries records on computer; the building of Yellowtail Dam.

INTERVIEWED BY ART WHITNEY, APRIL 19, 1994, HELENA.
1 TAPE: 30 MINUTES

OH 1614
RICHARD VINCENT INTERVIEW

Richard Vincent discusses: his childhood in Bozeman and in Garrison; his education in forestry at Montana State University in Bozeman; his first job for the Montana Department of Fish, Wildlife and Parks (FWP) as a student in the 1960s; large-river activities to establish population-estimate equipment and techniques; the development of systems to mark and to recapture fish;

experiments to evaluate the effects of stocking on wild species; public reaction to FWP experimentation with stocking; studies of the Madison River; public misunderstanding of the FWP's regulatory power (e.g., catch-and-release programs) to "fix" streams; the Clark's Fork River and the U.S. Environmental Protection Agency's "Superfund" cleanup.

INTERVIEWED BY ART WHITNEY, OCTOBER 26, 1994, BOZEMAN.

1 TAPE: 40 MINUTES

OH 1616
JOHN GAFFNEY INTERVIEW

John Gaffney depicts: his childhood in South Dakota on a dryland farm; enlisting in the U.S. Navy; his enchantment with fish and wildlife, gained through magazines during the 1930s and the 1940s; his study to gain a B.S. degree at the University of Montana in Missoula; his graduate work at Montana State University in Bozeman; his work with the Montana Department of Fish, Wildlife and Parks on a survey of public lands and the fish they contained; fish traps and other equipment; conflicts within the profession; difficulties in transferring families from one assignment to the next; the challenges of working in winter weather; problems involved with changing stream flow; troubles caused by inconsistent management policies; fish population-estimate techniques, especially shocking; fisheries-related controversies through the years.

INTERVIEWED BY ART WHITNEY, SEPTEMBER 29, 1993, BOZEMAN.

1 TAPE: 50 MINUTES

OH 1617
BOYD OPHEIM INTERVIEW

Boyd Opheim describes: his childhood in Minnesota; his service in World War II; his GI Bill education in fisheries management at the University of North Dakota in Grand Forks and at Utah State University in Logan; his first assignment as a creel-census monitor on the Madison River in Montana; working as an assistant fisheries biologist; his conflict with the Anaconda Company over the Clark's Fork River; working at the Red Lodge fish hatchery; building a cooperative relationship with the Montana Highway Department to ensure the better preservation of fish habitat during road construction; dichlorodiphenyltrichloroethane (DDT) spraying and the national lawsuit; his work on the Two Medicine River; the Marias River Rehabilitation Project; delivering toxicants to Montana river systems by airplane.

INTERVIEWED BY ART WHITNEY, SEPTEMBER 27, 1993, FLATHEAD LAKE.

2 TAPES: 1 HOUR, 15 MINUTES

OH 1618
KEITH SEABURG INTERVIEW

Miles City resident Keith Seaburg describes: his childhood in Grand Rapids, Michigan; his service in the U.S. Navy during World War II; his education at the University of Michigan in science; his relocation to Montana to work on the Marias River Rehabilitation Project; his duties in Missoula as a project coordinator for the Montana Department of Fish, Wildlife and Parks (FWP); the project to mitigate winterkill on Brown's Lake and on Georgetown Lake; his assignment as regional information officer, including work on publicity films; becoming the FWP regional supervisor in Miles City; studying the effects of coal development on the Yellowstone River and its tributaries; the South Sand Stone Project.

INTERVIEWED BY ART WHITNEY, SEPTEMBER 6, 1993, MILES CITY.

1 TAPE: 25 MINUTES

OH 1619
NELS THORESON INTERVIEW

Nels Thoreson, a resident of Belt, discusses: his childhood in Great Falls and in Belt; his education in fisheries management at Utah State University in Logan; his relocation to Montana to study farm ponds for the Montana Department of Fish, Wildlife and Parks; early fish biologists in the state; his appointment as a district biologist for the Belt area; challenges faced by the too-few biologists in the state trying to handle the entire region; difficulties encountered during the Marias River Rehabilitation Project; working conditions during field projects; the Kipp Lake Project to remove carp brought into the system via railroad reservoirs; equipment and weather conditions.

INTERVIEWED BY ART WHITNEY, SEPTEMBER 16, 1993, BELT.

1 TAPE: 45 MINUTES

OH 1621
MELVIN HUDSON INTERVIEW

Melvin Hudson discusses: his experiences growing up in Absorkee; daily life in CCC Camp 1998, Thompson Falls, and in Company F9, Haugen.

INTERVIEWED BY JODIE FOLEY, JUNE 23, 1995, THREE FORKS.

1 TAPE: 20 MINUTES

OH 1622
WILLIAM ADAMEK INTERVIEW
William Adamek describes: his childhood as the son of Czchechoslovakian immigrants; arriving at CCC Camp 1586, Squaw Creek; his work as a first-aid attendant at the camp infirmary, a camp bugler, a creosote plant supervisor, on roadside cleanup, and creating fire lines.
INTERVIEWED BY JODIE FOLEY, JUNE 23, 1995, THREE FORKS.
SUMMARY: 3 PAGES
2 TAPES: 1 HOUR, 15 MINUTES

OH 1623
LUCILLE T. OTTER INTERVIEW
Lucille Otter details: growing up near St. Ignatius on the Flathead Indian Reservation; gaining clerical training in the WPA; the Kicking Horse Job Corps; working for the Native American Division of the Montana CCC as a supply and payroll clerk for Headquarters at Dixon from 1935 to 1942; living conditions, social activities and politics at Headquarters.
INTERVIEWED BY JODIE FOLEY, JUNE 24, 1995, THREE FORKS.
SUMMARY: 4 PAGES
2 TAPES: 1 HOUR, 10 MINUTES

OH 1624
WILLIAM KEBSCHULL INTERVIEW
William Kebschull describes: his family life in Boyd during the 1930s Depression; life at Camp 1998, Thompson Falls, Camp F61, Neihart, and Camp F75, Flint Creek; his work constructing telephone lines, building roads, and fighting fires.
INTERVIEWED BY JODIE FOLEY, JUNE 24, 1995, THREE FORKS.
SUMMARY: 3 PAGES
1 TAPE: 45 MINUTES

OH 1625
ROBERT THORPE INTERVIEW
Robert Thorpe details: his early childhood in Pennsylvania; joining the CCC; work in an Arizona camp as a baker; fire fighting in Columbia Falls; recreation; discipline; pharmacy work in the Navy during World War II.
INTERVIEWED BY JODIE FOLEY, JUNE 24, 1995, THREE FORKS.
SUMMARY: 3 PAGES
1 TAPE: 45 MINUTES

OH 1626
ROBERT HALLIDAY INTERVIEW
Robert Halliday discusses: his experiences in the CCC Birch Creek camp; his duties as camp radio operator, camp maintenance, in the creosote treatment plant, and building roads; social life in camp; camp discipline.
INTERVIEWED BY JODIE FOLEY, JUNE 25, 1995, THREE FORKS.
SUMMARY: 3 PAGES
1 TAPE: 1 HOUR

OH 1627
MARGARET WIEDMAN CHRISTENSEN INTERVIEW
Margaret Wiedman Christensen recalls: her life at the Montana Children's Center in Twin Bridges from 1946 to 1948; daily routines; chores; education; special celebrations (especially Christmas gifts from the Anaconda Mining Company); the loss of her parents; health care; the Foster Care Program.
INTERVIEWED BY BRIAN SHOVERS, JULY 22, 1995, TWIN BRIDGES.
SUMMARY: 3 PAGES
1 TAPE: 50 MINUTES

OH 1628
MARTHA KLAR INTERVIEW
Martha Klar details: her experiences at the Montana Children's Center in Twin Bridges from 1960 to 1969; her siblings joining her over time at the center; Christmas celebrations; daily work and discipline; education; running away; her feelings about reestablishing orphanages.
INTERVIEWED BY BRIAN SHOVERS, JULY 22, 1995, TWIN BRIDGES.
SUMMARY: 2 PAGES
1 TAPE: 45 MINUTES

OH 1629
BILL HANLEY INTERVIEW
Bill Hanley (b. 1934) discusses: his experiences in the Montana Children's Center in Twin Bridges from 1938 to 1955; coming to the center as a four year old; daily routines and chores; discipline; getting Christmas gifts from the Anaconda Mining Company; education; the importance of the reunion; reaction to the debate over reopening orphanages.
INTERVIEWED BY BRIAN SHOVERS, JULY 22, 1995, TWIN BRIDGES.

SUMMARY: 3 PAGES
1 TAPE: 50 MINUTES

OH 1630
VICKIE GARRETT INTERVIEW

Vickie Garrett describes: her experiences in the Montana Children's Center in Twin Bridges 1960 to 1964; her life before coming to the center; daily routines and chores; education; relationships with children and staff; her work now as a teacher; her reaction to the debate over reopening orphanages.
INTERVIEWED BY BRIAN SHOVERS, JULY 22 1995, TWIN BRIDGES.
SUMMARY: 4 PAGES
1 TAPE: 50 MINUTES.

OH 1631
PAM ENGEBRETSON INTERVIEW

Pam Engebretson details: her experiences in the Montana Children's Center in Twin Bridges from 1953 to 1961; daily routines; relationships with matrons and other children; her family; the foster care system; her reactions to the debate over reopening orphanages.
INTERVIEWED BY JODIE FOLEY, JULY 21, 1995, TWIN BRIDGES.
SUMMARY: 5 PAGES
1 TAPE: 55 MINUTES

OH 1632
DONNA ENGEBRETSON FULLNER INTERVIEW

Donna Engebretson Fullner portrays: her experiences in the Montana Children's Center in Twin Bridges from 1953 to 1960; family conditions previous to coming to the center; daily routines and chores; special activities; relationships with staff and children; impact of life in the center on adulthood; her reactions to the debate over reopening orphanages.
INTERVIEWED BY JODIE FOLEY, JULY 22, 1995, TWIN BRIDGES.
SUMMARY: 7 PAGES
2 TAPES: 1 HOUR, 20 MINUTES

OH 1633
NOEL FREEDMAN INTERVIEW

Noel Freedman discusses: his experiences in the Montana Children's Center in Twin Bridges from 1938 to 1945; his experiences at Deaconess Children's Home in Helena; coming to the children's center; daily routines and chores; his relationship with children and staff; participation in sports; being released to serve in World

War II; the debate over reopening orphanages.
INTERVIEWED BY JODIE FOLEY, JULY 21 1995, TWIN BRIDGES.
SUMMARY: 6 PAGES
2 TAPES: 1 HOUR, 15 MINUTES

OH 1634
HAROLD FREEDMAN INTERVIEW

Harold Freedman describes: his experiences in the Montana Children's Center in Twin Bridges from 1935 to 1941; his experiences at the Deaconess Children's Home in Helena; coming to the center; daily life and chores; his mother (first female to enter the School of Mines in Butte); meals; education; sports; Christmas and Anaconda Mining Company gifts; nicknames; relationships with children and staff; raising his own children; reactions to the call to reopen orphanages.
INTERVIEWED BY JODIE FOLEY, JULY 21 1995, TWIN BRIDGES.
SUMMARY: 6 PAGES
2 TAPES: 1 HOUR, 15 MINUTES

OH 1635
FRED WENTZ INTERVIEW

Fred Wentz discusses: his experiences in the Montana Children's Center in Twin Bridges from 1933 to 1945; his family's situation before he came to the Center; chores and daily routines; discipline; his relationships with other children and matrons; raising his own children; effects on adult life; anger at "outsider" discussions about life in orphanages; the impact of the reunion on him.
INTERVIEWED BY JODIE FOLEY, JULY 22 1995, TWIN BRIDGES.
SUMMARY: 5 PAGES
1 TAPE: 45 MINUTES

OH 1636
ROSELLA TEMPLETON INTERVIEW

Rosella Templeton shares: her experiences in the Montana Children's Center in Twin Bridges from 1914 to 1916; the conditions that brought her to the center; daily chores; illnesses; runaways; friendships; education; returning to her family; her grandchild's experience at the center in the 1960s.
INTERVIEWED BY JODIE FOLEY, JULY 21 1995, TWIN BRIDGES.
TRANSCRIPT: 28 PAGES
1 TAPE: 45 MINUTES

OH 1637
MARY YOTHER INTERVIEW

Mary Yother details: her experiences in the Montana Children's Center in Twin Bridges; the circumstances that brought her there; daily routines; discipline; running away; relationship with Twin Bridges town people; raising her family; feelings about returning to the center for the reunion.

INTERVIEWED BY JODIE FOLEY, JULY 22 1995, TWIN BRIDGES.

SUMMARY: 3 PAGES
1 TAPE: 50 MINUTES.

OH 1638
EULA MAE HALL INTERVIEW

Eula Hall discusses: her experiences growing up around Helena; the Hall family ranch outside of White Sulphur Springs; Blackfeet and Crow Indians' interactions with her parents; moving to Helena; Helena residents; the history of many of Helena's historic homes and buildings, including the Warren Hotel, Sixth Street business district, Holter family home, the Tobin House; traveling throughout the world with the Holter family as a young woman.

INTERVIEWED BY DOUG DODGE, NOVEMBER 3 AND 5, 1994, HELENA.

2 TAPES: 1 HOUR, 35 MINUTES

OH 1639
ALBERT TONG INTERVIEW

Albert Tong (b. 1915) describes: his experiences in the CCC; daily life at Nine Mile, Goat Creek, St. Ignatius camps; his duties; family life after leaving the CCC. *[See also New Deal in Montana OH 1119.]*

INTERVIEWED BY JODIE FOLEY, JUNE 25 1995, THREE FORKS.

SUMMARY: 2 PAGES
1 TAPE: 25 MINUTES

OH 1640
CLIFFORD DALE ELERY INTERVIEW

Dale Elery portrays: his experiences in the Montana Children's Center in Twin Bridges from 1928 to 1935; his father's illness; coming to the center with his sister; daily routines and chores; education; playtime and holidays, especially Christmas and Anaconda Mining Company gifts; medical care; overall impact of living in the center.

INTERVIEWED BY CONNIE GEIGER, JULY 21 1995, TWIN BRIDGES.

SUMMARY: 2 PAGES
1 TAPE: 50 MINUTES.

OH 1641
JACK, WALT AND KEN PIIPO INTERVIEW

Jack, Walt and Ken Piipo share: their experiences in the Montana Children's Center in Twin Bridges in 1958; coming to the center from an alcoholic family in Butte; life in the dormitory; relationships with other children and staff members; education; their adult lives; their families; reactions to the debate over reopening orphanages.

INTERVIEWED BY CONNIE GEIGER, JULY 21 1995, TWIN BRIDGES.

SUMMARY: 3 PAGES
2 TAPES: 1 HOUR, 20 MINUTES

OH 1642
SHIRLEY SMITH KLATT INTERVIEW

Shirley Klatt discusses: her experiences in the Montana Children's Center in Twin Bridges from 1934 to 1960; coming to the home from Butte; treatment by staff; discipline; relationships with other children; running away; importance of religion; her adult life; feelings about the reunion.

INTERVIEWED BY CONNIE GEIGER, JULY 21 1995, TWIN BRIDGES.

SUMMARY: 3 PAGES
2 TAPES: 1 HOUR, 20 MINUTE

OH 1643
DOROTHY SCHOKNECHT INTERVIEW

Dorothy Schoknecht discusses: her family's experiences owning property on Lake McDonald in Glacier National Park, from the 1920s to date; transportation; the development of tourist accommodations; Going-to-the-Sun Highway; the fire of 1929; National Park Service Management; Glacier View Dam; the Flood of 1964.

INTERVIEWED BY KEN HOLSTE, AUGUST 5, 1995, KALISPELL.

SUMMARY: 2 PAGES
1 TAPE: 40 MINUTES

OH 1651
FRED PHILLIPS INTERVIEW

Fred Phillips details: hopping a freight train to Montana as a young man; working as a cowboy in the 1930s around Miles City; moving to the Pony area; guiding hunting groups; moving to Mammoth; packing fish into Lake Louise for stocking; accidents he had breaking horses and herding cattle; dealings with the Forest Ser-

vice; the Nicholson Mine; his wife Helen Walters Phillips.
INTERVIEWED BY BLANCHE UEHLING, SEPTEMBER 9, 1992,
PONY.
TRANSCRIPT: 11 PAGES
1 TAPE: 40 MINUTES

OH 1652
ART CARRIER INTERVIEW

Art Carrier describes: his childhood; attending Holy
Family Mission, a Catholic boarding school; working
on local ranches in the summers; Métis families Jocko,
Collins, LaRance, Nadeau, Azure, Sinclair, and
Belgardes; dances and playing the fiddle in homes around
Choteau; his education; hunting and preparing the meat
and hide; nicknames for family and friends; Moccasin
Flats in Choteau; making a dish called "bullets"; New
Year's Eve celebrations. [Donated by Métis Cultural
Recovery, Inc.]
INTERVIEWED BY SCARLETT SCHOCK, NOVEMBER 16, 1993,
CHOTEAU.
TRANSCRIPT: 42 PAGES

OH 1653
RICHARD KENCK INTERVIEW

Richard Kenck discusses: the loss of Métis language
(recalls a few words); his childhood home near the Diamond Bar X Ranch; his father's work as a dentist (unof-
ficial doctor and mortician of Augusta area); dances,
fiddle music, and alcohol; the New Year's dance; the Riel
Rebellion and local Canadian Métis; his mother's trip to
Cow Island in 1878; his grandmother's experience with
Sitting Bull; local Métis families Pocha and Jarvey; the
school at Bowman's Corner; Ole Bean and family; Catholic priests; St. Peter's Mission school; learning blacksmith techniques and related work during World War II
for the Air Corps. [Donated by Métis Cultural Recovery,
Inc.] [See also General Montana OH 1660.]
INTERVIEWED BY MELINDA LIVEZEY, JUNE 7, 1994,
CHOTEAU
TRANSCRIPT: 35 PAGES

OH 1654
JOSEPHINE LAMFROMBOISE INTERVIEW

Josephine Lamfromboise—a 93-year-old Métis
woman—discusses: coming to Box Elder in 1914; Turtle
Island Indian lands; her father's work as interpreter for
Chief Rocky Boy; Red River carts; the demise of the
buffalo; Box Elder families Collings, St. Germaine, and
Wiseman; her 13 children; Moccasin Flats and its growth
since 1935; the 1930s Depression; butchering elk and

deer; her work in the Beanery and other restaurants. [Do-
nated by Métis Cultural Recovery, Inc.]
INTERVIEWED BY BOB MCDONALD, JUNE 8, 1994,
CHOTEAU
TRANSCRIPT: 25 PAGES

OH 1655
MYRTLE BUSHMAN REARDON INTERVIEW

Myrtle Reardon details: growing up west of Choteau
on Battle Creek; her family's connection to the Riel Rebellion; food preparation and preservation, including
wine, bannack, and crushed cherries; sewing and clothes;
children's games; Red River carts; her parents speaking
French and Cree; New Year's dances and other dances;
her mother's marriage clothing; her mother making moc-
casins, gloves, and neckerchiefs; the 1910 forest fire; her
mother's childbirths. [Donated by Métis Cultural Recovery, Inc.] [See also Small Town Montana OH 757.]
INTERVIEWED BY MELINDA LIVEZEY, FEBRUARY 2, 1994,
CHOTEAU
TRANSCRIPT: 53 PAGES.

OH 1656
CECELIA WISEMAN INTERVIEW

Métis Cecelia Wiseman discusses: her work life from
the age of 12, including working 23 years in a nursing
home; living in a log house built by her father near the
South Fork of the Teton; other cabins in the area; trapping; food preparation and preservation of meat, pem-
mican, crushed cherries, bread, bannack, fry bread, various herbs and spices, and wine; draw knives; her parent's
Canadian background; baby hammocks; traditional medi-
cines and remedies. [Donated by Métis Cultural Recovery, Inc.] [See also General Montana OH 1661.]
INTERVIEWED BY MELINDA LIVEZEY, FEBRUARY 18, 1994,
CHOTEAU
TRANSCRIPT: 34 PAGES.

OH 1657
ROBERT ZION INTERVIEW

Robert Zion describes: his childhood in the Fort
Benton and Choteau areas; his education; winter weather;
A. B. Guthrie, Sr.; his mother's aid to ill neighbors;
Dr. Maynard; the 1930s Depression; discrimination
against the Métis; commodity distribution plan for sur-
plus food; going with the agent to distribute food to Métis
families south of Choteau; Riel Rebellion; Hill 57;
Lt. Pershing marching Métis through Choteau; Mocca-
sin Flats; the Bushman Cemetery; fighting at local dances.
[Donated by Métis Cultural Recovery, Inc.]

INTERVIEWED BY MELINDA LIVEZEY, JUNE 27, 1994, CHOTEAU.

TRANSCRIPT: 19 PAGES

OH 1658
ALFRED WISEMAN INTERVIEW

Alfred Wiseman discusses: his memories of Art Carrier and his family; Gilman in the 1930s; Métis families in Augusta, Sangrays, Poches, Swans, Thomas, and Lafromboise; Sophie Malatares' home and family; winter hardships; Art Carrier's fiddle playing; square dances and "jigging"; New Year's dances, food, and festivities; hunting; preserving meat; his life before and after World War II; the impact of cars and electrification; Métis heritage; his ranch work stacking haystacks, shocking, and threshing. [Donated by Métis Cultural Recovery, Inc.] *[See also General Montana OH 1659.]*

INTERVIEWED BY MELINDA LIVEZEY, NOVEMBER 29, 1993, CHOTEAU.

TRANSCRIPT: 33 PAGES.

OH 1659
ALFRED WISEMAN INTERVIEW

Alfred Wiseman discusses: his interest in carpentry; his interest in recording fiddle music (he began recording in 1962); his Chippewa-Cree heritage; growing up in Gilman; childhood chores; his father's work farming, breaking horses, and trapping on Deep Creek; coyotes; discipline as a child; building of cabins on the south fork of the Teton; the Circle 8 Ranch; traditional medicine for animals and humans; childhood games and sports. [Donated by Métis Cultural Recovery, Inc.] *[See also General Montana OH 1658.]*

INTERVIEWED BY MELINDA LIVEZEY, FEBRUARY 10, 1994, CHOTEAU.

TRANSCRIPT: 36 PAGES

OH 1660
RICHARD KENCK INTERVIEW

Richard Kenck details: growing up among Métis on the Dearborn River; tearing down cabins to build a road in the 1980s; settlement on Highway 287, old Birdtail Road, and Sullivan Pass; St. Peter's Mission and the Moran Family; the Dearborn Crossing; a muzzle-loader he found near Deadman Coulee; various families' entrance into the area, including the Fords, Cobbs, and Gosses; children keeping warm in winter without winter clothing; beadwork; a traditional Métis vest and tobacco pouch; mixing tobacco with kinnikinnick or tree bark; Métis clothing; childhood games and toys, including

things made from porcupine quills and horse hair; trapping; pack outfits. [Donated by Métis Cultural Recovery, Inc.] *[See also General Montana OH 1653.]*

INTERVIEWED BY MELINDA LIVEZEY, JUNE 22, 1994, CHOTEAU.

TRANSCRIPT: 24 PAGES

OH 1661
CECELIA WISEMAN INTERVIEW

Cecelia Wiseman depicts: her work in a nursing home; her father's work stacking hay; photos of family members and friends; straw tick; homesteads; square dances and fiddle music; being drug by a horse; the family cabin she grew up in; chores; coal oil lights; soap making; using a washboard; bathing; gardens and domestic animals; childhood games; catching coyote pups and gopher tails for bounty; gathering wool and collecting bones for money; dances; the Belleville School; town life; local place-names; women who served in the military during World War II. [Donated by Métis Cultural Recovery, Inc.] *[See also General Montana OH 1656.]*

INTERVIEWED BY MELINDA LIVEZEY, MARCH 1, 1994, CHOTEAU.

TRANSCRIPT: 47 PAGES

OH 1664
EVA LENARZ INTERVIEW

Eva Lenarz presents: her childhood in the Tobacco Valley, especially the communities of Eureka and Demers; local farms and residents; Cuffe and Phillips Creek Schools; rural electrification; "Jungle Town"; local dances; Eureka area orchards; making apple cider.

INTERVIEWED BY CATHRYN SCHROEDER, OCTOBER 25, 1995, EUREKA.

TRANSCRIPT: 9 PAGES

1 TAPE: 45 MINUTES

OH 1665
WELLINGTON D. RANKIN INTERVIEW

Wellington Rankin—rancher, attorney general and brother of Jeanette Rankin—discusses: Ms. Rankin's campaign for Congress in 1916; her reasons for running, primarily suffrage; difficulties of the campaign; her campaign capabilities; his work as campaign manager; work of their sisters Mary, Edna, and Grace on the campaign; union votes; poor press coverage; the Bull Moose Party and Theodore Roosevelt; the Anaconda Copper Mining Company; World War I and why he disagreed with her vote against the war; her failed reelection attempt in 1918; her strong sense of conviction; their mother and father.

INTERVIEWED BY V. W. STEELE, N.D., HELENA.
2 TAPES: 1 HOUR, 35 MINUTES

OH 1666
LEAH STUART BRICKETT INTERVIEW
Leah Brickett—daughter of Montana governor S. V. Stuart—briefly discusses: her family's early experiences in Virginia City before moving to Helena; life in the Original Governor's Mansion. *[See also General Montana OH 1669.]*
INTERVIEWED BY MARY HOFFSCHWELLE AND HARRIET MELOY, NOVEMBER 16, 1982, HELENA
TRANSCRIPT: 24 PAGES

OH 1669
LEAH STUART BRICKETT INTERVIEW
Leah Brickett, daughter of Montana governor S. V. Stuart, discusses: life in the Original Governor's Mansion in the 1910s; the Conrad family; her family; various servants (cooks, groundskeepers, cleaning staff); Prohibition; Helena area history; her mother's work as first lady; the World War I homefront; effects of a Butte miner's strike on her family; personal illnesses and Dr. Cooney; her recollections of other governors' families (the Tooles, Norths, and McDowells). *[See also General Montana OH 1666.]*

OH 1730
BOB CAMPBELL INTERVIEW
Bob Campbell—a delegate to the 1972 Montana Constitutional Convention and a member of the bill of rights committee—depicts: campaigning to become a delegate; fellow members of the Missoula delegation; his role in writing the bill of rights; the impact of the Warren Commission on the content of the Montana Constitution; chairman Leo Graybill; John C. Harrison and the role of the Supreme Court; the role of the LWV; promoting passage of the new constitution; the narrow vote margin; activities of those opposed to passage, primarily the Farm Bureau.
INTERVIEWED BY JODIE FOLEY, JANUARY 9, 1997, HELENA.
SUMMARY: 4 PAGES
2 TAPES: 1 HOUR 20 MINUTES

OH 1738
MERLIN MILLER INTERVIEW
Merlin Miller—son of Olive and Abraham Miller—discusses: his family's experiences living near CPS Camp 55 in Belton while his father served as a Conscientious Objector during World War II; his mother's stories about

hardships during the war years; his feelings about his father's service; his own faith system and military service.
INTERVIEWED BY JODIE FOLEY, JULY 27, 1996, CARDWELL.
1 TAPE: 25 MINUTES

OH 1739
JASPER ROTH INTERVIEW
Jasper Roth recounts: growing up and working on the family farm in Oregon; his Mennonite faith; his decision to declare Conscientious Objector status during World War II; life at Belton in Camp 55; feelings about his alternative service; possibilities for young people now to serve in the same manner.
INTERVIEWED BY JODIE FOLEY, JULY 27, 1996, CARDWELL.
1 TAPE: 35 MINUTES

OH 1740
DANIEL HEADINGS INTERVIEW
Daniel Headings discusses: growing up in an Amish Mennonite farming community; his decision to declare Conscientious Objector status during World War II; serving in Belton at Camp 55; his various duties in camp; leisure time activities [includes typed reminiscence].
INTERVIEWED BY JODIE FOLEY, JULY 27, 1996, CARDWELL.
1 TAPE: 45 MINUTES

OH 1741
LAWRENCE AND ALTA SCHROCK INTERVIEW
Lawrence and Alta Schrock describe: growing up in a Mennonite community; his decision to serve as a Conscientious Objector during World War II; his assignment to Camp 55 in Belton; camp life and work routines; his feelings about alternative military service programs.
INTERVIEWED BY JODIE FOLEY, JULY 27, 1996, CARDWELL.
1 TAPE: 50 MINUTES

OH 1742
ABRAHAM AND OLIVE MILLER INTERVIEW
Abraham and Olive Miller discuss: growing up in a conservative Mennonite community; his decision to serve as a Conscientious Objector during World War II; his assignment to Camp 55 in Belton; bringing his family to Montana to live during his service; camp life and work routines; his feelings about alternative military service programs.
INTERVIEWED BY JODIE FOLEY, JULY 27, 1996, CARDWELL.
2 TAPES: 1 HOUR, 15 MINUTES

OH 1743

CRIST BORNTRAGER INTERVIEW

Crist Borntrager recalls: growing up in an Amish community; his decision to serve as a Conscientious Objector during World War II; work in a mental institution; his assignment to Camp 55 in Belton; camp life and work routines; his feelings about alternative military service programs.

INTERVIEWED BY JODIE FOLEY, JULY 28, 1996, CARDWELL.

1 TAPE: 1 HOUR

OH 1744

ALVIN KLIEWER INTERVIEW

Alvin Kliewer depicts: growing up in a Mennonite community; deciding to serve as a Conscientious Objector during World War II; his assignment to Camp 55 in Belton; camp life and work routines; his feelings about alternative military service programs.

INTERVIEWED BY JODIE FOLEY, JULY 27, 1996, CARDWELL.

2 TAPES: 1 HOUR, 55 MINUTES

OH 1745

SIMON AND ESTA HERSHBERGER INTERVIEW

Simon and Esta Hershberger detail: his Amish Men–nonite upbringing; his decision to serve as a Conscien–tious Objector during World War II; his assignment to Camp 55 in Belton; camp life and work routines; his feelings about alternative military service programs and pacifism.

INTERVIEWED BY MARCELLA SHERFY, JULY 27, 1996, BELTON.

1 TAPE: 55 MINUTES

OH 1746

MELVIN AND LUCILLE GERIG INTERVIEW

Melvin and Lucille Gerig discuss: his Mennonite faith; his decision to serve as a Conscientious Objector during World War II; his service in Colorado and Michigan; his assignment to Camp 55 in Belton; camp life and work routines; his feelings about alternative military service programs and pacifism.

INTERVIEWED BY MARCELLA SHERFY, JULY 27, 1996, BELTON.

1 TAPE: 55 MINUTES

OH 1747

EARL KENNEL INTERVIEW

Earl Kennel discusses: his Mennonite faith; his decision to serve as a Conscientious Objector during World War II; his service in Idaho; his assignment to Camp 55 in Belton; camp life and work routines; his feelings about alternative military service programs and pacifism.

INTERVIEWED BY MARCELLA SHERFY, JULY 27, 1996, BELTON.

2 TAPES: 1 HOUR, 12 MINUTES

OH 1748

HENRY AND EVELYN MULLET INTERVIEW

Henry and Evelyn Mullet portray: his Mennonite faith; his decision to serve as a Conscientious Objector during World War II; his service in Colorado and Michigan; his assignment to Camp 55 in Belton; camp life and work routines; his feelings about alternative military service programs and pacifism.

INTERVIEWED BY MARCELLA SHERFY, JULY 27, 1996, BELTON.

1 TAPE: 40 MINUTES

OH 1749

DANIEL AND BETTY SCHRAG INTERVIEW

Daniel and Betty Schrag detail: his Mennonite faith; his decision to serve as a Conscientious Objector during World War II; his service in Nebraska; his assignment to Camp 55 in Belton; camp life and work routines; his feelings about alternative military service programs and pacifism.

INTERVIEWED BY JODIE FOLEY, JULY 27, 1996, BELTON.

1 TAPE: 25 MINUTES

OH 1750

JOHN GARBER INTERVIEW

John Garber discusses: his Mennonite faith; his decision to serve as a Conscientious Objector during World War II; service in Missoula as a smoke jumper; assignment to Camp 55 in Belton; camp life and work routines; his feelings about alternative military service programs and pacifism.

INTERVIEWED BY MARCELLA SHERFY, JULY 27, 1996, BELTON.

1 TAPE: 30 MINUTES

OH 1751

JAMES AND VERA WEAVER INTERVIEW

James and Vera Weaver talk about: his Mennonite faith; his decision to serve as a Conscientious Objector during World War II; service in Pennsylvania, and in a mental institution in Rhode Island; his assignment to Camp 55 in Belton; camp life and work routines; his feelings about alternative military service programs and pacifism.

INTERVIEWED BY MARCELLA SHERFY, JULY 26, 1996, BELTON.
1 TAPE: 50 MINUTES

OH 1752
HOWARD KING INTERVIEW

Howard King discusses: his Mennonite faith; his decision to serve as a Conscientious Objector during World War II; his assignment to Camp 55 in Belton; camp life and work routines; his feelings about alternative military service programs and pacifism.
INTERVIEWED BY MARCELLA SHERFY, JULY 27, 1996, BELTON.
TRANSCRIPT: 8 PAGES
1 TAPE: 50 MINUTES

OH 1753
PERRY AND AUDREY SCHROCK INTERVIEW

Perry and Audrey Schrock discuss: his Mennonite faith; his decision to serve as a Conscientious Objector during World War II; his service in Oregon; his assignment to Camp 55 in Belton; camp life and work routines; his feelings about alternative military service programs and pacifism.
INTERVIEWED BY MARCELLA SHERFY, JULY 26, 1996, BELTON.
1 TAPE: 40 MINUTES

OH 1754
JACOB AND PHOEBE GLANZER INTERVIEW

Jacob and Phoebe Glanzer detail: his Mennonite faith; his decision to serve as a Conscientious Objector during World War II; his service in Iowa; his assignment to Camp 55 in Belton; camp life and work routines; his feelings about alternative military service programs and pacifism.
INTERVIEWED BY MARCELLA SHERFY, JULY 27, 1996, BELTON.
1 TAPE: 20 MINUTES

OH 1755
AMOS GROFF INTERVIEW

Amos Groff describes: his Mennonite faith; his decision to serve as a Conscientious Objector during World War II; his service in Virginia; his assignment to Camp 55 in Belton; camp life and work routines; his feelings about alternative military service programs and pacifism.
INTERVIEWED BY DAVE WALTER, JULY 27, 1996, BELTON.
1 TAPE: 30 MINUTES

OH 1756
OSCAR ROTH INTERVIEW

Oscar Roth recounts: his Mennonite faith; his decision to serve as a Conscientious Objector during World War II; his assignment to Camp 55 in Belton; camp life and work routines; his feelings about alternative military service programs and pacifism.
INTERVIEWED BY DAVE WALTER, JULY 26, 1996, BELTON.
1 TAPE: 35 MINUTES

OH 1757
EMANUEL SCHLABACH INTERVIEW

Emanuel Schlabach describes: his Amish Mennonite faith; his decision to serve as a Conscientious Objector during World War II; service in Indiana and Virginia; his assignment to Camp 55 in Belton; camp life and work routines; his feelings about alternative military service programs and pacifism.
INTERVIEWED BY DAVE WALTER, JULY 26, 1996, BELTON.
1 TAPE: 45 MINUTES

OH 1758
GLENFORD AND RUTH KING INTERVIEW

Glenford and Ruth King present: his Mennonite faith; his decision to serve as a Conscientious Objector during World War II; his service in Indiana; his assignment to Camp 55 in Belton; bringing his wife to Montana (Ruth King discusses her work as a housekeeper); camp life and work routines; his feelings about alternative military service programs and pacifism.
INTERVIEWED BY DAVE WALTER, JULY 27, 1996, BELTON.
TRANSCRIPT: 14 PAGES
1 TAPE: 30 MINUTES

OH 1759
RALPH KAUFMAN INTERVIEW

Ralph Kaufman discusses: his Mennonite faith; his decision to serve as a Conscientious Objector during World War II; service in Colorado and Michigan; his assignment to Camp 55 in Belton; camp life and work routines; his feelings about alternative military service programs and pacifism.
INTERVIEWED BY DAVE WALTER, JULY 27, 1996, BELTON.
1 TAPE: 25 MINUTES

OH 1760
WILLARD NOFZIGER INTERVIEW

Willard Nofziger describes: his Mennonite faith; his decision to serve as a Conscientious Objector during World War II; service in Oregon in a mental institution;

his assignment to Camp 55 in Belton; camp life and work routines; his feelings about alternative military service programs and pacifism.
INTERVIEWED BY DAVE WALTER, JULY 28, 1996, BELTON.
1 TAPE: 23 MINUTES

OH 1761
HENRY ROGER FRIESEN INTERVIEW

Henry Friesen describes: his Mennonite faith; his decision to serve as a Conscientious Objector during World War II; his assignment to Camp 55 in Belton; camp life and work routines; his feelings about alternative military service programs and pacifism.
INTERVIEWED BY DAVE WALTER, JULY 27, 1996, BELTON.
1 TAPE: 30 MINUTES

OH 1762
MARVIN AND ESTHER FAST INTERVIEW

Marvin and Esther Fast discuss: his Mennonite faith; his decision to serve as a Conscientious Objector during World War II; his assignment to Camp 55 in Belton; camp life and work routines; his feelings about alternative military service programs and pacifism.
INTERVIEWED BY DAVE WALTER, JULY 28, 1996, BELTON.
1 TAPE: 50 MINUTES

OH 1763
JOHN K. "JACK" McDONALD INTERVIEW

Jack McDonald—chairman of the Montana Constitution Revision Commission that studied the 1889 Constitution and recommended to the 1971 legislature that it be revised—describes: the problems with the 1889 Constitution; some of the political maneuvering that led to the Constitutional Convention in 1972 and passage of the new constitution; the issues that pulled him into the debate, including the inadequacies of the amendment process and the need for referendum and initiative language in the Constitution. The latter he used in a political battle in Kalispell over pornography. He also discusses leaving the legislature as a result of reapportionment and ending his affiliation with the Democratic Party.
INTERVIEWED BY PAUL VERDON, OCTOBER 11, 1996, HELENA.
TRANSCRIPT: 27 PAGES
1 TAPE: 50 MINUTES

OH 1764
GEORGE HARPER INTERVIEW

George Harper—a longtime Helena-area minister and member of the 1972 Montana Constitutional Convention—discusses: his religious training; political philosophies, and how he viewed his work in the convention.
INTERVIEWED BY PAUL VERDON, NOVEMBER 1996, HELENA.
TRANSCRIPT: 24 PAGES
1 TAPE: 1 HOUR

Pioneer Collections

Pioneer Collections

This section contains oral reminiscences from the A. J. Noyes Reminiscences Collection, the William Wheeler Biographies Collection, and other miscellaneous interviews for which no tapes exist. The Noyes and Wheeler projects were conducted in an effort to gather information about Montana's earliest pioneer residents. These recollections are strong in mining, ranching, military, and frontier life anecdotes. The majority of these interviews predate the widespread use of tape recorders and thus are transcripts based on notes taken during interview sessions. Some of these transcripts are verbatim, taken from tapes that no longer exist.

A. J. Noyes Biographical Reminiscences Collection

SC 16
GEORGE B. HERENDEEN PAPERS

George Herendeen (1846–1919)—a Bozeman resident—served as: a pioneer; a cowboy; a prospector; an explorer; a scout for military expeditions, including the Battle of the Little Bighorn; a saloon keeper. The collection includes his outgoing correspondence (1872–1880) to his sister Jennie Cramton and to Emma Mount, the wife of his partner. His reminiscences concern his scouting experiences; family matters; day-to-day life on the frontier.
TYPESCRIPT: 7 PAGES

SC 86
JOSEPH HORSKY PAPERS

Joseph Horsky (1842–1930) became a pioneer in Helena, a placer miner who later operated a livery business, and an investor in local real estate. This collection contains an account book/daybook (1880–1881) for Horsky's feed-stable operations and a ten-page reminiscence (circa 1916) in which Horsky details his experiences in the West from 1861 to the 1890s.
TYPESCRIPT: 10 PAGES

SC 283
SHIRLEY CARTER ASHBY PAPERS

Helena resident Shirley Ashby worked as a local banker. This collection contains a diary (April 13–May 14, 1867) that details his journey up the Missouri River on the steamboat *Nile* and that includes "rules and regulations for freighting." An oral reminiscence (1916) addresses: his work for I. G. Baker and Company; trading with the Blackfeet; his business dealings in Helena from 1867 to 1889. *[The diary can also be found as Microfilm 99e.]*
TYPESCRIPT: 20 PAGES

SC 350
H. FRANK ADKINS REMINISCENCE

Frank Adkins—a native of Kentucky who arrived in Helena as a freighter in 1865—worked as a dry-goods clerk until 1868, when he returned to Kentucky. In 1881, Adkins moved permanently to Helena, where he worked as a postman until his retirement in 1913. This oral reminiscence (1915) addresses various aspects of Adkins's life and vigilante activities in Helena.
TYPESCRIPT: 7 PAGES

SC 372
CHARLES AVERY REMINISCENCE

Charles Avery participated in the 1874 Yellowstone prospecting expedition, which moved from Bozeman to the mouth of the Rosebud River, to Lame Deer, and back to Bozeman. This interview discusses the group's repeated encounters with Indians.
TYPESCRIPT: 4 PAGES

SC 373
FRANK LEEDY AND JEANNETTE MORROW
WHITEHEAD LEEDY REMINISCENCES
Frank Leedy (b. 1841) discusses: his travel from Salt Lake City, Utah Territory, to Helena in 1866; his subsequent work as a prospector and a miner. His wife, Jeannette Leedy (b. 1856), tells of her life in Montana during the 1860s and the 1870s, while married to her first husband, John C. Whitehead.
TYPESCRIPT: 5 PAGES

SC 380
THOMAS BAKER PAPERS
Thomas Baker addresses: his arrival in Montana Territory in 1863; his work as a miner; his subsequent career as the editor of the Virginia City *Madisonian*, to 1900. Also included in the collection is a copy of a letter from Baker to W. W. Cheely that explains the background of the old printing press located first at Bannack and subsequently at Virginia City.
TYPESCRIPT: 5 PAGES

SC 385
WRIGHT L. LILES REMINISCENCE
Wright Liles talks about his mining experiences in Helena and Butte from 1865 to 1875.
TYPESCRIPT: 4 PAGES

SC 386
WILLIAM BALL REMINISCENCE
Zortman resident William Ball worked as a pioneer freighter and trader. He discusses, in 1915: his experiences in the Little Rockies from 1873 to 1878; his encounters with Indians; the discovery of gold in the Little Rockies; Pike Landusky; Kid Curry.
TYPESCRIPT: 2 PAGES

SC 396
J. MILTON BARNHART REMINISCENCE
Milton Barnhart—a Butte resident—worked as a miner and a restaurant operator. He describes his experiences in Montana's early mining towns from approximately 1866 until 1880.
TYPESCRIPT: 3 PAGES

SC 404
SETH BAWDEN REMINISCENCE
Seth Bawden was a miner in the vicinity of Helena. He reflects on: his trip to Idaho and Montana in the early 1860s; his experiences while mining in several districts.
TYPESCRIPT: 4 PAGES

SC 406
DONALD W. BEECH REMINISCENCE
Helena resident Donald Beech recalls: his work as a livery operator and rancher near Helena; his experiences as a freighter in Utah and Colorado; his other business activities in Montana.
TYPESCRIPT: 6 PAGES

SC 419
WILLIAM R. McCOMAS REMINISCENCES
In two separate interviews, William McComas (1845–1931) discusses his work as a miner, a freighter, and a ranch hand in Alder Gulch and Helena.
TYPESCRIPT: 7 PAGES

SC 423
PAUL McCORMICK PAPERS
Paul McCormick (1845–1921) was a merchant and a cattle rancher in Yellowstone County as well as a member of the Baker expedition against the Piegan Indians in 1870. The collection consists of: an oral reminiscence; copies of two letters from Wilbur Fisk Sanders and Thomas C. Power; a January 1921 Montana House of Representatives resolution on the death of McCormick.
TYPESCRIPT: 1 PAGE

SC 449
BENJAMIN MALBEN REMINISCENCE
Benjamin Malben (b. 1845) describes: his experiences on the Fisk wagon expedition from Minnesota to Montana Territory in 1866; his life in Helena during the gold rush era.
TYPESCRIPT: 7 PAGES

SC 462
A. H. BRADLEY REMINISCENCE
A. H. Bradley, an early eastern Montana Territory resident, worked as a carpenter, a trader, and a freighter at several trading posts and Indian agencies. He describes (circa 1915): encounters with Indians; trading practices in Montana between 1869 to 1877.
TYPESCRIPT: 11 PAGES

SC 480
JAMES JACKSON BROWN REMINISCENCE
James Brown (b. 1844)—a rancher in the Hays area—worked as a freighter and scout in north central Mon-

tana. He recalls his early experiences in Montana, especially his encounters with Indians.
TYPESCRIPT: 6 PAGES

SC 481
WALLACE MILLIGAN REMINISCENC
Wallace Milligan addresses: his mining experiences in Bannack in 1864; running his own boarding house in Blackfoot City beginning in 1865; his later experiences farming in the Prickly Pear Valley, just north of Helena; serving as a Lewis and Clark County commissioner.
TYPESCRIPT: 7 PAGES

SC 530
NICHOLAS T. CHEMIDLIN REMINISCENCE
Nicholas Chemidlin details his trips across the plains to Montana Territory with the Fisk wagon expeditions of 1864 and 1866.
TYPESCRIPT: 6 PAGES

SC 535
MALCOLM MORROW REMINISCENCE
Malcolm Morrow (b. 1850) comments on his work as a miner and a rancher in Montana Territory from 1864 to 1882.
TYPESCRIPT: 4 PAGES

SC 537
WILLIAM T. MORROW REMINISCENCE
William Morrow (b. 1854) talks about: his childhood on the family farm in the Prickly Pear Valley, just north of Helena during the 1860s; his years as a Fort Benton rancher.
TYPESCRIPT: 8 PAGES

SC 541
GEORGE W. MORSE REMINISCENCE
George Morse (b. 1838) describes: his work as a placer miner in Reynolds City, Blackfoot City, and other Montana Territory gold-mining camps in the 1860s; cattle raising in the Rock Creek area in the 1870s.
TYPESCRIPT: 7 PAGES

SC 546
WILLIAM D. COCHRAN PAPERS
William Cochran worked as a placer miner, a freighter, and a fur trader in Montana Territory. He recalls (circa 1916): his early experiences in Montana;

encounters with Indians. Also included is a letter (1917) to Thomas Irvine.
TYPESCRIPT: 4 PAGES

SC 559
ANDREW J. MYERS REMINISCENCE
Andrew Myers recounts his meeting with fugitive Nez Perce Indians near his ranch in Horse Prairie during the summer of 1877. This collection also contains the reminiscences of Myers's unidentified friend "Max."
TYPESCRIPT: 8 PAGES

SC 560
SAMUEL S. COOK REMINISCENCE
Samuel Cook reflects on his work as a miner and a farmer in the Helena area from the early 1860s to 1900.
TYPESCRIPT: 4 PAGES

SC 574
FRANK COOK REMINISCENCE
Frank Cook explains (1916) his role in the capture and trial of Michael McAndrews, the murderer of the pioneer "Scotty" Mavor, circa 1877.
TYPESCRIPT: 2 PAGES

SC 589
ALVA JOSIAH "AJAX" NOYES WRITINGS
A. J. Noyes (1855–1917) worked as a Beaverhead County assessor and later as an oral historian for the Montana Historical Society in Helena. This collection consists of: a biographical sketch written, in 1963, of Noyes by his son Charles R. Noyes; collected reminiscences of several north central Montana pioneers.
TYPESCRIPT: 3 PAGES

SC 603
ELIZA WARING O'NEIL REMINISCENCE
Eliza O'Neil discusses: her wagon journey to Montana Territory in 1864 with her first husband, Robert P. Waring; her subsequent life in Diamond City and in Helena.
TYPESCRIPT: 4 PAGES

SC 624
WHEELER O. DEXTER REMINISCENCE
Fort Benton freighter and rancher Wheeler Dexter discusses: his trip to Montana with the 1866 Fisk expedition; his experiences in Montana from 1866 to 1878.
TYPESCRIPT: 5 PAGES

SC 631
OSCAR E. PENWELL PAPERS
Oscar Penwell—a Bannack placer miner—recalls his experiences prospecting and mining in western Montana Territory from 1863 to 1873. The collection also includes a poll-tax receipt (September 30, 1865) from Gallatin County.
TYPESCRIPT: 8 PAGES

SC 633
PETER PEYER REMINISCENCE
Peter Peyer describes his work as a miner, a stockman, a stage driver, and an operator of a hotel in Montana Territory from 1865 to 1882.
TYPESCRIPT: 2 PAGES

SC 666
JAMES C. EMERSON REMINISCENCE
James Emerson (b. 1845), who arrived in Montana Territory in 1864, tells, in 1915, about his work as a miner, a freighter, a rancher, a smelterman, a hotel operator, and a Cascade County undersheriff from 1864 to 1910.
TYPESCRIPT: 6 PAGES

SC 669
FRANCIS POWERS REMINISCENCE
Francis Powers (b. 1844) describes his placer mining experiences at Silver Bow and at other mining camps in western Montana Territory.
TYPESCRIPT: 3 PAGES

SC 672
BENJAMIN "UNCLE BEN" ERWAY
REMINISCENCE
Benjamin Erway (1834–1916) worked as a Pony Express rider, a placer miner, a freighter, and a clerk throughout the West from the late 1850s to 1890. He discusses especially his experiences as a miner in Montana Territory from 1862 to 1872.
TYPESCRIPT: 7 PAGES

SC 673
BENNETT PRICE REMINISCENCE
Bennett Price (b. 1842) describes: his work in Marysville as a miner and a general store owner; life in Marysville and surrounding mining camps from 1864 to 1886.
TYPESCRIPT: 2 PAGES

SC 677
HAROLD RASH REMINISCENCE
Harold Rash—a miner in the Little Rocky Mountains—reflects on: his mining experiences; the killing of "Rattlesnake Jake" Owen and Charles Fallon at Lewistown on July 4, 1884; the central Montana vigilante "Stranglers" of 1884; the 1885 Riel Rebellion in Canada.
TYPESCRIPT: 6 PAGES

SC 687
VENZLE CHARLES RINDA REMINISCENCE
V. C. Rinda (1846–1919)—a Helena hotel owner—recalls: his business experiences; his life in Montana from about 1870 to 1900.
TYPESCRIPT: 4 PAGES

SC 696
VAN HAYDEN FISK REMINISCENCE
Van Fisk worked as a rancher and as a partner in several Fisk Brothers enterprises in Helena. This collection comprises: an 1867 deed to a mining claim; an account of an incident witnessed during the 1864 Fisk expedition from Minnesota to Helena; biographical sketches of Van Hayden Fisk and his wife.
TYPESCRIPT: 22 PAGES

SC 729
LOUIS SHAMBOW REMINISCENCE
A longtime resident of the Milk River area of north central Montana, Louis Shambow (Chambeau), in 1916, addresses: his arrival in Montana Territory in 1865 with the Métis; his work as a scout and a hunter for the U.S. Army; his involvement in the Nez Perce Campaign in 1877; the Battle of the Bears Paw Mountains.
TYPESCRIPT: 8 PAGES

SC 732
JOSEPH GANS REMINISCENCE
Helena resident Joseph Gans comments on his experiences from 1862 to 1915: his work as a mercantile owner in Helena; investing in cattle operations; his experiences in Montana gold camps; his other business interests.
TYPESCRIPT: 5 PAGES

SC 739
THOMAS SHERRILL AND BUNCH SHERRILL
REMINISCENCES
Thomas Sherrill (1854–1927) and his brother Bunch

Sherrill served as two civilian volunteers accompanying U.S. Army troops in Montana Territory. They discuss, in 1916, their involvement in the Battle of the Big Hole against the Nez Perce Indians in August 1877.
TYPESCRIPT: 33 PAGES

SC 744
STEPHEN C. GILPATRICK AND LUELLA GILPATRICK REMINISCENCES

Stephen Gilpatrick and Luella Gilpatrick were two pioneers in Helena. Luella Gilpatrick describes (1915, revised 1923) her trip across the plains to Montana Territory in 1864. Stephen Gilpatrick recalls (1923) his 1863 steamboat trip up the Missouri River; his experiences as a miner.
TYPESCRIPT: 10 PAGES

SC 757
JAMES S. SMITH REMINISCENCE

James Smith (b. 1844) operated a stamp mill in Cable. He recounts (circa 1916): his 1868 trip to Montana; the problems involved with transporting the stamp mill to Cable in approximately 1870.
TYPESCRIPT: 4 PAGES

SC 762
F. S. GOSS REMINISCENCE

F. S. Goss reviews (circa 1915): his 1862–1865 experiences in Montana Territory; his encounter with the Virginia City sheriff and outlaw Henry Plummer.
TYPESCRIPT: 4 PAGES

SC 811
JEREMIAH SULLIVAN PAPERS

The Fort Benton hotel owner Jeremiah Sullivan (1844–1919) recalls (circa 1916): his 1865 Missouri River trip on the steamboats *Benton* and *Deer Lodge* to Fort Benton; his operation of hotels in Fort Shaw and in Fort Benton. The collection also includes letters (1865–1866) to his family written from the *Deer Lodge* and from Helena, describing his travel to and within the territory.
TYPESCRIPT: 4 PAGES

SC 814
WILLIAM H. HEALY REMINISCENCE

William Healy, in 1916, describes: his experiences since arriving in Montana Territory in 1869; his work as a rancher at Lodge Pole.
TYPESCRIPT: 2 PAGES

SC 949
COLES P. VAN WART REMINISCENCE

Coles Van Wart (b. 1833) tells of (circa 1916): his journey through Panama to San Francisco in 1855; his boat trip up the Fraser River in British Columbia, Canada, circa 1858; his work as a miner in Montana, in the years following 1868.
TYPESCRIPT: 5 PAGES

William Wheeler
Biographies Collection

MC 65
WILLIAM FLETCHER WHEELER PAPERS, 1859–1894

William Wheeler (1824–1894) served as a U.S. marshal and as the Montana Historical Society librarian in Helena. This collection includes: biographical writings—based on interviews and correspondence—addressing experiences of Montana pioneers. The listings below include the date each biography was written and the number of pages in the typed and/or handwritten version. *[Portions of the collection are duplicated on Microfilm 12.]*

Biographies

Baptiste Aeneas, 1885. Typescript: 6 pages; manuscript: 13 pages.

Louis Brown, 1885. Typescript: 2 pages; manuscript: 5 pages.

Joseph Cobell, ca. 1885. Typescript: 4 pages.

Walter W. de Lacy, ca. 1894. Typescript: 14 pages; manuscript: 47 pages.

Robert Dempsey, 1885. Typescript: 8 pages; manuscript: 5 pages.

James Gemmell, 1881. Manuscript: 16 pages.

Caleb Ewing Irvine, 1889. Manuscript: 5 pages.

William Kennedy, 1885. Typescript: 11 pages; manuscript: 41 pages.

Benjamin Keyser, 1889. Typescript: 3 pages; manuscript: 6 pages.

Mortimer H. Lott, 1885. Typescript: 5 pages; manuscript: 19 pages.

George W. Lovell, 1886. Typescript 27 pages; manuscript: 72 pages.

Angus McDonald, 1885. Typescript 4 pages; manuscript: 9 pages.

Eli W. McNeal, 1885. Typescript: 8 pages; manuscript: 31 pages.

Louis R. Maillet, ca. 1885. Manuscript: 80 pages.

Henry H. Mood, 1889. Manuscript: 8 pages.

Joseph O'Neill, 1885. Typescript: 4 pages; manuscript: 21 pages.

William H. Parkinson, 1884. Typescript: 2 pages; manuscript: 7 pages.

Henry Robert, 1884. Typescript: 2 pages; manuscript: 7 pages.

Francis L. Worden, 1885. Typescript: 3 pages; manuscript: 12 pages.

Personal histories of early pioneers of Chouteau County (notebook recording interviews of Charles Mercier, George Weippert, Louis Rivet, Joseph Cobell, Antoine Juneau, and Henry Robert). Typescript: 26 pages; manuscript: 78 pages.

Non-Taped Oral Interviews (transcripts only)

MF 64
JOHN J. HEALY INTERVIEW
John Healy worked as a fur trapper, an Indian trader, a miner, and a newspaper publisher in Montana Territory, in Canada, and in Alaska. He describes: his experiences with Indians; trapping; the conflicts between Indians and whites in 1866.
INTERVIEWED BY FORREST CRISSEY, MAY 2, 1899, CHICAGO, IL.
TRANSCRIPT: 113 PAGES

MF 159a
HAROLD A. LOUCKS AND LOIS MAY LOUCKS INTERVIEW
Harold Loucks and his wife, Lois Loucks, describe: homestead life in Sheridan County from 1909 to 1920; the formation of Sheridan County in 1913; local politics.
INTERVIEWED BY HOMER LOUCKS, DECEMBER 22, 1959, REDSTONE.
TRANSCRIPT: 41 PAGES

MF 159b
WILLIAM ARMINGTON INTERVIEW
William Armington—a rancher in the Malta area—addresses: early ranching in north central Montana; sheep raising; the history of Malta; local cowboys and ranchers from 1902 to 1935.
INTERVIEWED BY HOMER LOUCKS, DECEMBER 1, 1959, MALTA.
TRANSCRIPT: 105 PAGES

SC 105
PATRICIA HARD GROUND AND FANNIE STANDING ELK INTERVIEW
Patricia Hard Ground and Fannie Standing Elk, members of the Northern Cheyenne tribe, recall witnessing the deaths of Head Chief and Young Mule on the Northern Cheyenne Reservation on September 13, 1890.

INTERVIEWED BY MARGOT LIBERTY, NOVEMBER 2, 1957, BIRNEY.
TRANSCRIPT: 4 PAGES

SC 467
META GALLOW MEES INTERVIEW
Meta Mees comments on: her life on a homestead at Blue Creek (near Billings) in the early 1900s; her work on a Carterville dairy farm from 1910 to 1928.
INTERVIEWED BY ESTER JOHANSSON MURRAY, NOVEMBER 26, 1969, CODY, WY.
TRANSCRIPT: 6 PAGES

SC 608
GEORGE REED DAVIS INTERVIEW
George Davis reviews (1896) the circumstances surrounding the death of John Bozeman in 1867.
INTERVIEWED BY AN UNIDENTIFIED MAN, APRIL 21, 1896, FORT LARAMIE, WY.
TRANSCRIPT: 2 PAGES

SC 1252
ADELAIDE DAMPIERE MELTON INTERVIEW
Adelaide Melton—Montana's first state superintendent of music—discusses: teaching music at various Montana high schools; her European travels. [This interview is a component of the Historical Memoirs Project conducted by the Billings chapter of the AAUW.]
INTERVIEWED BY ESTER JOHANSSON MURRAY, APRIL, 1976, CODY, WY.
TRANSCRIPT: 4 PAGES

SC 1283
DORMAN JACKSON INTERVIEW
Dorman Jackson, a rancher in Fergus County, describes: Lewistown-area personalities; central Montana; his family, including his father, George Jackson.

INTERVIEWED BY FRANK W. WILEY, SEPTEMBER, 1968, LEWISTOWN.
TRANSCRIPT: 6 PAGES

SC 1285
FRED "SCOTTY" PALMER INTERVIEW

Scotty Palmer (1875–1969) reflects on events in his life from about 1894 to 1948, including: serving as a cabin boy at sea; mining in Alaska; ranching in Canada; supplying horses to the British; working for the Great Northern Railway in Montana.
INTERVIEWED BY FRANK W. WILEY, FEBRUARY, 1968, HELENA.
TRANSCRIPT: 13 PAGES

SC 1287
CHARLES M. DORSETT INTERVIEW

Charles Dorsett reviews: his work in Pacific Northwest sawmills, slaughter houses, and meat markets; his jobs freighting, ranching, and prospecting.
INTERVIEWED BY FRANK W. WILEY, MAY, 1968, CLARKSTON, WA.
TRANSCRIPT: 4 PAGES

SC 1338
MARY PEACHY COX INTERVIEW

Mary Cox considers life in Miles City during the 1880s and the 1890s.
INTERVIEWED BY FLOYD T. ALDERSEN, 1957, MILES CITY.
TRANSCRIPT: 8 PAGES

SC 1493
JOHN A. "RED" WOLRICH INTERVIEW

The Helena rancher Red Wolrich comments on: his experiences with the area stockman Henry Sieben; his own Lazy B Ranch near Helena; his work in the cattle-ranching business during the 1920s and the 1930s. [See also General Montana OH 621.]
INTERVIEWED BY DICK PACE AND BILL LANG, APRIL 4, 1978, HELENA.
TRANSCRIPT: 17 PAGES

SC 1510
EUGENE EDWARD WILSON INTERVIEWS

The former Helena resident Eugene Wilson (1887–1974) details: his career as a U.S. Navy officer and aviator; his employment, after retirement, as an officer and a director of several aviation companies.
INTERVIEWED BY COLUMBIA UNIVERSITY ORAL HISTORY PROGRAM, AUGUST-OCTOBER, 1962, ESSEX, CT.
TRANSCRIPT: 898 PAGES

SC 1512
WESLEY A. D'EWART INTERVIEW

Wesley D'Ewart speaks of: his success as a rancher near Wilsall during the 1920s drought and the 1930s Depression; his service as a Montana legislator; his terms as a U.S. Congressman (1945–1955); his work in the U.S. Departments of Agriculture and Interior during the second Eisenhower administration.
INTERVIEWED BY ROY HUFFMAN AND JEFF SAFFORD, JUNE 16 AND OCTOBER 19, 1972, WILSALL.
TRANSCRIPT: 39 PAGES

SC 1513
SAMUEL S. MACLAY AND DAVID J. MACLAY INTERVIEWS

Samuel Maclay and his brother David Maclay—ranchers near Lolo—discuss: ranching and farming during the 1920s drought and the 1930s Depression; cattle rustling; the relationship of the banking business to ranching.
INTERVIEWED BY K. ROSS TOOLE AND JEFF SAFFORD, JUNE 26 AND 28, 1972, LOLO.
TRANSCRIPT: 44 PAGES

SC 1514
ARTHUR R. DESCHAMPS, SR., INTERVIEW

Arthur Deschamps depicts: his successful hay and cattle operation at Grass Valley, west of Missoula, from 1900 into the 1940s; his family's farm-implement and meat-processing businesses.
INTERVIEWED BY JEFF SAFFORD, JULY 17, 1972, MISSOULA.
TRANSCRIPT: 25 PAGES

SC 1515
ERWIN MILLER AND LILLIAN MILLER WESTIN INTERVIEW

Erwin Miller and Lillian Westin—retired Chinook area ranchers—comment on: the Miller Brothers, Incorporated, ranch, one of the largest sheep ranches in the early 1900s and later a substantial cattle operation; the sale of the ranch to Wellington D. Rankin in 1958.
INTERVIEWED BY JEFF SAFFORD, OCTOBER 21, 1972, CHINOOK.
TRANSCRIPT: 36 PAGES

SC 1516

WILLIAM DAVIES INTERVIEW

William Davies recalls: working on the Thomas C. Power ranches; his employment on the J. L. Sprinkle ranches; his experiences as a lessee and as a ranch owner.

INTERVIEWED BY JEFF SAFFORD, OCTOBER 21, 1972, CHINOOK.

TRANSCRIPT: 27 PAGES

SC 1517

CHAUNCEY FLYNN INTERVIEW

Chauncey Flynn discusses: the failure of Montana homesteaders; the growth of the modern cattle industry; his experiences as an aircraft pilot.

INTERVIEWED BY JEFF SAFFORD, OCTOBER 21, 1972, CHINOOK.

TRANSCRIPT: 25 PAGES

SC 1518

JAMES McCANN INTERVIEW

North central Montana rancher James McCann describes: his two ranches, one in the Bears Paw Mountains and the other near Harlem; his relationships with the Montana Stockgrowers Association, with the Montana Agricultural Extension Service, and with the Montana Woolgrowers Association; his involvement with the Milk River Production Credit Association and with the Blaine County Commission.

INTERVIEWED BY JEFF SAFFORD, OCTOBER 21, 1972, CHINOOK.

TRANSCRIPT: 28 PAGES

SC 1519

HARRY L. BURNS INTERVIEW

The Chinook lawyer and ranch owner Harry Burns considers: his youth on his parents' homestead, circa 1910–1920; his years teaching at the Logie School, in Blaine County; his work as an irrigation lawyer after World War II.

INTERVIEWED BY JEFF SAFFORD, OCTOBER 21, 1972, CHINOOK.

TRANSCRIPT: 11 PAGES

SC 1520

MURDOCK MATHESON INTERVIEW

Murdock Matheson describes: his move from Canada to Chinook with his parents in 1890; the development of his ranch near Chinook from a small homestead into a large livestock operation; drought conditions, circa 1910–1920; problems with alkali soil; methods of training horses.

INTERVIEWED BY JEFF SAFFORD AND TOM ROSS, OCTOBER 22, 1972, CHINOOK.

TRANSCRIPT: 32 PAGES

SC 1521

RALPH MIRACLE INTERVIEW

Ralph Miracle (b. 1904)—a retired rancher, a member of the Montana Livestock Commission, and the executive secretary of the Montana Stockgrowers Association—summarizes: the development of the cattle industry in Montana from 1900 to 1970; geographical differences in the Montana industry; transportation and marketing problems; state and federal government involvement in the industry; state politics. [See also General Montana OH 13.]

INTERVIEWED BY JEFF SAFFORD, NOVEMBER 6, 1972, HELENA.

TRANSCRIPT: 24 PAGES

SC 1526

ROLAND R. RENNE INTERVIEW

Roland Renne served as the president of Montana State University in Bozeman (1943–1964) and as the assistant secretary of the U.S. Department of Agriculture under Presidents John Kennedy and Lyndon Johnson in the 1960s. He talks about the critical transitions that have occurred in the Montana agriculture and livestock-raising industries from the 1930s to 1975.

INTERVIEWED BY JEFF SAFFORD AND MIKE MALONE, JULY 8, 1975, BOZEMAN.

TRANSCRIPT: 19 PAGES

SC 1663

MARGARET SIEBEN HIBBARD INTERVIEW

Margaret Hibbard, a Helena resident, reviews: her collection of historical vehicles, including the "Copper King" Marcus Daly's show buggy, Frank S. Lusk's Landau carriage, and Charles A. Broadwater's sleigh; her discovery and purchase of the trap (carriage) once owned by Lillie Aston, the first madam of "The Castle"; prostitution in Helena. [See also General Montana OH 989.]

INTERVIEWED BY JAMES DION, DECEMBER, 1968, HELENA.

TRANSCRIPT: 6 PAGES

SC 1774
NATIONAL EXTENSION-HOMEMAKERS
COUNCIL INTERVIEWS
   Eight interviewees discuss their local Extension
Homemakers clubs and the ideas that they acquired from
club programs: Lora Foster of Portage; Marie Carlile of
Smith River; Daisy Taylor of Prairie Elk; Myra Daniel
and Lillie Badgley of Gallatin Gateway; Pearl Herndon
of Miles City; Louella Hardie of Birdseye; Elsie Rieger
of Clinton.
INTERVIEWED BY NATIONAL EXTENSION HOMEMAKERS
COUNCIL, 1981–1982, VARIOUS MONTANA LOCATIONS.
7 TRANSCRIPTS: 78 PAGES

SC 1992
RAYMOND LUCIER INTERVIEW
   Raymond Lucier (b. 1906) describes: ox teams and
20-horse teams arriving at the Hilger railhead; several
Missouri River ferries; the cattle-raising experiences of
his father, Peter Lucier.
INTERVIEWED BY CURTIS LUCIER, 1983, HILGER.
TRANSCRIPT: 4 PAGES

SC 1993
EMILY WILLIAMS SMITH INTERVIEW
   Emily Smith chronicles her childhood, spent living
at the Yellowstone County Poor Farm, where her father,
Elias Newston Williams, served as superintendent.
INTERVIEWED BY ESTER JOHANNSON MURRAY, JANUARY 3,
1990, BILLINGS.
TRANSCRIPT: 8 PAGES

Index of Interviewees

The following is an index of the people who gave the interviews that are described in this guide. The first number after an index entry is the page on which you can find the oral history summary; the number after the hyphen is the oral history or collection number itself. MC, SC, MF, or MM precede references to Manuscript Collections, Small Collections, Microfilm Collections, or Multimedia Collections; no letter abbreviations precede oral history numbers in the index (see page vii for further explanation on abbreviations.)

People who gave interviews (interviewees) may also have been the subject of other oral histories; for example, a woman might have been interviewed and have been a topic of her husband's oral history. Only the woman's interview would be referenced in the Index of Interviewees. *To find the interviews in which an individual was discussed, you must check the Subject Index.*

Subject Index

The following index references topics that are included in the oral histories themselves but that may not have been included in the summaries published in this guide. Thus, more people, places, and topics are listed below than may be mentioned in an entry's summary.

The first number after an index entry is the page on which you can find the oral history summary; the number following in parentheses is the oral history or collection number itself. MC, SC, MF, or MM precede references to Manuscript Collections, Small Manuscript Collections, Microfilm Collections, or Multimedia Collections; no letter abbreviations precede oral history numbers in the index (see page vii for further explanation on abbreviations.)

Interviewees are not included in this index unless they were also the subject of someone else's interview. *You must check the Index of Interviewees to find a specific individual's interview.* The towns in which particular businesses operated have been placed in parentheses after the business name to help with identification. All places are in Montana unless stated otherwise.

A

AAA. *See* United States Agricultural Adjustment Administration

AAUW. *See* American Association of University Women

A. J. Oliver and Company (Virginia City), 53 (355)

A. M. Holter Hardware Company (Helena), 181 (625)

Aberdeen-Angus cattle, 77 (660)

abortion, 21 (1348), 22 (1511), 115 (827)

Absaroka Indians. *See* Crow Indians

Absaroka National Forest, 66 (465)

Absaroka primitive area, 215 (1593)

Absorkee, 56 (376), 218 (1621)

Acton Funeral Home (Roundup), 45 (278)

Adair, Hugh Rogers, 162 (105)

Adel Ranch (Lewis and Clark County), 181 (621)

Aeneas, Baptiste, 235 (MC65)

aeronautics, 157 (69), 161 (101), 162 (104)

AFL-CIO, 50 (322), 159 (85), 198 (1409), 199 (1410, 1411)

African Americans, 27 (934), 60 (411, 412), 61 (417), 68 (483), 131 (1278), 132 (1279), 144 (1044), 145 (1545); education, 165 (124), 196 (1388); soldiers, 214 (1582)

Agricultural Adjustment Administration. *See* United States Agricultural Adjustment Administration

Agricultural College of the State of Montana (Bozeman) (1893–1913), 212 (1563)

agricultural experiment stations, 64 (445)

agricultural implements, 41 (247); trade and manufacture of, 35 (193), 41 (246), 59 (403), 98 (1168), 109 (773), 116 (837), 122 (885), 237 (SC1514)

agricultural laborers, 54 (362), 62 (427, 432), 110 (781), 112 (800), 183 (634). *See also* migrant workers

agricultural laws and legislation, 177 (589)

agricultural organizations and associations, 36 (197), 42 (249), 43 (259), 47 (296, 297), 49 (315), 71 (504), 73 (521), 77 (660), 110 (782, 788), 141 (1021), 159 (82, 83), 162 (108), 163 (114), 177 (591), 179 (611), 186 (697), 224 (1730), 238 (SC1518). *See also* Montana Farmer's Union; Montana Stockgrowers Association

agriculture, 119 (859), 135 (1526), 159 (82), 177 (589); aerial spraying and, 69 (493); in Baker, 51 (330); in Beaverhead County, 53 (354), 57 (387, 388), 172 (553), 175 (576), 182 (633); in Big Horn County, 49 (314), 52 (341, 342, 343, 344, 346), 53 (349), 56 (382), 57 (385), 71 (509), 72 (517), 75 (544); in the Bitterroot River Valley, 61 (422, 423), 62 (429), 203 (1444, 1445, 1447); in Blaine County, 47 (294, 295, 296, 299), 76 (548), 111 (794, 795); in Broadus, 122 (883); in Carbon County, 54 (362), 56 (375), 72 (513); in Cascade County, 44 (274), 61 (419); in Chinook, 47 (294, 296, 299), 111 (794, 795), 159 (82), 238 (SC1520); in Chouteau County, 44 (274), 79 (672), 106 (750), 108 (764, 768); in Custer County, 39 (226), 70 (502), 71 (503, 504), 72 (517), 75 (544), 93 (1131), 94 (1139); in Daniels County, 79 (672); in Fallon County, 51 (330, 331, 332, 333, 335, 336, 337), 172 (505); in Fergus County, 40 (233), 42 (253), 43 (258), 44 (271), 69 (488); in Flathead County, 50 (324), 79 (678), 103 (725); in Gallatin County, 39 (227), 74 (532); in Garfield County, 36 (200), 49 (311), 57 (384), 66 (464), 70 (502), 72 (519); in Glendive, 194 (1284); in Golden Valley County, 42 (249), 70 (501); in Granite County, 66 (462), 105 (739); in Hill County, 35 (189), 39 (227), 69 (492, 493), 187 (987); in Jefferson County, 66 (464), 74 (537); in Judith Basin County, 42 (249, 251, 255), 69 (490); in Lewis and Clark County, 36 (197), 65 (455), 78 (669); in Liberty County, 75 (544); in Madison County, 56 (381), 57 (388); in Meagher County, 43 (259, 260, 261), 49 (315), 53 (350); in McCone County, 37 (207, 208, 209); in Miles City, 94 (1137); in Mineral County, 63 (442), 67 (472); in Missoula County, 58 (397), 153 (39), 196 (1384), 237 (SC1514); in Musselshell County, 42 (252); in Pablo, 209 (1519); in Park County, 57 (389), 58 (395); in Phillips County, 42 (256), 46 (285), 71 (506), 72 (518), 151 (26), 157 (73), 210 (1546); in Plentywood, 121 (879); in Pondera County, 53 (351), 79 (673); in

E

Earls' Bar (Black Eagle), 33 (981)

East Glacier, 173 (562); social life and customs, 30 (961), 31 (962), 65 (457)

East Helena, 24 (912), 26 (927, 928, 930), 27 (931, 932), 29 (950), 31 (965), 32 (972), 33 (983), 200 (1421); commerce, 30 (961), 65 (453, 456); education, 33 (985); industries, 24 (911, 912), 25 (921, 922), 26 (927, 928, 929, 930), 27 (931, 932), 28 (944), 29 (950), 30 (961), 31 (962, 965), 32 (971), 33 (982, 983, 984, 985), 65 (455, 456, 457), 199 (1410); religious life and customs, 25 (922); social life and customs, 32 (973), 65 (456), 66 (466)

Eck, Dorothy, 163 (114)

Eddy, John R., 179 (610)

Edgar, 178 (601)

Edgerton, Mary Wright, 173 (556)

Edgerton, Sidney, 151 (27)

education: in Beaverhead County, 57 (388); in Big Horn County, 52 (341), 81 (1226), 82 (1232), 93 (1126, 1127); in Blaine County, 112 (804), 113 (805, 806), 238 (SC1519); in Broadwater County, 178 (600); in Carbon County, 54 (363), 204 (1478), 205 (1481, 1485, 1486), 206 (1487); in Daniels County, 101 (708); in Fergus County, 143 (1029); in Flathead County, 102 (721), 104 (731, 733, 735); in Gallatin County, 70 (500), 80 (680), 179 (608); in Garfield County, 66 (464); in Glacier County, 115 (823, 826); in Golden Valley County, 70 (501); in Granite County, 50 (319), 105 (739, 740); in Jefferson County, 66 (464), 184 (647); in Judith Basin County, 113 (806); in Lake County, 113 (806), 209 (1518); in Lewis and Clark County, 26 (928), 33 (985), 143 (1036); in Lincoln County, 53 (352), 78 (665), 101 (708, 709), 102 (717), 124 (1385), 170 (162), 184 (684), 185 (691), 198 (1404, 1405); in Madison County, 15 (1306), 184 (649); in Mineral County, 63 (439); in Missoula County, 40 (232), 58 (393), 82 (1237), 191 (1212), 212 (1563); in Musselshell County, 113 (809), 114 (815); in Powder River County, 112 (884, 888), 123 (893, 894); in Prairie County, 78 (667); in Ravalli County, 61 (423, 424); in Richland County, 110 (782), 111 (790); in Rosebud County, 101 (708), 118 (848); in Sanders County, 50 (319), 118 (852, 855, 856), 119 (857, 862, 863); in Sheridan County, 120 (867, 871); in Stillwater County, 54 (363), 55 (370, 371); in Teton County, 79 (672), 106 (749), 107 (755, 759), 108 (766); in Treasure County, 62 (432); in Valley County, 54 (363), 60 (410); vocational, 47 (294). See also African Americans; schools; teachers; Indians of North America, education; under specific school names; under specific professions

Egly, 34 (187)

electric utilities, 67 (471), 185 (693)

electrical engineering, 23 (907), 84 (1054)

Elkhorn, 39 (224), 151 (24), 176 (582)

emergency medical services, 17 (1317, 1318, 1319, 1321), 18 (1324, 1327, 1329, 1330), 19 (1331, 1335), 20 (1340), 21 (1342, 1345), 22 (1351), 195 (1320). See also airplane ambulances; ambulance services

Emergency Medical Technicians, 17 (1318, 1321), 20 (1340). See also emergency medical services

emigration and immigration, 34 (183), 36 (198), 37 (213), 39 (221, 224, 228), 44 (271), 46 (290), 52 (340), 53 (453), 55 (469), 141 (1014), 176 (582), 177 (593), 178 (604), 179 (609), 198 (1406, 1409), 199 (1411), 214 (1588)

Emory, 67 (474)

Enterprise Lumber Company (Flathead Valley), 38 (219)

environmental policy, state, 163 (110, 115), 164 (118), 165 (124), 166 (134), 172 (180), 210 (1548)

epidemics, 19 (1335), 54 (363), 55 (368), 69 (486), 100 (704), 142 (1028), 179 (605), 191 (1209). See also Spanish Influenza Epidemic (1918)

Episcopal Church, 142 (1028)

Equal Rights Amendment (ERA), 140 (1012), 143 (1036)

Etchart family (Glasgow), 163 (113)

Etchart Ranch (Valley County), 59 (400)

Ethnic History Symposium: (Butte, 1975), 150 (15); (Glendive, 1974), 150 (16)

Eureka, 185 (691), 197 (1398); commerce, 100 (702), 101 (712), 102 (714, 718), 109 (776), 124 (1194, 1386), 185 (689, 690); education, 101 (708), 124 (1385); industries, 38 (221), 78 (670), 101 (707); medical care, 101 (704), 109 (776), 124 (1194, 1385); politics and government, 100 (705), 124 (1385, 1386); social life and customs, 100 (701, 702, 703, 705, 706), 101 (709, 711, 713), 102 (715, 716, 717), 109 (775, 776), 124 (1194, 1386), 184 (684), 185 (688)

Eureka Lumber Company (Eureka), 38 (221), 78 (670)

F

Faddis-Spear Cattle Company (Big Horn County), 56 (382)

Fairfield, 142 (1026), 143 (1032)

Fallan, Ole, 35 (195)

Fallon County: agriculture, 51 (330, 331, 332, 333, 335, 336, 337), 71 (505); cattle raising, 51 (332, 337), 93 (1126); social life and customs, 51 (331)

Farell, H. G., 162 (105)

farm cooperatives. See agricultural organizations and associations

Farm Security Administration (FSA). See United States Farm Security Administration

Farmer-Labor Party, 121 (876)

farmers' organizations. See agricultural organizations and associations

Farmington, 106 (753), 108 (770)

farms and farming. See agriculture

Fay's Electric Shop (Columbia Falls), 30 (959)

Fechin, Nicolai Ivanovich, 168 (151)

Federal Bureau of Investigation (FBI). See United States Federal Bureau of Investigation

feminism, 139 (1004), 142 (1022)

Fergus County, 210 (1544); agriculture, 40 (233), 42 (253), 43 (258), 44 (271), 69 (488); cattle raising, 156 (66); education, 143 (1029); medical care, 16 (1316), 19 (1332, 1334, 1335, 1336), 142 (1024); social life and customs, 40 (233)

ferries, 170 (168, 169), 171 (171, 175). See also steamboats

Fewkes General Store (Rexford), 101 (710)

Finnish Americans, 42 (251), 48 (302, 303), 54 (357, 359), 55 (365), 78 (664), 150 (15), 215 (1600)

fire departments, 91 (1110), 98 (1170), 175 (578); volunteer, 24 (912), 103 (722, 724), 119 (858), 123 (890), 140 (1010). See also fire fighting, forest; smokejumpers

fire fighting, forest, 57 (391), 58 (399), 77 (662), 90 (1104), 91 (1107, 1109, 1110, 1113), 98 (1170), 185 (687), 186 (695), 219 (1624, 1625), 225 (1750). See also forest fires; smokejumpers

First Bank of Forsyth, 117 (839)

First County Creamery (Lewistown), 203 (1450)

First National Bank of Nashua (Nashua), 46 (289)

First National Bank of Plains (Plains), 118 (856), 119 (859, 861)

fish hatcheries, 217 (1610, 1611, 1612)

fishing, 90 (1104), 184 (646), 189 (1047), 216 (1606, 1607), 217 (1608, 1609, 1612, 1613, 1614), 218 (1616, 1617, 1618, 1619)

Fishtail, 55 (373), 84 (1152)

Fisk Expedition (1864), 232 (SC530), 233 (SC696); (1866), 231 (SC449), 232 (SC530, SC624)

Flaten's Dress Shop (Fort Peck), 90 (1101)

Flathead Cherry Growers Association, 186 (697)

Flathead County, 30 (959), 50 (324), 79 (678), 103 (722, 725), 195 (1299); agriculture, 50 (324), 103 (725), 186 (697); education, 102 (721), 104 (731, 733, 735); industries, 34 (184, 185), 35 (191), 38 (219), 103 (724), 186 (697); lumber trade, 29 (951), 34 (184, 185), 35 (191), 38 (217, 218, 219, 220, 221), 43 (262, 263, 264), 50 (321, 323, 325, 327), 51 (329), 79 (677), 102 (720), 104 (729), 169 (156), 174 (570); medical care, 20 (1340), 21 (1348). See also Flathead National Forest; Flathead Valley

Flathead Indian Reservation, 43 (262, 264, 265), 61 (420), 83 (1238, 1240), 160 (93), 209 (1519), 211 (1553). See also Confederated Salish-Kootenai tribes; Salish Indians

Flathead Indians. See Salish Indians

Flathead Lake, 50 (327), 216 (1607); medical care, 21 (1348)

Flathead National Forest, 194 (1290), 195 (1354)

170 (164), 197 (1398)

Jackson, George, 236 (SC1283)

Jackson, John G., 109 (772)

Japan, 132 (1453), 135 (1522)

Japanese Americans, 59 (402), 74 (531), 75 (538), 113 (809), 150 (15)

Jardine, 56 (378)

Jefferson County: agriculture, 66 (464), 74 (537); cattle raising, 159 (83); education, 66 (464), 184 (647); mines and mining, 184 (648)

Jennings, 170 (165)

jewelry trade, 53 (355), 103 (728)

Jewish Americans, 161 (98), 180 (615), 216 (1604)

John Birch Society, 110 (788), 164 (119)

Johnson, E. L., 118 (854)

Johnson's Cafe (Kalispell), 38 (217)

Jordan, 72 (520), 92 (1124)

Jordan, A. L., 73 (559), 102 (720)

Joseph Cafe, the (Forsyth), 117 (842)

journalism, 44 (272), 60 (408), 114 (815), 158 (81), 163 (114), 182 (630), 211 (1553), 231 (SC380). *See also* journalists; newspapers

journalists, 40 (232), 60 (413), 61 (425), 104 (735), 112 (799), 113 (812), 116 (831), 134 (1471), 137 (1564, 1566), 140 (1012), 152 (33), 187 (902). *See also* journalism; newspapers

Judge, Thomas L., 137 (1599), 163 (110, 115), 164 (117, 120), 177 (589, 591)

judges, 113 (807), 188 (998)

Judith Basin County, 42 (251), 49 (312), 166 (135); agriculture, 42 (249, 251, 255), 69 (490); education, 113 (806); medical care, 69 (489); social life and customs, 126 (1208)

Judith Gap, 132 (1376), 196 (1380)

Juneau, Antoine, 235 (MC65)

Jurcichs' Grocery Store (Anaconda), 32 (975)

K

KBLL (Helena), 155 (57), 158 (78)

KBMN (Bozeman), 158 (75)

KPWD-FM (Plentywood), 121 (880)

KSEN (Shelby), 158 (79)

KSEN Radio Broadcasts (1964), 158 (79)

Kaasch, Beatrice, 14 (1300)

Kaiser Hotel (Philipsburg), 104 (737)

Kalispell: commerce, 38 (217), 50 (323, 326), 51 (328), 79 (678), 190 (1193); industries, 38 (221), 50 (321); medical care, 20 (1340); social life and customs, 50 (324, 326), 51 (328), 79 (678), 129 (1259), 130 (1265), 140 (1011), 141 (1013)

Kalispell Lumber Company (Kalispell), 38 (221), 50 (321)

Kalispell Mercantile Company (Kalispell), 50 (326), 51 (328)

Kalispell Women's Center (Kalispell), 140 (1011)

Kallio's Bathhouse (Red Lodge), 54 (357)

Kanduch, Joe, 60 (415)

Karkanen, Hazel Beadle, 55 (367), 58 (392)

Karkanen Public Library (Milltown), 58 (392)

Karst Camp (Gallatin County), 194 (1291)

Karst, Pete, 194 (1291)

Kathan, A. E., 162 (105)

Keith, McCarty, 16 (1312)

Kelly Mine (Butte), 79 (674)

Kennedy, William, 235 (MC65)

Kent State University (Ohio), 153 (45)

Kerr Dam (Lake County), 91 (1112), 209 (1519), 211 (1553)

Kevin, 65 (459)

Kevin-Sunburst Oil Field (Toole County), 63 (436), 64 (450), 65 (459)

Keyser, Benjamin, 235 (MC65)

Keystone Mine (Broadwater County), 177 (595)

Kid Curry. *See* Logan, Harvey

King, Fred, 101 (707, 712)

King's X Bar (Anaconda), 27 (938)

Kinsey, 95 (1144, 1146)

Kinsey Irrigation Project (Custer), 71 (504)

Kip Lake, 218 (1619)

Kirch, Ann, 177 (593)

Kirch, Lewis, 177 (593)

Kitzenberg's Store (Plentywood), 60 (409)

Klaxton, John K., 162 (105)

Kleffner Ranch (East Helena), 27 (931)

Klein, 45 (279, 280), 65 (453), 114 (816)

Knees, 187 (986)

Knoop, Walter A., 109 (779)

Kohrs, Augusta, 186 (698)

Kohrs, Conrad, 186 (698)

Kootenai Lineage (Readers Theater), 172 (181)

Kootenai National Forest (Montana and Idaho), 61 (421), 160 (92), 169 (154), 215 (1595)

Kootenai River (Montana and British Columbia), 168 (153)

Kootenai Seminar (Libby, 1977–1979), 171 (178, 179), 172 (180)

Korean War (1950–1953): personal narratives, 131 (1273, 1275), 136 (1530, 1532, 1535), 161 (101)

Korell Grocery (Utica), 49 (312)

Korell's Guest Ranch (Judith Basin County), 49 (312)

Ksanka Lumber Company (Eureka), 101 (708)

Ku Klux Klan, 51 (328), 113 (812, 813)

L

La Pierre, Louis, 153 (39)

labor relations, 26 (929), 38 (221), 50 (322), 79 (674), 148 (1). *See* also unions

Lafavre, John, 164 (118)

Lake County, 91 (1112), 209 (1519), 211 (1553); education, 113 (806), 209 (1518); politics and government, 20 (1511)

Lake McDonald (Glacier National Park), 174 (565), 221 (1643)

Lakeview, 162 (103)

Lalonde, Jay, 111 (791)

Lame Deer, 22 (1352), 93 (1132), 95 (1147), 167 (141)

Lanart, 138 (1648)

landless Indians, 30 (954), 75 (542, 543), 107 (757). *See also* Chippewa Indians, Cree Indians

Landusky, Pike, 179 (607)

Latter Day Saints, Church of Jesus Christ of, 145 (1545), 212 (1558)

Laurel, 72 (512), 88 (1082), 200 (1417), 216 (1602)

Lavina, 70 (501); industries, 149 (6); politics and government, 149 (6)

law enforcement, 28 (945), 64 (446), 107 (761), 115 (825), 122 (887), 123 (896), 153 (42), 155 (58), 156 (66)

lawyers, 27 (936), 113 (807), 115 (824), 121 (877), 188 (998)

Lazy E 4 Ranch (Beaverhead County), 163 (116)

Lazy E L Ranch (Carbon County), 164 (122)

League of Women Voters of Montana, 140 (1006), 142 (1022), 143 (1036), 163 (115), 193 (1281), 224 (1730)

Leavens, Robert, 149 (7)

Leavitt, Scott, 58 (399)

Lebanese Americans, 200 (1420)

Lee Enterprises (Helena), 158 (81), 211 (1553)

legislators, 36 (200), 148 (5), 153 (41), 159 (87), 163 (115, 116), 164 (117, 118, 119, 120, 122), 181 (626), 182 (628, 629), 212 (1559). *See also* Montana Legislature

Leh, Clark, 75 (539)

Lehigh, 42 (257), 68 (489)

Leonard Mine (Butte), 67 (472)

Leonard's Barber Shop (Eureka), 102 (718)

Leslie, Preston H., 181 (623)

Lewis and Clark Caverns State Park, 189 (1190)

Lewis and Clark County, 34 (186); agriculture, 36 (197), 65 (455), 78 (669); cattle raising, 27 (931), 36 (197), 77 (660), 78 (669), 152 (36), 159 (84), 181 (621), 237 (SC1493); education, 26 (928), 33 (985), 143 (1036); medical care, 16 (1310, 1314), 21 (1342), 181 (622), 187 (989); industries, 40 (236); mines and mining, 11 (1181), 29 (950), 33 (982), 40 (236, 237), 65 (458), 79 (675), 151 (24), 197 (1399), 200 (1421), 231 (SC419, SC449), 232 (SC560), 233 (SC673), 234 (SC949)

Lewis and Clark Expedition (1804–1806), 157 (71), 160 (91, 92, 94), 162 (109)

Lewis and Clark National Historic Trail, 160 (89), 162 (109)

Lewis and Clark Trail Heritage Foundation, 160 (91)

Lewistown, 97 (1157), 154 (50), 203 (1450); clubs, 143 (1029, 1031); education, 143 (1029); medical care, 19 (1332, 1334, 1335, 1336), 142 (1024); social life and customs, 14 (1300), 236 (SC1283)

Libby, 18 (1329), 91 (1111), 92 (1123), 168 (152, 153), 169 (159), 170 (161, 162), 171 (179), 198 (1405), 212 (1560), 213 (1571, 1573, 1575, 1576); commerce, 153 (40), 170 (163), 171 (170, 177), 172 (180, 181); industries, 170 (166); lumber trade, 77 (657, 661), 78 (666), 101 (712), 169 (154, 159), 170 (164), 197 (1398); religious life and customs, 198 (1406), 204 (1475)

St. Luke's Community Hospital (Ronan), 22 (1428)
St. Mary, 169 (157), 173 (560)
St. Peter's Hospital (Helena), 15 (1309), 16 (1310, 1313), 19 (1335), 187 (989)
St. Regis, 64 (444), 79 (672)
St. Richard's Catholic Church (Columbia Falls), 103 (726)
Standard Oil Company, 66 (463), 186 (699)
State Bank and Trust Company (Dillon), 212 (1561)
steamboats, 34 (186), 51 (329), 78 (669), 230 (SC283), 234 (SC811)
steelworkers union. *See* United Steelworkers of America
Stevenson, Branson Graves, 182 (627), 202 (1434, 1441)
Stevensville, 148 (4), 206 (1488); clubs, 143 (1033)
Stillwater County, 55 (370); agriculture, 47 (294), 55 (369, 371, 372, 373), 56 (374, 377), 58 (394), 72 (515); cattle raising, 56 (377); education, 54 (363), 55 (370, 371); mines and mining, 56 (379), 58 (394); social life and customs, 55 (371)
Stockett, 66 (468); industries, 39 (222)
Stoltz Lumber Company (Columbia Falls), 104 (729)
stonemasons, 176 (584, 585, 586)
strikes and lockouts, 25 (919, 923, 924), 26 (925), 33 (983), 67 (472), 79 (674), 99 (1410, 1411, 1412, 1414, 1416), 198 (1409), 200 (1417, 1418, 1423)
Sts. Cyril and Methodius Catholic Church (East Helena), 27 (931), 31 (962), 33 (984, 985)
Stuart, Granville, 156 (66)
sugar beet industry, 47 (297), 49 (310), 62 (427, 430, 432), 71 (504), 72 (513), 109 (779), 110 (781, 782, 787), 111 (793, 795)
Sula, 189 (1050)
Summers, Naomi, 20 (1340)
Sun River, 32 (978)
Superior, 62 (432), 63 (440)
Superior Ranger District, 215 (1597)
surveyors, 86 (1067)
Swanhand Cattle Company (Wyoming), 36 (198)
Swedish Americans, 25 (920), 27 (938), 39 (228), 68 (477), 178 (604)
Sweet Grass County: agriculture, 56 (380)
Sweetgrass Hills, 193 (1282), 216 (1603)
Swims Under, Maggie, 153 (37)
swine breeding, 27 (931)
sylvanite, 167 (167), 184 (683)

T

T. C. Power and Brother Company, 214 (1588)
T. C. Power Ranch, 238 (SC1516)
taverns, 27 (938), 28 (941), 33 (981), 35 (196), 45 (284), 65 (453, 457), 75 (546), 87 (1077), 110 (783), 111 (796), 113 (810, 811), 120 (870), 123 (896), 175 (579), 176 (581), 195 (1296)
Taylor, Charles, 60 (408), 121 (879)

Taylor, Fred, 19 (1333)
Taylor Garage (Choteau), 106 (752)
Taylor Grazing Act. *See* United States Taylor Grazing Act
Taylor, Leroy E., 106 (752)
teachers, 26 (928), 34 (187), 35 (193), 36 (204), 37 (205, 208), 39 (229), 40 (232), 46 (287, 291), 47 (294, 295), 50 (319, 324), 52 (341), 53 (348, 352, 363), 55 (370), 57 (388, 390), 58 (392, 393), 59 (405, 406), 60 (410), 61 (424), 62 (432), 63 (439), 65 (452), 66 (464, 466), 69 (491), 70 (498), 72 (511, 519), 77 (665), 79 (672), 81 (1227, 1228, 1230), 82 (1231, 1232, 1233), 83 (1239), 96 (1153), 101 (708, 709), 102 (717, 721), 105 (740), 107 (758, 759), 108 (766), 109 (775), 111 (790), 113 (806, 809), 114 (815), 115 (823, 826), 118 (848, 855, 856), 119 (863), 120 (871), 122 (888), 123 (894), 126 (1220), 139 (1002), 141 (1016), 142 (1023, 1028), 144 (1041), 172 (551), 175 (571), 177 (594), 178 (601), 179 (612), 184 (685), 191 (1212), 196 (1379, 1380), 198 (1405), 205 (1482), 206 (1494), 208 (1509), 209 (1517), 213 (1571, 1575), 214 (1588), 216 (1603), 236 (SC1252), 238 (SC1519); unions, 60 (410)
Tee Bar Ranch (Augusta), 159 (84)
telegraphers, 73 (528), 169 (158), 175 (574), 178 (599)
telephone operators, 45 (283), 79 (675), 88 (1081), 97 (1156), 103 (725), 113 (808), 120 (872), 175 (577), 192 (1215)
television broadcasting, 93 (1129), 160 (90), 165 (130)
Templeton, Payne, 162 (105)
Ten Lakes Scenic Area, 185 (691)
Tesch Implement Company (Choteau), 109 (773)
Testlig, Sophia, 204 (1476)
Teton County, 143 (1032); agriculture, 32 (978), 34 (183), 39 (223), 40 (234), 106 (750), 107 (758), 108 (764, 768, 769); cattle raising, 39 (223), 106 (748), 107 (755), 108 (769); education, 79 (672), 106 (749), 107 (755, 759), 108 (766); medical care, 106 (762, 763), 107 (755); politics and government, 108 (768); social life and customs, 108 (766). *See also* Choteau
Teton County Council on Aging, 143 (1032)
Teton County Shipping Association, 108 (768)
Teton Nursing Home (Choteau), 108 (763)
Teton Steam Laundry (Choteau), 109 (772)
Tewey, Dan, 67 (475)
theater, amateur, 178 (602)
theaters, 62 (432), 75 (546), 100 (705), 105 (743), 106 (754), 112 (797)
Thompson, Emma, 106 (751)
Thompson Falls, 49 (318), 91 (1114), 218 (1621), 219 (1624), 221 (1639); industries, 49 (316, 317), 50 (320), 77 (658)
Thompson Falls Lumber Company (Thompson Falls), 49 (316)
Thorkelson, Jacob, 162 (105)
Three Calves (Blackfeet), 154 (48)
timber trade. *See* lumber trade
title companies, 75 (545)

Titter, Herb, 172 (182)
Tobacco Plains, 169 (160)
Tobacco Valley, 101 (707), 209 (1536, 1537), 210 (1538, 1539); agriculture, 100 (703)
Tobacco Valley Improvement Association, 101 (710), 102 (717)
Toggery, the (Sidney), 110 (784)
Tolan, Providencia, 145 (1545)
Tongue River Valley (Wyoming and Montana), 71 (507)
Tonrey-Baxter Orchestra (Dillon), 175 (572), 212 (1561)
Toole County, 65 (452), 158 (79); agriculture, 39 (228), 63 (434, 435), 64 (448, 449); cattle raising, 64 (449); industries, 63 (435, 436), 64 (450, 451), 65 (459)
Toole, Joseph K., 211 (1554)
Toole, Kenneth Ross, 150 (17), 153 (45), 159 (86), 165 (124), 181 (624), 197 (1389, 1390), 212 (1563)
Topping, Thomas, 152 (35)
Toston, 178 (599)
tourism, 122 (885). *See also* dude ranches; Glacier National Park, commerce; Yellowstone National Park, commerce
Towey Hotel (Butte), 37 (213)
Townsend, 212 (1557); social life and customs, 177 (594), 178 (596, 602, 603, 604)
trade unions. *See* unions
Trafton, Jesse, 71 (505)
train robberies, 152 (32), 179 (607)
tramps, 212 (1563)
trapping, 35 (190), 42 (257), 51 (336), 52 (338), 54 (368), 62 (433), 69 (490), 76 (650), 77 (655), 78 (666), 79 (637), 172 (554), 174 (570), 184 (649), 223 (1660), 236 (MF64)
Treasure State Labor Journal (Kalispell), 50 (322), 187 (902)
Triangle Telephone Company (Blaine County), 47 (296)
Trident, 70 (500), 73 (527), 75 (538); industries, 70 (499), 73 (524, 525, 526), 74 (529, 531, 532, 536), 75 (539, 540); social life and customs, 74 (531, 536)
Tripp, Leland Edmund, 209 (1537)
Tri-State T.V. Repeater Association, 165 (130)
Trout Creek, 17 (1322), 77 (655)
Troy, 78 (665), 162 (107), 169 (155), 172 (181); commerce, 162 (107); industries, 170 (164)
tuberculosis, 20 (1338)
turkey farms, 73 (524)
Twin Bridges, 15 (1306), 175 (571), 219 (1627, 1628, 1629), 220 (1630, 1631, 1632, 1633, 1634, 1635, 1636), 221 (1640, 1641, 1642); education, 184 (649); social life and customs, 57 (388)
Two Brothers Market (Black Eagle), 24 (909)
Two Eagle River School, 83 (1240)
Two Medicine River, 218 (1617)

U

U.S.S. *Helena*, 50 (327), 131 (1275)
Ulm, 61 (419)

undertakers and undertaking, 12 (1187), 29
(947), 45 (278), 54 (359), 175 (577), 212
(1562), 216 (1602)
Union Bank and Trust Company (Helena), 152
(29)
Union Market (Helena), 10 (1171)
Union Oil Company of California, 64 (451)
Union Pacific Railroad Company, 154 (47)
unions: aluminum, 29 (952), 32 (970), 103
(722); carpenters, 27 (938), 38 (215); cement
industry, 70 (500), 73 (525, 526, 527, 528),
74 (529, 530), 75 (540); electrical workers,
50 (320); farmers, 37 (207), 39 (249), 47
(296, 297), 49 (310), 55 (369), 59 (406), 73
(521), 79 (673), 110 (788), 162 (108), 177
(591); hotel and tavern workers, 27 (938), 28
(940), 115 (824); lumber industry, 49 (316),
50 (322), 53 (364, 365, 366), 54 (367), 63
(440), 77 (658); machinists, 23 (903), 33
(980), 68 (482); miners, 26 (929), 27 (933),
52 (338), 56 (378), 63 (440), 67 (472), 105
(745), 198 (1409), 199 (1410, 1411, 1412,
1413, 1414, 1415, 1416), 200 (1417, 1418,
1419, 1422), 201 (1424), 204 (1479); nurses,
20 (1511), 21 (1349); oil workers, 200
(1417); railroad, 68 (478, 482), 69 (487);
smelter workers, 23 (904, 905), 24 (913,
915), 25 (916, 923), 26 (924, 925, 930), 27
(934, 936, 937, 938), 28 (940, 943, 945), 29
(950), 32 (971), 33 (980, 982, 983), 38 (216),
60 (412), 199 (1412), 200 (1419, 1421, 1422,
1423), 201 (1424); teachers, 60 (410). See
also AFL-CIO; Industrial Workers of the
World; labor relations; United Mine Workers
of America
Unionville: industries, 40 (236)
United Brotherhood of Carpenters and Joiners of
America, 27 (938)
United Cement, Lime, Gypsum and Allied
Workers International Union, 70 (500), 73
(525, 526, 527), 74 (530), 75 (540)
United Mine Workers of America, 25 (916), 45
(281, 282), 48 (302, 305), 53 (356), 66 (468),
78 (668), 204 (1478, 1479)
United States Agricultural Adjustment
Administration (AAA), 94 (1139)
United States Air Force, 125 (1199), 126 (1221),
128 (1246, 1252), 129 (1254, 1259), 130
(1261, 1262, 1263), 135 (1534)
United States Army, 126 (1222), 127 (1242), 128
(1253), 130 (1260), 132 (1453), 137 (1587,
1599); cavalry, 133 (1464), 134 (1468), 165
(126); Corps of Engineers, 46 (292), 84
(1051); 18th Airborne Corps Artillery, 133
(1464); 163rd Infantry Regiment, 137
(1644), 138 (1645, 1646, 1647, 1648, 1649,
1650); 10th Mountain Division, 180 (616);
3rd Armored Calvary Regiment, 133 (1464),
134 (1468)
United States Bonneville Power Administration
(BPA), 30 (953)
United States Bureau of Indian Affairs (BIA), 43
(263), 70 (498), 82 (1237), 83 (1238, 1239).
See also United States Office of Indian
Affairs

United States Bureau of Reclamation, 46 (292)
United States Circuit Court, District of Montana,
188 (998)
United States Coast Guard, 129 (1257)
United States Congress, 237 (SC1512); House of
Representatives, 189 (1046), 194 (1288);
Senate, 149 (9)
United States Environmental Protection Agency
(EPA), 217 (1614)
United States Farm Security Administration, 71
(504)
United States Federal Bureau of Investigation
(FBI), 191 (1210)
United States Federal Land Bank, 46 (289), 69
(493)
United States First Special Service Force, 132
(1280, 1391)
United States Forest Service, 58 (398, 399), 61
(421), 62 (431, 433), 66 (465), 76 (650), 77
(657, 662), 79 (677), 100 (706), 103 (727),
105 (745), 119 (863, 865), 120 (866), 148 (2,
3, 4), 170 (164, 165), 185 (687), 186 (695),
190 (1191, 1193), 194 (1290), 195 (1354),
196 (1383), 208 (1510), 213 (1567), 215
(1593, 1594, 1595, 1596, 1597)
United States Immigration Border Patrol, 183
(636)
United States Marine Corps, 126 (1219), 129
(1254, 1255), 131 (1275), 132 (1376), 133
(1458)
United States National Park Service, 50 (323)
United States National Youth Administration
(NYA), 93 (1128), 95 (1140, 1141, 1147), 96
(1152)
United States Navy, 127 (1223), 128 (1251), 129
(1256), 130 (1265), 131 (1277), 132 (1279),
134 (1472)
United States Office of Indian Affairs, 75 (541).
See also United States Bureau of Indian
Affairs (BIA)
United States Postal Service, 50 (319), 104 (730)
United States Rural Electrification
Administration (REA), 37 (207), 59 (406),
61 (424), 102 (715), 181 (626), 185 (693)
United States Soil Conservation Service, 93
(1129, 1130)
United States Weather Bureau, 40 (233), 76
(654)
United States Works Progress Administration
(WPA), 41 (247), 42 (249, 257), 44 (269), 47
(297), 50 (323), 59 (405, 406), 62 (426), 65
(455), 93 (1125, 1130, 1132), 94 (1133,
1136), 95 (1140, 1142, 1143, 1144, 1145,
1146), 96 (1148, 1149, 1150, 1152), 97
(1158), 108 (765), 191 (1209), 192 (1214),
193 (1283), 207 (1497), 209 (1520), 219
(1623)
United Steelworkers of America, 24 (915), 25
(916, 919, 923), 26 (924, 925, 930), 27 (936,
938), 28 (945), 29 (950), 32 (971), 33 (982,
983), 114 (819), 199 (1413)
Unity Church, 40 (231)
universities and colleges, 14 (1302), 15 (1303,
1305, 1308), 20 (1337, 1511), 81 (1226), 82
(1236, 1237), 83 (1239, 1240, 1467), 132

(1279), 159 (86), 165 (124), 166 (133), 192
(1213), 201 (1431), 202 (1439), 205 (1482),
209 (1517), 212 (1563), 213 (1571), 214
(1589, 1590), 216 (1606, 1607)
University of Montana (Missoula) (1893–1913;
1965–), 82 (1237), 212 (1563)
Ural: commerce, 170 (168), 171 (171, 175)
Utah-Idaho Sugar Company, 111 (795), 112
(800)
Utica, 42 (257), 49 (312)

V

Valier: agriculture, 73 (521), 74 (533);
commerce, 53 (351)
Valley County: agriculture, 42 (249), 46 (286,
289, 291), 49 (315), 59 (400), 61 (423), 62
(429), 70 (501), 71 (507), 73 (521), 74 (533),
162 (108), 203 (1444, 1445, 1447); cattle
raising, 45 (284); education, 54 (363), 60
(410); politics and government, 73 (521)
Valley Hotel (Sidney), 109 (777)
Van Orsdel, William Wesley, 156 (63)
Vande Ven, George, 111 (796)
Variety Store (Red Lodge), 54 (357)
vermiculite, 168 (152), 170 (163), 172 (180)
veterans, societies, 154 (51)
Veterans and Pioneers Memorial Building
(Helena), 197 (1389)
veterinarians, 20 (1339, 1341)
Vicars, Joe, 113 (813)
Victor, 203 (1445)
Vienna Cafe (Roundup), 45 (276)
Vietnam War (1961–1973): personal narratives
of, 21 (1345), 126 (1219), 127 (1224), 128
(1251), 130 (1261, 1266), 131 (1274), 132
(1378), 133 (1458), 137 (1599), 193 (1268,
1269)
vigilantes, 156 (66), 230 (SC350), 233 (SC677)
Virginia City, 149 (14), 231 (SC380), 234
(SC762); commerce, 35 (196), 53 (355);
social life and customs, 231 (SC380)
Vogue, The (Plentywood), 121 (880)
volunteer ambulance services, 17 (1319), 18
(1329)
volunteer fire fighters, 24 (912), 103 (722, 724),
119 (858), 123 (890)
volunteers and volunteerism, 139 (1003), 140
(1009, 1010), 141 (1013, 1017), 142 (1022,
1024), 143 (1032, 1034, 1035), 144 (1043), 196
(1380); hospitals, 16 (1310), 142 (1024);
social services, 140 (1011), 187 (989). See
also volunteer ambulance services; volunteer
fire fighters
Voulkos, Peter, 202 (1434, 1435, 1441)

W

Wagner, John W., 154 (48)
waitresses, 28 (940). See also unions, hotel and
tavern workers
Walkerville, 199 (1416)
Walsh, Thomas James, 99 (1046), 152 (33)